INTERNATIONAL

ACCLAIM

IS

GLOBAL
VISION

Since 1955, International Schools Services has grown into a dynamic educational force in the overseas community. A nonprofit corporation dedicated to educational excellence for children attending international schools worldwide, International Schools Services is the world leader in providing a comprehensive range of quality educational services for schools, educators, families and corporations.

Headquartered in Princeton, New Jersey, International Schools Services is led by a team of professionals, each with decades of overseas educational experience. We pride ourselves in offering individualized assistance to international schools facing the many challenges unique to the overseas community.

Shore

■ ISS Management & Consulting

Multinational corporations turn to ISS Management & Consulting when they require expertise to establish and operate schools or to provide educational solutions for their employees' children in global settings.

From planning facilities and developing core curricula to hiring staff and purchasing supplies, our School Management division partners with corporations and local governmental officials to develop quality schools in an international context. Our Consulting services include educational site assessments, new school planning, specialized curriculum planning, recruitment assistance and financial forecasting.

ISS Management & Consulting strives to create or enhance educational operations to meet and exceed the expectations of the families who rely on their companies' schools.

■ ISS Educational Staffing

Finding qualified teachers and principals willing to relocate overseas is a challenge perpetually faced by international schools. ISS Educational Staffing helps meet that challenge by providing international schools with a large pool of highly qualified, dedicated educators who wish to teach overseas. Our professional staff members screen candidates' references and credentials, and also provide counseling on the overseas recruitment process. In addition to conducting year-round searches, ISS Educational Staffing hosts four annual International Recruitment Centers.

ISS Educational Staffing also assists international schools to recruit school heads. With our extensive knowledge of international education and well-established connections throughout the international school community, we help place superintendent and director candidates, ranging from newly certified administrators from the U.S. to seasoned superintendents with many years of international school experience.

ISS Information Services

ISS Information Services unites the international school community through its informative publications, interactive web site, conferences, seminars and other forums.

ISS Information Services annually publishes *The ISS Directory of International Schools*, a comprehensive guide to American and international schools worldwide, to help families make the best educational choices for their children. ISS also publishes a newspaper, *NewsLinks*, four times during the school year, which is distributed to more than 500 American and international schools.

ISS Purchasing

ISS Purchasing provides schools with greater access to American and internationally approved teaching materials and supplies, and helps institutions achieve administrative efficiencies and cost savings.

The School Supply department of ISS Purchasing provides complete purchasing services to international schools. From books to supplies to school equipment, School Supply helps schools streamline their procurement efforts and realize cost efficiencies.

The University Services department serves as the procurement arm of international universities, university satellite programs and teaching hospitals. Our staff is knowledgeable about regulations and guidelines, including those required by USAID/ASHA grants. From competitive bidding to consolidated shipping and final invoicing, University Services provides a complete purchasing service.

ISS Foundation Management

International schools that are incorporated in the United States as 501(c)3 nonprofit organizations avail themselves of greater fundraising, investment and tax savings opportunities.

Since 1968, ISS Foundation Management has served overseas schools by providing comprehensive financial services–including legal, financial, administrative and development expertise–to create and manage a school's foundation. In addition, ISS Foundation Management offers U.S.-based payroll processing, which may provide tax advantages for the school and access to several U.S. benefit options, including U.S. Social Security.

ISS Foundation Management manages the foundation and its programs on behalf of the school and provides comprehensive administrative support. Our professionals relieve a school of virtually all administrative responsibilities and report to the schools and foundation boards on the status of the foundation finances, programs and activities.

ISS Financial & Insurance Network

The ISS Financial & Insurance Network (ISSFIN) helps international schools meet their human resources and risk management objectives through the design and delivery of cost effective program solutions. In addition to giving its clients easy access to coverage from global insurance organizations such as ACE, AIG, Aetna, CIGNA and UNUMProvident, ISSFIN also created and manages EduCare International, a tailor made health insurance solution for international educators.

ISS Financial Network

ISS Financial Network is dedicated exclusively to meeting the financial service challenges of educational institutions worldwide by providing advice and services needed to achieve optimal financial performance.

ISS Financial Network offers the only comprehensive portfolio of financial services to international schools developed by international school experts, including cash and asset management, retirement plans, financial planning and capital financing. We customize financial packages to best meet the individual needs of international schools and their staff.

THE ISS DIRECTORY OF INTERNATIONAL SCHOOLS 2007–2008

"THE MOST COMPREHENSIVE RESOURCE GUIDE TO INTERNATIONAL SCHOOLS."

©2007 by International Schools Services, Inc.

Fees and other data are accurate as reported to International Schools Services by the individual schools as of August 2007. Readers are advised to obtain updated information from the individual schools. Inclusion in the Directory does not imply endorsement of any school or its programs by International Schools Services. Maps are representational and intended for general orientation only. Country information collected from The World Factbook at http://www.cia.gov/cia/publications/factbook/index.html.

Twenty-seventh edition, September 2007

ISBN - 10: 0-913663-23-9 paperback
ISBN - 13: 978-0-913663-24-0 paperback

Distributed by International Schools Services, 15 Roszel Road, PO Box 5910, Princeton, NJ 08543-5910, USA.

Cost: $49.95 plus shipping and handling

To order:
International Schools Services
Telephone: 1.609.452.0990
Fax: 1.609.452.2690
Email: directory@iss.edu
Web: www.iss.edu

Published annually since 1981 by
International Schools Services
PO Box 5910, Princeton, New Jersey 08543-5910, USA
Telephone: 1.609.452.0990
Fax: 1.609.452.2690
Email: iss@iss.edu
Website: www.iss.edu

Produced by Candace M. Hawkins Graphic Design, 1.609.575.1198

For advertising information contact: Becky Yurga, 1.609.259.6672

Printed in Canada

CONTENTS

ISS BOARD OF DIRECTORS / STAFF

DATA

INTERNATIONAL SCHOOLS

Total number of schools	520
Countries represented	153

Africa	57
Caribbean	18
Central America	20
East Asia/Pacific	135
Eastern Europe	48
Near East/South Asia/Middle East	68
North America	19
South America	51
Western Europe	104

STUDENTS

Total number of students	272,659

Students per school (average)	524
Percentage gaining college admission (average)	97%*

US	64,629
UK	14,080
Host country	93,125
Other nationalities	100,825

Class size (average)	
Elementary	17*
Secondary	17*

STAFF

Total full time staff	30,543
Total part time staff	3,367

Full time staff per school (average)	59
Part time staff per school (average)	7

US	11,497
UK	3,864
Host country	8,834
Other nationalities	8,862

.....as reported to ISS by the individual schools.
Some schools did not supply data in each category.
*Data from 2006/07 school year.

NOTES

Schools included in the Directory are primarily American and/or international with an English-language curriculum. They are arranged alphabetically, first by country, then by city or town, and finally by school name. Schools in rural areas are listed under the nearest town.

Accredited by: Accreditation is not mandatory, but many overseas schools elect to become accredited. U.S. and international accrediting organizations are listed in an appendix at the end of the Directory.

Boarding facilities: Schools with boarding services are identified within their entries.

Chief school officer: The name and title of each chief school officer is followed by up to eight academic division heads and other administrative staff. Chief school officers are listed alphabetically in the index.

Curriculum: Each school in the Directory provides an English-language curriculum alone or in combination with a host-national curriculum. Some offer the International Baccalaureate Diploma Programme (IB Diploma), a two-year course of study recognized by many colleges and universities, as well as the International Baccalaureate Middle Years Programme (IBMYP), and the International Baccalaureate Primary Years Programme (IBPYP). Schools offering the U.S. Advanced Placement (AP®) Program® are so noted.

Grade levels: The following abbreviations are used: N for Nursery; PreK for prekindergarten; K for kindergarten (usually 5- to 6-year-olds).

Nationalities of teaching staff and nationalities of student body: Teaching staff and students are defined by nationality groups. The United States, the United Kingdom, the host country, and other significant nationalities are noted.

Percentage of graduates attending college: Secondary schools were asked to list five colleges or universities recently attended by their graduates.

Regional organizations: Many schools are members of international regional organizations which provide professional development opportunities and other educational resources to their member schools. Organizations supporting international education are listed in an appendix at the end of the Directory.

School addresses: The street address may differ from the mailing address. When specifically provided, use the mailing address for correspondence.

APO and FPO are U.S. military mail services with strict regulations. No personal name may appear in an APO or FPO address. Use the title of the chief school officer, followed by the address. U.S. Department of State addresses may include personal names.

School governance: Most overseas schools are governed by a board of directors (or the host country's equivalent,) a company, religious organization, or individual proprietor. Sponsors or operators are listed when reported. Individual schools have identified themselves as falling within the following categories: coeducational, boarding, day, company-sponsored, church-related, proprietary, private nonprofit.

School year: Most schools in the directory follow a northern hemisphere calendar and are in session from September to June. Those following a southern hemisphere calendar from March to December are so noted.

Teaching staff: The number of both full- and part-time teaching staff members is listed.

Telephone and facsimile numbers: Numbers include the country and city codes (where applicable) followed by the telephone number.

Tuition: Most tuition figures are given in U.S. dollars. The currency used is noted in each school's entry. School charges other than tuition are also listed.

INTERNATIONAL SCHOOLS RESOURCE GUIDE

International Schools Services

Winter 2008
International
Recruitment Centers

ISS: Bangkok, Thailand
8-12 January 2008

ISS: New York, NY
17-21 February 2008
Administrative Recruitment Day—18 February

AAIE Conference to follow in NY: 21-24 February

CIS/ISS: Seattle, WA
25-28 February 2008

International Schools Services
PO Box 5910, Princeton, NJ 08543, USA
Phone 609.452.0990 • www.iss.edu

The Council of International Schools
21A Lavant Street, Petersfield, Hampshire, GU32 3EL, UK
Phone 44.1730.263131 • www.cois.org

Association for the Advancement of International Education
AAIE Office, Sheridan College, P.O. Box 1500, Sheridan, WY 82801-1500, USA
Phone 307-674-6446, ext 5201/5202 • www.aaie.org

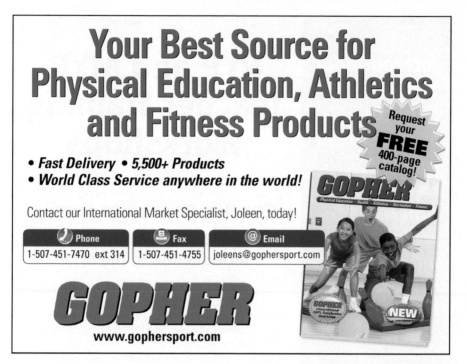
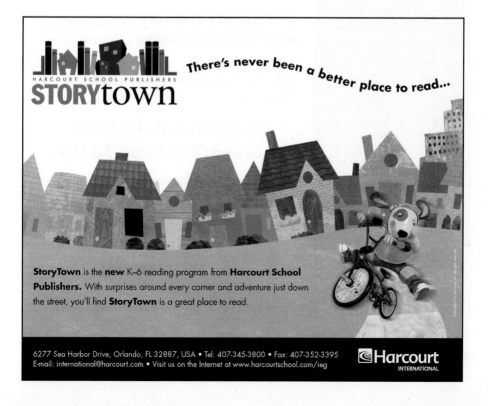

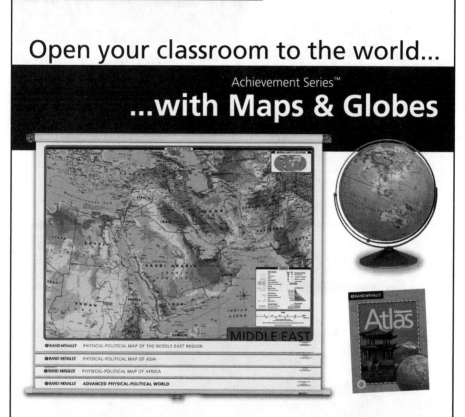

Meet Cicilia.

"I want to be a pediatrician."

Helping educate 100 million people. **Worldwide**.

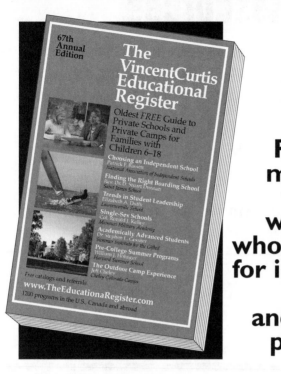

Index of Resources

Index of Resources

Harcourt International   A5
Joan Lucas
6277 Sea Harbor Drive
Orlando, Florida 32887
Tel: 407.345.3673
Fax: 407.352.3395
Email: international@harcourt.com
Web: www.harcourt.com

ISS Financial &
Insurance Network   A2
PO Box 5910
Princeton, NJ 08543-5910
Tel: 609.452.2490
Fax: 609.452.0117
Web: www.issfin.com

Office of International Programs,
College of Education,
Lehigh University   A8
Dr. Daphne P. Hobson
B308 International Programs
111 Research Drive
Bethlehem, PA 18015
Tel: 610.758.5737
Fax: 610.758.6223
Email: intlcoe@lehigh.edu
Web: www.lehigh.edu/lbl

Pearson Education   A9
International School Marketing
10 Bank Street
White Plains, NY 10606
Tel: 914.287.8020
Fax: 914.287.8484
Web: www.pearson.com

Rand McNally   A7
Educational Publishing
8255 Central Park Avenue
Skokie, IL 60076
Tel: 847.329.2100
Fax: 847.673.9935
Email: education@randmcnally.com
Web: www.randmcnally.com/education

Scholastic Inc.   A10
557 Broadway, 5th Floor
New York, NY 10012
Tel: 212.343.6783
Fax: 212.343.4714
Email: meo'neill@scholastic.com
Web: www.scholastic.com/international

Vincent Curtis
Educational Register   A11
Stanford B. Vincent
29 Simpson Lane
Tel: 508.457.6473
Fax: 508.457.6499
Email: register@vincentcurtis.com
Web: www.TheEducationalRegister.com

World of Reading, Ltd.   A12
Cindy Tracy–President
P.O. Box 13092
Atlanta, GA 30324-0092
Tel: 404.233.4042
Toll-Free 800.729.3703
Fax: 404.237.5511
Email: polyglot@wor.com
Web: www.wor.com

INTERNATIONAL SCHOOLS

SCHOOLS

BY COUNTRY

ALBANIA

Area:	28,748 sq km
Population:	3,600,523
Capital:	Tirana (Tirane)
Currency:	Lek (ALL)
Languages:	Albanian, Greek

TIRANA INTERNATIONAL SCHOOL

Phone	355 4 365239
Fax	355 4 377679
Email	tirana@qsi.org
Website	www.qsi.org
Address	Tre Vellezrit Kondi, Villa Germane #6, Tirana, Albania
Mailing address	Kutia Postare 1527, Tirana, Albania

STAFF

Director Scott A. D'Alterio
Teaching staff Full time 17; Part time 9; Total 26

Nationalities of teaching staff US 11; Albanian 12; Other(s) (Canadian, Pole) 3

INFORMATION

Grade levels PreK–12
School year September–June
School type coeducational, day, private non-profit
Year founded 1991
Governed by appointed Board of Directors
Sponsored by Quality Schools International (QSI)
Accredited by Middle States
Regional organizations CEESA
Enrollment PreK 28; Elementary K–5 50; Middle School 6–8 22; High School 9–12 25; Total 125

Nationalities of student body US 35; UK 2; Albanian 40; Other(s) (Italian, Dutch) 48
Tuition/fee currency US Dollar
Tuition range 4,200–13,500
Annual fees Registration 100; Capital Levy 1,600
Graduates attending college 100%
Graduates have attended Brock U, Drexel U, U of Belgrade, St. Andrews U, American U of Cairo

EDUCATIONAL PROGRAM

Curriculum US, AP
Average class size Elementary 10; Secondary 7
Language(s) of instruction English
Language(s) taught French, German, Italian, Spanish, Albanian
Staff specialists counselor
Special curricular programs art, instrumental music, computer/technology, physical education

Extra curricular programs community service, dance, drama, excursions/expeditions, literary magazine, newspaper
Sports basketball, martial arts, soccer
Examinations AP, Iowa

CAMPUS FACILITIES

Location Suburban
Campus 2 hectares, 9 buildings, 20 classrooms, 2 computer labs, 30 instructional computers, 7,000 library volumes, 1 auditorium, 1 cafeteria, 1 gymnasium, 4 playing fields, 1 science lab, air conditioning

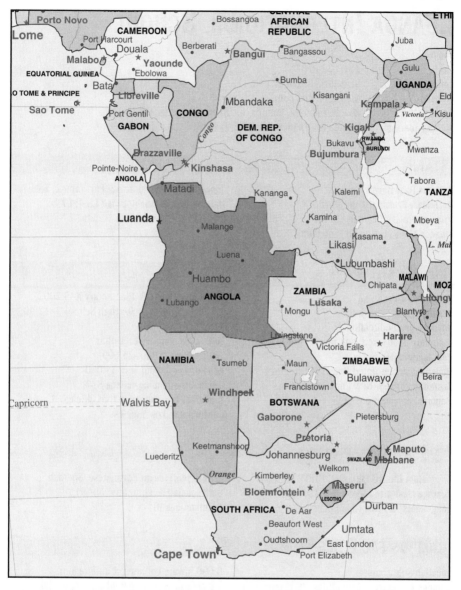

ANGOLA

Area:	1,246,700 sq km
Population:	12,263,596
Capital:	Luanda
Currency:	Kwanza (AOA)
Languages:	Portuguese

LUANDA INTERNATIONAL SCHOOL

Phone	244 222 46 0762
Fax	244 2 2246 0782
Email	Director@lisluanda.com
Website	www.lisluanda.com
Address	Rua da Talatona, Luanda Sul, Samba, Luanda, Angola
Mailing address	Luanda International School, Box 1566, Luanda, Angola

STAFF

Director Tony Baron
Secondary Principal Tony Martin
Primary Principal Felicity Hewitt
Finance Manager Ronald Hamalala

Teaching staff Full time 42; Part time 2; Total 44
Nationalities of teaching staff US 4; UK 8; Angolan 5; Other(s) (Australian) 27

INFORMATION

Grade levels PreK–12
School year August–June
School type coeducational, company-sponsored, day, private non-profit
Year founded 1996
Governed by appointed Board of Directors
Accredited by CIS, New England
Regional organizations ECIS

Enrollment PreK 25; Elementary K–5 200; Middle School 6–8 80; High School 9–12 40; Total 345
Tuition/fee currency US Dollar
Tuition range 9,000–25,000
Annual fees Capital Levy 25,000
Graduates attending college 82%
Graduates have attended U of Chicago, U of California in Los Angeles

EDUCATIONAL PROGRAM

Curriculum Intl, IB Diploma, IBPYP, IBMYP
Average class size Elementary 19; Secondary 18
Language(s) of instruction English

Language(s) taught Portuguese, Spanish
Staff specialists computer, librarian
Examinations IB

CAMPUS FACILITIES

Location Suburban
Campus 6 hectares, 7 buildings, 29 classrooms, 2 computer labs, 100 instructional computers,

6,600 library volumes, 1 auditorium, 1 cafeteria, 3 playing fields, 2 science labs, 2 pools, 1 tennis court, air conditioning

ARGENTINA

Area:	2,766,890 sq km
Population:	40,301,927
Capital:	Buenos Aires
Currency:	Argentine Peso (ARS)
Languages:	Spanish, English

LINCOLN, THE AMERICAN INTERNATIONAL SCHOOL OF BUENOS AIRES

Phone	54 11 4794 9400
Fax	54 11 4790 2117
Email	lincoln@lincoln.edu.ar
Website	www.lincoln.edu.ar
Address	Andrés Ferreyra 4073, B1637AOS, La Lucila, Buenos Aires, B1637AOS, Argentina

STAFF

Superintendent Philip T. Joslin
High School Principal Joele Basnight
Middle School Principal Jeff Voracek
Elementary School Principal Elizabeth Haddon
Assistant to the Superintendent Jane Lowery
Dean, Lincoln University College Ray McKay
Business/Finance Manager Carlos Alberto Patiño

Head of Technology Leandro Segura
Head of Library/Media Center Peggy Keough
Teaching staff Full time 94; Part time 2; Total 96
Nationalities of teaching staff US 38; UK 1; Argentine 49; Other(s) (Canadian, New Zealander) 8

INFORMATION

Grade levels PreK–12
School year August–June
School type coeducational, day
Year founded 1936
Governed by elected Board
Accredited by Southern
Regional organizations AASSA, ECIS
Enrollment PreK 17; Elementary K–5 306; Middle School 6–8 183; High School 9–12 198; Total 704

Nationalities of student body US 187; UK 30; Argentine 111; Other(s) (Brazilian, Venezuelan) 376
Tuition/fee currency US Dollar
Tuition range 12,500–15,200
Annual fees Registration 1,400; Busing 750; Lunch 540
One time fees Capital Levy 6,000
Graduates attending college 100%
Graduates have attended Boston U, U of British Columbia, Stanford U, Pomona Col, U of Pennsylvania

EDUCATIONAL PROGRAM

Curriculum US, National, AP, IB Diploma
Average class size Elementary 15; Secondary 15
Language(s) of instruction English, Spanish
Language(s) taught French, Spanish
Staff specialists counselor, ESL, librarian

Extra curricular programs community service, yearbook
Sports basketball, soccer, swimming, track and field, volleyball, track and field
Examinations ACT, AP, IB, SAT, SAT II, TOEFL

CAMPUS FACILITIES

Location Suburban
Campus 9 hectares, 6 buildings, 69 classrooms, 5 computer labs, 280 instructional computers, 47,059 library volumes, 2 auditoriums,

1 cafeteria, 1 covered play area, 2 gymnasiums, 1 infirmary, 3 playing fields, 7 science labs, 1 pool, 3 tennis courts, air conditioning

St. George's College

Phone	54 11 4257 3472
Fax	54 11 4253 0030
Email	info@stgeorge.com.ar
Website	www.stgeorge.com.ar
Address	Guido 800, Quilmes, Buenos Aires, B1878WAA, Argentina
Mailing address	Casilla de Correo N°2, B1878WAA Quilmes, Buenos Aires, Argentina

STAFF

Headmaster Robert S. Dillow
Deputy Headmaster Peter Ashton
Director Polimodal Oscar Piersanti
Director of Studies and IB Coordinator Gavin Horgan
EGB III Coordinator Roberto Prata

Middle Years Program Coordinator Lidia Frascarelli
General Manager María Cristina Gatica de Barr
Head of Technology Fabián Casas
Librarian Marisa Alonso de Lara

INFORMATION

Grade levels K–12
School year February–December
School type boarding, coeducational, day, private non-profit
Year founded 1898
Governed by elected Board of Governors

Tuition/fee currency US Dollar
Tuition range 2,350–10,688
Annual fees Boarding, 5-day 9,562; Boarding, 7-day 10,688; Insurance 110
Graduates attending college 95%

EDUCATIONAL PROGRAM

Curriculum UK, National, Intl, IB Diploma, IBPYP, IBMYP, IGCSE, SAT, PET
Average class size Elementary 24; Secondary 24
Language(s) of instruction English, Spanish
Language(s) taught English, Spanish, French
Staff specialists computer, ESL, librarian, nurse, psychologist, reading resource
Special curricular programs art, instrumental music, vocal music, computer/technology, physical education, carpentry

Extra curricular programs computers, community service, drama, environmental conservation, excursions/expeditions, literary magazine, newspaper, photography, yearbook, International Award for Young People (Duke of Edinburgh Award)
Sports basketball, cricket, cross-country, football, golf, hockey, rugby, soccer, softball, squash, swimming, tennis, track and field, handball
Examinations GCSE, IB, IGCSE, PSAT, SAT

CAMPUS FACILITIES

Location Suburban
Campus 27 hectares, 17 buildings, 50 classrooms, 3 computer labs, 90 instructional computers,

29,000 library volumes, 1 auditorium, 1 cafeteria, 2 covered play areas, 1 gymnasium, 2 infirmaries, 12 playing fields, 5 science labs, 2 pools, 5 tennis courts, air conditioning

Data from 2006/07 school year.

ARMENIA

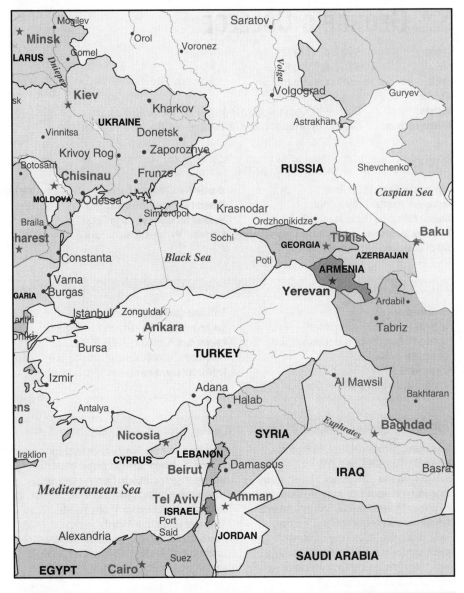

ARMENIA

Area:	29,800 sq km
Population:	2,971,650
Capital:	Yerevan
Currency:	Dram (AMD)
Languages:	Armenian

QSI INTERNATIONAL SCHOOL OF YEREVAN

Phone	374 10 391 030
Fax	374 10 397 599
Email	yerevan@qsi.org
Website	www.qsi.org/arm
Address	2A Caritas Building, Ashtarak Highway, Yerevan, 0088, Armenia
Mailing address	c/o American Embassy, Yerevan, Dept. of State, 7020 Yerevan Place, Washington, DC 20521-7020, USA

STAFF

Director Mark J. Hemphill
Teaching staff Full time 19; Part time 2; Total 21

Nationalities of teaching staff US 8; Armenian 9; Other(s) (Canadian, Australian) 4

INFORMATION

Grade levels PreK–12
School year August–June
School type coeducational, day, private non-profit
Year founded 1995
Governed by appointed Board of Directors
Regional organizations CEESA
Enrollment PreK 2; Elementary K–5 41; Middle School 6–8 18; High School 9–12 6; Total 67

Nationalities of student body US 31; UK 2; Other(s) (Indian, German) 34
Tuition/fee currency US Dollar
Tuition range 4,000–14,500
Annual fees Capital Levy 1,600
One time fees Registration 100
Graduates attending college 100%
Graduates have attended Tufts U, Col of William and Mary

EDUCATIONAL PROGRAM

Curriculum US
Average class size Elementary 10; Secondary 6
Language(s) of instruction English
Language(s) taught Russian, French, Armenian
Staff specialists computer, ESL, librarian

Special curricular programs art, instrumental music, computer/technology, distance learning, physical education
Extra curricular programs community service, dance, drama, yearbook
Sports basketball, cross-country, golf, soccer
Examinations Iowa

CAMPUS FACILITIES

Location Suburban
Campus 1 hectare, 1 building, 12 classrooms,

1 computer lab, 26 instructional computers, 4,414 library volumes, 1 playing field

ARUBA

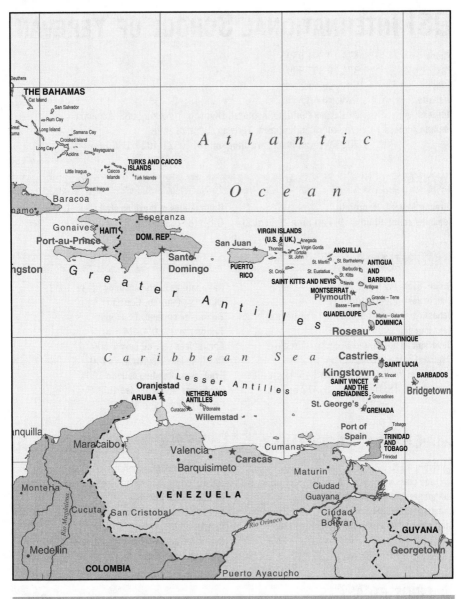

ARUBA

Area:	193 sq km
Population:	100,018
Capital:	Oranjestad
Currency:	Aruban Guilder/Florin (AWG)
Languages:	Papiamento, Spanish

INTERNATIONAL SCHOOL OF ARUBA

Phone	297 583 5040
Fax	297 583 6020
Email	intschool@setarnet.aw
Website	www.isaruba.com
Address	Wayaca 238A, Oranjestad, Aruba

STAFF

Head of School Paul Sibley, Ed.D.
Academic Dean Mary Sibley
Business Manager Jacqueline Juliao-Wong
Technology Coordinator Michael Lance

Head of Library Elena Musto
Teaching staff Full time 25; Part time 2; Total 27
Nationalities of teaching staff US 14; Aruban 4;
Other(s) (Dutch, Venezuelan) 9

INFORMATION

Grade levels PreK–12
School year August–June
School type coeducational, day, private non-profit
Year founded 1985
Governed by appointed International Schools
Services
Accredited by Southern
Regional organizations AASSA
Enrollment PreK 25; Elementary K–5 90; Middle
School 6–8 45; High School 9–12 40; Total 200

Nationalities of student body US 60; Aruban 50;
Other(s) (Dutch, Venezuelan) 90
Tuition/fee currency US Dollar
Tuition range 10,905–13,630
Annual fees Registration 1,395
One time fees Capital Levy 6,057
Graduates attending college 98%
Graduates have attended U of Florida,
Fashion Institute of Technology, Stetson U,
Daytona Community Col, York U

EDUCATIONAL PROGRAM

Curriculum US, Intl, AP
Average class size Elementary 14; Secondary 10
Language(s) of instruction English
Language(s) taught Spanish, Dutch
Staff specialists computer, counselor, ESL,
librarian
Special curricular programs art, vocal music,
computer/technology, distance learning,
physical education

Extra curricular programs computers, community
service, drama, environmental conservation,
yearbook
Sports basketball, soccer, softball, swimming,
tennis, volleyball
Examinations ACT, AP, Iowa, PSAT, SAT

CAMPUS FACILITIES

Location Suburban
Campus 3 hectares, 4 buildings, 32 classrooms,
2 computer labs, 70 instructional computers,
20,000 library volumes, 1 auditorium,

1 cafeteria, 1 covered play area, 1 gymnasium,
1 infirmary, 2 playing fields, 2 science labs,
1 tennis court, air conditioning

AUSTRALIA

AUSTRALIA

Area:	7,686,850 sq km
Population:	20,434,176
Capital:	Canberra
Currency:	Australian Dollar (AUD)
Languages:	English

THE KILMORE INTERNATIONAL SCHOOL

Phone	61 3 57 822 211
Fax	61 3 57 822 525
Email	info@kilmore.vic.edu.au
Website	www.kilmore.vic.edu.au
Address	40 White Street, Kilmore, Victoria, 3764, Australia

STAFF

Principal John M. Settle
Deputy Principal/IB Coordinator Neil McBurney
Head of Year 12 Rod Mumford
Head of Year 11 Diego Bertotto
Head of Year 10 Yan Ru Li
Head of Years 7–9 Sue Phillips

Business Manager Patricia Mahon
Head of Information Technology Jayne Logan
Librarian Shelley Frawley
Teaching staff Full time 43; Part time 17; Total 60
Nationalities of teaching staff UK 5;
Australian 38; Other(s) (Chinese, Indonesian) 17

INFORMATION

Grade levels 7–12
School year February–December
School type boarding, coeducational, day, private non-profit
Year founded 1990
Governed by appointed School Board
Enrollment Middle School 6–8 120; High School 9–12 310; Total 430
Nationalities of student body Australian 230; Other(s) (Chinese, Korean) 200
Tuition/fee currency Australian Dollar

Tuition range 10,500–20,900
Annual fees Boarding, 7-day 14,600; Insurance 402; Camps 1,200
One time fees Registration 220; IB Examination 1,000
Boarding program grades 7–12
Boarding program length 7-day **Boys** 100 **Girls** 100
Graduates attending college 100%
Graduates have attended Oxford U, London School of Economics, Imperial Col, Yale U, The U of Melbourne

EDUCATIONAL PROGRAM

Curriculum Intl, IB Diploma
Average class size Secondary 16
Language(s) of instruction English
Language(s) taught Chinese, Korean, Japanese, Thai, Indonesian, German, French, Hindi
Staff specialists computer, counselor, learning disabilities, librarian, math resource, nurse, physician, psychologist

Special curricular programs instrumental music, vocal music, computer/technology, physical education, vocational
Extra curricular programs community service, dance, drama, excursions/expeditions, literary magazine, newspaper, photography, yearbook
Sports basketball, cross-country, skiing, soccer, swimming, tennis, track and field
Examinations IB, SAT, SAT II, TOEFL

CAMPUS FACILITIES

Location Rural
Campus 6 hectares, 11 buildings, 30 classrooms, 2 computer labs, 50 instructional computers, 30,000 library volumes, 1 auditorium, 1 cafeteria, 3 covered play areas, 1 gymnasium, 1 infirmary, 2 playing fields, 4 science labs, 1 pool, 2 tennis courts, air conditioning

AUSTRALIAN SCHOOL FOR INTERNATIONAL EDUCATION

Phone	61 8 9285 1144
Fax	61 8 9285 1188
Email	info@asie.wa.edu.au
Website	www.asie.wa.edu.au
Address	22 Kalinda Drive, City Beach, Western Australia, 6015, Australia
Mailing address	PO Box 366, Floreat, WA 6014, Australia

STAFF

Principal Karyn M. Watt
Leadership Team/Director Admissions
Carrie Fischer
Administration Manager Rosina del a Mare

Teaching staff Full time 12; Part time 1; Total 13
Nationalities of teaching staff US 2; UK 2;
Australian 5; Other(s) (French, Chinese) 4

INFORMATION

Grade levels 3–12
School year July–June
School type coeducational, day, private non-profit
Year founded 2005
Governed by elected AAIE
Accredited by Western
Enrollment Elementary K–5 20; Middle School 6–8 15; High School 9–12 35; Total 70
Nationalities of student body US 30; UK 15; Australian 8; Other(s) (Venezuelan, Norwegian) 17

Tuition/fee currency Australian Dollar
Tuition range 9,500–13,500
Annual fees Lunch 1,260; Books 400; Technology 250; Advanced Placement 250; Art 50
One time fees Registration 3,475
Graduates attending college 100%
Graduates have attended Purdue U, Northwestern U, Cornell U, Rensselaer Polytechnic Institute, Berkeley U

EDUCATIONAL PROGRAM

Curriculum US, UK, Intl, AP
Average class size Elementary 8; Secondary 8
Language(s) of instruction English
Language(s) taught Spanish, French
Staff specialists computer, ESL
Special curricular programs art, computer/technology, physical education

Extra curricular programs community service, environmental conservation, yearbook
Sports baseball, basketball, cricket, football, martial arts, soccer, swimming, tennis
Clubs honors society, student council, Spanish club.
Examinations ACT, AP, PSAT, SAT, SAT II, ISA, WALNA

CAMPUS FACILITIES

Location Suburban
Campus 10 hectares, 3 buildings, 15 classrooms, 3 computer labs, 38 instructional computers,

2,500 library volumes, 1 cafeteria, 1 covered play area, 1 gymnasium, 1 playing field, 2 science labs, 1 pool, 1 tennis court

AMERICAN INTERNATIONAL SCHOOL– AUSTRALIA

Phone	61 2 9890 3488
Fax	61 2 9890 3499
Email	lcheetham@ais.thin-ed.net
Website	www.amschool.com.au
Address	216 Pennant Hills Road, Carlingford, Sydney, New South Wales, 2118, Australia
Mailing address	Locked Bag 204, Oatlands, NSW, 2117, Australia

STAFF

Head of School Lyn Cheetham
Admissions/Enrollment Officer Mary Nolan
Secondary School and IB Coordinator Shannan Godfrey
Business Officer Peter Taylor

Head of Technology Mirka Taras
Head of Library Harvey Cheetham
Teaching staff Full time 20; Part time 5; Total 25
Nationalities of teaching staff US 10; UK 1; Australian 4; Other(s) 4

INFORMATION

Grade levels PreK–12
School year August–June
School type coeducational, day, proprietary
Year founded 2000
Governed by appointed Board of Governors
Sponsored by The International School
Enrollment PreK 15; Elementary K–5 80; Middle School 6–8 60; High School 9–12 45; Total 200

Nationalities of student body US 80; UK 20; Australian 60; Other(s) 40
Tuition/fee currency Australian Dollar
Tuition range 11,850–21,850
One time fees Registration 2,010
Graduates attending college 100%
Graduates have attended Michigan State U, Boston U, Sydney U, Ball State U, Kingston U

EDUCATIONAL PROGRAM

Curriculum US, AP, IB Diploma
Average class size Elementary 14; Secondary 12

Language(s) of instruction English
Language(s) taught Spanish, French

CAMPUS FACILITIES

Location Suburban
Campus 2 hectares, 5 buildings, 22 classrooms, 1 computer lab, 55 instructional computers,

10,000 library volumes, 1 auditorium, 1 cafeteria, 1 playing field, 1 science lab, 1 tennis court, air conditioning

AUSTRIA

AUSTRIA

Area:	83,870 sq km
Population:	8,199,783
Capital:	Vienna
Currency:	Euro (EUR)
Languages:	German

AMERICAN INTERNATIONAL SCHOOL VIENNA

Phone	43 1 401320
Fax	43 1 401325
Email	info@ais.at
Website	www.ais.at
Address	Salmannsdorfer Strasse 47, Vienna, A-1190, Austria

STAFF

Director Ellen Stern
High School Principal Gregory Moncada, Ed.D.
Middle School Principal David Straffon, Ed.D.
Elementary School Principal Deena Tarleton, Ed.D.
Business/Finance Manager Russell Cooke

Head of Technology Christopher Rolfe
Head of Library/Media Center Theresa Rolfe
Teaching staff Full time 97; Part time 5; Total 102
Nationalities of teaching staff US 72; UK 4;
Austrian 8; Other(s) 18

INFORMATION

Grade levels PreK–12
School year August–June
School type coeducational, day, private non-profit
Year founded 1959
Governed by elected Board
Accredited by Middle States
Regional organizations CEESA, ECIS
Enrollment PreK 30; Elementary K–5 310;
Middle School 6–8 200; High School 9–12 260;
Total 800

Nationalities of student body US 260; UK 34;
Austrian 142; Other(s) (Korean, Israeli) 361
Tuition/fee currency Euro
Annual fees Busing 885
One time fees Registration 150;
Capital Levy 3,600; Enrollment 300
Graduates attending college 96%
Graduates have attended Stanford U, Brown U,
London School of Economics, Cambridge U,
John Hopkins U

EDUCATIONAL PROGRAM

Curriculum US, IB Diploma, Austrian Matura
Average class size Elementary 18; Secondary 16
Language(s) of instruction English
Language(s) taught German, French, Spanish
Staff specialists computer, counselor, ESL,
learning disabilities, librarian, nurse, reading
resource
Special curricular programs art, instrumental
music, vocal music, computer/technology,
physical education

Extra curricular programs dance, drama,
excursions/expeditions, newspaper,
photography, yearbook
Sports basketball, cross-country, gymnastics,
soccer, softball, swimming, tennis, track and
field, volleyball
Examinations ACT, AP, IB, Iowa, PSAT, SAT, SAT II

CAMPUS FACILITIES

Location Suburban
Campus 15 hectares, 6 buildings, 63 classrooms,
4 computer labs, 300 instructional computers,

25,000 library volumes, 1 auditorium,
1 cafeteria, 3 gymnasiums, 1 infirmary,
1 playing field, 6 science labs, 2 tennis courts

DANUBE INTERNATIONAL SCHOOL

Phone	43 1 720 3110
Fax	43 1 720 3110 40
Email	info@danubeschool.at
Website	www.danubeschool.at
Address	Josef Gall-Gasse 2, Vienna, A-1020, Austria

STAFF

Director Andrew R. Scott
Deputy Director and Secondary School Principal
Steven Ellis
Elementary School Principal Pamela Defty
IB MYP Coordinator Mark Brierley
IB Diploma Coordinator Giles Pope, Ph.D.

Business Manager F. W. Biber
Librarian Hadia Abushady
Teaching staff Full time 25; Part time 12; Total 37
Nationalities of teaching staff US 4; UK 12;
Austrian 7; Other(s) (Australian, Canadian) 14

INFORMATION

Grade levels K–12
School year August–June
School type coeducational, day, proprietary
Year founded 1992
Sponsored by Private Ownership
Regional organizations ECIS
Enrollment Elementary K–5 119; Middle School
6–8 80; High School 9–12 123; Total 322
Nationalities of student body US 13; UK 25;
Austrian 161; Other(s) (German,
Zimbabwean) 123

Tuition/fee currency Euro
Tuition range 8,876–15,714
Annual fees Activities and Trips 1,000
One time fees Registration 2,000; Application 100;
Deposit 365
Graduates attending college 100%
Graduates have attended U of Manchester,
U of Vienna, London School of Economics,
U of London, Vienna U for Economics/Business

EDUCATIONAL PROGRAM

Curriculum National, Intl, IB Diploma, IBMYP
Average class size Elementary 20; Secondary 20
Language(s) of instruction English
Language(s) taught German, French, Spanish
Staff specialists computer, counselor, ESL,
learning disabilities, librarian

Extra curricular programs community service,
dance, drama, excursions/expeditions
Sports badminton, martial arts, skiing, soccer,
swimming, tennis, volleyball
Examinations IB

CAMPUS FACILITIES

Location Urban
Campus 1 building, 22 classrooms,
1 computer lab, 40 instructional computers,

10,000 library volumes, 1 auditorium,
1 cafeteria, 1 gymnasium, 3 science labs

VIENNA INTERNATIONAL SCHOOL

Phone	43 1 203 5595
Fax	43 1 203 0366
Email	visinfo@vis.ac.at
Website	www.vis.ac.at
Address	Strasse der Menschenrechte 1, Vienna, A-1220, Austria

STAFF

Director James S. Walbran
Head of Secondary School Nancy J. Schupelius
Head of Primary School Philip Armstrong
Deputy Head of Secondary School Derrick Devenport
Deputy Head of Primary School Sharyn Rieger

Business Manager Rainer Dobianer
IT Manager Mark Crumby
Head of Secondary Library Marija Oblak
Teaching staff Full time 136; Part time 8; Total 144
Nationalities of teaching staff US 16; UK 61; Austrian 34; Other(s) (Australian, Canadian) 33

INFORMATION

Grade levels PreK–12
School year August–June
School type coeducational, day, private non-profit
Year founded 1978
Governed by appointed and elected Board of Governors
Accredited by CIS
Regional organizations CEESA, ECIS
Enrollment PreK 59; Elementary K–5 452; Middle School 6–8 322; High School 9–12 491; Total 1,324

Nationalities of student body US 111; UK 127; Austrian 265; Other(s) (Russian, German) 821
Tuition/fee currency Euro
Tuition range 4,576–14,604
One time fees Registration 2,500; Application 90; Deposit 370
Graduates attending college 95%
Graduates have attended Oxford U, Cambridge U, U of London, Harvard U, Stanford U

EDUCATIONAL PROGRAM

Curriculum IB Diploma, IBPYP
Average class size Elementary 25; Secondary 20
Language(s) of instruction English
Language(s) taught German, French, Spanish
Staff specialists computer, counselor, ESL, librarian, nurse, physician
Special curricular programs art, computer/technology, physical education

Extra curricular programs community service, dance, drama, environmental conservation, literary magazine, newspaper, yearbook
Sports basketball, cross-country, football, golf, hockey, rugby, skiing, soccer, swimming, track and field, volleyball
Examinations IB, PSAT, SAT, Austrian Matura Equivalence

CAMPUS FACILITIES

Location Urban
Campus 6 hectares, 1 building, 58 classrooms, 4 computer labs, 550 instructional computers, 50,000 library volumes, 1 auditorium, 1 cafeteria, 5 gymnasiums, 1 infirmary, 1 playing field, 8 science labs, 2 tennis courts

AZERBAIJAN

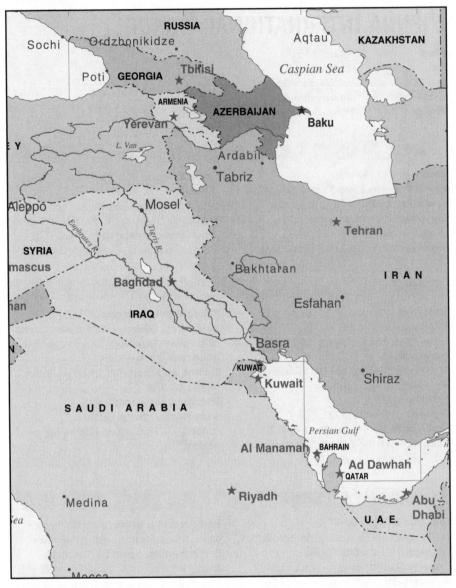

AZERBAIJAN

Area:	86,600 sq km
Population:	8,120,247
Capital:	Baku (Baki, Baky)
Currency:	Azerbaijani Manat (AZM)
Languages:	Azerbaijani

Baku International School

Phone	994 12 440 6616
Fax	994 12 440 6616
Email	scottroot@qsi.org
Website	www.qsi.org
Address	Darnagul Qasabasi, Str. Ajami Nakhchivani, Block 3097, Baku, 1108, Azerbaijan
Mailing address	c/o American Embassy, Baku, Dept. of State, 7050 Baku Place, Washington, DC 20521-7050, USA

STAFF

Director Scott E. Root
Teaching staff Full time 31; Part time 8; Total 39

Nationalities of teaching staff US 8; UK 5; Azerbaijani 22; Other(s) (Canadian) 4

INFORMATION

Grade levels N–12
School year September–June
School type coeducational, day, private non-profit
Year founded 1994
Governed by appointed Board of Directors
Sponsored by U.S. State Dept.
Accredited by Middle States
Regional organizations CEESA

Enrollment Nursery 25; PreK 20; Elementary K–5 55; Middle School 6–8 25; High School 9–12 22; Total 147
Nationalities of student body US 26; UK 18; Azerbaijani 18; Other(s) (Indian) 85
Tuition/fee currency US Dollar
Tuition range 4,000–12,400
Annual fees Capital Levy 1,600; Busing 1,080; Lunch 540
One time fees Registration 100

EDUCATIONAL PROGRAM

Curriculum US, AP
Average class size Elementary 12; Secondary 12
Language(s) of instruction English
Language(s) taught French, Russian, Azeri, Turkish
Staff specialists computer, ESL, librarian
Special curricular programs art, instrumental music, vocal music, computer/technology, physical education

Extra curricular programs computers, community service, dance, drama, environmental conservation, excursions/expeditions, newspaper, yearbook
Sports basketball, cross-country, gymnastics, martial arts

CAMPUS FACILITIES

Location Suburban
Campus 2 hectares, 1 building, 17 classrooms, 1 computer lab, 20 instructional computers, 5,000 library volumes, 1 auditorium, 1 cafeteria, 1 covered play area, 1 gymnasium, 1 infirmary, 1 playing field, 1 science lab, 1 tennis court, air conditioning

INTERNATIONAL SCHOOL OF AZERBAIJAN

Phone	994 12 973 028
Fax	994 12 972 194
Email	admin@tisa.az
Website	www.tisa.az
Address	Royal Park/Stonepay, Yeni Yassamal, Baku, Azerbaijan
Mailing address	c/o BP Azerbaijan, Chertsey Rd, Sunbury on Thames, Middlesex TW16 7LN, United Kingdom

STAFF

Director Peter Harding, Ed.D.
Secondary Principal Steven Scoble
Primary Principal David Tigchelaar
Admissions Officer Gayle Berger

Business Manager Larissa Sayaliyeva
Head of Technology Anne Kennedy
Head of Library/Media Center Samira Hajiyeva

INFORMATION

Grade levels N–12
School year August–June
School type coeducational, company-sponsored, day, private non-profit
Year founded 1996
Governed by appointed Board of Directors
Sponsored by BP/AIOC
Accredited by CIS
Regional organizations ECIS
Enrollment Nursery 37; PreK 31; Elementary K–5 203; Middle School 6–8 85; High School 9–12 73; Total 429

Nationalities of student body US 111; UK 136; Azerbaijani 51; Other(s) 131
Tuition/fee currency US Dollar
Tuition range 5,700–15,000
Annual fees Registration 500
One time fees Capital Levy 5,000
Graduates attending college 100%
Graduates have attended Stanford U, Parsons The New School for Design, Edinburgh U, Rutgers U, Texas A&M

EDUCATIONAL PROGRAM

Curriculum Intl, IB Diploma, IBPYP, IBMYP
Average class size Elementary 17; Secondary 15
Language(s) of instruction English
Language(s) taught French, Spanish, Russian, Azeri
Staff specialists computer, counselor, ESL, librarian, math resource, nurse
Special curricular programs art, computer/technology, physical education

Extra curricular programs computers, community service, dance, drama, environmental conservation, excursions/expeditions, literary magazine, photography
Sports basketball, cricket, gymnastics, rugby, soccer, softball, swimming, track and field, volleyball, fencing
Clubs Model UN, chess, film, garden, Turkish, French
Examinations ACT, IB, PSAT, SAT, ERB

CAMPUS FACILITIES

Location Suburban
Campus 8 hectares, 3 buildings, 23 classrooms, 2 computer labs, 53 instructional computers,

8,000 library volumes, 1 auditorium, 1 cafeteria, 1 gymnasium, 1 playing field, 3 science labs, air conditioning

Data from 2006/07 school year.

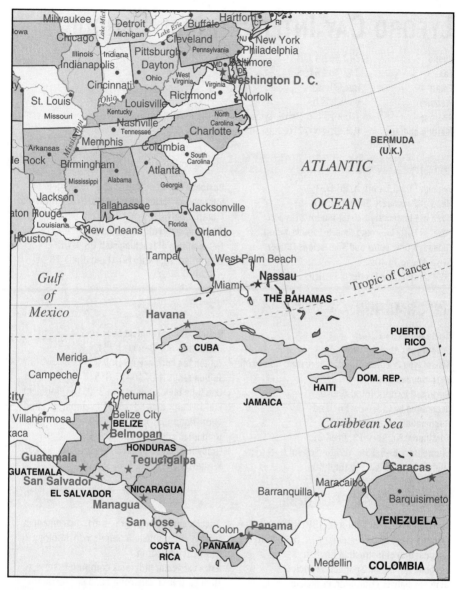

THE BAHAMAS

Area:	13,940 sq km
Population:	305,655
Capital:	Nassau
Currency:	Bahamian Dollar (BSD)
Languages:	English, Haitian

LYFORD CAY INTERNATIONAL SCHOOL

Phone	242 362 4774
Fax	242 362 5198
Email	info@lcis.bs
Website	www.lcis.bs
Address	1 Lyford Cay Drive, Lyford Cay, Nassau, The Bahamas
Mailing address	P.O. Box N-7776, Nassau, Bahamas

STAFF

Principal Paul Lieblich, Ed.D.
Head of Secondary School Kirti Joshi
Head of Elementary School Isadora Blyden
Head of Early Learning Centre Tamela Kemp
Guidance Counselor and Admissions Officer
Rose-Marie Taylor
MYP Coordinator Frederic Bournas

Business Manager Bathsheba Fernander
Information Technology Director Scott Gutowski
Librarian Lily Padykula
Teaching staff Full time 29; Part time 11; Total 40
Nationalities of teaching staff US 9; UK 5;
Bahamian 10; Other(s) (Canadian) 16

INFORMATION

Grade levels N–12
School year August–June
School type coeducational, day, private non-profit
Year founded 1960
Governed by appointed Board
Accredited by CIS, New England
Regional organizations ECIS
Enrollment Nursery 18; PreK 22;
Elementary K–5 154; Middle School 6–8 65;
High School 9–12 46; Total 305

Nationalities of student body US 25; UK 9;
Bahamian 40; Other(s) 231
Tuition/fee currency US Dollar
Tuition range 11,730–17,855
One time fees Registration 250; Development
Fund (Bahamian) 1,250; Development Fund
(non-Bahamian) 3,500
Graduates attending college 85%
Graduates have attended Brock U, Acadia U,
Western U, Trent U, U of Miami

EDUCATIONAL PROGRAM

Curriculum Intl, IB Diploma, IBPYP, IBMYP
Average class size Elementary 14; Secondary 14
Language(s) of instruction English
Language(s) taught Spanish, French
Staff specialists computer, counselor, ESL,
learning disabilities, librarian, math resource,
reading resource

Special curricular programs art, instrumental
music, vocal music, computer/technology,
physical education
Extra curricular programs community service,
dance, drama, environmental conservation,
excursions/expeditions, yearbook
Sports baseball, basketball, cricket, soccer,
softball, swimming, track and field, volleyball
Clubs Bahamas Football Association, Swift Swim
Examinations IB, PSAT, SAT, ERB

CAMPUS FACILITIES

Location Rural
Campus 10 hectares, 7 buildings, 27 classrooms,
1 computer lab, 250 instructional computers,

9,500 library volumes, 1 cafeteria, 1 covered
play area, 3 playing fields, 1 science lab,
1 pool, air conditioning

St. Andrew's School, The International School of The Bahamas

Phone	242 324 2621
Fax	242 324 0816
Email	BWade@st-andrews.com
Website	www.st-andrews.com
Address	PO Box EE 17340, Yamacraw Hill Road, Nassau, New Providence, EE 17340, The Bahamas

STAFF

Principal and CEO Robert F. Wade
Head of the Primary School Allison Collie
Head of the Secondary School Frank Coyle
Business Manager Marcus W. Moss

Chair of IT and Libraries Dept Mark Henderson
Secondary School Teacher and Librarian Jennifer Taylor

INFORMATION

Grade levels N–12
School year August–June
School type coeducational, day, private non-profit
Year founded 1948
Governed by elected Board
Accredited by CIS, New England
Regional organizations ECIS

Tuition/fee currency Bahamanian Dollar
Tuition range 4,605–11,815
Annual fees Yearbook 50
One time fees Registration 500; Capital Levy 2,000; Admission and testing 500
Graduates attending college 98%
Graduates have attended Yale U, Harvard U, Vassar Col, McGill U, Tufts U

EDUCATIONAL PROGRAM

Curriculum National, Intl, IB Diploma, IBPYP, BGCSE–Years 10, 11
Average class size Elementary 19; Secondary 19
Language(s) of instruction English
Language(s) taught Spanish, French
Staff specialists computer, learning disabilities, librarian, nurse

Special curricular programs art, instrumental music, vocal music, physical education, drama
Extra curricular programs community service, yearbook
Sports basketball, soccer, softball, swimming, volleyball
Examinations GCSE, IB, IGCSE, PSAT, SAT, SAT II

CAMPUS FACILITIES

Location Suburban
Campus 15 hectares, 10 buildings, 48 classrooms, 5 computer labs, 300 instructional computers, 16,000 library volumes, 1 auditorium, 1 cafeteria, 1 infirmary, 2 playing fields, 6 science labs, 1 pool, 2 tennis courts, air conditioning

BAHRAIN

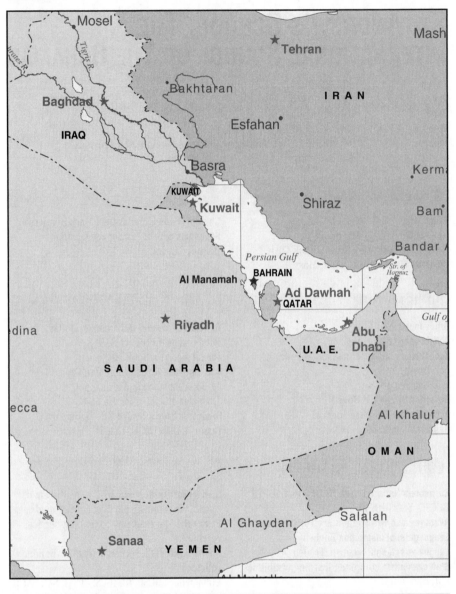

BAHRAIN

Area:	665 sq km
Population:	708,573
Capital:	Manama
Currency:	Bahraini Dinar (BHD)
Languages:	Arabic, English

BAHRAIN BAYAN SCHOOL

Phone	973 17 682 227
Fax	973 17 780 019
Email	bayanschool@bayan.edu.bh
Website	www.bayanschool.edu.bh
Address	Building No 230, Road 4111, Block No 841, Isa Town, Bahrain
Mailing address	PO Box 32411, Isa Town, Bahrain

STAFF

Director General Youssef Korfali
Primary School Principal Dorothy Loveland
Secondary Principal Ollis Miller, Ed.D.
Curriculum Coordinator Bridget Doogan
IB Coordinator and Assistant Principal Majdi Al Hajj
Secondary School Dean of Students Alan Morley

Business Office Manager Samar Nabhan
Network System Manager Saleh Al Shehabi
Librarian and Resource Specialist Norma Kashouh
Teaching staff Full time 88; Total 88
Nationalities of teaching staff US 12; UK 4;
Bahraini 32; Other(s) (Canadian, Australian) 40

INFORMATION

Grade levels N–12
School year September–June
School type coeducational, day, private non-profit
Year founded 1982
Governed by elected Board of Directors
Accredited by Middle States
Regional organizations ECIS, NESA
Enrollment Nursery 48; PreK 145;
Elementary K–5 364; Middle School 6–8 217;
High School 9–12 301; Total 1,075

Nationalities of student body US 11; Bahraini 986;
Other(s) (Saudi, Omani) 78
Tuition/fee currency Bahraini Dinar
Tuition range 1,285–2,625
Annual fees Books 40
One time fees Registration 200; Capital Levy 400;
Application 30
Graduates attending college 100%
Graduates have attended Harvard U, Tampa U,
Massachusetts Institute of Art, McGill U,
British Columbia U

EDUCATIONAL PROGRAM

Curriculum Intl, IB Diploma
Average class size Elementary 25; Secondary 25
Language(s) of instruction English
Language(s) taught Arabic
Staff specialists computer, counselor, learning
disabilities, librarian, nurse, reading resource
Special curricular programs art

Extra curricular programs computers, community
service, drama, environmental conservation,
excursions/expeditions, literary magazine,
newspaper, yearbook
Sports badminton, basketball, football, soccer,
squash, tennis, track and field, volleyball
Clubs Model UN, Trade Quest, Roots and
Shoots, globe
Examinations IB, PSAT, SAT, SAT II, TOEFL

CAMPUS FACILITIES

Location Suburban
Campus 1 hectare, 9 buildings, 78 classrooms,
4 computer labs, 141 instructional computers,

31,069 library volumes, 1 tennis court,
air conditioning

IBN KHULDOON NATIONAL SCHOOL

Phone	973 17 780 661
Fax	973 17 689 028
Email	staffing@ikns.edu.bh
Website	www.ikns.edu.bh
Address	Road 4111, Area 841, Isa Town Education Area, Isa Town, Bahrain
Mailing address	PO Box 20511, Manama, Kingdom of Bahrain

STAFF

President Samir J. Chammaa
Elementary School Principal Ghada Bou Zeineddine
Middle School Principal Douglas Joy
Secondary School Principal Chaouki Barake
Curriculum Coordinator George Rizkallah
Director of Human Resources Sandra Joy
Business Manager Hassan Radhi

Network Administrators Karima Matrook and Leslie Badalkar
Librarians Susan Gray and Taghreed Quti
Teaching staff Full time 150; Total 150
Nationalities of teaching staff US 13; UK 1; Bahraini 45; Other(s) (Lebanese) 91

INFORMATION

Grade levels PreK–12
School year September–June
School type coeducational, day, private non-profit
Year founded 1983
Governed by appointed Board
Accredited by Middle States
Regional organizations NESA
Enrollment PreK 98; Elementary K–5 611; Middle School 6–8 344; High School 9–12 434; Total 1,487

Nationalities of student body Bahraini 1,215; Other(s) (Lebanese) 272
Tuition/fee currency US Dollar
Tuition range 4,040–7,218
Annual fees Capital Levy 530; Busing 930; Lunch 185
One time fees Registration 265
Graduates attending college 98%
Graduates have attended Georgetown U, U of Pennsylvania, U of Miami, U College London, U of Warwick

EDUCATIONAL PROGRAM

Curriculum US, National, IB Diploma
Average class size Elementary 20; Secondary 20
Language(s) of instruction English, Arabic
Language(s) taught French
Staff specialists computer, counselor, librarian, nurse, speech/hearing
Special curricular programs art, vocal music, computer/technology, physical education

Extra curricular programs computers, community service, drama, environmental conservation, literary magazine, newspaper, yearbook
Sports badminton, basketball, cross-country, soccer, softball, tennis, track and field, volleyball
Clubs Heritage, Animal Lovers, debating, Community Caring, newspaper, Healthy Buddies
Examinations IB, PSAT, SAT, SAT II, TOEFL

CAMPUS FACILITIES

Location Suburban
Campus 5 hectares, 8 buildings, 150 classrooms, 6 computer labs, 300 instructional computers, 52,000 library volumes, 1 cafeteria, 3 covered play areas, 3 gymnasiums, 2 infirmaries, 4 playing fields, 6 science labs, 2 tennis courts, air conditioning

NASEEM INTERNATIONAL SCHOOL

Phone	973 17683 683
Fax	973 17687 166
Email	naseem@batelco.com.bh
Website	www.naseemschool.com.bh
Address	Muharraq Avenue, PO Box 28503, Bldg. 30, Road 18, Muharraq Ave. Riffa 922, Riffa, Bahrain

STAFF

President and Director Sameera A.J. Al-Kooheji
Director of Studies Christopher Connellan
Elementary School Principal Patricia Berry
Middle and High School Principal Bilal Okasha
IB Coordinator Fuad Prins

Accountant Anil Kumar
Head of IT Ameer Ali
Librarian Fawzia Bastaki
Teaching staff Full time 62; Total 62

INFORMATION

Grade levels N–12
School year September–June
School type coeducational, day
Year founded 1981
Governed by appointed Advisory Board
Accredited by Middle States
Regional organizations ECIS, NESA
Enrollment Nursery 12; PreK 46;
Elementary K–5 212; Middle School 6–8 175;
High School 9–12 363; Total 808

Tuition/fee currency Bahraini Dinar
Tuition range 1,240–2,440
One time fees Registration 200; Application and testing 30
Graduates attending college 100%
Graduates have attended U of Bahrain, McGill U, Montreal U, Royal Col of Surgeons, Bristol U

EDUCATIONAL PROGRAM

Curriculum US, National, Intl, IB Diploma, IBPYP, IBMYP
Average class size Elementary 20; Secondary 25
Language(s) of instruction English, Arabic
Staff specialists computer, counselor, ESL, librarian, nurse, reading resource

Special curricular programs art, instrumental music, vocal music, physical education
Extra curricular programs community service, excursions/expeditions, yearbook
Sports basketball, cross-country, football, track and field, volleyball
Examinations IB, SAT, TOEFL

CAMPUS FACILITIES

Location Suburban
Campus 4 hectares, 4 buildings, 58 classrooms, 3 computer labs, 75 instructional computers,

36,000 library volumes, 1 tennis court, air conditioning

BANGLADESH

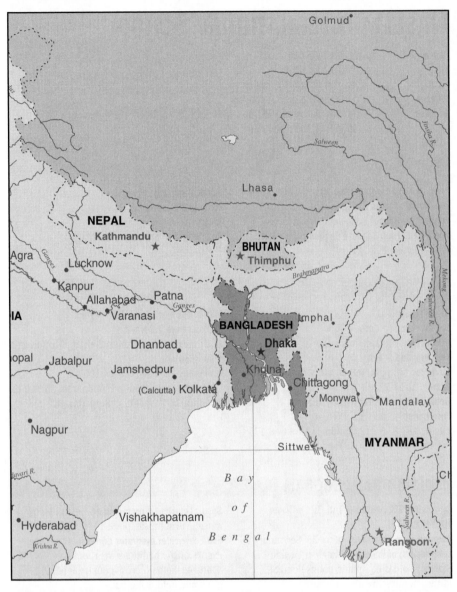

BANGLADESH

Area:	144,000 sq km
Population:	150,448,339
Capital:	Dhaka
Currency:	Taka (BDT)
Languages:	Bangla, English

CHITTAGONG GRAMMAR SCHOOL

Phone	880 31 622 472
Fax	880 31 632 001
Email	cgs.upper@gmail.com
Website	www.chittagonggrammarschool.com
Address	321/11 Sarson Road, Chittagong, Bangladesh

STAFF

Head of Upper School Mahine Khan
Academic Director Shereen Ispahani, Ed.D.
Director of Development Bilquis Dada
Head of Middle School Farida Chowdhury
Head of Lower School Munira Chowdhury
Head of Administration, Upper School Loretta Dias

Finance Director Farhat Khan
Head of IT Jalaluddin
Head of Library Philip Clump
Teaching staff Full time 265; Part time 7; Total 272
Nationalities of teaching staff UK 1;
Bangladeshi 232; Other(s) (Indian) 39

INFORMATION

Grade levels N–12
School year August–June
School type coeducational, day
Year founded 1992
Governed by appointed Board of Directors
Enrollment Nursery 124; PreK 124;
Elementary K–5 753; Middle School 6–8 291;
High School 9–12 165; Total 1,457
Nationalities of student body US 3; UK 15;
Bangladeshi 1,366; Other(s) (Sri Lankan, Korean) 73

Tuition/fee currency Bangladeshi Taka
Tuition range 72,000–114,000
Annual fees Lunch 10,000; Books 6,500
One time fees Registration 30,000
Graduates attending college 100%
Graduates have attended Havard U, Oxford U, Cambridge U, Bristol U, London School of Economics

EDUCATIONAL PROGRAM

Curriculum UK, CIPP (Cambridge International Primary Programme)
Average class size Elementary 20; Secondary 18
Language(s) of instruction English
Language(s) taught Bengali, French, Hindi
Staff specialists computer, counselor, ESL, librarian, math resource, reading resource
Special curricular programs art, instrumental music, vocal music, computer/technology, physical education, Christian studies, Islamic studies, debating, elocution, general knowledge
Extra curricular programs computers, community service, dance, drama, environmental conservation, excursions/expeditions, literary magazine, newspaper, photography, yearbook, arts and crafts, chess, embroidery, Bengali dance and music
Sports badminton, basketball, cricket, football, martial arts, soccer, swimming, track and field, volleyball, table tennis, aerobics, fitness training, Karate, yoga, Tae Kwon Do
Clubs science, publishing, youth, Boy Scouts, Girl Guides, Bengali Society, Young Readers, Nature Society, book
Examinations A-level GCE, GCSE, PSAT, SAT, SAT II, Cambridge Checkpoint, CIPP

CAMPUS FACILITIES

Location Urban
Campus 3 hectares, 5 buildings, 96 classrooms, 6 computer labs, 182 instructional computers, 37,000 library volumes, 1 auditorium, 2 cafeterias, 2 covered play areas, 4 gymnasiums, 5 playing fields, 4 science labs, air conditioning

AMERICAN INTERNATIONAL SCHOOL/DHAKA

Phone	880 2 882 2452
Fax	880 2 882 3175
Email	info@ais-dhaka.net
Website	www.ais-dhaka.net
Address	12 United Nations Road, Baridhara, Dhaka, 1212, Bangladesh
Mailing address	PO Box 6106, Gulshan, Dhaka 1212, Bangladesh

STAFF

Superintendent Walter Plotkin
Elementary School Principal Caroline Jacoby
Middle School Principal Tom Pado
High School Principal Brian Brumsickle
Assistant Principal Peter Janda
Chief Accountant Raquibul Husain

Technology Coordinator Drew Cover
Middle and High School Librarian Judyth Lessee
Teaching staff Full time 82; Part time 4; Total 86
Nationalities of teaching staff US 80; UK 1;
Bangladeshi 2; Other(s) (Australian, Korean) 3

INFORMATION

Grade levels PreK–12
School year August–June
School type coeducational, day, private non-profit
Year founded 1972
Governed by elected School Board
Accredited by CIS, New England
Regional organizations NESA
Enrollment PreK 48; Elementary K–5 284;
Middle School 6–8 147; High School 9–12 187;
Total 666

Nationalities of student body US 148; UK 61;
Bangladeshi 71; Other(s) (Korean, Indian) 386
Tuition/fee currency US Dollar
Tuition range 4,940–17,290
One time fees Registration 3,450; Capital Levy
1,000; Admissions 50
Graduates attending college 95%
Graduates have attended Bard Col, Bryn Mawr Col,
Haverford Col, Col of William and Mary,
Macalester Col

EDUCATIONAL PROGRAM

Curriculum US, Intl, AP, IB Diploma
Average class size Elementary 15; Secondary 15
Language(s) of instruction English
Language(s) taught French, Spanish
Staff specialists computer, counselor, ESL,
learning disabilities, librarian, nurse, physician,
reading resource
Special curricular programs art, instrumental
music, vocal music, computer/technology,
physical education, Senior Project

Extra curricular programs computers, community
service, drama, excursions/expeditions, literary
magazine, photography, yearbook, Habitat for
Humanity, Model UN, Boy and Girl Scouts
Sports basketball, cricket, football, soccer,
swimming, tennis, track and field, volleyball
Clubs Amnesty International, National Honor
Society, French Honor Society, Spanish Honor
Society, Student Council, debate, service
Examinations ACT, IB, PSAT, SAT

CAMPUS FACILITIES

Location Suburban
Campus 2 hectares, 4 buildings, 70 classrooms,
4 computer labs, 450 instructional computers,
25,000 library volumes, 1 auditorium, 1 cafeteria,

1 covered play area, 4 gymnasiums,
1 infirmary, 1 playing field, 6 science labs,
1 pool, air conditioning

INTERNATIONAL SCHOOL DHAKA

Phone	880 2 881 7101
Fax	880 2 988 3622
Email	info@isdbd.org
Website	www.isdbd.org
Address	Plot 80, Block E, Basundhara R/A, Dhaka, 1229, Bangladesh
Mailing address	c/o CIS, Dhaka Bag, 21 Lavant Street, Petersfield, Hants GU32 3EL, UK

STAFF

Director Stephen Murray
Secondary Principal Ross Hall
Primary Principal Paula Baxter
MYP Coordinator Liz Carrick
PYP Coordinator Kate Grant
DP Coordinator Steve Robson
Business Manager Sayed M. Babar

Technology Coordinator Richard Hawkins
Librarian Catherine DeLevay
Teaching staff Full time 68; Total 68
Nationalities of teaching staff US 5; UK 14; Bangladeshi 7; Other(s) (Australian, Canadian) 42

INFORMATION

Grade levels N–12
School year August–June
School type coeducational, day, proprietary
Year founded 1999
Governed by appointed Board
Sponsored by STS Educational Group
Accredited by CIS, New England
Enrollment Nursery 45; PreK 30; Elementary K–5 236; Middle School 6–8 129; High School 9–12 166; Total 606

Nationalities of student body US 51; UK 20; Bangladeshi 408; Other(s) (Indian, Sri Lankan) 127
Tuition/fee currency US Dollar
Tuition range 1,880–12,240
Annual fees Lunch 690; Annual (Kg –5) 630; Annual (6 –12) 890
One time fees Registration 100; Capital Levy 2,500
Graduates attending college 90%
Graduates have attended McGill U, U College of London, U of Toronto, Bard Col, U of Sussex

EDUCATIONAL PROGRAM

Curriculum Intl, IB Diploma, IBPYP, IBMYP
Average class size Elementary 20; Secondary 23
Language(s) of instruction English
Language(s) taught French, Bangla, Spanish
Staff specialists computer, counselor, ESL, learning disabilities, librarian, math resource, physician, reading resource
Special curricular programs art, instrumental music, computer/technology, physical education

Extra curricular programs computers, community service, drama, environmental conservation, excursions/expeditions, newspaper, yearbook, debating
Sports badminton, basketball, cricket, soccer, swimming, tennis, track and field, volleyball
Clubs Roots and Shoots, International Award, Model UN, school magazine, yearbook
Examinations IB, PSAT, SAT, SAT II, TOEFL, ACER ISA

CAMPUS FACILITIES

Location Urban
Campus 3.6 hectares, 6 buildings, 82 classrooms, 2 computer labs, 150 instructional computers, 22,000 library volumes, 1 auditorium,

1 cafeteria, 3 covered play areas, 1 gymnasium, 1 infirmary, 1 playing field, 4 science labs, 1 pool, 2 tennis courts, air conditioning

BELARUS

BELARUS

Area:	207,600 sq km
Population:	9,724,723
Capital:	Minsk
Currency:	Belarusian Ruble (BYB/BYR)
Languages:	Belarusian, Russian

INTERNATIONAL SCHOOL

Phone	375 17 234 3035
Fax	375 17 234 3035
Email	mis@open.by
Website	www.qsi.org
Address	Kropotkeena Str. 74, Minsk, 220002, Belarus
Mailing address	c/o American Embassy, Minsk, Dept. of State, 7010 Minsk Place, Washington, DC 20521-7010, USA

STAFF

Director Daniel Waterman
Teaching staff Full time 6; Part time 4; Total 10

Nationalities of teaching staff Belarusian 8; Other(s) (Canadian) 2

INFORMATION

Grade levels PreK–10
School year September–June
School type coeducational, day, private non-profit
Year founded 1993
Governed by appointed Board of Directors
Regional organizations CEESA

Enrollment PreK 4; Elementary K–5 13; Middle School 6–8 3; Total 20
Nationalities of student body US 3; Other(s) (German, Swede) 17
Tuition/fee currency US Dollar
Graduates attending college 100%

EDUCATIONAL PROGRAM

Curriculum US
Average class size Elementary 4; Secondary 2
Language(s) of instruction English
Language(s) taught Russian

Special curricular programs art, vocal music, computer/technology, physical education
Extra curricular programs computers, drama
Examinations Iowa

CAMPUS FACILITIES

Location Urban
Campus 1 building, 6 classrooms, 1 computer lab,

10 instructional computers, 3,600 library volumes, 1 auditorium, 1 gymnasium, 1 pool

BELGIUM

BELGIUM

Area:	30,528 sq km
Population:	10,392,226
Capital:	Brussels
Currency:	Euro (EUR)
Languages:	Dutch, French, German

ANTWERP INTERNATIONAL SCHOOL, VZW

Phone	32 3 543 93 00
Fax	32 3 541 82 01
Email	ais@ais-antwerp.be
Website	www.ais-antwerp.be
Address	Veltwijcklaan 180, Ekeren, 2180, Belgium

STAFF

Head of School Thomas Walters
Elementary School Principal Matthew Cox
Middle and High School Principal Stephen Petra
Business Administrator Patrick De Ceuster, Ed.D.
IT Coordinator Paul Candler

Librarian Barbara Noels
Teaching staff Full time 42; Part time 15; Total 57
Nationalities of teaching staff US 18; UK 16;
Belgian 11; Other(s) (Dutch, Canadian) 12

INFORMATION

Grade levels N–12
School year August–June
School type coeducational, day, private non-profit
Year founded 1967
Governed by appointed Board of Directors
Accredited by CIS, New England
Regional organizations ECIS
Enrollment Nursery 16; PreK 25;
Elementary K–5 187; Middle School 6–8 141;
High School 9–12 169; Total 538

Nationalities of student body US 75; UK 52;
Belgian 100; Other(s) (Indian, German) 311
Tuition/fee currency Euro
Tuition range 6,830–22,150
Annual fees Capital Levy 525; Busing 2,665
One time fees Registration 1,000
Graduates attending college 90%
Graduates have attended Columbia U,
Northwestern U, Cornell U, Occidental Col,
Michigan State U

EDUCATIONAL PROGRAM

Curriculum Intl, IB Diploma
Average class size Elementary 18; Secondary 18
Language(s) of instruction English

Language(s) taught French, Dutch, German,
Spanish

CAMPUS FACILITIES

Location Suburban
Campus 3 hectares, 6 buildings, 35 classrooms,
2 computer labs, 150 instructional computers,

10,000 library volumes, 1 auditorium,
2 cafeterias, 3 gymnasiums, 1 infirmary,
2 playing fields, 4 science labs, 1 tennis court

BEPS BRUSSELS

Phone	32 2 648 4311
Fax	32 2 646 1653
Email	info@beps.com
Website	www.beps.com
Address	23 Avenue Franklin Roosevelt, Brussels, 1050, Belgium

STAFF

Director Charles A. Gellar
Head of School Nicola Claire
Business/Finance Manager Poul Beck Sorensen

Teaching staff Full time 28; Part time 5; Total 33
Nationalities of teaching staff US 1; UK 20; Belgian 5; Other(s) 7

INFORMATION

Grade levels N–5
School year September–June
School type coeducational, day, proprietary
Year founded 1972
Governed by appointed Director
Regional organizations ECIS
Enrollment Nursery 50; PreK 36; Elementary K–5 145; Total 231

Nationalities of student body US 10; UK 50; Belgian 50; Other(s) 121
Tuition/fee currency Euro
Tuition range 7,800–17,900
Annual fees Busing 2,900
One time fees Registration 500; Capital Levy 500; Deposit 800

EDUCATIONAL PROGRAM

Curriculum Intl, IBPYP
Average class size Elementary 16
Language(s) of instruction English

Language(s) taught French
Staff specialists computer, ESL, librarian

CAMPUS FACILITIES

Location Urban
Campus 6 hectares, 2 buildings, 20 classrooms, 1 computer lab, 20 instructional computers,

9,000 library volumes, 1 covered play area, 1 gymnasium, 1 playing field

BEPS–WATERLOO

Phone	32 2 358 5606
Fax	32 2 358 3132
Email	waterloo@beps.com
Website	www.beps.com
Address	280 Chaussee de Waterloo, Rhode St. Genese, 1640, Belgium

STAFF

Director Charles A. Gellar
Head of School Henny de Waal
Business/Finance Manager Poul Beck Sorensen

Teaching staff Full time 5; Part time 5; Total 10
Nationalities of teaching staff UK 3; Caymanian 3; Other(s) 4

INFORMATION

Grade levels N–5
School year September–June
School type coeducational, day, proprietary
Year founded 1999
Governed by appointed Director
Regional organizations ECIS
Enrollment Nursery 8; PreK 16; Elementary K–5 40; Total 64

Nationalities of student body US 4; UK 8; Host 11; Other(s) 37
Tuition/fee currency Euro
Tuition range 7,800–17,900
One time fees Registration 500; Capital Levy 500; Deposit 800

EDUCATIONAL PROGRAM

Curriculum Intl
Average class size Elementary 12

Language(s) of instruction English
Language(s) taught French

CAMPUS FACILITIES

Location Suburban
Campus 8 hectares, 12 classrooms, 1 computer lab, 15 instructional computers,

3,000 library volumes, 1 covered play area, 1 gymnasium, 1 science lab

THE BRITISH INTERNATIONAL SCHOOL OF BRUSSELS

Phone	32 2 736 8981
Fax	32 2 736 8983
Email	schooloffice@bisb.org
Website	www.bisb.org
Address	163 Avenue Emile Max, B-1030, Brussels, Belgium

STAFF

Head Teacher Stephen Prescott
Deputy Head Sarah Barlow
Teaching staff Full time 11; Part time 3; Total 14

Nationalities of teaching staff US 2; UK 5;
Other(s) (Australian, Canadian) 7

INFORMATION

Grade levels N–5
School year September–July
School type coeducational, day, proprietary
Year founded 2000
Governed by elected Board
Regional organizations ECIS
Enrollment Nursery 18; PreK 18;
Elementary K–5 65; Total 101

Nationalities of student body US 10; UK 30;
Belgian 10; Other(s) (Indian, Japanese) 51
Tuition/fee currency Euro
Tuition range 10,450–13,000
Annual fees Busing 2,800
One time fees Registration 500

EDUCATIONAL PROGRAM

Curriculum UK
Average class size Elementary 16
Language(s) of instruction English
Language(s) taught French
Staff specialists ESL

Extra curricular programs dance, excursions/
expeditions
Sports hockey, martial arts, soccer
Clubs computers, puppet making, drama,
needlework, soccer, jazz ballet, touch typing

CAMPUS FACILITIES

Location Urban
Campus 1 hectare, 1 building, 6 classrooms,

1 computer lab, 24 instructional computers,
3,000 library volumes, air conditioning

THE INTERNATIONAL SCHOOL OF BRUSSELS

Phone	32 2 661 4211
Fax	32 2 661 4200
Email	admissions@isb.be
Website	www.isb.be
Address	Kattenberg 19, Brussels, 1170, Belgium

STAFF

Director Kevin Bartlett
Head of Early Childhood Center Caroline Nu'u
Head of Elementary School Anna Zeiders
Head of Middle School Michael Crowley, Ph.D.
Head of High School Ellen Lawsky
Finance Director Francis Trappeniers

Director of Technology Doug Stone
Librarians Katie Basha and Jeffrey Brewster
Teaching staff Full time 160; Part time 41; Total 201
Nationalities of teaching staff US 62; UK 30; Belgian 47; Other(s) (Canadian) 62

INFORMATION

Grade levels N–13
School year August–June
School type coeducational, day
Year founded 1951
Governed by appointed Board of Trustees
Accredited by CIS, Middle States
Regional organizations ECIS
Enrollment Nursery 36; PreK 40; Elementary K–5 512; Middle School 6–8 349; High School 9–12 472; Grade 13 5; Total 1,414

Nationalities of student body US 396; UK 92; Belgian 98; Other(s) (Japanese, Dutch) 828
Tuition/fee currency Euro
Tuition range 11,400–25,000
Annual fees Busing 2,100
One time fees Registration 1,000
Graduates attending college 98%
Graduates have attended Imperial Col, Harvard Col, Boston U, Queen's U, Maastricht U

EDUCATIONAL PROGRAM

Curriculum US, Intl, AP, IB Diploma
Average class size Elementary 22; Secondary 18
Language(s) of instruction English
Language(s) taught Dutch, French, German, Spanish
Staff specialists computer, counselor, ESL, learning disabilities, librarian, nurse, psychologist
Special curricular programs art, instrumental music, vocal music, computer/technology, physical education

Extra curricular programs computers, dance, drama, environmental conservation, literary magazine, newspaper, photography, yearbook
Sports badminton, baseball, basketball, cross-country, football, golf, hockey, soccer, softball, swimming, tennis, track and field, volleyball
Examinations AP, IB, PSAT, SAT, SAT II, TOEFL, AP International

CAMPUS FACILITIES

Location Rural
Campus 40 hectares, 7 buildings, 110 classrooms, 11 computer labs, 947 instructional computers, 56,000 library volumes, 1 auditorium,

3 cafeterias, 2 gymnasiums, 1 infirmary, 3 playing fields, 10 science labs, 2 tennis courts

St Paul's British Primary School

Phone	32 2 767 3098
Fax	32 2 767 0351
Email	info@britishprimary.com
Website	www.britishprimary.com
Address	Stationsstraat 3, Vossem, Tervuren, 3080, Belgium

STAFF

Headteacher Katie Tyrie
Bursar Roger Morgan
Admissions Director Chris Start
Administrator Angela Phanopoulos

Librarian Lynda Skinner
Teaching staff Full time 5; Part time 7; Total 12
Nationalities of teaching staff UK 11; Other(s) (Canadian) 1

INFORMATION

Grade levels N–5
School year September–July
School type coeducational, church-affiliated, day, proprietary
Year founded 1975
Governed by appointed Board of Directors
Sponsored by St Paul's Anglican Church, Tervuren, Belgium

Regional organizations ECIS
Enrollment Nursery 20; PreK 15; Elementary K–5 40; Total 75
Nationalities of student body US 12; UK 38; Other(s) (German, Italian) 25
Tuition/fee currency Euro
Tuition range 6,050–16,500
One time fees Registration 600

EDUCATIONAL PROGRAM

Curriculum UK
Average class size Elementary 15

Language(s) of instruction English
Language(s) taught French

CAMPUS FACILITIES

Location Suburban
Campus 2 buildings, 8 classrooms, 1 computer lab, 25 instructional computers, 1 playing field

St. John's International School

Phone	32 2 352 0610
Fax	32 2 352 0630
Email	Admissions@stjohns.be
Website	www.stjohns.be
Address	Drève Richelle 146, Waterloo, Brabant Walloon, 1410, Belgium

STAFF

Director Joseph H. Doenges, Ed.D.
High School Principal Nicholas Miller, Ph.D.
Middle School Principal Mandy Macleod
Elementary School Principal Johanna Bambridge
Director of Admissions Judith Hoskins
Director of Community Relations Marcia de Wolf
Business Manager Richard Katherman

Director of IT Jean-Louis Cornez
Librarian Veronica Cunningham
Teaching staff Full time 101; Part time 44; Total 145
Nationalities of teaching staff US 24; UK 46; Belgian 26; Other(s) (Irish, Dutch) 49

INFORMATION

Grade levels N–13
School year August–June
School type coeducational, church-affiliated, day, private non-profit
Year founded 1964
Governed by appointed Religious Congregation & Board
Accredited by CIS, Middle States
Regional organizations ECIS
Enrollment Nursery 20; PreK 40; Elementary K–5 340; Middle School 6–8 200; High School 9–12 298; Grade 13 2; Total 900

Nationalities of student body US 290; UK 110; Belgian 60; Other(s) (Swede, French) 440
Tuition/fee currency Euro
Tuition range 7,000–25,500
Annual fees Busing 2,350
One time fees Registration 1,000
Graduates attending college 95%
Graduates have attended Harvard U, Yale U, U of Cambridge, Oxford U, Massachusetts Institute of Technology

EDUCATIONAL PROGRAM

Curriculum US, AP, IB Diploma, IBPYP
Average class size Elementary 19; Secondary 19
Language(s) of instruction English
Language(s) taught French, German, Spanish, Dutch, Swedish
Staff specialists computer, counselor, ESL, learning disabilities, librarian, nurse, psychologist, reading resource

Special curricular programs art, instrumental music, vocal music, computer/technology, physical education
Extra curricular programs community service, dance, drama, excursions/expeditions, yearbook
Sports baseball, basketball, cross-country, golf, soccer, softball, swimming, tennis, track and field, volleyball
Clubs chess
Examinations ACT, AP, IB, Iowa, PSAT, SAT

CAMPUS FACILITIES

Location Suburban
Campus 7 hectares, 9 buildings, 50 classrooms, 5 computer labs, 280 instructional computers, 40,000 library volumes, 1 auditorium,

1 cafeteria, 1 covered play area, 3 gymnasiums, 1 infirmary, 3 playing fields, 7 science labs, 3 tennis courts

BERMUDA

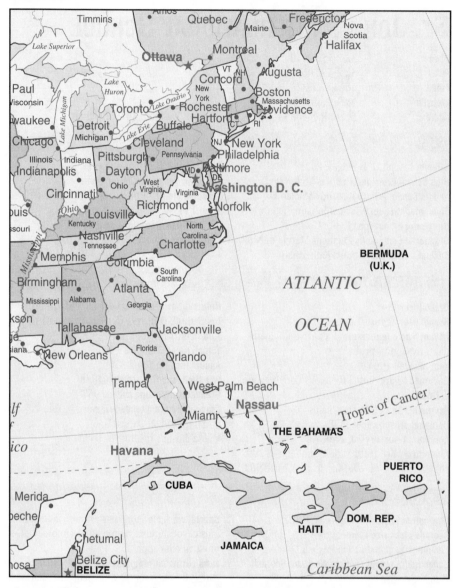

BERMUDA

Area:	53.3 sq km
Population:	66,163
Capital:	Hamilton
Currency:	Bermudian Dollar (BMD)
Languages:	English, Portuguese

BERMUDA INSTITUTE OF SEVENTH-DAY ADVENTISTS

Phone	441 238 1566
Fax	441 238 1309
Email	jansmith@bermudainstitute.bm
Website	www.bermudainstitute.bm
Address	234 Middle Road, Southampton, SN 04, Bermuda
Mailing address	PO Box SN 114, Southampton, Bermuda SN BX

STAFF

Superintendent Sheila V. Holder
Principal Lois Tucker, Ed.D.
Registrar/Vice Principal Kathleen Wilson-Allers
Vice Principal Gregory Outerbridge

Development Officer/Public Relations
Frigga Simmons
Business Manager Tanya Dickinson
Librarian Janet King

INFORMATION

Grade levels K–12
School year August–June
School type coeducational, church-affiliated, day, private non-profit
Year founded 1947
Governed by appointed School Board
Sponsored by Bermuda Conference of S.D.A.
Enrollment Elementary K–5 118; Middle School 6–8 114; High School 9–12 139; Total 371
Nationalities of student body US 6; UK 2;

Bermudian 349; Other(s) 14
Tuition/fee currency Bermudian Dollar
Tuition range 8,580–9,000
Annual fees Registration 30; Books 600; Graduation 8 & 12 100; Band Instrument 50; Choir Robe Rental 25
Graduates attending college 95%
Graduates have attended Bermuda Col, Oakwood Col, Atlantic Union Col, Andrews U, Columbia Union Col

EDUCATIONAL PROGRAM

Curriculum US
Average class size Elementary 15; Secondary 17
Language(s) of instruction English
Language(s) taught Spanish
Staff specialists computer, counselor, learning disabilities, librarian, math resource, reading resource
Special curricular programs art, instrumental music, vocal music, computer/technology, physical education, vocational, family studies, speech & debate, literary analysis, cooking, international relations

Extra curricular programs computers, community service, drama, excursions/expeditions, newspaper, photography, yearbook, campus beautification, standarized test preparation
Sports badminton, basketball, cricket, cross-country, golf, hockey, soccer, softball, swimming, track and field, volleyball, soccer
Clubs student association, Science, Spanish, drama
Examinations ACT, Iowa, PSAT, SAT, TOEFL

CAMPUS FACILITIES

Location Suburban
Campus 1 hectare, 5 buildings, 25 classrooms, 2 computer labs, 55 instructional computers,

12,700 library volumes, 1 auditorium, 1 cafeteria, 1 gymnasium, 1 infirmary, 2 playing fields, 3 science labs, air conditioning

Data from 2006/07 school year.

BOLIVIA

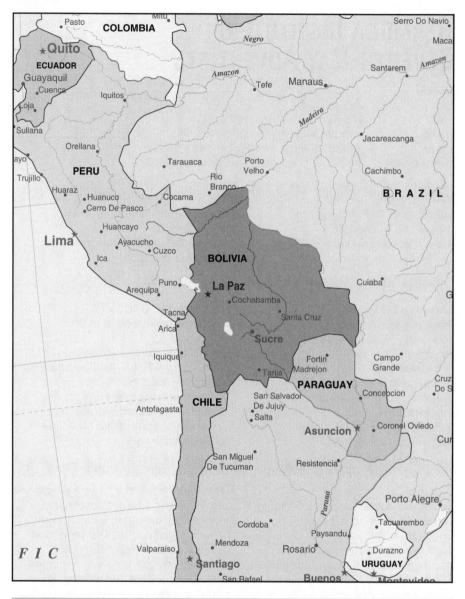

BOLIVIA

Area:	1,098,580 sq km
Population:	9,119,152
Capital:	La Paz
Currency:	Boliviano (BOB)
Languages:	Spanish

THE AMERICAN INTERNATIONAL SCHOOL OF BOLIVIA

Phone 591 442 88577
Fax 591 442 88576
Email admin@aisb.edu.bo
Website www.aisb.edu.bo
Address Av. Ecologica Km. 1 1/2, Zona Linde-Tiquipaya, Cochabamba, Bolivia
Mailing address PO Box 5309, Cochabamba, Bolivia

STAFF

Director General Silke Marina Schöler, Ph.D.
Secondary Coordinator Paola Villarroel
Elementary Coordinator Patricia Valderrama
Curriculum Coordinator Jim Jansen
Discipline Coordinator Augustine Corcoran
Director of Finances Tatiana Jimenez

Computer Technology Edwin Velasco
Library Coordinator Jorge Sejas
Teaching staff Full time 25; Part time 5; Total 30
Nationalities of teaching staff US 4; Bolivian 16; Other(s) (German, Argentine) 10

INFORMATION

Grade levels PreK–12
School year August–June
School type coeducational, day, private non-profit
Year founded 1993
Governed by appointed Board of Directors
Accredited by Southern
Regional organizations AASSA, ECIS
Enrollment PreK 15; Elementary K–5 120; Middle School 6–8 60; High School 9–12 80; Total 275

Nationalities of student body US 70; UK 5; Bolivian 100; Other(s) (Korean, Dutch) 100
Tuition/fee currency US Dollar
Tuition range 1,155–3,355
Annual fees Insurance 23; Busing 29; Yearbook 30
One time fees Registration 1,160; Senior Graduation 150
Graduates attending college 95%
Graduates have attended U of Pennsylvania, Bentley Col, U of North Florida, Suffolk U, Nova Southeastern U

EDUCATIONAL PROGRAM

Curriculum US, National, Intl, AP, IB Diploma
Average class size Elementary 20; Secondary 20

Language(s) of instruction English
Language(s) taught Spanish, French, German

CAMPUS FACILITIES

Location Urban
Campus 5 hectares, 9 buildings, 18 classrooms, 1 computer lab, 28 instructional computers, 15,000 library volumes, 1 auditorium,

1 cafeteria, 1 covered play area, 6 playing fields, 2 science labs, 1 pool, 1 tennis court, air conditioning

COCHABAMBA COOPERATIVE SCHOOL

Phone	591 4 4490 605
Fax	591 4 4490 609
Email	cbbacoopschool@yahoo.com
Website	www.ccs.edu.bo
Address	Av. Circunvalacion, Cochabamba, Bolivia
Mailing address	Casilla 1395, Cochabamba, Bolivia

STAFF

Director William Cattelle
Counseling Services Director Polly McFerren
Finance Manager Elizabeth Fiorilo

Teaching staff Full time 29; Part time 1; Total 30
Nationalities of teaching staff US 14; Bolivian 16

INFORMATION

Grade levels PreK–12
School year August–June
School type coeducational, day, proprietary
Year founded 1957
Governed by elected School Board
Accredited by Southern
Regional organizations AASSA
Enrollment PreK 24; Elementary K–5 162; Middle School 6–8 56; High School 9–12 72; Total 314

Nationalities of student body US 10; Bolivian 294; Other(s) (Chinese) 10
Tuition/fee currency US Dollar
Tuition range 900–3,180
Annual fees Capital Levy 78; Insurance 15
One time fees Registration 500
Graduates attending college 100%
Graduates have attended U of Pennsylvania, Brigham Young U, Emerson Col, Michigan State U, Tulane U

EDUCATIONAL PROGRAM

Curriculum US, National, AP
Average class size Elementary 15; Secondary 20
Language(s) of instruction English
Language(s) taught Spanish
Staff specialists computer, counselor, ESL, librarian

Special curricular programs art, vocal music, computer/technology, physical education
Extra curricular programs drama, yearbook
Sports basketball, soccer, track and field, volleyball
Clubs National Honor Society
Examinations Iowa, PSAT, SAT, SAT II

CAMPUS FACILITIES

Location Suburban
Campus 5 hectares, 10 buildings, 40 classrooms, 2 computer labs, 55 instructional computers,

15,000 library volumes, 1 auditorium, 1 cafeteria, 1 covered play area, 1 gymnasium, 3 playing fields, 1 science lab

AMERICAN COOPERATIVE SCHOOL

Phone	591 2 2792 302
Fax	591 2 2797 218
Email	acs@acslp.org
Website	www.acslp.org
Address	Calle 10 y Pasaje Kantutas, Calacoto, La Paz, Bolivia
Mailing address	c/o American Embassy, La Paz, Bolivia

STAFF

Superintendent and Secondary Principal Peter Zeitoun, Ph.D.
Elementary Principal Marcene Pareja
Middle School Coordinator Samuel McKibben
Elementary Counselor Jessica Delgado
Secondary Counselor Rachel Siegel

Business Manager Walter Pena
Head of Technology Marcelo Pacheco
Head of Library/Media Center Gaila Chambi
Teaching staff Full time 42; Part time 2; Total 44
Nationalities of teaching staff US 29; UK 1; Bolivian 14

INFORMATION

Grade levels PreK–12
School year August–May
School type coeducational, day, private non-profit
Year founded 1955
Governed by elected Board of Trustees
Accredited by Southern
Regional organizations AASSA
Enrollment PreK 8; Elementary K–5 160; Middle School 6–8 80; High School 9–12 152; Total 400

Nationalities of student body US 160; UK 5; Bolivian 155; Other(s) (Dutch, Peruvian) 80
Tuition/fee currency US Dollar
Tuition range 2,900–11,350
Annual fees Busing 500
One time fees Registration 10,000
Graduates attending college 100%
Graduates have attended Harvard U, American U, Yale U, Tufts U, U of Notre Dame

EDUCATIONAL PROGRAM

Curriculum US, AP, Bolivian Bachillerato
Average class size Elementary 15; Secondary 15
Language(s) of instruction English
Language(s) taught Spanish, French
Staff specialists computer, counselor, ESL, librarian, nurse
Special curricular programs art, instrumental music, vocal music, computer/technology, physical education

Extra curricular programs community service, drama, excursions/expeditions, newspaper, yearbook
Sports basketball, soccer, track and field, volleyball
Examinations AP, Iowa, PSAT, SAT, SAT II, TOEFL

CAMPUS FACILITIES

Location Rural
Campus 7 hectares, 9 buildings, 50 classrooms, 4 computer labs, 120 instructional computers, 24,000 library volumes, 2 auditoriums,

1 cafeteria, 1 covered play area, 1 gymnasium, 1 infirmary, 3 playing fields, 4 science labs, 1 pool, 2 tennis courts

SANTA CRUZ COOPERATIVE SCHOOL

Phone	591 3 3530 808
Fax	591 3 3526 993
Email	wmckelligott@sccs.edu.bo
Website	www.sccs.edu.bo
Address	Calle Barcelona #1, Barrio Las Palmas, Santa Cruz, Bolivia
Mailing address	Casilla 753, Calle Barcelona #1, Santa Cruz, Bolivia, South America

STAFF

Director William J. McKelligott
Elementary Principal Susan Zapata
Secondary Principal Cory Carson
Elementary Counselor Vanessa Krewiec
Secondary Counselor Michale Vande Loo
Learning Resource Specialist Valerie Kyllmann

Administrative/Finance Manager Patricia Vilela
Technology Coordinator Heath Kendro
Media Specialist/Librarian Josie Hannenman
Teaching staff Full time 51; Total 51
Nationalities of teaching staff US 32; Bolivian 14;
Other(s) 5

INFORMATION

Grade levels PreK–12
School year August–June
School type coeducational, day, private non-profit
Year founded 1959
Governed by elected Board of Directors
Accredited by Southern
Regional organizations AASSA
Enrollment PreK 36; Elementary K–5 243;
Middle School 6–8 110; High School 9–12 135;
Total 524

Nationalities of student body US 63; Bolivian
424; Other(s) 37
Tuition/fee currency US Dollar
Tuition range 2,668–4,987
Annual fees Insurance 25; Busing 336; Lunch 345;
Technology 100; Scholarship Fund 218
One time fees Capital Levy 6,000
Graduates attending college 99%
Graduates have attended Cornell U, U of Notre
Dame, Harvard U, Stanford U, U of Miami

EDUCATIONAL PROGRAM

Curriculum US, National, AP
Average class size Elementary 20; Secondary 23
Language(s) of instruction English, Spanish
Language(s) taught French
Staff specialists computer, counselor, ESL,
learning disabilities, librarian, physician,
psychologist
Special curricular programs art, instrumental
music, vocal music, computer/technology,
physical education

Extra curricular programs community service,
drama, excursions/expeditions, newspaper,
yearbook
Sports basketball, soccer, track and field,
volleyball
Clubs National Honor Society, student
goverment, Helping Hands, knowledge bowl,
science fair, senior projects
Examinations ACT, AP, Iowa, PSAT, SAT, SAT II,
TOEFL, ERB

CAMPUS FACILITIES

Location Urban
Campus 4 hectares, 6 buildings, 48 classrooms,
3 computer labs, 14125 instructional computers,

14,000 library volumes, 1 cafeteria, 3 covered
play areas, 1 gymnasium, 1 infirmary, 2 playing
fields, 4 science labs, air conditioning

BOSNIA AND HERZEGOVINA

Area:	51,129 sq km
Population:	4,552,198
Capital:	Sarajevo
Currency:	Konvertibilna Marka (convertible mark) (BAM)
Languages:	Bosnian, Croatian

QSI INTERNATIONAL SCHOOL OF SARAJEVO

Phone	387 33 424 450
Fax	387 33 424 450
Email	sarajevo@qsi.org
Website	www.qsi.org
Address	Omladinska #12, 71320 Vogosca, Sarajevo, Bosnia and Herzegovina

STAFF

Director Jay Hamric
Director of Instruction Reza Keivanzadeh
Business Manager Sladana Hrelja
Librarian Elvira Kajevic

Teaching staff Full time 20; Part time 4; Total 24
Nationalities of teaching staff US 14; UK 2; Bosnian 5; Other(s) (Canadian) 3

INFORMATION

Grade levels PreK–12
School year September–June
School type coeducational, day, private non-profit
Year founded 1997
Governed by appointed Board of Directors
Sponsored by Quality Schools International
Accredited by Middle States
Regional organizations CEESA
Enrollment PreK 15; Elementary K–5 85; Middle School 6–8 30; High School 9–12 15; Total 145

Nationalities of student body US 35; UK 10; Bosnian 15; Other(s) 85
Tuition/fee currency US Dollar
Tuition 14,100–14,100
Annual fees Busing 1,800; Lunch 600
One time fees Registration 100
Graduates attending college 100%
Graduates have attended Saint Mary's U, U of Stirling

EDUCATIONAL PROGRAM

Curriculum US
Average class size Elementary 10; Secondary 3
Language(s) of instruction English
Language(s) taught French, Bosnian, German
Staff specialists computer, ESL
Special curricular programs art, vocal music, computer/technology, distance learning, physical education

Extra curricular programs computers, community service, dance, drama, excursions/expeditions, yearbook
Sports basketball, skiing, soccer, track and field, volleyball
Clubs French, German, Bosnian
Examinations AP, Iowa, PSAT, SAT II, Stanford

CAMPUS FACILITIES

Location Suburban
Campus 2 hectares, 1 building, 10 classrooms, 1 computer lab, 24 instructional computers,

5,000 library volumes, 1 cafeteria, 1 playing field, 1 science lab

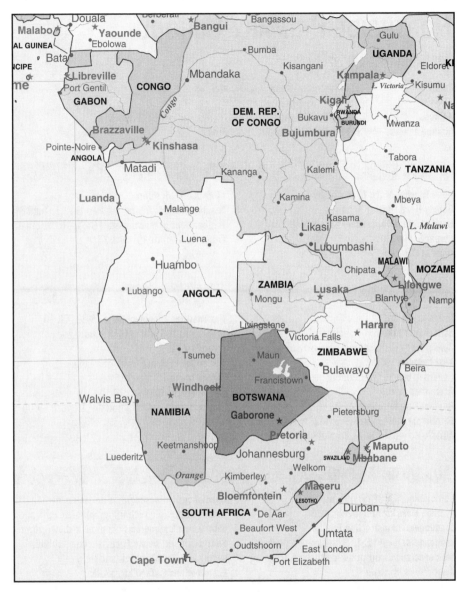

BOTSWANA

Area:	600,370 sq km
Population:	1,815,508
Capital:	Gaborone
Currency:	Pula (BWP)
Languages:	Setswana

NORTHSIDE PRIMARY SCHOOL

Phone	267 3952 440
Fax	267 3953 573
Email	administration@northsideschool.net
Website	www.northsideschool.net
Address	Plot 2786, Tshekedi Crescent, Ext. 9, Gaborone, Botswana
Mailing address	PO Box 897, Gaborone, Botswana

STAFF

Head Teacher Mark L. McCarthy
Deputy Head Garth Kitching
Head of Infant Department Nicola Major
Bursar S. Masolotate
Head of IT J. Gard

Librarian J. McMinn
Teaching staff Full time 30; Part time 5; Total 35
Nationalities of teaching staff UK 4; Motswana 4;
Other(s) (South African) 27

INFORMATION

Grade levels K–7
School year January–December
School type coeducational, day, private non-profit
Year founded 1974
Governed by elected Council
Accredited by CIS
Regional organizations AISA, ECIS
Enrollment Elementary K–5 342;
Middle School 6–8 89; Total 431

Nationalities of student body US 22; UK 30;
Motswana 165; Other(s) (South African,
Indian) 214
Tuition/fee currency Botswana Pula
Tuition range 7,950–8,550
One time fees Registration 200;
Capital Levy 1,500; Refundable Deposit 3,000

EDUCATIONAL PROGRAM

Curriculum UK, IBPYP, International
Average class size Elementary 23
Language(s) of instruction English
Language(s) taught ESL, Setswana, French
Staff specialists computer, counselor, learning
disabilities, librarian

Special curricular programs art, instrumental
music, computer/technology, physical education
Extra curricular programs computers, dance, drama
Sports cricket, martial arts, soccer, softball,
swimming, tennis, track and field
Examinations CAT, NFER, NARE,

CAMPUS FACILITIES

Location Suburban
Campus 3 hectares, 7 buildings, 22 classrooms,
1 computer lab, 60 instructional computers,
12,000 library volumes, 1 auditorium,

1 cafeteria, 1 gymnasium, 1 infirmary, 1 playing
field, 1 science lab, 1 pool, 2 tennis courts,
air conditioning

WESTWOOD INTERNATIONAL SCHOOL

Phone	267 3906 736
Fax	267 3906 734
Email	westwood@info.bw
Website	www.westwood.ac.bw
Address	Plot 22978 Mmakgwedi Road, Gaborone West, Gaborone, Botswana
Mailing address	PO Box 2446, Gaborone, Botswana

STAFF

Director Michael C. Francis
Head of Primary School Juliette van Eerdewijk
Head of Secondary School Christopher Edmunds
Deputy Head of Secondary School Jannie Kleynhans
Admissions Officer Shireen Melamu
School Counselor Sian Griffiths

Head of Administration and Finance John Abraham
IT Coordinator Graham Fleet
Librarian Joy Mnjama
Teaching staff Full time 53; Part time 3; Total 56
Nationalities of teaching staff US 1; UK 9; South African 5; Other(s) (Australian) 41

INFORMATION

Grade levels K–13
School year January–December
School type coeducational, day, private non-profit
Year founded 1988
Governed by appointed and elected School Council
Accredited by CIS, New England
Regional organizations AISA
Enrollment Elementary K–5 225; Middle School 6–8 153; High School 9–12 160; Grade 13 38; Total 576

Nationalities of student body US 15; UK 30; South African 140; Other(s) (Zimbabwean, Chinese) 391
Tuition/fee currency Botswana Pula
Tuition range 8,500–15,000
One time fees Capital Levy 8,500
Graduates attending college 85%
Graduates have attended U of Edinburgh, Brown U, Melbourne U, U of Cape Town, U of Pretoria

EDUCATIONAL PROGRAM

Curriculum Intl, IB Diploma, IBPYP, IGCSE
Average class size Elementary 25; Secondary 25
Language(s) of instruction English
Language(s) taught French, Setswana, Spanish, Afrikaans
Staff specialists computer, counselor, ESL, learning disabilities, librarian, nurse
Special curricular programs art, vocal music, computer/technology, physical education
Extra curricular programs computers, community service, dance, drama, environmental

conservation, excursions/expeditions, photography, yearbook
Sports badminton, basketball, cricket, gymnastics, hockey, rugby, soccer, softball, swimming, tennis, track and field, wall climbing, canoeing
Clubs guitar, Latin dance, self defense, aerobics, Judo, Model UN, choir, band, student council, painting
Examinations GCSE, IB, IGCSE

CAMPUS FACILITIES

Location Suburban
Campus 5 hectares, 14 buildings, 39 classrooms, 2 computer labs, 95 instructional computers, 14,000 library volumes, 1 auditorium,

1 cafeteria, 1 covered play area, 1 infirmary, 2 playing fields, 3 science labs, 2 pools, 3 tennis courts, air conditioning

BRAZIL

BRAZIL

Area:	8,511,965 sq km
Population:	190,010,647
Capital:	Brasilia
Currency:	Real (BRL)
Languages:	Portuguese, Spanish, English

AMAZON VALLEY ACADEMY

Phone	55 91 3245 2566
Fax	55 91 3245 7202
Email	avab@amazon.com.br
Website	www.nics.org/belem
Address	BR316 Km3 Tr. Tenri No. 132, Guanabara, Belem, Para, 67113-120, Brazil
Mailing address	Caixa Postal 5170, Agencia Cabanagem, 66613-970 Belem, PA, Brazil

STAFF

Principal Ernest W. Underwood, Ph.D.
Vice-Principal of Jr. High & High School
Trevor Collazo

Vice-Principal of Elementary School Linda Storms

INFORMATION

Grade levels PreK–12
School year August–June
School type coeducational, day, private non-profit
Year founded 1958
Governed by elected School Board
Sponsored by Network of International
 Christian Schools

Accredited by Southern
Tuition/fee currency US Dollar
Tuition range 3,050–6,700
One time fees Registration 500; Capital Levy 1,000
Graduates attending college 100%
Graduates have attended Prairie Bible Col,
Cedarville Col, Moody Bible Col, Grace Col

EDUCATIONAL PROGRAM

Curriculum US
Average class size Elementary 10; Secondary 10
Language(s) of instruction English
Language(s) taught Portuguese, German
Staff specialists computer, ESL, learning
disabilities, math resource
Special curricular programs art, instrumental
music, computer/technology, physical education

Extra curricular programs excursions/expeditions,
yearbook
Sports badminton, baseball, basketball,
football, soccer, softball, swimming, tennis,
track and field, volleyball
Examinations ACT, PSAT, SAT, Stanford

CAMPUS FACILITIES

Location Suburban
Campus 12 hectares, 5 buildings,
16 classrooms, 1 computer lab, 6 instructional
computers, 2,000 library volumes,

1 auditorium, 1 covered play area,
1 gymnasium, 1 infirmary, 2 playing fields,
1 science lab, 1 pool, 1 tennis court,
air conditoning

Data from 2006/07 school year.

Escola Americana de Belo Horizonte

Phone	55 31 3378 6700
Fax	55 31 3378 6878
Email	eabh@eabh.com.br
Website	www.eabh.com.br
Address	Av. Deputado Cristovan Chiardia, 120, Belo Horizonte, Minas Gerais, 30575 815, Brazil

STAFF

Director Bill Shell
Business Manager Leonardo Cordeiro
Computer Teacher Gustavo Salviano

Librarian Gilda Silva
Teaching staff Full time 26; Total 26
Nationalities of teaching staff US 8; Brazilian 18

INFORMATION

Grade levels PreK–12
School year August–June
School type coeducational, day, private non-profit
Year founded 1956
Governed by elected Board of Directors
Accredited by Southern
Regional organizations AASB, AASSA
Enrollment PreK 28; Elementary K–5 45; Middle School 6–8 30; High School 9–12 59; Total 162

Nationalities of student body US 15; Brazilian 80; Other(s) (Australian, Chilean) 67
Tuition/fee currency US Dollar
Tuition range 1,500–1,800
Graduates attending college 100%
Graduates have attended Georgetown U, Boston U, Pennsylvania State U, Colorado State U, American U

EDUCATIONAL PROGRAM

Curriculum US, AP, IB Diploma, IBPYP, IBMYP
Average class size Elementary 14; Secondary 14
Language(s) of instruction English
Language(s) taught Portuguese
Staff specialists librarian

Special curricular programs art, vocal music, computer/technology, physical education
Extra curricular programs computers, community service
Sports basketball, soccer, volleyball
Examinations Iowa

CAMPUS FACILITIES

Location Suburban
Campus 3 hectares, 6 buildings, 16 classrooms, 1 computer lab, 40 instructional computers,

10,000 library volumes, 1 cafeteria, 1 gymnasium, 1 infirmary, 2 playing fields, 2 science labs

AMERICAN SCHOOL OF BRASILIA

Phone	55 61 3442 9700
Fax	55 61 3244 4303
Email	cjohnson@eabdf.br
Website	www.eabdf.br
Address	SGAS 605, Conjunto E, Lotes 34/37, Brasilia, DF, 70200-650, Brazil

STAFF

Head of School Craig A. Johnson
Lower School Principal JoAnne Rehberg
Director of Brazilian Program Darcy Sullivan
Upper School Principal Derrick des Vignes, Ph.D.
Business Manager Alessandra Gonzalves

Technology Coordinator Daniel De Moraes
Head Librarian Anna Maria Machado
Teaching staff Full time 62; Total 62
Nationalities of teaching staff US 32;
Brazilian 23; Other(s) (Canadian) 7

INFORMATION

Grade levels PreK–12
School year August–June
School type coeducational, day, private non-profit
Year founded 1961
Governed by Self Perpetuated Board
Accredited by Southern
Regional organizations AASB, AASSA
Enrollment PreK 46; Elementary K–5 200;
Middle School 6–8 120; High School 9–12
160; Total 526

Nationalities of student body US 90; UK 12;
Brazilian 305; Other(s) (Korean,
South African) 119
Tuition/fee currency Brazilian Real
Tuition range 27,936–33,528
One time fees Registration 150;
Capital Levy 18,000
Graduates attending college 95%
Graduates have attended U of Michigan,
U of Wisconsin, Miami University of Ohio,
American U, U of Pennsylvania

EDUCATIONAL PROGRAM

Curriculum US, National, AP, IB Diploma
Average class size Elementary 22; Secondary 22
Language(s) of instruction English
Language(s) taught Portuguese, Spanish,
French, Mandarin
Staff specialists computer, counselor, ESL,
learning disabilities, librarian, math resource,
nurse, psychologist, reading resource

Special curricular programs art, instrumental
music, vocal music, computer/technology,
physical education, digital film making
Extra curricular programs computers,
community service, dance, drama, excur-
sions/expeditions, photography, yearbook
Sports badminton, baseball, basketball,
football, gymnastics, hockey, martial arts,
soccer, softball, track and field, volleyball
Examinations ACT, AP, IB, Iowa, PSAT, SAT, SAT II

CAMPUS FACILITIES

Location Suburban
Campus 2 hectares, 6 buildings, 50 classrooms,
3 computer labs, 95 instructional computers,
17,000 library volumes, 1 auditorium,

2 cafeterias, 1 covered play area, 1 gymnasium,
1 infirmary, 3 playing fields, 4 science labs,
air conditioning

AMERICAN SCHOOL OF CAMPINAS

Phone	55 19 2102 1000
Fax	55 19 2102 1016
Email	steve_herrera@eac.com.br
Website	www.eac.com.br
Address	Rua Cajamar, 35, Chacara da Barra, Campinas, São Paulo, 13090-860, Brazil
Mailing address	PO Box 978, 13012-970 Campinas, São Paulo, Brazil

STAFF

Superintendent Stephen A. Herrera
Upper School Principal Davi Sanchez Neto
Technology and Curriculum Coordinator
Christopher Kuczynski
Elementary School Principal Luciane Garcia
Brazilian Program Director Maria Celia de Oliveira

Business Manager Luiz Percico
Librarian Lais Martins
Teaching staff Full time 73; Part time 3; Total 76
Nationalities of teaching staff US 14;
Brazilian 60; Other(s) (Canadian, Bahraini) 2

INFORMATION

Grade levels PreK–12
School year August–June
School type coeducational, day, private non-profit
Year founded 1956
Governed by elected Board of Directors
Accredited by Southern
Regional organizations AASB, AASSA
Enrollment PreK 90; Elementary K–5 218;
Middle School 6–8 96; High School 9–12 87;
Total 491

Nationalities of student body US 68; UK 5;
Brazilian 333; Other(s) (Argentine, Korean) 85
Tuition/fee currency US Dollar
Tuition 21,000
Annual fees Lunch 1,000; Transportation 1,000
One time fees Registration 15,000
Graduates attending college 100%
Graduates have attended Emory U, Tufts U,
Georgetown U, U of Chicago, Villanova U

EDUCATIONAL PROGRAM

Curriculum US, National, AP
Average class size Elementary 20; Secondary 18
Language(s) of instruction English, Portuguese
Staff specialists computer, counselor, ESL,
librarian, nurse, psychologist, reading resource
Special curricular programs art, instrumental
music, computer/technology, physical education

Extra curricular programs computers, community
service, drama, excursions/expeditions,
newspaper, photography, yearbook
Sports basketball, football, martial arts, soccer,
softball, volleyball
Examinations ACT, AP, PSAT, SAT, SAT II, ERBs
CTP-IV

CAMPUS FACILITIES

Location Urban
Campus 14 hectares, 13 buildings, 38 classrooms,
2 computer labs, 75 instructional computers,

20,000 library volumes, 1 auditorium,
1 cafeteria, 1 gymnasium, 1 infirmary,
2 playing fields, 3 science labs

INTERNATIONAL SCHOOL OF CURITIBA

Phone	55 41 3364 7400
Fax	55 41 3364 9663
Email	isc.employment@iscbrazil.com
Website	www.iscbrazil.com
Address	Av. Dr. Eugênio Bertolli, 3900, Santa Felicidade, Curitiba, Paraná, 82410-530, Brazil

STAFF

Superintendent Bill R. Pearson
Secondary Principal Paul D. Combs
Elementary Principal Elizabeth Silva
Early Childhood Principal Marizete Bolzani
Curriculum Coordinator Rebeca Heinerici
Brazilian Program Coordinator
Claudia Lebiedziejewski

Business Manager Carla Jacobs
Technology Coordinator Fabio Rocco
Librarian Sandra Sparremberger
Teaching staff Full time 51; Part time 3; Total 54
Nationalities of teaching staff US 10;
Brazilian 43; Other(s) (Canadian) 1

INFORMATION

Grade levels N–12
School year August–June
School type coeducational, day, private non-profit
Year founded 1959
Governed by elected Board of Directors
Accredited by Southern
Regional organizations AASB, AASSA
Enrollment Nursery 48; PreK 25;
Elementary K–5 149; Middle School 6–8 64;
High School 9–12 90; Total 376

Nationalities of student body US 45; UK 5;
Brazilian 204; Other(s) (French, Argentine) 122
Tuition/fee currency Brazilian Real
Tuition range 56,781–64,402
Annual fees Lunch 2,200; Development Fund
1,000; ESL 3,000
One time fees Registration 2,700;
Capital Levy 13,390
Graduates attending college 99%
Graduates have attended Washington U,
U of Rochester, Georgia Institute of Technology,
Lehigh U, Wake Forest U

EDUCATIONAL PROGRAM

Curriculum US, National, Intl, IB Diploma
Average class size Elementary 16; Secondary 16
Language(s) of instruction English
Language(s) taught Portuguese, Spanish
Staff specialists computer, learning disabilities,
librarian, reading resource
Special curricular programs art, instrumental
music, vocal music, computer/technology,
distance learning, physical education, vocational

Extra curricular programs community service,
dance, drama, environmental conservation,
excursions/expeditions, literary magazine,
newspaper, yearbook, music
Sports basketball, cross-country, soccer,
volleyball
Clubs National Honor Society, Junior National
Honor Society, student council, junior student
council, Ecoclub
Examinations IB, Iowa, PSAT, SAT, SAT II, ERB, DRA

CAMPUS FACILITIES

Location Suburban
Campus 8 hectares, 19 buildings, 47 classrooms,
4 computer labs, 190 instructional computers,

55,461 library volumes, 2 cafeterias, 2 covered
play areas, 2 gymnasiums, 2 infirmaries,
4 playing fields, 3 science labs, air conditioning

PAN AMERICAN SCHOOL OF PORTO ALEGRE

Phone	55 51 3334 5866
Fax	55 51 3334 5866
Email	school@panamerican.com.br
Website	www.panamerican.com.br
Address	Rua Joao Paetzel 440, Porto Alegre, RS, 91330280, Brazil

STAFF

Director Caryl Brayton Toole
Brazilian Program Coordinator Clarisa Sassi
PYP Coordinator Sharon Wallsh
Math Coordinator Matt McCormick

Science Coordinator Carlos Schroeder
Business Manager Sergio Nunes
IT Coordinator Frederick Krautz
Librarian Andrew Sassi

INFORMATION

Grade levels N–12
School year August–June
School type coeducational, day, private non-profit
Year founded 1966
Governed by elected Board
Accredited by Southern

Regional organizations AASB, AASSA
Tuition/fee currency US Dollar
Tuition range 8,064–14,400
Annual fees Capital Levy 4,000; Activity 527
One time fees Registration 360
Graduates attending college 90%

EDUCATIONAL PROGRAM

Curriculum US, National, Intl, IBPYP
Average class size Elementary 20; Secondary 6
Language(s) of instruction English
Language(s) taught Portuguese
Staff specialists computer, counselor, ESL, librarian, psychologist, speech/hearing
Special curricular programs art, vocal music, computer/technology, distance learning, physical education

Extra curricular programs computers, community service, drama, excursions/expeditions, newspaper, yearbook
Sports basketball, gymnastics, martial arts, soccer, swimming, volleyball
Clubs Capoeira, judo, basketball, drumming, cooking, guitar, soccer, computer, science
Examinations AP, Iowa, SAT, SAT II

CAMPUS FACILITIES

Location Suburban
Campus 1 hectare, 3 buildings, 16 classrooms, 1 computer lab, 30 instructional computers,

8,000 library volumes, 1 cafeteria, 1 covered play area, 1 gymnasium, 1 playing field, 1 science lab, air conditioning

Data from 2006/07 school year.

AMERICAN SCHOOL OF RECIFE

Phone	55 81 3341 4716
Fax	55 81 3341 0142
Email	info@ear.com.br
Website	www.ear.com.br
Address	Rua Sa e Souza 408, Boa Viagem, Recife, PE, 51030 060, Brazil
Mailing address	American School of Recife–Superintendent, US Consulate Recife, Unit 3503, APO AA34030-3503

STAFF

Superintendent George G. Takacs, Ph.D.
Principal William Whitaker
Brazilian Studies Director Gloria Souza
Guidance Counselor Charles Hodges
Business Manager Agnaldo Camara

Technology Coordinator Tedy Ander
Librarian Solange Carneiro
Teaching staff Full time 18; Part time 17; Total 35
Nationalities of teaching staff US 12;
Brazilian 20; Other(s) (French, Serb) 3

INFORMATION

Grade levels N–12
School year August–June
School type coeducational, day, private non-profit
Year founded 1957
Governed by elected Board of Directors
Accredited by Southern
Regional organizations AASB, AASSA
Enrollment Nursery 11; PreK 8; Elementary K–5 86; Middle School 6–8 51; High School 9–12 51; Total 207

Nationalities of student body US 25; Brazilian 144; Other(s) (Argentine, Japanese) 38
Tuition/fee currency US Dollar
Tuition range 4,368–9,240
Annual fees Registration 164; Books 1,300
One time fees Capital Levy 1,500
Graduates attending college 98%
Graduates have attended Harvard U, U of California in Los Angeles, Purdue U, U of Kansas, Oberlin Col

EDUCATIONAL PROGRAM

Curriculum US, National, AP
Average class size Elementary 20; Secondary 20
Language(s) of instruction English
Language(s) taught French, Spanish, Portuguese
Staff specialists computer, counselor, ESL, librarian, math resource, nurse, psychologist, reading resource

Special curricular programs art, instrumental music, vocal music, physical education
Extra curricular programs dance, excursions/expeditions, photography, yearbook
Sports basketball, hockey, soccer, track and field, volleyball, Capoeira
Examinations ACT, AP, PSAT, SAT, Stanford

CAMPUS FACILITIES

Location Urban
Campus 8 hectares, 4 buildings, 32 classrooms, 2 computer labs, 55 instructional computers,

20,000 library volumes, 1 auditorium, 1 cafeteria, 1 covered play area, 1 infirmary, 3 playing fields, 2 science labs, air conditioning

ESCOLA AMERICANA DO RIO DE JANEIRO

Phone	55 21 2125 9002
Fax	55 21 2259 4722
Email	katia.veiga@earj.com.br
Website	www.earj.com.br
Address	Estrada da Gavea, 132, Gavea, Rio de Janeiro, 22451 263, Brazil

STAFF

Head of School Robert Werner
Upper School Principal Joe Santos
Middle School Principal Shaysann Kaun
Lower School Principal Julie Hunt
Business Manager Emilia Ferreira
Information Technology Manager Rodrigo Brasil

Librarian Flavita Cotrim
Teaching staff Full time 105; Part time 1; Total 106
Nationalities of teaching staff US 31; UK 1;
Brazilian 66; Other(s) (British Virgin Islander,
Canadian) 8

INFORMATION

Grade levels N–12
School year August–June
School type coeducational, day, private non-profit
Year founded 1937
Governed by appointed and elected Board of
Directors
Accredited by Southern
Regional organizations AASB, AASSA
Enrollment Nursery 25; PreK 25; Elementary
K–5 270; Middle School 6–8 185;
High School 9–12 235; Total 740

Nationalities of student body US 90; UK 7;
Brazilian 483; Other(s) (Argentine,
Colombian) 160
Tuition/fee currency US Dollar
Tuition range 10,188–22,877
Annual fees Busing 1,575; Lunch 1,125
One time fees Capital Levy 6,500
Graduates attending college 99%
Graduates have attended U of Pennsylvania,
Yale U, Stanford U, U of Miami, Vanderbilt U

EDUCATIONAL PROGRAM

Curriculum US, National, IB Diploma
Average class size Elementary 20; Secondary 18
Language(s) of instruction English, Portuguese
Language(s) taught French, Spanish
Staff specialists computer, counselor, ESL,
learning disabilities, librarian, nurse,
psychologist, speech/hearing
Special curricular programs art, instrumental
music, vocal music, computer/technology,
physical education, experiential education,
video production

Extra curricular programs computers, community
service, dance, drama, environmental
conservation, excursions/expeditions, literary
magazine, newspaper, photography, yearbook,
National Honor Society, Model UN
Sports baseball, basketball, rugby, soccer,
softball, track and field, volleyball
Clubs yearbook, newspaper, chess, drama
Examinations ACT, IB, SAT, SAT II

CAMPUS FACILITIES

Location Suburban
Campus 5 hectares, 9 buildings, 75 classrooms,
5 computer labs, 260 instructional computers,
33,000 library volumes, 1 auditorium,

1 cafeteria, 3 covered play areas, 1 gymnasium,
1 infirmary, 1 playing field, 8 science labs,
air conditioning

INTERNATIONAL CHRISTIAN SCHOOL

Phone	55 91 2431 1239
Fax	55 21 2431 1239
Email	info@ics-rio.com
Website	www.ics-rio.com
Address	Ave Prefeito Dulcìdio Cardoso 4351-Barra da Tijuca, Rio de Janeiro, RJ, 22793-011, Brazil
Mailing address	Caixa Postal 37.725 Barra Shopping, Barra da Tijuca, RJ 22642-970, Brazil

STAFF

Director Teresa Stamler
Brazilian Director Mara Lene Rangel

Marketing Director Larry Stamler
Financial Manager Marcelo Coutinho

INFORMATION

Grade levels N–12
School year August–June
School type coeducational, day
Year founded 2000
Governed by appointed Board

Sponsored by Network of International Christian Schools
Tuition/fee currency Brazilian Real
Tuition range 23,700–28,776
One time fees Registration 350; Capital Levy 9,000
Graduates attending college 98%

EDUCATIONAL PROGRAM

Curriculum US, National
Average class size Elementary 7; Secondary 6
Language(s) of instruction English, Portuguese
Language(s) taught Portuguese
Staff specialists ESL
Special curricular programs art, instrumental music, vocal music, computer/technology, physical education

Extra curricular programs computers, drama, excursions/expeditions, yearbook
Sports baseball, basketball, soccer, swimming, tennis, volleyball
Examinations SAT, Stanford

CAMPUS FACILITIES

Location Suburban
Campus 1 hectare, 2 buildings, 10 classrooms, 1 computer lab, 20 instructional computers,

850 library volumes, 1 auditorium, 1 cafeteria, 1 covered play area, 1 playing field, 1 science lab, 1 pool, 1 tennis court, air conditioning

Data from 2006/07 school year.

PAN AMERICAN SCHOOL OF BAHIA

Phone	55 71 3367 9099
Fax	55 71 3367 9090
Email	info@escolapanamericana.com
Website	www.escolapanamericana.com
Address	Loteamento Patamares s/n Patamares, Salvador, Bahia, 41680-060, Brazil
Mailing address	Cx. Postal 231, 40.001-970, Salvador, Bahia, Brazil

STAFF

Director Dennis M. Klumpp
Elementary Principal Joseph Miller
Secondary Principal Thomas Burgess
Brazilian Program Coordinator
Maria Elena Kravchychyn
Business and Finance Manager Marina Skelton

Technology Coordinator Leonardo Orrico
School Media Specialist Lêda Smith
Teaching staff Full time 45; Part time 11; Total 56
Nationalities of teaching staff US 22; UK 1;
Brazilian 30; Other(s) (Canadian, Dutch) 3

INFORMATION

Grade levels N–12
School year August–June
School type coeducational, day, private non-profit
Year founded 1960
Governed by elected Board of Directors
Accredited by Southern
Regional organizations AASB, AASSA
Enrollment Nursery 61; PreK 33;
Elementary K–5 242; Middle School 6–8 75;
High School 9–12 71; Total 482

Nationalities of student body US 37; UK 6;
Brazilian 377; Other(s) (French, German) 62
Tuition/fee currency US Dollar
Tuition range 5,000–12,000
Annual fees Capital Levy 500; Portuguese as a
Second Language 800; ESL 2,500;
After School Activities 300
One time fees Registration 1,500
Graduates attending college 98%
Graduates have attended Harvard U, Brown U,
Yale U, American U of London,
U of North Carolina

EDUCATIONAL PROGRAM

Curriculum US, National, AP
Average class size Elementary 20; Secondary 18
Language(s) of instruction English
Language(s) taught Portuguese, Spanish
Staff specialists computer, counselor, ESL,
learning disabilities, librarian, nurse,
reading resource

Special curricular programs art, computer/
technology, distance learning, physical education
Extra curricular programs community service,
drama, excursions/expeditions, yearbook
Sports basketball, soccer, swimming, volleyball
Clubs Model UN
Examinations ACT, AP, Iowa, PSAT, SAT, SAT II,
TOEFL, ERB

CAMPUS FACILITIES

Location Suburban
Campus 8 hectares, 5 buildings, 49 classrooms,
2 computer labs, 89 instructional computers,

17,000 library volumes, 2 cafeterias, 2 covered
play areas, 1 gymnasium, 1 infirmary, 3 playing
fields, 2 science labs, 1 pool, air conditioning

Associação Escola Graduada de São Paulo

Phone	55 11 3747 4800
Fax	55 11 3742 9358
Email	lpeixoto@graded.br
Website	www.graded.br
Address	Av. Pres. Giovanni Gronchi, 4710, São Paulo, SP, 05724-002, Brazil
Mailing address	Caixa Postal 1976, 01059-970 São Paulo, SP, Brazil

STAFF

Superintendent Richard M. Detwiler
High School Principal Barry Dequanne
Middle School Principal James Urquhart
Lower School Principal Paige Geiger
Director of Admissions Lisa Peixoto
Brazilian Studies Director Angelina Fregonesi

Business Manager Jose Carlos Cardozo
Director of Technology Derrel Fincher
Upper School Librarian Hillary Marshall
Teaching staff Full time 125; Part time 7; Total 132
Nationalities of teaching staff US 46; UK 3;
Brazilian 68; Other(s) (Canadian) 15

INFORMATION

Grade levels N–12
School year August–June
School type coeducational, day, private non-profit
Year founded 1920
Governed by appointed Board of Directors
Accredited by Southern
Regional organizations AASB, AASSA, ECIS
Enrollment Nursery 54; PreK 50;
Elementary K–5 467; Middle School 6–8 254;
High School 9–12 326; Total 1,151
Nationalities of student body US 238; UK 13;
Brazilian 545; Other(s) 355

Tuition/fee currency US Dollar
Tuition range 12,885–25,280
Annual fees Busing 2,982
One time fees Registration 150;
Capital Levy 13,500;
Testing Services 564; Follow up Testing 283
Graduates attending college 100%
Graduates have attended Tufts U, U of
Pennsylvania, IBMEC in São Paulo, Stanford U,
ESPM in São Paulo

(Continued)

Associação Escola Graduada de São Paulo (Continued)

EDUCATIONAL PROGRAM

Curriculum US, National, IB Diploma
Average class size Elementary 22; Secondary 17
Language(s) of instruction English
Language(s) taught Portuguese, Spanish, French
Staff specialists computer, counselor, ESL, learning disabilities, librarian, math resource, nurse, physician, psychologist, reading resource
Special curricular programs art, instrumental music, vocal music, computer/technology, distance learning, physical education

Extra curricular programs computers, community service, dance, drama, environmental conservation, excursions/expeditions, literary magazine, newspaper, photography, yearbook
Sports basketball, soccer, softball, tennis, track and field, volleyball, cheerleading, indoor soccer
Clubs National Honor Society, astronomy, chess, computer, ecology, photography, community service, Knowledge Bowl, forensics, Model UN
Examinations ACT, AP, IB, PSAT, SAT, SAT II, ERB

CAMPUS FACILITIES

Location Suburban
Campus 7 hectares, 10 buildings, 90 classrooms, 10 computer labs, 700 instructional computers, 50,000 library volumes, 2 auditoriums,

1 cafeteria, 2 covered play areas, 2 gymnasiums, 1 infirmary, 2 playing fields, 4 science labs, 4 tennis courts

Chapel (Escola Maria Imaculada)

Phone	55 11 2101 7400
Fax	55 11 5521 7763
Email	chapel@chapelschool.com
Website	www.chapelschool.com
Address	Rua Vigário João de Pontes, 537, São Paulo, SP, 04748-000, Brazil
Mailing address	Caixa Postal 21.293, Brooklin, 04602-970, São Paulo, Brazil

STAFF

Superintendent John T. Ciallelo
High School Principal Sarah Colgrove
Elementary Principal Liza Baker
Brazilian Program Director Cristina Muller Calil
Early Childhood Coordinator Lorraine Brotero
Learning Resource Coordinator Jean Rheims

Oblate Treasurer Antonio Borges Mesquita
Department Head Jimmy Lin
Head Librarian Lucia Paranhos
Teaching staff Full time 69; Total 69
Nationalities of teaching staff US 22;
Brazilian 41; Other(s) (Canadian) 6

INFORMATION

Grade levels N–12
School year August–June
School type coeducational, church-affiliated,
day, private non-profit, proprietary
Year founded 1947
Governed by appointed Board of Directors
Sponsored by Oblates of Mary Immaculate
Accredited by Southern
Regional organizations AASB, AASSA
Enrollment Nursery 32; PreK 32;
Elementary K–5 285; Middle School 6–8 140;
High School 9–12 156; Total 645

Nationalities of student body US 75; UK 5;
Brazilian 400; Other(s) (Korean, Argentine) 165
Tuition/fee currency Brazilian Real
Tuition range 1,770–3,510
Annual fees Books 1,650
One time fees Registration 4,980; Admissions
Exam 200
Graduates attending college 100%
Graduates have attended Boston Col,
U of British Columbia, Savannah Col of Art and
Design, Georgetown U, U of Notre Dame

EDUCATIONAL PROGRAM

Curriculum US, National, Intl, IB Diploma
Average class size Elementary 25; Secondary 20
Language(s) of instruction English, Portuguese
Language(s) taught French, Spanish
Staff specialists computer, counselor, ESL,
learning disabilities, librarian, math resource,
nurse, reading resource
Special curricular programs art, vocal music,
computer/technology, physical education

Extra curricular programs community service,
dance, drama, environmental conservation,
excursions/expeditions, literary magazine,
newspaper, yearbook, student council,
Knowledge Bowl, Math Counts, Model UN,
Destination Imagination
Sports basketball, soccer, softball, volleyball
Clubs National Honor Society, community
service, retreats, chess
Examinations ACT, IB, Iowa, PSAT, SAT, SAT II,
TOEFL, ERB

CAMPUS FACILITIES

Location Suburban
Campus 3 hectares, 6 buildings, 55 classrooms,
3 computer labs, 225 instructional computers,
30,000 library volumes, 1 auditorium,

1 cafeteria, 2 covered play areas, 2 gymnasiums,
1 infirmary, 1 playing field, 3 science labs,
1 tennis court

BRITISH VIRGIN ISLANDS

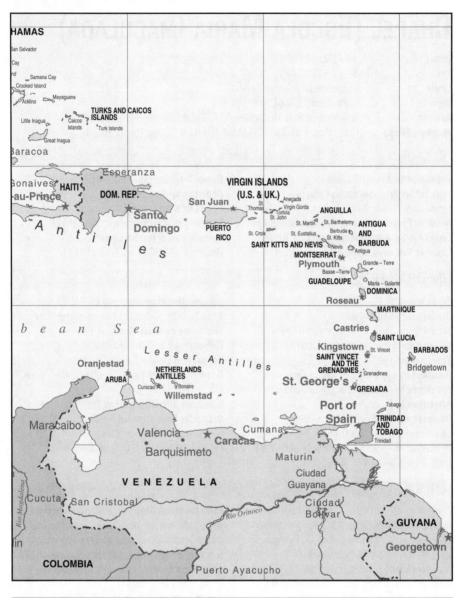

BRITISH VIRGIN ISLANDS

Area:	153 sq km
Population:	23,552
Capital:	Road Town
Currency:	US Dollar (USD)
Languages:	English

CEDAR SCHOOL

Phone	284 494 5262
Fax	284 495 9695
Email	cedaradmin@surfbvi.com
Website	www.cedarschoolbvi.com
Address	Kingston, Road Town, Tortola, British Virgin Islands
Mailing address	PMB 5000, PO Box 8309, Cruz Bay, United States Virgin Islands 00831

STAFF

Head of School Janet Tennikait, Ed.D.
Assistant Head of School Seamus Hennessy
Head of Primary School Jonathan Bridgeman
Head of Kindegarten Rachel Bridgeman

Business Manager Natasha Nicholas
Computer Teacher Deborah Maddox
Librarian Ryan Robinson

INFORMATION

Grade levels N–12
School year September–June
School type coeducational, day, private non-profit
Year founded 1987
Governed by appointed Board of Trustees
Accredited by Middle States

Tuition/fee currency US Dollar
Tuition range 4,050–7,850
One time fees Registration 100
Graduates have attended Spelman Col,
U of Portsmouth, Devry U

EDUCATIONAL PROGRAM

Curriculum US
Average class size Elementary 14; Secondary 10
Language(s) of instruction English
Language(s) taught Spanish
Staff specialists computer, librarian, math
resource, reading resource
Special curricular programs art, vocal music,
computer/technology, physical education, music

Extra curricular programs community service,
dance, drama, environmental conservation,
excursions/expeditions, newspaper, yearbook
Sports basketball, rugby, soccer, swimming,
track and field, volleyball
Clubs art, recorder, gardening, crafts, scuba,
surfing, cheerleading, band, sports
Examinations SAT, Stanford

CAMPUS FACILITIES

Location Rural
Campus 2 hectares, 1 building, 16 classrooms,
1 computer lab, 30 instructional computers,

5,500 library volumes, 1 auditorium,
1 covered play area, 1 infirmary, 1 playing field,
1 science lab, air conditioning

Data from 2006/07 school year.

BULGARIA

BULGARIA

Area:	110,910 sq km
Population:	7,322,858
Capital:	Sofia
Currency:	Lev (BGL)
Languages:	Bulgarian

THE AMERICAN COLLEGE OF SOFIA

Phone	359 2 975 3695
Fax	359 2 974 3129
Email	acs@acs.bg
Website	www.acs.bg
Address	Floyd Black Lane, Sofia, Mladost 2, 1799, Bulgaria
Mailing address	PO Box 873, Sofia 1000, Bulgaria

STAFF

President Louis J. Perske, Ed.D.
Deputy Director Maria Angelova
Dean of Students and International Student Coordinator Karen Hillis
College Counselor Tracy Muilenberg

Business Manager Slaveja Milanova
Chairman of Computer Department Mark Reynolds
Teaching staff Full time 70; Part time 5; Total 75
Nationalities of teaching staff US 21; UK 2; Bulgarian 39; Other(s) (Canadian) 8

INFORMATION

Grade levels 8–12
School year September–June
School type boarding, coeducational, day, private non-profit
Year founded 1860
Governed by appointed Sofia American Schools Board of Trustees
Accredited by Middle States
Regional organizations CEESA
Enrollment Middle School 6–8 142; High School 9–12 497; Total 639

Nationalities of student body US 2; UK 1; Bulgarian 604; Other(s) 32
Tuition/fee currency Euro
Tuition range 2,200–12,000
Annual fees Boarding, 7-day 5,000
One time fees Registration 300
Boarding program grades 8–12
Boarding program length 7-day **Boys** 12 **Girls** 17
Graduates attending college 100%
Graduates have attended Princeton U, Yale U, Harvard U, Stanford U, Massachusetts Institute of Technology

EDUCATIONAL PROGRAM

Curriculum US, National, Intl, IB Diploma
Average class size Secondary 20
Language(s) of instruction English
Language(s) taught French, Spanish, German, Bulgarian
Staff specialists computer, counselor, ESL, librarian, nurse, physician, psychologist
Special curricular programs art, vocal music, computer/technology, physical education

Extra curricular programs computers, community service, dance, drama, environmental conservation, excursions/expeditions, literary magazine, newspaper, photography, yearbook
Sports badminton, basketball, skiing, soccer, softball, swimming, tennis, track and field, volleyball
Examinations AP, IB, PSAT, SAT, SAT II, TOEFL

CAMPUS FACILITIES

Location Suburban
Campus 22 hectares, 14 buildings, 55 classrooms, 4 computer labs, 90 instructional computers,

15,000 library volumes, 1 auditorium, 1 cafeteria, 1 gymnasium, 1 infirmary, 3 playing fields, 4 science labs, 2 tennis courts

THE ANGLO-AMERICAN SCHOOL OF SOFIA

Phone	359 2 923 8810/11
Fax	359 2 923 8859
Email	mmihailova@aas-sofia.org
Website	www.aas-sofia.org
Address	c/o The American Embassy, 16 Koziak Street, Sofia, 1407, Bulgaria
Mailing address	Dept. of State, 5740 Sofia Place, Washington, DC 20521-5740, USA

STAFF

Director Eric E. Larson
Deputy Director William Corey
Athletic Director Murray Te Huki
Business Manager Marchella Ignatova
ICT Manager Linda Dimitrov

Librarian Angela Browne
Teaching staff Full time 30; Part time 3; Total 33
Nationalities of teaching staff US 14; UK 1;
Bulgarian 10; Other(s) (Canadian) 8

INFORMATION

Grade levels PreK–10
School year August–June
School type coeducational, day, private non-profit
Year founded 1967
Governed by appointed School Board
Accredited by CIS, New England
Regional organizations CEESA, ECIS

Enrollment PreK 16; Elementary K–5 160;
Middle School 6–8 50; High School 9–12 26;
Total 252
Nationalities of student body US 44; UK 16;
Bulgarian 41; Other(s) (Indian, Dutch) 151
Tuition/fee currency Euro
Tuition range 4,120–13,640
Annual fees Capital Levy 2,209; Busing 900
One time fees Registration 698; Entrance 1,103

EDUCATIONAL PROGRAM

Curriculum US, UK, Intl
Average class size Elementary 20; Secondary 15
Language(s) of instruction English
Language(s) taught French, Bulgarian, Spanish
Staff specialists computer, counselor, ESL,
librarian, math resource, nurse, reading
resource, speech/hearing
Special curricular programs art, instrumental
music, vocal music, computer/technology,
physical education

Extra curricular programs computers, community
service, dance, drama, environmental
conservation, excursions/expeditions,
newspaper, photography, mountain climbing,
horse riding, tennis
Sports basketball, cross-country, football, golf,
gymnastics, skiing, soccer, softball, squash,
swimming, tennis, volleyball

CAMPUS FACILITIES

Location Suburban
Campus 7 hectares, 1 building, 50 classrooms,
1 computer lab, 70 instructional computers,

10,000 library volumes, 1 auditorium,
1 cafeteria, 1 gymnasium, 1 infirmary, 1 playing
field, 1 science lab, 2 tennis courts

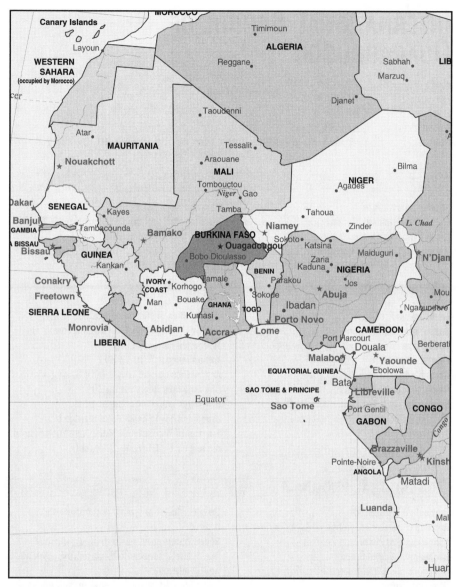

BURKINA FASO

Area:	274,200 sq km
Population:	14,326,203
Capital:	Ouagadougou
Currency:	Communaute Financiere Africaine Franc (XOF)
Languages:	French

INTERNATIONAL SCHOOL OF OUAGADOUGOU

Phone	226 50 362 143
Fax	226 50 362 228
Email	iso@iso.bf
Website	www.iso.bf
Address	s/c Ambassade des Etats Unis, 01 BP 35, Ouagadougou, 01, Burkina Faso

STAFF

Director Larry Ethier
Elementary Principal Kim Overton
Finance Manager Kadia Kamano
Information Technology Coordinator Marcel Niampa

Librarian Neil Caves
Teaching staff Full time 21; Part time 5; Total 26
Nationalities of teaching staff US 13;
Burkinabe 3; Other(s) (Canadian, French) 10

INFORMATION

Grade levels PreK–12
School year August–June
School type coeducational, day, private non-profit
Year founded 1976
Accredited by Middle States
Regional organizations AISA
Enrollment PreK 16; Elementary K–5 85;
Middle School 6–8 35; High School 9–12 45;
Total 181

Nationalities of student body US 40; UK 5;
Burkinabe 26; Other(s) (Indian, Dutch) 110
Tuition/fee currency Euro
Tuition range 3,750–12,805
Annual fees Capital Levy 1,000; Busing 450
One time fees Registration 205
Graduates attending college 100%
Graduates have attended Cambridge U,
The Col of William and Mary, New York School
of Design, U of Toronto, Drexel U

EDUCATIONAL PROGRAM

Curriculum US, Intl, AP
Average class size Elementary 13; Secondary 14
Language(s) of instruction English
Language(s) taught French
Staff specialists computer, counselor, ESL,
librarian, nurse
Special curricular programs art, vocal music,
computer/technology, physical education,
Week Without Walls, drama, dance, Quest,
journalism, Senior Seminar

Extra curricular programs community service,
drama
Sports badminton, basketball, gymnastics,
martial arts, soccer, softball, tennis, track and
field, volleyball
Clubs Model UN, Batik, cooking, student
government, Writer's Workshop, computer
games, pottery
Examinations ACT, AP, PSAT, SAT, SAT II,
TOEFL, ISA

CAMPUS FACILITIES

Location Suburban
Campus 3 hectares, 10 buildings, 16 classrooms,
1 computer lab, 70 instructional computers,

9,500 library volumes, 1 cafeteria, 1 covered
play area, 1 infirmary, 1 playing field, 1 science
lab, 1 pool, 2 tennis courts, air conditioning

CAMBODIA

Area:	181,040 sq km
Population:	13,995,904
Capital:	Phnom Penh
Currency:	Riel (KHR)
Languages:	Khmer, French, English

INTERNATIONAL SCHOOL OF PHNOM PENH

Phone   855 23 213 103
Fax   855 23 213 104
Email   ispp@ispp.edu.kh
Website   www.ispp.edu.kh
Address   146 Norodom Boulevard, PO Box 138, Phnom Penh, Cambodia

STAFF

Director Rob Mockrish, Ph.D.
Secondary Principal Jim Canavan
Elementary Principal Diane O'Connell
IB Coordinator Tammy Rodabaugh
MYP Coordinator Brian Webster
PYP Coordinator Rosemary Wright

Business Manager Sally Relph
Head of Technology Mallie Hardie
K–12 Library/Media Center David Edson
Teaching staff Full time 53; Part time 6; Total 59
Nationalities of teaching staff US 15; UK 10;
Cambodian 1; Other(s) (Canadian, Australian) 33

INFORMATION

Grade levels N–12
School year August–June
School type coeducational, day, private non-profit
Year founded 1989
Governed by elected Board of Directors
Accredited by CIS, Western
Regional organizations EARCOS, ECIS
Enrollment Nursery 66; PreK 37;
Elementary K–5 144; Middle School 6–8 90;
High School 9–12 114; Total 451

Nationalities of student body US 56; UK 30;
Cambodian 92; Other(s) (Korean, Australian) 273
Tuition/fee currency US Dollar
Tuition range 3,780–12,070
Annual fees Capital Levy 1,200
One time fees Registration 25,000
Graduates attending college 98%
Graduates have attended Michigan State U,
Loyola Col, U of California, U of London, York Col

EDUCATIONAL PROGRAM

Curriculum IB Diploma, IBPYP, IBMYP
Average class size Elementary 18; Secondary 11
Language(s) of instruction English
Language(s) taught French, Khmer, other local
dialects program
Staff specialists computer, counselor, ESL,
learning disabilities, librarian, nurse, reading
resource
Special curricular programs art, instrumental
music, vocal music, computer/technology,
physical education

Extra curricular programs computers, community service, dance, drama,
excursions/expeditions, literary magazine,
newspaper, yearbook
Sports basketball, golf, gymnastics, martial arts,
rugby, soccer, softball, swimming, track and
field, volleyball
Clubs chess
Examinations AP, IB, PSAT, SAT, SAT II, TOEFL, ISA

CAMPUS FACILITIES

Location Urban
Campus 2 hectares, 7 buildings, 35 classrooms,
2 computer labs, 105 instructional computers,
25,000 library volumes, 1 auditorium,

1 covered play area, 1 gymnasium, 1 infirmary,
3 playing fields, 2 science labs, 1 pool,
air conditioning

NORTHBRIDGE INTERNATIONAL SCHOOL CAMBODIA

Phone	855 23 886 000
Fax	855 23 886 009
Email	Info@NISCambodia.com
Website	www.NISCambodia.com
Address	Corner of Northbridge Street and International School Street, Phnom Penh, Cambodia
Mailing address	PO Box 2042, Phnom Penh 3, Cambodia

STAFF

Head of School David E. Eaton
Principal and Counselor/Student Advocate (grades 6 to 12) Annette Meeuwse
Registrar and Administrative Assistant Margie Gomez
CFO Mae Sirichindakul

Technology Coordinator Jim Cuthill
Librarian Wanda Creeger
Teaching staff Full time 25; Part time 8; Total 33
Nationalities of teaching staff US 15; Cambodian 2; Other(s) (Australian, Canadian) 16

INFORMATION

Grade levels N–12
School year August–June
School type coeducational, company-sponsored, day, proprietary
Year founded 1997
Governed by appointed Board of Trustees
Sponsored by The Royal Group Cambodia
Accredited by Western
Regional organizations EARCOS
Enrollment Nursery 19; PreK 15; Elementary K–5 123; Middle School 6–8 61; High School 9–12 68; Total 286

Nationalities of student body US 53; UK 6; Cambodian 59; Other(s) (Korean, Japanese) 168
Tuition/fee currency US Dollar
Tuition range 3,000–9,950
Annual fees Capital Levy 2,000; Busing 800; Excursions 150; ESL 3,200
One time fees Registration 2,500
Graduates attending college 100%
Graduates have attended Duke U, Ohio State U, U of California in Irvine, U of South Australia, Reed Col

(Continued)

Northbridge International School Cambodia (Continued)

EDUCATIONAL PROGRAM

Curriculum US, AP
Average class size Elementary 20; Secondary 18
Language(s) of instruction English
Language(s) taught French, Khmer, Spanish, Mandarin
Staff specialists computer, counselor, ESL, learning disabilities, librarian, math resource, reading resource

Special curricular programs art, instrumental music, vocal music, computer/technology, physical education
Extra curricular programs computers, community service, drama, excursions/expeditions, photography, yearbook
Sports basketball, soccer, softball, swimming, volleyball
Clubs Habitat for Humanity, Operation Smile
Examinations AP, Iowa, PSAT, SAT, SAT II, TOEFL

CAMPUS FACILITIES

Location Suburban
Campus 7 hectares, 4 buildings, 26 classrooms, 2 computer labs, 100 instructional computers, 8,000 library volumes, 1 auditorium, 1 cafeteria, 2 covered play areas, 1 gymnasium, 1 infirmary, 3 playing fields, 2 science labs, 1 pool, 3 tennis courts, air conditioning

CAMEROON

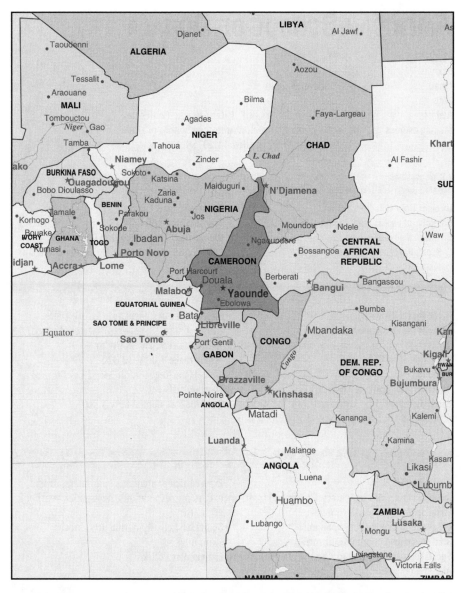

CAMEROON

Area:	475,440 sq km
Population:	18,060,382
Capital:	Yaounde
Currency:	Communaute Financiere Africaine Franc (XAF)
Languages:	African, English, French

AMERICAN SCHOOL OF DOUALA

Phone	237 342 1437
Fax	237 342 8393
Email	asd@asddouala.com
Website	www.asddouala.com
Address	767, Ave. De Palmiers, B.P. 1909, Douala, Cameroon
Mailing address	Dr. Robert Voruz, Director, American School of Douala, 2520 Yaounde Place, Dulles, VA 20189

STAFF

Director Robert L. Voruz, Ed.D.
Administrative Assistant Bernadette Ebata
Business Manager James Besong
IT Specialist Charles Azong

Librarian Helen Elonge
Teaching staff Full time 15; Part time 4; Total 19
Nationalities of teaching staff US 6; UK 1;
Cameroonian 8; Other(s) (Romanian, Belgian) 4

INFORMATION

Grade levels PreK–10
School year December–June
School type coeducational, day, private non-profit
Year founded 1978
Governed by elected Board of Directors
Regional organizations AISA, ECIS
Enrollment PreK 14; Elementary K–5 76; Middle
School 6–8 34; High School 9–12 16; Total 140

Nationalities of student body US 15; UK 6;
Cameroonian 28; Other(s) (Dutch, French) 91
Tuition/fee currency US Dollar
Tuition range 4,006–12,320
Annual fees Registration 336; PTA 100;
Yearbook 20
One time fees Capital Levy 3,360

EDUCATIONAL PROGRAM

Curriculum US, Intl
Average class size Elementary 12; Secondary 9
Language(s) of instruction English
Language(s) taught French, Spanish
Staff specialists computer, librarian
Special curricular programs computer/technology,
physical education, drama, journalism

Extra curricular programs computers, drama,
excursions/expeditions, newspaper, yearbook,
art, music
Sports basketball, martial arts, soccer,
swimming
Examinations ERB

CAMPUS FACILITIES

Location Suburban
Campus 1 hectare, 6 buildings, 13 classrooms,
1 computer lab, 35 instructional computers,

10,000 library volumes, 1 auditorium,
1 covered play area, 1 playing field,
1 science lab, air conditioning

AMERICAN SCHOOL OF YAOUNDE

Phone	237 223 0421
Fax	237 223 6011
Email	school@asoy.org
Website	www.asoy.org
Address	Rue Martin Paul Samba, Carrefour EMIA, BP 7475, Yaounde, Cameroon
Mailing address	Department of State, 2520 Yaounde Place, Washington, DC 20521-2520, USA

STAFF

Director Nanci L. Shaw, Ph.D.
Counselor Peter Schmitt
Registrar Jennifer J. Mbombo-Njoya
Assistant Director Valerie Ngolle

Business Manager Valerie Ngolle
IT Coordinator Peter Rock
Librarian Claudette Bristol

INFORMATION

Grade levels N–12
School year August–June
School type boarding, coeducational, day, private non-profit
Year founded 1964
Governed by elected Board of Directors
Accredited by CIS, Middle States
Regional organizations AISA, ECIS
Enrollment Nursery 6; PreK 7; Elementary K–5 70; Middle School 6–8 39; High School 9–12 63; Total 185
Nationalities of student body US 41; UK 3; Cameroonian 39; Other(s) 89

Tuition/fee currency US Dollar
Tuition range 3,200–11,900
Annual fees Boarding, 7-day 9,000; Busing 1,250; Lunch 850; ESL 1,500; Special Needs 2,000
One time fees Registration 300; Capital Levy 3,000
Boarding program grades 1–12
Boarding program length 5-day and 7-day
Boys 8 **Girls** 9
Graduates attending college 100%
Graduates have attended U of Delaware, Boston U, Drake U, Syracuse U, Carlton U

EDUCATIONAL PROGRAM

Curriculum US, AP
Average class size Elementary 15; Secondary 11
Language(s) of instruction English
Language(s) taught French
Staff specialists computer, counselor, ESL, learning disabilities, librarian, nurse
Special curricular programs art, instrumental music, vocal music, computer/technology, physical education

Extra curricular programs computers, community ervice, drama, excursions/expeditions, newspaper, photography, yearbook, Mt. Cameroon Climb; MS and HS student council
Sports baseball, basketball, football, martial arts, soccer, swimming, tennis, volleyball
Clubs student council, chess, yearbook, NHS, NJHS
Examinations AP, Iowa, PSAT, SAT, SAT II, TOEFL, ERBS

CAMPUS FACILITIES

Location Urban
Campus 4 hectares, 5 buildings, 20 classrooms, 2 computer labs, 34 instructional computers,

16,000 library volumes, 1 cafeteria, 1 covered play area, 1 infirmary, 1 playing field, 1 science lab, 1 pool, 4 tennis courts, air conditioning

Data from 2006/07 school year.

CAYMAN ISLANDS

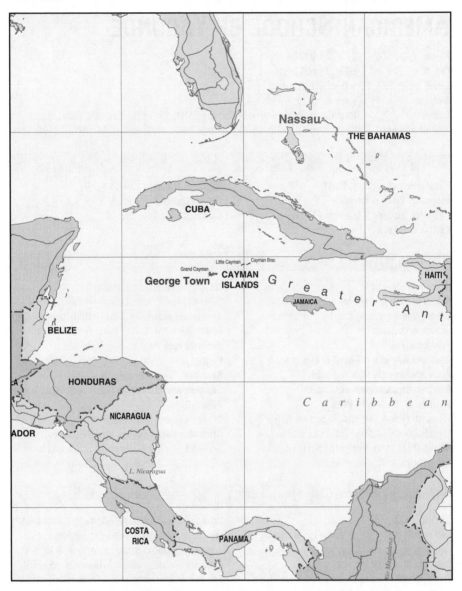

CAYMAN ISLANDS

Area:	262 sq km
Population:	46,600
Capital:	George Town
Currency:	Caymanian Dollar (KYD)
Languages:	English

CAYMAN INTERNATIONAL SCHOOL

Phone	345 945 4664
Fax	345 945 4650
Email	cayis@candw.ky
Website	www.CaymanInternationalSchool.org
Address	95 Minerva Drive, Camana Bay, Grand Cayman, Cayman Islands KY1-1206
Mailing address	PO Box 31364 Grand Cayman KY1-1206, Cayman Islands

STAFF

Director Jean Caskey
Vice Principal Nimmi Sekhar
Guidance/Admissions Andrea Kilam-Higgo
Office Manager Wendy Foreman

Librarian Katherine Field
Teaching staff Full time 45; Part time 1; Total 46
Nationalities of teaching staff US 12; UK 2;
Caymanian 2; Other(s) (Canadian) 30

INFORMATION

Grade levels N–12
School year September–June
School type coeducational, day, proprietary
Year founded 1994
Governed by International Schools Services, Inc.
Accredited by Middle States
Regional organizations AASCA, ACCAS

Enrollment Nursery 35; PreK 90; Elementary
K–5 108; Middle School 6–8 30;
High School 9–12 21; Total 284
Nationalities of student body US 40; UK 10;
Other(s) (Canadian, Swiss) 234
Tuition/fee currency Cayman Islands Dollar
Tuition range 6,500–12,600
One time fees Registration 300

EDUCATIONAL PROGRAM

Curriculum US, Intl
Average class size Elementary 15; Secondary 15
Language(s) of instruction English
Language(s) taught Spanish
Staff specialists computer, counselor, learning
disabilities, librarian
Special curricular programs art, instrumental
music, vocal music, computer/technology,
distance learning, physical education

Extra curricular programs computers, community
service, drama, excursions/expeditions,
newspaper, photography, yearbook
Sports basketball, soccer, swimming, tennis,
track and field
Examinations Iowa, PSAT, SAT

CAMPUS FACILITIES

Location Suburban
Campus 8 buildings, 22 classrooms, 2 computer
labs, 70 instructional computers, 15,000
library volumes, 1 auditorium, 1 cafeteria,

1 covered play area, 1 gymnasium, 1 infirmary,
1 playing field, 2 science labs, 1 pool, 2 tennis
courts, air conditioning

CHAD

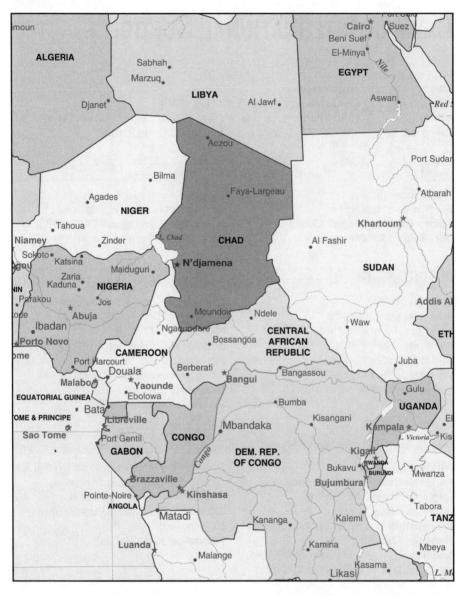

CHAD

Area:	1.284 million sq km
Population:	9,885,661
Capital:	N'Djamena
Currency:	Communaute Financiere Africaine Franc (XAF)
Languages:	French, Arabic

AMERICAN INTERNATIONAL SCHOOL OF N'DJAMENA

Phone	235 52 2103
Fax	235 51 5654
Email	aisn@aisn.org
Website	www.aisn.org
Address	BP 413, N'Djamena, Chad
Mailing address	U.S. State Dept., 2410 N'Djamena Place, Washington, DC 20521-2410

STAFF

Interim Director Angela E. Adamu
Teaching staff Full time 7; Part time 1; Total 8

Nationalities of teaching staff Chadian 3;
Other(s) (Nigerian, Filipino) 5

INFORMATION

Grade levels PreK–9
School year August–June
School type coeducational, day, private non-profit
Year founded 1986
Governed by appointed and elected Board of Directors
Regional organizations AISA

Enrollment PreK 10; Elementary K–5 6;
Middle School 6–8 2; Total 18
Nationalities of student body US 4; Chadian 10;
Other(s) (Swede, French) 4
Tuition/fee currency US Dollar
Tuition range 3,500–11,500
Annual fees Registration 125; Busing 1,200
One time fees Capital Levy 1,000

EDUCATIONAL PROGRAM

Curriculum US
Average class size Elementary 8
Language(s) of instruction English
Language(s) taught French
Staff specialists computer, librarian, math resource
Special curricular programs art, computer/technology, distance learning, physical education

Extra curricular programs computers, dance, drama, yearbook
Sports badminton, basketball, football, soccer, track and field, volleyball
Clubs African ballet, modern dance, arts and crafts, Calabash painting, math
Examinations International Schools Assessment

CAMPUS FACILITIES

Location Suburban
Campus 1 building, 7 classrooms, 1 computer lab, 15 instructional computers,

2,500 library volumes, 1 cafeteria, 1 playing field, 1 science lab, air conditioning

CHILE

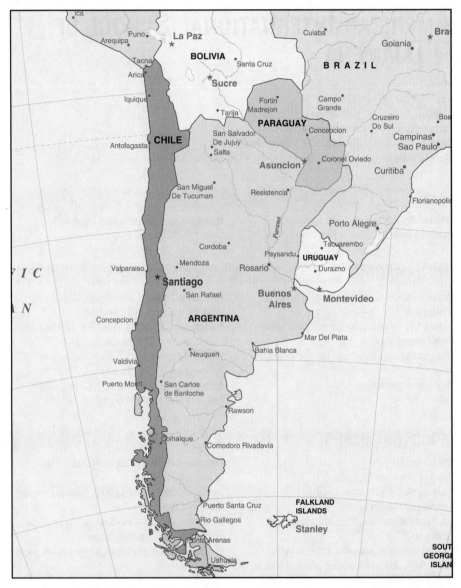

CHILE

Area:	756,950 sq km
Population:	16,284,741
Capital:	Santiago
Currency:	Chilean Peso (CLP)
Languages:	Spanish

Santiago **CHILE**

THE GRANGE SCHOOL

Phone	56 2 586 0100
Fax	56 2 227 1204
Email	rectoria@grange.cl
Website	www.grange.cl
Address	Principe de Gales 6154-La Reina, Santiago, 6870671, Chile
Mailing address	Casilla 218, Correo 12, Santiago, Chile

STAFF

Interim Head of School and Deputy Head–Pastoral Office (yrs. 11 & 12) Hernan Rivas
Deputy Head of Pastoral Office (years 7 to 10) Lance Baguley
Head of the Preparatory School Michael Freeman
Deputy Head of the Upper Preparatory School Carolina Varela

Deputy Head of the Lower Preparatory School Jocelyn Everett
Bursar Pubill Cristian
Head of IT Department Sandra Zapata
Head of Senior Library Paula Jorquera
Teaching staff Full time 106; Part time 13; Total 119

INFORMATION

Grade levels PreK–12
School year March–December
School type coeducational, day, private non-profit
Year founded 1928
Governed by appointed Board of Directors

Regional organizations ECIS
Tuition/fee currency Chilean Peso
Graduates attending college 99%
Graduates have attended U Catolica de Chile, U de Chile, U College of London, U of York

EDUCATIONAL PROGRAM

Curriculum National, Intl, IGCSE, U of Cambridge AICE Diploma
Average class size Elementary 20; Secondary 25

Language(s) of instruction English, Spanish
Language(s) taught French

CAMPUS FACILITIES

Location Urban
Campus 9 hectares, 18 buildings, 94 classrooms, 6 computer labs, 172 instructional computers, 50,000 library volumes, 2 auditoriums, 2 cafeterias, 1 covered play area, 3 gymnasiums, 1 infirmary, 5 playing fields, 7 science labs, 1 pool

THE INTERNATIONAL PREPARATORY SCHOOL

Phone	56 2 321 5800
Fax	56 2 321 5821
Email	info@tipschile.com
Website	www.tipschile.com
Address	Pastor Fernandez 16001, Lo Barnechea, Santiago, N/A, Chile

STAFF

Head of School Lesley A. Easton-Allen
Curriculum Coordinator Pamela Van Arsdale, Ed.D.
General Manager, Partner and Business/Finance Manager Carlos Willson Marin
Head of Technology Pablo Saba, Ed.D.

Head of Library/Media Center Maria Ines Strappa, Ed.D.
Teaching staff Full time 15; Part time 6; Total 21
Nationalities of teaching staff US 1; UK 2; Chilean 13; Other(s) (Irish, New Zealander) 5

INFORMATION

Grade levels N–12
School year March–December
School type coeducational, day, private non-profit, proprietary
Year founded 1975
Governed by appointed Parents' Advisory Committee
Sponsored by Easton & Cia. Ltda
Enrollment Nursery 8; PreK 14; Elementary K–5 67; Middle School 6–8 22; High School 9–12 11; Grade 13 2; Total 124

Nationalities of student body US 25; UK 18; Chilean 24; Other(s) (Australian, Finn) 57
Tuition/fee currency US Dollar
Tuition range 5,000–9,500
Annual fees Insurance 100; Lunch 1,000; Extra Curricular 300
One time fees Registration 80; Books 800
Graduates have attended Bristol U, U Finis Terrae, U of Colorado

EDUCATIONAL PROGRAM

Curriculum UK, IGCSE, A Levels
Average class size Elementary 8; Secondary 10
Language(s) of instruction English
Language(s) taught Spanish, French
Staff specialists computer, counselor, ESL, librarian, math resource, psychologist, speech/hearing
Special curricular programs art, instrumental music, vocal music, computer/technology, physical education

Extra curricular programs computers, community service, dance, drama, excursions/expeditions, newspaper, photography, yoga
Sports baseball, basketball, gymnastics, martial arts, skiing, soccer, swimming, tennis, track and field, volleyball
Examinations A-level GCE, GCSE, IGCSE

CAMPUS FACILITIES

Location Suburban
Campus 2 hectares, 5 buildings, 13 classrooms, 1 computer lab, 20 instructional computers,

25,000 library volumes, 1 auditorium, 1 covered play area, 1 infirmary, 1 playing field, 1 science lab, 1 tennis court

THE INTERNATIONAL SCHOOL NIDO DE AGUILAS

Phone	56 2 339 8100
Fax	56 2 216 7603
Email	abattistoni@nido.cl
Website	www.nido.cl
Address	Avenida El Rodeo 14200, Lo Barnechea, Santiago, Chile
Mailing address	Casilla 162, Correo La Dehesa, Lo Barnechea, Santiago, Chile

STAFF

Head of School Don Bergman, Ed.D.
High School Principal Nathan Walker
Middle School Principal Matt Beata
Elementary School Principal Michael Allen
IB Coordinator Claudia Rose
Chilean National Program Coordinator Maria Teresa Villa

Business Manager Alfredo Rebolar
Director of Technology Anne Croocker
Director Library and Media Center Linda Strauss
Teaching staff Full time 129; Part time 2; Total 131
Nationalities of teaching staff US 55; UK 3; Chilean 61; Other(s) (Canadian) 12

INFORMATION

Grade levels N–12
School year July–June
School type coeducational, day, private non-profit
Year founded 1934
Governed by elected Board of Directors
Accredited by Southern
Regional organizations AASSA
Enrollment Nursery 50; PreK 75; Elementary K–5 557; Middle School 6–8 273; High School 9–12 340; Total 1,295

Nationalities of student body US 239; UK 7; Chilean 637; Other(s) (Korean, Canadian) 412
Tuition/fee currency US Dollar
Tuition 12,760–12,760
Annual fees Registration 650; Busing 1,100
One time fees Capital Levy 8,500
Graduates attending college 99%
Graduates have attended Harvard U, Yale U, Stanford U, Princeton U, Johns Hopkins U

EDUCATIONAL PROGRAM

Curriculum US, National, IB Diploma
Average class size Elementary 20; Secondary 17
Language(s) of instruction English
Language(s) taught Spanish, French
Staff specialists computer, counselor, ESL, learning disabilities, librarian, math resource, nurse, psychologist, reading resource
Special curricular programs art, instrumental music, vocal music, computer/technology, physical education

Extra curricular programs computers, community service, dance, drama, environmental conservation, excursions/expeditions, newspaper, yearbook
Sports baseball, basketball, rugby, soccer, tennis, track and field, volleyball, field hockey, indoor soccer, cheerleading, dance
Clubs Model UN, chess, art, drama, languages, cultural dance, math, science
Examinations ACT, AP, IB, Iowa, PSAT, SAT, TOEFL

CAMPUS FACILITIES

Location Suburban
Campus 63 hectares, 14 buildings, 100 classrooms, 4 computer labs, 400 instructional computers,

38,000 library volumes, 2 auditoriums, 1 cafeteria, 1 gymnasium, 1 infirmary, 9 playing fields, 6 science labs, 4 tennis courts

SANTIAGO COLLEGE EDUCATIONAL FOUNDATION

Phone	56 2 751 3800
Fax	56 2 751 3802
Email	master@scollege.cl
Website	www.scollege.cl
Address	Lota 2465, Providencia, Santiago, 130-D, Chile

STAFF

Director Lorna Prado Scott, Ed.D.
High School Principal Ximena Susaeta, Ed.D.
Upper School Principal Peter Barnett, Ed.D.
Middle School Principal Robert Jones, Ed.D.
Lower School Principal Annabella Farba, Ed.D.
Infant School Principal Claudia Ribalta, Ph.D.
Business Manager Roberto Ternero

IT Administrator Oscar Padilla
Librarian Francisca Concha
Teaching staff Full time 132; Part time 43;
Total 175
Nationalities of teaching staff US 10; UK 5;
Chilean 154; Other(s) (Indian, Spaniard) 6

INFORMATION

Grade levels PreK–12
School year March–December
School type coeducational, day, private non-profit
Year founded 1880
Governed by elected Local Directing Council
Accredited by CIS, New England
Regional organizations ECIS
Enrollment PreK 134; Elementary K–5 796;
Middle School 6–8 397;
High School 9–12 513; Total 1,840

Nationalities of student body US 68; UK 10;
Chilean 1,668; Other(s) (Argentine, Spaniard) 94
Tuition/fee currency US Dollar
Tuition 6,025–6,025
One time fees Registration 3,451
Graduates attending college 97%
Graduates have attended U of Chile, U Catolica
de Chile, Massachusetts Institute of Technology,
U Diego Portales, U Los Andes

EDUCATIONAL PROGRAM

Curriculum National, Intl, IB Diploma, IBPYP,
IBMYP, DELF
Average class size Elementary 24; Secondary 24
Language(s) of instruction English, Spanish
Language(s) taught French
Staff specialists computer, counselor, ESL,
learning disabilities, librarian, nurse,
psychologist

Special curricular programs art, instrumental
music, vocal music, computer/technology,
physical education
Extra curricular programs community service,
drama, yearbook
Sports basketball, cross-country, gymnastics,
hockey, rugby, skiing, soccer, swimming,
tennis, track and field, volleyball
Examinations IB, PSAT, SAT

CAMPUS FACILITIES

Location Urban
Campus 14 hectares, 12 buildings, 80 classrooms,
5 computer labs, 120 instructional computers,

32,000 library volumes, 2 auditoriums,
2 cafeterias, 2 covered play areas, 3 gymnasiums,
2 infirmaries, 6 playing fields, 8 science labs

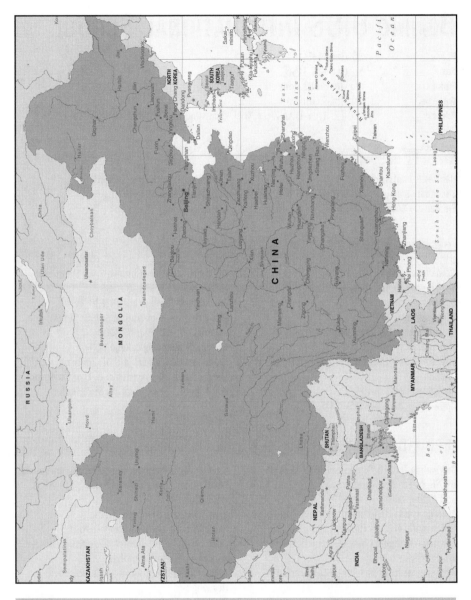

CHINA

Area:	9,596,960 sq km
Population:	1,321,851,888
Capital:	Beijing
Currency:	Yuan (CNY); Note–also referred to as the Renminbi (RMB)
Languages:	Chinese, Mandarin

Beijing BISS International School

Phone 86 10 6443 3151
Fax 86 10 6443 3156
Email afowles@biss.com.cn
Website www.biss.com.cn
Address No. 17, Area 4, An Zhen Xi Li, Chaoyang District, Beijing, 100029, China

STAFF

Head of School Anne Fowles
Secondary School Principal Raymond Williams
Elementary School Principal Wayne Demnar

Counselor, K–12 Karen Nelson
Chief Accountant Valerie Ong
Librarian Jacque Peterson

INFORMATION

Grade levels PreK–12
School year August–June
School type coeducational, day, proprietary
Year founded 1994
Governed by appointed Committee of Management
Sponsored by Int'l School Singapore Holdings Pte Ltd
Accredited by Western
Regional organizations EARCOS, ECIS

Tuition/fee currency Chinese Yuan Renminbi
Tuition range 33,575–64,385
Annual fees Capital Levy 14,220
One time fees Registration 3,950; Refundable Deposit 39,500; ESL 15,800
Graduates attending college 90%
Graduates have attended U of California in San Diego, Stanford U, Carleton U, U of California in Los Angeles, U of California in Berkeley

EDUCATIONAL PROGRAM

Curriculum Intl, IB Diploma, IBPYP, IBMYP, IGCSE, Alternative Academic Program for 11th and 12th grades
Average class size Elementary 20; Secondary 15
Language(s) of instruction English
Language(s) taught Chinese, French, Spanish, Korean
Staff specialists counselor, ESL, librarian

Special curricular programs instrumental music, vocal music, computer/technology, physical education
Extra curricular programs drama, excursions/expeditions, newspaper
Sports badminton, basketball, cricket, hockey, soccer, volleyball, handball
Clubs Model UN, Roots and Shoots, yoga, drawing
Examinations IB

CAMPUS FACILITIES

Location Urban
Campus 1 hectare, 1 building, 30 classrooms, 2 computer labs, 155 instructional computers, 17,324 library volumes, 1 auditorium, 1 cafeteria, 1 infirmary, 1 playing field, 3 science labs, 1 tennis court, air conditioning

Beijing   **CHINA**

Beijing City International School

Phone	86 10 87717171
Fax	86 10 87717778
Email	info@bcis.cn
Website	www.bcis.cn
Address	No.77, Baiziwan Nan Er Road, Chaoyang, Beijing, Chaoyang District, 100022, China

STAFF

Head of School Nicholas Bowley
Elementary School Principal Julie Todd
Upper School Principal Frank Davis
Guidance Counselor Anthony Carman
Administration Director Lawrence Tan

IT Coordinator Bruce Roadside
Teaching staff Full time 63; Part time 1; Total 64
Nationalities of teaching staff US 11; UK 7; Chinese 11; Other(s) (Australian, Canadian) 35

INFORMATION

Grade levels PreK–11
School year August–June
School type coeducational, day, private non-profit
Year founded 2005
Governed by appointed School Board
Sponsored by LandGent Group
Regional organizations EARCOS, ECIS

Enrollment PreK 32; Elementary K–5 180; Middle School 6–8 65; High School 9–12 38; Total 315
Nationalities of student body US 42; UK 35; Chinese 45; Other(s) (Korean, Canadian) 193
Tuition/fee currency Chinese Yuan Renminbi
Tuition range 80,000–128,000
Annual fees Capital Levy 32,000; Busing 8,000
One time fees Registration 8,000

EDUCATIONAL PROGRAM

Curriculum Intl, IB Diploma, IBPYP, IBMYP
Average class size Elementary 20; Secondary 22
Language(s) of instruction English
Language(s) taught Chinese
Staff specialists computer, counselor, ESL, learning disabilities, librarian, nurse
Special curricular programs art, computer/technology, physical education, general music

Extra curricular programs computers, community service, drama, environmental conservation, excursions/expeditions, yearbook
Sports badminton, basketball, football, gymnastics, hockey, martial arts, skiing, soccer, swimming, track and field
Examinations IB

CAMPUS FACILITIES

Location Urban
Campus 14 hectares, 3 buildings, 50 classrooms, 5 computer labs, 200 instructional computers, 15,000 library volumes, 1 auditorium,

2 cafeterias, 1 gymnasium, 1 infirmary, 1 playing field, 7 science labs, 1 pool, 1 tennis court, air conditioning

INTERNATIONAL SCHOOL OF BEIJING

Phone	86 10 8149 2345
Fax	86 10 8046 2002
Email	communications@isb.bj.edu.cn
Website	www.isb.bj.edu.cn
Address	No. 10 An Hua Street, Shunyi District, Beijing, 101318, China

STAFF

Head of School Thomas L. Hawkins, Ed.D.
High School Principal Rodney Fagg
Middle School Principal Dale Cox
Upper Elementary School Principal Greg Smith
Lower Elementary School Principal Sandra Hite
Chinese Program Principal Theresa Chao
CFO and COO Jim Kerrigan

Information Technology Director Russell Layton
High School Librarian Steve Anichowski
Teaching staff Full time 193; Part time 14; Total 207
Nationalities of teaching staff US 91; UK 13; Chinese 12; Other(s) (Canadian, Australian) 91

INFORMATION

Grade levels PreK–12
School year August–June
School type coeducational, day, private non-profit
Year founded 1980
Governed by elected Board of Trustees
Accredited by CIS, New England
Regional organizations EARCOS, ECIS
Enrollment Nursery 16; PreK 28; Elementary K–5 692; Middle School 6–8 525; High School 9–12 616; Total 1,877

Nationalities of student body US 809; UK 80; Other(s) (Korean, Canadian) 988
Tuition/fee currency US Dollar
Tuition range 7,500–18,970
Annual fees Capital Levy 2,585; Busing 960
One time fees Registration 200
Graduates attending college 99%
Graduates have attended Northwestern U, Brown U, Boston U, U of Chicago, Duke U

(Continued)

THE INTERNATIONAL SCHOOL OF BEIJING (Continued)

EDUCATIONAL PROGRAM

Curriculum Intl, IB Diploma
Average class size Elementary 18; Secondary 22
Language(s) of instruction English
Language(s) taught Chinese, French, Spanish
Staff specialists computer, counselor, ESL, learning disabilities, librarian, math resource, nurse, psychologist, reading resource, speech/hearing
Special curricular programs art, instrumental music, vocal music, computer/technology, physical education

Extra curricular programs computers, community service, dance, drama, environmental conservation, excursions/expeditions, literary magazine, newspaper, photography, yearbook
Sports badminton, baseball, basketball, cross-country, martial arts, rugby, soccer, softball, swimming, tennis, track and field, volleyball, community ice hockey, gymnastics, golf, cricket
Clubs stamp, debate, chess, Dragon Pride, running, swim team, Habitat for Humanity, Interact, golf, Roots and Shoots
Examinations ACT, AP, IB, Iowa, PSAT, SAT, SAT II, ISA

CAMPUS FACILITIES

Location Suburban
Campus 6 hectares, 1 building, 138 classrooms, 10 computer labs, 1200 instructional computers, 71,000 library volumes, 1 auditorium,

2 cafeterias, 3 covered play areas, 3 gymnasiums, 2 infirmaries, 6 playing fields, 12 science labs, 1 pool, 6 tennis courts, air conditioning

WESTERN ACADEMY OF BEIJING

Phone	86 10 8456 4155
Fax	86 10 6437 5936
Email	wabinfo@wab.edu
Website	www.wab.edu
Address	PO Box 8547, No. 10 Lai Guang Ying Dong Lu, Chao Yang District, Beijing, 100103, China

STAFF

Interim Director and Elementary School Principal
Karen O'Connell
Middle School Principal Donna Connolly
High School Principal Rena Mirkin
Admissions and Development Manager
Sinead Collins
Business Manager Wang Yan

Finance and Administration Manager
Dariusz Zarebinski
IT Manager Martin Leicht
Teacher and Librarian Jane Edgar
Teaching staff Full time 181; Part time 8; Total 189
Nationalities of teaching staff US 26; UK 27;
Chinese 15; Other(s) (Canadian, Australian) 121

INFORMATION

Grade levels N–12
School year August–June
School type coeducational, day, private non-profit
Year founded 1994
Governed by appointed and elected Board of
Governors
Accredited by CIS, New England
Regional organizations EARCOS, ECIS
Enrollment Nursery 42; PreK 70;
Elementary K–5 625; Middle School 6–8 315;
High School 9–12 440; Total 1,492

Nationalities of student body US 273; UK 97;
Other(s) (Korean, Canadian) 1,146
Tuition/fee currency Chinese Yuan Renminbi
Tuition range 67,520–137,855
Annual fees Capital Levy 30,666; Busing 8,133
One time fees Registration 1,660
Graduates have attended U of Illinois, Boston U,
Oxford U, Imperial Col London, U of Toronto

(Continued)

WESTERN ACADEMY OF BEIJING (Continued)

EDUCATIONAL PROGRAM

Curriculum Intl, IB Diploma, IBPYP, IBMYP
Average class size Elementary 21; Secondary 21
Language(s) of instruction English
Language(s) taught Chinese, French, Spanish, Dutch, Korean, Danish
Staff specialists computer, counselor, ESL, learning disabilities, librarian, nurse, psychologist, speech/hearing
Special curricular programs art, instrumental music, vocal music, computer/technology, physical education

Extra curricular programs computers, community service, dance, drama, environmental conservation, excursions/expeditions, photography, yearbook
Sports badminton, basketball, cross-country, football, gymnastics, martial arts, rugby, skiing, soccer, swimming, tennis, track and field, volleyball
Examinations ACT, IB, PSAT, SAT, TOEFL

CAMPUS FACILITIES

Location Suburban
Campus 7 hectares, 6 buildings, 106 classrooms, 6 computer labs, 1032 instructional computers, 75,000 library volumes, 3 auditoriums, 7 cafeterias, 3 gymnasiums, 3 infirmaries, 2 playing fields, 10 science labs, 1 pool, 5 tennis courts, air conditioning

QSI INTERNATIONAL SCHOOL OF CHENGDU

Phone 86 028 851 13852
Fax 86 028 851 98393
Email chengdu@qsi.org
Website www.qsi.org
Address #188 South, 3rd Ring Road, American Garden, Chengdu, 610041, China

STAFF

Director Karin Noll, Ed.D.
Administrative Assistant Irene Feng
Teaching staff Full time 11; Part time 3; Total 14

Nationalities of teaching staff US 5; UK 1;
Chinese 5; Other(s) (Canadian, Australian) 3

INFORMATION

Grade levels N–11
School year August–June
School type coeducational, day, private non-profit
Year founded 2002
Governed by appointed Board of Directors
Sponsored by Quality Schools International
Enrollment Nursery 10; PreK 10;
Elementary K–5 30; Middle School 6–8 6;
High School 9–12 5; Total 61

Nationalities of student body US 25; UK 1;
Other(s) (Malaysian, Finn) 35
Tuition/fee currency US Dollar
Tuition 16,500–16,500
Annual fees Capital Levy 1,600; Busing 1,200;
Lunch 450
One time fees Registration 100

EDUCATIONAL PROGRAM

Curriculum US, AP
Average class size Elementary 7
Language(s) of instruction English
Language(s) taught Mandarin
Staff specialists computer, counselor, ESL,
librarian
Special curricular programs instrumental music,
vocal music, computer/technology, physical
education

Extra curricular programs computers, drama,
excursions/expeditions, yearbook
Sports badminton, basketball, hockey, soccer,
swimming, tennis, volleyball
Clubs Roots and Shoots
Examinations AP, Iowa, WrAP

CAMPUS FACILITIES

Location Suburban
Campus 1 building, 14 classrooms,
1 computer lab, 30 instructional computers,

4,000 library volumes, 1 cafeteria, 1 infirmary,
1 playing field, 1 science lab, 1 tennis court,
air conditioning

DALIAN AMERICAN INTERNATIONAL SCHOOL

Phone	86 411 8757 2000
Fax	86 411 8791 5656
Email	admissions@daischina.org
Website	www.daischina.org
Address	No.2 Dianchi Road, Golden Pebble National Resort, Development Area, Dalian, 116650, China

STAFF

Director Brian D. Berneking
Administrative Manager Dawei Cui
Teaching staff Full time 10; Total 10

Nationalities of teaching staff US 7; Chinese 1; Other(s) (Peruvian, Romanian) 2

INFORMATION

Grade levels K–8
School year August–June
School type proprietary
Year founded 2006
Sponsored by Dalian American Int'l School Co; Managed by International Schools Services, Inc.
Regional organizations EARCOS
Enrollment Elementary K–5 40; Middle School 6–8 10; Total 50

Nationalities of student body US 8; Other(s) (Korean, Taiwanese) 42
Tuition/fee currency US Dollar
Tuition range 10,000–15,000
Annual fees Busing 1,200; Lunch 700; Technology 300
One time fees Registration 150; Capital Levy 2,600

EDUCATIONAL PROGRAM

Curriculum US, Intl
Average class size Elementary 12; Secondary 6
Language(s) of instruction English
Language(s) taught Mandarin
Staff specialists computer, ESL, librarian, nurse

Special curricular programs art, vocal music, computer/technology, distance learning, physical education
Extra curricular programs computers, community service, chess, art
Sports badminton, basketball, soccer, swimming, track and field, volleyball

CAMPUS FACILITIES

Location Suburban
Campus 39 hectares, 1 building, 10 classrooms, 1 computer lab, 30 instructional computers,

1 cafeteria, 1 covered play area, 1 gymnasium, 1 playing field, 1 science lab, 1 pool, 1 tennis court, air conditioning

AMERICAN INTERNATIONAL SCHOOL OF GUANGZHOU

Phone	86 20 8735 3393
Fax	86 20 8735 3339
Email	info@aisgz.edu.cn
Website	www.aisgz.edu.cn
Address	No. 3, Yan Yu Street South, Er Sha Island, Yuexiu District, Guangzhou, 510105, China

STAFF

Director F. Joseph Stucker
Elementary School Principal Gary MacPhie
Middle School Principal Ken Roy
High School Principal Judy Hunter
Director of Admissions Barbara MacPhie
High School Counselor Kathy Ortman

Business Manager Ann Tay
Technology Coordinator Robert Bauer
Librarian Kathy Turner
Teaching staff Full time 82; Part time 3; Total 85
Nationalities of teaching staff US 48; UK 4; Chinese 2; Other(s) (Australian, Canadian) 31

INFORMATION

Grade levels PreK–12
School year August–June
School type coeducational, day, private non-profit
Year founded 1981
Governed by elected School Board
Accredited by Western
Regional organizations EARCOS
Enrollment PreK 45; Elementary K–5 395; Middle School 6–8 215; High School 9–12 240; Total 895

Nationalities of student body US 180; UK 30; Other(s) (Korean, Canadian) 685
Tuition/fee currency US Dollar
Tuition range 10,400–13,800
Annual fees Capital Levy 2,500
One time fees Registration 250
Graduates attending college 95%
Graduates have attended U of Virginia, Harvard U, Brown U, Stanford U, Princeton U

EDUCATIONAL PROGRAM

Curriculum US, Intl, AP, IB Diploma, IBPYP
Average class size Elementary 20; Secondary 17
Language(s) of instruction English
Language(s) taught Mandarin, French, Spanish
Staff specialists computer, counselor, learning disabilities, librarian, nurse
Special curricular programs art, instrumental music, vocal music, computer/technology, physical education

Extra curricular programs computers, community service, dance, drama, environmental conservation, excursions/expeditions, literary magazine, newspaper, photography, yearbook
Sports badminton, basketball, rugby, soccer, softball, tennis, track and field, volleyball
Clubs Habitat for Humanity, Roots and Shoots, Amnesty International, National Honor Society, Model UN
Examinations AP, IB, Iowa, PSAT, SAT, SAT II

CAMPUS FACILITIES

Location Suburban
Campus 12 hectares, 2 buildings, 110 classrooms, 4 computer labs, 450 instructional computers,

30,000 library volumes, 2 auditoriums, 1 cafeteria, 3 gymnasiums, 1 infirmary, 2 playing fields, 7 science labs, air conditioning

Guangzhou

CHINA

QSI INTERNATIONAL SCHOOL OF DONGGUAN

Phone	86 769 22300131
Fax	86 769 22300130
Email	dongguan@qsi.org
Website	www.qsi.org
Address	Block A2, Dongcheng Center, Dongguan, China

STAFF

Director Karen Hall, Ed.D.
Teaching staff Full time 15; Part time 1; Total 16

Nationalities of teaching staff US 8; Chinese 5; Other(s) (Canadian) 3

INFORMATION

Grade levels PreK–10
School year August–June
School type coeducational, day, private non-profit
Year founded 2004
Governed by appointed QSI Executive Board
Sponsored by Quality Schools International
Regional organizations ACCAS

Enrollment PreK 25; Elementary K–5 35; Middle School 6–8 8; High School 9–12 2; Total 70
Nationalities of student body US 8; UK 2; Other(s) (Chinese, Korean) 60
Tuition/fee currency US Dollar
Tuition range 4,000–11,500
Annual fees Capital Levy 1,600; Busing 1,160
One time fees Registration 100; Lunch 450

EDUCATIONAL PROGRAM

Curriculum US, Intl
Average class size Elementary 8
Language(s) of instruction English
Language(s) taught Chinese
Staff specialists computer, ESL, reading resource

Special curricular programs art, vocal music, computer/technology, physical education
Extra curricular programs community service, dance, drama, excursions/expeditions, yearbook
Examinations Iowa, PSAT, SAT

CAMPUS FACILITIES

Location Urban
Campus 2 buildings, 15 classrooms, 2 computer labs, 17 instructional computers,

2,500 library volumes, 2 cafeterias, 1 playing field, 1 science lab, 2 pools, air conditioning

HANGZHOU INTERNATIONAL SCHOOL

Phone	86 571 8669 0045
Fax	86 571 8669 0044
Email	bhorvath@scischina.org
Website	www.scischina.org/hangzhou
Address	80 Dongxin Street, Binjiang District, Hangzhou, 310053, China

STAFF

Principal Brian Horvath, Ed.D.
Finance Manager Andy Seng
Teaching staff Full time 35; Part time 2; Total 37

Nationalities of teaching staff Other(s)
(Canadian, Cameroonian) 37

INFORMATION

Grade levels N–12
School year August–June
School type coeducational, day, private non-profit
Year founded 2002
Governed by appointed Board of Governors
Sponsored by International School Development
Foundation
Accredited by Western
Regional organizations EARCOS

Enrollment Nursery 8; PreK 14;
Elementary K–5 120; Middle School 6–8 33;
High School 9–12 15; Total 190
Nationalities of student body US 20; UK 1;
Other(s) (Japanese, Korean) 169
Tuition/fee currency Chinese Yuan Renminbi
Tuition range 40,500–133,200
Annual fees Busing 8,200
One time fees Registration 1,700

EDUCATIONAL PROGRAM

Curriculum US, AP
Average class size Elementary 12; Secondary 6
Language(s) of instruction English
Language(s) taught Mandarin
Staff specialists computer, ESL, librarian,
nurse, psychologist
Special curricular programs art, instrumental
music, vocal music, computer/technology,
distance learning, physical education

Extra curricular programs computers, community
service, dance, drama, environmental
conservation, excursions/expeditions, literary
magazine, yearbook
Sports basketball, football, soccer, track and
field, volleyball
Examinations PSAT, SAT, NWEA MAP

CAMPUS FACILITIES

Location Urban
Campus 3 hectares, 3 buildings, 18 classrooms,
3 computer labs, 55 instructional computers,
5,000 library volumes, air conditioning

Data from 2006/07 school year.

CARMEL JEWISH DAY SCHOOL

Phone	852 296 41600
Fax	852 281 34121
Email	admin@carmel.edu.hk
Website	www.carmel.edu.hk
Address	10 Borrett Road, Mid Levels, Hong Kong, China

STAFF

Head of School Edwin I. Epstein, Ed.D.
Principal Lauren Goldman Brown
Business Manager Kaisha Chow
IT Teacher and Coordinator Mark Davidson

Librarian Susan Morrison
Teaching staff Full time 50; Part time 8; Total 58
Nationalities of teaching staff US 4; UK 8;
Chinese 15; Other(s) (Israeli, Canadian) 31

INFORMATION

Grade levels N–8
School year August–June
School type coeducational, church-affiliated,
day, private non-profit
Year founded 1991
Governed by appointed and elected Board of
Trustees
Accredited by Western
Regional organizations EARCOS

Enrollment Nursery 32; PreK 16; Elementary
K–5 121; Middle School 6–8 40; Total 209
Nationalities of student body US 50; UK 36;
Chinese 5; Other(s) (Israeli, Canadian) 118
Tuition/fee currency Hong Kong Dollar
Tuition range 59,820–112,880
Annual fees On-going Expense Fund 2,000
One time fees Registration 1,000

EDUCATIONAL PROGRAM

Curriculum US, Intl
Average class size Elementary 20; Secondary 13
Language(s) of instruction English, Hebrew
Language(s) taught French, Putonghua
Staff specialists computer, counselor, ESL,
learning disabilities, librarian, math resource,
reading resource
Special curricular programs art, instrumental
music, computer/technology, physical education

Extra curricular programs computers, dance,
newspaper, photography, yearbook,
modern language
Sports football, gymnastics, swimming
Clubs Book Lovers, cooking, drawing, Flight
Simulation Club, GBG Dance Team, Jewish arts
and crafts, photography, Putonghua (school
publications), Spanish
Examinations Stanford

CAMPUS FACILITIES

Location Urban
Campus 1 hectare, 2 buildings, 20 classrooms,
1 computer lab, 30 instructional computers,

5,000 library volumes, 1 auditorium, 2 cafeterias,
1 covered play area, 1 gymnasium, 1 playing
field, 1 science lab, 1 pool, air conditioning

CHINESE INTERNATIONAL SCHOOL

Phone	852 251 25918
Fax	852 251 07378
Email	cis_info@cis.edu.hk
Website	www.cis.edu.hk
Address	1 Hau Yuen Path, Braemar Hill, Hong Kong, China

STAFF

Head of School Theodore S. Faunce, Ph.D.
Head of Secondary School Barry Drake, Ph.D.
Head of Primary School Tonya Porter
Business Manager Monica Vallor
Director of Information and Communication Head of Technology Tommy Svinhufvud

Librarian Phoebe Wong
Teaching staff Full time 114; Part time 6; Total 120
Nationalities of teaching staff US 27; UK 35; Chinese 24; Other(s) (Australian, Canadian) 54

INFORMATION

Grade levels PreK–12
School year September–June
School type coeducational, day, private non-profit
Year founded 1983
Governed by appointed Board of Governors
Accredited by CIS, New England
Regional organizations EARCOS, ECIS
Enrollment PreK 88; Elementary K–5 528; Middle School 6–8 360; High School 9–12 430; Total 1,406

Nationalities of student body US 316; UK 329; Chinese 260; Other(s) (Australian, Canadian) 501
Tuition/fee currency Hong Kong Dollar
Tuition range 82,400–130,700
Annual fees Capital Levy 7,500; Busing 13,000; Lunch 4,000; Books 3,000
One time fees Registration 1,000
Graduates attending college 100%
Graduates have attended Princeton U, Stanford U, U of Pennsylvania, Cambridge U, London School of Economics

EDUCATIONAL PROGRAM

Curriculum Intl, IB Diploma, IBMYP
Average class size Elementary 22; Secondary 20
Language(s) of instruction English, Putonghua
Language(s) taught English, Putonghua, French, Spanish
Staff specialists counselor, ESL, learning disabilities, librarian, nurse, reading resource, speech/hearing

Special curricular programs art, instrumental music, computer/technology, physical education
Extra curricular programs community service, drama, literary magazine, yearbook
Sports basketball, cross-country, football, golf, gymnastics, hockey, rugby, soccer, squash, swimming, tennis, track and field, volleyball
Examinations IB, SAT

CAMPUS FACILITIES

Location Urban
Campus 1 hectare, 7 buildings, 115 classrooms, 7 computer labs, 600 instructional computers, 60,000 library volumes, 1 auditorium,

2 cafeterias, 4 gymnasiums, 1 infirmary, 1 playing field, 8 science labs, 1 pool, air conditioning

HONG KONG ACADEMY

Phone	852 2575 8282
Fax	852 2891 4460/1
Email	office@hkacademy.edu.hk
Website	www.hkacademy.edu.hk
Address	4/F Chung On Hall, 15 Stubbs Road, Hong Kong, China

STAFF

Director and CEO Andy Page-Smith, Ed.D.
Elementary Principal Virginia Hunt
Middle School Principal and Curriculum Cooordinator Merris Page-Smith
Business and Operation Manager Anna Wong

IT Integration Coordinator Timothy Lower
Librarian Virginia Hand
Teaching staff Full time 34; Part time 10; Total 44
Nationalities of teaching staff US 14; UK 5; Chinese 7; Other(s) (Australian, Canadian) 18

INFORMATION

Grade levels PreK–8
School year August–June
School type coeducational, day, private non-profit
Year founded 2000
Governed by appointed and elected Board of Management
Accredited by Western
Regional organizations EARCOS

Enrollment PreK 61; Elementary K–5 185; Middle School 6–8 27; Total 273
Nationalities of student body US 91; UK 40; Chinese 17; Other(s) (Australian, Canadian) 125
Tuition/fee currency Hong Kong Dollar
Tuition 109,800–109,800
Annual fees Capital Levy 10,000; Scholarship Levy 2,500
One time fees Registration 1,500

EDUCATIONAL PROGRAM

Curriculum Intl, IBPYP
Average class size Elementary 16; Secondary 15
Language(s) of instruction English
Language(s) taught Mandarin, Spanish, French
Staff specialists computer, learning disabilities, librarian, speech/hearing
Special curricular programs art, instrumental music, vocal music, computer/technology, physical education

Extra curricular programs computers, community service, dance, drama, environmental conservation, excursions/expeditions, literary magazine, newspaper, arts and crafts
Sports badminton, basketball, golf, hockey, martial arts, rugby, soccer, volleyball
Clubs chess, papermaking, ice skating, running, guitar

CAMPUS FACILITIES

Location Urban
Campus 2 buildings, 20 classrooms, 80 instructional computers,

9,000 library volumes, 1 auditorium, 1 covered play area, 1 gymnasium, 1 science lab, air conditioning

HONG KONG INTERNATIONAL SCHOOL

Phone	852 3149 7000
Fax	852 2813 4293
Email	oia@hkis.edu.hk
Website	www.hkis.edu.hk
Address	1 Red Hill Road, Tai Tam, Hong Kong, China

STAFF

Head of School Richard W. Mueller
High School Principal Patricia Klekamp
Middle School Principal Wil Chan, Ph.D.
Upper Primary Principal Bruce Kelsh, Ph.D.
Lower Primary Principal Madeleine Heide
Director of Admissions Vicky Seehafer

CFO Ken Fowler
Director of Information Technology Francis Thong
Librarian David Elliott
Teaching staff Full time 493; Total 493
Nationalities of teaching staff US 242; UK 35;
Chinese 35; Other(s) (Canadian, Australian) 181

INFORMATION

Grade levels PreK–12
School year August–June
School type coeducational, church-affiliated,
day, private non-profit
Year founded 1966
Governed by appointed Board of Managers
Sponsored by Mr. Jeong Jin Park, Board President
Accredited by Western
Regional organizations EARCOS
Enrollment PreK 153; Elementary K–5 954;
Middle School 6–8 600; High School 9–12 843;
Total 2,550

Nationalities of student body US 1,250; UK 230;
Chinese 200; Other(s) (Canadian, Australian) 820
Tuition/fee currency Hong Kong Dollar
Tuition range 137,200–157,100
Annual fees Capital Levy 12,000
One time fees Registration 1,500
Graduates attending college 99%
Graduates have attended Havard U, Princeton U,
Stanford U, Yale U, Duke U

(Continued)

HONG KONG INTERNATIONAL SCHOOL (Continued)

EDUCATIONAL PROGRAM

Curriculum US, AP
Average class size Elementary 17–20; Secondary 19–22
Language(s) of instruction English
Language(s) taught Mandarin, French, Spanish
Staff specialists computer, counselor, ESL, librarian, math resource, nurse, psychologist, reading resource
Special curricular programs art, instrumental music, vocal music, computer/technology

Extra curricular programs computers, community service, dance, drama, environmental conservation, excursions/expeditions, literary magazine, photography, yearbook
Sports badminton, basketball, football, golf, gymnastics, hockey, martial arts, rugby, soccer, swimming, tennis, track and field, volleyball
Clubs photography, interact, film
Examinations SAT, SAT II, Stanford

CAMPUS FACILITIES

Location Rural
Campus 4 buildings, 1200 instructional computers, 110,000 library volumes, 2 auditoriums, 3 cafeterias, 2 covered play areas, 4 gymnasiums, 3 infirmaries, 1 playing field, 10 science labs, 2 pools, 2 tennis courts, air conditioning

INTERNATIONAL CHRISTIAN SCHOOL

Phone   852 2304 6808
Fax   852 2336 6114
Email   ics@ics.edu.hk
Website   www.ics.edu.hk
Address   1 On Muk Lane, Shek Mun, New Territories, Hong Kong, China

STAFF

Headmaster Ben H. Norton
Director of Curriculum and Instruction
Ed Tackett, Ed.D.
Director of Admissions and Student Services
Jerry Buckner
Director of Advancement To be announced
Academic Dean Brian VanTassel

Curriculum Coordinator Jeff Auty
Director of Finance and Administration LC Wan
Director of Information Technology Hillman Lai
Head Librarian Phil McBrayer, Ph.D.
Teaching staff Full time 90; Part time 5; Total 95
Nationalities of teaching staff US 65; UK 2;
Chinese 7; Other(s) (Canadian) 16

INFORMATION

Grade levels PreK–12
School year August–June
School type coeducational, day, private non-profit
Year founded 1992
Governed by appointed and elected Board of
Trustees
Accredited by Western
Regional organizations EARCOS
Enrollment PreK 96; Elementary K–5 450;
Middle School 6–8 195; High School 9–12 200;
Total 941

Nationalities of student body US 480; UK 10;
Chinese 280; Other(s) (Canadian, Korean) 171
Tuition/fee currency Hong Kong Dollar
Tuition range 59,000–92,500
Annual fees Busing 5,400
One time fees Registration 1,000;
Capital Levy 10,000; Books 500
Graduates attending college 77%
Graduates have attended U of Toronto, U of
California in Berkeley, Oxford U, Hong Kong U,
U of California in Los Angeles

EDUCATIONAL PROGRAM

Curriculum US, AP
Average class size Elementary 25; Secondary 22
Language(s) of instruction English
Language(s) taught Mandarin, French
Staff specialists computer, counselor, ESL,
learning disabilities, librarian, nurse,
psychologist
Special curricular programs art, instrumental
music, vocal music, computer/technology,
physical education, Week without Walls,
Madrigals, drama

Extra curricular programs community service,
drama, excursions/expeditions, newspaper,
photography, yearbook
Sports badminton, basketball, cross-country,
soccer, swimming, tennis, track and field,
volleyball
Clubs chess, Chinese Culture, marketing,
ceramics, production studio
Examinations AP, PSAT, SAT, SAT II, Stanford

CAMPUS FACILITIES

Location Urban
Campus 2 hectares, 2 buildings, 48 classrooms,
3 computer labs, 212 instructional computers,
23,000 library volumes, 1 auditorium,

1 cafeteria, 1 covered play area, 2 gymnasiums,
1 infirmary, 5 science labs, 1 pool,
air conditioning

THE INTERNATIONAL MONTESSORI SCHOOL

Phone	852 2861 0339
Fax	852 3006 2950
Email	info@montessori.edu.hk
Website	www.montessori.edu.hk
Address	1/F, 29 Queen's Road East, Hong Kong, China
Mailing address	4/F 6-8 Salvation Army Street, Wanchai, Hong Kong SAR

STAFF

Principal Karin Ann
Vice Principal James Park
School Business Manager and School Supervisor Anne Sawyer

Librarian Doug Gordon
Teaching staff Full time 18; Part time 2; Total 20
Nationalities of teaching staff US 2; Chinese 10; Other(s) (Irish, Canadian) 8

INFORMATION

Grade levels N–8
School year September–June
School type coeducational, day, private non-profit
Year founded 2001
Governed by appointed Board of Directors
Sponsored by The International Montessori Education Foundation Limited
Enrollment Nursery 50; PreK 50; Elementary K–5 95; Middle School 6–8 5; Total 200

Nationalities of student body US 56; UK 24; Chinese 40; Other(s) (Canadian, German) 80
Tuition/fee currency Hong Kong Dollar
Tuition range 70,000–108,000
Annual fees Busing 10,000
One time fees Registration 1,000;
Capital Levy 50,000
Curriculum US, UK, Intl, Montessori
Average class size Elementary 25

EDUCATIONAL PROGRAM

Language(s) of instruction English
Language(s) taught Mandarin
Staff specialists computer, ESL, learning disabilities, librarian, math resource, psychologist, reading resource
Special curricular programs art, vocal music, computer/technology, physical education
Extra curricular programs computers, community service, drama, environmental conservation,
excursions/expeditions
Sports baseball, basketball, cricket, football, gymnastics, martial arts, soccer
Examinations Stanford, British National Curriculum Key Stage Tests

CAMPUS FACILITIES

Location Urban
Campus 2 buildings, 11 classrooms, 1 computer lab, 20 instructional computers, 5,000
library volumes, 1 auditorium, 1 cafeteria, 1 covered play area, 1 gymnasium, 1 infirmary, 1 playing field, air conditioning

ISLAND SCHOOL

Phone	852 2524 7135
Fax	852 2840 1673
Email	school@mail.island.edu.hk
Website	www.island.edu.hk
Address	20 Borrett Road, Mid-levels, Hong Kong, China

STAFF

Principal Michelle J. Hughes, Ed.D.
Admission Officer Dilip Sandhu
School Bursar Rebecca Yip

Head of IT Andy Statham
Librarian Eva Bannon
Teaching staff Full time 150; Total 150

INFORMATION

Grade levels 7–13
School year August–June
School type coeducational, day
Year founded 1967
Governed by elected English Schools Foundation

Tuition/fee currency Hong Kong Dollar
Tuition 85,000–85,000
Graduates attending college 95%
Graduates have attended Oxford U,
Cambridge U, Yale U, Stanford U, Princeton U

EDUCATIONAL PROGRAM

Curriculum UK, IB Diploma, IGCSE, GenCSE
Average class size Secondary 30
Language(s) of instruction English
Language(s) taught Chinese, French, Spanish, Japanese
Staff specialists counselor
Special curricular programs art, instrumental music, vocal music, computer/technology

Extra curricular programs computers, community service, drama, environmental conservation, yearbook
Sports cricket, softball, volleyball, Karate, sailing, netball
Clubs juggling, Scrabble, debating, Mandarin
Examinations GCSE, IB, IGCSE, SAT

CAMPUS FACILITIES

Location Urban
Campus 1 hectare, 6 buildings, 42 classrooms, 8 computer labs, 240 instructional computers, 25,000 library volumes, 1 auditorium, 1 covered play area, 1 gymnasium, 1 infirmary, 10 science labs, 1 pool, 1 tennis court, air conditioning

NORWEGIAN INTERNATIONAL SCHOOL

Phone	852 2658 0341
Fax	852 2651 0050
Email	principal@nis.edu.hk
Website	www.nis.edu.hk
Address	175 Kwong Fuk Road, Tai Po, N.T., Hong Kong, China

STAFF

Principal John Lok

INFORMATION

Grade levels PreK–6
School year August–June
School type church-affiliated, private non-profit
Year founded 1984

Governed by Norwegian Lutheran Mission
Sponsored by Norwegian Lutheran Mission
Tuition/fee currency Hong Kong Dollar
Tuition range 3,900–6,150

EDUCATIONAL PROGRAM

Curriculum Intl, International Primary Curriculum
Average class size Elementary 10–15

Language(s) of instruction English
Language(s) taught Mandarin
Staff specialists ESL

CAMPUS FACILITIES

Location Suburban

Campus air conditioning

Data from 2006/07 school year.

SCHOOL OF THE NATIONS (MACAU)

Phone	853 701 759
Fax	853 701 724
Email	admin@schoolofthenations.com
Website	www.schoolofthenations.com
Address	Rua Louis G Gomes #136, Edif Lei San, 4 Andar, Macau SAR, China

STAFF

Director Saba Payman

INFORMATION

Grade levels PreK–11
School year September–June
School type coeducational, day, private non-profit
Year founded 1988

Governed by Badi Foundation
Tuition/fee currency US Dollar
Graduates attending college 90%

EDUCATIONAL PROGRAM

Curriculum Intl, IGCSE
Average class size Elementary 19; Secondary 15
Language(s) of instruction English
Language(s) taught Mandarin
Special curricular programs art, computer/technology

Extra curricular programs community service, excursions/expeditions, yearbook
Sports basketball
Examinations GCSE, IGCSE

CAMPUS FACILITIES

Location Urban

Campus 10,000 library volumes, air conditioning

Data from 2006/07 school year.

NANJING INTERNATIONAL SCHOOL

Phone	86 25 85899111
Fax	86 25 85899222
Email	recruitment@nanjing-school.com
Website	www.nanjing-school.com
Address	Nanjing International School, Xue Heng Lu 8, Xian Lin College and University Town, Qi Xia District, Nanjing, 210046, China

STAFF

Director Gez Hayden
K–12 Principal Richard Swart
IB Diploma Coordinator Phil Harrington
IB MYP Coordinator Arden Tyoschin
IB PYP Coordinator Karen Campbell
Assistant IB PYP Coordinator Luke Schoff
Operations and Finance Manager Arek Owczarek

Information Technology Coordinator / Design Technology Coordinator
Theresa Jenkins / Steven Edkins
Head of Library/Media Center Neil Kilah
Teaching staff Full time 70; Total 70
Nationalities of teaching staff US 7; UK 10; Chinese 7; Other(s) (Australian, New Zealander) 46

INFORMATION

Grade levels PreK–12
School year August–July
School type coeducational, day, private non-profit
Year founded 1990
Governed by elected Parent-elected Board
Accredited by CIS, New England
Regional organizations EARCOS
Enrollment PreK 16; Elementary K–5 220; Middle School 6–8 107; High School 9–12 89; Total 432

Nationalities of student body US 43; UK 19; Other(s) (Korean, German) 371
Tuition/fee currency Chinese Yuan Renminbi
Tuition range 118,275–158,530
One time fees Registration 830
Graduates attending college 100%
Graduates have attended Michigan State U, New York U, U of California in Los Angeles, U of New South Wales, U of Birmingham

EDUCATIONAL PROGRAM

Curriculum IB Diploma, IBPYP, IBMYP
Average class size Elementary 16; Secondary 16
Language(s) of instruction English

Language(s) taught Mandarin, French
Staff specialists computer, counselor, ESL, learning disabilities, librarian, nurse

CAMPUS FACILITIES

Location Suburban
Campus 7 hectares, 1 building, 54 classrooms, 3 computer labs, 260 instructional computers, 23,900 library volumes, 1 auditorium,

1 cafeteria, 1 covered play area, 1 gymnasium, 1 infirmary, 2 playing fields, 4 science labs, 2 tennis courts, air conditioning

QINGDAO INTERNATIONAL SCHOOL

Phone 86 532 8890 8000
Fax 86 532 8890 8950
Email jdfisch47@yahoo.com
Website www.qischina.org
Address Middle Sector, Songling Road, Qingdao, Shandong, 266061, China

STAFF

Director Jeffrey D. Fischmann
Upper School Principal Peter Burnside
Lower School Principal Tim Green
Counselor and Director of Admissions David Addicott
Athletic Director Jim Erber

Business and Finance Manager Dana Wang
IT Coordinator David Casler
Head of Library Greg Ellis
Teaching staff Full time 36; Total 36
Nationalities of teaching staff US 18; UK 2; Chinese 5; Other(s) (Canadian) 11

INFORMATION

Grade levels PreK–12
School year August–June
School type coeducational, day, proprietary
Year founded 1998
Governed by appointed Owners
Sponsored by Qingdao Education Bureau
Accredited by Western
Enrollment PreK 15; Elementary K–5 90; Middle School 6–8 60; High School 9–12 60; Total 225

Nationalities of student body US 20; UK 10; Korean 10; Other(s) (Italian, Swede) 195
Tuition/fee currency Chinese Yuan Renminbi
Tuition range 82,000–120,000
Annual fees Registration 4,500; Busing 6,000; Lunch 4,500
One time fees Capital Levy 20,000
Graduates attending college 90%
Graduates have attended Waseda U, National Seoul U, Hanyang U, Fudan U, George Washington U

EDUCATIONAL PROGRAM

Curriculum Intl
Average class size Elementary 15; Secondary 17
Language(s) of instruction English
Language(s) taught Mandarin, Chinese
Staff specialists computer, counselor, ESL, nurse
Special curricular programs art, vocal music, computer/technology, distance learning, physical education

Extra curricular programs computers, community service, dance, drama, environmental conservation, excursions/expeditions, literary magazine, newspaper, photography, yearbook, media studies
Sports badminton, basketball, gymnastics, rugby, soccer, swimming, track and field, volleyball

CAMPUS FACILITIES

Location Suburban
Campus 20 hectares, 2 buildings, 20 classrooms, 3 computer labs, 60 instructional computers,

1 cafeteria, 1 gymnasium, 1 infirmary, 3 playing fields, 1 science lab, air conditioning

CONCORDIA INTERNATIONAL SCHOOL SHANGHAI

Phone	86 21 589 90380
Fax	86 21 589 91685
Email	jimk@ciss.com.cn
Website	www.ciss.com.cn
Address	999 Mingyue Road, JinQiao, Pudong, Shanghai, 201206, China

STAFF

Head of School Jim M. Koerschen
Elementary School Principal Louise S. Weber
Middle School Principal Mark Lewis
High School Principal David Harris
Curriculum Coordinator Kristin Kappelmann
Business Administrator Curtiss Larson

Director of Technology Michael Weber
School Librarian Kim Gertz
Teaching staff Full time 81; Part time 4; Total 85
Nationalities of teaching staff US 57; Chinese 6; Other(s) (Canadian, Australian) 22

INFORMATION

Grade levels PreK–12
School year August–June
School type coeducational, church-affiliated, day, private non-profit
Year founded 1998
Governed by appointed Board of Directors
Accredited by Western
Regional organizations EARCOS
Enrollment PreK 60; Elementary K–5 415; Middle School 6–8 209; High School 9–12 156; Total 840

Nationalities of student body US 526; UK 25; Chinese 54; Other(s) (Canadian, Korean) 235
Tuition/fee currency US Dollar
Tuition range 18,150–24,200
Annual fees Busing 1,307
One time fees Registration 200; Lunch 3
Graduates attending college 100%
Graduates have attended Boston U, Virginia Polytechnic Institute, U of Michigan, Wheaton Col, Waseda U

EDUCATIONAL PROGRAM

Curriculum US, Intl, AP
Average class size Elementary 17; Secondary 18
Language(s) of instruction English
Language(s) taught Chinese, Spanish, French
Staff specialists computer, counselor, librarian, nurse
Special curricular programs art, instrumental music, vocal music, computer/technology, physical education

Extra curricular programs computers, community service, drama, excursions/expeditions, photography, yearbook
Sports badminton, basketball, martial arts, rugby, soccer, volleyball
Examinations AP, PSAT, SAT, SAT II, CTP4

CAMPUS FACILITIES

Location Suburban
Campus 466 instructional computers, 18,000 library volumes, 5 auditoriums, 2 cafeterias, 5 covered play areas, 3 gymnasiums, 1 infirmary, 2 playing fields, 3 science labs, air conditioning

SHANGHAI AMERICAN SCHOOL

Phone	86 21 6221 1445
Fax	86 21 6221 1269
Email	info@saschina.org
Website	www.saschina.org
Address	258 Jin Feng Lu, Zhudi Town, Minhang District, Shanghai, 201107, China

STAFF

Superintendent Dennis Larkin, Ed.D.
Puxi High School Principal Alan Knobloch
Puxi Elementary Principal Mary Lane
Puxi Middle School Principal Bernadette Carmody
Deputy Superintendent Andrew Torris
Pudong High School Principal
Jonathan Borden, Ed.D.

Business Services Manager/Finance Manager
Himmat Sandhu/Rosanna Lee
Technology Manager Orion Weber
High School Librarian Jeff Barons
Teaching staff Full time 344; Part time 3; Total 347
Nationalities of teaching staff US 208; UK 2;
Chinese 29; Other(s) (Canadian, Australian) 108

INFORMATION

Grade levels PreK–12
School year August–June
School type coeducational, day, private non-profit
Year founded 1912
Governed by appointed and elected Board of
Directors
Sponsored by USA Consulate in Shanghai
Accredited by Western
Regional organizations EARCOS, ECIS
Enrollment PreK 69; Elementary K–5 1,062;
Middle School 6–8 756; High School 9–12
1,018; Total 2,905

Nationalities of student body US 1,250; UK 58;
Chinese 40; Other(s) (Canadian, Korean) 1,557
Tuition/fee currency US Dollar
Tuition range 12,750–21,250
Annual fees Capital Levy 4,250; Busing 980
One time fees Registration 250
Graduates attending college 98%
Graduates have attended Massachusetts Institute
of Technology, London School of Economics,
Cornell U, Johns Hopkins U, Duke U

EDUCATIONAL PROGRAM

Curriculum US, AP, IB Diploma
Average class size Elementary 18; Secondary 18
Language(s) of instruction English
Language(s) taught Mandarin, French, Spanish
Staff specialists computer, counselor, ESL,
librarian, math resource, nurse, psychologist,
reading resource

Special curricular programs art, instrumental
music, vocal music, computer/technology,
physical education
Extra curricular programs computers, community
service, drama, excursions/expeditions,
newspaper, photography, yearbook
Sports baseball, basketball, hockey, soccer,
swimming, tennis, track and field
Examinations AP, IB, PSAT, SAT

CAMPUS FACILITIES

Location Suburban
Campus 22 hectares, 17 buildings,
176 classrooms, 8 computer labs, 825
instructional computers,

50,000 library volumes, 1 auditorium, 3
cafeterias, 2 covered play areas, 4 gymnasiums,
4 infirmaries, 4 playing fields, 10 science labs,
1 pool, air conditioning

SHANGHAI COMMUNITY INTERNATIONAL SCHOOLS

Phone   86 21 6261 4338
Fax   86 21 6261 4639
Email   info@scischina.org
Website   www.scischina.org
Address   1161 Hongqiao Road, Shanghai, 200051, China

STAFF

Head of School William R. Parker, Ph.D.
Deputy Head and Director of Technology and Assessment Jon Zurfluh
Principals at Hong Qiao Campus Michael Donaldson, Stacey Gailey and Jeffery Stubbs
Principals at Pudong Campus Jane Queen and Derek Luebbe

Director of Admission Susan Schulman
Director of Curriculum Bronwyn Weale
Business Manager Andy Seng
Teaching staff Full time 130; Part time 20; Total 150
Nationalities of teaching staff US 70; UK 5; Chinese 25; Other(s) (Australian, Canadian) 50

INFORMATION

Grade levels N–12
School year August–June
School type coeducational, day, private non-profit
Year founded 1996
Governed by appointed Board of Directors
Sponsored by International School Foundation
Accredited by Western
Regional organizations EARCOS
Enrollment Nursery 44; PreK 91; Elementary K–5 755; Middle School 6–8 265; High School 9–12 250; Total 1,405

Nationalities of student body US 350; UK 40; Other(s) (Dutch, Korean) 1,015
Tuition/fee currency US Dollar
Tuition range 8,333–25,000
One time fees Registration 215
Graduates attending college 100%
Graduates have attended U of London, Pennsylvania State U, U of Edinburgh, Smith Col, Boston U

(Continued)

SHANGHAI COMMUNITY INTERNATIONAL SCHOOLS (Continued)

EDUCATIONAL PROGRAM

Curriculum US, Intl, AP
Average class size Elementary 16; Secondary 18
Language(s) of instruction English
Language(s) taught Mandarin, French, Spanish
Staff specialists computer, counselor, ESL, librarian, nurse, psychologist
Special curricular programs art, instrumental music, vocal music, computer/technology, physical education, drama

Extra curricular programs computers, community service, dance, drama, environmental conservation, excursions/expeditions, newspaper, yearbook
Sports basketball, cross-country, football, rugby, soccer, swimming, volleyball
Examinations AP, PSAT, SAT, NWEA-MAP

CAMPUS FACILITIES

Location Urban
Campus 12 hectares, 7 buildings, 90 classrooms, 12 computer labs, 320 instructional computers, 20,000 library volumes, 1 auditorium, 2 cafeterias, 4 covered play areas, 4 gymnasiums, 2 infirmaries, 3 playing fields, 6 science labs, 2 pools, 1 tennis court, air conditioning

YEW CHUNG INTERNATIONAL SCHOOL OF SHANGHAI

Phone	86 21 6219 5910
Fax	86 21 6219 0675
Email	inquiry@ycef.com
Website	www.ycef.com
Address	Hongqiao Campus: 11 Shui Cheng Road, Gubei Campus: 18 Rong Hua Xi Road, Pudong Campus: 1817 Hua Mu Road, Shanghai, 200336, China
Mailing address	11 Shui Cheng Road, 200336 Shanghai, China

STAFF

Director Betty Chan Po-King, Ph.D.
Superintendent Tom Ulmet
Co-Principal, Pudong Campus Margaret Fler
Co-Principal, Pudong Campus Cherry Chen
Co-Principal, Gubei Campus James Fielding

Co-Principal, Hong Qiao Campus Zhang Hong
Head, Accounts Division Jin Yi Wu
Head, IT Division Roy Wong
Head, Library Services Annick Wong

INFORMATION

Grade levels N–13
School year August–June
School type boarding, coeducational, day, private non-profit
Year founded 1993
Governed by appointed Yew Chung Education Foundation
Accredited by CIS, New England
Regional organizations ECIS

Tuition/fee currency Chinese Yuan Renminbi
Tuition range 33,000–174,000
Boarding program grades 4–13
Boarding program length 5-day **Boys** 6 **Girls** 5
Graduates attending college 95%
Graduates have attended Central Saint Martins Col, Imperial Col, Michigan State U, London School of Economics, Instituto Marangoni

EDUCATIONAL PROGRAM

Curriculum UK, Intl, IB Diploma, IGCSE
Average class size Elementary 21; Secondary 18
Language(s) of instruction English, Mandarin
Staff specialists computer, counselor, librarian, nurse

Sports badminton, basketball, hockey, soccer, softball, swimming, track and field, volleyball
Examinations GCSE, IB, IGCSE, PSAT, SAT, SAT II

CAMPUS FACILITIES

Location Urban
Campus 3 buildings, 95 classrooms, 4 computer labs, 3 auditoriums, 3 cafeterias, 3 covered play areas, 2 gymnasiums, 3 infirmaries, 3 playing fields, 4 science labs, air conditioning

QSI INTERNATIONAL SCHOOL OF SHEKOU

Phone	86 755 2667 6031
Fax	86 755 2667 6030
Email	shekou@qsi.org
Website	www.qsi.org/shk
Address	8 Tai Zi Road, Bitao Center, Shekou, Guangdong, 518067, China

STAFF

Director Britt Brantley, Ed.D.
Director of Instruction Ron Duffy
Upper School Coordinator Robb Bouma
Lower School Coordinator Kees Riemens
Resource Coordinator Melissa Stalker
Counselor Justin Walker, Ph.D.

Accountant Joy Bonsol
Technology Coordinator Tim Winterfeld
Librarian Chris LoFrumento
Teaching staff Full time 89; Part time 11; Total 100
Nationalities of teaching staff US 79; UK 2;
Chinese 8; Other(s) (Canadian, Australian) 11

INFORMATION

Grade levels N–12
School year August–June
School type coeducational, day, private non-profit
Year founded 2001
Governed by appointed Board of Directors
Enrollment Nursery 30; PreK 110;
Elementary K–5 300; Middle School 6–8 160;
High School 9–12 120; Grade 13 5; Total 725
Nationalities of student body US 150; UK 15;
Other(s) (Korean, Brazilian) 560

Tuition/fee currency US Dollar
Tuition range 4,200–11,500
Annual fees Capital Levy 1,600; Busing 900;
Lunch 400
One time fees Registration 100
Graduates attending college 100%
Graduates have attended U of Oregon,
U of Michigan, Ohio State U, U of Portland,
U of San Francisco

EDUCATIONAL PROGRAM

Curriculum US, Intl, AP
Average class size Elementary 12; Secondary 9
Language(s) of instruction English
Language(s) taught Chinese, French, German
Staff specialists computer, counselor, ESL,
learning disabilities, librarian, nurse, reading
resource, speech/hearing
Special curricular programs art, instrumental
music, vocal music, computer/technology,
physical education

Extra curricular programs computers, community
service, drama, excursions/expeditions,
yearbook
Sports badminton, basketball, football, martial
arts, rugby, soccer, track and field, volleyball
Clubs Model UN, Odyssey of the Mind
Examinations AP, PSAT, SAT, SAT II

CAMPUS FACILITIES

Location Urban
Campus 1 hectare, 1 building, 42 classrooms,
3 computer labs, 190 instructional computers,

11,000 library volumes, 1 covered play area,
1 gymnasium, 1 infirmary, 1 playing field,
3 science labs, 1 tennis court, air conditioning

SHEKOU INTERNATIONAL SCHOOL

Phone	86 755 2669 3669
Fax	86 755 2667 4099
Email	rdunseth@sis.org.cn
Website	www.sis.org.cn
Address	Jing Shan Villas, Nan Hai Boulevard, Shekou-Shenzhen, Guangdong, 518067, China

STAFF

Director Robert Dunseth
Curriculum and Admissions Coordinator Treena Casey
Counselor Andrea Callaway
Assistant Principal of Middle and High School Mike Neeland
Assistant Principal of Elementary School Brian Tuia

Government Relations Manager Lisa Ge
Technology Coordinator Carol Neeland
Senior Librarian Mary Alice Osborne
Teaching staff Full time 88; Part time 6; Total 94
Nationalities of teaching staff US 37; UK 2; Chinese 29; Other(s) (Canadian, New Zealander) 26

INFORMATION

Grade levels N–12
School year August–June
School type coeducational, day
Year founded 1988
Governed by International Schools Services, Inc.
Sponsored by Academic Information Consulting (Shenzhen) Ltd.
Accredited by Western
Regional organizations EARCOS

Enrollment Nursery 30; PreK 90; Elementary K–5 230; Middle School 6–8 95; High School 9–12 75; Total 520
Nationalities of student body US 135; UK 15; Other(s) (Canadian, Korean) 370
Tuition/fee currency Chinese Yuan Renminbi
Tuition range 32,000–156,000
One time fees Capital Levy 36,000; Busing 10,000
Graduates attending college 100%

EDUCATIONAL PROGRAM

Curriculum US, Intl, AP
Average class size Elementary 15; Secondary 15
Language(s) of instruction English
Language(s) taught Mandarin, French
Staff specialists computer, counselor, ESL, librarian, nurse, psychologist
Special curricular programs art, instrumental music, vocal music, computer/technology, distance learning, physical education, drama
Extra curricular programs computers, community service, dance, drama, environmental conservation, excursions/expeditions, literary magazine, newspaper, photography, yearbook
Sports badminton, basketball, martial arts, rugby, soccer, softball, squash, swimming, tennis, track and field, volleyball
Clubs Model UN, global issues, chess, cooking, intramural sports, bowling, student government, Roots and Shoots
Examinations AP, SAT, SAT II, ISA (International Schools Assessment)

CAMPUS FACILITIES

Location Suburban
Campus 10 hectares, 12 buildings, 60 classrooms, 3 computer labs, 250 instructional computers, 15,000 library volumes, 2 auditoriums, 1 cafeteria, 1 covered play area, 2 gymnasiums, 1 infirmary, 2 playing fields, 6 science labs, 2 pools, 3 tennis courts, air conditioning

TEDA INTERNATIONAL SCHOOL

Phone 86 22 66226158
Fax 86 22 62001818
Email info@tedainternationalschool.net
Website www.tedainternationalschool.net
Address 72 Third Avenue, Teda, Tianjin, 300457, China

STAFF

Principal Andrew F. Watts
Bursar Isabella Fan
Computer Teacher Allan Fowler
Librarian Louise Salter

Teaching staff Full time 39; Total 39
Nationalities of teaching staff US 5; UK 3;
Other(s) (Canadian, Australian) 31

INFORMATION

Grade levels N–12
School year August–June
School type coeducational, day, private non-profit
Year founded 1995
Governed by appointed Steering Committee
Sponsored by Song Kuojun
Accredited by Western
Regional organizations EARCOS
Enrollment Nursery 10; PreK 20;
Elementary K–5 80; Middle School 6–8 80;
High School 9–12 80; Total 270

Nationalities of student body US 15; UK 5;
Other(s) (Canadian, Korean) 250
Tuition/fee currency US Dollar
Tuition 12,000–12,000
Annual fees Busing 425
One time fees Registration 260
Graduates attending college 100%
Graduates have attended U of Waterloo,
U of Guelph, U of Nebraska,
U of British Columbia

EDUCATIONAL PROGRAM

Curriculum Intl, AP
Average class size Elementary 15; Secondary 15
Language(s) of instruction English
Language(s) taught Chinese
Staff specialists computer, counselor, ESL,
librarian, nurse
Special curricular programs art, instrumental
music, vocal music, computer/technology,
physical education

Extra curricular programs computers, community
service, dance, excursions/expeditions,
newspaper, photography, yearbook
Sports badminton, basketball, cross-country,
martial arts, rugby, soccer, swimming, tennis,
track and field, volleyball
Examinations AP, PSAT, SAT

CAMPUS FACILITIES

Location Suburban
Campus 5 hectares, 6 buildings, 40 classrooms,
3 computer labs, 120 instructional computers,
15,000 library volumes, 1 auditorium,

1 cafeteria, 1 covered play area, 1 gymnasium,
1 infirmary, 1 playing field, 2 science labs,
air conditioning

INTERNATIONAL SCHOOL OF TIANJIN

Phone	86 22 2859 2001
Fax	86 22 2859 2007
Email	info@istianjin.net
Website	www.istianjin.org
Address	Weishan Road Shuanggang, Jinnan Economic Development Zone, Jinnan District, Tianjin, 300350, China

STAFF

Interim Director and Elementary Principal Steve Moody
Secondary Principal Cathy Jones
Business Director Jay Myers
Information Technology Coordinator Kleber Quevedo

Librarian Beth Gourley
Teaching staff Full time 51; Part time 6; Total 57
Nationalities of teaching staff US 14; UK 8; Chinese 6; Other(s) (Australian, New Zealander) 29

INFORMATION

Grade levels N–12
School year August–June
School type coeducational, day, private non-profit
Year founded 1994
Governed by appointed Board of Governors
Accredited by CIS, Western
Regional organizations EARCOS
Enrollment Nursery 14; PreK 14; Elementary K–5 198; Middle School 6–8 128; High School 9–12 116; Total 470

Nationalities of student body US 30; UK 16; Other(s) (Korean, Australian) 424
Tuition/fee currency Chinese Yuan Renminbi
Tuition range 49,700–126,900
Annual fees Capital Levy 24,900; Busing 7,200
One time fees Registration 1,700; Grade 12 IB Diploma Exam 5,200
Graduates attending college 95%
Graduates have attended Sarah Lawrence Col, Purdue U, Pennsylvania State U, U of Southern California, Seoul National U

EDUCATIONAL PROGRAM

Curriculum Intl, IB Diploma, IBPYP, IBMYP
Average class size Elementary 15; Secondary 16
Language(s) of instruction English
Language(s) taught Chinese, French, Korean, Spanish, Japanese
Staff specialists computer, counselor, ESL, learning disabilities, librarian, nurse
Special curricular programs art, instrumental music, vocal music, computer/technology, physical education

Extra curricular programs computers, community service, dance, drama, environmental conservation, excursions/expeditions, newspaper, yearbook, Model UN, choir, band
Sports badminton, basketball, soccer, softball, swimming, track and field, volleyball
Clubs ACAMIS and ISAC Sports Leagues, student council, International Award Scheme, chess, cooking
Examinations ACT, IB, PSAT, SAT, SAT II, TOEFL

CAMPUS FACILITIES

Location Suburban
Campus 5 hectares, 3 buildings, 38 classrooms, 2 computer labs, 140 instructional computers, 19,000 library volumes, 1 cafeteria, 1 covered play area, 1 gymnasium, 1 infirmary, 1 playing field, 3 science labs, air conditioning

AMERICAN INTERNATIONAL SCHOOL OF WUXI

Phone	86 510 8552 3468
Fax	86 510 8552 3313
Email	info@aisw.org
Website	www.aisw.org
Address	No. 1 Wanghu Road Meiyuan, Wuxi, Jiangsu, 214066, China

STAFF

Director / Principal Lila Leung
Teaching staff Full time 8; Total 8

Nationalities of teaching staff US 6; Chinese 2

INFORMATION

Grade levels K–6
School year August–June
School type boarding, coeducational, day, private non-profit
Year founded 2006
Governed by appointed Board of Directors
Sponsored by Guanghua Educational Co., Managed by International Schools Services, Inc.

Enrollment Elementary K–5 50; Total 50
Tuition/fee currency US Dollar
Tuition 15,000
Annual fees Boarding, 5-day 5,000; Busing 900
One time fees Registration 200
Boarding program grades 1–5
Boarding program length 5-day

EDUCATIONAL PROGRAM

Curriculum US, Intl, IBPYP, PYP candidate
Average class size Elementary 20
Language(s) of instruction English
Language(s) taught Chinese
Staff specialists ESL

Special curricular programs art, instrumental music, computer/technology, physical education
Extra curricular programs community service, dance, excursions/expeditions

CAMPUS FACILITIES

Location Suburban
Campus 1 building, 35 classrooms, 1 computer lab, 1 auditorium, 1 cafeteria, 1 gymnasium,

1 infirmary, 4 playing fields, 1 pool, 4 tennis courts, air conditioning

XIAMEN INTERNATIONAL SCHOOL

Phone	86 592 625 6581
Fax	86 592 6072900
Email	askxis@hotmail.com
Website	www.xischina.com
Address	Jiu Tian Hu, Xinglin District, Xiamen, Fujian Province, 361022, China

STAFF

Head of School John M. Godwin
Principal, K–12 Patricia Puia
Deputy Head David Wei
Personnel Director David Huang
Counselor Tim Wilson
Adminstrative Assistant Celeste Zou

Director of Accounting Linda Lin
IT Coordinator Betsy Pickering
Director of Library Services Janet Wright
Teaching staff Full time 45; Total 45
Nationalities of teaching staff US 21; UK 3; Chinese 12; Other(s) (Filipino) 9

INFORMATION

Grade levels PreK–12
School year August–June
School type coeducational, day, private non-profit
Year founded 1997
Governed by appointed and elected Board of Directors
Accredited by Western
Regional organizations EARCOS
Enrollment PreK 20; Elementary K–5 95; Middle School 6–8 65; High School 9–12 95; Total 275

Nationalities of student body US 50; UK 10; Host 5; Other(s) (Chinese, Korean) 210
Tuition/fee currency US Dollar
Tuition range 10,000–14,650
Annual fees Busing 450; Activities 300
One time fees Registration 200
Graduates attending college 100%
Graduates have attended Concordia U, Pennsylvania State U, U of Nottingham, Harvard U, Boston Col

EDUCATIONAL PROGRAM

Curriculum US, Intl, IB Diploma, IBPYP, IBMYP
Average class size Elementary 15; Secondary 15
Language(s) of instruction English
Language(s) taught Mandarin, French
Staff specialists computer, counselor, ESL, librarian, nurse

Special curricular programs art, instrumental music, vocal music, computer/technology, physical education
Extra curricular programs community service, dance, yearbook
Sports basketball, soccer, swimming, volleyball
Examinations ACT, IB, PSAT, SAT, SAT II, TOEFL

CAMPUS FACILITIES

Location Suburban
Campus 3 hectares, 3 buildings, 11 classrooms, 2 computer labs, 120 instructional computers, 15,000 library volumes, 1 cafeteria, 1 covered play area, 1 gymnasium, 1 infirmary, 2 playing fields, 2 science labs, 1 pool, 1 tennis court, air conditioning

QSI International School of Zhuhai

Phone   86 756 815 6134
Fax   86 756 815 6134
Email   zhuhai@qsi.org
Website   www.qsi.org
Address   2 Langxing St., Villa #105, Gongbei, Zhuhai, 519020, China

STAFF

Director Robert H. Tower, Ed.D.
Teaching staff Full time 13; Part time 1; Total 14

Nationalities of teaching staff US 5; Chinese 5; Other(s) (Canadian, Portuguese) 4

INFORMATION

Grade levels PreK–10
School year August–June
School type coeducational, day, private non-profit
Year founded 1999
Governed by appointed Board of Directors
Accredited by Middle States
Enrollment PreK 10; Elementary K–5 30; Middle School 6–8 25; High School 9–12 5; Total 70

Nationalities of student body US 10; UK 4; Other(s) (German, Dane) 56
Tuition/fee currency US Dollar
Tuition range 5,700–14,500
Annual fees Capital Levy 1,600
One time fees Registration 100

EDUCATIONAL PROGRAM

Curriculum US
Average class size Elementary 8; Secondary 0
Language(s) of instruction English
Language(s) taught Chinese
Staff specialists computer, ESL

Special curricular programs art, vocal music, computer/technology, physical education
Extra curricular programs dance, drama, yearbook
Sports badminton, martial arts, soccer, volleyball
Examinations Iowa, ERB WrAP

CAMPUS FACILITIES

Location Urban
Campus 1 hectare, 1 building, 10 classrooms, 1 computer lab, 10 instructional computers,

3,000 library volumes, 1 cafeteria, 1 covered play area, 1 playing field, 1 pool, 1 tennis court, air conditioning

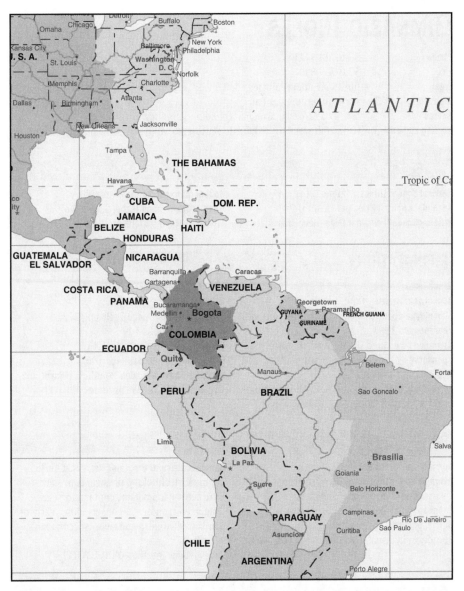

COLOMBIA

Area:	1,138,910 sq km
Population:	44,379,598
Capital:	Bogota
Currency:	Colombian Peso (COP)
Languages:	Spanish

GIMNASIO INGLES

Phone	57 6 749 5111
Fax	57 6 749 8446
Email	jurazan@gimnasioingles.edu.co
Website	www.gimnasioingles.edu.co
Address	Km 3 Via Circasia, Armenia, Quindio, Colombia
Mailing address	Calle 20 Norte #14-19 Edificio Barlovento, Apto 204, Armenia, Colombia

STAFF

General School Director Jaime A. Urazan
Secondary School Principal Heath Hough
Primary School Principal Olga Mercedes Forero

School Manager Xandra Jaramillo
Head of Technology Isabel Sarmiento
Librarian Martha Elena Medina

INFORMATION

Grade levels N–12
School year August–June
School type coeducational, day, private non-profit
Year founded 1991
Governed by elected Board of Directors
Sponsored by Fundacion Gimnasio Ingles
Regional organizations ACCAS
Enrollment Elementary K–5 340; Middle School 6–8 137; High School 9–12 134; Total 611

Tuition/fee currency US Dollar
Tuition range 1,150–1,866
Annual fees Insurance 7; Busing 272; Lunch 325; Books 109
One time fees Registration 1,133
Graduates attending college 100%
Graduates have attended Pontificia U Javeriana, Wichita State U, U de Los Andes, U EAFIT

EDUCATIONAL PROGRAM

Curriculum US, National
Average class size Elementary 20; Secondary 19
Language(s) of instruction English, Spanish
Language(s) taught English, Spanish
Staff specialists computer, counselor, ESL, librarian, physician, psychologist, speech/hearing

Special curricular programs art, vocal music, computer/technology, physical education
Extra curricular programs community service, drama, environmental conservation, yearbook
Sports basketball, gymnastics, soccer, tennis, volleyball
Examinations Iowa, PSAT, SAT, TOEFL

CAMPUS FACILITIES

Location Suburban
Campus 4 hectares, 5 buildings, 35 classrooms, 2 computer labs, 29 instructional computers, 6,000 library volumes, 1 cafeteria, 1 infirmary, 6 playing fields, 2 science labs

Data from 2006/07 school year.

COLEGIO ALBANIA

Phone	57 5 350 5648
Fax	57 5 777 4969
Email	coalbadirector@mushaisa.com
Website	www.mushaisa.com/coalbania.html
Address	A.A. 51973, Barranquilla, Colombia
Mailing address	c/o Cerrejon, PO Box 02-5573, Miami, FL 33102, USA

STAFF

Director Ruth Allen
Secondary School Principal Luis Monroy
Upper Primary School Principal
Juan Carlos Rodriguez
Lower Primary School Principal Rosita Payan
Business Manager Jose Rafael Barrios

Computer Teacher Carlos Herrera
Library Director Gladys Arias
Teaching staff Full time 72; Total 72
Nationalities of teaching staff US 7; UK 3;
Colombian 60; Other(s) (Canadian) 2

INFORMATION

Grade levels PreK–12
School year August–June
School type coeducational, company-sponsored,
day, private non-profit, proprietary
Year founded 1983
Governed by appointed Board of Trustees
Sponsored by Cerrejon
Accredited by Southern
Regional organizations ACCAS, AASSA

Enrollment PreK 21; Elementary K–5 166;
Middle School 6–8 143; High School 9–12
208; Total 538
Nationalities of student body US 4; UK 1;
Colombian 533
Tuition/fee currency Colombian Peso
Graduates attending college 100%
Graduates have attended Pontificia U Javeriana,
U de los Andes, U of Phoenix, Concordia U, U
La Sorbona

EDUCATIONAL PROGRAM

Curriculum US, National, Intl
Average class size Elementary 25; Secondary 25
Language(s) of instruction English, Spanish
Language(s) taught English, Spanish
Staff specialists computer, counselor, ESL,
learning disabilities, librarian, nurse,
psychologist, speech/hearing
Special curricular programs art, instrumental
music, computer/technology, physical education

Extra curricular programs community service,
dance, drama, environmental conservation,
newspaper, yearbook
Sports baseball, basketball, football, golf,
soccer, softball, swimming, tennis, track and
field, volleyball, chess, Tae Kwon Do
Clubs robotics, Model UN, Young Scientists,
technical drawing, weight lifting, astronomy,
Business Enterprise, Young Congress, theatre
Examinations Iowa, SAT, TOEFL

CAMPUS FACILITIES

Location Rural
Campus 5 hectares, 5 buildings, 54 classrooms,
2 computer labs, 114 instructional computers,
20,000 library volumes, 1 auditorium,

1 cafeteria, 2 covered play areas, 1 gymnasium,
1 infirmary, 3 playing fields, 3 science labs,
2 pools, 2 tennis courts, air conditioning

COLEGIO KARL C. PARRISH

Phone 57 5 359 8929
Fax 57 5 359 8828
Email mail@kcparrish.edu.co
Website www.kcparrish.edu.co
Address KM. 2 Antigua Via a Puerto Colombia, Barranquilla, Atlantico, Colombia
Mailing address A.A. 52962, Barranquilla, Colombia

STAFF

Director Laura Horbal, Ed.D.
Elementary School Principal Hectalina Donado, Ed.D.
Secondary School Principal Alex Partos, Ed.D.
Business Manager Mauricio Naranjo
Information Technology Coordinator Myriam Rosado
Teaching staff Full time 54; Part time 10; Total 64
Nationalities of teaching staff US 11; Colombian 48; Other(s) (Canadian) 5

INFORMATION

Grade levels N–12
School year August–June
School type coeducational, day, private non-profit
Year founded 1938
Governed by appointed Board of Directors
Accredited by Southern
Regional organizations ACCAS, AASSA
Enrollment Nursery 51; PreK 46; Elementary K–5 322; Middle School 6–8 142; High School 9–12 163; Total 724
Nationalities of student body US 58; Colombian 640; Other(s) (Costa Rican, Italian) 26
Tuition/fee currency US Dollar
Tuition range 4,155–6,000
Annual fees Insurance 23; Books 211; Activities 150; Optimal Resource Center 735; Parent Teachers Association 33
One time fees Registration 6,130
Graduates attending college 100%
Graduates have attended Georgia Institute of Technology, U of Connecticut, Columbia U, Boston U, Cornell U

EDUCATIONAL PROGRAM

Curriculum US, AP, Colombian Bachillerato
Average class size Elementary 26; Secondary 26
Language(s) of instruction English, Spanish
Staff specialists computer, counselor, learning disabilities, librarian, math resource, nurse, physician, psychologist
Special curricular programs art, instrumental music, vocal music, computer/technology
Extra curricular programs community service, drama, yearbook
Sports baseball, basketball, soccer, softball, swimming, volleyball
Clubs Model UN, Mu Alpha Theta, student council, Junior Honor Society, National Honor Society
Examinations AP, PSAT, SAT, Stanford, TOEFL, Metropolitan Readiness Test

CAMPUS FACILITIES

Location Suburban
Campus 10 hectares, 9 buildings, 40 classrooms, 4 computer labs, 100 instructional computers, 25,000 library volumes, 1 auditorium, 2 cafeterias, 1 covered play area, 1 gymnasium, 1 infirmary, 4 playing fields, 3 science labs, 1 pool, 2 tennis courts, air conditioning

COLEGIO NUEVA GRANADA

Phone	57 1 212 3511
Fax	57 1 211 3720
Email	zgomez@cng.edu
Website	www.cng.edu
Address	Carrera 2 Este No. 70-20, Rosales, Bogota, Cundinamarca, Colombia

STAFF

Director Barry L. McCombs, Ph.D.
Deputy Director Michael Adams, Ed.D.
High School Principal Dwight Mott
Middle School Principal Keith Bookwalter, Ph.D.
Elementary School Principal Natalia Hernández
Primary School Principal Barry Gilman
General Manager Maria I. Wiesner, Ed.D.

Technology Director Susie Faccini
Head Librarian Kandy Szymusiak
Teaching staff Full time 238; Part time 10; Total 248
Nationalities of teaching staff US 36; UK 2; Colombian 194; Other(s) (Canadian, Chilean) 16

INFORMATION

Grade levels K–12
School year August–June
School type coeducational, day, private non-profit
Year founded 1938
Governed by elected Board of Directors
Accredited by Southern
Regional organizations ACCAS, AASSA
Enrollment PreK 103; Elementary K–5 900; Middle School 6–8 411; High School 9–12 454; Total 1,868

Nationalities of student body US 411; UK 19; Colombian 1,214; Other(s) (Brazilian, Israeli) 224
Tuition/fee currency US Dollar
Tuition range 12,225–19,630
Graduates attending college 98%
Graduates have attended Babson Col, Brandeis U, Loyola U, Pennsylvania State U, Purdue U

EDUCATIONAL PROGRAM

Curriculum US, AP, Colombian Baccalaureate
Average class size Elementary 18; Secondary 22
Language(s) of instruction English, Spanish
Language(s) taught French, Mandarin
Staff specialists computer, counselor, ESL, learning disabilities, librarian, math resource, nurse, psychologist, reading resource, speech/hearing
Special curricular programs art, instrumental music, vocal music, computer/technology, physical education, vocational

Extra curricular programs community service, dance, excursions/expeditions, literary magazine, newspaper, photography, yearbook, gymnastics, martial arts, wall climbing
Sports baseball, basketball, football, gymnastics, hockey, soccer, track and field, dancing, cheerleading, ping pong
Clubs chess, cooking, Batik, ballet, cartoon drawing, skating, carpentry.
Examinations AP, Iowa, MAT, PSAT, SAT, ICFES

CAMPUS FACILITIES

Location Urban
Campus 8 hectares, 9 buildings, 80 classrooms, 5 computer labs, 155 instructional computers,

40,000 library volumes, 1 auditorium, 1 cafeteria, 2 gymnasiums, 1 infirmary, 4 playing fields, 6 science labs

COLEGIO PANAMERICANO

Phone	577 638 6213
Fax	577 639 8970
Email	panamericano@panamericano.edu.co
Website	www.panamericano.edu.co
Address	Calle 34 #8-73, Canaveral Alto, Floridablanca, Santander, Colombia
Mailing address	A.A. 522, Bucaramanga, Colombia

STAFF

Director Jeffrey M. Jurkovac
Preschool/Elementary Principal J. Zeb Johnson
Preschool Coordinator Blanca C. Gutierrez
Interim High School Principal Brian C. Hartman
Director of Finance Gueyler Elena Blanco

Technology Coordinator Andres Amaya
Head of Library Gloria Gomez
Teaching staff Full time 57; Part time 13; Total 70
Nationalities of teaching staff US 13;
Colombian 55; Other(s) (Canadian) 2

INFORMATION

Grade levels N–12
School year August–June
School type coeducational, day, private non-profit
Year founded 1963
Governed by elected School Board
Accredited by Southern
Regional organizations ACCAS
Enrollment Nursery 25; PreK 35;
Elementary K–5 275; Middle School 6–8 125;
High School 9–12 130; Total 590
Nationalities of student body US 18;
Colombian 560; Other(s) (Venezuelan) 12

Tuition/fee currency US Dollar
Tuition range 1,500–2,000
Annual fees Registration 175; Busing 300;
Lunch 250; Books 150
One time fees Capital Levy 3,000; Materials 50
Graduates attending college 100%
Graduates have attended Boston U, Tulane U,
Ohio State U, U de Los Andes,
U of California in Los Angeles

(Continued)

134

COLEGIO PANAMERICANO (Continued)

EDUCATIONAL PROGRAM

Curriculum US, National, AP, AP, Colombian Ministry of Education
Average class size Elementary 24; Secondary 22
Language(s) of instruction English, Spanish
Staff specialists computer, counselor, ESL, learning disabilities, librarian, nurse, psychologist, reading resource, speech/hearing
Special curricular programs art, instrumental music, computer/technology, physical education, values education (Tribes/Vyda)

Extra curricular programs computers, community service, environmental conservation, excursions/expeditions, literary magazine, yearbook, home reading program, band/orchestra, cheerleading
Sports basketball, football, golf, martial arts, soccer, tennis, horseback riding, ultimate frisbee
Clubs Sunshine, Model UN, National Honor Society, Junior National Honor Society, student council, Boy and Girl Scouts, pre-band
Examinations AP, SAT, SAT II, Stanford

CAMPUS FACILITIES

Location Suburban
Campus 3 hectares, 11 buildings, 42 classrooms, 2 computer labs, 100 instructional computers, 20,000 library volumes, 1 auditorium, 1 cafeteria, 2 covered play areas, 1 gymnasium, 1 infirmary, 3 playing fields, 4 science labs, air conditioning

COLEGIO BOLIVAR

Phone	57 2 555 2039
Fax	57 2 555 2041
Email	admisiones@colegiobolivar.edu.co
Website	www.colegiobolivar.edu.co
Address	Calle 5 #122-21, via a Pance, Cali, Valle del Cauca, Colombia
Mailing address	Apartado Aereo 26300, Cali, Colombia

STAFF

Director Joseph J. Nagy, Ed.D.
High School Principal Steven Hupp, Ed.D.
Middle School Principal Robert Sims, Ed.D.
Primary Principal David Fayad, Ed.D.
Pre-Primary Principal Carla Ravassa, Ed.D.
Director of Finances Teresa Tapiero

Technology Coordinator Rodrigo Navia
Head of Library Thomas Rompf
Teaching staff Full time 150; Total 150
Nationalities of teaching staff US 25;
Colombian 125

INFORMATION

Grade levels N–12
School year August–June
School type coeducational, company-sponsored, day, private non-profit
Year founded 1947
Governed by appointed Board of Directors
Sponsored by Bondholder Companies
Accredited by Southern
Regional organizations ACCAS, AASSA
Enrollment PreK 89; Elementary K–5 572;
Middle School 6–8 281;
High School 9–12 312; Total 1,254

Nationalities of student body US 92; Colombian 1,118; Other(s) (Italian, Venezuelan) 44
Tuition/fee currency Colombian Peso
Tuition range 10,611,419–16,610,240
Annual fees Insurance 38,200; Busing 2,172,000
One time fees Registration 80,000;
Capital Levy 16,485,000
Graduates attending college 99%
Graduates have attended Clark U, Lynn U, Boston U, Wingate U, Tulane U

EDUCATIONAL PROGRAM

Curriculum US, National, AP, Colombian Ministry of Education
Average class size Elementary 20; Secondary 18
Language(s) of instruction English, Spanish, French
Staff specialists computer, counselor, ESL, learning disabilities, librarian, nurse, physician, psychologist, reading resource, speech/hearing

Special curricular programs art, computer/technology, physical education
Extra curricular programs community service, dance, drama, environmental conservation, literary magazine, newspaper, yearbook
Sports baseball, basketball, gymnastics, soccer, swimming, track and field, volleyball
Examinations AP, Iowa, PSAT, SAT, TOEFL, ICFES

CAMPUS FACILITIES

Location Suburban
Campus 15 hectares, 16 buildings, 98 classrooms, 3 computer labs, 340 instructional computers, 49,000 library volumes, 2 auditoriums,

4 cafeterias, 2 covered play areas, 2 gymnasiums, 1 infirmary, 8 playing fields, 9 science labs, 2 pools

COLEGIO JORGE WASHINGTON

Phone	57 5 665 3136
Fax	57 5 665 6447
Email	director@cojowa.edu.co
Website	www.cojowa.edu.co
Address	Carrera 1 #12-120, Bocagrande, Cartagena, Colombia
Mailing address	A.A. 2899, Cartagena, Colombia

STAFF

Director Pete W. Nonnenkamp, Ed.D.
Curriculum Coordinator Jack Jackson
Elementary School Principal Miriam Angulo
Guidance Counselor and Assistant Principal
Luz Elena Carvajal

Business Manager Moraima Lequerica
Technology Coordinator Bernarda Baquero
Head Librarian Lizette Cepeda
Teaching staff Full time 64; Part time 2; Total 66
Nationalities of teaching staff US 21; Croatian 45

INFORMATION

Grade levels N–12
School year August–June
School type coeducational, day, private non-profit
Year founded 1952
Governed by elected Board of Directors
Accredited by Southern
Regional organizations ACCAS
Enrollment Nursery 18; PreK 48;
Elementary K–5 280; Middle School 6–8 140;
High School 9–12 180; Total 666

Nationalities of student body US 26; Colombian
640; Other(s) (Venezuelan) 2
Tuition/fee currency US Dollar
Tuition 4,050–4,050
One time fees Registration 5,000; Lunch 2;
technology 30; PTA 35
Graduates attending college 100%
Graduates have attended Yale U, Georgia
Institute of Technology, U of Miami, Texas
Christian U, Babson Col

EDUCATIONAL PROGRAM

Curriculum US, National, AP, GenCSE,
Colombian Bachillerato
Average class size Elementary 24; Secondary 24
Language(s) of instruction English
Language(s) taught Spanish, French
Staff specialists computer, counselor, learning
disabilities, librarian, nurse, psychologist,
reading resource

Special curricular programs art, instrumental
music, vocal music, computer/technology,
distance learning, physical education
Extra curricular programs community service,
dance, drama, environmental conservation,
excursions/expeditions, literary magazine,
newspaper, photography, yearbook
Sports baseball, basketball, soccer, softball,
volleyball
Examinations Iowa, SAT, SAT II

CAMPUS FACILITIES

Location Urban
Campus 3 hectares, 4 buildings, 34 classrooms,
5 computer labs, 100 instructional computers,

18,000 library volumes, 1 cafeteria,
1 infirmary, 1 playing field, 1 science lab,
2 tennis courts, air conditioning

COLEGIO GRANADINO

Phone	57 6 874 9066
Fax	57 6 874 6066
Email	rsims@granadino.edu.co
Website	www.granadino.edu.co
Address	A.A. 2138, Verda La Florida, Manizales, Colombia

STAFF

General Director Robert Sims
Early Childhood/Elementary Principal
David D'ercole
Secondary School Principal Patricia Jaramillo Mejia
K–12 Curriculum Coordinator Gloria Gonzales

Business Manager
María Mercedes Londoño de Gutiérrez
Technology Coordinator Patricia Jaramillo Sanint
School Librarian Patricia Quintero
Teaching staff Full time 54; Part time 9; Total 63
Nationalities of teaching staff US 10; UK 1;
Colombian 43; Other(s) (Canadian) 9

INFORMATION

Grade levels PreK–12
School year August–June
School type coeducational, day, private non-profit
Year founded 1980
Governed by elected Board of Directors and
School Director
Accredited by Southern
Regional organizations ACCAS
Enrollment PreK 62; Elementary K–5 285;
Middle School 6–8 141; High School 9–12 134;
Total 622

Nationalities of student body Colombian 622
Tuition/fee currency Colombian Peso
Tuition range 6,615,400–746,000
Annual fees Busing 960,000; Lunch 1,019,000;
Books 737,600
One time fees Registration 746,000
Graduates attending college 100%
Graduates have attended Savannah Col of
Design, Central Florida U, U of South Florida,
U de los Andes, Pontificia U Javeriana

EDUCATIONAL PROGRAM

Curriculum US, National, Intl
Average class size Elementary 25; Secondary 20

Language(s) of instruction English, Spanish
Examinations TOEFL, Melicet

CAMPUS FACILITIES

Location Suburban
Campus 9 hectares, 6 buildings, 37 classrooms,
2 computer labs, 60 instructional computers,

12,500 library volumes, 3 auditoriums,
1 cafeteria, 2 covered play areas, 1 gymnasium,
1 infirmary, 8 playing fields, 4 science labs

Medellin   **COLOMBIA**

THE COLUMBUS SCHOOL

Phone	574 386 1122, ext. 125
Fax	574 386 11 33
Email	superintendent@columbus.edu.co
Website	www.columbus.edu.co
Address	Alto de las Palmas, Kilometro 16, Envigado, Antioquia, Colombia
Mailing address	Apartado Aereo 60562, Medellin, Colombia, South America

STAFF

Superintendent David E. Cardenas
Director of Curriculum/Professional Development Susan Jaramillo
High School Principal Alexander Bennett
Middle School Principal Jane Losada, Ph.D.
Upper and Lower Elementary Principal Barbara Alken

Business Plant Manager Juan Ricardo García
Technology Director Willem Neumann
Librarians Jane Atkinson and Constanza Gonzalez
Teaching staff Full time 141; Part time 2; Total 143
Nationalities of teaching staff US 60; Colombian 83

INFORMATION

Grade levels K–12
School year August–June
School type coeducational, day, private non-profit
Year founded 1947
Governed by elected School Board
Accredited by Southern
Regional organizations ACCAS, AASSA
Enrollment Elementary K–5 762; Middle School 6–8 317; High School 9–12 401; Total 1,480

Nationalities of student body US 85; Colombian 1,395
Tuition/fee currency US Dollar
Tuition range 4,500–5,300
One time fees Registration 6,500
Graduates attending college 100%
Graduates have attended Massachusetts Institute of Technology, Emory U, U of Miami, U of Florida, Michigan State U

EDUCATIONAL PROGRAM

Curriculum US, National, AP, Colombian High School Diploma
Average class size Elementary 22; Secondary 22
Language(s) of instruction English, Spanish
Language(s) taught French
Staff specialists computer, counselor, ESL, learning disabilities, librarian, math resource, nurse, physician, psychologist, reading resource, speech/hearing

Special curricular programs art, instrumental music, vocal music, computer/technology, physical education, vocational
Extra curricular programs community service
Sports baseball, basketball, football, soccer, softball, track and field, volleyball
Examinations ACT, AP, Iowa, PSAT, SAT, SAT II, DRA

CAMPUS FACILITIES

Location Suburban
Campus 21 hectares, 8 buildings, 83 classrooms, 8 computer labs, 350 instructional computers,

21,651 library volumes, 2 cafeterias, 3 gymnasiums, 1 infirmary, 6 playing fields, 6 science labs

DEMOCRATIC REPUBLIC OF CONGO

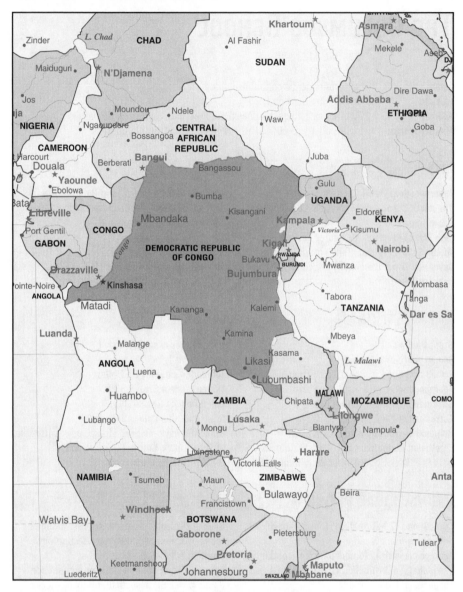

DEMOCRATIC REPUBLIC OF CONGO

Area:	2,345,410 sq km
Population:	65,751,512
Capital:	Kinshasa
Currency:	Congolese Franc (CDF)
Languages:	French

THE AMERICAN SCHOOL OF KINSHASA

Phone	243 88 46619
Fax	646 616 4231
Email	tasokinquiries@yahoo.com
Website	www.tasok.cd
Address	Route de Matadi, Ngaliema, Kinshasa, Democratic Republic of Congo
Mailing address	American Embassy-Kinshasa, Unit 31550, APO AE 09828, USA

STAFF

Superintendent Irene Epp, Ph.D.
Principal Gregory Hughes, Ed.D.
Business Manager Fiona Merali
Librarian Chantal Harte

Teaching staff Full time 28; Total 28
Nationalities of teaching staff US 22; Congolese 1; Other(s) 5

INFORMATION

Grade levels K–12
School year August–June
School type coeducational, day, private non-profit
Year founded 1961
Governed by elected School Board
Accredited by Middle States
Regional organizations AISA, ECIS
Enrollment Elementary K–5 110; Middle School 6–8 55; High School 9–12 75; Total 240

Nationalities of student body US 65; Congolese 30; Other(s) 145
Tuition/fee currency US Dollar
Tuition range 5,250–11,750
One time fees Registration 2,500; Application 250
Graduates attending college 95%
Graduates have attended State U of New York, Johns Hopkins U, Ithaca Col, Rose-Hulman Institute of Technology, Syracuse U

EDUCATIONAL PROGRAM

Curriculum US, AP
Average class size Elementary 15; Secondary 16
Language(s) of instruction English
Language(s) taught French
Staff specialists computer, ESL, librarian, nurse
Special curricular programs art, instrumental music, vocal music, computer/technology, physical education

Extra curricular programs computers, community service, dance, drama, literary magazine, newspaper, photography
Sports basketball, golf, martial arts, soccer, swimming, tennis, track and field, volleyball
Clubs Model UN
Examinations ACT, AP, PSAT, SAT, SAT II, Stanford

CAMPUS FACILITIES

Location Suburban
Campus 17 hectares, 22 buildings, 40 classrooms, 2 computer labs, 60 instructional computers, 20,000 library volumes, 1 auditorium, 1 covered play area, 1 infirmary, 2 playing fields, 4 science labs, 1 pool, 1 tennis court, air conditioning

COSTA RICA

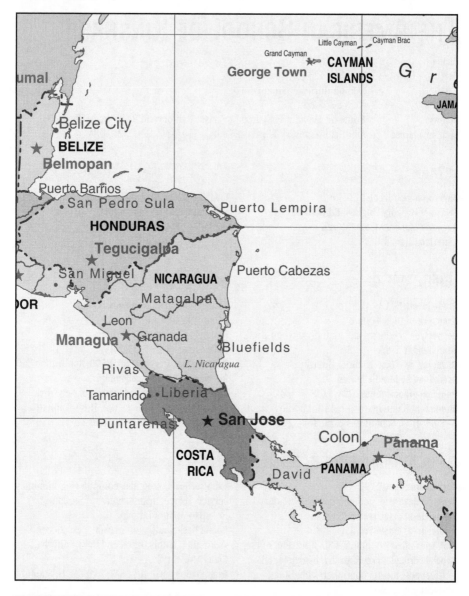

COSTA RICA

Area:	51,100 sq km
Population:	4,133,884
Capital:	San Jose
Currency:	Costa Rican Colon (CRC)
Languages:	Spanish, English

San Jose

COSTA RICA

COUNTRY DAY SCHOOL

Phone	506 289 0919
Fax	506 228 2076
Email	codasch@racsa.co.cr
Website	www.cds.ed.cr
Address	Del Banco Nacional de Costa Rica, 2 cuadras al oeste y 2 cuadras al sur, Escazu, San José, Costa Rica
Mailing address	Apartado 1139-1250, Escazu, San José, Costa Rica

STAFF

Director Robert W. Trent
High School Principal and Deputy Director Gloria Doll, Ed.D.
Middle School Principal Harry Grzelewski
Elementary School Principal William Large
Early Childhood Principal Katie DesChenes
Admissions and Community Relations Coordinator Maria Fernanda Cardona

Business Manager Dora Sevilla
Technology Coordinator Michael Parreles
Head of Library/Media Center Jo Reinmiller
Teaching staff Full time 78; Part time 12; Total 90
Nationalities of teaching staff US 42; Costa Rican 41; Other(s) 7

INFORMATION

Grade levels N–12
School year August–June
School type coeducational, day, proprietary
Year founded 1963
Sponsored by Shareholders
Accredited by Middle States
Regional organizations AASCA
Enrollment Nursery 40; PreK 41; Elementary K–5 472; Middle School 6–8 171; High School 9–12 160; Total 884

Nationalities of student body US 320; UK 13; Costa Rican 281; Other(s) (Mexican, Canadian) 270
Tuition/fee currency US Dollar
Tuition range 3,260–9,130
Annual fees Matriculation 825
One time fees Registration 1,000
Graduates attending college 100%
Graduates have attended U of Pennsylvania, Trinity U, Purdue U, Boston U, Tufts U

EDUCATIONAL PROGRAM

Curriculum US, AP
Average class size Elementary 18; Secondary 15
Language(s) of instruction English
Language(s) taught Spanish, French
Staff specialists computer, counselor, ESL, learning disabilities, librarian, nurse, psychologist

Special curricular programs art, instrumental music, vocal music, computer/technology, physical education
Extra curricular programs community service, drama, environmental conservation, excursions/expeditions, literary magazine, newspaper, photography, yearbook
Sports basketball, soccer, softball, swimming, volleyball
Examinations AP, Iowa, PSAT, SAT

CAMPUS FACILITIES

Location Suburban
Campus 3 hectares, 9 buildings, 54 classrooms, 3 computer labs, 95 instructional computers, 25,000 library volumes, 1 auditorium, 1 cafeteria, 1 covered play area, 1 gymnasium, 1 infirmary, 2 playing fields, 6 science labs, 1 pool

Marian Baker School

Phone	506 273 0024
Fax	506 273 4609
Email	lniehaus@mbs.ed.cr
Website	www.mbs.ed.cr
Address	San Ramon de Tres Rios, 200 meters east and 200 meters south from the Catholic Church, San José, 4269-1000, Costa Rica
Mailing address	Marian Baker School, SJO 751, PO Box 025331, Miami, FL 33102-5331, USA

STAFF

General Director Linda A. Niehaus
High and Middle School Principal Sylvia E. Soto
Business Manager Bonnie Heigold
Head of Technology Guiselle D'Avanzo

Head Librarian Lorrie Satterwaithe
Teaching staff Full time 33; Part time 1; Total 34
Nationalities of teaching staff US 12; Other(s)
(Costa Rican, Venezuelan) 22

INFORMATION

Grade levels PreK–12
School year August–June
School type coeducational, day, proprietary
Year founded 1984
Governed by elected Board
Accredited by Southern
Regional organizations AASCA
Enrollment PreK 17; Elementary K–5 74; Middle School 6–8 49; High School 9–12 60; Total 200

Nationalities of student body US 47; Other(s)
(Costa Rican, Chinese) 153
Tuition/fee currency US Dollar
Tuition range 5,650–8,500
Annual fees Registration 750; busing 875;
Elementary ESL 1,875; Upper School ESL 2,250
Graduates attending college 100%
Graduates have attended Louisville U,
Pennsylvania State U, Ohio Wesleyan U,
Virginia Institute of Technology, McGill U

EDUCATIONAL PROGRAM

Curriculum US, National, AP
Average class size Elementary 15; Secondary 18
Language(s) of instruction English
Language(s) taught Spanish
Staff specialists computer, counselor, ESL, librarian

Special curricular programs art, vocal music, computer/technology, physical education
Extra curricular programs computers, community service, drama, photography, yearbook
Sports basketball, soccer, volleyball
Examinations AP, Iowa, SAT

CAMPUS FACILITIES

Location Suburban
Campus 2 hectares, 6 buildings, 29 classrooms, 1 computer lab, 35 instructional computers, 9,000 library volumes, 1 auditorium,

1 cafeteria, 1 covered play area, 1 gymnasium, 1 infirmary, 2 playing fields, 1 science lab, 1 tennis court

Lincoln School

Phone	506 247 6600
Fax	506 247 6700
Email	director@lincoln.ed.cr
Website	www.lincoln.ed.cr
Address	Barrio Socorro. In front of the Catholic Church, Heredia, Santo Domingo, Costa Rica
Mailing address	Lincoln School, Apdo 1919-1000, San Josè, Costa Rica

STAFF

Director General Jack J. Bimrose, Ed.D.
Elementary School Principal Iris Prada
Secondary School Principal Charles E. Prince
Preschool Assistant Sylvia Montero
Middle School Dean Silvia Barahona
Secondary School Assistant Principal Charles Benavage

Finance/Business Manager Carlos Rodríguez
Technology Coordinator Victor Roman
Secondary School Librarian Martha Rubì
Teaching staff Full time 104; Part time 11; Total 115
Nationalities of teaching staff US 24; Costa Rican 84; Other(s) 7

INFORMATION

Grade levels N–12
School year August–June
School type coeducational, day, private non-profit
Year founded 1945
Governed by elected Board of Directors
Accredited by Southern
Regional organizations AASCA
Enrollment Nursery 142; PreK 85; Elementary K–5 363; Middle School 6–8 253; High School 9–12 347; Total 1,190

Nationalities of student body US 98; UK 4; Costa Rican 1,023; Other(s) 65
Tuition/fee currency US Dollar
Tuition range 3,391–5,694
Annual fees Registration 50; Insurance 16; Busing 1,000; Books 186; Physical Plant 444
One time fees Capital Levy 1,000
Graduates attending college 100%
Graduates have attended Harvard U, Cornell U, Georgetown U, U of Notre Dame, Ohio State U

EDUCATIONAL PROGRAM

Curriculum US, National, IB Diploma
Average class size Elementary 20; Secondary 23
Language(s) of instruction English
Language(s) taught Spanish, French
Staff specialists computer, counselor, ESL, learning disabilities, librarian, nurse, physician, psychologist, reading resource
Special curricular programs art, instrumental music, vocal music, computer/technology, physical education

Extra curricular programs computers, community service, dance, drama, environmental conservation, excursions/expeditions, newspaper, yearbook
Sports badminton, basketball, gymnastics, martial arts, soccer, swimming, tennis, volleyball
Clubs cooking, international relations, knowledge bowl, swimming, French
Examinations ACT, IB, PSAT, SAT, SAT II, Stanford

CAMPUS FACILITIES

Location Suburban
Campus 7 hectares, 8 buildings, 96 classrooms, 4 computer labs, 250 instructional computers,

10,000 library volumes, 1 auditorium, 1 cafeteria, 1 covered play area, 2 gymnasiums, 1 infirmary, 2 playing fields, 4 science labs

COUNTRY DAY SCHOOL GUANACASTE

Phone	506 654 5042
Fax	506 654 5044
Email	info@cds.ed.cr
Website	www.cdsgte.com
Address	400 metros sur del, Hotel Melia Conchal, Brasilito, Guanacaste, Costa Rica
Mailing address	Country Day School Guanacaste, Apartado 1139-1250, Escazu, Costa Rica

STAFF

Director General Robert W. Trent
Campus Principal Stephen Butler
Operations Director Patrick Brown
Business Manager Dora Sevilla
Technology Consultant Rogers Bestgem

Librarian and College Counselor Shannon Porter
Teaching staff Full time 27; Part time 2; Total 29
Nationalities of teaching staff US 21;
Costa Rican 3; Other(s) (Canadian, German) 5

INFORMATION

Grade levels PreK–12
School year August–June
School type boarding, coeducational, day, proprietary
Year founded 2000
Sponsored by Shareholders
Accredited by Middle States
Regional organizations AASCA
Enrollment PreK 5; Elementary K–5 95; Middle School 6–8 35; High School 9–12 46; Total 181
Nationalities of student body US 96; Costa Rican 23; Other(s) (Canadian, French) 62
Tuition/fee currency US Dollar

Tuition range 3,210–7,460
Annual fees Boarding, 5-day 15,030; Boarding, 7-day 23,780; matriculation 650
One time fees Registration 800; Refundable Deposit/Boarding 5-day 500; Refundable Deposit/Boarding 7-day 1,000
Boarding program grades 7–12
Boarding program length 5-day and 7-day
Boys 7 **Girls** 4
Graduates attending college 95%
Graduates have attended U of California in San Diego, Cuesta Col, Georgia Institute of Technology, U of Nevada at Las Vegas, U of Victoria British Columbia

EDUCATIONAL PROGRAM

Curriculum US, AP
Average class size Elementary 14; Secondary 12
Language(s) of instruction English
Language(s) taught Spanish
Staff specialists ESL, librarian, psychologist
Special curricular programs art, vocal music, physical education

Extra curricular programs community service, dance, drama, environmental conservation, excursions/expeditions, yearbook
Sports basketball, soccer, swimming, volleyball
Examinations ACT, AP, Iowa, PSAT, SAT, SAT II

CAMPUS FACILITIES

Location Rural
Campus 15 hectares, 5 buildings, 20 classrooms, 1 computer lab, 20 instructional computers,

6,000 library volumes, 1 cafeteria, 1 covered play area, 1 gymnasium, 2 playing fields, 1 science lab, 1 pool, air conditioning

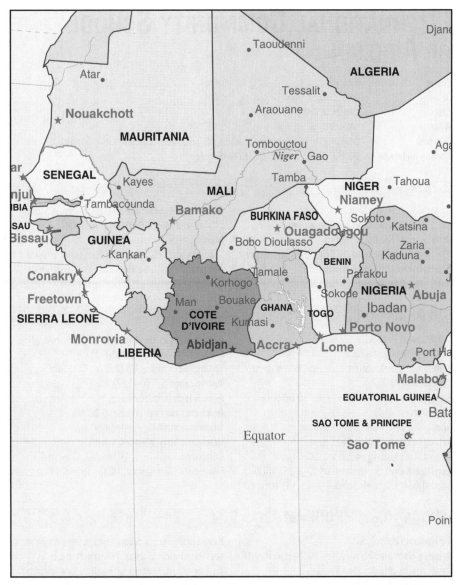

COTE D'IVOIRE

Area:	322,460 sq km
Population:	18,013,409
Capital:	Yamoussoukro
Currency:	Communaute Financiere Africaine Franc (XOF)
Languages:	French

INTERNATIONAL COMMUNITY SCHOOL OF ABIDJAN

Phone	225 22 471 152
Fax	225 22 471 996
Email	rwalbridge@icsa.ac.ci
Website	www.icsa.ac.ci
Address	c/o American Embassy-Abidjan, Riviera-Golf, Abidjan, Cote d'Ivoire
Mailing address	06 B.P. 544, Abidjan 06, Cote d'Ivoire

STAFF

Director Rob Walbridge
Assistant to the Director for Curriculum Development Gloria Freeman
Assistant to the Director for Strategic Planning and Development Lauryne Clarke, Ed.D.
Business Office Manager Annie Kimou Koffi

Technology Coordinator, K–12 Lawrence Morris
Library and Media Center Coordinator Mamadou Soro
Teaching staff Full time 10; Part time 3; Total 13
Nationalities of teaching staff US 5; Ivorian 4; Other(s) (Canadian, Liberian) 4

INFORMATION

Grade levels PreK–12
School year August–June
School type coeducational, day, private non-profit
Year founded 1972
Governed by appointed and elected Board of Directors
Sponsored by US Embassy/Abidjan
Accredited by CIS, Middle States
Regional organizations AISA, ECIS
Enrollment PreK 5; Elementary K–5 25; Middle School 6–8 15; High School 9–12 15; Total 60

Nationalities of student body US 5; Ivorian 30; Other(s) (Indian, Korean) 25
Tuition/fee currency US Dollar
Tuition range 5,750–11,900
Annual fees Registration 370
One time fees Capital Levy 5,000
Graduates attending college 80%
Graduates have attended York U, Concordia University (Canada), Concordia University (Minnesota, USA), Toronto University

EDUCATIONAL PROGRAM

Curriculum US, Intl, AP
Average class size Elementary 10; Secondary 10
Language(s) of instruction English
Language(s) taught French
Staff specialists computer, ESL
Special curricular programs art, instrumental music, vocal music, computer/technology, distance learning, physical education, Blackboard Virtual School

Extra curricular programs computers, community service, dance, drama, environmental conservation, literary magazine, newspaper, yearbook
Sports basketball, football, gymnastics, soccer, softball, swimming, tennis, volleyball
Examinations ACT, AP, PSAT, SAT, SAT II, TOEFL

CAMPUS FACILITIES

Location Suburban
Campus 1 hectare, 3 buildings, 12 classrooms, 1 computer lab, 50 instructional computers,

12,000 library volumes, 1 cafeteria, 1 covered play area, 2 playing fields, 1 science lab, 1 pool, air conditioning

CROATIA

Area:	56,542 sq km
Population:	4,493,312
Capital:	Zagreb
Currency:	Kuna (HRK)
Languages:	Croatian

AMERICAN INTERNATIONAL SCHOOL OF ZAGREB

Phone	385 1 468 0133
Fax	385 1 468 0171
Email	aisz@aisz.hr
Website	www.aisz.hr
Address	Vocarska 106, Zagreb, 10000, Croatia
Mailing address	Dept. of State, 5080 Zagreb Pl., Washington, DC 20189-5080, USA

STAFF

Director James Swetz
Upper School Principal Harry Houlis
Elementary School Principal Erika Saravanja
IB Coordinator Melanie Swetz

Counselor Alemka Berliner
Business Manager Lidija Jelacic
Computer Teacher/Technician Neven Soric
Librarian/Media Specialist Joan Cobb

INFORMATION

Grade levels PreK–12
School year August–June
School type coeducational, day, private non-profit
Year founded 1966
Governed by appointed and elected School Board
Accredited by Middle States
Regional organizations CEESA, ECIS

Enrollment PreK 9; Elementary K–5 96;
Middle School 6–8 36; High School 9–12 33;
Total 174
Nationalities of student body US 45; UK 14;
Croatian 27; Other(s) 88
Tuition/fee currency US Dollar
Tuition range 5,900–17,600
Annual fees IB Exam 750
One time fees Capital Levy 2,000;
Admissions 500; Graduation 300

EDUCATIONAL PROGRAM

Curriculum US, IB Diploma
Average class size Elementary 17; Secondary 7
Language(s) of instruction English
Language(s) taught French, German
Staff specialists computer, counselor, ESL,
librarian, nurse
Special curricular programs art, computer/
technology, physical education, music, drama

Extra curricular programs computers, community
service, dance, drama, excursions/expeditions,
newspaper, yearbook, student council, Math
Counts, Knowledge Bowl
Sports basketball, cross-country, skiing, soccer,
tennis, track and field, volleyball
Clubs chess, cooking, pottery
Examinations IB, PSAT, SAT, WRAP

CAMPUS FACILITIES

Location Urban
Campus 2 buildings, 20 classrooms,
2 computerlabs, 60 instructional computers,

5,000 library volumes, 1 auditorium,
1 cafeteria, 1 gymnasium, 1 infirmary,
2 playing fields, 1 science lab, 1 tennis court

Data from 2006/07 school year.

CUBA

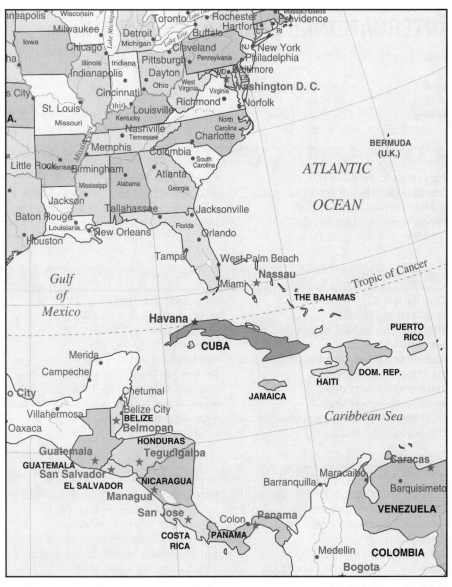

CUBA

Area:	110,860 sq km
Population:	11,394,043
Capital:	Havana
Currency:	Cuban Peso (CUP) and Convertible Peso (CUC)
Languages:	Spanish

INTERNATIONAL SCHOOL OF HAVANA

Phone	537 204 2540
Fax	537 204 2723
Email	office@ish.co.cu
Website	www.ishav.org
Address	Calle 18 #315 e/ 3ra y 5ta., Miramar, Playa, Ciudad de la Habana, 11300, Cuba

STAFF

Principal Ian R. Morris, Ed.D.
Secondary School Head Richard Fluit, Ed.D.
Lower School Head Heidi Cavanagh, Ed.D.
Finance/Accounting Maria Morell, Ed.D.
IT Manager Juan Rodríguez, Ed.D.

Librarian Yudexy Lleonart
Teaching staff Full time 39; Part time 3; Total 42
Nationalities of teaching staff UK 1; Cuban 33; Other(s) 8

INFORMATION

Grade levels N–12
School year August–June
School type coeducational, day, private non-profit
Year founded 1965
Governed by appointed Board of Directors
Accredited by CIS, New England
Regional organizations ECIS
Enrollment Nursery 21; PreK 20; Elementary K–5 86; Middle School 6–8 40; High School 9–12 30; Total 197

Nationalities of student body US 19; UK 10; Other(s) (Spaniard, Italian) 168
Tuition/fee currency US Dollar
Tuition range 3,490–10,674
Annual fees Capital Levy 1,500
One time fees Registration 4,000
Graduates attending college 100%
Graduates have attended International Florida U, Atlanta U, U of Queensland

EDUCATIONAL PROGRAM

Curriculum US, UK, Intl, IB Diploma, IGCSE, IPC
Average class size Elementary 15; Secondary 8
Language(s) of instruction English
Language(s) taught Spanish
Staff specialists computer, ESL, learning disabilities, librarian, nurse, psychologist
Special curricular programs art, instrumental music, computer/technology, physical education

Extra curricular programs computers, community service, dance, drama, environmental conservation, excursions/expeditions, newspaper, photography, yearbook
Sports basketball, football, hockey, martial arts, soccer, swimming, tennis, volleyball
Clubs homework, cooking
Examinations GCSE, IB, IGCSE, SAT, SAT II

CAMPUS FACILITIES

Location Urban
Campus 1 hectare, 4 buildings, 31 classrooms, 3 computer labs, 110 instructional computers, 6,884 library volumes, air conditioning

CURACAO

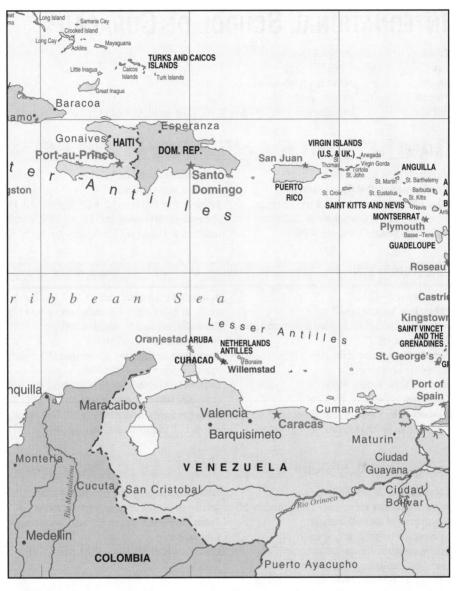

CURACAO

Area:	444 sq km
Population:	150,000
Capital:	Willemstad
Currency:	Netherlands Antillean Guilder
Languages:	Dutch

INTERNATIONAL SCHOOL OF CURAÇAO

Phone 5 999 737 3633
Fax 5 999 737 3142
Email iscmec@attglobal.net
Website www.isc.an
Address Koninginnelaan z/n, PO Box 3090, Willemstad, Curacao

STAFF

Director Margie Elhage, Ph.D.
High School Principal Gustavo Sever
Middle School Coordinator Douglas Vaughan
Elementary School Coordinator Annia Duran
Business Manager Emma van Delden

IT Coordinator Angelica Galicia
Librarian Stuart Crouch
Teaching staff Full time 52; Part time 3; Total 55
Nationalities of teaching staff US 19; UK 2; Dutch
Antillean 8; Other(s) (Dutch, Venezuelan) 26

INFORMATION

Grade levels N–12
School year August–June
School type coeducational, day, private non-profit
Year founded 1972
Governed by appointed Board
Accredited by Southern
Regional organizations AASSA
Enrollment Nursery 24; PreK 24;
Elementary K–5 166; Middle School 6–8 93;
High School 9–12 143; Total 450

Nationalities of student body US 41; UK 4; Dutch
Antillean 230; Other(s) (Dutch, Venezuelan) 175
Tuition/fee currency NL Antillian Guilder
Tuition range 6,000–18,100
Annual fees Registration 2,500; Gym 500;
Parent Teacher Association 50
One time fees Capital Levy 10,000; Senior year 500
Graduates attending college 99%
Graduates have attended Stanford U, U of Miami,
Emory U, U of Richmond, Babson Col

EDUCATIONAL PROGRAM

Curriculum US, AP, IB Diploma
Average class size Elementary 18; Secondary 17
Language(s) of instruction English
Language(s) taught Dutch, Spanish
Staff specialists computer, counselor, ESL,
learning disabilities, librarian, psychologist
Special curricular programs art, instrumental
music, computer/technology, physical education

Extra curricular programs community service,
drama, excursions/expeditions, yearbook
Sports basketball, soccer, softball, swimming,
volleyball
Examinations AP, IB, Iowa, PSAT, SAT, SAT II,
TOEFL

CAMPUS FACILITIES

Location Suburban
Campus 2 hectares, 11 buildings, 37 classrooms,
1 computer lab, 26 instructional computers,

10,000 library volumes, 1 auditorium,
1 covered play area, 1 gymnasium, 3 playing
fields, 3 science labs, air conditioning

CYPRUS

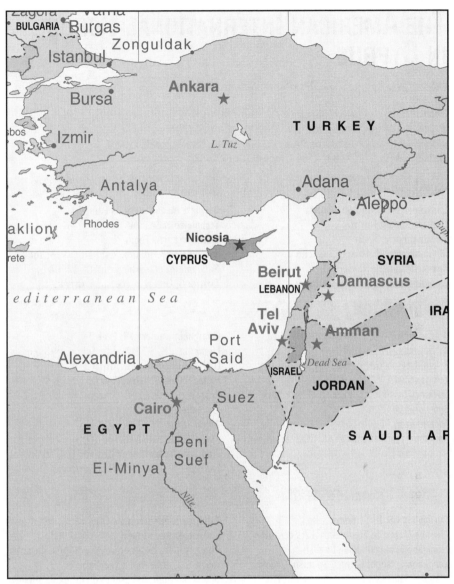

CYPRUS

Area:	9,250 sq km
Population:	788,457
Capital:	Nicosia (Lefkosia)
Currency:	Cypriot Pound (CYP)
Languages:	Greek, Turkish, English

THE AMERICAN INTERNATIONAL SCHOOL IN CYPRUS

Phone	357 22 316 345
Fax	357 22 316 549
Email	aisc@aisc.ac.cy
Website	www.aisc.ac.cy
Address	11 Kassos Street, PO Box 23847, Nicosia, 1686, Cyprus
Mailing address	PO Box 23847, Nicosia, Cyprus 1686

STAFF

Superintendent Walid Abushakra
Director Ronald Joron
Principal Edric Olsen
IB Coordinator Christiane Camacho
Counselor Sangita Vakis
Activities Director Arno Morales

Business Manager Kokos Pantelides
Technician Dale Esau
Librarian Lorna Flynn
Teaching staff Full time 44; Part time 3; Total 47
Nationalities of teaching staff US 22; UK 6; Cypriot 6; Other(s) (German, Greek) 13

INFORMATION

Grade levels N–12
School year August–June
School type coeducational, day, proprietary
Year founded 1987
Governed by appointed Board of Directors
Sponsored by ESOL
Accredited by Middle States
Regional organizations CEESA, ECIS, MAIS, NESA

Enrollment Nursery 13; PreK 14; Elementary K–5 77; Middle School 6–8 63; High School 9–12 112; Total 279
Nationalities of student body US 47; UK 30; Cypriot 108; Other(s) (Israeli, Swede) 94
Tuition/fee currency Cyprus Pound
Tuition range 1,760–5,540
Graduates attending college 100%
Graduates have attended Grinnell Col, Trinity Col, Lawrence U, U of York, U of Newcastle

EDUCATIONAL PROGRAM

Curriculum US, IB Diploma
Average class size Elementary 12; Secondary 15
Language(s) of instruction English
Language(s) taught French, Spanish, Greek
Staff specialists computer, counselor, ESL, learning disabilities, librarian, nurse, psychologist
Special curricular programs art, instrumental music, vocal music, computer/technology, physical education

Extra curricular programs computers, community service, dance, drama, environmental conservation, excursions/expeditions, literary magazine, newspaper, yearbook
Sports badminton, basketball, football, hockey, rugby, soccer, softball, swimming, tennis, track and field, volleyball
Examinations IB, Iowa, PSAT, SAT, TOEFL, Cognitive Abilities Test, ERB Writing Assessment

CAMPUS FACILITIES

Location Urban
Campus 4 hectares, 3 buildings, 32 classrooms, 2 computer labs, 45 instructional computers, 12,000 library volumes, 1 auditorium, 1 cafeteria, 1 covered play area, 1 infirmary, 1 playing field, 3 science labs, 1 pool, 2 tennis courts, air conditioning

CZECH REPUBLIC

Area:	78,866 sq km
Population:	10,228,744
Capital:	Prague
Currency:	Czech Koruna (CZK)
Languages:	Czech

INTERNATIONAL SCHOOL OF PRAGUE

Phone	420 220 384 111
Fax	420 220 384 555
Email	ispmail@isp.cz
Website	www.isp.cz
Address	Nebusicka 700, Prague, 6, 164 00, Czech Republic

STAFF

Director Robert Landau
Upper School Principal Peter Dawson
Middle School Principal Kevin Hawkins
Elementary School Principal Cynthia Gause-Vega
Assistant Elementary School Principal
Katherine Hawkins

Business and Operations Manager Barry Freckmann
Director of Information Technology John Mikton
Elementary School Librarian Linda Marti
Teaching staff Full time 87; Part time 8; Total 95
Nationalities of teaching staff US 68; UK 6;
Czech 3; Other(s) (Canadian, Israeli) 18

INFORMATION

Grade levels PreK–12
School year August–June
School type coeducational, day, private non-profit
Year founded 1948
Governed by appointed and elected Nine Board
Members
Accredited by CIS, New England
Regional organizations CEESA, ECIS
Enrollment PreK 50; Elementary K–5 300;
Middle School 6–8 190; High School 9–12 240;
Total 780

Nationalities of student body US 190; UK 52;
Japanese 60; Other(s) (Russian, Israeli) 478
Tuition/fee currency US Dollar
Tuition range 10,100–17,800
Annual fees Capital Levy 3,000
One time fees Registration 1,100
Graduates attending college 96%
Graduates have attended Harvard U,
London School of Economics, Cambridge U,
Yale U

EDUCATIONAL PROGRAM

Curriculum US, IB Diploma
Average class size Elementary 16; Secondary 15
Language(s) of instruction English
Language(s) taught French, German, Spanish,
Czech

Staff specialists computer, counselor, ESL,
librarian, nurse
Extra curricular programs dance
Sports basketball, soccer, softball, tennis,
volleyball
Examinations IB, Iowa, SAT

CAMPUS FACILITIES

Location Suburban
Campus 6 hectares, 1 building, 56 classrooms,
3 computer labs, 180 instructional computers,
30,000 library volumes, 1 auditorium,

1 cafeteria, 1 covered play area, 2 gymnasiums,
1 infirmary, 1 playing field, 4 science labs,
4 tennis courts

DENMARK

DENMARK

Area:	43,094 sq km
Population:	5,468,120
Capital:	Copenhagen
Currency:	Danish Krone (DKK)
Languages:	Danish

COPENHAGEN INTERNATIONAL SCHOOL

Phone	45 3946 3300
Fax	45 3961 2230
Email	cis@cisdk.dk
Website	www.cis-edu.dk
Address	Hellerupvej 22-26, Hellerup, Copenhagen, 2900, Denmark

STAFF

Director Claes-Göran Widlund
Senior School Principal Peter Wellby
Primary and Middle School Principal
Elisabeth Stanners

Admissions Officer Thomas M. Nielsen
Business/Finance Manager Poul Michael Fanøe
Head of Technology Dan Palomares
Head of Library/Media Center Urania Sobrinho

INFORMATION

Grade levels PreK–12
School year August–June
School type coeducational, day, private non-profit
Year founded 1963
Governed by elected School Board
Accredited by CIS, New England
Regional organizations ECIS
Enrollment PreK 84; Elementary K–5 214; Middle School 6–8 122; High School 9–12 172; Total 592

Nationalities of student body US 118; UK 70; Dane 90; Other(s) 314
Tuition/fee currency Danish Krone
Tuition range 66,000–99,000
Annual fees Busing 26,000; Application 2,500
One time fees Registration 22,500; Compulsory 22–102
Graduates attending college 95%
Graduates have attended Oxford U, Cambridge U, Harvard U, Dartmouth Col, Queens Col

EDUCATIONAL PROGRAM

Curriculum Intl, IB Diploma, IBPYP, IBMYP
Average class size Elementary 20; Secondary 18
Language(s) of instruction English
Language(s) taught English, French, German, Danish, Swedish, Norwegian, Polish, Dutch
Staff specialists computer, counselor, ESL, learning disabilities, librarian, math resource, nurse, psychologist
Special curricular programs art, vocal music, computer/technology, physical education, writing, house system

Extra curricular programs computers, community service, dance, drama, excursions/expeditions, literary magazine, newspaper, photography, yearbook, charity, Model UN
Sports badminton, basketball, rugby, soccer, softball, swimming, track and field, volleyball
Clubs math, chemistry
Examinations AP, GCSE, IB, PSAT, SAT

CAMPUS FACILITIES

Location Suburban
Campus 1 hectare, 2 buildings, 40 classrooms, 3 computer labs, 120 instructional computers,

15,000 library volumes, 1 auditorium, 1 cafeteria, 1 gymnasium, 1 infirmary, 2 playing fields, 4 science labs, 1 tennis court

Data from 2006/07 school year.

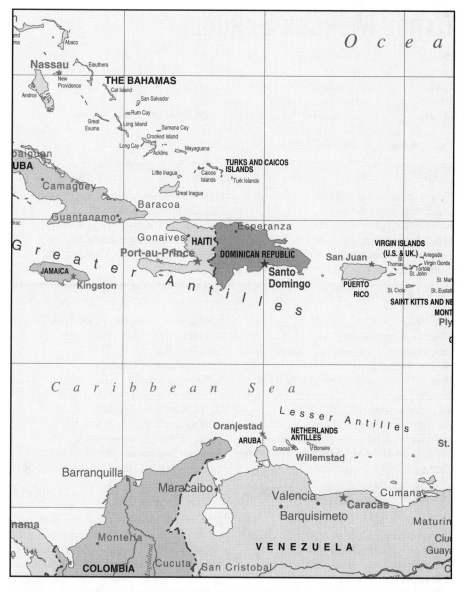

DOMINICAN REPUBLIC

Area:	48,730 sq km
Population:	9,365,818
Capital:	Santo Domingo
Currency:	Dominican Peso (DOP)
Languages:	Spanish

CAROL MORGAN SCHOOL

Phone	809 947 1000
Fax	809 533 9222
Email	headmaster@cms.edu.do
Website	www.cms.edu.do
Address	Ave. Sarasota esq. Nunez de Caceres, Bella Vista, Santo Domingo, Dominican Republic
Mailing address	EPS-P-2379, PO Box 02-5261, Miami, FL 33102-5261, USA

STAFF

Head of School Jack L. Delman
Deputy Head Ernest Peterson
High School Principal Ken Axelson
Middle School Principal Rick Bunnell
Elementary Principal Brien McCall
Business Manager Ariel Villaba

Academic Technology Director Mark Picketts
Head Librarian Laura Peabody
Teaching staff Full time 123; Total 123
Nationalities of teaching staff US 67;
Dominican 35; Other(s) (Canadian) 21

INFORMATION

Grade levels PreK–12
School year August–June
School type coeducational, day, private non-profit
Year founded 1933
Governed by elected Eight Member Board of Directors
Accredited by Southern
Regional organizations ACCAS
Enrollment PreK 63; Elementary K–5 496;
Middle School 6–8 247; High School 9–12 308;
Total 1,114

Nationalities of student body US 341; UK 1;
Dominican 612; Other(s) (Spaniard, Canadian) 160
Tuition/fee currency US Dollar
Tuition range 4,195–10,489
Annual fees Registration 464; Optimal Learning Center 800; Capital Fund 875
One time fees Capital Levy 3,000; Entrance 5,150
Graduates attending college 100%
Graduates have attended Duke U, Tufts U, U of Pennsylvania, Georgetown U, John Hopkins U

EDUCATIONAL PROGRAM

Curriculum US, AP
Average class size Elementary 20; Secondary 18
Language(s) of instruction English
Language(s) taught Spanish, Mandarin
Staff specialists computer, counselor, ESL, learning disabilities, librarian, math resource, nurse, physician, reading resource, speech/hearing
Special curricular programs art, instrumental music, vocal music, computer/technology, distance learning, physical education

Extra curricular programs computers, community service, drama, excursions/expeditions, literary magazine, newspaper, photography, yearbook
Sports baseball, basketball, football, golf, gymnastics, soccer, softball, track and field, volleyball
Clubs band, choir, drama, Model UN, ecology, Destination Imagination
Examinations ACT, AP, Iowa, PSAT, SAT, SAT II, TOEFL

CAMPUS FACILITIES

Location Suburban
Campus 6 hectares, 10 buildings, 80 classrooms, 6 computer labs, 300 instructional computers,

25,000 library volumes, 1 cafeteria, 2 covered play areas, 2 gymnasiums, 1 infirmary, 3 playing fields, 9 science labs, air conditioning

INTERNATIONAL SCHOOL OF SOSUA

Phone	809 571 3271
Fax	809 571 1904
Email	issosua@gmail.com
Website	www.issosua.com
Address	International School of Sosua, La Mulata #1, El Batey, Sosua, Dominican Republic
Mailing address	BM 30042, 6911 NW 87th Avenue, Miami FL 33178, USA

STAFF

Principal Michael Sayer
Business Manager Gina Gonzales
Teaching staff Full time 20; Part time 3; Total 23

Nationalities of teaching staff US 3; UK 3; Dominican 7; Other(s) (Canadian) 7

INFORMATION

Grade levels N–12
School year September–June
School type coeducational, day, private non-profit
Year founded 1989
Governed by appointed Board of Directors
Accredited by Southern
Regional organizations ACCAS
Nationalities of student body Dominican 48; Other(s) 112

Tuition/fee currency US Dollar
Tuition range 2,200–5,200
Annual fees Capital Levy 180
One time fees Registration 500; Admission 500
Graduates attending college 100%
Graduates have attended Fairleigh Dickinson U, Pontifical Catholic U Mother and Teacher

EDUCATIONAL PROGRAM

Curriculum US, National, Intl, AP
Average class size Elementary 14; Secondary 10
Language(s) of instruction English, Spanish
Staff specialists computer, ESL

Special curricular programs art, computer/ technology, physical education
Sports baseball, basketball, soccer, track and field, volleyball, ultimate frisbee
Examinations SAT

CAMPUS FACILITIES

Location Rural
Campus 6 hectares, 9 buildings, 18 classrooms, 1 computer lab, 18 instructional computers,

4,000 library volumes, 1 playing field, 1 science lab

EAST TIMOR

EAST TIMOR

Area:	15,007 sq km
Population:	1,084,971
Capital:	Dili
Currency:	US Dollar (USD)
Languages:	Tetum, Portuguese

QSI INTERNATIONAL SCHOOL OF DILI

Phone	670 332 2389
Email	dili@qsi.org
Website	www.qsi.org
Address	Aldea 04 Marconi, Suco Fatu, Sub Distrito Dom Aleixo, Dili, East Timor
Mailing address	8250 Dili Place, Dulles, VA 20189-8250, USA

STAFF

Director Jo Ellen Fuller
Administrative Assistant Jose Magbanua
IT Teacher Emily Brotherton

Teaching staff Full time 3; Part time 4; Total 7
Nationalities of teaching staff US 4; Timorese 1; Other(s) (Filipino) 2

INFORMATION

Grade levels K–9
School year August–June
School type private non-profit
Year founded 2005
Sponsored by Quality Schools International
Enrollment Elementary K–5 17; Middle School 6–8 6; High School 9–12 2; Total 25

Nationalities of student body US 3; Timorese 1; Other(s) (Australian) 21
Tuition/fee currency US Dollar
Tuition 12,500
Annual fees Capital Levy 1,600
One time fees Registration 100

EDUCATIONAL PROGRAM

Curriculum US
Language(s) of instruction English
Language(s) taught Tetum
Staff specialists computer
Special curricular programs art, computer/

technology, distance learning, physical education
Extra curricular programs computers, drama, excursions/expeditions, newspaper
Sports badminton, basketball, gymnastics, martial arts, swimming, tennis, volleyball

CAMPUS FACILITIES

Location Urban
Campus 2 buildings, 4 classrooms, 1 computer lab, 13 instructional computers,

300 library volumes, 1 covered play area, air conditioning

ECUADOR

ECUADOR

Area:	283,560 sq km
Population:	13,755,680
Capital:	Quito
Currency:	US Dollar (USD)
Languages:	Spanish

AMERICAN SCHOOL OF GUAYAQUIL

Phone	5934 226-1893
Fax	5934 2250 453
Email	info@colegioamericano.edu.ec
Website	www.colegioamericano.edu.ec
Address	Avenida Juan Tanca Marengo–KM 6 1/2, Guayaquil, Ecuador
Mailing address	PO Box 09-01-3304, Guayaquil, Ecuador

STAFF

Director General Keith J. D. Miller
High School Principal
Patricia Ayala de Coronel, Ph.D.
Elementary School Principal
Guisella Zevallos de Amaya
Preschool Principal Mariana HiFong de Camchong

Athletic Director Billy Dwyer
Financial Administrative Manager
Carolina Garzon Reyes
Head of the Computer Department Dino Herrera
Head Librarian Laura Marcillo

INFORMATION

Grade levels PreK–12
School year April–January
School type coeducational, day, private non-profit
Year founded 1942
Governed by elected Board of Directors
Regional organizations AASSA
Enrollment PreK 220; Elementary K–5 680;
Middle School 6–8 300; High School 9–12
350; Total 1,550

Nationalities of student body US 50; UK 10;
Ecuadorian 1,440; Other(s)
(Chinese, Korean) 50
Tuition/fee currency US Dollar
Tuition range 2,300–2,840
One time fees Registration 170; Insurance 35;
Yearbook 25; Pictures 5
Graduates attending college 90%
Graduates have attended State U of New York,
Tecnologico de Monterrey, Mexico, U of
Colorado, U of New Orleans, Purdue U

EDUCATIONAL PROGRAM

Curriculum National, IB Diploma, IBMYP
Average class size Elementary 30; Secondary 30
Language(s) of instruction English, Spanish
Language(s) taught English, Spanish
Staff specialists computer, counselor, ESL,
learning disabilities, librarian, math resource,
psychologist, reading resource
Special curricular programs art, instrumental
music, vocal music, computer/technology,
physical education, vocational

Extra curricular programs computers, community
service, dance, drama, environmental
conservation, excursions/expeditions, literary
magazine, newspaper, yearbook
Sports baseball, basketball, football, gymnastics,
soccer, track and field, volleyball
Clubs chess, cheerleading, guitar, band
Examinations IB

CAMPUS FACILITIES

Location Suburban
Campus 13 hectares, 20 buildings, 70 classrooms,
4 computer labs, 128 instructional computers,

9,100 library volumes, 1 auditorium,
2 cafeterias, 3 infirmaries, 6 playing fields,
4 science labs, air conditioning

Data from 2006/07 school year.

INTER-AMERICAN ACADEMY

Phone	593 4 287 1790
Fax	593 4 287 3358
Email	admin@interamerican.edu.ec
Website	www.interamerican.edu.ec
Address	Puerto Azul, km 10 1/2, Via de la Costa, Guayaquil, Guayas, Ecuador
Mailing address	8424 NW 56 St., Suite GYE 1096, Miami, FL 33166

STAFF

Executive Director Robert Gronniger
Guidance Counselor Marcela Doylet
High School and Middle School Principal Belinda McRoberts
Athletic Director Bob Jonson
Chief Accountant Humberto Acosta

Network Manager Joe McRoberts
Educational Media Coordinator Monica Aguiar
Teaching staff Full time 22; Part time 2; Total 24
Nationalities of teaching staff US 11; Ecuadorian 9; Other(s) 4

INFORMATION

Grade levels N–12
School year August–May
School type coeducational, day, private non-profit
Year founded 1979
Governed by elected Board of Directors
Accredited by Southern
Regional organizations AASSA
Enrollment Nursery 19; PreK 12; Elementary K–5 88; Middle School 6–8 40; High School 9–12 71; Total 230

Nationalities of student body US 50; Ecuadorian 93; Other(s) 87
Tuition/fee currency US Dollar
Tuition range 2,210–10,190
One time fees Registration 150; Capital Levy 2,800
Graduates attending college 100%
Graduates have attended Boston Col, Purdue U, Rutgers U, New York U, Mt. Holyoke Col

EDUCATIONAL PROGRAM

Curriculum US, AP
Average class size Elementary 15; Secondary 16
Language(s) of instruction English
Language(s) taught Spanish, French
Staff specialists computer, counselor, ESL, learning disabilities, librarian, nurse

Special curricular programs art, computer/ technology, distance learning, physical education
Extra curricular programs community service, yearbook
Sports basketball, soccer, swimming, volleyball
Examinations ACT, Iowa, PSAT, SAT, SAT II

CAMPUS FACILITIES

Location Suburban
Campus 7 hectares, 9 buildings, 24 classrooms, 2 computer labs, 90 instructional computers, 15,000 library volumes, 1 cafeteria, 1 covered play area, 1 gymnasium, 1 infirmary, 2 science labs, 1 pool, 1 tennis court, air conditioning

ACADEMIA COTOPAXI AMERICAN INTERNATIONAL SCHOOL

Phone	593 2 246 7373
Fax	593 2 244 5195
Email	director@cotopaxi.k12.ec
Website	www.cotopaxi.k12.ec
Address	De las Higuerillas y Alondras (Monteserrin), Quito, PO Box 17-11-6510, Ecuador
Mailing address	Casilla 17-11-6510, Quito, Ecuador

STAFF

Director William Johnston, Ed.D.
Elementary School Principal Larry May, Ed.D.
Secondary School Principal Juanita Burch-Clay
Administrative Officer Patricia de Marin
Curriculum Coordinator Anne Ray
Director of Admissions and Outreach Paola Pereira
Business Manager Mauricio Mera, Ph.D.

Technology Coordinator Aland Russell
Librarian Ana Soria
Teaching staff Full time 61; Part time 4; Total 65
Nationalities of teaching staff US 41; UK 2; Ecuadorian 14; Other(s) (Canadian, Uruguayan) 8

INFORMATION

Grade levels N–12
School year August–June
School type coeducational, day, private non-profit
Year founded 1959
Governed by elected Board of Directors
Accredited by Southern
Regional organizations AASSA, ECIS
Enrollment PreK 53; Elementary K–5 206; Middle School 6–8 110; High School 9–12 120; Total 489

Nationalities of student body US 141; UK 1; Ecuadorian 166; Other(s) (Colombian, Brazilian) 181
Tuition/fee currency US Dollar
Tuition range 5,910-13,274
Annual fees Busing 540
One time fees Registration 300; Capital Levy 4,000
Graduates attending college 96%
Graduates have attended Yale U, U of Miami, Clark U, Boston U, Cornell U

EDUCATIONAL PROGRAM

Curriculum US, National, Intl, IB Diploma, IBPYP
Average class size Elementary 16; Secondary 16
Language(s) of instruction English, Spanish
Staff specialists computer, counselor, ESL, learning disabilities, librarian, nurse, psychologist, reading resource
Special curricular programs art, instrumental music, vocal music, computer/technology, physical education

Extra curricular programs computers, community service, dance, drama, environmental conservation, excursions/expeditions, literary magazine, photography, yearbook
Sports baseball, basketball, football, gymnastics, soccer, softball, swimming, volleyball
Examinations IB, Iowa, PSAT, SAT, TOEFL

CAMPUS FACILITIES

Location Urban
Campus 6 hectares, 6 buildings, 80 classrooms, 12 computer labs, 261 instructional computers,

32,000 library volumes, 1 auditorium, 2 cafeterias, 1 gymnasium, 1 infirmary, 4 playing fields, 4 science labs, 1 pool

ALLIANCE ACADEMY INTERNATIONAL

Phone	593 2 226 6985
Fax	593 2 226 4350
Email	hyandun@alliance.k12.ec
Website	www.alliance.k12.ec
Address	Villalengua 789, Quito, Ecuador
Mailing address	Casilla 17-11-06186, Quito, Ecuador

STAFF

Director Rohn D. Peterson, Ed.D.
High School Principal Kurt Peterson
Elementary Principal Jack Vegter
Skills Center Director Carolyn Eumurian
Assistant to the Director Helga Yandun

Business/Finance Manager
Helga Yandun/Keith Newburn
High School Computer Sciences Department Head
Gary Roedding
Learning Resource Center Coordinator
Renee Sheppard

INFORMATION

Grade levels PreK–12
School year August–June
School type boarding, coeducational, company-sponsored, church-affiliated, day, private non-profit
Year founded 1929
Governed by appointed and elected School Board
Accredited by Southern
Regional organizations AASSA
Enrollment PreK 15; Elementary K–5 137; Middle School 6–8 95; High School 9–12 161; Total 408

Nationalities of student body US 191; UK 6; Ecuadorian 145; Other(s) (Canadian, Korean) 66
Tuition/fee currency US Dollar
Tuition range 6,675–7,630
Annual fees Insurance 35
One time fees Registration 50
Boarding program grades 7–12
Boarding program length 7-day **Boys** 9 **Girls** 11
Graduates attending college 95%
Graduates have attended Harvard U, Wheaton Col, John Brown U, Crown Col, Nyack Col

EDUCATIONAL PROGRAM

Curriculum US, AP
Average class size Elementary 15; Secondary 20
Language(s) of instruction English
Language(s) taught French, Spanish
Staff specialists computer, counselor, ESL, learning disabilities, librarian, nurse, psychologist, reading resource, speech/hearing
Special curricular programs art, instrumental music, vocal music, computer/technology, physical education, vocational, photography, journalism, home economics, typing

Extra curricular programs computers, community service, drama, excursions/expeditions, newspaper, photography, yearbook
Sports badminton, basketball, soccer, softball, volleyball
Clubs National Honor Society, student council, music ensemble, Christian Service Organization, mountain climbing, gardening, video
Examinations ACT, AP, PSAT, SAT, Stanford

CAMPUS FACILITIES

Location Urban
Campus 2 hectares, 9 buildings, 52 classrooms, 4 computer labs, 120 instructional computers,

32,000 library volumes, 1 auditorium, 1 cafeteria, 2 covered play areas, 1 gymnasium, 1 infirmary, 2 playing fields, 3 science labs

Data from 2006/07 school year.

AMERICAN SCHOOL OF QUITO

Phone	593 2 2472 974
Fax	593 2 2472 972
Email	sbarba@fcaq.k12.ec
Website	www.fcaq.k12.ec
Address	Manuel Benigno Cueva N 80-190, Quito, Ecuador
Mailing address	Director-ASQ, c/o US Embassy Quito, Unit 5372 Box 004, APO AA 34039, USA

STAFF

Director General Susan A. Barba
High School Principal-National Section
Susana Hervas
Director-International Program Susan Montalvo
Elementary Principal-National Section
Theresa Barrera
Middle Years Coordinator Leah Yepez

Elementary Coordinator-International Section
Amy Surillo
Financial Manager Gonzalo Luna
Technology Coordinator Leonardo Castro
Media Center Director Judy Williams
Teaching staff Full time 228; Total 228
Nationalities of teaching staff US 46;
Ecuadorian 160; Other(s) (Canadian) 22

INFORMATION

Grade levels PreK–12
School year September–June
School type coeducational, day, private non-profit
Year founded 1940
Governed by elected Board of Administration
Accredited by Southern
Regional organizations ACCAS, AASSA
Enrollment PreK 130; Elementary K–5 1,000;
Middle School 6–8 484; High School 9–12 600;
Total 2,214

Nationalities of student body US 80; Ecuadorian
2,043; Other(s) (Colombian, Peruvian) 91
Tuition/fee currency US Dollar
Tuition range 4,750–7,660
Annual fees Registration 378; Busing 500;
Materials 411
One time fees Equipment 750
Graduates attending college 96%
Graduates have attended Brown U, Yale U,
Princeton U, Mount Holyoke Col, Smith Col

EDUCATIONAL PROGRAM

Curriculum US, National, Intl, IB Diploma, IBMYP
Average class size Elementary 22; Secondary 25
Language(s) of instruction English, Spanish
Staff specialists computer, counselor, ESL,
librarian, nurse, physician, psychologist
Special curricular programs art, instrumental
music, vocal music, computer/technology,
physical education, vocational

Extra curricular programs computers, community
service, drama, environmental conservation,
excursions/expeditions, newspaper
Sports basketball, gymnastics, hockey, martial
arts, soccer, track and field, volleyball
Clubs ecology, newspaper, drama, Model UN,
Organization of American States, garden,
Girl Scouts, recycling
Examinations IB, Iowa, PSAT, SAT, SAT II, TOEFL

CAMPUS FACILITIES

Location Urban
Campus 12 hectares, 19 buildings, 188 classrooms,
7 computer labs, 223 instructional computers,
72,000 library volumes, 1 auditorium,

1 cafeteria, 2 covered play areas, 1 gymnasium,
1 infirmary, 7 playing fields, 8 science labs,
1 tennis court

EGYPT

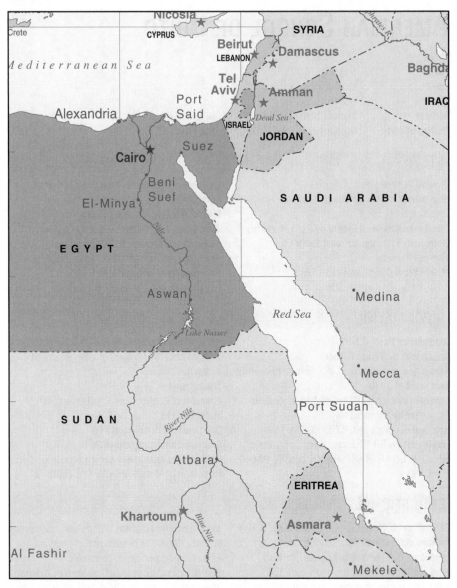

EGYPT

Area:	1,001,450 sq km
Population:	80,335,036
Capital:	Cairo
Currency:	Egyptian Pound (EGP)
Languages:	Arabic

Alexandria **EGYPT**

SCHUTZ AMERICAN SCHOOL

Phone	20 3 574 1435
Fax	20 3 576 0229
Email	headmaster@schutzschool.org.eg
Website	www.schutzschool.org.eg
Address	51 Schutz Street, Alexandria, 21111, Egypt
Mailing address	PO Box 1000, Alexandria, Egypt 21111

STAFF

Head of School Anthony Spencer, Ed.D.
Elementary/Middle School Principal
Nada Collins, Ph.D.
Secondary Principal Massimo Laterza
Registrar Omneya El Naggar
Chief Financial Officer Mona Henry

Technology Coordinator Mark McCright
Librarian Catherine Inchmore
Teaching staff Full time 28; Part time 3; Total 31
Nationalities of teaching staff US 19; Egyptian 9;
Other(s) (New Zealander, Canadian) 3

INFORMATION

Grade levels PreK–12
School year August–June
School type coeducational, day, private non-profit
Year founded 1924
Governed by appointed Board of Trustees
Accredited by CIS, New England
Regional organizations CEESA, ECIS, NESA
Enrollment PreK 24; Elementary K–5 91;
Middle School 6–8 54; High School 9–12 75;
Total 244

Nationalities of student body US 49;
Egyptian 110; Other(s) (Indian, Turk) 85
Tuition/fee currency US Dollar
Tuition range 3,500–10,750
Annual fees Busing 400; Lunch 500;
Facilities 200; Technology 125
One time fees Registration 2,000
Graduates attending college 100%
Graduates have attended Dartmouth Col, George
Washington U, Boston Col, U of Virginia, Boston U

EDUCATIONAL PROGRAM

Curriculum US, AP
Average class size Elementary 15; Secondary 19
Language(s) of instruction English
Language(s) taught French, Arabic
Staff specialists computer, ESL, librarian, nurse
Special curricular programs art, instrumental
music, vocal music, computer/technology,
distance learning, physical education, drama,
student publications

Extra curricular programs community service,
drama, environmental conservation,
excursions/expeditions, yearbook
Sports badminton, basketball, soccer,
swimming, tennis, volleyball
Clubs student council, National Junior Honor
Society, National Honor Society, MathCounts
Examinations AP, Iowa, PSAT, SAT, SAT II

CAMPUS FACILITIES

Location Urban
Campus 2 hectares, 9 buildings, 27 classrooms,
2 computer labs, 46 instructional computers,
20,000 library volumes, 1 auditorium,
1 cafeteria, 1 covered play area, 1 gymnasium,
1 infirmary, 2 playing fields, 1 science lab,
1 pool, 1 tennis court, air conditioning

CAIRO AMERICAN COLLEGE

Phone	20-2-2755 5555
Fax	20-2-2519 6584
Email	support@cacegypt.org
Website	www.cacegypt.org
Address	1 Midan Digla, Road 253, Digla, Maadi, Cairo, 11431, Egypt
Mailing address	PO Box 39, Digla, Maadi, 11431, Cairo, Egypt

STAFF

Superintendent Monica N. Greeley
High School Principal Robert DeWolf
Middle School Principal Michael Popinchalk
Elementary School Principal Seamus Marriott
Business Manager Larry Kraut

Director of Information Services Cheryl Bohn
Head Librarian Paul Bartos
Teaching staff Full time 152; Part time 23; Total 175
Nationalities of teaching staff US 106; UK 9;
Egyptian 26; Other(s) (Canadian, Australian) 34

INFORMATION

Grade levels PreK–12
School year August–June
School type coeducational, day, private non-profit
Year founded 1945
Governed by appointed and elected Board of
Trustees
Accredited by Middle States
Regional organizations ECIS, NESA
Enrollment PreK 30; Elementary K–5 520;
Middle School 6–8 350; High School 9–12 500;
Total 1,400

Nationalities of student body US 660; UK 60;
Egyptian 200; Other(s) (Korean, Canadian) 480
Tuition/fee currency US Dollar
Tuition range 8,650–13,780
Annual fees Busing 1,700; ESL 1,200
One time fees Capital Levy 5,500; Application 350
Graduates attending college 95%
Graduates have attended Columbia U, McGill U,
Massachusetts Institute of Technology, Stanford
U, U of London

EDUCATIONAL PROGRAM

Curriculum US, IB Diploma
Average class size Elementary 18; Secondary 18
Language(s) of instruction English
Language(s) taught Arabic, French, Spanish
Staff specialists computer, counselor, ESL,
librarian, math resource, nurse, psychologist,
reading resource, speech/hearing
Special curricular programs art, instrumental
music, vocal music, computer/technology,
physical education
Extra curricular programs computers, community
service, dance, drama, environmental

conservation, excursions/expeditions, literary
magazine, newspaper, photography, yearbook
Sports baseball, basketball, cross-country,
soccer, softball, swimming, tennis, track and
field, volleyball, wrestling
Clubs National Honor Society, Model UN,
student government, academic games, peer
support, Arab, Green Team, Thespians
Examinations ACT, AP, IB, Iowa, PSAT, SAT,
SAT II, TOEFL

CAMPUS FACILITIES

Location Suburban
Campus 5 hectares, 12 buildings, 126 classrooms,
15 computer labs, 700 instructional computers,
70,000 library volumes, 1 auditorium,

1 cafeteria, 2 gymnasiums, 1 infirmary,
2 playing fields, 12 science labs, 1 pool,
3 tennis courts, air conditioning

MODERN ENGLISH SCHOOL

Phone	20 2 617 0005 11
Fax	20 2 617 0020
Email	mescairo@mescairo.com
Website	www.mescairo.com
Address	PO Box 5, Tagamoa Khamis, Cairo, 11835, Egypt

STAFF

Managing Director Sawsan L. Dajani
Principal Peter Godfrey
American High School Principal
Virginia Dahlstrom, Ed.D.
Primary Head Teacher Key Stage 1
Catherine Symonds
Primary Head Teacher Key Stage 2 Carole Godfrey

Head of Secondary School Diana Perry
Financial Controller Shaker Beltagi
Head of Secondary IT Department Filip Rafaneli
Secondary Librarian Samia Beltagi
Teaching staff Full time 119; Part time 4; Total 123
Nationalities of teaching staff US 14; UK 94;
Egyptian 5; Other(s) (French, Canadian) 10

INFORMATION

Grade levels PreK–12
School year September–June
School type coeducational, day, proprietary
Year founded 1990
Governed by appointed Board of Trustees
Accredited by Middle States
Regional organizations ECIS, MAIS, NESA
Enrollment PreK 182; Elementary K–5 704;
Middle School 6–8 288; High School 9–12 476;
Total 1,650

Nationalities of student body US 34; UK 36;
Egyptian 1,464; Other(s) (Syrian, Jordanian) 116
Tuition/fee currency British Pound
Tuition range 1,850-4,800
One time fees Registration 600
Graduates attending college 100%
Graduates have attended Massachusetts Institute
of Technology, Bath U, Cornell U,
American U in Cairo, McGill U

(Continued)

MODERN ENGLISH SCHOOL (Continued)

EDUCATIONAL PROGRAM

Curriculum US, UK, Intl, AP, IB Diploma, IBMYP, IGCSE, GenCSE
Average class size Elementary 25; Secondary 16
Language(s) of instruction English, Arabic, French
Language(s) taught Spanish
Staff specialists computer, counselor, ESL, librarian, nurse, physician
Special curricular programs art, instrumental music, vocal music, computer/technology, physical education

Extra curricular programs computers, community service, dance, drama, environmental conservation, excursions/expeditions, photography, yearbook
Sports basketball, football, skiing, soccer, swimming, track and field, volleyball
Clubs Ultimate Games, strategy gaming, pantomime, darts, needlework, dance, movie, arts and crafts, cricket, card making
Examinations A-level GCE, AP, GCSE, IB, IGCSE, PSAT, SAT, SAT II

CAMPUS FACILITIES

Location Suburban
Campus 3 hectares, 3 buildings, 90 classrooms, 5 computer labs, 225 instructional computers, 21,000 library volumes, 2 auditoriums, 1 covered play area, 1 gymnasium, 1 infirmary, 3 playing fields, 6 science labs, 2 pools, 1 tennis court, air conditioning

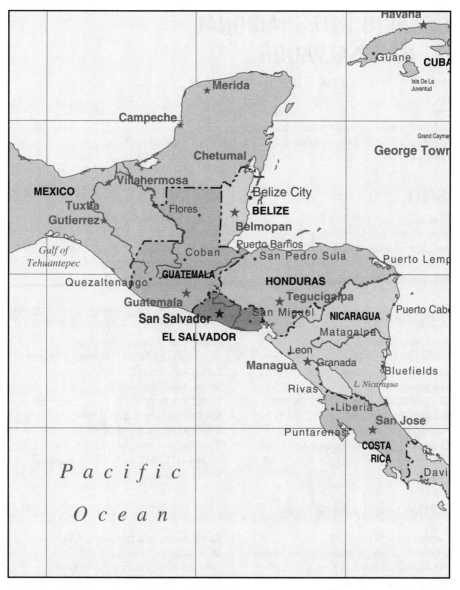

EL SALVADOR

Area:	21,040 sq km
Population:	6,948,073
Capital:	San Salvador
Currency:	US Dollar (USD)
Languages:	Spanish

COLEGIO INTERNACIONAL DE SAN SALVADOR

Phone	503 2 224 1330
Fax	503 2 223 7335
Email	c_stemp@intschoolsansal.com
Website	www.intschoolsansal.com
Address	Calle La Reforma 169, San Salvador, El Salvador
Mailing address	VIPSAL 1214, Box 02-5364, Miami, FL 33101, USA

STAFF

Head of School Chester S. Stemp
Head of Primary, 1–6 Amy Delgado
Head of Pre-School, PreK–K Carole Castillo
Head of Secondary, 7–12 Dennis Miller
Business Manager Nora Stemp

Technology Coordinator Marisabel Barahona
Librarian Tania Guardado
Teaching staff Full time 25; Part time 5; Total 30
Nationalities of teaching staff US 14;
Salvadoran 14; Other(s) 2

INFORMATION

Grade levels PreK–12
School year August–June
School type coeducational, day, proprietary
Year founded 1979
Governed by appointed Board of Owners
Sponsored by Owners
Regional organizations AASCA
Enrollment PreK 23; Elementary K–5 140;
Middle School 6–8 70; High School 9–12 90;
Total 323

Nationalities of student body US 80;
Salvadoran 130; Other(s) (Korean, Mexican) 113
Tuition/fee currency US Dollar
Tuition range 3,800-4,600
Annual fees Books 300
One time fees Registration 1,000
Graduates attending college 100%
Graduates have attended U of Notre Dame,
Texas A&M U, Indiana U, Michigan State U,
Loyola U Chicago

EDUCATIONAL PROGRAM

Curriculum US, National, AP
Average class size Elementary 24; Secondary 24
Language(s) of instruction English, Spanish
Language(s) taught French
Staff specialists computer, counselor, ESL,
librarian, psychologist

Special curricular programs art, computer/
technology, physical education
Extra curricular programs dance, drama,
environmental conservation, newspaper,
yearbook
Sports basketball, swimming, volleyball
Clubs cheerleaders, ecology, student council
Examinations Iowa, SAT

CAMPUS FACILITIES

Location Urban
Campus 1 hectare, 12 buildings, 15 classrooms,
1 computer lab, 25 instructional computers,

5,000 library volumes, 1 auditorium,
1 gymnasium, 1 science lab, 1 pool

ESCUELA AMERICANA

Phone	503 2528 8300
Fax	503 2528 8321
Email	iss.recruiting@amschool.edu.sv
Website	www.amschool.edu.sv
Address	Colonia y Calle La Mascota, Final Pasaje #3, San Salvador, El Salvador
Mailing address	PO Box 025364, VIPSAL #1352, Miami, FL 33102-5364, USA

STAFF

General Director Charles H. Skipper, Ph.D.
Upper School Director Ramon Morales
Middle School Director Bob Sinnett
Lower School Director Cristina Lima
Athletic Director Raquel Rodriguez
Director of Finance and Operations
Patricia de Zaldivar

Technology Department Manager Salvador Canjura
Head Librarian Nora de Hirlemann
Teaching staff Full time 187; Part time 2; Total 189
Nationalities of teaching staff US 45; Salvadoran 134; Other(s) (Canadian, Guatemalan) 10

INFORMATION

Grade levels PreK–12
School year August–June
School type coeducational, day, private non-profit
Year founded 1946
Governed by elected Board of Directors
Accredited by Southern
Regional organizations AASCA
Enrollment PreK 125; Elementary K–5 775; Middle School 6–8 380; High School 9–12 480; Total 1,760

Nationalities of student body US 260; Salvadoran 1,382; Other(s) (Guatemalan, Korean) 118
Tuition/fee currency US Dollar
Tuition range 3,526–8,100
One time fees Registration 3,708
Graduates attending college 100%
Graduates have attended Harvard U, Yale U, U of Pennsylvania, Cornell U, Princeton U

EDUCATIONAL PROGRAM

Curriculum US, National, AP
Average class size Elementary 24; Secondary 21
Language(s) of instruction English, Spanish
Language(s) taught French
Staff specialists computer, counselor, ESL, learning disabilities, librarian, math resource, nurse, psychologist, reading resource, speech/hearing
Special curricular programs art, instrumental music, computer/technology, physical education

Extra curricular programs computers, community service, drama, environmental conservation, excursions/expeditions, literary magazine, newspaper, photography, yearbook
Sports basketball, golf, soccer, squash, track and field, volleyball, wall climbing, team handball
Clubs ecology, Teens United for Health, drama, chess, MathCounts, knowledge bowl, social service, art
Examinations ACT, AP, PSAT, SAT, SAT II, Stanford, TOEFL

CAMPUS FACILITIES

Location Suburban
Campus 35 hectares, 20 buildings, 134 classrooms, 8 computer labs, 357 instructional computers,

31,500 library volumes, 2 auditoriums, 2 cafeterias, 2 covered play areas, 2 gymnasiums, 2 infirmaries, 2 playing fields, 8 science labs

ERITREA

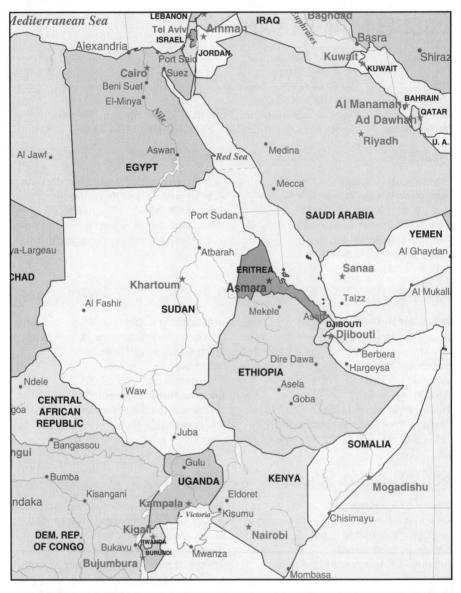

ERITREA

Area:	121,320 sq km
Population:	4,906,585
Capital:	Asmara (Asmera)
Currency:	Nakfa (ERN)
Languages:	Afar, Arabic

ASMARA INTERNATIONAL COMMUNITY SCHOOL

Phone	291 1 161 705
Fax	291 1 161 705
Email	aics@aics.org.er
Website	www.aicsasmara.com
Address	117-19 Street #6, Asmara, Eritrea
Mailing address	PO Box 4941, Asmara, Eritrea

STAFF

Director Paul S. Johnston
Business Manager Akeza Kidane
Librarian Kristine Anderson

Teaching staff Full time 12; Part time 1; Total 13
Nationalities of teaching staff US 7; UK 1; Eritrean 4; Other(s) (Australian) 1

INFORMATION

Grade levels PreK–12
School year August-June
School type coeducational, day, private non-profit
Year founded 1994
Governed by appointed and elected Board of Governors
Accredited by Middle States
Regional organizations AISA
Enrollment PreK 15; Elementary K–5 57; Middle School 6–8 30; High School 9–12 25; Total 127

Nationalities of student body US 21; UK 4; Eritrean 73; Other(s) (Dutch, Zimbabwean) 29
Tuition/fee currency US Dollar
Tuition range 7,500-16,500
One time fees Registration 100; Capital Levy 2,800
Graduates attending college 100%
Graduates have attended Catholic U, U of Maryland, U of Connecticut, U of Richmond, U of Tulsa

EDUCATIONAL PROGRAM

Curriculum US, Intl, IBPYP
Average class size Elementary 12; Secondary 12
Language(s) of instruction English
Language(s) taught French
Staff specialists computer, ESL, librarian, nurse

Special curricular programs art, vocal music, distance learning, physical education
Extra curricular programs drama, newspaper, yearbook
Examinations AP, Iowa, PSAT, SAT, TOEFL

CAMPUS FACILITIES

Location Urban
Campus 1 hectare, 2 buildings, 17 classrooms, 1 computer lab, 35 instructional computers,

7,500 library volumes, 1 auditorium, 1 infirmary, 1 playing field, 1 science lab

ESTONIA

ESTONIA

Area:	45,226 sq km
Population:	1,315,912
Capital:	Tallinn
Currency:	Estonian Kroon (EEK)
Languages:	Estonian, Russian

INTERNATIONAL SCHOOL OF ESTONIA

Phone   372 666 4380
Fax   372 666 43 83
Email   office@ise.edu.ee
Website   www.ise.edu.ee
Address   Juhkentali 18, Tallinn, 10132, Estonia

STAFF

Director Sharon A. Sperry, Ed.D.
Deputy Director and MYP Coordinator
Don Fitzmahan, Ed.D.
PYP Coordinator Dee Broussard, Ed.D.
Diploma Coordinator Randy Eplin, Ed.D.
Business/Finance Manager Katre Pohlak

IT Coordinator Marcel Ideler
Head of Library/Media Center Kadri Tompson
Teaching staff Full time 22; Part time 1; Total 23
Nationalities of teaching staff US 6; UK 2;
Estonian 9; Other(s) (French) 5

INFORMATION

Grade levels PreK–12
School year August–June
School type coeducational, day, private non-profit
Year founded 1995
Governed by elected Board
Accredited by CIS, New England
Regional organizations CEESA, ECIS
Enrollment PreK 25; Elementary K–5 45;
Middle School 6–8 35; High School 9–12 10;
Total 115

Nationalities of student body US 10; UK 5;
Estonian 15; Other(s) (Swede, Pole) 85
Tuition/fee currency Euro
Tuition range 2,347-14,747
One time fees Capital Levy 2,000
Graduates attending college 100%
Graduates have attended Whitman Col,
U of Warsaw, Portobello Col,
Ecole Hotelier De Lausanne, U of Moscow

EDUCATIONAL PROGRAM

Curriculum Intl, IB Diploma, IBPYP, IBMYP
Average class size Elementary 9; Secondary 8
Language(s) of instruction English
Language(s) taught French, German, Estonian
Staff specialists computer, counselor, ESL,
learning disabilities, librarian, nurse
Special curricular programs art, computer/
technology, physical education

Extra curricular programs computers, community
service, excursions/expeditions, literary
magazine, yearbook
Clubs cooking, art, dance, Karate, homework,
cricket, soccer
Examinations IB, PSAT, SAT, SAT II, TOEFL, MAP

CAMPUS FACILITIES

Location Urban
Campus 1 hectare, 1 building, 19 classrooms,
1 computer lab, 35 instructional computers,

7,000 library volumes, 1 cafeteria,
1 gymnasium, 1 infirmary, 1 playing field,
1 science lab

ETHIOPIA

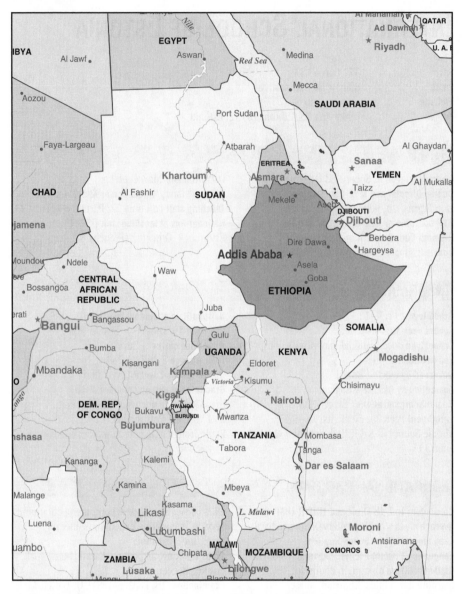

ETHIOPIA

Area:	1,127,127 sq km
Population:	76,511,887
Capital:	Addis Ababa
Currency:	Birr (ETB)
Languages:	Amharic, Oromigna

INTERNATIONAL COMMUNITY SCHOOL OF ADDIS ABABA

Phone	251 11 371 0870
Fax	251 11 371 0722
Email	info@icsaddis.edu.et
Website	www.icsaddis.edu.et
Address	Mauritania Road, Addis Ababa, Shoa, Ethiopia
Mailing address	PO Box 70282, Addis Ababa, Ethiopia

STAFF

Director Stephen E. Plisinski
Secondary Principal James Laney, Jr.
Elementary Principal/Curriculum Coordinator
Barbara Parker
Business Manager Wondwossen G. Egziabeher

IT Director Robert Vicknair
Librarian Douglas Glenn
Teaching staff Full time 47; Part time 2; Total 49
Nationalities of teaching staff US 30; UK 1;
Ethiopian 5; Other(s) 13

INFORMATION

Grade levels PreK–12
School year August–June
School type coeducational, day
Year founded 1964
Governed by elected Parents
Accredited by Middle States
Regional organizations AISA, ECIS
Enrollment PreK 33; Elementary K–5 27;
Middle School 6–8 49; High School 9–12 84;
Grade 13 139; Total 332

Nationalities of student body US 112; UK 23;
Ethiopian 43; Other(s) 254
Tuition/fee currency US Dollar
Tuition range 5,590-15,650
Annual fees Registration 500; Capital Levy 800;
Extended Days for PreK 2,000
One time fees Capital Levy 2,200
Graduates attending college 98%
Graduates have attended Yale U, Stanford U,
Massachusetts Institute of Technology,
Cornell U, Brandeis U

EDUCATIONAL PROGRAM

Curriculum US, IB Diploma
Average class size Elementary 18; Secondary 18
Language(s) of instruction English
Language(s) taught French, Spanish
Staff specialists counselor, ESL, librarian, nurse
Special curricular programs art, instrumental
music, computer/technology, physical education

Extra curricular programs Model UN, National
Honor Society
Sports basketball, cricket, soccer, tennis, track
and field, volleyball
Examinations ACT, IB, PSAT, SAT, SAT II, TOEFL,
ISA, PLAN

CAMPUS FACILITIES

Location Suburban
Campus 5 hectares, 10 buildings, 42 classrooms,
3 computer labs, 140 instructional computers,
15,000 library volumes, 3 auditoriums,

2 cafeterias, 1 covered play area, 1 gymnasium,
1 infirmary, 6 playing fields, 5 science labs,
4 tennis courts

FINLAND

FINLAND

Area:	338,145 sq km
Population:	5,238,460
Capital:	Helsinki
Currency:	Euro (EUR)
Languages:	Finnish

THE ENGLISH SCHOOL

Phone 358 9 477 1123
Fax 358 9 477 1980
Email english.school@edu.hel.fi
Website www.eschool.edu.hel.fi
Address Mantytie, 14, Helsinki, 00270, Finland

STAFF

Principal Juhani Kulmala, Ph.D.
Assistant Principal Riitta Pajuniemi

Proxy of the Board of Trustees Maijaliisa Aho
Head of Library/Media Center Marjatta Kurtén

INFORMATION

Grade levels PreK–12
School year August–June
School type coeducational, day, private non-profit
Year founded 1945
Governed by elected Board

Enrollment PreK 80; Elementary K–5 180;
Middle School 6–8 108; High School 9–12 90;
Total 458
Tuition/fee currency Euro
Tuition range 508–678
One time fees Registration 10

EDUCATIONAL PROGRAM

Curriculum US, UK, National, AP
Average class size Elementary 36; Secondary 35
Language(s) of instruction English, Finnish
Language(s) taught Finnish, English, Swedish,
German, French, Spanish, Italian, Russian
Staff specialists computer, counselor, learning
disabilities, psychologist, speech/hearing
Special curricular programs distance learning

Extra curricular programs computers, dance,
drama, excursions/expeditions, photography,
yearbook
Sports baseball, basketball, football, golf,
gymnastics, skiing, soccer, squash, swimming,
tennis, volleyball
Clubs French, German, technical work, band,
textile
Examinations AP, PSAT, SAT, Finnish
Matriculation Exams

CAMPUS FACILITIES

Location Urban
Campus 1 hectare, 2 buildings, 1 classroom,
1 computer lab, 31 instructional computers,

9,600 library volumes, 1 auditorium,
1 cafeteria, 1 gymnasium, 2 science labs,
air conditioning

Data from 2006/07 school year.

INTERNATIONAL SCHOOL OF HELSINKI

Phone	358 9 686 6160
Fax	358 9 685 6699
Email	mainoffice@ish.edu.hel.fi
Website	www.ish.edu.hel.fi
Address	Selkämerenkatu 11, Helsinki, 00180, Finland

STAFF

Head of School Robert W. Woods, Ed.D.
Lower School Principal Taina Wilson
Upper School Principal Debbie Brook

Business Manager Lars Forsell
Computer Coordinator Kirsi Tapola
Head of Library Inga-Britt Jäske

INFORMATION

Grade levels PreK–12
School year August–June
School type coeducational, day, private non-profit
Year founded 1963
Governed by elected Parent Association
Accredited by CIS, New England
Regional organizations CEESA, ECIS
Enrollment PreK 10; Elementary K–5 120;
Middle School 6–8 70; High School 9–12 95;
Total 295

Nationalities of student body US 43; UK 22;
Finn 48; Other(s) (Japanese, Russian) 177
Tuition/fee currency Euro
Tuition range 10,344–13,517
Annual fees Capital Levy 1,000
One time fees Registration 3,000
Graduates attending college 95%
Graduates have attended Oxford U,
Charleston U, Queen Mary's Col,
London School of Economics, U of Pennsylvania

EDUCATIONAL PROGRAM

Curriculum Intl, IB Diploma, IBPYP, IBMYP
Average class size Elementary 15; Secondary 15
Language(s) of instruction English
Language(s) taught French, Finnish, Spanish,
Swedish
Staff specialists computer, counselor, ESL,
learning disabilities, librarian, nurse
Special curricular programs art, vocal music,
computer/technology, physical education

Extra curricular programs computers, community
service, drama, environmental conservation,
excursions/expeditions, literary magazine,
newspaper, photography, yearbook
Sports badminton, baseball, basketball,
gymnastics, hockey, skiing, soccer, softball,
swimming, tennis, track and field, volleyball
Examinations GCSE, IB, Iowa, PSAT, SAT,
SAT II, ISA

CAMPUS FACILITIES

Location Urban
Campus 1 hectare, 1 building, 25 classrooms,
3 computer labs, 100 instructional computers,

12,000 library volumes, 1 auditorium,
1 cafeteria, 1 gymnasium, 1 infirmary,
1 playing field, 2 science labs

Data from 2006/07 school year.

FRANCE

FRANCE

Area:	643,427 sq km
Population:	63,713,926
Capital:	Paris
Currency:	Euro (EUR)
Languages:	French

BORDEAUX INTERNATIONAL SCHOOL

Phone	33 557 870 211
Fax	33 556 790 047
Email	bis@bordeaux-school.com
Website	www.bordeaux-school.com
Address	252 Rue Judaïque, Bordeaux, 33000, France

STAFF

Director Christine Cussac
Secondary Head A. J. Woodcock

Primary Head Judith Huguenin
Head of Library/Media Center Alex Desmond

INFORMATION

Grade levels N–13
School year September–June
School type boarding, coeducational, day, private non-profit
Year founded 1988
Governed by appointed Cooperative
Accredited by CIS
Regional organizations ECIS
Enrollment Nursery 12; PreK 15; Elementary K–5 23; Middle School 6–8 5; High School 9–12 14; Grade 13 9; Total 78

Nationalities of student body US 5; UK 29; French 30; Other(s) (Canadian) 14
Tuition/fee currency Euro
Tuition range 2,019–12,700
Annual fees Boarding, 5-day 4,620; Boarding, 7-day 6,860; Equipment 470
One time fees Registration 540; Host Family 160
Boarding program grades 8–13
Boys 7 **Girls** 6
Graduates attending college 95%
Graduates have attended U of Bristol, U of Sussex, U College London, McGill U, U of Bordeaux

EDUCATIONAL PROGRAM

Curriculum UK, National, IGCSE, French
Average class size Elementary 7; Secondary 7
Language(s) of instruction English, French
Language(s) taught English, French, Spanish, Italian
Staff specialists computer, counselor, ESL, learning disabilities, librarian, math resource, reading resource

Special curricular programs art, instrumental music, vocal music, computer/technology
Extra curricular programs community service, dance, drama, excursions/expeditions, literary magazine, newspaper, photography
Sports basketball, football, golf, martial arts, rugby, soccer, squash, swimming, tennis, volleyball, local clubs
Examinations A-level GCE, GCSE, IGCSE, TOEFL

CAMPUS FACILITIES

Location Urban
Campus 3 buildings, 20 classrooms, 1 computer lab, 12 instructional computers,

1,000 library volumes, 1 cafeteria, 1 covered play area, 1 science lab

Data from 2006/07 school year.

C.I.V. INTERNATIONAL SCHOOL OF SOPHIA ANTIPOLIS

Phone	33 0 4 92381720
Fax	33 0 4 92381721
Email	admissions@issa.net
Website	www.issa.net
Address	BP 97, Rue du Vallon, Sophia Antipolis, 06560, France

STAFF

Director Andrew P. Derry
High School Principal Robin Tyner
Middle School Principal David Shandley
IB Coordinator Nicholas Francis

MYP Coordinator Paul Cawthorne
Bursar Brigitte Véron
Head of Technology Nigel Ward

INFORMATION

Grade levels 1–13
School year September–June
School type boarding, coeducational, day, private non-profit
Year founded 1979
Governed by elected Board of Governors (ASEICA)
Regional organizations ECIS
Tuition/fee currency Euro

Tuition 9,500
Annual fees Boarding, 5-day 10,500; Boarding, 7-day 10,500
One time fees Registration 1,500; Books 98; IB Application 350
Graduates attending college 95%
Graduates have attended Oxford U, Cambridge U, Columbia U, Princeton U, Yale U

EDUCATIONAL PROGRAM

Curriculum National, Intl, IB Diploma, French Baccalaureate
Average class size Elementary 21; Secondary 20
Language(s) of instruction English, French
Language(s) taught Spanish, German, Italian, Russian, Swedish, Arabic, Chinese
Staff specialists computer, ESL, librarian, math resource, nurse
Special curricular programs art, computer/technology, physical education

Extra curricular programs computers, community service, dance, drama, excursions/expeditions, newspaper, photography, yearbook, Model UN, theater/film festival visits
Sports basketball, football, golf, hockey, martial arts, rugby, skiing, soccer, squash, swimming, tennis, track and field, volleyball, Judo, sailing
Examinations IB, SAT, French Baccalaureate-International Option, Brevet du College

CAMPUS FACILITIES

Location Rural
Campus 40 hectares, 14 buildings, 70 classrooms, 2 computer labs, 100 instructional computers, 10,000 library volumes, 1 auditorium, 2 cafeterias, 1 gymnasium, 1 infirmary, 4 playing fields, 6 science labs, 1 pool, 8 tennis courts, air conditioning

Data from 2006/07 school year.

MOUGINS SCHOOL

Phone 33 493 901 547
Fax 33 493 753 140
Email information@mougins-school.com
Website www.mougins-school.com
Address 615 Avenue Dr. Maurice Donat, Font De L'Orme, BP 401, Mougins, 06251, France

STAFF

Head of School Brian G. Hickmore
Deputy Head and Careers Officer Jane Hart
Examinations Officer Catherine Wright
Head of Studies Joanna Povall
Primary School Coordinator David Gifford

Head of Technology Rob Charlton
Head of Library Denise Aughton
Teaching staff Full time 41; Part time 8; Total 49
Nationalities of teaching staff UK 40; French 7;
Other(s) (Irish, Spaniard) 2

INFORMATION

Grade levels N–12
School year September–June
School type coeducational, day, private non-profit
Year founded 1964
Governed by elected Board of Governors
Enrollment Nursery 16; PreK 20;
Elementary K–5 142; Middle School 6–8 114;
High School 9–12 162; Total 454

Nationalities of student body US 9; UK 62;
French 38; Other(s) (Dane, German) 345
Tuition/fee currency Euro
Tuition range 4,700–12,800
Annual fees Lunch 760
One time fees Registration 600
Graduates attending college 85%
Graduates have attended Oxford U, Kent U,
Imperial Col, U of Provence, McGill U

EDUCATIONAL PROGRAM

Curriculum UK, IGCSE, AS and A Levels
Average class size Elementary 22; Secondary 22
Language(s) of instruction English
Language(s) taught French, German, Spanish
Staff specialists computer, ESL, learning
disabilities, librarian, nurse
Special curricular programs art, instrumental
music, vocal music, computer/technology,
physical education

Extra curricular programs computers, dance,
drama, excursions/expeditions, yearbook
Sports badminton, basketball, cross-country,
football, gymnastics, hockey, track and field,
volleyball
Clubs chess, computer, drama, dance, football,
basketball, volleyball, ultimate frisbee, art,
instrumental music
Examinations A-level GCE, GCSE, IGCSE

CAMPUS FACILITIES

Location Suburban
Campus 3 hectares, 6 buildings, 32 classrooms,
2 computer labs, 30 instructional computers,

9,000 library volumes, 1 auditorium,
1 cafeteria, 1 gymnasium, 1 infirmary,
1 playing field, 3 science labs, air conditioning

INTERNATIONAL SCHOOL OF NICE

Phone 33 493 210 400
Fax 33 493 218 490
Email edwige.roussel@cote-azur.cci.fr
Website www.isn-nice.org
Address 15 Avenue Claude Debussy, Nice, 06200, France

STAFF

Director Michael Wylie, Ed.D.
Principal Katherine Gandolfo
IB Coordinator Eugene Stevelberg, Ph.D.
Middle School Coordinator Nalinka Kalder
Lower School Coordinator Jackie Tindle

Guidance Counselors David Johnson and Katherine Gandolfo
Librarian Victoria Tabuteau
Teaching staff Full time 32; Part time 11; Total 43

INFORMATION

Grade levels PreK–12
School year September–June
School type coeducational, day, private non-profit
Year founded 1977
Governed by appointed and elected School Council
Sponsored by French Riviera Chamber of Commerce
Accredited by CIS, Middle States
Regional organizations ECIS

Enrollment Elementary K–5 121; Middle School 6–8 87; High School 9–12 112; Total 320
Tuition/fee currency Euro
Tuition range 9,162–12,840
Annual fees Capital Levy 1,250; Busing 2,273
Boarding program grades PreK–12
Boys 169 **Girls** 151
Graduates attending college 98%
Graduates have attended London School of Economics, Cambridge U, U of London, Tufts U, Boston U

EDUCATIONAL PROGRAM

Curriculum US, UK, Intl, AP, IB Diploma, IGCSE
Average class size Elementary 22; Secondary 22
Language(s) of instruction English
Language(s) taught French
Staff specialists computer, counselor, ESL, learning disabilities, librarian, speech/hearing
Special curricular programs art, instrumental music, vocal music, computer/technology, physical education

Extra curricular programs computers, community service, drama, yearbook
Sports badminton, basketball, football, gymnastics, soccer, swimming, tennis, track and field, volleyball
Examinations AP, GCSE, IB, IGCSE, PSAT, SAT, SSAT, ACT, ABRSM

CAMPUS FACILITIES

Location Suburban
Campus 2 hectares, 1 building, 24 classrooms, 1 computer lab, 19 instructional computers,

5,000 library volumes, 1 auditorium, 1 cafeteria, 1 covered play area, 1 gymnasium, 1 infirmary, 2 playing fields, 2 science labs

AMERICAN SCHOOL OF PARIS

Phone	33 1 411 28282
Fax	33 1 460 22390
Email	admissions@asparis.fr
Website	www.asparis.org
Address	41, rue Pasteur, Saint Cloud, 92210, France

STAFF

Head of School Pilar Cabeza de Vaca
Assistant Head and Upper School Director
Aaron Hubbard
Middle School Director Jim Ferguson
Lower School Director Margaret Coleman
Director of Finance and Human Resources
Joyce Kearney

IT Coordinator Chad Fairey
Librarian Krysha Papillon
Teaching staff Full time 72; Part time 35; Total 107
Nationalities of teaching staff US 52; UK 13;
French 32; Other(s) (Canadian) 10

INFORMATION

Grade levels K–12
School year August–June
School type coeducational, day, private non-profit
Year founded 1946
Governed by elected Board of Trustees
Accredited by CIS, Middle States
Regional organizations CEESA, ECIS, MAIS
Enrollment Elementary K–5 242; Middle School
6–8 180; High School 9–12 350; Total 772

Nationalities of student body US 348; UK 23;
French 58; Other(s) (Canadian, Korean) 371
Tuition/fee currency Euro
Tuition range 14,130–22,070
Annual fees Security 550; ESL 3,200;
Special Needs 6,550
One time fees Registration 760; Capital Levy 7,700
Graduates attending college 98%
Graduates have attended Yale U, Columbia U,
Stanford U, Tufts U, Cornell U

EDUCATIONAL PROGRAM

Curriculum US, AP, IB Diploma
Average class size Elementary 20; Secondary 20
Language(s) of instruction English
Language(s) taught French, Spanish
Staff specialists computer, counselor, ESL,
learning disabilities, librarian, nurse,
psychologist, reading resource
Special curricular programs art, instrumental
music, vocal music, computer/technology,
physical education

Extra curricular programs computers, community
service, dance, drama, environmental
conservation, excursions/expeditions, literary
magazine, newspaper, photography, yearbook
Sports baseball, basketball, cross-country,
football, golf, soccer, softball, swimming,
tennis, track and field, volleyball
Clubs film, Model UN, Harvard Model Congress,
Amnesty International
Examinations ACT, AP, IB, PSAT, SAT, SAT II

CAMPUS FACILITIES

Location Suburban
Campus 7 hectares, 6 buildings, 50 classrooms,
3 computer labs, 200 instructional computers,

38,000 library volumes, 1 auditorium,
2 cafeterias, 1 covered play area, 2 gymnasiums,
1 infirmary, 1 playing field, 5 science labs

INTERNATIONAL SCHOOL OF PARIS

Phone	33 1 422 40954
Fax	33 1 452 71593
Email	info@isparis.edu
Website	www.isparis.edu
Address	6 rue Beethoven, Paris, 75016, France

STAFF

Head of School Gareth F. Jones
Primary School Principal Audrey Peverrelli
Secondary School Principal Ian Piper
Business Manager Isabelle Giraud-Carrier
Head of Technology Stephanie Goring

Librarian Emma Dornan
Teaching staff Full time 70; Part time 19; Total 89
Nationalities of teaching staff US 12; UK 34;
French 18; Other(s) (Canadian, Irish) 25

INFORMATION

Grade levels N–12
School year September–June
School type coeducational, day, private non-profit
Year founded 1964
Governed by appointed and elected Trustees
Accredited by CIS, New England
Regional organizations ECIS
Enrollment Nursery 20; PreK 30;
Elementary K–5 180; Middle School 6–8 145;
High School 9–12 289; Total 664

Nationalities of student body US 106; UK 41;
French 54; Other(s) (Japanese, Indian) 463
Tuition/fee currency Euro
Tuition range 14,500–20,500
Annual fees Insurance 30; Busing 3,500
One time fees Capital Levy 5,000
Graduates attending college 99%
Graduates have attended Cambridge U,
Columbia U, Barnard U, Oxford U, Waseda U

EDUCATIONAL PROGRAM

Curriculum Intl, IB Diploma, IBPYP, IBMYP
Average class size Elementary 16; Secondary 16
Language(s) of instruction English
Language(s) taught French, Spanish, German,
Hindi, Japanese, Korean
Staff specialists computer, counselor, ESL,
learning disabilities, librarian, psychologist
Special curricular programs art, instrumental
music, computer/technology, physical education

Extra curricular programs computers, community
service, drama, environmental conservation,
excursions/expeditions, literary magazine,
yearbook
Sports baseball, basketball, soccer, softball,
swimming, tennis, volleyball
Examinations IB, PSAT, SAT, SAT II

CAMPUS FACILITIES

Location Suburban
Campus 8 hectares, 12 classrooms,
1 computer lab, 15 instructional computers,

3,000 library volumes, 1 covered play area,
1 gymnasium, 1 science lab

MARYMOUNT SCHOOL

Phone	33 0 1 462 41051
Fax	33 0 1 462 49326
Email	info@marymount.fr
Website	www.marymount.fr
Address	72 Blvd de la Saussaye, Neuilly-sur-Seine, 92200, France

STAFF

Head of School Sister Anne Marie Hill, Ph.D.
Principal Adrian Ash
Business Manager Annie Auvray
Technology Coordinator Maurice Chan

Librarian Mary Lumsden
Teaching staff Full time 50; Part time 25; Total 75
Nationalities of teaching staff US 15; UK 20; French 10; Other(s) 30

INFORMATION

Grade levels PreK–8
School year September–June
School type coeducational, day, private non-profit
Year founded 1923
Governed by appointed Marymount School Association
Accredited by CIS, Middle States
Regional organizations ECIS, MAIS

Enrollment PreK 23; Elementary K-5 290; Middle School 6-8 80; Total 393
Nationalities of student body US 160; UK 12; Host 32; Other(s) 196
Tuition/fee currency Euro
Tuition range 14,700-19,000
Annual fees Lunch 1,100
One time fees Registration 700; Capital Levy 6,000

EDUCATIONAL PROGRAM

Curriculum US
Average class size Elementary 18; Secondary 14
Language(s) of instruction English
Language(s) taught French, Spanish, Latin, Chinese
Staff specialists computer, counselor, ESL, learning disabilities, librarian, math resource, nurse, physician, psychologist, reading resource, speech/hearing

Special curricular programs art, instrumental music, vocal music, computer/technology, physical education
Extra curricular programs computers, community service, drama, environmental conservation, excursions/expeditions, newspaper, yearbook
Sports baseball, basketball, football, gymnastics, hockey, martial arts, rugby, soccer, softball, swimming, tennis, track and field, volleyball
Examinations Iowa

CAMPUS FACILITIES

Location Urban
Campus 1 hectare, 5 buildings, 42 classrooms, 1 computer lab, 70 instructional computers,

12,000 library volumes, 1 auditorium, 1 cafeteria, 1 gymnasium, 1 infirmary, 3 playing fields, 1 science lab

INTERNATIONAL SCHOOL OF BÉARN

Phone	33 6 12 56 68 67
Fax	33 5 59 90 09 74
Email	isbearn@wanadoo.fr
Website	www.isbearn.com
Address	Rue des Fougeres, Morlaas (Pau), 64160, France

STAFF

Head of School Maria Elias
Head of Primary School Steve Hayman
**Head of Secondary School and Business/
Finance Manager** Mike Kirby
ICT Coordinator Ludovic Bernard

Head of Library and Media Center Patsy Hayman
Teaching staff Full time 16; Part time 3; Total 19
Nationalities of teaching staff UK 13; French 4;
Other(s) (Venezuelan, Russian) 2

INFORMATION

Grade levels N–9
School year September–June
School type coeducational, day, private non-profit
Year founded 2003
Enrollment Nursery 14; PreK 14;
Elementary K–5 70; Middle School 6–8 42;
High School 9–12 14; Total 154

Nationalities of student body US 15; UK 41;
French 20; Other(s) (Indonesian, Nigerian) 78
Tuition/fee currency Euro
Tuition range 2,960–11,630
Annual fees Lunch 946; Clubs 600
One time fees Registration 200; Capital Levy 1,600;
Entry 650

EDUCATIONAL PROGRAM

Curriculum UK, National
Average class size Elementary 14; Secondary 14
Language(s) of instruction English
Language(s) taught French, Spanish
Staff specialists computer, ESL, librarian
Special curricular programs art, instrumental
music, computer/technology

Extra curricular programs computers, dance, drama
Sports basketball, football, rugby, soccer,
swimming, tennis, horse riding
Clubs chess, fencing, Judo, board games,
computer, art and crafts, film
Examinations SAT

CAMPUS FACILITIES

Location Suburban
Campus 3 buildings, 9 classrooms,
1 computer lab, 15 instructional computers,

1 library volumes, 1 cafeteria, 1 covered play
area, 1 gymnasium, 2 playing fields,
air conditioning

LYCÉE INTERNATIONAL, AMERICAN SECTION

Phone	33 1 34 51 74 85
Fax	33 1 30 87 00 49
Email	american.lycee.intl@wanadoo.fr
Website	www.lycee-intl-american.org
Address	BP 5230, rue du Fer à Cheval, St. Germain-en-Laye, Cedex, 78175, France

STAFF

Director Sean Lynch
Primary Principal Barbara Moross
Middle School Principal Adrienne Covington
Director of Admissions Mary Friel
Business Manager Alain Ginsbach

Head Librarian Madolyn Nichols
Teaching staff Full time 16; Part time 2; Total 18
Nationalities of teaching staff US 16; Other(s) (Canadian) 2

INFORMATION

Grade levels PreK–12
School year September–June
School type coeducational, day
Year founded 1952
Governed by elected ASALI Board
Regional organizations ECIS
Enrollment Nursery 16; PreK 16; Elementary K–5 225; Middle School 6–8 190; High School 9–12 240; Total 687

Nationalities of student body US 313; UK 13; French 309; Other(s) 52
Tuition/fee currency Euro
Tuition range 1,490–6,250
One time fees Membership 800
Graduates attending college 100%
Graduates have attended Princeton U, New York U, McGill U, London School of Economics, Imperial Col London

EDUCATIONAL PROGRAM

Curriculum US, National, International Option of French Baccalaureate
Average class size Elementary 18; Secondary 20
Language(s) of instruction English, French
Language(s) taught Spanish, German, Latin, Russian, Italian
Staff specialists librarian, nurse, psychologist

Extra curricular programs community service, drama, excursions/expeditions, literary magazine, yearbook, Model UN, a capella
Sports soccer
Examinations AP, PSAT, SAT, International Option French Baccalaureate

CAMPUS FACILITIES

Location Suburban
Campus 3 hectares, 6 buildings, 1 computer lab, 100,000 library volumes, 1 auditorium,

2 cafeterias, 1 gymnasium, 1 infirmary, 1 playing field, 1 science lab, 1 tennis court

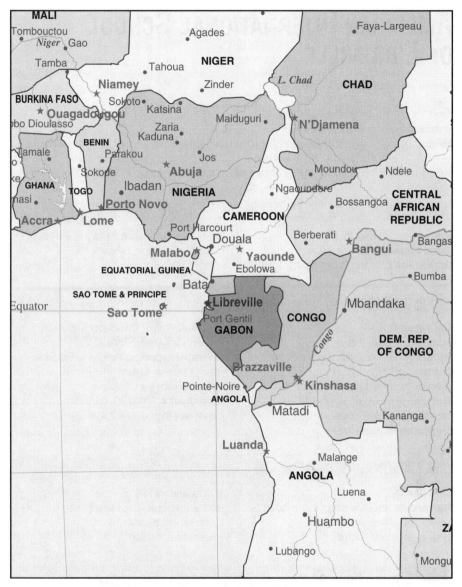

GABON

Area:	267,667 sq km
Population:	1,454,867
Capital:	Libreville
Currency:	Communaute Financiere Africaine Franc (XAF)
Languages:	French

AMERICAN INTERNATIONAL SCHOOL OF LIBREVILLE

Phone	241 724 556
Fax	241 745 240
Email	aisl@aislgabon.net
Website	www.aislgabon.net
Address	Ecole Américaine, Boulevard du Bord de la Mer, Quartier Glass, Libreville, Estuaire, BP4000, Gabon
Mailing address	AISL Director, 2270 Libreville Place, Washington, DC 20521-2270, USA

STAFF

Director James Moras, Ph.D.
Business Manager Shreedevi Rao
Teaching staff Full time 7; Part time 3; Total 10

Nationalities of teaching staff US 6; Gabonese 1; Other(s) (Togolese, Lebanese) 3

INFORMATION

Grade levels PreK–8
School year August–June
School type coeducational, day, private non-profit
Year founded 1975
Governed by elected Board of Directors
Sponsored by US Overseas School
Accredited by Middle States
Regional organizations AISA

Enrollment PreK 5; Elementary K–5 20; Middle School 6–8 12; Total 37
Nationalities of student body US 8; Gabonese 4; Other(s) (Irish, Lebanese) 25
Tuition/fee currency US Dollar
Tuition range 6,700–15,000
Annual fees Registration 250

EDUCATIONAL PROGRAM

Curriculum US
Average class size Elementary 8; Secondary 8
Language(s) of instruction English
Language(s) taught French

Staff specialists ESL
Extra curricular programs newspaper, yearbook
Sports soccer, tennis
Examinations Stanford

CAMPUS FACILITIES

Location Urban
Campus 1 hectare, 1 building, 7 classrooms, 1 computer lab, 6 instructional computers,

5,000 library volumes, 1 covered play area, 1 playing field, 1 science lab, air conditioning

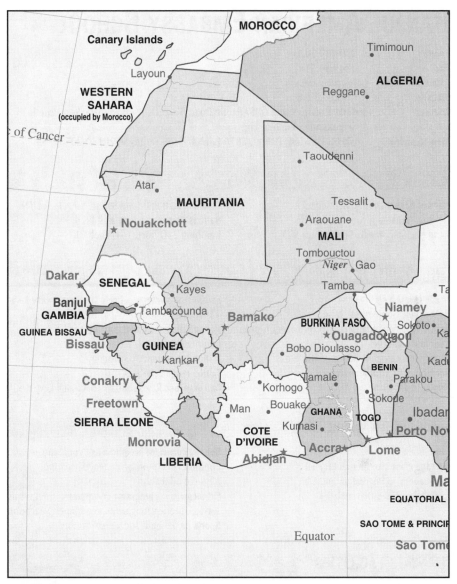

THE GAMBIA

Area:	11,300 sq km
Population:	1,688,359
Capital:	Banjul
Currency:	Dalasi (GMD)
Languages:	English

Banjul American Embassy School

Phone	220 449 5920
Fax	220 449 7181
Email	baes@qanet.gm
Website	www.baes.gm
Address	Sutay Bojang Street (off Atlantic Road, Fajara), PO Box 2596, Serrekunda, Serrekunda, Gambia, The
Mailing address	c/o US Embassy, Banjul, 2070 Banjul Place, Dulles VA 20189-2070, USA

STAFF

Head of School Dianne Zemichael
Head of Technology Amal Abou-Alfa
Head of Library/Media Center Kura N'Djai

Teaching staff Full time 8; Part time 1; Total 9
Nationalities of teaching staff US 5; UK 1; Gambian 2; Other(s) (French) 1

INFORMATION

Grade levels N–9
School year September–June
School type coeducational, day, private non-profit
Year founded 1984
Governed by elected Board of Directors
Accredited by Middle States
Regional organizations AISA

Enrollment Nursery 7; PreK 20; Elementary K–5 42; Middle School 6–8 11; Total 80
Nationalities of student body US 18; UK 18; Gambian 5; Other(s) (Lebanese) 39
Tuition/fee currency US Dollar
Tuition range 2,800–8,750
One time fees Registration 150; Capital Levy 1,600

EDUCATIONAL PROGRAM

Curriculum US
Average class size Elementary 10
Language(s) of instruction English
Language(s) taught French

Special curricular programs art, vocal music, computer/technology, distance learning, physical education
Extra curricular programs computers, community service, literary magazine, newspaper, yearbook
Sports basketball, soccer, swimming

CAMPUS FACILITIES

Location Suburban
Campus 4 buildings, 12 classrooms, 1 computer lab, 16 instructional computers,

10,000 library volumes, 2 playing fields, 1 science lab

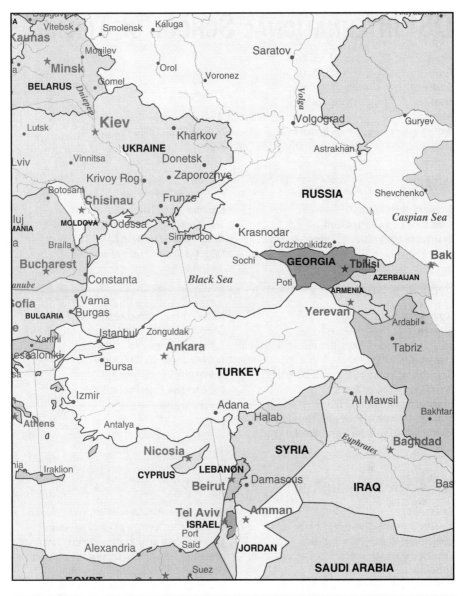

GEORGIA

Area:	69,700 sq km
Population:	4,646,003
Capital:	T'bilisi
Currency:	Lari (GEL)
Languages:	Georgian

QSI INTERNATIONAL SCHOOL OF TBILISI

Phone	995 32 537 674
Fax	995 32 322 607
Email	tbilisi@qsi.org
Website	www.qsi.org/grg
Address	4 King Parnavas Sq., Dighomi, Tbilisi, Georgia
Mailing address	c/o US Embassy, Tbilisi, Dept. of State, 7060 Tbilisi Place, Washington, DC 20521-7060, USA

STAFF

Director Robert Hinman
Accountant Inga Chalagashvili
Information and Technology Support Manager Shota Khoperia

Librarian Nino Chavchavadze
Teaching staff Full time 25; Total 25
Nationalities of teaching staff US 11; Georgian 7; Other(s) (Dane, South African) 7

INFORMATION

Grade levels N–12
School year September–June
School type coeducational, day, private non-profit
Year founded 1995
Governed by appointed Board of Directors
Accredited by Middle States
Regional organizations CEESA
Enrollment Nursery 4; PreK 15; Elementary K–5 78; Middle School 6–8 24; High School 9–12 26; Total 147

Nationalities of student body US 39; UK 10; Georgian 13; Other(s) (German, French) 85
Tuition/fee currency US Dollar
Tuition range 4,500–15,500
Annual fees Capital Levy 3,200
One time fees Registration 100
Graduates have attended U of Chicago

EDUCATIONAL PROGRAM

Curriculum US
Average class size Elementary 14; Secondary 6
Language(s) of instruction English
Language(s) taught French, Russian, Georgian, Spanish
Staff specialists computer, counselor, ESL, librarian, nurse, physician, reading resource

Special curricular programs art, vocal music, computer/technology, physical education
Extra curricular programs computers, community service, dance, drama, excursions/expeditions, newspaper, photography, yearbook
Sports baseball, basketball, cross-country, football, skiing, soccer, track and field, volleyball
Examinations AP, PSAT, SAT, Stanford

CAMPUS FACILITIES

Location Urban
Campus 5 hectares, 1 building, 22 classrooms, 1 computer lab, 65 instructional computers, 7,000 library volumes, 1 auditorium,

1 cafeteria, 1 covered play area, 1 gymnasium, 1 infirmary, 1 playing field, 2 science labs, 1 tennis court, air conditioning

GERMANY

Area:	357,021 sq km
Population:	82,400,996
Capital:	Berlin
Currency:	Euro (EUR)
Languages:	German

BERLIN BRANDENBURG INTERNATIONAL SCHOOL

Phone	49 33203 80 36 0
Fax	49 33203 80 36 21
Email	office@bbis.de
Website	www.bbis.de
Address	Am Hochwald 30, Kleinmachnow, Brandenburg, 14532, Germany

STAFF

Director Thomas Schädler
High School Principal Richard Bartlett
Middle School Principal Benedict Kestner
Elementary School Principal Mark Hansen
IB Diploma Coordinator Karin Schnoor
Head of Student Support Services
Christina Limbird, Ph.D.

Business Manager and Geschäftsführer
Burkhard Dolata
IT Coordinator Harry Klooster
Teacher Librarian Annie Pyers
Teaching staff Full time 71; Part time 13; Total 84
Nationalities of teaching staff US 35; UK 23;
German 17; Other(s) (Australian, French) 9

INFORMATION

Grade levels PreK–12
School year August–June
School type coeducational, day, private non-profit
Year founded 1990
Governed by appointed and elected Supervisory Board
Accredited by CIS, Middle States
Regional organizations ECIS
Enrollment PreK 70; Elementary K–5 210;
Middle School 6–8 130; High School 9–12 150;
Total 560

Nationalities of student body US 70; UK 20;
German 230; Other(s) (Dutch, Korean) 240
Tuition/fee currency Euro
Tuition range 7,900–12,800
Annual fees Busing 1,000
One time fees Registration 3,000
Graduates attending college 85%
Graduates have attended U of Pennsylvania,
Harvard U, Columbia U, Princeton U,
London School of Economics

EDUCATIONAL PROGRAM

Curriculum IB Diploma, IBPYP, IBMYP
Average class size Elementary 16; Secondary 18
Language(s) of instruction English
Language(s) taught German, French, Spanish
Staff specialists computer, counselor, ESL,
learning disabilities, librarian, math resource,
psychologist
Special curricular programs art, instrumental
music, vocal music, computer/technology,
physical education
Extra curricular programs dance, drama,
excursions/expeditions, newspaper, art outings,
still-life drawing, BBIS band, choir, instrumental
ensemble, jazz ensemble, Paper Creation
Station, arts and crafts, Recipe Fun, BBIS zoo
Sports badminton, baseball, basketball,
cross-country, football, gymnastics, soccer,
swimming, tennis, track and field, volleyball,
sailing, rowing, Karate, horseback riding, biking
Clubs drama, sailing, human rights, dancing,
junior math, senior math, chess, German,
Model UN
Examinations IB

CAMPUS FACILITIES

Location Suburban
Campus 2 buildings, 43 classrooms, 2 computer
labs, 50 instructional computers,
8,000 library volumes, 1 auditorium,
1 cafeteria, 1 playing field, 3 science labs

BERLIN INTERNATIONAL SCHOOL

Phone	49 30 82 00 77 90
Fax	49 30 82 00 77 99
Email	office@berlin-international-school.de
Website	www.berlin-international-school.de
Address	Lentzeallee 8/14, Berlin, 14195, Germany

STAFF

Head of School Peggy Bleyberg-Shor
Principal, Elementary School Hubert Keulers
Principal, Secondary School Herbert Krüger, Ph.D.
Principal, Early Childhood Center, Kita
International Kiersten Leang

IB Coordinator/University Admissions Counselor
Derek M. Bleyberg, Ph.D.
Counselor Steven Gregory
Superintendent Andreas Wegener
IT Coordinator Garret Tynan
Librarian Cyril Compeyron

INFORMATION

Grade levels N–13
School year August–July
School type coeducational, day, private non-profit
Year founded 1998
Governed by appointed Private Kant-Schule e.V.
Regional organizations ECIS
Enrollment Nursery 60; PreK 60;
Elementary K–5 380; Middle School 6–8 140;
High School 9–12 165; Grade 13 8; Total 813

Nationalities of student body US 41; UK 32;
German 350; Other(s) (Korean, Pakistani) 377
Tuition/fee currency Euro
Tuition range 7,500–9,000
Annual fees Busing 1,200
One time fees Registration 400; IB Exam 1,000;
IGCSE Exams 450
Graduates attending college 100%
Graduates have attended Humboldt U Berlin,
Imperial Col London, McGill U, Canada,
Georgetown U, Freie U Berlin

EDUCATIONAL PROGRAM

Curriculum National, Intl, IB Diploma, IBPYP,
IGCSE
Average class size Elementary 21; Secondary 21
Language(s) of instruction English
Language(s) taught French, Latin, Spanish,
English, German
Staff specialists computer, counselor, ESL,
librarian
Special curricular programs art, instrumental
music, vocal music, computer/technology,
physical education

Extra curricular programs computers, community
service, dance, drama, excursions/expeditions,
newspaper, photography, yearbook, Model UN
Sports basketball, cricket, cross-country,
football, golf, soccer, swimming, tennis, track
and field, running
Examinations GCSE, IB, IGCSE, TOEFL, Bilingual
German Abitur (German/English)

CAMPUS FACILITIES

Location Urban
Campus 3 buildings, 50 classrooms,
2 computer labs, 80 instructional computers,

7,000 library volumes, 2 cafeterias,
2 gymnasiums, 1 infirmary, 1 playing field,
3 science labs

Data taken from 2006/07 school year.

JOHN F. KENNEDY SCHOOL

Phone	49 30 90299 5758
Fax	49 30 90299 6868
Email	jfkschool@t-online.de
Website	www.jfks.de
Address	Teltower Damm 87-93, Berlin, 14167, Germany

STAFF

Managing Principal Ulrich Schuermann
American Elementary School Principal
Kandace Williams, Ed.D.
American High School Principal
Mark Olderog, Ed.D.
German High School Principal
Ulrich Schuermann

Business/Finance Manager Marina Wöpke
Head of Technology Horst Kuschnerow, Ph.D.
High School Librarians
Erik Scherer and Suzanne Thompson
Teaching staff Full time 139; Part time 17;
Total 156
Nationalities of teaching staff US 79; UK 1;
German 76

INFORMATION

Grade levels K–13
School year August–July
School type coeducational, day
Year founded 1960
Governed by appointed and elected State of Berlin
Accredited by CIS, New England
Regional organizations ECIS

Enrollment Elementary K–5 704;
Middle School 6–8 403; High School 9–12
518; Grade 13 76; Total 1,701
Nationalities of student body US 567; UK 59;
German 970; Other(s) (Canadian) 105
Tuition/fee currency US Dollar
Graduates attending college 90%
Graduates have attended Stanford U, Harvard U,
Michigan State U, Cambridge U, Oxford U

EDUCATIONAL PROGRAM

Curriculum US, National, AP
Average class size Elementary 24; Secondary 26
Language(s) of instruction English, German
Language(s) taught French, Spanish, Latin
Staff specialists computer, counselor, librarian,
math resource, reading resource
Special curricular programs art, instrumental
music, vocal music, computer/technology,
physical education

Extra curricular programs computers, community
service, drama, excursions/expeditions, literary
magazine, newspaper, photography, yearbook
Sports badminton, baseball, basketball, soccer,
swimming, track and field, volleyball
Examinations ACT, AP, PSAT, SAT, SAT II, Stanford

CAMPUS FACILITIES

Location Suburban
Campus 4 hectares, 6 buildings, 135 classrooms,
3 computer labs, 120 instructional computers,

70,000 library volumes, 2 auditoriums,
1 cafeteria, 2 gymnasiums, 1 infirmary,
3 playing fields, 9 science labs

BONN INTERNATIONAL SCHOOL

Phone	49 228 30854 151
Fax	49 228 30854 250
Email	admin@bis.bonn.org
Website	www.bis.bonn.org
Address	Martin-Luther-King Strasse 14, Bonn, 53175, Germany

STAFF

Director Peter M.J. Murphy
Secondary School Principal Diane Lewthwaite
Primary School Principal Simon Davidson
Business Manager Sabine Schattenberg
IT Coordinator Francis Morin

Media Center Manager Poonam Sanwal
Teaching staff Full time 50; Part time 8; Total 58
Nationalities of teaching staff US 10; UK 17; German 10; Other(s) (Canadian, Australian) 21

INFORMATION

Grade levels PreK–12
School year August–June
School type coeducational, day, private non-profit
Year founded 1997
Governed by elected Board of Trustees
Enrollment PreK 40; Elementary K–5 180; Middle School 6–8 100; High School 9–12 140; Total 460
Nationalities of student body US 60; UK 40; German 115; Other(s) (Dutch) 245

Tuition/fee currency Euro
Tuition range 6,500–14,500
Annual fees Capital Levy 1,050
One time fees Registration 1,600
Graduates attending college 98%
Graduates have attended Cambridge U, St. Andrews U, Princeton U, Wharton School of Business, McGill U

EDUCATIONAL PROGRAM

Curriculum Intl, IB Diploma, IBPYP, IBMYP
Average class size Elementary 16; Secondary 18
Language(s) of instruction English
Language(s) taught German, French, Spanish
Staff specialists computer, counselor, ESL, learning disabilities, librarian, nurse
Special curricular programs art, instrumental music, physical education

Extra curricular programs community service, drama, newspaper, yearbook
Sports basketball, cross-country, gymnastics, soccer, track and field
Clubs dance, rocket, Model UN, global issues, bike
Examinations IB, PSAT, SAT, SAT II, ISA

CAMPUS FACILITIES

Location Suburban
Campus 10 hectares, 1 building, 60 classrooms, 2 computer labs, 120 instructional computers,

18,000 library volumes, 1 cafeteria, 1 gymnasium, 2 playing fields, 4 science labs

INTERNATIONAL SCHOOL OF BREMEN

Phone	49 04 21 337 9272
Fax	49 04 21 337 9273
Email	office@isbremen.de
Website	www.isbremen.de
Address	Thomas-Mann-Strasse 6-8, Bremen, 28213, Germany

STAFF

Director Malcolm Davis
Head of Secondary School Jeff Ellis
Head of Elementary School Sussana Bergmann
IB Coordinator Daniela Otto-Zierold
IGCSE Coordinator Susan Turner
Business/Finance Manager Brigitta Siemoneit

Coordinator Andrew Fielding
Librarian Ruth Holsten
Teaching staff Full time 26; Part time 7; Total 33
Nationalities of teaching staff US 7; UK 8;
German 6; Other(s) (Australian) 12

INFORMATION

Grade levels N–12
School year August–June
School type coeducational, company-sponsored,
day, private non-profit
Year founded 1998
Governed by appointed Board of Directors
Sponsored by Multinational Corporations
Accredited by Middle States
Regional organizations ECIS

Enrollment Nursery 10; PreK 15;
Elementary K–5 90; Middle School 6–8 35;
High School 9–12 55; Total 205
Nationalities of student body US 10; UK 8;
German 50; Other(s) 137
Tuition/fee currency Euro
Tuition range 7,400–10,900
Annual fees Lunch 450
One time fees Registration 1,000;
Capital Levy 2,000
Graduates attending college 95%

EDUCATIONAL PROGRAM

Curriculum Intl, IB Diploma, IGCSE,
International Primary Curriculum
Average class size Elementary 16; Secondary 10
Language(s) of instruction English

Language(s) taught German, Spanish, French
Staff specialists computer, ESL, librarian
Examinations A-level GCE, GCSE, IB, IGCSE,
PSAT, SAT, TOEFL

CAMPUS FACILITIES

Location Urban
Campus 1 hectare, 1 building, 20 classrooms,
1 computer lab, 40 instructional computers,

10,000 library volumes, 1 auditorium,
1 cafeteria, 2 science labs

DRESDEN INTERNATIONAL SCHOOL

Phone	0049 351 340 0428
Fax	0049 351 340 0430
Email	dis@dresden-is.de
Website	www.dresden-is.de
Address	Goetheallee 18, Dresden, Saxony, 01309, Germany

STAFF

Director Geoffrey Clark
Secondary School Principal Steven Ellis
Primary School Principal Joyce Larson
Assistant for Communications
Konstanze Gensmann
Office Manager Luise Heyne

Business Manager Andrea Harnisch
Head of Technology Jennifer Janesko
Librarian Sharon Larner
Teaching staff Full time 60; Part time 11; Total 71
Nationalities of teaching staff US 16; UK 6;
German 24; Other(s) (Canadian, Australian) 25

INFORMATION

Grade levels PreK–12
School year August–June
School type coeducational, day, private non-profit
Year founded 1996
Governed by appointed Board
Regional organizations ECIS

Enrollment PreK 62; Elementary K–5 264;
Middle School 6–8 137; High School 9–12 69;
Total 532
Nationalities of student body US 56; UK 19;
German 307; Other(s) 150
Tuition/fee currency Euro
Tuition range 5,400–9,570
One time fees Registration 50

EDUCATIONAL PROGRAM

Curriculum Intl, IB Diploma, IBPYP, IBMYP
Average class size Elementary 16; Secondary 16
Language(s) of instruction English, German
Language(s) taught English, German, French,
Japanese

Staff specialists computer, counselor, ESL,
learning disabilities, librarian
Extra curricular programs drama, yearbook
Sports badminton, football, soccer, swimming,
track and field

CAMPUS FACILITIES

Location Urban
Campus 4 buildings, 46 classrooms,
2 computer labs, 60 instructional computers,

12,000 library volumes, 2 cafeterias,
1 science lab

INTERNATIONAL SCHOOL OF DÜSSELDORF E.V.

Phone	49 211 94066
Fax	49 211 408 0774
Email	info@isdedu.de
Website	www.isdedu.de
Address	Niederrheinstrasse 336, Düsseldorf, 40489, Germany

STAFF

Director Neil A. McWilliam
Senior School Principal Michael Coffey
Development Director Beatrice Caston
Elementary School Principal Carol Esposito
Business Manager Dieter Kapteina

Teaching staff Full time 111; Part time 15; Total 126
Nationalities of teaching staff US 27; UK 26; German 16; Other(s) (Japanese, Azerbaijani) 57

INFORMATION

Grade levels N–13
School year August–June
School type coeducational, day, private non-profit
Year founded 1968
Governed by elected Board of Trustees
Accredited by CIS, New England
Regional organizations ECIS
Enrollment Nursery 16; PreK 30; Elementary K–5 431; Middle School 6–8 180; High School 9–12 303; Total 960

Nationalities of student body US 195; UK 92; German 203; Other(s) (Japanese, Korean) 470
Tuition/fee currency Euro
Tuition range 2,740–10,560
Annual fees Membership 4,800
Graduates attending college 98%
Graduates have attended Oxford U, Cambridge U, Cornell U, Massachusetts Institute of Technology, Waseda U

EDUCATIONAL PROGRAM

Curriculum Intl, IB Diploma, IBPYP, IBMYP
Average class size Elementary 16; Secondary 16
Language(s) of instruction English
Language(s) taught French, German, Japanese, Spanish, Korean
Staff specialists computer, counselor, ESL, learning disabilities, librarian, nurse, physician
Special curricular programs art, instrumental music, vocal music, computer/technology, physical education, vocational

Extra curricular programs community service, dance, drama, environmental conservation, excursions/expeditions, newspaper, yearbook
Sports basketball, gymnastics, rugby, soccer, softball, swimming, tennis, track and field, volleyball
Examinations IB, SAT, SAT II, TOEFL

CAMPUS FACILITIES

Location Urban
Campus 19 hectares, 7 buildings, 84 classrooms, 3 computer labs, 100 instructional computers, 65,000 library volumes, 1 auditorium, 2 cafeterias, 2 gymnasiums, 2 infirmaries, 3 playing fields, 7 science labs, 1 tennis court

FRANKFURT INTERNATIONAL SCHOOL / INTERNATIONAL SCHOOL WIESBADEN

Phone	49 6171 20240
Fax	49 6171 202 4384
Email	mark_ulfers@fis.edu
Website	www.fis.edu
Address	An der Waldlust 15, Oberursel, 61440, Germany

STAFF

Head of School Mark E. Ulfers, Ed.D.
Upper School Principal Rhiannon Wood
Elementary School Principal Peter Baker
Primary School Principal Teresa Dupre
Principal of International School of Wiesbaden
Chris Bayliss

Business Manager Detlev Siebrecht
Teaching staff Full time 172; Part time 23;
Total 195
Nationalities of teaching staff US 58; UK 46;
Other(s) (German, Canadian) 91

INFORMATION

Grade levels N–12
School year August–June
School type coeducational, day, private non-profit
Year founded 1961
Governed by appointed and elected Board of
Trustees
Accredited by CIS, New England
Regional organizations ECIS
Enrollment Nursery 36; PreK 57;
Elementary K–5 812; Middle School 6–8 393;
High School 9–12 468; Total 1,766

Nationalities of student body US 352; UK 97;
German 298; Other(s) (Japanese, Korean) 306
Tuition/fee currency Euro
Tuition range 14,300–16,980
Annual fees Registration 500; Busing 2,140;
Capital Assessment 7,000; Re-enrollment 130
Graduates attending college 90%
Graduates have attended U of Cambridge,
U of Oxford, Cornell U, Stanford U,
Georgetown U

EDUCATIONAL PROGRAM

Curriculum US, UK, IB Diploma, IBPYP
Average class size Elementary 20; Secondary 18
Language(s) of instruction English
Language(s) taught German, French, Spanish,
Japanese
Staff specialists computer, counselor, ESL,
learning disabilities, librarian, nurse

Special curricular programs art, instrumental
music, vocal music, computer/technology,
physical education
Extra curricular programs computers, community
service, drama, yearbook
Sports baseball, basketball, cross-country, soccer,
softball, tennis, track and field, volleyball
Examinations ACT, IB, PSAT, SAT, SAT II

CAMPUS FACILITIES

Location Suburban
Campus 16 hectares, 4 buildings, 112 classrooms,

7 computer labs, 600 instructional computers,
80,000 library volumes

INTERNATIONALE SCHULE FRANKFURT-RHEIN-MAIN

Phone	49 69 954 3190
Fax	49 69 954 31920
Email	isf@sabis.net
Website	www.isf-net.de
Address	Verwaltungs-GmbH, Strasse zur Internationalen Schule 33, Frankfurt am Main, Hesse, 65931, Germany

STAFF

Director Angus Slesser
Lower Primary School Coordinator Carrington Lundquist
Upper Primary School Coordinator Usha Srivastava
Secondary School Coordinator Buddy Tobias
SABISÆ Student Life Organization Coordinator Stéphan Michaud
Student Management Coordinator Wayne May

Business Manager Theo Kreuz
Computer Center and Examinations Coordinator Gilmour Lothian
Head of Library Arienne van den Biggelaar
Teaching staff Full time 84; Part time 4; Total 88
Nationalities of teaching staff US 27; UK 10; German 19; Other(s) (Canadian, Australian) 32

INFORMATION

Grade levels PreK–13
School year August–June
School type coeducational, day, proprietary
Year founded 1995
Sponsored by SABISÆ School Network
Accredited by North Central
Regional organizations ECIS
Enrollment Nursery 20; PreK 50; Elementary K–5 490; Middle School 6–8 243; High School 9–12 235; Grade 13 2; Total 1,040

Nationalities of student body US 130; UK 45; German 352; Other(s) (Korean, French) 513
Tuition/fee currency Euro
Tuition range 11,850–15,420
Graduates attending college 100%
Graduates have attended Cambridge U, Imperial Col, U of Chicago, London School of Economics, U of Southern California

EDUCATIONAL PROGRAM

Curriculum AP, IB Diploma, IGCSE, SABISÆ, A-Level
Average class size Elementary 25; Secondary 20
Language(s) of instruction English
Language(s) taught German, Spanish, French
Special curricular programs art, instrumental music, vocal music, computer/technology, physical education

Extra curricular programs computers, community service, dance, drama, environmental conservation, excursions/expeditions, literary magazine, newspaper, photography, yearbook
Sports basketball, gymnastics, soccer, swimming, tennis, track and field, volleyball
Examinations A-level GCE, ACT, AP, GCSE, IGCSE, PSAT, SAT, SAT II, TOEFL

CAMPUS FACILITIES

Location Suburban
Campus 1 hectare, 1 building, 52 classrooms, 2 computer labs, 35 instructional computers,

9,000 library volumes, 1 auditorium, 1 cafeteria, 2 gymnasiums, 1 infirmary, 1 playing field, 3 science labs, 1 pool, 2 tennis courts

INTERNATIONAL SCHOOL HAMBURG

Phone	49 40 883 0010
Fax	49 40 881 1405
Email	info@international-school-hamburg.de
Website	www.international-school-hamburg.de
Address	Holmbrook 20, Hamburg, 22605, Germany

STAFF

Head of School Peter R. Gittins
Deputy Head and Junior School Director Nick Ronai
Secondary School Head Martin Hague
Senior School Head Anthony Martin
Business Manager Rüdiger Wrobel
Head of IT Department Anthony Lawrence

Librarian Patricia Hayward
Teaching staff Full time 78; Part time 33; Total 111
Nationalities of teaching staff US 17; UK 42; German 19; Other(s) (Canadian, New Zealander) 33

INFORMATION

Grade levels N–12
School year August–June
School type coeducational, day, private non-profit
Year founded 1957
Governed by elected Board of Directors
Accredited by CIS, New England
Regional organizations ECIS
Enrollment Nursery 20; PreK 28; Elementary K–5 277; Middle School 6–8 148; High School 9–12 177; Total 650
Nationalities of student body US 113; UK 74; German 190; Other(s) (Dutch, Japanese) 273

Tuition/fee currency Euro
Tuition range 8,300–16,200
Annual fees Busing 800; Primary School Admission 1,000
One time fees Registration 100; Capital Grades 1–12 5,250
Graduates attending college 90%
Graduates have attended U of Michigan, U of British Colombia, U of Illinois, Boston Col, U of Guelph

EDUCATIONAL PROGRAM

Curriculum IB Diploma, IBPYP, IBMYP
Average class size Elementary 20; Secondary 18
Language(s) of instruction English
Language(s) taught German, French, Spanish, Japanese
Staff specialists computer, counselor, ESL, learning disabilities, librarian, nurse

Special curricular programs art, instrumental music, vocal music, computer/technology, physical education
Extra curricular programs computers, community service, dance, drama, newspaper, yearbook
Sports basketball, gymnastics, rugby, skiing, soccer, softball, swimming, tennis, track and field, volleyball
Examinations ACT, IB, PSAT, SAT, SAT II

CAMPUS FACILITIES

Location Suburban
Campus 1 hectare, 2 buildings, 2 computer labs, 200 instructional computers, 30,000

library volumes, 1 auditorium, 1 cafeteria, 1 gymnasium, 1 infirmary, 1 playing field, 5 science labs, 2 tennis courts

INTERNATIONAL SCHOOL HANNOVER REGION

Phone	49 511 270 416 50
Fax	49 511 270 416 51
Email	adminoffice@is-hr.de
Website	www.is-hr.de
Address	Bruchmeisterallee 6, Hannover, 30169, Germany

STAFF

Director Patricia Baier
Head of Upper School Chris Collins
Head of Lower School Tony Pearson
Head of Early Childhood Cathy de Castro
IB Coordinator Meera Phatarfod
Academic Counsellor Karla Schmidt

Business Manager Steffen Stegemann
Head of IT Kathy Snow
Library Manager Barbara O'Brien
Teaching staff Full time 55; Part time 8; Total 63
Nationalities of teaching staff US 13; UK 13;
German 13; Other(s) (Australian, Canadian) 24

INFORMATION

Grade levels PreK–12
School year August–June
School type coeducational, day, private non-profit
Year founded 1996
Governed by appointed and elected Board
Regional organizations ECIS
Enrollment PreK 52; Elementary K–5 217;
Middle School 6–8 84; High School 9–12 119;
Total 472

Nationalities of student body US 56; UK 35;
German 220; Other(s) (French, Japanese) 161
Tuition/fee currency Euro
Tuition range 6,150–10,990
One time fees Registration 2,500
Graduates attending college 98%
Graduates have attended Cambridge U,
St. Andrews U, Durham U, U of Warwick,
Dartmouth Col

EDUCATIONAL PROGRAM

Curriculum Intl, IB Diploma, IBPYP, IBMYP
Average class size Elementary 18; Secondary 18
Language(s) of instruction English
Language(s) taught German, French, Spanish ,
Japanese
Staff specialists computer, counselor, ESL,
learning disabilities, librarian, math resource,
nurse, reading resource
Special curricular programs art, instrumental
music, vocal music, computer/technology,
physical education

Extra curricular programs computers, community
service, dance, drama, photography, yearbook
Sports badminton, baseball, basketball, golf,
gymnastics, hockey, martial arts, soccer,
swimming, track and field, volleyball, fencing,
archery
Clubs drama, choir, media, yearbook, global
issues, sports
Examinations IB, SAT

CAMPUS FACILITIES

Location Suburban
Campus 4 hectares, 4 buildings, 40 classrooms,
2 computer labs, 110 instructional computers,

14,000 library volumes, 1 auditorium,
1 cafeteria, 2 gymnasiums, 1 infirmary,
1 playing field, 3 science labs

BAVARIAN INTERNATIONAL SCHOOL

Phone	49 8133 917 111
Fax	49 8133 917 115
Email	r.bock@bis-school.com
Website	www.bis-school.com
Address	Hauptstrasse 1, Schloss Haimhausen, Haimhausen, Bavaria, 85778, Germany

STAFF

Director Matthew G. Mills, Ed.D.
Upper School Principal Thomas D. Connolly
Middle School Principal Michelle Hiteman
Lower School Principal Bryan Nixon
Assistant Lower School Principal Angela Hoelzl
Deputy Director Uwe Schweneke

ICT Manager Thomas Singbartl
Librarian Jacquelyn Zimmermann
Teaching staff Full time 66; Total 66
Nationalities of teaching staff US 20; UK 20;
German 10; Other(s) (Austrian, Canadian) 16

INFORMATION

Grade levels PreK–12
School year August–June
School type coeducational, day, private non-profit
Year founded 1991
Governed by elected BIS Association-Board
Accredited by CIS, New England
Regional organizations ECIS
Enrollment PreK 21; Elementary K–5 296;
Middle School 6–8 158;
High School 9–12 183; Total 658

Nationalities of student body US 118; UK 100;
German 162; Other(s) (Spaniard, Italian) 278
Tuition/fee currency Euro
Tuition range 10,100–13,000
Annual fees Registration 1,000
One time fees Capital Levy 8,000
Graduates attending college 100%
Graduates have attended American U of Paris,
Emerson Col, U of Glasgow, Durham U,
Northwestern U

EDUCATIONAL PROGRAM

Curriculum Intl, IB Diploma, IBPYP, IGCSE,
Mittlere Reife
Average class size Elementary 23; Secondary 23
Language(s) of instruction English
Language(s) taught German, Japanese, French,
Spanish
Staff specialists counselor, ESL, learning
disabilities, librarian, nurse, psychologist

Special curricular programs art, instrumental
music, computer/technology, physical
education, vocational, drama
Extra curricular programs community service,
yearbook
Sports badminton, basketball, cross-country,
golf, skiing, soccer, swimming, tennis, track
and field, volleyball
Examinations GCSE, IB, IGCSE, SAT, SAT II

CAMPUS FACILITIES

Location Rural
Campus 5 hectares, 4 buildings, 60 classrooms,
3 computer labs, 200 instructional computers,

1 auditorium, 2 cafeterias, 1 gymnasium,
1 infirmary, 2 playing fields, 4 science labs,
1 tennis court

MUNICH INTERNATIONAL SCHOOL

Phone	49 8151 366 0
Fax	49 8151 366 129
Email	admissions@mis-munich.de
Website	www.mis-munich.de
Address	Schloss Buchhof, Starnberg, Bavaria, D-82319, Germany

STAFF

Head of School Mary Seppala, Ed.D.
Senior School Principal Martin Ward
Middle School Principal Eifion Phillips
Junior School Principal Gary Langenhuizen, Ph.D.
Chief Operations Officer Leonne Francot

IT Director Steve Druggan
Librarians David Veinot and Emily Schoenbeck
Teaching staff Full time 142; Total 142
Nationalities of teaching staff US 40; UK 32; German 19; Other(s) (Canadian, Australian) 51

INFORMATION

Grade levels PreK–12
School year August–June
School type coeducational, day, private non-profit
Year founded 1966
Governed by elected Board of Directors
Accredited by CIS, New England
Regional organizations ECIS
Enrollment PreK 40; Elementary K–5 553; Middle School 6–8 310; High School 9–12 398; Total 1,301

Nationalities of student body US 297; UK 155; German 442; Other(s) (Canadian, Dutch) 407
Tuition/fee currency Euro
Tuition range 11,680–14,350
Graduates attending college 95%
Graduates have attended Brown U, Columbia U, Stanford U, U of Warwick, Oxford U

EDUCATIONAL PROGRAM

Curriculum IB Diploma, IBPYP, IBMYP, IGCSE
Average class size Elementary 20; Secondary 21
Language(s) of instruction English
Language(s) taught German, French, Spanish, Japanese, Italian
Staff specialists computer, counselor, ESL, learning disabilities, librarian, nurse, physician
Special curricular programs art, instrumental music, vocal music, computer/technology, distance learning, physical education

Extra curricular programs community service, dance, drama, environmental conservation, excursions/expeditions, yearbook
Sports basketball, cross-country, golf, martial arts, skiing, soccer, softball, swimming, tennis, track and field, volleyball
Examinations IB, PSAT, SAT, SAT II, TOEFL

CAMPUS FACILITIES

Location Rural
Campus 10 hectares, 5 buildings, 76 classrooms, 3 computer labs, 100 instructional computers, 33,000 library volumes, 3 auditoriums, 1 cafeteria, 3 gymnasiums, 1 infirmary, 4 playing fields, 7 science labs, 3 tennis courts

INTERNATIONAL SCHOOL OF STUTTGART

Phone	49 711 769 6000
Fax	49 711 769 60010
Email	iss@issev.de
Website	www.international-school-stuttgart.de
Address	Sigmaringer Str. 257, Stuttgart, Baden-Württemberg, 70597, Germany

STAFF

Director John Foulkes-Jones
Upper School Principal Stephen Castledine
Lower School Principal Paul Morris
Head of School, Sindelfingen Campus Sarah Kupke
Finance Director Rainer Raupp

Librarian Mark Lawrence
Teaching staff Full time 54; Part time 20; Total 74
Nationalities of teaching staff US 20; UK 12; German 20; Other(s) 22

INFORMATION

Grade levels N–12
School year September–June
School type coeducational, day, private non-profit
Year founded 1985
Governed by elected Board of Directors
Accredited by CIS, New England
Regional organizations ECIS
Enrollment Nursery 28; PreK 36; Elementary K–5 250; Middle School 6–8 126; High School 9–12 160; Total 600

Nationalities of student body US 210; UK 60; German 150; Other(s) 180
Tuition/fee currency Euro
Tuition range 8,400–13,350
Annual fees Registration 300
One time fees Capital Levy 5,400
Graduates have attended Imperial Col, U of Oxford, Col of William and Mary, U of Toronto, U of Michigan

EDUCATIONAL PROGRAM

Curriculum Intl, IB Diploma, IBPYP, IBMYP
Average class size Elementary 22; Secondary 22
Language(s) of instruction English
Language(s) taught German, French, Spanish
Staff specialists computer, counselor, ESL, learning disabilities, librarian, nurse, psychologist

Special curricular programs art, computer/technology, physical education
Extra curricular programs community service, drama, excursions/expeditions, photography, yearbook
Sports basketball, soccer, swimming, tennis, volleyball
Examinations IB, PSAT, SAT

CAMPUS FACILITIES

Location Suburban
Campus 3 hectares, 2 buildings, 46 classrooms, 2 computer labs, 100 instructional computers,

1 auditorium, 1 cafeteria, 1 covered play area, 1 gymnasium, 1 infirmary, 1 playing field, 3 science labs, 1 tennis court

GHANA

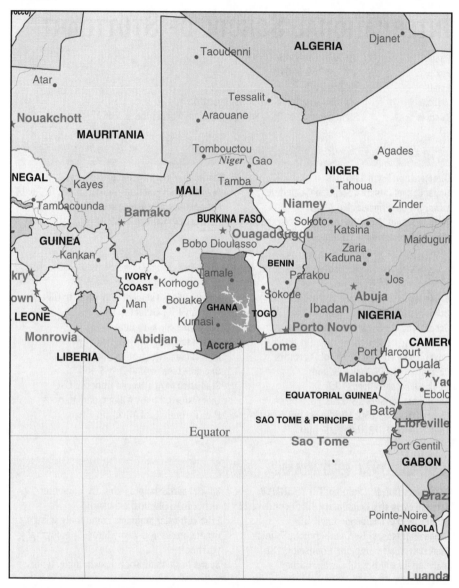

GHANA

Area:	239,460 sq km
Population:	22,931,299
Capital:	Accra
Currency:	Cedi (GHC)
Languages:	Asante

GHANA INTERNATIONAL SCHOOL

Phone 233 21 777 163
Fax 233 21 774 379
Email prinoffice@gisedu.com
Website www.gis.edu.gh
Address PO Box GP 2856, 2nd Circular Road, Cantonments, Accra, Ghana

STAFF

Principal Diana Nyatepe-Coo
Vice Principal, Upper Secondary David Arku
Vice Principal, Lower Secondary Diana Nyatepe-Coo
Vice Principal, Junior School Mary Ocansey
Vice Principal, Infant School Heidi Owu

Business Manager/Financial Controller
Joscelyn Barnor
Systems Administrator James Nkansah
Senior Librarian Elfrida Adablah

INFORMATION

Grade levels N–12
School year September–June
School type coeducational, day, private non-profit
Year founded 1955
Governed by appointed Board of Directors/Governors
Regional organizations AISA, ECIS

Tuition/fee currency US Dollar
Tuition range 6,000–9,600
One time fees Registration 75; Admission 5,500
Graduates attending college 95%
Graduates have attended Oxford U, Cambridge U, U of London, U of Texas, Legon U

EDUCATIONAL PROGRAM

Curriculum UK, IGCSE, GenCSE
Average class size Elementary 22; Secondary 17
Language(s) of instruction English
Language(s) taught French, Spanish
Staff specialists computer, counselor, ESL, librarian, nurse
Special curricular programs art, vocal music, computer/technology, physical education

Extra curricular programs computers, community service, dance, drama, excursions/expeditions, yearbook, Model UN, math, IT
Sports basketball, cricket, golf, gymnastics, rugby, soccer, softball, swimming, tennis, volleyball
Clubs Key, French, Spanish, honor society, ethics, debate
Examinations A-level GCE, GCSE, IGCSE, SAT, SAT II, British SAT

CAMPUS FACILITIES

Location Urban
Campus 25 hectares, 20 buildings, 71 classrooms, 3 computer labs, 280 instructional computers,

20,000 library volumes, 2 auditoriums, 2 cafeterias, 3 covered play areas, 2 infirmaries, 3 playing fields, 7 science labs, 2 tennis courts, air conditioning

Data from 2006/07 school year.

LINCOLN COMMUNITY SCHOOL

Phone	233 21 774 018
Fax	233 21 780 985
Email	lincoln@lincoln.edu.gh
Website	www.lincoln.edu.gh
Address	N 126/21 Dedeibaa Street, Abelemkpe, Accra, Ghana
Mailing address	c/o American Embassy, Accra, Postal 194, Accra, Ghana

STAFF

Superintendent John S. Roberts
Elementary School Principal Elsa Donohue
Secondary School Principal Douglas Musco
Business Manager Emmanuel Asiedu-Appiah
Technology Coordinator Sherrie Buchner

Learning Resources Coordinator Mary-Ellen Scribner
Teaching staff Full time 62; Part time 5; Total 67
Nationalities of teaching staff US 29; UK 5;
Ghanaian 11; Other(s) (Canadian, German) 22

INFORMATION

Grade levels N–12
School year August–June
School type coeducational, day, private non-profit
Year founded 1968
Governed by appointed and elected Nine
Member Board of Directors
Accredited by Middle States
Regional organizations AISA, ECIS
Enrollment Nursery 17; PreK 32;
Elementary K–5 229; Middle School 6–8 129;
High School 9–12 178; Total 585

Nationalities of student body US 113; UK 33;
Ghanaian 75; Other(s) (Dutch, Korean) 364
Tuition/fee currency US Dollar
Tuition range 4,200–14,150
Annual fees Capital Levy 750
One time fees Registration 6,000;
 Application 125
Graduates attending college 95%
Graduates have attended Cornell U, Stanford U,
McGill U, George Washington U,
American U of Beirut

EDUCATIONAL PROGRAM

Curriculum Intl, IB Diploma, IBPYP, IBMYP
Average class size Elementary 19; Secondary 18
Language(s) of instruction English
Language(s) taught French, Spanish
Staff specialists counselor, librarian
Special curricular programs art, instrumental
music, computer/technology, physical education

Extra curricular programs computers, community
service, dance, excursions/expeditions, yearbook
Sports basketball, golf, soccer, swimming,
tennis, track and field, yoga
Clubs National Honor Society, Girl Scouts,
Model UN, guitar, language, cooking, outdoor
Examinations IB, SAT

CAMPUS FACILITIES

Location Suburban
Campus 4 hectares, 14 buildings, 63 classrooms,
3 computer labs, 160 instructional computers,
18,080 library volumes, air conditioning

GREECE

Area:	131,940 sq km
Population:	10,706,290
Capital:	Athens
Currency:	Euro (EUR)
Languages:	Greek

THE AMERICAN COLLEGE OF GREECE (PIERCE COLLEGE)

Phone	30 210 600 9800
Fax	30 210 600 9811
Email	acg@acg.edu
Website	www.acg.edu
Address	6 Gravias Street, GR-153 42 Aghia Paraskevi, Athens, Greece

STAFF

President John S. Bailey
Principal and Chair, English Department
Olga Elaine Julius
Director of Gymnasium Kleomenis Petrochilos
Director of Lykeion Pericles Photopoulos
Assistant Principal Pericles Photopoulos
Assistant Principal George Drakopoulos

Controller Gabriel Alexopoulos
Senior VP/VP for Information Resources
Management Theodore Lyras
Dean of Library Resources Vicky Tseroni
Teaching staff Full time 79; Part time 29; Total 108
Nationalities of teaching staff US 11; Greek 89;
Other(s) (Australian, Canadian) 8

INFORMATION

Grade levels 7–12
School year September–June
School type coeducational, day, private non-profit
Year founded 1875
Governed by elected Board of Trustees
Regional organizations ECIS, NESA
Enrollment Middle School 6–8 363; High
School 9–12 483; Total 846
Nationalities of student body US 1; Greek 845

Tuition/fee currency Euro
Tuition range 6,012–7,518
Annual fees Busing 1,200; Sports 340;
French 1,485
One time fees Registration 85
Graduates attending college 93%
Graduates have attended Cornell U,
Virginia Polytechnic Institute, Wellesley Col,
Mt. Holyoke Col, Vassar Col

EDUCATIONAL PROGRAM

Curriculum US, National, Greek High School
Average class size Secondary 25
Language(s) of instruction English, Greek
Language(s) taught French, German
Staff specialists computer, counselor, learning
disabilities, librarian, nurse, physician,
psychologist
Special curricular programs art, instrumental
music, vocal music, computer/technology,
physical education, vocational, enviromental
Extra curricular programs computers, community
service, dance, drama, environmental

conservation, excursions/expeditions, literary
magazine, newspaper, photography, yearbook,
Greek and English forensics
Sports badminton, baseball, basketball, football,
gymnastics, martial arts, skiing, soccer, softball,
swimming, tennis, track and field, volleyball,
handball, fencing, table tennis
Clubs decoration, debate, astronomy, orchestra,
photography, biology, sports, English, choir
Examinations SAT, State Panhellenic
Examinations

CAMPUS FACILITIES

Location Suburban
Campus 65 hectares, 1 building, 57 classrooms,
4 computer labs, 22 instructional computers,
30,000 library volumes, 1 auditorium,

1 cafeteria, 2 covered play areas, 1 gymnasium,
1 infirmary, 4 playing fields, 3 science labs,
1 pool, 4 tennis courts

AMERICAN COMMUNITY SCHOOLS OF ATHENS

Phone	30 210 639 3200
Fax	30 210 639 0051
Email	acs@acs.gr
Website	www.acs.gr
Address	129 Aghias Paraskevis Street, Ano Halandri, Athens, 15234, Greece

STAFF

Head of School Stefanos Gialamas, Ph.D.
Academy Principal Steve Medeiros, Ed.D.
Elementary School Principal Dina Pappas
Middle School Principal Mary Ann Augoustatos
Director of Academic and Student Affairs
Peggy Pelonis

Director of Athletics Affairs Annie Constantinides
Business Manager Stephanos Kakaris
Head of Library Kathlene O'Donoghue
Teaching staff Full time 77; Part time 15; Total 92
Nationalities of teaching staff US 88; UK 2;
Greek 9; Other(s) 1

INFORMATION

Grade levels PreK–12
School year September–June
School type coeducational, day, private non-profit
Year founded 1945
Governed by elected Board of Education
Accredited by Middle States
Regional organizations NESA

Enrollment Nursery 40; PreK 42;
Elementary K–5 200; Middle School 6–8 156;
High School 9–12 287; Total 725
Tuition/fee currency Euro
Tuition range 7,000–11,000
Graduates attending college 99%
Graduates have attended Stanford U,
Georgetown U, U of California in Los Angeles,
Cornell U, Nortwestern U

EDUCATIONAL PROGRAM

Curriculum US, IB Diploma, IBPYP, IBMYP
Average class size Elementary 18; Secondary 20
Language(s) of instruction English
Language(s) taught Greek, German, Arabic,
Spanish, French
Staff specialists computer, counselor, ESL,
learning disabilities, librarian, math resource,
nurse, psychologist, reading resource

Special curricular programs art, instrumental
music, vocal music, computer/technology,
physical education
Extra curricular programs computers, community
service, dance, drama, environmental
conservation, excursions/expeditions, literary
magazine, newspaper, photography, yearbook
Sports basketball, martial arts, skiing, soccer,
swimming, tennis, track and field, volleyball
Examinations ACT, IB, PSAT, SAT, SAT II, TOEFL

CAMPUS FACILITIES

Location Suburban
Campus 3 hectares, 7 buildings, 77 classrooms,
5 computer labs, 275 instructional computers,
27,900 library volumes, 1 auditorium,

2 cafeterias, 2 gymnasiums, 1 infirmary,
3 playing fields, 8 science labs, 1 pool,
3 tennis courts, air conditioning

INTERNATIONAL SCHOOL OF ATHENS

Phone	30 210 623 3888
Fax	30 210 623 3160
Email	info@isa.edu.gr
Website	www.isa.edu.gr
Address	Xenias & Artemidos Streets, Kifissia, Greece
Mailing address	PO Box 51051, GR-145 10 Kifissia, Greece

STAFF

Director Costis N. Dardoufas
Secondary School Principal Chris Tragas
Primary School Principal Chris Grant-Bear
Director, Center for Counseling and Career Services Gina Thanopoulou
Director of Admissions Betty Haniotakis
Financial Manager Fanis Malakondas

IT Coordinator Paskalis Matsoukas
Librarian Kathy Petri
Teaching staff Full time 49; Part time 3; Total 52
Nationalities of teaching staff US 22; UK 3; Greek 11; Other(s) (Australian, Canadian) 16

INFORMATION

Grade levels N–12
School year September–June
School type coeducational, day, proprietary
Year founded 1979
Governed by appointed Board of Governors
Sponsored by Daskalakis Educational Group
Accredited by Middle States
Enrollment Nursery 8; PreK 70; Elementary K–5 95; Middle School 6–8 45; High School 9–12 82; Total 300

Nationalities of student body US 35; UK 20; Greek 85; Other(s) (Australian, Canadian) 160
Tuition/fee currency Euro
Tuition range 4,200–10,300
Annual fees Busing 1,200
One time fees Registration 900
Graduates attending college 95%
Graduates have attended U of Rochester, U of Manchester, U College London, U of Reading, American Col of Greece

EDUCATIONAL PROGRAM

Curriculum US, AP, IB Diploma
Average class size Elementary 15; Secondary 15
Language(s) of instruction English
Language(s) taught French, Spanish, Greek, Arabic
Staff specialists computer, counselor, ESL, learning disabilities, librarian, math resource, reading resource

Special curricular programs art, instrumental music, computer/technology, physical education
Extra curricular programs community service, excursions/expeditions, yearbook
Sports basketball, soccer, swimming, track and field, volleyball
Examinations AP, IB, Iowa, PSAT, SAT, SAT II

CAMPUS FACILITIES

Location Suburban
Campus 2 buildings, 29 classrooms, 2 computer labs, 35 instructional computers,

12,000 library volumes, 1 auditorium, 1 cafeteria, 1 infirmary, 4 playing fields, 4 science labs

ANATOLIA COLLEGE

Phone	30 2310 398 201
Fax	30 2310 327 500
Email	georgiad@ac.anatolia.edu.gr
Website	www.anatolia.edu.gr
Address	PO Box 21021, Pylea, Thessaloniki, 55510, Greece

STAFF

Vice President for Secondary Education
Panagiota Georgiadou
Dean of 'B' Lyceum Christos Plousios
Dean of 'A' Lyceum Ioannis Lalatsis

English Department Chair Phillip Holland, Ph.D.
Executive Vice President and Chief Operations Officer Panos Kanellis, Ph.D.
Head of Library/Media Center Paraskevi Tantanozi

INFORMATION

Grade levels 7–12
School year September–June
School type boarding, coeducational, day, private non-profit
Year founded 1886
Governed by elected Board of Trustees
Tuition/fee currency Euro

Tuition 4,721
Annual fees Boarding, 7-day 6,495; Insurance 50; Busing 663
One time fees Registration 50
Graduates attending college 95%
Graduates have attended Harvard U, Grinnell Col, Mt. Holyoke Col, Yale U, U of Pennsylvania

EDUCATIONAL PROGRAM

Curriculum US, National
Average class size Secondary 32
Language(s) of instruction English, Greek
Language(s) taught English, French, German, Spanish (IB only)
Staff specialists computer, counselor, ESL, math resource, psychologist
Special curricular programs art, instrumental music, vocal music, computer/technology, physical education, vocational, IB CAS Program
Extra curricular programs computers, community service, dance, drama, environmental conservation, excursions/expeditions, literary magazine, newspaper, photography, yearbook, forensics, Model UN, European Youth, parliament, chess, fashion design, mass media, Ancient Greek technology
Sports baseball, basketball, cross-country, gymnastics, soccer, softball, tennis, track and field, volleyball, handball, aerobics
Clubs Greek dancing, drama, Greek theater
Examinations IB, PSAT, SAT, TOEFL, TSE, EGPE, GRE (subject), Greek University Leaving Certificate

CAMPUS FACILITIES

Location Rural
Campus 45 hectares, 23 buildings, 60 classrooms, 6 computer labs, 132 instructional computers, 30,000 library volumes, 3 auditoriums, 1 cafeteria, 1 covered play area, 1 gymnasium, 1 infirmary, 11 playing fields, 9 science labs, 2 tennis courts

Data from 2006/07 school year.

PINEWOOD–THE INTERNATIONAL SCHOOL OF THESSALONIKI

Phone	30 231 0 301 221
Fax	30 231 0 323 196
Email	leoruberto@pinewood.gr
Website	www.pinewood.gr
Address	P.O. 21001, 555 10 Pilea, Thessaloniki, 55510, Greece

STAFF

Director Leo Ruberto, Ph.D.
Secondary Academic Coordinator Mary Tsoulfa
Technology Instructor Natalie Pinakidou

Teaching staff Full time 25; Part time 7; Total 32
Nationalities of teaching staff US 3; UK 3; Greek 26

INFORMATION

Grade levels N–12
School year September–June
School type boarding, coeducational, day, private non-profit
Year founded 1950
Governed by elected School Board
Accredited by Middle States
Regional organizations NESA
Enrollment Nursery 30; PreK 5; Elementary K–5 45; Middle School 6–8 25; High School 9–12 65; Total 170

Nationalities of student body US 40; UK 5; Greek 100; Other(s) (Bulgarian, Ukrainian) 25
Tuition/fee currency Euro
Tuition range 5,000–8,250
Annual fees Busing 500
One time fees Capital Levy 1,400
Boarding program grades 9–12
Boarding program length 7-day **Boys** 3 **Girls** 5
Graduates attending college 85%
Graduates have attended Georgia Tech U, Macalester U, Cornell U, U of Virginia, Boston U

EDUCATIONAL PROGRAM

Curriculum US, IB Diploma
Average class size Elementary 10; Secondary 13
Language(s) of instruction English
Language(s) taught Modern Greek, French
Staff specialists computer, ESL

Special curricular programs art, computer/technology, physical education
Sports soccer
Examinations IB, Iowa, SAT, SAT II

CAMPUS FACILITIES

Location Suburban
Campus 2 hectares, 3 buildings, 21 classrooms, 1 computer lab, 25 instructional computers,

17,000 library volumes, 1 auditorium, 1 gymnasium, 1 playing field, 1 science lab

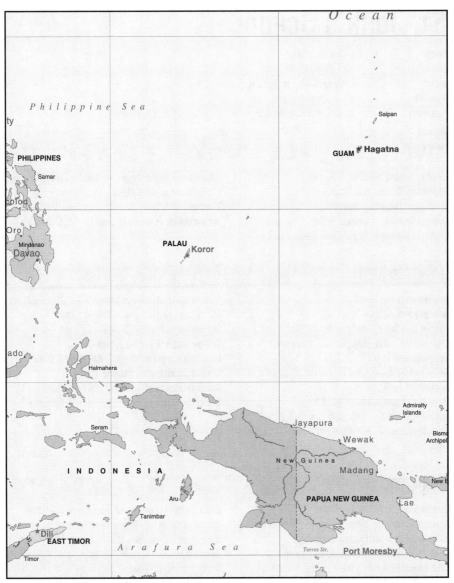

GUAM

Area:	541.3 sq km
Population:	173,456
Capital:	Hagatna (Agana)
Currency:	US Dollar (USD)
Languages:	English

St. John's School

Phone	671 646 8080
Fax	671 649 1055
Email	jshimizu@stjohnsguam.com
Website	www.stjohnsguam.com
Address	911 North Marine Corps Drive, Tumon, 96913, Guam

STAFF

Head of School Imelda D. Santos
Secondary School Principal
Hauhouot Diambra-Odi, Ph.D.
College Counselor Robert Kelley
Business Manager Rebecca D. Hernandez

Educational Technology Coordinator Rolly Maiquez
Librarian Margaret Mesa
Teaching staff Full time 60; Part time 10; Total 70
Nationalities of teaching staff US 63; Other(s) 7

INFORMATION

Grade levels PreK–12
School year August–June
School type boarding, coeducational,
church-affiliated, day, private non-profit
Year founded 1962
Governed by appointed Board of Trustees
Accredited by Western
Regional organizations EARCOS
Enrollment PreK 67; Elementary K–5 215;
Middle School 6–8 147; High School 9–12 96;
Total 525

Nationalities of student body US 341; Guamanian
16; Other(s) (Korean, Chinese) 168
Tuition/fee currency US Dollar
Tuition range 9,100–13,100
Boarding program length 7-day **Boys** 3 **Girls** 5
Graduates attending college 100%
Graduates have attended Cornell U, Stanford U,
Berkeley Col, Princeton U, Johns Hopkins U

EDUCATIONAL PROGRAM

Curriculum US, AP, IB Diploma
Average class size Elementary 15; Secondary 13
Language(s) of instruction English
Language(s) taught Spanish, Japanese
Staff specialists computer, counselor, ESL,
librarian, math resource, reading resource
Special curricular programs art, instrumental
music, vocal music, computer/technology,
physical education

Extra curricular programs community service,
dance, drama, environmental conservation,
excursions/expeditions, photography, yearbook
Sports basketball, cross-country, golf, rugby,
soccer, softball, tennis, paddling
Clubs art, National Forensic League, mock trial,
student council, boy and girl scouts, Model UN,
National Honor Society, handbells, glee
Examinations AP, IB, PSAT, Stanford

CAMPUS FACILITIES

Location Urban
Campus 3 hectares, 12 buildings, 61 classrooms,
4 computer labs, 200 instructional computers,
30,000 library volumes, 1 auditorium,

3 covered play areas, 1 gymnasium,
1 infirmary, 3 playing fields, 4 science labs,
air conditioning

GUATEMALA

Area:	108,890 sq km
Population:	12,728,111
Capital:	Guatemala
Currency:	Quetzal (GTQ), US Dollar (USD)
Languages:	Spanish

AMERICAN SCHOOL OF GUATEMALA

Phone	502 2 3688543
Fax	502 23698335
Email	cagadm@cag.edu.gt
Website	www.cag.edu.gt
Address	11 Calle 15-79, Zona 15, Vista Hermosa 111, Guatemala City, 01015, Guatemala
Mailing address	Section 1783, PO Box 25339, Miami, Florida 33102, USA

STAFF

General Director Ettie Zilber, Ed.D.
Elementary School Principal Tracy Berry-Lazo
Middle School Principal Sheryl Salem
Secondary Principal Fabio Corvaglia
Early Childhood Principal Jennifer Ashton-Lilo
Business Manager Cesar Garcia

Technology Coordinator Claudia Estrada
Head of Library/Educational Resource Center Carol Hunter
Teaching staff Full time 147; Total 147
Nationalities of teaching staff US 48; Guatemalan 88; Other(s) (Canadian) 11

INFORMATION

Grade levels K–12
School year August–June
School type coeducational, day, private non-profit
Year founded 1945
Governed by appointed Board of Directors
Accredited by New England
Regional organizations AASCA
Enrollment Elementary K–5 790; Middle School 6–8 217; High School 9–12 442; Total 1,449
Nationalities of student body US 188; Guatemalan 1,105; Other(s) 156

Tuition/fee currency US Dollar
Tuition range 4,870–5,290
Annual fees Busing 270; Security and Traffic Control 290; Technology 245; Educational Materials and Activities 229
One time fees Registration 2,500; Insurance 27
Graduates attending college 99%
Graduates have attended Georgetown U, Harvard U, U of Pennsylvania, U of Virginia, U of Notre Dame

EDUCATIONAL PROGRAM

Curriculum US, National, AP
Average class size Elementary 22; Secondary 24
Language(s) of instruction English, Spanish
Language(s) taught French, German, Italian
Staff specialists computer, counselor, learning disabilities, librarian, physician, psychologist
Special curricular programs art, computer/technology, physical education
Extra curricular programs community service, drama, newspaper, photography, yearbook, school community performances, painting, drawing
Sports badminton, baseball, basketball, soccer, softball, swimming, tennis, track and field, volleyball, fencing
Clubs chorus, orchestra, instruments, student council, Model UN, National Honor Society, Junior National Honor Society, Destination Imagination
Examinations ACT, AP, PSAT, SAT, Stanford

CAMPUS FACILITIES

Location Urban
Campus 52 hectares, 22 buildings, 75 classrooms, 4 computer labs, 210 instructional computers, 29,000 library volumes, 1 gymnasium, 3 infirmaries, 10 playing fields, 6 science labs, 1 pool

COLEGIO INTERAMERICANO

Phone	502 2385 7088
Fax	502 2364 1779
Email	migularte@interamericano.edu.gt
Website	www.interamericano.edu.gt
Address	Blvd. La Montaña, Finca El Socorro, Zona 16, Guatemala City, Guatemala, 01016, Guatemala
Mailing address	Section 4134, PO Box 02-5339, Miami, Fl 33102-5339, USA

STAFF

General Director Robert Michael Farr, Ph.D.
High School Principal Conrad Pholar
Elementary Principal Mayra de Cifuentes
Middle School Principal Jaime Tres

Technology Coordinator William Gatica
Library/Media Center Coordinator Odette de Rodriguez

INFORMATION

Grade levels PreK–12
School year August–June
School type coeducational, day, private non-profit
Year founded 1975
Governed by appointed Board of Directors
Sponsored by Fundación Educativa Guatemala
Accredited by Southern
Regional organizations AASCA
Enrollment PreK 60; Elementary K–5 480;
Middle School 6–8 240;
High School 9–12 322; Total 1,102

Nationalities of student body US 21;
Guatemalan 1,008; Other(s) (Korean) 73
Tuition/fee currency Guatemalan Quetzal
Tuition range 16,100–23,300
Annual fees Registration 2,500; Insurance 375;
Busing 4,700; Books 3,175;
Complementary Services 5,350
One time fees Capital Levy 10,000
Graduates attending college 98%
Graduates have attended Duke U,
Wellesley Col, U of Michigan, U of Notre Dame,
U Del Valle de Guatemala

EDUCATIONAL PROGRAM

Curriculum US, National, AP
Average class size Elementary 22; Secondary 24
Language(s) of instruction English, Spanish
Language(s) taught English, Spanish
Staff specialists computer, counselor, ESL,
learning disabilities, librarian, math resource,
nurse, psychologist
Special curricular programs art, instrumental
music, vocal music, computer/technology,
physical education

Extra curricular programs computers, community
service, drama, environmental conservation,
excursions/expeditions, photography,
yearbook, Model UN, Destination Imagination,
Knowledge Bowl, Science/Math Olympics
Sports basketball, soccer, softball, track and
field, volleyball
Clubs hand crafts, recycling, theatre, chess,
Origami, cooking, photography
Examinations AP, Iowa, MAT, PSAT, SAT, TOEFL

CAMPUS FACILITIES

Location Suburban
Campus 4 hectares, 7 buildings, 62 classrooms,
4 computer labs, 142 instructional computers,

17,000 library volumes, 1 cafeteria,
2 covered play areas, 1 infirmary,
4 playing fields, 4 science labs

Data from 2006/07 school year.

COLEGIO MAYA/THE AMERICAN INTERNATIONAL SCHOOL OF GUATEMALA

Phone	502 2365 0037
Fax	502 2365 0116
Email	info@cm.edu.gt
Website	www.cm.edu.gt
Address	Km. 12.5, Carretera a El Salvador, Guatemala City, 01073, Guatemala
Mailing address	Section 0280, PO Box 02-5289, Miami, FL 33102-5289, USA

STAFF

Director and Elementary Principal Sherry Miller, Ed.D.
Secondary Principal Maribel Maldonado
Business Manager Aida Tsuji
Head of Technology Ruth Rosenfeld

Head of Library Kate Dunigan-AtLee
Teaching staff Full time 45; Total 45
Nationalities of teaching staff US 32; Guatemalan 10; Other(s) (Brazilian, Canadian) 3

INFORMATION

Grade levels PreK–12
School year August–June
School type coeducational, day, private non-profit
Year founded 1958
Governed by elected Board of Directors
Accredited by Southern
Regional organizations AASCA
Enrollment PreK 12; Elementary K–5 160; Middle School 6–8 68; High School 9–12 98; Total 338

Nationalities of student body US 85; UK 2; Guatemalan 61; Other(s) (Korean, Venezuelan) 190
Tuition/fee currency US Dollar
Tuition range 8,846–9,368
Annual fees Busing 1,000; ESL 800; Learning Resource 800
One time fees Registration 6,000
Graduates attending college 97%
Graduates have attended Harvard U, U of Richmond, Georgetown U, Brigham Young U, U of Virginia

EDUCATIONAL PROGRAM

Curriculum US, AP
Average class size Elementary 15; Secondary 16
Language(s) of instruction English, Spanish
Staff specialists computer, counselor, ESL, learning disabilities, librarian, nurse
Special curricular programs art, instrumental music, vocal music, computer/technology, distance learning, physical education

Extra curricular programs community service, drama, excursions/expeditions, photography
Sports basketball, soccer, volleyball
Clubs National Honor Society, National Junior Honor Society
Examinations AP, Terra Nova

CAMPUS FACILITIES

Location Suburban
Campus 12 hectares, 9 buildings, 42 classrooms, 2 computer labs, 150 instructional computers, 20,000 library volumes, 1 auditorium, 1 cafeteria, 2 covered play areas, 1 gymnasium, 1 infirmary, 3 playing fields, 2 science labs, 2 tennis courts

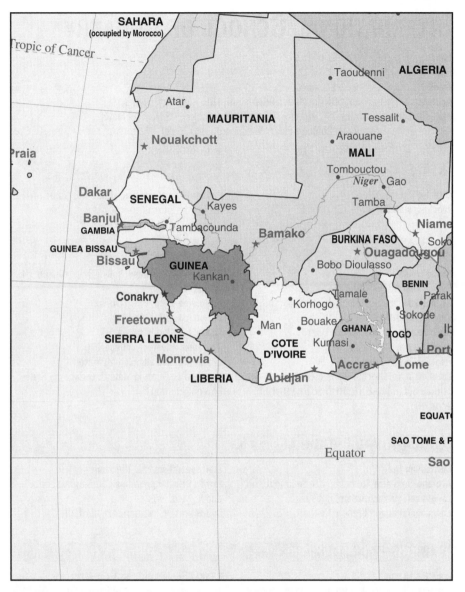

GUINEA

Area:	245,857 sq km
Population:	9,947,814
Capital:	Conakry
Currency:	Guinean Franc (GNF)
Languages:	French

INTERNATIONAL SCHOOL OF CONAKRY

Phone	224 12 661535
Fax	224 41 15 22
Email	isc@biasy.net
Address	BP 603 Corniche Sud, Matam, Lido, Conakry, Guinea
Mailing address	Attn: ISC Director, US Embassy Conakry, US Dept. of State, 2110 Conakry Place, Washington, DC 20521-2110, USA

STAFF

Director Phillip Dale
Teaching staff Full time 12; Total 12

Nationalities of teaching staff US 3; Guinean 1; Other(s) (Sierra Leonean) 8

INFORMATION

Grade levels N–12
School year August–June
School type coeducational, day, private non-profit
Year founded 1966
Governed by elected School Board
Accredited by Middle States
Regional organizations AISA, ECIS
Enrollment Nursery 2; PreK 2; Elementary K–5 15; Middle School 6–8 15; High School 9–12 6; Total 40

Nationalities of student body US 5; Guinean 10; Other(s) 25
Tuition/fee currency US Dollar
Tuition range 2,200–11,000
Annual fees Registration 500
Graduates attending college 100%
Graduates have attended McMaster U, Marshall U, Georgia State U, Oklahoma State U, Korean National U

EDUCATIONAL PROGRAM

Curriculum Intl
Average class size Elementary 8; Secondary 6
Language(s) of instruction English
Language(s) taught French

Staff specialists ESL, librarian
Extra curricular programs community service, dance, yearbook
Sports soccer, swimming, volleyball

CAMPUS FACILITIES

Location Urban
Campus 1 hectare, 2 buildings, 10 classrooms, 1 computer lab, 25 instructional computers,

6,000 library volumes, 1 cafeteria, 1 covered play area, 1 playing field, 1 science lab, air conditioning

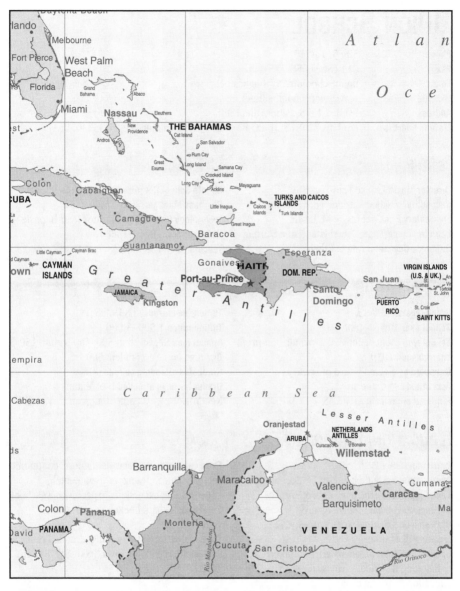

HAITI

Area:	27,750 sq km
Population:	8,706,497
Capital:	Port-au-Prince
Currency:	Gourde (HTG)
Languages:	French, Creole

UNION SCHOOL

Phone	509 511-4715
Fax	011 (866) 688-7754
Email	unionschooldirect@hughes.net
Website	www.unionschoolhaiti.net
Address	PO Box 1175, PetionVille, Haiti
Mailing address	c/o Lynx Air/UNSCH, PO Box 407134, Ft. Lauderdale, FL 33340, USA

STAFF

Director Marie France Jean-Baptiste
Secondary Principal Marlene Ford Nicolas
Elementary Principal Jessye M. Bazile
Learning Center/Math Coordinator Nadia Durban
Guidance Counselor Ana L. Ribeiro

Middle School Coordinator Dominique Pierre
Business Manager Wisnel Milien
Technology Coordinator Mesidor Jean-Baptiste
Head Librarian Janice Hall
Teaching staff Full time 28; Part time 2; Total 30

INFORMATION

Grade levels PreK–12
School year August–June
School type coeducational, day, private non-profit
Year founded 1919
Governed by elected Board of Trustees
Accredited by Southern
Regional organizations ACCAS

Tuition/fee currency US Dollar
Tuition range 1,500–5,000
Annual fees Registration 300; Application 150
One time fees New Student 500
Graduates attending college 99%
Graduates have attended U of Miami,
New York U, West Point, American U, McGill U

EDUCATIONAL PROGRAM

Curriculum US, AP
Average class size Elementary 17; Secondary 17
Language(s) of instruction English, French
Language(s) taught French, Spanish
Staff specialists computer, counselor, ESL,
learning disabilities
Special curricular programs art, computer/
technology, distance learning, physical
education, learning center

Extra curricular programs computers, community
service, dance, drama, environmental
conservation, excursions/expeditions, yearbook
Sports basketball, hockey, soccer, tennis,
volleyball
Clubs debate, creative writing, drama, French
Examinations ACT, AP, Iowa, PSAT, SAT, SAT II,
TOEFL, TAP

CAMPUS FACILITIES

Location Suburban
Campus 2 hectares, 2 buildings, 38 classrooms,
2 computer labs, 40 instructional computers,

12,000 library volumes, 1 infirmary,
2 playing fields, 2 science labs

Data from 2006/07 school year.

HONDURAS

Area:	112,090 sq km
Population:	7,483,763
Capital:	Tegucigalpa
Currency:	Lempira (HNL)
Languages:	Spanish

MAZAPAN SCHOOL

Phone	504 443 2716
Fax	504 443 3559
Email	enufio@la.dole.com
Website	www.mazapanschool.org
Address	Zona Mazapan, La Ceiba, Atlantida, Honduras
Mailing address	SFCO Honduras, MIA 951, PO Box 025365, Miami, FL 33102-5365, USA

STAFF

Superintendent Martha V. Counsil, Ed.D.
Guidance Counselor/Registrar Enma Nufio
Honduran Director Mirta Martinez
High School Principal Donna Dixon

Business Manager Ninoska Coto
Technology Coordinator Jason Boyd
Media Specialist Sharon Davis

INFORMATION

Grade levels 1–12
School year August–June
School type coeducational, company-sponsored, day, private non-profit
Year founded 1928
Governed by appointed Dole Fruit International Managers
Sponsored by Dole Fruit International
Accredited by Southern
Regional organizations AASCA
Enrollment Elementary K–5 120; Middle School 6–8 75; High School 9–12 100; Total 295

Nationalities of student body US 24; Honduran 239; Other(s) 32
Tuition/fee currency US Dollar
Tuition range 283–312
Annual fees Registration 312
One time fees Entrance 1–3 1,000; Entrance 4–8 2,000; Entrance 9–12 2,400
Graduates attending college 100%
Graduates have attended York U, Rochester Institute of Technology, U of Central Arkansas, U of the Ozarks, U of New Orleans

EDUCATIONAL PROGRAM

Curriculum US, National, Honduran
Average class size Elementary 25; Secondary 28
Language(s) of instruction English, Spanish
Language(s) taught English, Spanish, French
Staff specialists computer, counselor, librarian, math resource
Special curricular programs art, instrumental music, vocal music, computer/technology, physical education, vocational, college prep

Extra curricular programs computers, community service, dance, drama, environmental conservation, excursions/expeditions, newspaper, photography, yearbook, Knowledge Bowl, Model UN, island survival
Sports baseball, basketball, soccer, softball, swimming, tennis, track and field, volleyball
Clubs National Honor Society, student council, chess, ecology,
Examinations ACT, PSAT, SAT, Stanford, TOEFL, MRT6

CAMPUS FACILITIES

Location Urban
Campus 5 hectares, 7 buildings, 16 classrooms, 2 computer labs, 28 instructional computers, 8,000 library volumes, 1 auditorium,

1 cafeteria, 1 covered play area, 2 gymnasiums, 3 playing fields, 2 science labs, air conditioning

Data from 2006/07 school year.

ESCUELA BILINGUE SANTA BARBARA

Phone	504 659 3052
Fax	504 659 3059
Email	mochitoschool@breakwater.hn
Address	Apdo. 342-El Mochito, San Pedro Sula, Honduras

STAFF

Principal Daniel M. Wilkerson

INFORMATION

Grade levels K–8
School year August–June
School type coeducational, company-sponsored, day

Sponsored by AMPAC
Tuition/fee currency Honduran Lempira

EDUCATIONAL PROGRAM

Curriculum US, National
Average class size Elementary 10; Secondary 10

Language(s) of instruction English, Spanish

CAMPUS FACILITIES

Location Rural
Campus 1 building, 5 classrooms, 1 computer lab, 8 instructional computers, 2,000 library volumes, 1 covered play area, 1 infirmary, 3 playing fields, 1 pool, 1 tennis court

ESCUELA INTERNACIONAL SAMPEDRANA

Phone	504 566 2722
Fax	504 566 1458
Email	rvair@seishn.com
Website	www.seishn.org
Address	500 Metros arriba del Hospital Mario Rivas, San Pedro Sula, Cortes, Honduras
Mailing address	7339 NW 54 Street, Suite HNS-29, Miami, FL 33166, USA

STAFF

Superintendent Ronald J. Vair, Ed.D.
High School Principal Thomas Litecky
Elementary School Principal Gina Rietti de Larach
Principal of La Lima School Dennis Spencer
Middle School Principal Ximena Silva
Preschool Principal Lilliam Nasser

Director of Finance Omar Cardona
Manager of Technology Edwin Cabrera
Library Director Elsa Barrios
Teaching staff Full time 334; Part time 2; Total 336
Nationalities of teaching staff US 40;
Honduran 266; Other(s) (Canadian) 30

INFORMATION

Grade levels N–12
School year August–July
School type coeducational, day, private non-profit
Year founded 1953
Governed by elected Board of Directors
Accredited by Southern
Regional organizations AASCA, AASSA
Enrollment Nursery 120; PreK 116;
Elementary K–5 775; Middle School 6–8 376;
High School 9–12 450; Total 1,837

Nationalities of student body US 23;
Honduran 1,774; Other(s) (Korean) 40
Tuition/fee currency Honduran Lempira
Tuition range 53,600–66,240
Annual fees Registration 9,933
Graduates attending college 95%
Graduates have attended Harvard U,
Mount Holyoke Col, Duke U, Loyola U,
Texas A&M U

EDUCATIONAL PROGRAM

Curriculum US, AP, Honduran
Average class size Elementary 20; Secondary 25
Language(s) of instruction English, Spanish
Staff specialists computer, counselor, ESL,
librarian, psychologist, reading resource,
speech/hearing
Special curricular programs art, instrumental
music, vocal music, computer/technology,
physical education, vocational

Extra curricular programs computers, community
service, drama, environmental conservation,
excursions/expeditions
Sports basketball, soccer, volleyball
Examinations ACT, AP, Iowa, PSAT, SAT, TOEFL,
PLAN, CogAT

CAMPUS FACILITIES

Location Urban
Campus 25 hectares, 12 buildings, 64 classrooms,

3 computer labs, 45 instructional computers,
18,000 library volumes

THE AMERICAN SCHOOL OF TEGUCIGALPA

Phone	504 239 3333
Fax	504 239 6162
Email	info@amschool.org
Website	www.amschool.org
Address	Avenida Republica Dominicana, Colonia Lomas del Guijarro, Tegucigalpa, MDC, Honduras
Mailing address	IMC TGU Dept. 227, PO Box 025320, Miami, FL 33102-5320, USA

STAFF

Superintendent Liliana F. Jenkins
High School Principal Matthew Blake
Middle School Principal Robert Rinaldo
Elementary School Principal Elcenora Martinez
Preschool Principal Claudia Pereira
Business Manager David Mendoza

Coordinator of Instructional Technology Support
Jose Manuel Mendoza
Librarians Rosa Chinchilla/Janine Cervantes
Teaching staff Full time 80; Total 80
Nationalities of teaching staff US 25; Honduran 55

INFORMATION

Grade levels N–12
School year August–June
School type coeducational, day, private non-profit
Year founded 1946
Governed by elected Board of Directors
Accredited by Southern
Regional organizations AASCA
Enrollment Nursery 75; PreK 75; Elementary K–5 465; Middle School 6–8 234; High School 9–12 300; Total 1,149

Nationalities of student body US 59; Honduran 1,040; Other(s) 50
Tuition/fee currency US Dollar
Tuition range 1,800–5,800
One time fees Registration 2,500; Capital Levy 2,500
Graduates attending college 99%
Graduates have attended Boston Col, Loyola U, Babson Col, U of Notre Dame, Georgetown U

EDUCATIONAL PROGRAM

Curriculum US, National, IB Diploma
Average class size Elementary 25; Secondary 25
Language(s) of instruction English, Spanish
Staff specialists computer, counselor, learning disabilities, librarian, nurse, psychologist, speech/hearing
Special curricular programs art, instrumental music, vocal music, computer/technology, physical education

Extra curricular programs community service, newspaper, yearbook
Sports basketball, soccer, volleyball
Clubs student government, National Honor Society, Operation Smile, Hacia Democracy, ecology, Junior State of America, Model UN
Examinations ACT, IB, Iowa, PSAT, SAT, SAT II, TOEFL, SSAT

CAMPUS FACILITIES

Location Urban
Campus 5 hectares, 7 buildings, 45 classrooms, 3 computer labs, 90 instructional computers,

30,000 library volumes, 1 auditorium, 1 cafeteria, 1 covered play area, 1 gymnasium, 1 infirmary, 4 playing fields, 5 science labs

DISCOVERY SCHOOL

Phone	504 239-4454
Fax	504 269-4451
Email	dsoffice@mundo123.hn
Website	www.discoveryschool.edu.hn
Address	Zona el Molinon, Anillo Periferico, Antes Salida de Valle de Angeles, Tegucigalpa, Honduras
Mailing address	TGU 00015, PO Box 025387, Miami, FL 33102-5387, USA

STAFF

Director Glenn F. Jones, Ed.D.
Secondary Principal Gloria Palacios
Primary Coordinator Cristiana Banegas
Business Manager Reina Salgado
Technology Coordinator Carlos Ferrera

Librarian Carlos Echevarria
Teaching staff Full time 32; Part time 1; Total 33
Nationalities of teaching staff US 15; Honduran 16; Other(s) (Brazilian, Puerto Rican) 2

INFORMATION

Grade levels N–12
School year August–June
School type coeducational, day, private non-profit
Year founded 1995
Governed by elected Board of Directors
Accredited by Southern
Regional organizations AASCA
Enrollment Nursery 8; PreK 16; Elementary K–5 130; Middle School 6–8 50; High School 9–12 50; Total 254

Nationalities of student body US 81; Honduran 83; Other(s) (Dutch, German) 90
Tuition/fee currency US Dollar
Tuition range 4,100–5,600
Annual fees Busing 550
One time fees Registration 2,500
Graduates attending college 100%
Graduates have attended Mercyhurst Col, U of Bath, U of Texas, U Nacional Autonoma de Honduras, U Catholica de Honduras

EDUCATIONAL PROGRAM

Curriculum US, National, AP
Average class size Elementary 13; Secondary 8
Language(s) of instruction English
Language(s) taught Spanish
Staff specialists computer, counselor, ESL, librarian
Special curricular programs art, instrumental music, vocal music, computer/technology, physical education

Extra curricular programs community service, dance, drama, environmental conservation, excursions/expeditions, yearbook
Sports basketball, soccer, track and field
Examinations ACT, AP, Iowa, PSAT, SAT, SAT II, TOEFL

CAMPUS FACILITIES

Location Urban
Campus 3 hectares, 9 buildings, 32 classrooms, 1 computer lab, 35 instructional computers,

6,000 library volumes, 1 cafeteria, 1 covered play area, 1 gymnasium, 1 infirmary, 2 playing fields, 2 science labs

HUNGARY

Area:	93,030 sq km
Population:	9,956,108
Capital:	Budapest
Currency:	Forint (HUF)
Languages:	Hungarian

AMERICAN INTERNATIONAL SCHOOL OF BUDAPEST

Phone	36 26 556 000
Fax	36 26 556 003
Email	rhollidayb@nk.aisb.hu
Website	www.aisb.hu
Address	Kakukk utca 1-3, Budapest, 1121, Hungary
Mailing address	PO Box 53, 1525 Budapest, Hungary

STAFF

Director Raymond Holliday-Bersegeay
High School Principal Grant Fiedler
Middle School Principal Paul Ducharme
Elementary Principal Donna Kelley
Business Manager Zoltan Karaszy

Technology Coordinator Michael Meyer
Librarian Coralie Clark
Teaching staff Full time 90; Part time 20; Total 110
Nationalities of teaching staff US 69; UK 12; Hungarian 5; Other(s) (Canadian) 24

INFORMATION

Grade levels PreK–12
School year August–June
School type coeducational, day, private non-profit
Year founded 1973
Governed by appointed and elected Board of Directors
Accredited by CIS, Middle States
Regional organizations CEESA, ECIS
Enrollment PreK 25; Elementary K–5 335; Middle School 6–8 185; High School 9–12 225; Total 770

Nationalities of student body US 140; UK 18; Hungarian 121; Other(s) (Korean, Dutch) 491
Tuition/fee currency US Dollar
Tuition range 10,900–18,850
Annual fees Capital Levy 2,500
One time fees Registration 500
Graduates attending college 99%
Graduates have attended Georgetown U, Ottawa U, Boston U, U of Kent, Baylor U

EDUCATIONAL PROGRAM

Curriculum US, IB Diploma
Average class size Elementary 15; Secondary 14
Language(s) of instruction English
Language(s) taught French, German, Spanish
Staff specialists computer, counselor, ESL, learning disabilities, librarian, math resource, nurse, psychologist, reading resource
Special curricular programs art, instrumental music, vocal music, computer/technology, physical education, drama, Hungarian culture

Extra curricular programs computers, community service, dance, drama, environmental conservation, excursions/expeditions, literary magazine, photography, yearbook
Sports basketball, cross-country, golf, martial arts, soccer, softball, swimming, tennis, track and field, volleyball
Clubs National Honor Society, service
Examinations ACT, IB, Iowa, PSAT, SAT, TOEFL

CAMPUS FACILITIES

Location Suburban
Campus 14 hectares, 2 buildings, 63 classrooms, 6 computer labs, 256 instructional computers, 32,000 library volumes, 3 auditoriums,

2 cafeterias, 3 gymnasiums, 2 infirmaries, 4 playing fields, 6 science labs, 2 pools, 5 tennis courts

BRITANNICA INTERNATIONAL SCHOOL

Phone	36 1 466 9794
Fax	36 1 466 9794
Email	contact@britannicaschool.hu
Website	www.britannicaschool.hu
Address	Aga Utca 10, Budapest, H-1113, Hungary

STAFF

Head of School David J. Clapp, Ed.D.
Business Manager Agnes Clapp
Teaching staff Full time 12; Part time 5; Total 17

Nationalities of teaching staff US 3; UK 8;
Hungarian 3; Other(s) (French) 3

INFORMATION

Grade levels 5–12
School year September–June
School type coeducational, day
Year founded 1993
Governed by appointed School Board
Enrollment Elementary K–5 10; Middle School
6–8 50; High School 9–12 60; Total 120

Tuition/fee currency Hungarian Forint
Tuition range 1,600,000–2,200,000
Graduates attending college 100%
Graduates have attended U of Sussex,
U of Manchester, U of Liverpool, U of London

EDUCATIONAL PROGRAM

Curriculum UK, IGCSE, AS Level and Advanced
Level (CIE- University of Cambridge)
Average class size Elementary 12; Secondary 15
Language(s) of instruction English
Language(s) taught Spanish, French, German
Staff specialists computer, ESL, librarian, nurse
Special curricular programs art, computer/
technology, physical education

Extra curricular programs dance, drama,
excursions/expeditions, newspaper,
photography
Sports badminton, basketball, gymnastics,
hockey, skiing, soccer, swimming, tennis,
volleyball, skating
Clubs art, photography, guitar, investment,
French, basketball, football, volleyball, tennis
Examinations A-level GCE, GCSE, IGCSE, ECDL

CAMPUS FACILITIES

Location Suburban
Campus 1 building, 12 classrooms, 1 computer
lab, 24 instructional computers, 1 cafeteria,

1 gymnasium, 1 playing field, 1 science lab,
3 tennis courts

ICELAND

ICELAND

Area:	103,000 sq km
Population:	301,931
Capital:	Reykjavik
Currency:	Icelandic Krona (ISK)
Languages:	Icelandic

REYKJAVIK INTERNATIONAL SCHOOL

Phone	354 694 3341
Fax	354 585 2701
Email	int.school.iceland@gmail.com
Website	www.internationalschool.is
Address	v/Sjalandsskoli, Langalina 8, Gardabaer, 112, Iceland

STAFF

Teaching Principal Berta L. Faber
Teaching staff Full time 4; Part time 3; Total 7

Nationalities of teaching staff US 3; Icelander 3; Other(s) (German) 1

INFORMATION

Grade levels K–7
School year August–June
School type coeducational, day, private non-profit
Year founded 2004
Governed by appointed and elected School Board

Enrollment Elementary K–5 22; Middle School 6–8 5; Total 27
Nationalities of student body US 10; Icelander 6; Other(s) (German, Dane) 5
Tuition/fee currency US Dollar
Tuition 10,000

EDUCATIONAL PROGRAM

Curriculum US, Intl
Average class size Elementary 9; Secondary 9
Language(s) of instruction English, Icelandic

Staff specialists ESL
Special curricular programs art, physical education

CAMPUS FACILITIES

Location Suburban
Campus 1 hectare, 1 building, 2 classrooms, 1 computer lab, 30 instructional computers,

3,000 library volumes, 1 cafeteria, 1 gymnasium

INDIA

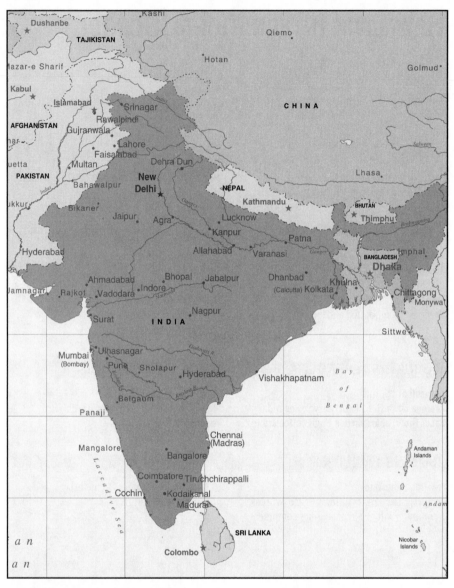

INDIA

Area:	3,287,590 sq km
Population:	1,129,866,154
Capital:	New Delhi
Currency:	Indian Rupee (INR)
Languages:	English, Hindi

CANADIAN INTERNATIONAL SCHOOL, INDIA

Phone	91 80 6451 4001
Email	principal@cisb.org.in
Website	www.cisb.org.in
Address	4 & 20 Manchenahalli Village, Yelahanka Hobli, Bangalore, Karnataka, 560 064, India

STAFF

Principal James H. Leahy
Vice Principal Michael Filip
IB Coordinator Craig Patterson
Director of Admissions & Development
Penny Abraham, Ph.D.

Business Manager Catherine Charles
Head Librarian Elizabeth Mathew
Teaching staff Full time 46; Part time 6; Total 52
Nationalities of teaching staff US 5; UK 2;
Indian 29; Other(s) 16

INFORMATION

Grade levels PreK–12
School year September–June
School type boarding, coeducational, day, proprietary
Year founded 1997
Governed by appointed Board of Directors
Sponsored by Sastri Family
Regional organizations ECIS
Enrollment PreK 7; Elementary K–5 195; Middle School 6–8 78; High School 9–12 118; Total 398
Nationalities of student body US 82; UK 22; Indian 44; Other(s) 250

Tuition/fee currency Indian Rupee
Tuition 450,000–450,000
Annual fees Boarding, 7-day 190,000;
Busing 12,000; IB 15,000; Lab 8,000
One time fees Registration 20,000;
Books 35,000
Boarding program grades 7–12
Boys 15 **Girls** 4
Graduates attending college 100%
Graduates have attended U of California in Los Angeles, Johns Hopkins U, Boston U, McGill U, London School of Economics

EDUCATIONAL PROGRAM

Curriculum National, IB Diploma, Ontario Ministry Education
Average class size Elementary 20; Secondary 20
Language(s) of instruction English
Language(s) taught French, Spanish, German, Hindi
Staff specialists computer, counselor, ESL, librarian, nurse, psychologist
Special curricular programs art, vocal music, computer/technology, physical education

Extra curricular programs computers, community service, dance, drama, environmental conservation, excursions/expeditions, literary magazine, newspaper, yearbook
Sports baseball, basketball, cricket, football, hockey, rugby, soccer, swimming, track and field, volleyball
Clubs Model UN, horseback riding, math, computer, cookery, fitness, yearbook
Examinations IB, PSAT, SAT, OSSD/Certificate

CAMPUS FACILITIES

Location Suburban
Campus 7 hectares, 4 buildings, 26 classrooms, 2 computer labs, 40 instructional computers,

12,000 library volumes, 1 auditorium, 1 cafeteria, 1 covered play area, 1 infirmary, 1 playing field, 3 science labs, 1 pool

AMERICAN INTERNATIONAL SCHOOL– CHENNAI

Phone	91 44 2254 9000
Fax	91 44 2254 9001
Email	headofschool@aisch.org
Website	www.aisch.org
Address	100 Feet Road, Taramani, Chennai, Tamil Nadu, 600 113, India

STAFF

Head of School Barry L. Clough
Principal of Elementary and High Schools
James R. Fellabaum, Ed.D.
Principal of Middle School Michele Dirksen
Guidance Counselor Karen Kinsella
Elementary Curriculum Coordinator Marci Carrel

Finance Manager Seetha Lakshmi
Director of Information Technology Frank Gardner
Head Librarian K. P. Indrasimhan
Teaching staff Full time 58; Part time 1; Total 59
Nationalities of teaching staff US 18; UK 3;
Indian 30; Other(s) (French) 8

INFORMATION

Grade levels PreK–12
School year August–June
School type coeducational, day, private non-profit
Year founded 1995
Governed by appointed and elected Board of
Directors
Accredited by CIS, Middle States
Regional organizations ECIS, NESA
Enrollment PreK 40; Elementary K–5 202;
Middle School 6–8 94; High School 9–12 124;
Total 460

Nationalities of student body US 95; UK 17;
Indian 48; Other(s) (Korean, Japanese) 300
Tuition/fee currency US Dollar
Tuition range 3,350–17,750
One time fees Registration 3,000;
Capital Levy 1,000
Graduates attending college 99%
Graduates have attended McGill U,
Pennsylvania State U, Purdue U, George
Washington U, Rutgers U

EDUCATIONAL PROGRAM

Curriculum US, Intl, AP, IB Diploma
Average class size Elementary 15; Secondary 8
Language(s) of instruction English
Language(s) taught French, Spanish
Staff specialists computer, counselor, ESL, learning
disabilities, librarian, math resource, nurse
Special curricular programs art, instrumental
music, vocal music, computer/technology,
physical education

Extra curricular programs computers, community
service, dance, drama, excursions/expeditions,
newspaper, photography, yearbook
Sports badminton, basketball, martial arts,
rugby, soccer, swimming, tennis, track and
field, volleyball
Clubs student council, chess, computer, drama,
SAT math
Examinations AP, IB, Iowa, PSAT, SAT, TOEFL

CAMPUS FACILITIES

Location Suburban
Campus 4 hectares, 3 buildings, 44 classrooms,
2 computer labs, 169 instructional computers,
17,285 library volumes, 1 auditorium,

1 cafeteria, 1 covered play area, 1 gymnasium,
1 infirmary, 1 playing field, 4 science labs,
1 pool, 4 tennis courts, air conditioning

WOODSTOCK SCHOOL

Phone	91 135 263-5900
Fax	91 135 263-2885
Email	mail@woodstock.ac.in
Website	www.woodstock.ac.in
Address	Landour, Mussoorie, Uttarakhand, 248179, India

STAFF

Principal Kaye V. Aoki
Vice Principal Philip Jacob
Head of High School Chris Cooke
Head of Middle School Sanjaya Mark
ICT Director Jeff Rollins

School Librarian Susan Swanson
Teaching staff Full time 121; Part time 4; Total 125
Nationalities of teaching staff US 45; UK 4; Indian 55; Other(s) (Canadian, New Zealander) 21

INFORMATION

Grade levels PreK–12
School year July–June
School type boarding, coeducational, day, private non-profit
Year founded 1854
Governed by appointed Board of Directors
Accredited by Middle States
Regional organizations ECIS, NESA
Enrollment PreK 5; Elementary K–5 80; Middle School 6–8 140; High School 9–12 275; Total 500

Nationalities of student body US 55; UK 10; Indian 245; Other(s) (Korean, Nepalese) 190
Tuition/fee currency US Dollar
Tuition range 13,250–16,250
One time fees Capital Levy 1,100
Boarding program grades 3–12
Boarding program length 7-day **Boys** 215 **Girls** 200
Graduates attending college 95%
Graduates have attended New York U, Columbia U, U of Warwick, McGill U, Webster U

EDUCATIONAL PROGRAM

Curriculum US, UK, National, AP, IGCSE
Average class size Elementary 15; Secondary 20
Language(s) of instruction English
Language(s) taught French, Hindi
Staff specialists computer, counselor, ESL, learning disabilities, librarian, nurse
Special curricular programs art, instrumental music, vocal music, computer/technology, physical education

Extra curricular programs community service, drama, environmental conservation, excursions/expeditions, newspaper, yearbook
Sports basketball, cricket, cross-country, hockey, soccer, track and field, volleyball
Examinations AP, GCSE, IGCSE, PSAT, SAT

CAMPUS FACILITIES

Location Rural
Campus 136 hectares, 12 buildings, 30 classrooms, 5 computer labs, 188 instructional computers, 40,000 library volumes,

3 auditoriums, 2 cafeterias, 1 covered play area, 1 gymnasium, 1 infirmary, 4 playing fields, 4 science labs, 1 pool, 2 tennis courts

INTERNATIONAL SCHOOL OF HYDERABAD

Phone	90 40 2335 1110
Fax	91 40 2339 5065
Email	ish@ishhyd.com
Website	www.ishhyd.com
Address	6-3-346, Road #1, Banjara Hills, Hyderabad, Andhra Pradesh, 500034, India

STAFF

Principal Helge H. Gallinger
Secondary School Coordinator James Raw
Elementary School Coordinator Sunita Verghese
IB/IGCSE Coordinator Vasundhara Bhalla
Accountant Hanumanth Rao

Technology Teacher Rama Kumar
Teaching staff Full time 27; Part time 10; Total 37
Nationalities of teaching staff US 3; UK 4; Indian 20; Other(s) (Australian, Canadian) 10

INFORMATION

Grade levels N–12
School year August–June
School type coeducational, company-sponsored, day, private non-profit
Year founded 1982
Governed by appointed and elected Advisory Board
Sponsored by ICRISAT
Accredited by CIS, New England
Regional organizations NESA

Enrollment Nursery 15; PreK 15; Elementary K–5 87; Middle School 6–8 32; High School 9–12 28; Total 177
Nationalities of student body US 46; UK 36; Indian 27; Other(s) (Malaysian, French) 68
Tuition/fee currency Indian Rupee
Tuition range 195,000–390,000
One time fees Registration 4,000; Capital Levy 85,000

EDUCATIONAL PROGRAM

Curriculum Intl, IB Diploma, IGCSE
Average class size Elementary 15; Secondary 10
Language(s) of instruction English
Language(s) taught French
Staff specialists computer, counselor, ESL, learning disabilities, librarian, nurse, psychologist
Special curricular programs art, instrumental music, vocal music, computer/technology, physical education

Extra curricular programs computers, community service, dance, drama, environmental conservation, excursions/expeditions, newspaper, yearbook
Sports badminton, baseball, basketball, cricket, cross-country, football, golf, hockey, martial arts, soccer, squash, swimming, tennis, track and field, volleyball
Examinations GCSE, IB, IGCSE

CAMPUS FACILITIES

Location Urban
Campus 11 hectares, 5 buildings, 29 classrooms, 2 computer labs, 45 instructional computers, 25,000 library volumes, 2 auditoriums, 2 cafeterias, 1 covered play area, 1 gymnasium, 2 infirmaries, 4 playing fields, 3 science labs, 1 pool, 3 tennis courts, air conditioning

KODAIKANAL INTERNATIONAL SCHOOL

Phone	91 4542 247 500
Fax	91 4542 241 109
Email	contact@kis.in
Website	www.kis.in
Address	Seven Roads Junction, PO Box 25, Kodaikanal, Tamil Nadu, 624 101, India

STAFF

Principal Arthur Geoffrey F. Fisher
Academic Vice Principal Greg Faddegon
High School Coordinator Margaret Das
Middle School Coordinator Asha Hariharan
Elementary School Coordinator Brian Nelsen
Dean of Students Garry DeJong

Finance Director Samraj Ganga Christus, Ph.D.
Information Systems Manager Rudy Wuthrich
Head Librarian S. P. Pawate
Teaching staff Full time 70; Part time 10; Total 80
Nationalities of teaching staff US 14; UK 3; Indian 47; Other(s) (Canadian, Australian) 16

INFORMATION

Grade levels N–12
School year July–May
School type boarding, coeducational, private non-profit
Year founded 1901
Governed by elected Association and Council of Directors
Accredited by Middle States
Regional organizations NESA
Enrollment Nursery 8; Elementary K–5 53; Middle School 6–8 105; High School 9–12 318; Total 484

Nationalities of student body US 41; UK 17; Indian 245; Other(s) (Korean, Bhutanese) 181
Tuition/fee currency US Dollar
Tuition range 698–6,395
Annual fees Boarding, 7-day 8,606; Lunch 465; Additional Music Tuition 140
One time fees Registration 70; Capital Levy 1,163
Boarding program grades 4–12
Boarding program length 7-day **Boys** 182 **Girls** 170
Graduates attending college 100%
Graduates have attended Massachusetts Institute of Technology, Stanford U, London School of Economics, U of Sydney, McGill U

(Continued)

KODAIKANAL INTERNATIONAL SCHOOL (Continued)

EDUCATIONAL PROGRAM

Curriculum US, Intl, IB Diploma, IBMYP
Average class size Elementary 15; Secondary 22
Language(s) of instruction English
Language(s) taught French, German, Spanish, Tamil, Hindi, Dzongkha
Staff specialists computer, counselor, ESL, learning disabilities, librarian, nurse, physician, reading resource
Special curricular programs art, instrumental music, vocal music, computer/technology, physical education

Extra curricular programs computers, community service, dance, drama, environmental conservation, excursions/expeditions, newspaper, photography, yearbook
Sports badminton, baseball, basketball, cricket, cross-country, football, golf, gymnastics, hockey, soccer, softball, squash, tennis, track and field, volleyball
Clubs video production, table tennis, movie, frisbee, hip-hop, canoe, chess
Examinations ACT, IB, Iowa, PSAT, SAT, SAT II, TOEFL, SSAT, RSM, BMAT

CAMPUS FACILITIES

Location Rural
Campus 62 hectares, 169 buildings, 80 classrooms, 5 computer labs, 225 instructional computers,

42,228 library volumes, 4 auditoriums, 3 cafeterias, 3 covered play areas, 1 gymnasium, 1 infirmary, 3 playing fields, 6 science labs, 10 tennis courts

THE AMERICAN SCHOOL OF BOMBAY

Phone	91 22 2652 1111
Fax	91 22 2652 1234
Email	ASB@asbindia.org
Website	www.asbindia.org
Address	SF2, G Block, Bandra Kurla Complex Road, Bandra East, Mumbai, Maharashtra, 400 098, India
Mailing address	Management Officer, American School of Bombay, 6240 Mumbai Place, Washington, DC 20521-6240, USA

STAFF

Superintendent Paul M. Fochtman, Ed.D.
High School Principal Devin Pratt
Middle School Principal Andrew Hoover
Elementary School Principal Joe Atherton
Director of Special Projects Joseph Cubas
High School Counselor Bernie Longboy

Director Finance and Operations Joydeep Kar
Director of Technology Shabbi Luthra, Ph.D.
Head Librarian Ann Krembs
Teaching staff Full time 70; Part time 2; Total 72
Nationalities of teaching staff US 38; UK 2; Indian 22; Other(s) (Canadian, New Zealander) 10

INFORMATION

Grade levels PreK–12
School year August–July
School type coeducational, day, private non-profit
Year founded 1981
Governed by elected Board of Trustees
Sponsored by Embassy of the U.S.A.
Accredited by Middle States
Regional organizations ECIS, NESA
Enrollment PreK 48; Elementary K–5 306; Middle School 6–8 160; High School 9–12 190; Total 704

Nationalities of student body US 180; UK 70; Indian 100; Other(s) (Australian, French) 354
Tuition/fee currency US Dollar
Tuition range 5,000–21,280
Annual fees Capital Levy 20,000
One time fees Registration 200
Graduates attending college 99%
Graduates have attended U of Pennsylvania, U of Michigan, U of Wisconsin Madison, Emory U, U of Virginia

EDUCATIONAL PROGRAM

Curriculum US, AP, IB Diploma, IBPYP
Average class size Elementary 18; Secondary 18
Language(s) of instruction English
Language(s) taught French, Spanish
Staff specialists computer, counselor, ESL, learning disabilities, librarian, nurse
Special curricular programs art, instrumental music, vocal music, computer/technology, physical education

Extra curricular programs computers, community service, drama, excursions/expeditions, yearbook
Sports badminton, gymnastics, martial arts, soccer, swimming, tennis, track and field, volleyball, climbing, table tennis
Examinations ACT, IB, Iowa, PSAT, SAT, SAT II

CAMPUS FACILITIES

Location Suburban
Campus 1 hectare, 1 building, 86 classrooms, 2 computer labs, 450 instructional computers, 25,000 library volumes, 1 auditorium, 1 cafeteria, 1 covered play area, 1 gymnasium, 1 infirmary, 1 playing field, 6 science labs, 2 pools, 2 tennis courts, air conditioning

AMERICAN EMBASSY SCHOOL

Phone	91 11 2688 8854
Fax	91 11 2687 3320
Email	aesindia@aes.ac.in
Website	www.aes.ac.in
Address	Chandragupta Marg, Chanakyapuri, New Delhi, 110021, India
Mailing address	Dept. of State/AES, 9000 New Delhi Place, Washington, DC 20521-9000

STAFF

Director Robert W. Hetzel, Ph.D.
High School Principal Uwe Bagnato
Middle School Principal Barbara Sirotin, Ed.D.
Elementary School Principal Susan Young
Curriculum Coordinator Jan Patten
Admissions Director Beth Miller-Manchester
Business Manager Martin Tromburg

Director of Educational Technology Warren Apel
Middle School and High School Librarian Melinda Kehe
Teaching staff Full time 143; Part time 18; Total 161
Nationalities of teaching staff US 124; UK 8; Indian 20; Other(s) (Canadian) 9

INFORMATION

Grade levels PreK–12
School year August–May
School type coeducational, day, private non-profit
Year founded 1952
Governed by elected Board of Governors
Accredited by Middle States
Regional organizations NESA
Enrollment PreK 60; Elementary K–5 648; Middle School 6–8 300; High School 9–12 370; Total 1,378

Nationalities of student body US 482; UK 124; Indian 41; Other(s) (Canadian) 731
Tuition/fee currency US Dollar
Tuition range 5,850–16,000
Annual fees Busing 890; Lunch 360
One time fees Registration 5,750; Application 200
Graduates attending college 93%
Graduates have attended Boston U, Brown U, George Washington U, New York U, U of Virginia

EDUCATIONAL PROGRAM

Curriculum US, AP, IB Diploma
Average class size Elementary 18; Secondary 18
Language(s) of instruction English
Language(s) taught Spanish, French
Staff specialists computer, counselor, ESL, learning disabilities, librarian, nurse, physician, psychologist, reading resource
Special curricular programs art, instrumental music, vocal music, computer/technology, physical education

Extra curricular programs computers, community service, dance, drama, environmental conservation, excursions/expeditions, literary magazine, newspaper, photography, yearbook
Sports badminton, baseball, basketball, cricket, soccer, softball, swimming, tennis, track and field, volleyball
Clubs chess, fitness, gamers, rock climbing, Amnesty International, Reach Out
Examinations ACT, AP, IB, Iowa, PSAT, SAT, SAT II

CAMPUS FACILITIES

Location Urban
Campus 13.8 hectares, 11 buildings, 100 classrooms, 31 computer labs, 568 instructional computers, 66,501 library volumes,

1 auditorium, 2 cafeterias, 1 gymnasium, 1 infirmary, 3 playing fields, 8 science labs, 3 pools, 5 tennis courts, air conditioning

INDONESIA

Area:	1,919,440 sq km
Population:	234,693,997
Capital:	Jakarta
Currency:	Indonesian Rupiah (IDR)
Languages:	Bahasa Indonesia

BALI INTERNATIONAL SCHOOL

Phone	62 361 288 770
Fax	62 361 285 103
Email	hkanan@baliis.net
Website	www.baliinternationalschool.com
Address	Jl. Danau Buyan IV #15, Sanur, Bali, Indonesia
Mailing address	PO Box 3259, Denpasar, Bali, Indonesia

STAFF

Director Hana Kanan, Ed.D.
Assistant Administrator Riki Teteina
High School Academic Coordinator Russell McGrath
Guidance Counselor Alfonso de Falco
Network Engineer Franky Edwin
Executive Secretary Lea Widiarti
Business Manager Anna Waruwu

MYP Coordinator Werner Paetzold
Librarian Kathryn Bruce
Teaching staff Full time 33; Part time 2; Total 35
Nationalities of teaching staff US 2; UK 3; Indonesian 3; Other(s) (Australian, New Zealander) 27

INFORMATION

Grade levels PreK–12
School year August–June
School type coeducational, day, private non-profit
Year founded 1986
Governed by elected Eight Member School Board
Accredited by Western
Regional organizations EARCOS, ECIS
Enrollment PreK 18; Elementary K–5 111; Middle School 6–8 87; High School 9–12 106; Total 322

Nationalities of student body US 44; UK 29; Indonesian 26; Other(s) (Australian, French) 223
Tuition/fee currency US Dollar
Tuition range 4,284–10,732
Annual fees Capital Levy 900
One time fees Registration 500
Graduates attending college 100%
Graduates have attended U of Heidelberg, U of Technology in Sydney, Wesleyan Col, International U of Bremen

EDUCATIONAL PROGRAM

Curriculum Intl, IB Diploma, IBPYP, IBMYP
Average class size Elementary 18; Secondary 20
Language(s) of instruction English
Language(s) taught Indonesian, French
Staff specialists computer, counselor, ESL librarian, math resource, nurse, reading resource
Special curricular programs art, instrumental music, vocal music, computer/technology, physical education

Extra curricular programs community service, dance, drama, environmental conservation, newspaper
Sports badminton, basketball, football, gymnastics, martial arts, rugby, soccer, softball, swimming, tennis, track and field, volleyball
Examinations IB, PSAT, SAT, SAT II

CAMPUS FACILITIES

Location Suburban
Campus 3 hectares, 10 buildings, 18 classrooms, 2 computer labs, 110 instructional computers, 31,518 library volumes, 1 auditorium, 1 covered play area, 1 gymnasium, 1 infirmary, 2 playing fields, 2 science labs, 1 pool, 2 tennis courts, air conditioning

PASIR RIDGE INTERNATIONAL SCHOOL

Phone	62 542 543 474
Fax	62 542 767 126
Email	rickbowden@chevron.com
Address	Chevron Indonesia Company, Pasir Ridge, PO Box 276, Balikpapan, East Kalimantan, 76102, Indonesia

STAFF

Director Richard J. Bowden
Head of Technology Larry Brown

Head of Library Brent Fullerton
Teaching staff Full time 15; Part time 3; Total 18

INFORMATION

Grade levels PreK–8
School year August–June
School type coeducational, company-sponsored, day
Year founded 1975
Governed by Chevron Pacific Indonesia

Sponsored by Chevron Pacific Indonesia; Managed by International Schools Services, Inc.
Accredited by Western
Regional organizations EARCOS
Tuition/fee currency US Dollar

EDUCATIONAL PROGRAM

Curriculum US, Intl
Average class size Elementary 9; Secondary 5
Language(s) of instruction English
Language(s) taught Bahasa, French
Staff specialists computer, librarian

Special curricular programs art, vocal music, computer/technology, physical education
Extra curricular programs community service, dance, drama, excursions/expeditions
Sports baseball, basketball, football, golf, martial arts, soccer, squash, swimming, tennis

CAMPUS FACILITIES

Location Urban
Campus 3 hectares, 5 buildings, 12 classrooms, 1 computer lab, 60 instructional computers, 17,000 library volumes, 1 auditorium,

1 cafeteria, 1 covered play area, 1 gymnasium, 1 playing field, 1 science lab, 1 pool, 4 tennis courts, air conditioning

BANDUNG ALLIANCE INTERNATIONAL SCHOOL

Phone	62 22 203 1844
Fax	62 22 203 4202
Email	info@baisedu.org
Website	www.baisedu.org
Address	Jalan Gunung Agung 14, Ciumbuleuit, Bandung, West Java, 40142, Indonesia

STAFF

Director/Principal Joseph W. Beeson II
Assistant Principal Jeannie Sung
Business Manager Welly Wijaya
System Administrator Tobin Schroeder

Librarian Karen Paese
Teaching staff Full time 29; Part time 2; Total 31
Nationalities of teaching staff US 23; UK 1; Indonesian 3; Other(s) (Canadian, French) 2

INFORMATION

Grade levels PreK–12
School year August–June
School type coeducational, day, private non-profit, proprietary
Year founded 1956
Governed by appointed NICS School Board
Sponsored by Network of International Christian Schools
Accredited by Western
Regional organizations EARCOS

Enrollment PreK 15; Elementary K–5 87; Middle School 6–8 49; High School 9–12 62; Total 213
Nationalities of student body US 72; UK 5; Indonesian 56; Other(s) (Korean, Canadian) 87
Tuition/fee currency US Dollar
Tuition range 2,722–9,600
Annual fees Capital Levy 800; Computer 375; Student Activity 125; Graduation 125
One time fees Registration 100
Graduates attending college 100%

EDUCATIONAL PROGRAM

Curriculum US, AP
Average class size Elementary 15; Secondary 15
Language(s) of instruction English
Language(s) taught Indonesian, French, Spanish, Latin, Mandarin
Staff specialists computer, counselor, ESL, librarian, nurse, speech/hearing

Special curricular programs art, instrumental music, computer/technology, physical education
Extra curricular programs dance, yearbook
Sports badminton, basketball, football, gymnastics, hockey, soccer, swimming, volleyball
Examinations ACT, AP, PSAT, SAT, SAT II, Stanford, TOEFL

CAMPUS FACILITIES

Location Rural
Campus 1 hectare, 5 buildings, 27 classrooms, 2 computer labs, 80 instructional computers,

16,000 library volumes, 1 auditorium, 1 cafeteria, 1 gymnasium, 1 infirmary, 1 playing field, 1 science lab

BANDUNG INTERNATIONAL SCHOOL

Phone   62 22 201 4995
Fax   62 22 201 2688
Email   bisadmin@bisdragons.com
Website   www.bisdragons.com
Address   Jl. Prof. Drg. Suria Sumantri no. 61, Bandung, West Java, 40164, Indonesia
Mailing address   PO Box 1167, Bandung 40011, West Java, Indonesia

STAFF

Head of School Oscar S. Nilsson, Ed.D.
Secondary Principal and IB Coordinator
Henri Bemelmans
Elementary Principal Angela Speirs
PYP Coordinator and Early Childhood Coordinator
Carren Barlow
College Guidance Counselor Jan Russell

Business Manager Pak Suwardi
IT Coordinator Rod Murphy
Librarian Any Fauzianie
Teaching staff Full time 25; Part time 5; Total 30
Nationalities of teaching staff US 5; UK 9;
Indonesian 4; Other(s) (Australian) 12

INFORMATION

Grade levels N–12
School year August–June
School type coeducational, day, private non-profit
Year founded 1972
Governed by elected Board of Directors
Accredited by CIS, New England
Regional organizations EARCOS
Enrollment Nursery 15; PreK 15;
Elementary K–5 100; Middle School 6–8 61;
High School 9–12 72; Total 263

Nationalities of student body US 20; UK 22;
Indonesian 50; Other(s) (Korean, Indian) 171
Tuition/fee currency US Dollar
Tuition range 3,700–10,700
Annual fees Capital Levy 1,250
One time fees Registration 100
Graduates attending college 100%
Graduates have attended American U of Paris,
U of New South Wales, U of Victoria, Boston U,
Kwansei Gakuin U

EDUCATIONAL PROGRAM

Curriculum Intl, IB Diploma, IBPYP
Average class size Elementary 15; Secondary 18
Language(s) of instruction English
Language(s) taught Indonesian, French, Mandarin
Staff specialists computer, counselor, ESL,
learning disabilities, librarian, nurse
Special curricular programs art, instrumental
music, computer/technology, physical education

Extra curricular programs computers, community
service, dance, drama, environmental
conservation, excursions/expeditions, literary
magazine, newspaper, photography, yearbook
Sports badminton, basketball, cricket, football,
gymnastics, hockey, martial arts, soccer,
softball, squash, swimming, tennis, track and
field, volleyball
Examinations ACT, AP, IB, PSAT, SAT, SAT II, TOEFL

CAMPUS FACILITIES

Location Suburban
Campus 2 hectares, 8 buildings, 25 classrooms,
2 computer labs, 60 instructional computers,

15,000 library volumes, 1 auditorium,
1 cafeteria, 1 covered play area, 1 infirmary,
1 playing field, 2 science labs, 1 pool

PENABUR INTERNATIONAL SCHOOL

Phone 62 22 4217792
Email Cynthia@bpkpenabur.or.id
Website www.bpkpenabur-bdg.sch.id/intschool
Address Jl. Banda no.19, Bandung, Jawa Barat, Indonesia

STAFF

Executive Director Jason A. Gaunt
Principal Cynthia Uri
Assistant Principal Fransisca

Curriculum Coordinator Veronica
Teaching staff Full time 41; Part time 8; Total 49

INFORMATION

Grade levels N–1
School year July–June
School type church-affiliated, private non-profit
Governed by GKI Foundation
Regional organizations EARCOS

Enrollment Nursery 30; PreK 40;
Elementary K–5 90; Total 160
Tuition/fee currency US Dollar
Tuition range 2,142–2,448
Annual fees Lunch 245; Uniforms 450
One time fees Registration 2,806; Books 50

EDUCATIONAL PROGRAM

Curriculum IBPYP
Average class size Elementary 23
Language(s) of instruction English
Language(s) taught Mandarin
Staff specialists ESL, physician

Special curricular programs art, vocal music,
physical education
Extra curricular programs dance
Examinations IB

CAMPUS FACILITIES

Location Urban
Campus 1 auditorium, 1 cafeteria,

1 covered play area, 1 gymnasium, 1 infirmary,
1 science lab, 1 pool

INTERNATIONAL SCHOOL OF BOGOR

Phone	62 251 324 360
Fax	62 251 328 512
Email	isb@isbogor.org
Website	www.isbogor.org
Address	Jl Papandayan 7, PO Box 258, Jl Papandayan No 7, Bogor, West Java, 16151, Indonesia

STAFF

Principal Christine E. Rawlins
PYP Coordinator Lizette Turnbull, Ed.D.
IT and Sports Coordinator Simon Turnbull, Ed.D.
Early Childhood Coordinator Edna Olaso, Ed.D.
Office Manager Yulianti Agustina

Technology Coordinator Simon Turnbull, Ed.D.
Library Instructor and Technician Ibu Lesmina Sari
Teaching staff Full time 8; Part time 2; Total 10
Nationalities of teaching staff Indonesian 4; Other(s) (Australian, New Zealander) 6

INFORMATION

Grade levels N–8
School year August–June
School type coeducational, day, private non-profit
Year founded 1974
Governed by elected Board
Regional organizations EARCOS
Enrollment Nursery 5; PreK 20; Elementary K–5 51; Middle School 6–8 8; Total 84

Nationalities of student body Indonesian 20; Other(s) (Canadian, Australian) 64
Tuition/fee currency US Dollar
Tuition range 1,900–9,500
Annual fees Capital Levy 500
One time fees Registration 100

EDUCATIONAL PROGRAM

Curriculum IBPYP
Average class size Elementary 13–18
Language(s) of instruction English
Language(s) taught Indonesian, French, Mandarin, Spanish
Staff specialists ESL, librarian

Special curricular programs art, instrumental music, vocal music, computer/technology, physical education
Extra curricular programs computers, community service, dance, drama, photography
Sports basketball, cricket, martial arts, soccer, swimming, volleyball
Examinations ISA

CAMPUS FACILITIES

Location Urban
Campus 1 hectare, 2 buildings, 8 classrooms, 30 instructional computers,

10,000 library volumes, 1 auditorium, 1 covered play area, 1 playing field, 1 science lab, air conditioning

THE BRITISH INTERNATIONAL SCHOOL

Phone	62 21 745 1670
Fax	62 21 745 1671
Email	Enquiries@bis.or.id
Website	www.bis.or.id
Address	JL Raya Jombang Ciledug, Bintaro Jaya Sektor 9, Pondok Aren, Jakarta, 15227, Indonesia
Mailing address	PO Box 4120 CPA POE, Ciputat 15224, Jakarta, Indonesia

STAFF

CEO and Principal Peter J. Derby-Crook
Head of Secondary School Thomas Sherrington
Head of Primary School Kevin Rae
Head of Academics Paul Starkie
Business Administration Director John Slack

Head of Art and Technology Katie Deacon
Head of Library Services Monica Mayers
Teaching staff Full time 100; Part time 15; Total 115
Nationalities of teaching staff UK 70; Indonesian 15; Other(s) 30

INFORMATION

Grade levels N–13
School year September–July
School type coeducational, day, private non-profit
Year founded 1973
Governed by elected Board of Governors
Accredited by CIS
Regional organizations ECIS
Enrollment Nursery 21; PreK 68; Elementary K–5 449; Middle School 6–8 279; High School 9–12 311; Grade 13 58; Total 1,186

Nationalities of student body US 25; UK 280; Indonesian 300; Other(s) (Korean, Australian) 581
Tuition/fee currency US Dollar
Tuition range 6,100–14,970
Annual fees Capital Levy 3,000; Busing 1,692
One time fees Registration 150
Graduates attending college 100%
Graduates have attended Oxford U, Imperial Col, London School of Economics, Monash U, U of London

EDUCATIONAL PROGRAM

Curriculum UK, Intl, IB Diploma, IGCSE
Average class size Elementary 18; Secondary 20
Language(s) of instruction English
Language(s) taught French, German, Indonesian, Spanish, Japanese
Staff specialists computer, ESL, librarian

Extra curricular programs computers, dance, drama
Sports badminton, basketball, football, gymnastics, soccer, swimming, tennis, volleyball
Examinations A-level GCE, GCSE, IB, IGCSE, SAT, SAT II

CAMPUS FACILITIES

Location Suburban
Campus 18 hectares, 8 computer labs, 350 instructional computers, 39,000 library volumes, 1 auditorium, 1 cafeteria,

2 gymnasiums, 3 infirmaries, 5 playing fields, 8 science labs, 2 pools, 3 tennis courts, air conditioning

JAKARTA INTERNATIONAL SCHOOL

Phone	62 21 769 2555
Fax	62 21 765 7852
Email	jcornacchio@jisedu.or.id
Website	www.jisedu.org
Address	Jalan Terogong Raya 33, Cilandak, Jakarta, 12430, Indonesia
Mailing address	PO Box 1078 JKS, Jakarta 12010, Indonesia

STAFF

Head of School David P. Cramer, Ed.D.
Deputy Head of School Ian H. Deakin
High School Principal Timothy S. Stuart, Ed.D.
Middle School Principal Geoffrey L. Smith
Pondok Indah Elementary Principal Diann D. Osterlund
Pattimura Elementary Principal Paul M. Buckley
Business Manager Guy M. Robinson

Technology Director Joseph A. Cornacchio
Middle School Librarian Kate Hodgson
Teaching staff Full time 173; Part time 26; Total 199
Nationalities of teaching staff US 95; UK 20; Indonesian 12; Other(s) (Australian, Canadian) 72

INFORMATION

Grade levels PreK–13
School year August–June
School type coeducational, day, private non-profit
Year founded 1951
Governed by elected School Council
Accredited by CIS, Western
Regional organizations EARCOS, ECIS, NESA
Enrollment PreK 96; Elementary K–5 831; Middle School 6–8 567; High School 9–12 990; Grade 13 2; Total 2,486

Nationalities of student body US 522; UK 75; Indonesian 398; Other(s) (Korean, Australian) 1,491
Tuition/fee currency US Dollar
Tuition range 12,500–17,300
Annual fees Capital Levy 3,000; Busing 1,800; Facilities 1,000
One time fees Registration 100
Graduates attending college 95%
Graduates have attended Columbia U, Princeton U, Cambridge U, Seoul National U, U of Melbourne

(Continued)

JAKARTA INTERNATIONAL SCHOOL (Continued)

EDUCATIONAL PROGRAM

Curriculum Intl, AP, IB Diploma
Average class size Elementary 18; Secondary 19
Language(s) of instruction English
Language(s) taught Dutch, German, Korean, Japanese, Spanish, Indonesian, French, Mandarin
Staff specialists computer, counselor, ESL, learning disabilities, librarian, math resource, nurse, psychologist, reading resource, speech/hearing
Special curricular programs art, instrumental music, vocal music, computer/technology, physical education, vocational

Extra curricular programs computers, community service, dance, drama, environmental conservation, excursions/expeditions, literary magazine, photography, yearbook
Sports badminton, basketball, cross-country, rugby, soccer, softball, swimming, tennis, track and field, volleyball
Clubs French, world cinema, Emmanuel's, Books on Wheels, magic, basketball, badminton, ski/snowboard camp, rock climbing, international travel
Examinations ACT, AP, IB, PSAT, SAT, TOEFL, International Schools Assessment

CAMPUS FACILITIES

Location Suburban
Campus 19 hectares, 46 buildings, 206 classrooms, 7 computer labs, 593 instructional computers, 100,000 library volumes,

4 auditoriums, 3 cafeterias, 4 gymnasiums, 4 infirmaries, 5 playing fields, 19 science labs, 3 pools, 3 tennis courts, air conditioning

THE NEW ZEALAND
INTERNATIONAL SCHOOL

Phone	62 21 788 41225
Fax	62 21 780 5541
Email	principal@nzis.net
Website	www.nzis.net
Address	Jalan Benda No 78, Kemang Jakarta Selatan, Jakarta, 12710, Indonesia

STAFF

Principal Linda M. Holdaway-Howard
Head of Primary Campus Raewyn Ashby
Head of Secondary Campus Michael Morey

Teaching staff Full time 14; Part time 4; Total 18
Nationalities of teaching staff US 3; UK 1; New Zealander 5; Other(s) (Australian, Indonesian) 9

INFORMATION

Grade levels K–13
School year January–December
School type coeducational, day
Year founded 2002
Governed by appointed Foundation
Sponsored by NZIS, Auckland
Enrollment PreK 20; Elementary K–5 80; Middle School 6–8 50; High School 9–12 54; Grade 13 6; Total 210

Nationalities of student body US 20; UK 20; Indonesian 40; Other(s) (New Zealander, Australian) 130
Tuition/fee currency US Dollar
Tuition range 4,800–13,500
Annual fees Busing 2,200
One time fees Registration 150
Graduates attending college 100%
Graduates have attended Auckland U, U of Papua New Guinea, U of London

EDUCATIONAL PROGRAM

Curriculum Intl, IGCSE, GenCSE, New Zealand
Average class size Elementary 15; Secondary 12
Language(s) of instruction English
Language(s) taught Indonesian, Mandarin, French
Staff specialists computer, ESL, learning disabilities, librarian, math resource, nurse, reading resource
Special curricular programs art, computer/technology

Extra curricular programs computers, dance, drama, excursions/expeditions, yearbook, dance, Tae Kwon Do, arts and crafts, cooking, swimming, sports, chess, drawing, Mad Science
Sports badminton, basketball, martial arts, rugby, soccer, swimming, tennis, volleyball
Examinations A-level GCE, GCSE, IGCSE, ICAS

CAMPUS FACILITIES

Location Suburban
Campus 1 hectare, 4 buildings, 17 classrooms, 2 computer labs, 32 instructional computers,

1 auditorium, 2 cafeterias, 1 covered play area, 1 infirmary, 1 science lab, 1 pool, 2 tennis courts, air conditioning

NORTH JAKARTA INTERNATIONAL SCHOOL

Phone	62 21 450 0683
Fax	62 21 450 0682
Email	info@njis.or.id
Website	www.njis.org
Address	Jalan Raya Kelapa Nias, Kelapa Gading Permai, PO Box 6759-JKUKP, Jakarta, 14250, Indonesia

STAFF

Head of School Samuel D. Cook
Deputy Head of School Barbara Forslund
Director of Admission Anna Rangkuti
Director of Finance and Operations Kristy D. Seng
Technology Coordinator Brandon Hoover

Librarian Laura Wray
Teaching staff Full time 34; Total 34
Nationalities of teaching staff US 17; UK 1; Indonesian 3; Other(s) (Canadian, South African) 13

INFORMATION

Grade levels PreK–10
School year August–June
School type coeducational, day, private non-profit
Year founded 1990
Governed by appointed Board of Governors
Sponsored by International School Development Foundation
Accredited by Western
Regional organizations EARCOS

Enrollment PreK 6; Elementary K–5 145; Middle School 6–8 126; High School 9–12 20; Total 297
Nationalities of student body US 12; UK 3; Indonesian 89; Other(s) (Korean, Indian) 193
Tuition/fee currency US Dollar
Tuition range 7,350–12,700
Annual fees Capital Levy 2,500; Busing 1,500
One time fees Registration 100

EDUCATIONAL PROGRAM

Curriculum US, Intl
Average class size Elementary 16; Secondary 18
Language(s) of instruction English
Language(s) taught French, Bahasa, Mandarin
Staff specialists computer, ESL, librarian, nurse
Special curricular programs art, instrumental music, vocal music, computer/technology, physical education

Extra curricular programs computers, community service, drama, environmental conservation, excursions/expeditions, literary magazine, newspaper, yearbook, student council
Sports badminton, basketball, cricket, cross-country, football, golf, soccer, softball, squash, swimming, tennis, track and field, volleyball, climbing wall
Examinations International Schools Assessment

CAMPUS FACILITIES

Location Suburban
Campus 2 hectares, 7 buildings, 35 classrooms, 2 computer labs, 120 instructional computers, 16,000 library volumes, 1 auditorium, 1 cafeteria, 2 covered play areas, 1 gymnasium, 1 infirmary, 1 playing field, 2 science labs, 1 pool, air conditioning

Jayapura INDONESIA

HILLCREST INTERNATIONAL SCHOOL

Phone 62 967 591 460
Fax 62 967 591 673
Email director@hismk.org
Website www.hismk.org
Address Jalan HIS, Sentani, Papua, 99352, Indonesia
Mailing address PO Box 249, Sentani 99352, Papua, Indonesia

STAFF

Director Timothy Cripe
Principal Alyssa Taylor
Business/Finance Manager Michael Werner
Head of Technology Wes Gardner
Librarian Barbara Dukes

INFORMATION

Grade levels K–12
School year August–May
School type boarding, coeducational, day, private non-profit
Year founded 1987
Governed by elected Board
Accredited by Western
Regional organizations EARCOS
Enrollment Elementary K–5 60; Middle School 6–8 40; High School 9–12 55; Total 155

Nationalities of student body US 100; Indonesian 10; Other(s) (Korean, Dutch) 45
Tuition/fee currency US Dollar
Tuition range 1,200–6,250
Annual fees Boarding, 7-day 2,185–3,335; Capital Levy 50–3,000
Boarding program grades 6–12
Boarding program length 7-day **Boys** 8 **Girls** 10
Graduates attending college 92%
Graduates have attended LeTourneau U, Seattle Pacific U, North Carolina State U, Washington State U, Wheaton Col

EDUCATIONAL PROGRAM

Curriculum US, AP
Average class size Elementary 12; Secondary 15
Language(s) of instruction English
Language(s) taught Indonesian, French
Staff specialists computer, counselor, ESL, learning disabilities, librarian, nurse, physician, speech/hearing

Special curricular programs art, instrumental music, vocal music, computer/technology, physical education, vocational
Extra curricular programs community service, excursions/expeditions, yearbook
Sports basketball, football, soccer, track and field, volleyball
Examinations ACT, AP, PSAT, SAT, SAT II, Stanford, Otis-Lennon

CAMPUS FACILITIES

Location Suburban
Campus 12 hectares, 11 buildings, 20 classrooms, 2 computer labs, 40 instructional computers, 20,000 library volumes, 2 tennis courts, air conditioning

Data from 2006/07 school year.

271

Makassar International School

Phone	62 411 872 591
Fax	62 411 873 903
Email	mischool@indosat.net.id
Website	www.mi-school.org
Address	Jalan Kasuari No.15, Makassar, Sulawesi Selatan, 90125, Indonesia
Mailing address	PO Box 1327, Makassar, Sulawesi Selatan, Indonesia

STAFF

Principal Stephen James Keighran
Preschool and Kindergarten Teacher/Coordinator Maria Gayla G. Escanillas
Office Manager Joyce Gani

IT/CCA Coordinator Rhoderick F. Escanillas
Teaching staff Full time 7; Part time 1; Total 8
Nationalities of teaching staff Indonesian 5; Other(s) (Australian, Filipino) 3

INFORMATION

Grade levels PreK–9
School year August–June
School type coeducational, private non-profit
Year founded 1991
Governed by appointed Board of MIS
Regional organizations EARCOS

Enrollment PreK 10; Elementary K–5 16; Middle School 6–8 2; Total 28
Nationalities of student body Indonesian 25; Other(s) (Australian, Belgian) 3
Tuition/fee currency US Dollar
Tuition range 3,000–9,000
One time fees Registration 250

EDUCATIONAL PROGRAM

Curriculum Intl
Average class size Elementary 15
Language(s) of instruction English

Special curricular programs art, instrumental music, computer/technology
Extra curricular programs computers, excursions/expeditions, yearbook

CAMPUS FACILITIES

Location Urban
Campus 1 hectare, 1 building, 3 classrooms, 10 instructional computers,

5,027 library volumes, 1 playing field, 1 science lab, air conditioning

BATU HIJAU INTERNATIONAL SCHOOL

Phone   62 372 635318, ext. 48424
Fax   62 372 635399
Email   dave.forbes@newmont.com
Website   www.batuhijauschool.org
Address   Jl Raya Ketimus 387, Townsite, Batu Hijau Project, Sumbawa, NTB, Indonesia
Mailing address c/o Newmont Gold Company, PMB 1040, 8533 Church Ranch Blvd #150, Westminster, CO 80021-5541, USA

STAFF

Principal Dave Forbes
Vice Principal Sally Sar'i
Administration Manager Wiwit Tirayoh
Head of IT Bruce Pohlmann, Ph.D.
Head of Library Lorelle Peterson

Teaching staff Full time 10; Part time 2; Total 12
Nationalities of teaching staff US 2; UK 1; Indonesian 1; Other(s) (Australian, New Zealander) 8

INFORMATION

Grade levels PreK–8
School year July–June
School type coeducational, company-sponsored, day, private non-profit
Year founded 1997
Governed by appointed and elected School Board
Sponsored by PT Newmont
Accredited by CIS

Regional organizations EARCOS, ECIS
Enrollment PreK 6; Elementary K–5 40; Middle School 6–8 11; Total 57
Nationalities of student body US 15; Other(s) (Australian, Japanese) 42
Tuition/fee currency US Dollar
Tuition 18,000

EDUCATIONAL PROGRAM

Curriculum Intl
Average class size Elementary 10; Secondary 8
Language(s) of instruction English
Language(s) taught Bahasa, Indonesia
Extra curricular programs computers, community service, dance, drama, excursions/expeditions, newspaper

Sports badminton, baseball, basketball, cricket, football, golf, martial arts, rugby, soccer, swimming
Examinations Iowa, SAT

CAMPUS FACILITIES

Location Rural
Campus 2 hectares, 4 buildings, 10 classrooms, 1 computer lab, 40 instructional computers, 10,000 library volumes, 3 covered play areas,

1 gymnasium, 1 infirmary, 1 playing field, 1 science lab, 1 pool, 2 tennis courts, air conditioning

MEDAN INTERNATIONAL SCHOOL

Phone	62 61 836 1894
Fax	62 61 836 1894
Email	mndkirby@hotmail.com
Website	www.medanis.org
Address	Jl Letjend Jamin Ginting Km10, Medan, North Sumatra, Indonesia
Mailing address	PO Box 1190, Medan 20111, Indonesia

STAFF

Principal/Head of School Matthew N.D. Kirby
IB MYP Coordinator Lisa Kopf
IB PYP Coordinator Ashley Penny
Office Manager Pak Alpian Hasibuan

Librarian Wendy Lewis
Teaching staff Full time 11; Part time 2; Total 13
Nationalities of teaching staff US 3; UK 1;
Indonesian 4; Other(s) (Australian, Canadian) 4

INFORMATION

Grade levels PreK–10
School year August–June
School type coeducational, day, private non-profit
Year founded 1969
Governed by elected Board of Directors
Accredited by Western
Regional organizations EARCOS

Enrollment PreK 7; Elementary K–5 40;
Middle School 6–8 30; High School 9–12 10;
Total 87
Nationalities of student body US 5; UK 6;
Indonesian 19; Other(s) 57
Tuition/fee currency US Dollar
Tuition range 4,900–9,800
One time fees Registration 1,500

EDUCATIONAL PROGRAM

Curriculum US, Intl, IBPYP, IBMYP
Average class size Elementary 15; Secondary 13
Language(s) of instruction English
Language(s) taught Bahasa, French, Mandarin
Staff specialists computer, ESL, librarian
Special curricular programs art, computer/
technology, physical education

Extra curricular programs computers, community
service, drama, environmental conservation,
excursions/expeditions, newspaper, yearbook
Sports badminton, basketball, martial arts,
rugby, soccer, softball, swimming, track and
field, volleyball
Examinations ISA

CAMPUS FACILITIES

Location Suburban
Campus 2 hectares, 7 buildings, 14 classrooms,
3 computer labs, 30 instructional computers,
9,000 library volumes, 1 auditorium,
1 gymnasium, 1 playing field, 1 science lab,
2 pools, air conditioning

CALTEX AMERICAN SCHOOL

Phone	62 765 995 301
Fax	62 765 996 321
Email	jpdehner@yahoo.com
Address	PT Chevron Pacific Indonesia, Rumbai, Pekanbaru, 28271, Indonesia
Mailing address	c/o AMOSEAS (CAS-Duri or Rumbai), #1 Scotts Road, #22-07 Shaw Center, Singapore, 228208, Republic of Singapore

STAFF

Superintendent James Dehner
Teaching Principal Alba Carollo
Technology Coordinator –Duri Campus Dave Neudorf
Librarian–Duri Campus Connie Freeman

Teaching staff Full time 27; Total 27
Nationalities of teaching staff US 15; Canadian 2; Other(s) (Australian) 10

INFORMATION

Grade levels PreK–8
School year August–June
School type coeducational, company-sponsored, day
Year founded 1953
Governed by appointed and elected CPI Management

Sponsored by PT Chevron Pacific Indonesia; Managed by International Schools Services, Inc
Accredited by Western
Regional organizations EARCOS
Enrollment PreK 19; Elementary K–5 67; Middle School 6–8 34; Total 120
Nationalities of student body US 78; UK 10; Other(s) (Canadian, Filipino) 32

EDUCATIONAL PROGRAM

Curriculum US
Average class size Elementary 8; Secondary 7
Language(s) of instruction English
Language(s) taught Bahasa
Staff specialists computer, counselor, librarian

Special curricular programs instrumental music, vocal music, computer/technology, physical education
Extra curricular programs dance, drama, newspaper, photography, sports, Boy and Girl Scouts
Examinations Iowa

CAMPUS FACILITIES

Location Rural
Campus 5 hectares, 3 buildings, 22 classrooms, 2 computer labs, 143 instructional computers,

30,000 library volumes, 2 gymnasiums, 2 playing fields, 2 science labs

SURABAYA INTERNATIONAL SCHOOL

Phone	62 31 741 4300
Fax	62 31 741 4334
Email	suptsis@sisedu.net
Website	www.sisedu.net
Address	Citra Raya International Village, Tromol Pos 2/SBDK, Surabaya, East Java, 60225, Indonesia

STAFF

Superintendent Lawrence W. Jones
Elementary Principal Robert Broekman, Ed.D.
Counselor Gina Cuthbert
Middle School Coordinator Harold Brown
Middle School Coordinator and Athletic Director Jason Cuthbert

Senior Business Manager Hestiawati Soeharjono
Librarian Barbara Kieran
Teaching staff Full time 32; Total 32
Nationalities of teaching staff US 23; Indonesian 3; Other(s) (Indian, Australian) 6

INFORMATION

Grade levels N–12
School year August–June
School type coeducational, day, private non-profit
Year founded 1971
Governed by elected School Board
Accredited by Western
Regional organizations EARCOS
Enrollment Nursery 6; PreK 6; Elementary K–5 80; Middle School 6–8 55; High School 9–12 80; Total 227

Nationalities of student body US 11; UK 3; Indonesian 65; Other(s) (Indian, Korean) 148
Tuition/fee currency US Dollar
Tuition range 2,962–11,760
Annual fees Capital Levy 2,200
One time fees Registration 1,650
Graduates attending college 98%
Graduates have attended U of Virginia, U of Illinois, U of British Columbia, Rochester Institute of Technology, Carnegie Mellon U

EDUCATIONAL PROGRAM

Curriculum US, Intl, AP
Average class size Elementary 15; Secondary 17
Language(s) of instruction English
Language(s) taught French, Bahasa, Mandarin
Staff specialists counselor, ESL, librarian, nurse
Special curricular programs art, instrumental music, vocal music, computer/technology, physical education, drama , 1-1 laptop computing Gr. 6–12

Extra curricular programs computers, community service, drama, excursions/expeditions, literary magazine, yearbook
Sports badminton, basketball, soccer, swimming, volleyball
Clubs Model UN, National Junior Honor Society, National Honor Society, student government
Examinations ACT, AP, Iowa, PSAT, SAT, SAT II, TOEFL

CAMPUS FACILITIES

Location Suburban
Campus 5 hectares, 4 buildings, 54 classrooms, 4 computer labs, 170 instructional computers, 20,000 library volumes, 1 auditorium,

1 cafeteria, 1 covered play area, 1 gymnasium, 1 infirmary, 1 playing field, 3 science labs, 1 pool, air conditioning

MT. ZAAGHAM INTERNATIONAL SCHOOL

Phone	62 901 40761
Fax	62 901 403170
Email	Mel_Soffe@fmi.com
Website	mzis.org
Address	PT Freeport Indonesia, PO Box 7100, Tembagapura, Timika, Irian Jaya, 99930, Indonesia
Mailing address	c/o PT Freeport Indonesia, 5th Floor Jl H.R.Rasuna Said Kav., X-7 No 6 Jakarta 12940, Indonesia

STAFF

Superintendent Mel J. Soffe
Principal Richard Ledger
PYP Coordinator Susan Ledger
Consultant and Executive Chairman Joe Cuthbertson, Ph.D.
Manager Corporate Planning and Integration John Laing

Technology Coordinator Patrick MacCormick
Librarian Michael Monchlov
Teaching staff Full time 15; Part time 3; Total 18
Nationalities of teaching staff US 7; Indonesian 2; Other(s) (Australian, New Zealander) 9

INFORMATION

Grade levels N–8
School year August–June
School type coeducational, company-sponsored, day
Year founded 1972
Governed by appointed Company School
Sponsored by PT Freeport

Accredited by Western
Regional organizations EARCOS
Enrollment Nursery 8; PreK 12; Elementary K–5 59; Middle School 6–8 17; Total 96
Nationalities of student body US 26; UK 1; Other(s) (Australian, South African) 69
Tuition/fee currency US Dollar

EDUCATIONAL PROGRAM

Curriculum Intl, IBPYP
Average class size Elementary 7
Language(s) of instruction English
Language(s) taught Bahasa
Staff specialists computer, librarian
Special curricular programs instrumental music, vocal music, computer/technology

Extra curricular programs computers, community service, dance, drama, environmental conservation, excursions/expeditions, literary magazine, newspaper, yearbook
Sports basketball, golf, martial arts, soccer, softball, squash, swimming, tennis, track and field
Examinations Iowa, ACER ISA

CAMPUS FACILITIES

Location Rural
Campus 5 hectares, 4 buildings, 12 classrooms, 2 computer labs, 30 instructional computers, 25,000 library volumes, 2 covered play areas, 2 playing fields, 2 science labs, 2 pools, 4 tennis courts, air conditioning

YOGYAKARTA INTERNATIONAL SCHOOL

Phone	62 274 586 067
Fax	62 274 586 067
Email	info@yis-yog.sch.id
Website	www.yisedu.org
Address	Jl Kaliurang KM 5, Pogung Baru Block A-18, Yogyakarta, Yogyakarta Special Territory, 55284, Indonesia
Mailing address	PO BOX 1175, Yogyakarta 55011, Indonesia

STAFF

Principal Mark E. Massion
Administrator Supriyanto
IT Coordinator Singgih Puji Yuwono
Library Head Rahman

Teaching staff Full time 9; Total 9
Nationalities of teaching staff US 3;
Indonesian 5; Other(s) (Australian) 1

INFORMATION

Grade levels N–8
School year August–June
School type coeducational, day, private non-profit
Year founded 1989
Governed by elected School Board
Regional organizations EARCOS

Enrollment Nursery 4; PreK 2; Elementary K–5
30; Middle School 6–8 10; Total 46
Nationalities of student body US 4; Indonesian
10; Other(s) (Australian, Dutch) 32
Tuition/fee currency US Dollar
Tuition range 1,650–6,600
Annual fees ESL 400

EDUCATIONAL PROGRAM

Curriculum US, Intl, NSW
Average class size Elementary 12–15
Language(s) of instruction English
Language(s) taught Bahasa
Staff specialists computer, ESL, librarian

Special curricular programs art, instrumental
music, vocal music, computer/technology,
distance learning, physical education
Extra curricular programs dance, drama,
newspaper
Sports badminton, basketball, soccer, volleyball

CAMPUS FACILITIES

Location Suburban
Campus 3 buildings, 4 classrooms,
12 instructional computers,

3,000 library volumes, 2 covered play areas,
2 playing fields, 1 science lab, air conditioning

IRELAND

Area:	70,280 sq km
Population:	4,109,086
Capital:	Dublin
Currency:	Euro (EUR)
Languages:	English, Gaelic

ST. ANDREW'S COLLEGE

Phone	353 1 288 2785
Fax	353 1 283 1627
Email	information@st-andrews.ie
Website	www.st-andrews.ie
Address	Booterstown Avenue, Blackrock, Dublin, Ireland

STAFF

Head of School Arthur Godsil
Vice Principal Brendan McArdle
Vice Principal Ronnie Hay
Vice Principal Joan Kirby

Bursar Jonathan Taylor
IT Coordinator Geoffrey Reeves
Librarian Susan Miller

INFORMATION

Grade levels K–12
School year September–June
School type coeducational, church-affiliated, day
Year founded 1894
Governed by appointed Board
Accredited by CIS, New England
Regional organizations ECIS

Tuition/fee currency Euro
Tuition 4,015
One time fees Registration 95
Graduates attending college 99%
Graduates have attended Trinity Col Dublin, U Col Dublin, National U of Ireland

EDUCATIONAL PROGRAM

Curriculum National, IB Diploma
Average class size Elementary 20; Secondary 24
Language(s) of instruction English
Language(s) taught Irish, French, Spanish, German
Staff specialists computer, counselor, learning disabilities, librarian, math resource, nurse, reading resource
Special curricular programs art, instrumental music, vocal music, computer/technology, physical education

Extra curricular programs computers, drama, excursions/expeditions, literary magazine, newspaper, photography, yearbook
Sports badminton, basketball, cricket, football, golf, gymnastics, hockey, martial arts, rugby, skiing, soccer, swimming, tennis, track and field, volleyball
Examinations IB, SAT, Junior and Leaving Certificate

CAMPUS FACILITIES

Location Suburban
Campus 5 hectares, 1 building, 60 classrooms, 3 computer labs, 70 instructional computers,
10,000 library volumes, 1 auditorium, 1 cafeteria, 1 gymnasium, 1 infirmary, 4 playing fields, 4 science labs, 10 tennis courts

Data from 2006/07 school year.

Dublin **IRELAND**

SUTTON PARK SCHOOL

Phone	353 1 832 2940
Fax	353 1 832 5929
Email	info@sps.ie
Website	www.suttonparkschool.com
Address	St. Fintan's Road, Sutton, Dublin, 13, Ireland

STAFF

Head Of School Michael Moretta
Deputy Principal, Senior School Raymond Russell
Principal, Junior School Geraldine McGuire
Business Director Emer Crowley
Director of IT James Bramich

Chief Librarian Valerie Richmond
Teaching staff Full time 29; Part time 8; Total 37
Nationalities of teaching staff UK 6; Irish 28; Other(s) 8

INFORMATION

Grade levels K–13
School year September–June
School type boarding, coeducational, day, private non-profit
Year founded 1957
Governed by appointed Board of Governors
Accredited by CIS, New England
Regional organizations ECIS
Enrollment Nursery 18; PreK 18; Elementary K–5 18; Middle School 6–8 60; High School 9–12 290; Grade 13 50; Total 454

Tuition/fee currency Euro
Tuition range 5,460–7,970
Annual fees Boarding, 7-day 14,500; Busing 440
Boarding program grades 10–13
Boarding program length 7-day **Boys** 10 **Girls** 7
Graduates attending college 97%
Graduates have attended Harvard U, Trinity Col, U College Dublin, Dublin City U

EDUCATIONAL PROGRAM

Curriculum National, Irish Department of Education and Science Curriculum
Average class size Elementary 21; Secondary 22
Language(s) of instruction English
Language(s) taught Irish, French, German, Italian, Spanish
Staff specialists computer, counselor, ESL, learning disabilities, librarian, math resource, nurse, reading resource

Special curricular programs art, instrumental music, vocal music, computer/technology, physical education
Extra curricular programs computers, community service, drama, excursions/expeditions, yearbook
Sports badminton, baseball, basketball, cross-country, football, golf, gymnastics, hockey, martial arts, skiing, swimming, tennis
Examinations GCSE

CAMPUS FACILITIES

Location Suburban
Campus 6 hectares, 6 buildings, 30 classrooms, 2 computer labs, 60 instructional computers, 9,000 library volumes, 2 auditoriums,

1 cafeteria, 1 covered play area, 1 gymnasium, 1 infirmary, 2 playing fields, 3 science labs, 1 pool, 1 tennis court

ISRAEL

ISRAEL

Area:	20,770 sq km
Population:	6,426,679
Capital:	Jerusalem
Currency:	New Israeli shekel (ILS)
Languages:	Hebrew, Arabic

ANGLICAN INTERNATIONAL SCHOOL JERUSALEM

Phone	972 2 567 7200
Fax	972 2 538 4874
Email	shermanj@aisj.co.il
Website	www.aisj.co.il
Address	82 HaNeviim Street, PO Box 191, Jerusalem, 91001, Israel

STAFF

Director Phil R. Billing
Secondary Principal Matthew Dufty
Elementary Principal Conita Cramer
Business Manager Wes Minor
Design and Technology/IT Coordinator Daniel Novich

Head of Library Marjorie Mendelson
Teaching staff Full time 31; Part time 17; Total 48
Nationalities of teaching staff US 7; UK 12; Israeli 20; Other(s) 9

INFORMATION

Grade levels N–12
School year August–June
School type coeducational, day, private non-profit
Year founded 1960
Governed by appointed School Board
Accredited by Middle States
Regional organizations ECIS, NESA
Enrollment Nursery 20; PreK 22; Elementary K–5 62; Middle School 6–8 33; High School 9–12 35; Total 172

Nationalities of student body US 39; UK 16; Israeli 43; Other(s) 127
Tuition/fee currency US Dollar
Tuition range 6,500–12,500
One time fees Registration 200
Graduates attending college 95%
Graduates have attended Yale U, Oxford U, Hebrew U, U of Tampere

EDUCATIONAL PROGRAM

Curriculum IB Diploma, IBPYP, IBMYP, Internationa Primary Curriculum (IPC)
Average class size Elementary 15; Secondary 15
Language(s) of instruction English
Language(s) taught Hebrew, Arabic, French
Staff specialists counselor, ESL, librarian, nurse
Special curricular programs art, instrumental music, computer/technology, physical education

Extra curricular programs computers, community service, drama, excursions/expeditions, newspaper, yearbook
Sports baseball, basketball, football, gymnastics, rugby, soccer, swimming, tennis
Examinations IB, SAT, TOEFL

CAMPUS FACILITIES

Location Urban
Campus 8 hectares, 5 buildings, 3 computer labs, 60 instructional computers,

13,000 library volumes, 1 auditorium, 1 cafeteria, 1 gymnasium, 1 infirmary, 3 playing fields, 2 science labs, air conditioning

THE WALWORTH BARBOUR AMERICAN INTERNATIONAL SCHOOL IN ISRAEL

Phone	972 9 980 1000
Fax	972 9 9801001
Email	aisrael@wbais.org
Website	www.wbais.org
Address	65 Hashomron Street, PO Box 484, Even Yehuda, 40500, Israel
Mailing address	PO Box 484, Even Yehuda, Israel, 40500

STAFF

Superintendent Marsha L. Aaronson
Elementary School Principal Michael Levinson
Middle School Principal Paul Petit
High School Principal Neal Jacover
Administrative Manager Neville Berman

Technology Coordinator Steve Roberts
Director of Library and Media Services
Margaret Knudson
Teaching staff Full time 57; Part time 16; Total 73
Nationalities of teaching staff US 53; Israeli 20

INFORMATION

Grade levels K–12
School year August–June
School type coeducational, private non-profit
Year founded 1958
Governed by elected School Board
Accredited by Middle States
Regional organizations NESA
Enrollment Elementary K–5 184;
Middle School 6–8 130; High School 9–12
172; Total 486

Nationalities of student body US 180; UK 14;
Israeli 72; Other(s) (Indian, Korean) 220
Tuition/fee currency US Dollar
Tuition range 15,200–17,500
Annual fees Busing 1,800; Building Fund
Levy 1,900
One time fees Registration 3,300
Graduates attending college 95%
Graduates have attended Harvard U,
Massachusetts Institute of Technology, Yale U,
Brown U, New York U

EDUCATIONAL PROGRAM

Curriculum US, AP
Average class size Elementary 16; Secondary 15
Language(s) of instruction English
Language(s) taught French, Hebrew, Spanish
Staff specialists computer, counselor, ESL,
learning disabilities, librarian, math resource,
nurse, reading resource
Special curricular programs art, instrumental
music, vocal music, computer/technology,
physical education

Extra curricular programs computers, community
service, dance, drama, environmental
conservation, excursions/expeditions, literary
magazine, newspaper, yearbook
Sports baseball, basketball, cross-country,
football, hockey, martial arts, soccer, softball,
swimming, tennis, track and field
Clubs ecology, chess, Spanish, learning
differences
Examinations AP, PSAT, SAT, SAT II

CAMPUS FACILITIES

Location Suburban
Campus 7 hectares, 7 buildings, 61 classrooms,
4 computer labs, 350 instructional computers,
25,000 library volumes, 1 auditorium,

1 cafeteria, 1 covered play area, 1 gymnasium,
1 infirmary, 2 playing fields, 7 science labs,
1 pool, 4 tennis courts, air conditioning

ITALY

Area:	301,230 sq km
Population:	58,147,733
Capital:	Rome
Currency:	Euro (EUR)
Languages:	Italian

QSI International School of Brindisi

Phone   39 0831 446003
Fax   39 0831 446005
Email   scottmastroianni@qsi.org
Website   www.qsi.org/brd/
Address   via Benvenuto Cellini, Brindisi, 72100, Italy

STAFF

Director Scott Mastroianni, Ed.D.
Teaching staff Full time 6; Total 6

Nationalities of teaching staff US 3; Italian 2;
Other(s) (French Polynesian) 1

INFORMATION

Grade levels N–9
School year August–June
School type private non-profit
Year founded 2005

Governed by appointed Advisory Board
Sponsored by UNLB
Tuition/fee currency US Dollar
One time fees Application 100

EDUCATIONAL PROGRAM

Curriculum US
Average class size Elementary 6
Language(s) of instruction English, Italian
Staff specialists computer, librarian

Special curricular programs art, instrumental
music, computer/technology
Extra curricular programs computers, community
service, excursions/expeditions

CAMPUS FACILITIES

Location Suburban
Campus 1 hectare, 1 building, 8 classrooms,
1 computer lab, 10 instructional computers,

1,000 library volumes, 1 playing field,
 air conditioning

INTERNATIONAL SCHOOL OF COMO

Phone	39 039 57 61 86
Fax	39 031 57 22 89
Email	info@iscomo.com
Website	www.iscomo.com
Address	Via per Cernobbio 19, Como, 22100, Italy

STAFF

Head of School Lawrence Buck, Ph.D.
Business Manager Pierfranco Ortelli
Teaching staff Full time 10; Part time 8; Total 18

Nationalities of teaching staff US 2; UK 5; Italian 5; Other(s) (South African) 4

INFORMATION

Grade levels N–6
School year September–June
School type coeducational, day, proprietary
Year founded 2002
Governed by appointed Board of Directors
Sponsored by International Schools of Italy srL
Regional organizations ECIS

Enrollment Nursery 10; PreK 10; Elementary K–5 80; Middle School 6–8 10; Total 110
Nationalities of student body US 10; UK 15; Italian 35; Other(s) 40
Tuition/fee currency Euro
Tuition range 3,500–5,000
Annual fees Registration 500

EDUCATIONAL PROGRAM

Curriculum Intl, IBPYP
Average class size Elementary 15
Language(s) of instruction English
Language(s) taught Italian
Staff specialists physician

Special curricular programs art, vocal music, physical education
Extra curricular programs dance, excursions/expeditions
Sports gymnastics, soccer, swimming, canoeing

CAMPUS FACILITIES

Location Suburban
Campus 4 hectares, 2 buildings, 12 classrooms, 1 computer lab, 20 instructional computers,

3,000 library volumes, 1 cafeteria, 2 gymnasiums, 1 infirmary, 1 playing field

INTERNATIONAL SCHOOL OF FLORENCE

Phone	39 055 646 1007
Fax	39 055 644 226
Email	admin.gat@isfitaly.org
Website	www.isfitaly.org
Address	via del Carota 23/25, Bagno a Ripoli, 50012, Italy
Mailing address	Middle/Upper School Campus, viuzzo di Gattaia, 9, 50123 Firenze, Italia

STAFF

Head of School Christopher Maggio, Ed.D.
Junior School Principal Debra Rader, Ed.D.
Deputy Head Paul Cook, Ed.D.
Business Manager Marie Jose Manzini
IT Coordinator Jeff Richardson

Librarian Sharon Allen
Teaching staff Full time 46; Part time 10; Total 56
Nationalities of teaching staff US 18; UK 14;
Italian 12; Other(s) (Australian, Canadian) 12

INFORMATION

Grade levels PreK–12
School year September–June
School type coeducational, day, private non-profit
Year founded 1952
Governed by elected Board of Directors
Accredited by CIS, Middle States
Regional organizations ECIS, MAIS
Enrollment PreK 24; Elementary K–5 154;
Middle School 6–8 95; High School 9–12 130;
Total 403

Nationalities of student body US 130; UK 40;
Italian 150; Other(s) (French, Spaniard) 83
Tuition/fee currency Euro
Tuition range 8,500–13,500
Annual fees Busing 2,400; Lunch 1,300
One time fees Registration 1,300;
Capital Levy 1,300
Graduates attending college 100%
Graduates have attended Boston U, U of Chicago,
U of London, McGill U, U of Bocconi

EDUCATIONAL PROGRAM

Curriculum US, National, IB Diploma, IBPYP,
IBMYP
Average class size Elementary 15; Secondary 15
Language(s) of instruction English
Language(s) taught Italian, French
Staff specialists computer, counselor, ESL,
learning disabilities, librarian
Special curricular programs art, vocal music,
computer/technology, physical education, Drama

Extra curricular programs community service,
dance, drama, environmental conservation,
yearbook
Sports badminton, baseball, basketball,
cross-country, soccer, tennis, track and field,
volleyball
Clubs Model UN, Habitat for Humanity, Tuscan
cooking, chess, knitting, math
Examinations IB, PSAT, SAT, SAT II, TOEFL, ACER

CAMPUS FACILITIES

Location Urban
Campus 11 hectares, 2 buildings, 35 classrooms,
2 computer labs, 50 instructional computers,

15,000 library volumes, 2 cafeterias, 1 covered
play area, 3 playing fields, 3 science labs

THE AMERICAN INTERNATIONAL SCHOOL IN GENOA

Phone	39 010 386 528
Fax	39 010 398 700
Email	info@aisge.it
Website	www.aisge.it
Address	Via Quarto 13-C, Genoa, 16148, Italy

STAFF

Director Anthony Mazzullo, Ed.D.
IB Diploma Program Coordinator
Elizabeth Rosser Boiardi
Early Childhood Coordinator Maria Teresa Mongardi
Admissions Officer Patrizia Palla

Technology Coordinator Gregory Read
Librarian Chantal Seys
Teaching staff Full time 31; Part time 10; Total 41
Nationalities of teaching staff US 17; Italian 22;
Other(s) (Australian, Canadian) 2

INFORMATION

Grade levels N–12
School year September–June
School type coeducational, day, private non-profit
Year founded 1966
Governed by elected Board of Directors
Accredited by CIS, New England
Regional organizations ECIS, MAIS
Enrollment Nursery 30; PreK 28;
Elementary K–5 147; Middle School 6–8 42;
High School 9–12 25; Total 272

Nationalities of student body US 20; UK 11;
Italian 188; Other(s) (Israeli, Dane) 53
Tuition/fee currency Euro
Tuition range 6,000–11,000
One time fees Membership 520; Capital 350
Graduates attending college 100%
Graduates have attended U of Genoa, U of York,
U of Southampton, New York U

EDUCATIONAL PROGRAM

Curriculum US, National, Intl, IB Diploma
Average class size Elementary 24; Secondary 9
Language(s) of instruction English
Language(s) taught Italian, French
Staff specialists computer, ESL, learning
disabilities, librarian
Special curricular programs art, vocal music,
computer/technology, physical education

Extra curricular programs computers, community
service, dance, environmental conservation,
excursions/expeditions, yearbook
Sports basketball, football, hockey, soccer,
tennis, track and field, volleyball
Examinations IB, PSAT, SAT

CAMPUS FACILITIES

Location Urban
Campus 1 hectare, 6 buildings, 24 classrooms,
1 computer lab, 45 instructional computers,

6,000 library volumes, 1 cafeteria, 1 gymnasium,
1 playing field, 2 science labs, 1 tennis court

AMERICAN SCHOOL OF MILAN

Phone	39 02 530 0001
Fax	39 02 576 06274
Email	director@asmilan.org
Website	www.asmilan.org
Address	Via C. Marx, 14, Noverasco di Opera, Milan, 20090, Italy
Mailing address	Via C. Marx, 14, 20090 Noverasco di Opera, Milano, Italy

STAFF

Director Alan P. Austen, Ed.D.
Elementary Principal Day Jones
High School Principal Samer Khoury
Middle School Principal Elizabeth Beatty-Khoury
Associate Director for Business Luisa G. Linzani

Director of Technology Stephen Reiach
Teaching staff Full time 69; Part time 2; Total 71
Nationalities of teaching staff US 35; UK 3;
Italian 16; Other(s) (French, Jordanian) 17

INFORMATION

Grade levels N–13
School year September–June
School type coeducational, day, private non-profit
Year founded 1962
Governed by elected Board of Trustees
Accredited by Middle States
Regional organizations ECIS, MAIS, SGIS
Enrollment Nursery 45; PreK 20;
Elementary K–5 210; Middle School 6–8 125;
High School 9–12 180; Total 580

Nationalities of student body US 190; UK 15;
Italian 195; Other(s) (Korean, Saudi) 185
Tuition/fee currency Euro
Tuition range 12,000–17,000
Graduates attending college 100%
Graduates have attended Massachusetts Institute
of Technology, Columbia U, U of Pennsylvania,
Cambridge U, New York U

EDUCATIONAL PROGRAM

Curriculum US, Intl, IB Diploma, IBMYP
Average class size Elementary 18; Secondary 18
Language(s) of instruction English
Language(s) taught Italian, French, Spanish
Staff specialists computer, counselor, ESL,
librarian, math resource, nurse, reading
resource

Special curricular programs art, instrumental
music, vocal music, computer/technology,
physical education
Extra curricular programs community service,
dance, drama, environmental conservation,
excursions/expeditions, newspaper, yearbook
Sports basketball, cross-country, soccer, tennis,
volleyball
Examinations AP, IB, PSAT, SAT, SAT II, TOEFL

CAMPUS FACILITIES

Location Suburban
Campus 14 hectares, 3 buildings, 37 classrooms,
2 computer labs, 60 instructional computers,

22,000 library volumes, 1 cafeteria, 1 covered
play area, 1 gymnasium, 1 infirmary, 3 playing
fields, 5 science labs, 2 tennis courts

INTERNATIONAL SCHOOL OF MILAN

Phone	39 02 42290577
Fax	39 02 4235428
Email	ismhigh@ism-ac.it
Website	www.ism-ac.it
Address	via Vespri Siciliani 88, Milan, 20146, Italy

STAFF

Head of School Terence F. Haywood
High School Principal Mark Dawson
Middle School Principal Mike Kirby
Lower School Principal Helen Cardani
Director of First School Sarah Ford
Principal of Monza Section Rachel Caldwell
Director General Franco Formiga

IT Coordinator Liz Collins
High School Librarian Olga Glussich
Teaching staff Full time 115; Part time 18; Total 133
Nationalities of teaching staff US 6; UK 107; Italian 11; Other(s) (Australian) 9

INFORMATION

Grade levels N–12
School year September–June
School type coeducational, day, proprietary
Year founded 1958
Governed by appointed Board
Sponsored by I.S.E. Srl
Regional organizations ECIS
Enrollment Nursery 60; PreK 190; Elementary K–5 520; Middle School 6–8 260; High School 9–12 250; Total 1,280

Nationalities of student body US 70; UK 100; Italian 700; Other(s) (Japanese) 410
Tuition/fee currency Euro
Tuition range 7,200–14,100
Annual fees Registration 500; Capital Levy 1,500; Busing 2,300; Lunch 1,100
Graduates attending college 99%
Graduates have attended Oxford U, Cambridge U, U of Notre Dame, Emory U, London School of Economics

EDUCATIONAL PROGRAM

Curriculum Intl, IB Diploma, IBPYP, IBMYP
Average class size Elementary 22; Secondary 15
Language(s) of instruction English
Language(s) taught French, German, Italian, Spanish, Chinese
Staff specialists computer, counselor, ESL, learning disabilities, librarian, math resource, nurse, psychologist, reading resource
Special curricular programs art, instrumental music, vocal music, computer/technology, physical education

Extra curricular programs computers, community service, drama, environmental conservation, excursions/expeditions, literary magazine, newspaper, yearbook, Global Issues Network, Model UN
Sports badminton, basketball, cross-country, gymnastics, hockey, martial arts, skiing, soccer, squash, swimming, track and field, volleyball
Examinations IB, IB MYP

CAMPUS FACILITIES

Location Urban
Campus 8 hectares, 6 buildings, 80 classrooms, 5 computer labs, 280 instructional computers,

35,000 library volumes, 4 auditoriums, 6 cafeterias, 5 covered play areas, 5 gymnasiums, 6 infirmaries, 5 playing fields, 7 science labs

SIR JAMES HENDERSON SCHOOL

Phone	39 02 210941
Fax	39 02 2109 4225
Email	trevor.church@sjhschool.com
Website	www.SJHSchool.com
Address	Via Pisani Dossi 16, Lambrate, Milan, Lombardia, 20134, Italy

STAFF

Principal Trevor J. Church
Head of Upper School Gregory Wright
Head of Lower School Angela Dean
Deputy Head Lower School David Bown
Principal Secretary Juliet Vanni

Director Post 16 Studies Hilary Furey
Bursar Guieseppina Bogani
Upper School Resource Centre Coordinator
J de Panizza

INFORMATION

Grade levels N–13
School year September–June
School type coeducational, day, private non-profit
Year founded 1969
Governed by elected Governors

Regional organizations ECIS
Tuition/fee currency US Dollar
Graduates attending college 99%
Graduates have attended Oxford U,
U of Chicago, Boston U, Emory U

EDUCATIONAL PROGRAM

Curriculum UK
Average class size Elementary 18; Secondary 15
Language(s) of instruction English
Language(s) taught Italian, French, Spanish,
German
Staff specialists computer, ESL, learning
disabilities, math resource, nurse, reading resource
Special curricular programs art, instrumental
music, computer/technology, physical education,
vocational

Extra curricular programs computers, dance,
drama, excursions/expeditions, yearbook
Sports badminton, basketball, cricket, football,
golf, hockey, rugby, skiing, soccer, swimming,
tennis, track and field, volleyball
Clubs art, languages, sports, craft, judo, karate,
Irish dancing, cooking, ballet
Examinations A-level GCE, GCSE,
Royal College of Music

CAMPUS FACILITIES

Location Urban
Campus 1 building, 65 classrooms, 2 computer
labs, 80 instructional computers, 1 auditorium,
1 cafeteria, 1 gymnasium, 1 infirmary,
1 playing field, 5 science labs, air conditioning

Data from 2006/07 school year.

THE INTERNATIONAL SCHOOL OF NAPLES

Phone 39 081 721 2037
Fax 39 081 570 0248
Email isn@na.cybernet.it
Website www.intschoolnaples.it
Address Viale della Liberazione, 1, Bagnoli, Napoli, Naples, 80125, Italy

STAFF

Principal Josephine A. Sessa
Vice Principal Patricia Montesano

Business Manager Maria Elizabeth Fusco
Head of Library/Media Center Eleonora Bonnici

INFORMATION

Grade levels PreK–12
School year September–June
School type coeducational, day, private non-profit
Year founded 1964
Governed by elected Board of Governors
Regional organizations ECIS
Enrollment PreK 5; Elementary K–5 81; Middle School 6–8 72; High School 9–12 75; Total 233
Nationalities of student body US 18; Italian 81; Other(s) (Spaniard, Turk) 134

Tuition/fee currency Euro
Tuition range 4,368–6,077
Annual fees Registration 77; Lunch 1,000; Books 500; Nato 75; Italian State Course 15,192
One time fees Admission (new students only) 258
Graduates attending college 90%
Graduates have attended U of Granada, U of Athens, U of Maryland, U of Madrid

EDUCATIONAL PROGRAM

Curriculum US
Average class size Elementary 15; Secondary 25
Language(s) of instruction English
Language(s) taught French, Italian
Staff specialists computer, counselor, ESL
Special curricular programs art, computer/technology, distance learning, physical education

Extra curricular programs computers, community service, dance, drama, excursions/expeditions, newspaper, photography, yearbook
Sports baseball, basketball, football, golf, soccer, softball, tennis, track and field, volleyball
Clubs student council, National Honor Society
Examinations PSAT, SAT, SAT II

CAMPUS FACILITIES

Location Urban
Campus 3 buildings, 15 classrooms, 1 computer lab, 15 instructional computers, 1 cafeteria,

1 gymnasium, 1 playing field, 1 science lab, 1 tennis court, air conditioning

Data from 2006/07 school year.

THE ENGLISH INTERNATIONAL SCHOOL OF PADUA

Phone	39 049 80 22 50 3
Fax	39 049 80 20 66 0
Email	eisp@eisp01.com
Website	www.eisp01.com
Address	Via Forcellini 168, Padova, 35128, Italy

STAFF

Director Lucio Rossi, Ph.D.
Head of Early Years Sharron Noakes
Head of Elementary Angela Barlow
Head of Middle School Jean Bampfield

Head of High School Silvester Fassari, Ph.D.
IB DP Coordinator Gregory Kremer
ICT Teacher William Walter
Foreign Languages Teacher Ross Gilli

INFORMATION

Grade levels N–12
School year September–June
School type coeducational
Year founded 1987
Regional organizations ECIS
Enrollment Nursery 72; PreK 24; Elementary K–5 340; Middle School 6–8 179; High School 9–12 75; Total 690
Nationalities of student body US 119; UK 130; Italian 392; Other(s) (Canadian, German) 49
Tuition/fee currency Euro

Tuition range 5–10
Annual fees Boarding, 5-day 3,500; Boarding, 7-day 3,700; Busing 1,800; Lunch 1,700; Books 900
One time fees Registration 600
Boarding program grades 9–12
Boarding program length 5-day and 7-day
Boys 3 **Girls** 2
Graduates attending college 100%
Graduates have attended U Bocconi, U of Cambridge

EDUCATIONAL PROGRAM

Curriculum Intl, IB Diploma
Average class size Elementary 20; Secondary 20
Language(s) of instruction English
Language(s) taught Italian, Spanish, French, German
Staff specialists computer, counselor, ESL, learning disabilities, librarian, math resource, nurse, physician, psychologist, reading resource, speech/hearing

Special curricular programs art, instrumental music, vocal music, computer/technology, physical education
Extra curricular programs computers, community service, dance, drama, photography, yearbook
Sports badminton, basketball, cricket, skiing, soccer, swimming, volleyball
Clubs drama, foreign languages, art, choir
Examinations IB, SAT, SAT II

CAMPUS FACILITIES

Location Suburban
Campus 3 hectares, 3 buildings, 54 classrooms, 3 computer labs, 85 instructional computers, 12,000 library volumes, 1 auditorium, 2 cafeterias, 1 covered play area, 2 gymnasiums, 2 infirmaries, 3 playing fields, 3 science labs, air conditioning

Data from 2006/07 school year.

AMBRIT ROME INTERNATIONAL SCHOOL

Phone	39 06 559 5305
Fax	39 06 559 5309
Email	ambrit@ambrit-rome.com
Website	www.ambrit-rome.com
Address	Via Filippo Tajani, 50, Rome, 00149, Italy

STAFF

Director Bernard C. Mullane
Assistant Director Loretta Nannini
8th Grade Dean of Students Robin Gilbody
Primary Principal Pascale Salomon
Early Childhood Principal Jennifer Level
Bursar Connie Mawer

Head of Technology Graham Bell
Head of Library Amy Ronning
Teaching staff Full time 64; Part time 1; Total 65
Nationalities of teaching staff US 10; UK 20; Italian 15; Other(s) (Irish, Swede) 23

INFORMATION

Grade levels N–8
School year September–June
School type coeducational, day, proprietary
Year founded 1996
Sponsored by Bernard C. Mullane
Regional organizations MAIS
Enrollment Nursery 20; PreK 25; Elementary K–5 315; Middle School 6–8 140; Total 500

Nationalities of student body US 100; UK 20; Italian 140; Other(s) (Indian, Swede) 240
Tuition/fee currency Euro
Tuition range 8,200–13,500
Annual fees Busing 2,100; Lunch 700
One time fees Registration 1,300; Capital Levy 1,500

EDUCATIONAL PROGRAM

Curriculum National, Intl
Average class size Elementary 20; Secondary 20
Language(s) of instruction English, Italian
Language(s) taught French, Spanish
Staff specialists computer, counselor, ESL, learning disabilities, librarian, nurse, reading resource
Special curricular programs art, instrumental music, vocal music, computer/technology, physical education

Extra curricular programs computers, community service, drama, excursions/expeditions, literary magazine, newspaper, yearbook
Sports badminton, basketball, gymnastics, soccer, tennis
Clubs chess, computer, ceramics, student council, film making

CAMPUS FACILITIES

Location Urban
Campus 4 hectares, 2 buildings, 30 classrooms, 2 computer labs, 40 instructional computers, 14,000 library volumes, 1 auditorium,

1 cafeteria, 1 covered play area, 1 gymnasium, 1 infirmary, 3 playing fields, 1 science lab, 2 tennis courts

AMERICAN OVERSEAS SCHOOL OF ROME

Phone	39 06 334 381
Fax	39 06 332 62608
Email	headmaster@aosr.org
Website	www.aosr.org
Address	Via Cassia, 811, Rome, 00189, Italy

STAFF

Head of School Beth Pfannl, Ph.D.
Principal Matt Neely
Director of Admissions Donald Levine

Financial Consultant Elisa Bruno
Director of Technology Geoff Miller
Head of Library Molly Bianchini

INFORMATION

Grade levels PreK–13
School year September–June
School type coeducational, day, private non-profit
Year founded 1946
Governed by elected Board of Trustees
Accredited by Middle States
Regional organizations ECIS, MAIS
Enrollment PreK 30; Elementary K–5 228; Middle School 6–8 149; High School 9–12 203; Total 610

Nationalities of student body US 170; UK 10; Italian 190; Other(s) (Israeli, Chinese) 240
Tuition/fee currency Euro
Tuition range 8,200–17,200
Annual fees Busing 2,400; Lunch 800; ESL 700
One time fees Registration 500; Capital Levy 3,500
Graduates attending college 100%
Graduates have attended Stanford U, Georgetown U, Cornell U, California Institute of Techology, U of Cambridge

EDUCATIONAL PROGRAM

Curriculum US, AP, IB Diploma
Average class size Elementary 18; Secondary 18
Language(s) of instruction English
Language(s) taught Italian, French, Latin, Spanish
Staff specialists computer, counselor, ESL, learning disabilities, librarian, nurse, reading resource, speech/hearing

Special curricular programs art, instrumental music, vocal music, computer/technology, physical education
Extra curricular programs computers, community service, drama, literary magazine, newspaper, yearbook
Sports basketball, cross-country, soccer, swimming, tennis, volleyball, wrestling
Examinations ACT, AP, IB, PSAT, SAT, SAT II, TOEFL, ERB Writing Test

CAMPUS FACILITIES

Location Urban
Campus 2 hectares, 5 buildings, 55 classrooms, 3 computer labs, 150 instructional computers, 22,000 library volumes, 1 auditorium, 1 cafeteria, 1 gymnasium, 1 infirmary, 1 playing field, 4 science labs, 2 tennis courts, air conditioning

Data from 2006/07 school year.

CASTELLI INTERNATIONAL SCHOOL

Phone	39 06 943 15779
Fax	39 06 943 15779
Email	maryac@castelli-international.it
Website	www.castelli-international.it
Address	Via Degli Scozzesi 13, Grottaferrata, Rome, 00046, Italy

STAFF

Director of Studies Marianne Palladino, Ph.D.
Administrative Assistant Christine Dryden

Head of Technology Paul Magee
Head of Library/Media Center Marianne Palladino

INFORMATION

Grade levels 1–8
School year September–June
School type coeducational, day, private non-profit
Year founded 1977
Governed by appointed Board of Directors

Tuition/fee currency Euro
Tuition range 5,950–7,750
Annual fees Registration 500; Busing 1,900; Lunch 860
One time fees Capital Levy 1,000

EDUCATIONAL PROGRAM

Curriculum US, UK, National, IBPYP, Italian Ministerial
Average class size Elementary 15; Secondary 15
Language(s) of instruction English, Italian
Language(s) taught Latin, French
Staff specialists computer, ESL, librarian, math resource, psychologist, reading resource
Special curricular programs art, instrumental music, vocal music, computer/technology, physical education

Extra curricular programs computers, community service, dance, drama, excursions/expeditions, photography, yearbook
Sports basketball, skiing, soccer, softball, tennis, track and field, volleyball, ping pong
Clubs Boy and Girl Scouts, chess
Examinations Italian State Exams

CAMPUS FACILITIES

Location Rural
Campus 5 hectares, 4 buildings, 8 classrooms, 1 computer lab, 10 instructional computers, 5,000 library volumes, 1 cafeteria, 1 covered play area, 1 gymnasium, 2 playing fields, 1 science lab, 1 tennis court

Data from 2006/07 school year.

MARYMOUNT INTERNATIONAL SCHOOL

Phone	39 06 362 9101
Fax	39 06 363 01738
Email	marymount@marymountrome.org
Website	www.marymountrome.org
Address	Via di Villa Lauchli, 180, Rome, 00191, Italy

STAFF

Head of School Yvonne Hennigan, Ed.D.
Secondary School Principal Terrence McAndrews
Elementary School Principal Sister Paulita Kuzy
IB Coordinator James Romano

Development Director James Dunn
Business Manager Priscilla Marenzi
Head of Technology Francesca Fava
Secondary School Librarian Chiara Canepa

INFORMATION

Grade levels PreK–12
School year September–June
School type coeducational, church-affiliated, day
Year founded 1946
Governed by appointed Religious Board of Trustees
Accredited by CIS, New England
Regional organizations ECIS, MAIS
Enrollment PreK 57; Elementary K–5 349;
Middle School 6–8 147;
High School 9–12 214; Total 767

Nationalities of student body US 125; UK 15;
Italian 430; Other(s) 197
Tuition/fee currency Euro
Tuition range 8,100–15,600
Annual fees Busing 2,700; Lunch 900;
Re-enrollment 300
One time fees Registration 350; Capital Levy 3,000
Graduates attending college 98%
Graduates have attended Boston U, New York U,
Col of William and Mary, U College of London,
Queen Mary U

EDUCATIONAL PROGRAM

Curriculum US, AP, IB Diploma
Average class size Elementary 22; Secondary 16
Language(s) of instruction English
Language(s) taught French, Spanish, Italian, Latin
Staff specialists computer, counselor, ESL,
learning disabilities, librarian, nurse, psychologist
Special curricular programs art, computer/
technology, physical education

Extra curricular programs computers, community
service, drama, excursions/expeditions,
newspaper, photography, yearbook
Sports basketball, cross-country, martial arts,
soccer, tennis, track and field, volleyball,
cheerleading
Clubs chess, robotics
Examinations AP, IB, Iowa, PSAT, SAT, TOEFL

CAMPUS FACILITIES

Location Suburban
Campus 6 hectares, 4 buildings, 50 classrooms,
4 computer labs, 84 instructional computers,

18,000 library volumes, 1 auditorium,
1 cafeteria, 1 infirmary, 1 playing field,
4 science labs, 2 tennis courts

Data from 2006/07 school year.

ST. STEPHEN'S SCHOOL

Phone	39 06 575 0605
Fax	39 06 574 1941
Email	ststephens@ststephens-rome.com
Website	www.ststephens-rome.com
Address	Via Aventina 3, Rome, 00153, Italy

STAFF

Head of School Philip Allen
Director of Studies Deborah Dostert
IB Coordinator Lesley Murphy
Asstistant Business Manager Luca Derito
Technology Coordinator Fausto Di Marco

Librarian Sarah Yates
Teaching staff Full time 26; Part time 13; Total 39
Nationalities of teaching staff US 22; UK 6; Italian 1; Other(s) (French, Australian) 10

INFORMATION

Grade levels 9–13
School year September–June
School type boarding, coeducational, day, private non-profit
Year founded 1964
Governed by elected Board of Trustees
Accredited by CIS, New England
Regional organizations ECIS
Enrollment High School 9–12 217; Grade 13 4; Total 221
Nationalities of student body US 90; UK 16; Italian 47; Other(s) (French, German) 68

Tuition/fee currency Euro
Tuition 17,900–17,900
Annual fees Boarding, 7-day 11,650; Lunch 1,050; Capital Assessment–Returning Students 450
One time fees Capital Assessment–New Students 850; IB 470
Boarding program grades 9–13
Boarding program length 7-day **Boys** 18 **Girls** 22
Graduates attending college 95%
Graduates have attended Brown U, Georgetown U, McGill U, Oxford U, Yale U

EDUCATIONAL PROGRAM

Curriculum US, AP, IB Diploma
Average class size Secondary 13
Language(s) of instruction English
Language(s) taught Italian, French, Latin
Staff specialists computer, counselor, librarian, nurse, psychologist
Special curricular programs art, vocal music, computer/technology

Extra curricular programs community service, dance, drama, environmental conservation, excursions/expeditions, literary magazine, newspaper, photography, yearbook, Model UN
Sports basketball, soccer, softball, tennis, track and field, volleyball, yoga
Clubs Bengt (political and social discussion group), Italian, chess, cooking
Examinations AP, IB, PSAT, SAT, SAT II

CAMPUS FACILITIES

Location Urban
Campus 1 hectare, 1 building, 13 classrooms, 2 computer labs, 30 instructional computers,

14,500 library volumes, 1 auditorium, 1 cafeteria, 1 gymnasium, 2 playing fields, 3 science labs, 1 tennis court

INTERNATIONAL SCHOOL OF TRIESTE

Phone	39 040 211 452
Fax	39 040 213 122
Email	info@istrieste.org
Website	www.istrieste.org
Address	Via Conconello 16, Trieste, 34151, Italy

STAFF

Director James Pastore
Elementary School Coordinator Carla Beltramini
Middle School Academic Dean Matthew Schvaneveldt

Early Childhood Coordinator Betty Ravalico
Business Manager Paola Zonta
Nationalities of teaching staff US 16; UK 5; Ukrainian 2

INFORMATION

Grade levels N–8
School year September–June
School type coeducational, day, private non-profit
Year founded 1964
Governed by appointed and elected Board of Directors

Accredited by Middle States
Regional organizations ECIS, MAIS
Tuition/fee currency Euro
Tuition range 4,850–6,450
Annual fees Busing 600
One time fees Registration 335

EDUCATIONAL PROGRAM

Curriculum US, Intl
Average class size Elementary 24; Secondary 17
Language(s) of instruction English
Language(s) taught Italian, German, French, Spanish, Latin
Staff specialists computer, ESL, learning disabilities, librarian

Special curricular programs art, computer/technology, physical education
Extra curricular programs computers, community service, drama, excursions/expeditions, newspaper, yearbook, choir
Sports basketball, soccer, volleyball
Examinations Iowa

CAMPUS FACILITIES

Location Suburban
Campus 4 hectares, 1 building, 13 classrooms, 1 computer lab, 32 instructional computers, 10,000 library volumes, 1 cafeteria, 1 gymnasium, 2 playing fields, 1 science lab

Data from 2006/07 school year.

UNITED WORLD COLLEGE OF THE ADRIATIC

Phone	39 040 3739 111
Fax	39 040 3739 225
Email	uwcad@uwcad.it
Website	www.uwcad.it
Address	Via Trieste n. 29, Duino (TS), 34011, Italy

STAFF

Head of School Marc Abrioux
Deputy Head/Director of Studies Sandy Thomas
IB Coordinator Peter Howe
Head of Guidance Anne Brearley
Bursar Colin Thompson

Head of IT Julius Krajnak
Head of Library/Media Center Henry Thomas
Teaching staff Full time 26; Part time 1; Total 27
Nationalities of teaching staff US 1; UK 9;
Italian 6; Other(s) 11

INFORMATION

Grade levels 12–13
School year September–May
School type boarding, coeducational, private
non-profit
Year founded 1982
Governed by appointed Council of
Administration
Regional organizations ECIS

Enrollment High School 9–12 100;
Grade 13 100; Total 200
Nationalities of student body US 6; UK 2;
Italian 26; Other(s) 166
Tuition/fee currency US Dollar
Graduates attending college 100%
Graduates have attended Princeton U, Oxford U,
London School of Economics, U Bocconi,
Utrecht U

EDUCATIONAL PROGRAM

Curriculum IB Diploma
Average class size Secondary 15
Language(s) of instruction English, Italian
Language(s) taught German, Spanish
Special curricular programs instrumental music

Sports basketball, football, martial arts, skiing,
soccer, swimming, volleyball, aerobics,
kayaking, sailing, climbing, orienteering
Examinations IB, SAT

CAMPUS FACILITIES

Location Urban
Campus 17 buildings, 19 classrooms,
1 computer lab, 30 instructional computers,

20,000 library volumes, 1 cafeteria,
1 infirmary, 4 science labs

A.C.A.T.–
INTERNATIONAL SCHOOL OF TURIN

Phone	39 011 645 967
Fax	39 011 643 298
Email	info@acat-ist.it
Website	www.acat-ist.it
Address	Vicolo Tiziano, 10, Moncalieri, 10024, Italy

STAFF

Head of School Jonathan Cramb
Lower School Dean Rachel Caldwell
Upper School Dean Cathryn Townsend
IB Coordinator/College Counselor Cy Webber
PYP Coordinator Claire Muir

Business/Finance Manager Maria Recrosio
Head of ICT James Mackay
Teaching staff Full time 33; Part time 6; Total 39
Nationalities of teaching staff US 9; UK 19;
Italian 5; Other(s) (Canadian, Irish) 6

INFORMATION

Grade levels N–12
School year September–June
School type coeducational, day
Year founded 1974
Governed by elected Board of Directors
Accredited by CIS, New England
Regional organizations ECIS
Enrollment Nursery 5; PreK 22;
Elementary K–5 163; Middle School 6–8 88;
High School 9–12 70; Total 348

Nationalities of student body US 32; UK 36;
Italian 207; Other(s) (German, Japanese) 73
Tuition/fee currency Euro
Tuition range 3,500–10,500
Annual fees Registration 1,000; Busing 1,100;
Lunch 1,200
One time fees School Development Fund 800
Graduates attending college 95%
Graduates have attended Boston U,
U of Rochester, London School of Economics,
U of Plymouth, U Bocconi

EDUCATIONAL PROGRAM

Curriculum Intl, IB Diploma, IBPYP
Average class size Elementary 23; Secondary 18
Language(s) of instruction English
Language(s) taught Italian, French, Spanish
Staff specialists computer, counselor, ESL

Special curricular programs art, instrumental
music, computer/technology, physical education
Extra curricular programs community service,
drama, newspaper, yearbook
Sports soccer, swimming, tennis, volleyball
Examinations PSAT, SAT

CAMPUS FACILITIES

Location Suburban
Campus 6 buildings, 28 classrooms,
1 computer lab, 45 instructional computers,

15,000 library volumes, 1 auditorium,
1 cafeteria, 1 gymnasium, 2 playing fields,
2 science labs

THE UDINE INTERNATIONAL SCHOOL

Phone	39 0432 541119
Fax	39 0432 411088
Email	info@udineis.org
Website	www.udineis.org
Address	Via Martignacco 187, Udine, 33100, Italy

STAFF

Director James Pastore
Principal Palmira Metzger
Teaching staff Full time 25; Part time 5; Total 30

Nationalities of teaching staff US 4; UK 4; Italian 5; Other(s) (Canadian, Australian) 17

INFORMATION

Grade levels N–8
School year September–June
School type coeducational, day, private non-profit
Year founded 2003
Governed by appointed and elected Board of Directors
Regional organizations ECIS, MAIS

Enrollment Nursery 45; PreK 25; Elementary K–5 95; Middle School 6–8 25; Total 190
Nationalities of student body UK 4; Italian 180; Other(s) (Korean, Australian) 6
Tuition/fee currency Euro
Tuition range 5,850–7,100
Annual fees Registration 335

EDUCATIONAL PROGRAM

Curriculum US, Intl
Average class size Elementary 20; Secondary 10
Language(s) of instruction English
Language(s) taught Italian, French, German, Latin
Staff specialists computer, ESL, librarian
Special curricular programs art, instrumental music, vocal music, computer/technology, physical education

Extra curricular programs dance, drama, excursions/expeditions
Sports baseball, basketball, football, gymnastics, rugby, soccer, swimming, track and field, volleyball
Examinations Iowa

CAMPUS FACILITIES

Location Suburban
Campus 600 hectares, 3 buildings, 16 classrooms, 1 computer lab, 12 instructional computers,

2,500 library volumes, 1 auditorium, 2 cafeterias, 1 gymnasium, 2 playing fields, 1 pool

JAMAICA

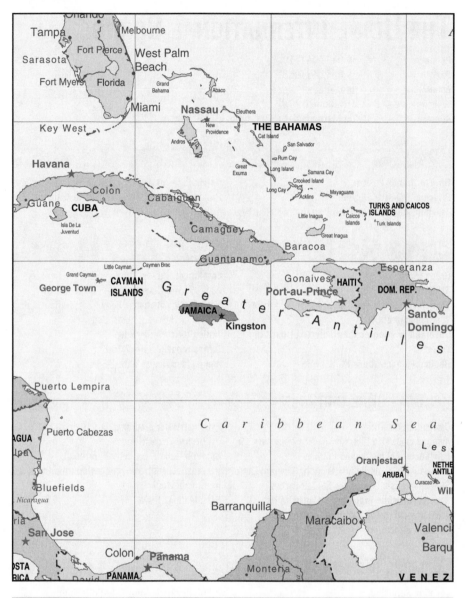

JAMAICA

Area:	10,991 sq km
Population:	2,780,132
Capital:	Kingston
Currency:	Jamaican Dollar (JMD)
Languages:	English

AMERICAN INTERNATIONAL SCHOOL OF KINGSTON

Phone	876 755 2634 6
Fax	876 925 4749
Email	office@aisk.com
Website	www.aisk.com
Address	1a Olivier Road, Kingston 8, Jamaica

STAFF

Director Paul Pescatore, Ed.D.
Assistant Director for Early Childhood and Elementary School Anna Wallace, Ed.D.
Administrative Coordinator LeeAnne Sherman
Assistant Director for Middle School Matthew Gaetano, Ed.D.

Business Manager Janet Stoddart-Allen
Technology Coordinator Mitch Saliba, Ed.D.
Librarian Peggy Pescatore, Ed.D.
Teaching staff Full time 31; Part time 3; Total 34
Nationalities of teaching staff US 12; UK 3; Jamaican 15; Other(s) (Canadian, Spaniard) 4

INFORMATION

Grade levels PreK–12
School year August–June
School type coeducational, day, private non-profit
Year founded 1994
Governed by elected Nine Member Board
Accredited by Southern
Enrollment PreK 7; Elementary K–5 112; Middle School 6–8 63; High School 9–12 54; Total 236

Nationalities of student body US 80; UK 16; Jamaican 58; Other(s) (Canadian, Belgian) 82
Tuition/fee currency US Dollar
Tuition range 5,548–12,058
Annual fees Capital Levy 1,500
One time fees Registration 4,500
Graduates attending college 100%
Graduates have attended U of Richmond, Macalester Col, Col of William and Mary, Trinity U, U of Guelph

EDUCATIONAL PROGRAM

Curriculum US, AP
Average class size Elementary 16; Secondary 16
Language(s) of instruction English
Language(s) taught Spanish, French
Staff specialists computer, counselor, ESL, librarian
Special curricular programs art, instrumental music, vocal music, computer/technology, physical education

Extra curricular programs community service, dance, drama, excursions/expeditions, photography, yearbook
Sports badminton, cricket, golf, martial arts, soccer, swimming, tennis, volleyball, water polo
Examinations AP, Iowa, PSAT, SAT, SAT II

CAMPUS FACILITIES

Location Urban
Campus 2 hectares, 5 buildings, 22 classrooms, 1 computer lab, 60 instructional computers, 5,000 library volumes, air conditioning

BELAIR SCHOOL

Phone	876 962 2168
Fax	876 962 3396
Email	general@belairschool.com
Website	www.belairschool.com
Address	43 DeCarteret Road, Mandeville, Manchester, Jamaica
Mailing address	PO Box 156, Mandeville, Jamaica

STAFF

Director/Principal Trevor Brown
Vice Principal Willemina Prinsen
Operations Manager Karen Charcharos

Computer/Support Specialist Othneil Brissett
Librarian Norma Ricketts

INFORMATION

Grade levels K–12
School year September–June
School type coeducational, day
Year founded 1967

Governed by appointed and elected Board of Governors
Tuition/fee currency Jamaican Dollar
One time fees Application 750; Yearbook 600; Caution 750

EDUCATIONAL PROGRAM

Curriculum National
Language(s) of instruction English
Language(s) taught Spanish, French
Staff specialists computer, learning disabilities, reading resource
Special curricular programs art, computer/technology, physical education
Extra curricular programs computers, dance, drama, environmental conservation, excursions/expeditions, yearbook, Tae Kwan Do

Sports badminton, basketball, cricket, football, swimming, tennis, track and field, netball
Clubs Scouts, debate, Guides, science, Key, first aid, Beavers, School Challenge Quiz, Interschool Christian Fellowship
Examinations A-level GCE, SAT, Caribbean Examination Council

CAMPUS FACILITIES

Location Rural
Campus 5 hectares, 12 buildings, 18 classrooms, 2 computer labs, 38 instructional computers,

5,751 library volumes, 1 auditorium, 1 cafeteria, 1 infirmary, 2 playing fields, 3 science labs, 3 tennis courts

Data from 2006/07 school year.

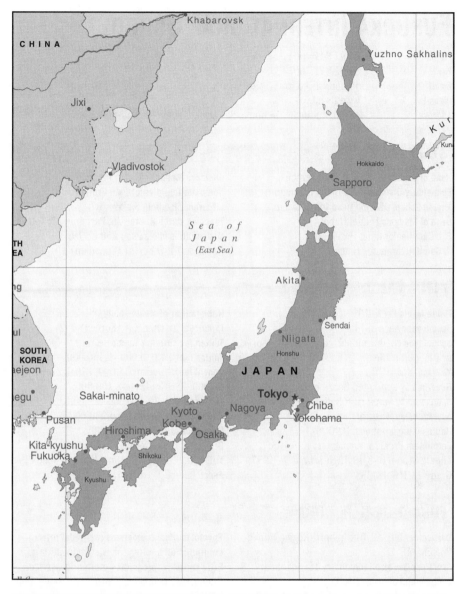

JAPAN

Area:	377,835 sq km
Population:	127,433,494
Capital:	Tokyo
Currency:	Yen (JPY)
Languages:	Japanese

FUKUOKA INTERNATIONAL SCHOOL

Phone	81 92 841 7601
Fax	81 92 841 7602
Email	admin@fis.ed.jp
Website	www.fis.ed.jp
Address	18-50 Momochi, 3-chome, Sawara-ku, Fukuoka, 814-0006, Japan

STAFF

Head of School Michael E. Saffarewich
Elementary Division Head Brian Freeman
Middle School Division Head John Savage
Dean of Students Daniel Habel
ESL Coordinator Janet Hazeltine
IB Coordinator James Hatch

Business Manager Masao Iguchi
Computer Coordinator Paul Fradale
Librarian Elizabeth Saffarewich
Teaching staff Full time 26; Part time 17; Total 43
Nationalities of teaching staff US 19;
Japanese 14; Other(s) (Canadian) 10

INFORMATION

Grade levels PreK–13
School year August–June
School type coeducational, company-sponsored,
private non-profit
Year founded 1972
Governed by appointed Board of Directors
Sponsored by Seven Host Nation Corporations
Accredited by Western
Regional organizations EARCOS
Enrollment PreK 24; Elementary K–5 103;
Middle School 6–8 48; High School 9–12 57;
Grade 13 1; Total 233

Nationalities of student body US 17; UK 4;
Japanese 70; Other(s) (Korean) 142
Tuition/fee currency Japanese Yen
Tuition range 1,060,000–1,360,000
Annual fees Insurance 3,000; ESL Grades 1–5
60,000; ESL Grades 6–8 100,000;
ESL Grades 9–10 120,000
One time fees Registration 230,000
Graduates attending college 90%
Graduates have attended Carlton U, Brigham
Young U, U of Washington, Michigan State U,
Asia Pacific U

EDUCATIONAL PROGRAM

Curriculum Intl, AP, IB Diploma, Reggio Emilia
Preschool
Average class size Elementary 16; Secondary 15
Language(s) of instruction English
Language(s) taught Japanese, French, Korean,
Spanish
Staff specialists computer, counselor, ESL,
librarian

Special curricular programs art, vocal music,
computer/technology, physical education
Extra curricular programs community service,
drama, excursions/expeditions, yearbook, budo
Sports basketball, volleyball
Clubs water sports, ensemble, choir, French,
cooking, Korean, student council, quilting,
Ikebana, soccer
Examinations AP, IB, PSAT, SAT, SAT II, IST ACER

CAMPUS FACILITIES

Location Urban
Campus 1 hectare, 3 buildings, 22 classrooms,
2 computer labs, 22 instructional computers,

8,700 library volumes, 1 cafeteria, 1 covered
play area, 1 gymnasium, 1 playing field,
1 science lab, air conditioning

HIROSHIMA INTERNATIONAL SCHOOL

Phone	81 82 843 4111
Fax	81 82 843 6399
Email	hisadmin@hiroshima-is.ac.jp
Website	www.hiroshima-is.ac.jp
Address	3-49-1 Kurakake, Asakita-ku, Hiroshima, 739-1743, Japan

STAFF

Principal Peter MacKenzie
PYP Coordinator John McPherson
IB Coordinator Peter MacKenzie
Business and Operations Manager Wayne Addis
IT and MYP Coordinator Nigel Barker

Librarian Freya Vaughn
Teaching staff Full time 20; Part time 1; Total 21
Nationalities of teaching staff US 3; UK 7;
Japanese 5; Other(s) (Australian, Canadian) 6

INFORMATION

Grade levels N–12
School year August–June
School type coeducational, day, private non-profit
Year founded 1962
Governed by appointed Board of Directors,
Board of Trustees
Accredited by CIS, New England
Regional organizations EARCOS

Enrollment Nursery 7; PreK 12;
Elementary K–5 82; Middle School 6–8 34;
High School 9–12 28; Total 163
Nationalities of student body US 20; UK 15;
Japanese 50; Other(s) (Korean) 78
Tuition/fee currency Japanese Yen
Tuition range 800,000–1,900,000
Annual fees Capital Levy 25,000; Busing 200,000
One time fees Registration 300,000
Graduates attending college 100%

EDUCATIONAL PROGRAM

Curriculum Intl, IB Diploma, IBPYP, IBMYP
Average class size Elementary 15; Secondary 10
Language(s) of instruction English
Language(s) taught Japanese
Staff specialists computer, ESL, learning
disabilities, librarian
Special curricular programs instrumental music

Extra curricular programs community service,
dance, environmental conservation,
newspaper, yearbook
Sports basketball, skiing, soccer, track and
field, volleyball
Examinations IB, PSAT, SAT

CAMPUS FACILITIES

Location Suburban
Campus 2 hectares, 1 building, 9 classrooms,
1 computer lab, 35 instructional computers,

8,000 library volumes, 1 gymnasium,
1 infirmary, 1 playing field, 1 science lab,
air conditioning

CANADIAN ACADEMY

Phone	81 78 857 0100
Fax	81 78 857 3250
Email	hdmstr@mail.canacad.ac.jp
Website	www.canacad.ac.jp
Address	4-1 Koyo-cho Naka, Higashinada-ku, Kobe, 658-0032, Japan

STAFF

Head of School Frederic F. Wesson
Elementary School Principal Matthew Flinchum
High School Principal Gerad Carrier
Middle School Principal Michael Colaianni
Elementary School Assistant Principal
Jonathan Schatzky
Assistant Head of School Charles A. Kite, Ph.D.

Director of Technology Rhonda Carrier
Media Services Coordinators Jeanie Colaianni
and Celia Schatzky
Teaching staff Full time 80; Part time 7; Total 87
Nationalities of teaching staff US 43; UK 1;
Japanese 16; Other(s) (Canadian,
New Zealander) 27

INFORMATION

Grade levels PreK–13
School year August–June
School type boarding, coeducational, private
non-profit
Year founded 1913
Governed by appointed Board of Trustees
Accredited by Western
Regional organizations EARCOS
Enrollment PreK 35; Elementary K–5 310;
Middle School 6–8 185; High School 9–12 250;
Total 780
Nationalities of student body US 126; UK 11;
Japanese 179; Other(s) (Korean, Indian) 464

Tuition/fee currency Japanese Yen
Tuition range 1,267,000–1,747,000
Annual fees Boarding, 7-day 850,000;
Capital Levy 152,000
One time fees Registration 310,000;
Application 55,000; ESOL 500,000
Boarding program grades 9–12
Boarding program length 7-day **Boys** 8 **Girls** 12
Graduates attending college 92%
Graduates have attended Stanford U,
Northwestern U, McGill U, Waseda U,
U of Queensland

EDUCATIONAL PROGRAM

Curriculum US, AP, IB Diploma
Average class size Elementary 18; Secondary 15
Language(s) of instruction English
Language(s) taught French, Japanese, Spanish
Staff specialists computer, counselor, ESL,
librarian, nurse

Special curricular programs art, instrumental
music, vocal music, computer/technology,
physical education
Extra curricular programs community service,
drama, yearbook, Habitat for Humanity
Sports badminton, baseball, basketball, soccer,
softball, tennis, volleyball
Examinations ACT, AP, IB, Iowa, PSAT, SAT, SAT II

CAMPUS FACILITIES

Location Rural
Campus 5 hectares, 1 building, 56 classrooms,
3 computer labs, 600 instructional computers,
35,000 library volumes, 1 auditorium,

1 cafeteria, 1 covered play area, 2 gymnasiums,
1 infirmary, 2 playing fields, 5 science labs,
2 tennis courts, air conditioning

MARIST BROTHERS INTERNATIONAL SCHOOL

Phone	81 78 732 6266
Fax	81 78 732 6268
Email	info@marist.ac.jp
Website	www.marist.ac.jp
Address	1-2-1 Chimori-cho, Suma-ku, Kobe, 654-0072, Japan

STAFF

Supervising Principal Rudy Maharaj
Vice Principal Geraldo de Couto
Montessori Coordinator Mark Pilgrim
Business Manager Jerry Ochs
IT Head Stephen Winter

Librarian Elbert Shitamoto
Teaching staff Full time 38; Part time 3; Total 41
Nationalities of teaching staff US 16; UK 1;
Japanese 5; Other(s) (Canadian, Antiguan,
Barbudan) 19

INFORMATION

Grade levels PreK–12
School year August–June
School type coeducational, day, private non-profit
Year founded 1951
Governed by appointed School Board
Accredited by Western
Regional organizations EARCOS

Enrollment PreK 30; Elementary K–5 140;
Middle School 6–8 65; High School 9–12 65;
Total 300
Tuition/fee currency Japanese Yen
One time fees Application 20,000
Graduates attending college 96%
Graduates have attended U of British Columbia,
New York U, Pennsylvania State U,
U of California in Los Angeles, York U

EDUCATIONAL PROGRAM

Curriculum US, AP
Average class size Elementary 25; Secondary 25
Language(s) of instruction English
Language(s) taught Japanese, French
Staff specialists computer, counselor, ESL,
librarian, nurse
Special curricular programs art, instrumental
music, computer/technology, physical
education, Japanese culture

Extra curricular programs community service,
drama, excursions/expeditions, photography,
yearbook
Sports basketball, soccer, softball, volleyball
Clubs Model UN, student council, National
Honor Society
Examinations AP, SAT, TOEFL

CAMPUS FACILITIES

Location Suburban
Campus 1 hectare, 3 buildings, 22 classrooms,
2 computer labs, 70 instructional computers,
30,000 library volumes, 1 auditorium,

1 cafeteria, 1 covered play area, 1 gymnasium,
1 infirmary, 1 playing field, 2 science labs,
air conditioning

St. Michael's International School

Phone 81 78 231 8885
Fax 81 78 231 8899
Email head@smis.org
Website www.smis.org
Address 3-17-2 Nakayamate-dori, Chuo-ku, Kobe, Hyogo-ken, 650 0004, Japan

STAFF

Head of School Hugh J. Mawby
Deputy Head of School Pauline Irvin-Hunter
English Language School Coordinator

Tazu Makino
Head of Library/Media Center Steve Lewington

INFORMATION

Grade levels N–5
School year September–June
School type coeducational, church-affiliated, day, private non-profit
Year founded 1946
Governed by appointed School Council
Regional organizations EARCOS, ECIS
Enrollment Nursery 20; PreK 24; Elementary K–5 120; Total 164

Nationalities of student body US 10; UK 9; Host 36; Other(s) 105
Tuition/fee currency Japanese Yen
Tuition range 880,000–950,000
Annual fees Insurance 3,000; Busing 100,000; Maintenance 75,000; Milk 15,000; PTA 4,000
One time fees Registration 150,000

EDUCATIONAL PROGRAM

Curriculum UK
Average class size Elementary 16
Language(s) of instruction English
Language(s) taught English, Japanese, French
Staff specialists computer, ESL, learning disabilities, librarian, nurse, reading resource
Special curricular programs art, computer/technology, physical education

Extra curricular programs computers, community service, dance, drama, environmental conservation, excursions/expeditions, literary magazine, newspaper, photography, yearbook, girls and boys clubs
Sports basketball, cricket, gymnastics, soccer, swimming, volleyball
Clubs arts and crafts, chess, physical fitness, cooking, gymnastics, soccer, literacy, music, creative dancing
Examinations SAT, QCA

CAMPUS FACILITIES

Location Urban
Campus 1 hectare, 2 buildings, 10 classrooms, 1 computer lab, 20 instructional computers,

3,000 library volumes, 1 auditorium, 1 covered play area, 1 gymnasium, 1 infirmary, 2 playing fields, air conditioning

Data from 2006/07 school year.

KYOTO INTERNATIONAL SCHOOL

Phone	81 75 451 1022
Fax	81 75 451 1023
Email	kis@kyoto-is.org
Website	www.kyoto-is.org
Address	317 Kitatawara-cho, Nakadachiuri-sagaru, Yoshiyamachi-dori, Kamigyo-ku, Kyoto, 602 8247, Japan

STAFF

Head of School Annette D. Levy
Business Manager Nobuko Nishimura
Computer Teacher Dana Del Raye
Librarian Izumi Hirai

Teaching staff Full time 11; Part time 6; Total 17
Nationalities of teaching staff US 4; Japanese 8; Other(s) (Canadian, Filipino) 5

INFORMATION

Grade levels N–8
School year August–June
School type coeducational, day, private non-profit
Year founded 1957
Governed by appointed Board of Governors
Accredited by Western
Regional organizations EARCOS
Enrollment Nursery 9; PreK 9; Elementary K–5 47; Middle School 6–8 12; Total 77

Nationalities of student body US 8; UK 4; Japanese 36; Other(s) (Korean, German) 29
Tuition/fee currency Japanese Yen
Tuition range 808,000–1,107,000
Annual fees Capital Levy 130,000; Books 51,000; Physical Education 10,000; Middle School 360,000
One time fees Registration 150,000

EDUCATIONAL PROGRAM

Curriculum Intl, IBPYP
Average class size Elementary 15
Language(s) of instruction English
Language(s) taught Japanese
Staff specialists computer, ESL, librarian
Special curricular programs art, instrumental music, vocal music, computer/technology, physical education

Extra curricular programs dance, drama, excursions/expeditions
Sports soccer, swimming, tennis, netball
Clubs chess, Chinese, French, Aikido, band, piano, cooking,

CAMPUS FACILITIES

Location Urban
Campus 1 hectare, 1 building, 7 classrooms, 1 computer lab, 24 instructional computers,

6,000 library volumes, 1 gymnasium, 1 playing field

NAGOYA INTERNATIONAL SCHOOL

Phone	81 52 736 2025
Fax	81 52 736 3883
Email	info@nis.ac.jp
Website	www.nis.ac.jp
Address	2686 Minamihara, Nakashidami, Moriyama-ku, Nagoya, Aichi, 463 0002, Japan
Mailing address	headmaster@nis.ac.jp

STAFF

Head of School Robert P. Risch
Elementary Principal Paul Ketko
Secondary Principal William Kneadler
Director of Development Erik Olson-Kikuchi
Counselor Kay Troxler, Ph.D.
Business Manager Hiroshi Sakai

IT Coordinator Jeff Genest
Librarian Karen Genest
Teaching staff Full time 30; Part time 6; Total 36
Nationalities of teaching staff US 18; UK 3; Japanese 9; Other(s) (Canadian, New Zealander) 6

INFORMATION

Grade levels PreK–12
School year August–June
School type coeducational, day, private non-profit
Year founded 1964
Governed by elected Board of Directors
Accredited by Western
Regional organizations EARCOS
Enrollment PreK 17; Elementary K–5 142; Middle School 6–8 72; High School 9–12 73; Total 304

Nationalities of student body US 73; UK 10; Japanese 120; Other(s) (Korean, Canadian) 101
Tuition/fee currency Japanese Yen
Tuition range 1,337,000–1,507,000
Annual fees Capital Levy 100,000; Busing 280,000; Lunch 107,250
One time fees Registration 200,000; Application 20,000; Building 400,000
Graduates attending college 100%
Graduates have attended American U, Carleton Col, Waseda U, Vanderbilt U, Yale U

EDUCATIONAL PROGRAM

Curriculum US, AP
Average class size Elementary 17; Secondary 10
Language(s) of instruction English
Language(s) taught Japanese, Spanish
Staff specialists computer, counselor, ESL, librarian, nurse, reading resource
Special curricular programs art, vocal music, computer/technology, distance learning, physical education

Extra curricular programs community service, drama, excursions/expeditions, newspaper, photography, yearbook
Sports badminton, baseball, basketball, gymnastics, soccer, softball, tennis, track and field, volleyball
Clubs Model UN, Habitat for Humanity, National Honor Society
Examinations ACT, AP, Iowa, PSAT, SAT, SAT II

CAMPUS FACILITIES

Location Suburban
Campus 7 hectares, 3 buildings, 28 classrooms, 1 computer lab, 80 instructional computers, 18,000 library volumes, 1 cafeteria, 1 covered play area, 1 gymnasium, 1 infirmary, 1 playing field, 2 science labs, 2 tennis courts, air conditioning

KATOH SCHOOL

Phone	81 55 924 3322
Fax	81 55 924 3352
Email	bostwick@gol.com
Website	www.bi-lingual.com
Address	1361-1 Nakamiyo, Numazu, Shizuoka, 410 0011, Japan

STAFF

Executive Director Mike Bostwick, Ed.D.
Kindergarten Co-Coordinator Alina Gavel
Elementary Director Chikae Hirayama
Director Jr and Sr High School Nobuko Wendfeldt
MYP Coordination Darryl Mann
DP Coordinator Craig Sutton

Head Office Manager Sadao Hasegawa
IT Coordinator/Site Manager Kazuhiro Horie
Head Librarian Natsuko Katoh
Teaching staff Full time 70; Part time 5; Total 75
Nationalities of teaching staff US 13; UK 2;
Japanese 38; Other(s) (Canadian, Australian) 22

INFORMATION

Grade levels PreK–12
School year April–March
School type coeducational, day, proprietary
Year founded 1926
Governed by appointed Board of Directors
Sponsored by Masahide Katoh
Regional organizations EARCOS
Enrollment PreK 100; Elementary K–5 290;
Middle School 6–8 100; High School 9–12 70;
Total 560

Nationalities of student body US 1; UK 1;
Japanese 555; Other(s) (Canadian, Australian) 3
Tuition/fee currency Japanese Yen
Tuition range 600,000–1,000,000
Annual fees Books 50,000; Class 70,000
One time fees Registration 200,000;
Uniform 80,000
Graduates attending college 100%
Graduates have attended Harvard U, Yale U,
Duke U, Massachusetts Institute of Technology,
McGill U

EDUCATIONAL PROGRAM

Curriculum National, Intl, IB Diploma, IBMYP
Average class size Elementary 20; Secondary 22
Language(s) of instruction English, Japanese
Language(s) taught Chinese
Staff specialists computer, counselor, librarian,
reading resource
Special curricular programs art, instrumental
music, vocal music, computer/technology,
physical education

Extra curricular programs computers, community
service, environmental conservation,
excursions/expeditions, study abroad
Sports basketball, martial arts, soccer, tennis,
track and field, volleyball
Examinations IB, PSAT, SAT, SAT II, TOEFL

CAMPUS FACILITIES

Location Suburban
Campus 10 hectares, 5 buildings, 40 classrooms,
3 computer labs, 120 instructional computers,

12,000 library volumes, 2 auditoriums,
2 gymnasiums, 3 infirmaries, 3 playing fields,
3 science labs, 6 tennis courts, air conditioning

315

OSAKA INTERNATIONAL SCHOOL

Phone	81 72 727 5050
Fax	81 72 727 5055
Email	kcaffin@senri.ed.jp
Website	www.senri.ed.jp
Address	4-4-16 Onohara-nishi, Mino-shi, Osaka-fu, 562 0032, Japan

STAFF

Head of School Karin M. Caffin, Ed.D.
Elementary Principal Rod Adam
Middle/High School Principal Gwyn Underwood
Business Manager Jim Schell
Director of Technology Steve Lewis

Head Librarian Clarence Coombs, Ph.D.
Teaching staff Full time 38; Part time 1; Total 39
Nationalities of teaching staff US 12; UK 4;
Japanese 6; Other(s) (Australian, Canadian) 17

INFORMATION

Grade levels PreK–12
School year September–June
School type coeducational, company-sponsored, day, private non-profit
Year founded 1991
Governed by appointed Board of Trustees/Board of Directors
Sponsored by Hankyu Corporation
Accredited by Western
Regional organizations EARCOS, ECIS

Enrollment PreK 8; Elementary K–5 106; Middle School 6–8 65; High School 9–12 56; Total 235
Nationalities of student body US 70; UK 10; Japanese 120; Other(s) (Korean, Australian) 35
Tuition/fee currency Japanese Yen
Tuition range 1,150,000–1,675,000
Annual fees Busing 80,000; Lunch 85,000
One time fees Registration 250,000
Graduates attending college 95%
Graduates have attended Oxford U, Wesleyan U, U of Southern California, Queen's U, Rice U

EDUCATIONAL PROGRAM

Curriculum US, Intl, IB Diploma, IBPYP, IBMYP
Average class size Elementary 19; Secondary 20
Language(s) of instruction English
Language(s) taught Japanese, Spanish, Chinese, German
Staff specialists computer, counselor, ESL, librarian, nurse
Special curricular programs art, instrumental music, vocal music, computer/technology, physical education

Extra curricular programs community service, drama, photography, yearbook, student government
Sports badminton, baseball, basketball, cross-country, rugby, soccer, softball, tennis, volleyball
Examinations IB, PSAT, SAT, SAT II, ISA

CAMPUS FACILITIES

Location Suburban
Campus 2 hectares, 1 building, 33 classrooms, 3 computer labs, 80 instructional computers, 55,000 library volumes, 1 auditorium, 1 cafeteria, 1 gymnasium, 1 infirmary, 1 playing field, 4 science labs, 1 pool, 1 tennis court, air conditioning

HOKKAIDO INTERNATIONAL SCHOOL

Phone	81 11 816 5000
Fax	81 11 816 2500
Email	his@his.ac.jp
Website	www.his.ac.jp
Address	1-55 5-jo 19-chome, Hiragishi, Toyohira-ku, Sapporo, 062-0935, Japan

STAFF

Head of School Richard Branson
Elementary Coordinator Margaret Shibuya
Technology Coordinator Glenn McKinney
Outdoor Activities Coordinator David Piazza
Secondary Coordinator Troy Gibbs
Business Manager Eri Kashiwabara

Technology Coordinator Glenn McKinney
Head Librarian Kathleen Riggins
Teaching staff Full time 20; Part time 2; Total 22
Nationalities of teaching staff US 15; Japanese 3; Other(s) (Canadian) 4

INFORMATION

Grade levels PreK–12
School year August–June
School type boarding, coeducational, private non-profit
Year founded 1958
Governed by appointed Member Board
Accredited by Western
Regional organizations EARCOS
Enrollment PreK 15; Elementary K–5 75; Middle School 6–8 40; High School 9–12 60; Total 190
Nationalities of student body US 20; UK 5; Japanese 65; Other(s) (Korean, Chinese) 100

Tuition/fee currency Japanese Yen
Tuition range 945,000–1,065,000
Annual fees Boarding, 7-day 640,000; Insurance 3,000; Busing 90,000; PTA 5,000
One time fees Registration 200,000; Application 15,000
Boarding program grades 7–12
Boarding program length 7-day **Boys** 8 **Girls** 8
Graduates attending college 90%
Graduates have attended New York U, Knox Col, Sarah Lawrence Col, Lewis and Clark Col, Purdue U

EDUCATIONAL PROGRAM

Curriculum US, AP, International Primary Curriculum
Average class size Elementary 15; Secondary 14
Language(s) of instruction English
Language(s) taught Spanish, Japanese
Staff specialists computer, ESL, librarian
Special curricular programs art, instrumental music, vocal music, physical education

Extra curricular programs community service, newspaper
Sports basketball, soccer, volleyball
Clubs outdoor, skiiing/snowboarding, student council
Examinations AP, PSAT, SAT, TOEFL, ACER—ISA

CAMPUS FACILITIES

Location Urban
Campus 2 hectares, 2 buildings, 16 classrooms, 1 computer lab, 45 instructional computers,

9,000 library volumes, 1 auditorium, 1 cafeteria, 1 gymnasium, 1 playing field, 1 science lab

TOHOKU INTERNATIONAL SCHOOL

Phone	81 22 348 2468
Fax	81 22 348 2467
Email	admin@tisweb.net
Website	www.tisweb.net
Address	7-101-1 Yakata, Izumi-Ku, Sendai, Miyagi, 981-3214, Japan

STAFF

Head of School Joan H Larsen, Ph.D.
Head Teacher Karina Eskajeda
Business/Finance Manager Yuko Kubo
Technology Coordinator Nicholas Schirmer

Library Coordinator Karina Eskajeda
Teaching staff Full time 10; Part time 7; Total 17
Nationalities of teaching staff US 7; Japanese 5; Other(s) (Austrian, Taiwanese) 5

INFORMATION

Grade levels N–12
School year August–June
School type coeducational, company-sponsored, day, private non-profit
Year founded 1950
Governed by appointed TIS Council
Sponsored by Nanko Educational Corporation
Accredited by Western
Regional organizations EARCOS
Enrollment Nursery 16; PreK 20; Elementary K–5 20; Middle School 6–8 20; High School 9–12 15; Total 91

Nationalities of student body US 5; Japanese 53; Other(s) (Korean, Pakistani) 33
Tuition/fee currency Japanese Yen
Tuition range 800,000–1,080,000
One time fees Registration 250,000
Graduates attending college 100%
Graduates have attended Indiana U, Hawai'i Pacific U, North Dakota State U, Ringling School of Art and Design, U of Pittsburgh

EDUCATIONAL PROGRAM

Curriculum US, Intl, AP
Average class size Elementary 10; Secondary 9
Language(s) of instruction English, Japanese
Staff specialists computer, ESL

Extra curricular programs drama, yearbook
Sports golf
Clubs Model UN, community action, film

CAMPUS FACILITIES

Location Suburban
Campus 2 hectares, 2 buildings, 12 classrooms, 1 computer lab, 40 instructional computers,

7,000 library volumes, 1 cafeteria, 1 gymnasium, 1 infirmary, 2 playing fields, 2 tennis courts, air conditioning

THE AMERICAN SCHOOL IN JAPAN

Phone	81 422 34 5300
Fax	81 422 34 5308
Email	info@asij.ac.jp
Website	www.asij.ac.jp
Address	1-1-1, Nomizu, Chofu-shi, Tokyo, 182-0031, Japan

STAFF

Head of School Timothy S. Carr
High School Principal Rick Weinland
Middle School Principal E. Scott Adams, Ed.D.
Elementary School Principal Daniel J. Bender
Early Learning Center Director Judy Beneventi
Director of Curriculum, Instruction and Assessment Patricia Butz

Director of Business Affairs Timothy L. Thornton, Ed.D.
Director of Information Technology Eugene Witt
High School Librarian Linda Hayakawa
Teaching staff Full time 166; Part time 6; Total 172
Nationalities of teaching staff US 116; UK 5; Japanese 18; Other(s) 33

INFORMATION

Grade levels N–12
School year August–June
School type coeducational, day, private non-profit
Year founded 1902
Governed by appointed Board of Trustees
Accredited by Western
Regional organizations EARCOS
Enrollment Nursery 150; Elementary K–5 536; Middle School 6–8 349; High School 9–12 546; Total 1,581

Nationalities of student body US 1,082; Japanese 251; Other(s) 248
Tuition/fee currency Japanese Yen
Tuition 2,020,000
Annual fees Capital Levy 100,000; Busing 325,000
One time fees Registration 300,000; Building Maintenance 500,000; Application 20,000
Graduates attending college 99%
Graduates have attended Stanford U, Yale U, Columbia U, Harvard U, Princeton U

EDUCATIONAL PROGRAM

Curriculum US, AP
Average class size Elementary 22; Secondary 17
Language(s) of instruction English
Language(s) taught Japanese, French, Spanish
Staff specialists computer, counselor, ESL, librarian, math resource, nurse, reading resource, speech/hearing
Special curricular programs art, instrumental music, vocal music, computer/technology, physical education, Japanese studies, outdoor education, television production

Extra curricular programs computers, community service, dance, drama, environmental conservation, excursions/expeditions, literary magazine, newspaper, photography, yearbook
Sports badminton, baseball, basketball, cross-country, football, golf, gymnastics, hockey, martial arts, soccer, softball, swimming, tennis, track and field, volleyball
Clubs Habitat for Humanity, Model UN, Amnesty International, kyogen theater, speech, debate, Animal Advocates, Media Production Network
Examinations ACT, AP, PSAT, SAT, SAT II, TOEFL, ERB

CAMPUS FACILITIES

Location Suburban
Campus 14 hectares, 8 buildings, 100 classrooms, 8 computer labs, 750 instructional computers, 60,000 library volumes, 1 auditorium, 1 cafeteria, 3 gymnasiums, 1 infirmary, 2 playing fields, 8 science labs, 1 pool, 4 tennis courts, air conditioning

AOBA-JAPAN INTERNATIONAL SCHOOL– SUGINAMI CAMPUS

Phone 81 3 3335 6620
Fax 81 3 3332 6930
Email info@a-jis.com
Website www.a-jis.com
Address 2-10-7 Miyamae, Suginami-ku, Tokyo, 168-0081, Japan

STAFF

Founding Director and Head of School Regina M. Doi
Vice President Adam Doi
International Education Consultant Roberto L. Gomez, Sr., Ed.D.
Middle School Principal Neal Dilk
Intensive Division Principal Phillip Carlo
Kindergarten and Elementary Principal Paul Wright
Senior Vice President and Director of Finance Chiharu Uemura
IT Manager Horace White
Head Librarian Ferdinand Licuanan
Teaching staff Full time 55; Total 55
Nationalities of teaching staff US 15; UK 5; Japanese 14; Other(s) (Australian, Gambian) 21

INFORMATION

Grade levels PreK–9
School year September–June
School type coeducational, day, private non-profit, proprietary
Year founded 1980
Governed by appointed and elected Board
Sponsored by Regina Doi
Accredited by CIS, New England
Regional organizations EARCOS, ECIS
Enrollment PreK 18; Elementary K–5 272; Middle School 6–8 148; Total 438
Nationalities of student body US 45; UK 15; Japanese 174; Other(s) (Korean, Saudi) 204
Tuition/fee currency Japanese Yen
Tuition range 1,900,000–2,500,000
Annual fees Lunch 92,000
One time fees Registration 300,000

EDUCATIONAL PROGRAM

Curriculum US, Intl
Average class size Elementary 20; Secondary 18
Language(s) of instruction English
Language(s) taught Japanese
Staff specialists computer, ESL, learning disabilities, librarian, math resource, nurse, physician, reading resource
Special curricular programs art, instrumental music, vocal music, computer/technology, physical education
Extra curricular programs computers, community service, dance, drama, excursions/expeditions, literary magazine, newspaper, photography, yearbook
Sports basketball, martial arts, soccer, swimming, volleyball
Clubs art, computer, choir, orchestra, Japanese dance, hand bell choir, Aikido, Junior Jaguars sports, team sports
Examinations TOEFL, ITBS, Gates-Macginitie

CAMPUS FACILITIES

Location Urban
Campus 2 buildings, 45 classrooms, 2 computer labs, 80 instructional computers, 55,000 library volumes, 1 cafeteria, 1 covered play area, 1 gymnasium, 1 infirmary, 1 playing field, 1 science lab, 1 pool, 1 tennis court, air conditioning

CHRISTIAN ACADEMY IN JAPAN

Phone	81 42 471 0022
Fax	81 42 476 2200
Email	infodesk@caj.or.jp
Website	www.caj.or.jp
Address	1-2-14 Shinkawa-cho, Higashi Kurume-shi, Tokyo, 203-0013, Japan

STAFF

Head of School Calvin W. Johnston
Elementary School Principal Jacquie Willson
Middle School Principal Tanya Hall
High School Principal Brian Vander Haak
Director of Educational Support Services
Flossie Epley

Business Manager Rick Seely
Technology Coordinator Dan Rudd
Librarian Lois Seely
Teaching staff Full time 41; Part time 19; Total 60
Nationalities of teaching staff US 35; Japanese 10;
Other(s) (Canadian) 15

INFORMATION

Grade levels K–12
School year August–June
School type boarding, coeducational,
church-affiliated, day
Year founded 1950
Governed by appointed Board of Directors
Accredited by Western
Regional organizations EARCOS
Enrollment Elementary K–5 155; Middle School
6–8 136; High School 9–12 184; Total 475
Nationalities of student body US 176; UK 10;
Japanese 166; Other(s) (Korean) 123

Tuition/fee currency Japanese Yen
Tuition range 965,000–1,450,000
Annual fees Registration 45,000; Boarding,
5-day 920,000; Boarding, 7-day 1,100,000;
Capital Levy 70,000
One time fees Entrance 300,000
Boarding program grades 6–12
Boarding program length 5-day and 7-day
Boys 8 **Girls** 8
Graduates attending college 90%
Graduates have attended Bethel Col, Biola U,
Calvin Col, Azusa Pacific U, Wheaton Col

EDUCATIONAL PROGRAM

Curriculum US, AP
Average class size Elementary 20; Secondary 17
Language(s) of instruction English
Language(s) taught Japanese, French, Spanish
Staff specialists computer, counselor, ESL,
learning disabilities, librarian, math resource,
nurse, reading resource
Special curricular programs art, instrumental music,
vocal music, computer/technology, physical
education, vocational, digital arts, yearbook

Extra curricular programs community service,
drama, excursions/expeditions
Sports basketball, cross-country, soccer, tennis,
track and field, volleyball, wrestling, field
hockey
Clubs girls soccer, boys volleyball, drama,
chess, jazz ensemble, chapel band
Examinations ACT, AP, Iowa, PSAT, SAT, SAT II,
TOEFL

CAMPUS FACILITIES

Location Urban
Campus 2 hectares, 7 buildings, 30 classrooms,
2 computer labs, 70 instructional computers,
23,450 library volumes, 1 auditorium,

1 cafeteria, 2 gymnasiums, 1 infirmary,
1 playing field, 3 science labs, 3 tennis courts,
air conditioning

INTERNATIONAL SCHOOL OF THE SACRED HEART

Phone	81 3 3400 3951
Fax	81 3 3400 3496
Email	info@issh.ac.jp
Website	www.issh.ac.jp
Address	4-3-1 Hiroo, Shibuya-ku, Tokyo, 150-0012, Japan

STAFF

Head of School Masako Egawa
High School Principal Yvonne Hayes
Middle School Principal Narelle English
Kindergarten and Junior School Principal
Kristen Moriarty
Curriculum Coordinator K–12 Mary Beth Luttrell

Business Manager Naruhiko Soga
Head Librarian Suzanne Gordon
Teaching staff Full time 67; Part time 23; Total 90
Nationalities of teaching staff US 15; UK 12;
Japanese 20; Other(s) (Australian, Canadian) 43

INFORMATION

Grade levels K–12
School year August–June
School type coeducational, church-affiliated,
day, girls only
Year founded 1908
Governed by appointed Society of the Sacred
Heart Corporation
Accredited by CIS, Western
Regional organizations EARCOS
Enrollment Elementary K–5 291;
Middle School 6–8 135; High School 9–12
151; Total 577

Nationalities of student body US 192; UK 23;
Japanese 56; Other(s) (Korean, Australian) 306
Tuition/fee currency Japanese Yen
Tuition range 1,100,000–1,980,000
Annual fees Capital Levy 70,000
One time fees Registration 250,000; Application
20,000; Placement Test 10,000; Educational
Enhancement 400,000
Graduates attending college 100%
Graduates have attended Columbia U,
Georgetown U, John Hopkins U,
U of Pennsylvania, London School of Economics

(Continued)

INTERNATIONAL SCHOOL OF THE SACRED HEART (Continued)

EDUCATIONAL PROGRAM

Curriculum US, UK, Intl, AP, International Primary Curriculum
Average class size Elementary 18; Secondary 15
Language(s) of instruction English
Language(s) taught French, Japanese
Staff specialists computer, counselor, ESL, learning disabilities, librarian, nurse
Special curricular programs art, instrumental music, vocal music, computer/technology, physical education

Extra curricular programs computers, dance, drama, excursions/expeditions, literary magazine, yearbook, student council, boosters, Social Service Council
Sports basketball, cross-country, soccer, swimming, tennis, track and field, volleyball
Examinations AP, PSAT, SAT

CAMPUS FACILITIES

Location Urban
Campus 2 hectares, 3 buildings, 49 classrooms, 4 computer labs, 200 instructional computers, 50,000 library volumes, 2 auditoriums, 1 cafeteria, 2 covered play areas, 1 gymnasium, 1 infirmary, 1 playing field, 4 science labs, 2 tennis courts, air conditioning

K. INTERNATIONAL SCHOOL TOKYO

Phone	+81-(0)3-3642-9993
Fax	+81-(0)3-3642-9994
Email	info@kist.ed.jp
Website	www.kist.ed.jp
Address	1-5-15 Shirakawa, Koto-ku, Tokyo, 135-0021, Japan

STAFF

Principal and Head of Primary Sasha Marshall
Head of Secondary Damian Rentoule
Head of Early Childhood and Vice Principal
Mary Christie
PYP Coordinator Terance Tiplady
MYP Coordinator Paul Workman
DP Coordinator Ashish Trivedi

Assistant School Director Takako Komaki
Computer Systems Supervisor Toshi Naito
Teacher and Librarian Anne Green
Teaching staff Full time 55; Total 55
Nationalities of teaching staff US 6; UK 7;
Japanese 8; Other(s) (Australian) 34

INFORMATION

Grade levels PreK–12
School year September–June
School type coeducational, company-sponsored,
day
Year founded 1997
Governed by appointed Seven Board Members
Sponsored by Komaki Corporation
Regional organizations ECIS
Enrollment PreK 77; Elementary K–5 233;
Middle School 6–8 64; High School 9–12 33;
Total 407

Nationalities of student body US 64; UK 15;
Japanese 150; Other(s) (Indian, Korean) 178
Tuition/fee currency Japanese Yen
Tuition range 960,000–1,350,000
Annual fees Building Maintenance 50,000
One time fees Enrollment 200,000; Facilities
Upgrade 200,000
Graduates attending college 50%

EDUCATIONAL PROGRAM

Curriculum IB Diploma, IBPYP, IBMYP
Average class size Elementary 20; Secondary 18
Language(s) of instruction English
Language(s) taught Japanese
Staff specialists computer, counselor, ESL,
librarian

Special curricular programs art, physical education
Extra curricular programs community service
Sports baseball, basketball, cross-country, soccer
Examinations IB

CAMPUS FACILITIES

Location Urban
Campus 1 hectare, 2 buildings, 24 classrooms,
1 computer lab, 50 instructional computers,

12,000 library volumes, 1 auditorium,
1 cafeteria, 1 covered play area, 1 gymnasium,
1 playing field, 1 science lab, air conditioning

NISHIMACHI INTERNATIONAL SCHOOL

Phone	81 3 3451 5520
Fax	81 3 3456 0197
Email	info@nishimachi.ac.jp
Website	www.nishimachi.ac.jp
Address	2-14-7 Moto Azabu, Minato-ku, Tokyo, 106-0046, Japan

STAFF

Head of School Terence M. Christian
Middle School Principal James O' Connor
Elementary Principal Julie Jackson-Jin
Director of Admissions Mariko Laabs
Director of Development Philippe Eymard
Director of Administration and External Affairs
Shusuke Ishida

Education Technology Coordinator Phillip Matz
Director of Media Center John Kolosowski
Teaching staff Full time 56; Part time 4; Total 60
Nationalities of teaching staff US 12; UK 5;
Japanese 20; Other(s) (Australian, Canadian) 23

INFORMATION

Grade levels K–9
School year August–June
School type coeducational, day, private non-profit
Year founded 1949
Governed by appointed Board of Directors
Accredited by CIS, Western
Regional organizations EARCOS, ECIS
Enrollment Elementary K–5 308; Middle School
6–8 114; High School 9–12 21; Total 443

Nationalities of student body US 234; UK 5;
Japanese 100; Other(s) (Australian,
New Zealander) 104
Tuition/fee currency Japanese Yen
Tuition 1,972,000
Annual fees Educational Enhancement 100,000
One time fees Registration 300,000; Capital Levy
500,000; Application 20,000
Graduates attending college 99%

EDUCATIONAL PROGRAM

Curriculum US, National, Intl
Average class size Elementary 20; Secondary 15
Language(s) of instruction English, Japanese
Staff specialists counselor, librarian, nurse,
speech/hearing
Special curricular programs art, physical
education, drama

Extra curricular programs dance, drama,
excursions/expeditions, photography, yearbook
Sports badminton, basketball, cross-country,
hockey, martial arts, skiing, soccer, softball,
track and field, volleyball

CAMPUS FACILITIES

Location Urban
Campus 1 hectare, 7 buildings, 36 classrooms,
2 computer labs, 150 instructional computers,

15,000 library volumes, 1 auditorium,
1 covered play area, 1 gymnasium, 1 infirmary,
2 science labs, air conditioning

SEISEN INTERNATIONAL SCHOOL

Phone   81 3 3704 2661
Fax   81 3 3701 1033
Email   sisinfo@seisen.com
Website   www.seisen.com
Address   12-15 Yoga 1-chome, Setagaya-ku, Tokyo, 158-0097, Japan

STAFF

Head of School Virginia A. Villegas
High School Principal Suzanne Kawasumi
Elementary School Principal Carmelita Nussbaum
Kindergarten Principal Sheila O'Donoghue
Assistant High School Principal Dinah Seno

IT Coordinator Douglas Jansen
Teaching staff Full time 62; Part time 16; Total 78
Nationalities of teaching staff US 23; UK 7;
Japanese 16; Other(s) (Canadian, Filipino) 32

INFORMATION

Grade levels K–12
School year August–June
School type church-affiliated, day, girls only
Year founded 1962
Governed by appointed Seisen Jogakuin
Educational Foundation
Accredited by CIS, New England
Regional organizations EARCOS
Enrollment Elementary K–5 412; Middle School
6–8 143; High School 9–12 165; Total 720

Nationalities of student body US 218; UK 42;
Japanese 146; Other(s) (Korean, Indian) 314
Tuition/fee currency Japanese Yen
Tuition range 1,035,000–1,940,000
Annual fees Building Maintenance 100,000
One time fees Registration 300,000;
Capital Levy 300,000
Graduates attending college 100%
Graduates have attended Cornell U, London
School of Economics, U of California in San
Diego, Keio U, St. Martin's Col

EDUCATIONAL PROGRAM

Curriculum US, Intl, IB Diploma, IGCSE
Average class size Elementary 21; Secondary 23
Language(s) of instruction English
Language(s) taught Japanese, Spanish, French
Staff specialists computer, counselor, ESL,
learning disabilities, librarian, math resource,
nurse, reading resource
Special curricular programs art, instrumental
music, vocal music, computer/technology,
physical education

Extra curricular programs computers, community
service, dance, drama, environmental
conservation, excursions/expeditions, yearbook
Sports badminton, basketball, cross-country,
skiing, soccer, swimming, tennis, track and
field, volleyball
Clubs Model UN, National Honor Society,
Boosters, Adventurers, debate, speech, drama,
math, Brainbowl, ensemble, middle and high
school choirs
Examinations GCSE, IB, IGCSE, Iowa, PSAT, SAT

CAMPUS FACILITIES

Location Suburban
Campus 2 buildings, 43 classrooms,
2 computer labs, 166 instructional computers,

22,000 library volumes, 1 cafeteria,
1 gymnasium, 1 infirmary, 3 science labs,
2 tennis courts, air conditioning

St. Mary's International School

Phone	81 3 3709 3411
Fax	81 3 3707 1950
Email	jutras@inter.net
Website	www.smis.ac.jp
Address	1-6-19 Seta, Setagaya-ku, Tokyo, 158-8668, Japan

STAFF

Head of School Michel Jutras
High School Principal Saburo Kagei
Middle School Principal Stephen Wilson
Elementary School Principal
Br. Lawrence Guy Lambert
Elementary School Assistant Principal
Michael DiMuzio

Curriculum Coordinator Linda Wayne
Business Manager Kunihiko Takamichi
IT Program Manager DJ Feldmeyer
Head Librarian Anna Fernicola
Teaching staff Full time 90; Part time 20; Total 110
Nationalities of teaching staff US 39; UK 5;
Japanese 22; Other(s) (Canadian, Australian) 44

INFORMATION

Grade levels K–12
School year August–June
School type boys only, church-affiliated, day,
private non-profit
Year founded 1954
Governed by appointed School Board
Accredited by CIS, Western
Regional organizations EARCOS
Enrollment Elementary K–5 447; Middle School
6–8 245; High School 9–12 291; Total 983
Nationalities of student body US 240; UK 42;
Japanese 261; Other(s) (Korean, Australian) 440

Tuition/fee currency Japanese Yen
Tuition 1,980,000
Annual fees Busing 300,000; Lunch 121,000;
Building Development 70,000; IB 160,000
One time fees Registration 300,000; Building
Maintenance 400,000
Graduates attending college 99%
Graduates have attended U of British Columbia,
Princeton U, U of Pennsylvania, Brown U,
U of Notre Dame

EDUCATIONAL PROGRAM

Curriculum US, IB Diploma
Average class size Elementary 23; Secondary 22
Language(s) of instruction English
Language(s) taught Japanese, Spanish, French
Staff specialists computer, counselor, ESL,
librarian, nurse
Special curricular programs art, instrumental
music, vocal music, computer/technology,
physical education

Extra curricular programs dance, drama,
excursions/expeditions, newspaper,
photography, yearbook
Sports baseball, basketball, cross-country,
hockey, skiing, soccer, swimming, tennis,
track and field
Examinations IB, SAT, TOEFL

CAMPUS FACILITIES

Location Urban
Campus 9 hectares, 2 buildings, 38 classrooms,
2 computer labs, 250 instructional computers,
40,000 library volumes, 1 cafeteria,

1 covered play area, 1 gymnasium, 1 infirmary,
2 playing fields, 4 science labs, 1 pool,
4 tennis courts

TOKYO INTERNATIONAL SCHOOL

Phone	81 35484 1160
Fax	81 0 5484 1139
Email	tis@tokyois.com
Website	www.tokyois.com
Address	3-4-22 Mita Minato-Ku, Tokyo, 108 0073, Japan

STAFF

Office Manager Atsumi Fujii
Head of School Desmond Hurst, Ed.D.
Deputy Head of School Lorraine Izzard, Ed.D.
Founder Patrick Newell
Business Manager Shigeo Otsu

Macintosh Computer Technician and Support Allan Tsuda
Library Teacher Leanne Windsor, Ed.D.
Teaching staff Full time 39; Total 39
Nationalities of teaching staff US 5; UK 2; Japanese 6; Other(s) (Australian, Canadian) 26

INFORMATION

Grade levels PreK–8
School year August–June
School type coeducational, day, proprietary
Year founded 1996
Governed by Patrick Newell
Sponsored by Tokyo International School Corporation
Accredited by CIS, New England
Regional organizations EARCOS, ECIS
Enrollment PreK 20; Elementary K–5 275; Middle School 6–8 49; Total 344

Nationalities of student body US 109; UK 16; Japanese 92; Other(s) (Australian, New Zealander) 127
Tuition/fee currency Japanese Yen
Tuition range 2,000,000–2,970,000
Annual fees Busing 320,000; IT 50,000; Building Maintenance 100,000
One time fees Registration 300,000; Building Development 350,000

EDUCATIONAL PROGRAM

Curriculum Intl, IBPYP, IBMYP
Average class size Elementary 16
Language(s) of instruction English
Language(s) taught Japanese
Staff specialists computer, counselor, ESL, librarian, nurse, reading resource
Special curricular programs art, vocal music, computer/technology, physical education

Extra curricular programs computers, community service, dance, drama, newspaper, photography
Sports basketball, cricket, cross-country, football, gymnastics, hockey, martial arts, skiing, soccer, swimming, tennis, track and field
Clubs cooking, computer, tennis, Aikido, Karate, drama, Spanish, photography, floor hockey, dance

CAMPUS FACILITIES

Location Urban
Campus 2 hectares, 1 building, 23 classrooms, 2 computer labs, 200 instructional computers, 1,000 library volumes, 1 auditorium, 1 gymnasium, 1 playing field, 1 science lab, 1 pool, 1 tennis court, air conditioning

SAINT MAUR INTERNATIONAL SCHOOL

Phone	81 45 641 5751
Fax	81 45 641 6688
Email	office@stmaur.ac.jp
Website	www.stmaur.ac.jp
Address	83 Yamate-cho, Naka-ku, Yokohama, 231-8654, Japan

STAFF

School Head Jeanette K. Thomas
Deputy School Head/Student Services
Catherine O. Endo
Coordinating Principal Richard B. Rucci
Secondary School Principal Matthew Parr
**Elementary School Principal and Montessori
Liaison** Yong-Lang Kwan

College Guidance Counselor Glenn Scoggins
Business Manager Marie Kawamura
Head of Technology Ray Owen
Head Librarian Jennifer Schumacher
Teaching staff Full time 52; Part time 10; Total 62
Nationalities of teaching staff US 15; UK 13;
Japanese 10; Other(s) (Australian, Canadian) 24

INFORMATION

Grade levels PreK–12
School year August–June
School type coeducational, church-affiliated,
day, private non-profit
Year founded 1872
Governed by appointed Board of Directors
Accredited by CIS, New England
Regional organizations EARCOS, ECIS
Enrollment PreK 58; Elementary K–5 174;
Middle School 6–8 106;
High School 9–12 122; Total 460

Nationalities of student body US 106; UK 16;
Japanese 185; Other(s) (Indian, Korean) 153
Tuition/fee currency Japanese Yen
Tuition range 1,070,000–1,985,000
Annual fees Building and Maintenance Fund
200,000
One time fees Registration 300,000
Graduates attending college 99%
Graduates have attended Yale U, Georgetown U,
Bryn Mawr Col, Brown U, Stanford U

EDUCATIONAL PROGRAM

Curriculum US, UK, Intl, AP, IB Diploma, IGCSE,
Trinity College of Music, IPC-International
Primary Curriculum
Average class size Elementary 16; Secondary 24
Language(s) of instruction English
Language(s) taught French, Spanish, Japanese
Staff specialists computer, counselor, ESL,
learning disabilities, librarian, math resource,
nurse, reading resource
Special curricular programs art, instrumental
music, vocal music, computer/technology,
physical education

Extra curricular programs computers, community
service, dance, drama, excursions/expeditions,
literary magazine, newspaper, yearbook
Sports baseball, basketball, cross-country,
martial arts, soccer, tennis, track and field,
volleyball
Examinations AP, GCSE, IB, IGCSE, Iowa, PSAT,
SAT, SAT II, TOEFL, Trinity International Music
Examinations

CAMPUS FACILITIES

Location Rural
Campus 1 hectare, 5 buildings, 30 classrooms,
5 computer labs, 124 instructional computers,
22,767 library volumes, 1 auditorium,

1 cafeteria, 2 covered play areas, 1 gymnasium,
1 infirmary, 1 playing field, 3 science labs,
1 tennis court, air conditioning

YOKOHAMA INTERNATIONAL SCHOOL

Phone	81 45 622 0084
Fax	81 45 621 0379
Email	yis@yis.ac.jp
Website	www.yis.ac.jp
Address	258 Yamate-cho, Naka-ku, Yokohama, 231-0862, Japan

STAFF

Head of School Simon Taylor
High School Principal Dennis Stanworth
Deputy Head of School James MacDonald
Middle School Principal Russell Brown
Elementary School Principal Paul Neary
Business Manager Chiyoka Kurahone

Information Technology Director Brian Lockwood
Head Librarian Anthony Tilke
Teaching staff Full time 74; Part time 13; Total 87
Nationalities of teaching staff US 14; UK 22;
Japanese 13; Other(s) (Australian, Canadian) 38

INFORMATION

Grade levels N–12
School year August–June
School type coeducational, day, private non-profit
Year founded 1924
Governed by elected Board of Directors
Accredited by CIS, New England
Regional organizations EARCOS, ECIS
Enrollment Nursery 30; PreK 30;
Elementary K–5 299; Middle School 6–8 167;
High School 9–12 220; Total 746

Nationalities of student body US 176; UK 97;
Japanese 167; Other(s) (Dutch, Swede) 306
Tuition/fee currency Japanese Yen
Tuition range 1,440,000–2,135,000
One time fees Registration 700,000; Graduation
50,000; Application 20,000
Graduates attending college 90%
Graduates have attended Harvard U,
Nottingham U, Waseda U, Yale U,
U of British Columbia

EDUCATIONAL PROGRAM

Curriculum Intl, AP, IB Diploma, IBPYP, IGCSE,
Humankind Curriculum
Average class size Elementary 20; Secondary 20
Language(s) of instruction English
Language(s) taught Japanese, French, Spanish,
Dutch, German, Chinese
Staff specialists computer, counselor, librarian,
math resource, nurse, reading resource
Special curricular programs art, instrumental
music, vocal music, computer/technology,
physical education, film, business studies,

studio technology, Japanese instrumental music
Extra curricular programs community service,
dance, drama, excursions/expeditions, literary
magazine, photography, yearbook, astronomy,
Brainbowl
Sports baseball, basketball, cross-country,
football, hockey, soccer, track and field, volleyball
Clubs Model UN
Examinations AP, GCSE, IB, IGCSE, PSAT, SAT,
SAT II, ISA

CAMPUS FACILITIES

Location Suburban
Campus 1 hectare, 8 buildings, 66 classrooms,
1 computer lab, 280 instructional computers,

27,000 library volumes, 1 auditorium,
1 cafeteria, 1 gymnasium, 1 infirmary,
2 playing fields, 4 science labs, air conditioning

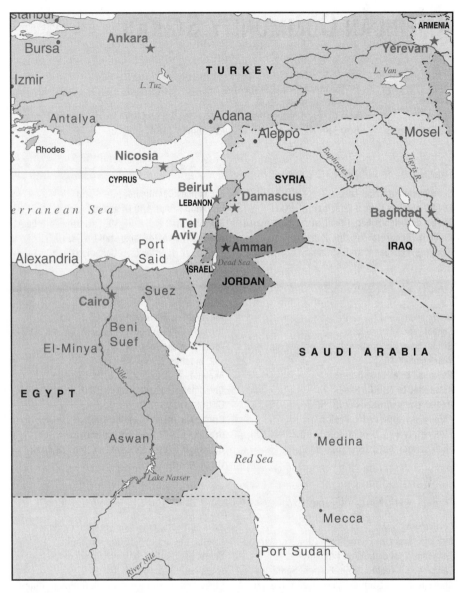

JORDAN

Area:	92,300 sq km
Population:	6,053,193
Capital:	Amman
Currency:	Jordanian Dinar (JOD)
Languages:	Arabic, English

AMERICAN COMMUNITY SCHOOL

Phone	962 6 581 3944
Fax	962 6 582 3357
Email	school@acsamman.edu.jo
Website	www.acsamman.edu.jo
Address	Next to Royal Automobile Club, Between 7th and 8th Circle, Amman, Jordan
Mailing address	Box 310, Dahiat Al-Amir Rashid, Amman 11831, Jordan

STAFF

Superintendent Brian Lahan
ECE/Elementary School Principal Julie Cox
Middle and High School Principal Steve Mancuso
Guidance Counselor Kristine Raggio
Business Manager Hamdi Hamdi

Technology Coordinator Nael Faraj
Librarian Samar Abu Ghazaleh
Teaching staff Full time 39; Part time 7; Total 46
Nationalities of teaching staff US 32; UK 1;
Jordanian 9; Other(s) (Canadian) 4

INFORMATION

Grade levels N–12
School year August–June
School type coeducational, day, private non-profit
Year founded 1957
Governed by elected Board
Accredited by Middle States
Regional organizations ECIS, NESA
Enrollment Nursery 15; PreK 23;
Elementary K–5 166; Middle School 6–8 106;
High School 9–12 135; Total 445

Nationalities of student body US 116; UK 8;
Jordanian 77; Other(s) (Korean, Canadian) 244
Tuition/fee currency US Dollar
Tuition range 2,965–11,815
Annual fees Registration 1,000; Busing 1,200
One time fees Capital Levy 3,000; Yearbook 45;
Graduation 95
Graduates attending college 95%
Graduates have attended American U,
California State U, Northwestern U, Duke U,
Brigham Young U

EDUCATIONAL PROGRAM

Curriculum US, AP
Average class size Elementary 20; Secondary 18
Language(s) of instruction English
Language(s) taught Arabic, French, Spanish
Staff specialists computer, counselor, ESL,
librarian, nurse, reading resource
Special curricular programs art, instrumental
music, vocal music, physical education

Extra curricular programs computers, dance,
drama, literary magazine, yearbook
Sports badminton, basketball, soccer, tennis,
track and field, volleyball
Clubs Arabic, student council, National Junior
Honor Society, National Honor Society, Model
UN, leadership, literary magazine, forensics
and debate, Spanish, drama
Examinations ACT, AP, Iowa, PSAT, SAT

CAMPUS FACILITIES

Location Rural
Campus 9 hectares, 6 buildings, 39 classrooms,
5 computer labs, 100 instructional computers,

24,000 library volumes, 1 auditorium,
1 gymnasium, 1 infirmary, 2 playing fields,
2 science labs, 2 tennis courts, air conditioning

AMMAN BACCALAUREATE SCHOOL

Phone	962 6 541 1572
Fax	962 6 541 2603
Email	proffice@abs.edu.jo
Website	www.abs.edu.jo
Address	P.O. Box 441, Sweileh, Amman, 11910, Jordan

STAFF

Principal Samia Al Farra, Ed.D.
Vice Principal Dermot Keegan
In-Service Director Riham Kawar
Head of IB College Cathy Souob
Head of Middle Years School Bassma Nimri
Head of Junior School Nora Shrydeh

Finance Manager Yousef Beitawi
IT Manager Ounis Zoubir
Head of Library/Media Center Maysa Al Haddadeh
Teaching staff Full time 152; Part time 4; Total 156
Nationalities of teaching staff US 15; UK 13;
Jordanian 107; Other(s) (Canadian, Irish) 21

INFORMATION

Grade levels K–12
School year September–June
School type coeducational, day, private non-profit
Year founded 1981
Governed by appointed Board of Trustees
Sponsored by Hashemite Society for Education
Accredited by CIS, New England
Regional organizations ECIS, NESA
Enrollment Elementary K–5 399; Middle School
6–8 230; High School 9–12 342; Total 971

Nationalities of student body US 88; UK 8;
Jordanian 875; Other(s) (Canadian, Iraq
Tuition/fee currency Jordanian Dinar
Tuition range 2,295–7,800
Annual fees Busing 430; Lunch 325
One time fees Registration 30
Graduates attending college 100%
Graduates have attended Harvard U,
Massachusetts Institute of Technology,
Standford U, Cambridge U, Brown U

EDUCATIONAL PROGRAM

Curriculum National, Intl, IB Diploma, IBMYP
Average class size Elementary 25; Secondary 22
Language(s) of instruction English, Arabic
Language(s) taught French
Staff specialists computer, counselor, librarian,
math resource, nurse, physician, psychologist,
reading resource
Special curricular programs art, instrumental
music, vocal music, computer/technology,
physical education

Extra curricular programs computers, community
service, dance, drama, environmental
conservation, excursions/expeditions, literary
magazine, newspaper, photography, yearbook
Sports badminton, basketball, football,
gymnastics, rugby, soccer, softball, tennis,
track and field, volleyball
Examinations IB, SAT, SAT II

CAMPUS FACILITIES

Location Suburban
Campus 9 hectares, 5 buildings, 57 classrooms,
4 computer labs, 155 instructional computers,
50,000 library volumes, 1 auditorium,

2 cafeterias, 1 covered play area, 1 gymnasium,
1 infirmary, 8 playing fields, 7 science labs,
3 tennis courts

Modern American School

Phone	962 6 5862779
Fax	962 6 5816860
Email	admin@modernamericanschool.com
Website	www.modernamericanschool.com
Address	P.O. Box 950553 Sweifieh, Code No 11195, Bakhit Issa Street # 27, Amman-Sweifieh, Jordan, 11195, Jordan

STAFF

School Principal Omaya Zamel
Deputy Director Jacqueline Al-Mufty
Director of Curriculum Roy Colquitt
Assistant Principal Samuel K. Davis
Director of International Office and Admissions Rumiana Nuseibeh

Head of Elementary Alia Husseini
Head of IT Hala El-A's
Chief Librarian Mary Shaban
Teaching staff Full time 93; Part time 7; Total 100
Nationalities of teaching staff US 20; UK 15; Jordanian 55; Other(s) (Canadian, Australian) 10

INFORMATION

Grade levels N–12
School year September–June
School type coeducational, day, proprietary
Year founded 1985
Governed by appointed Board of Trustees
Sponsored by Zamel Group
Accredited by North Central
Regional organizations ECIS, NESA
Enrollment Nursery 21; PreK 115; Elementary K–5 347; Middle School 6–8 199; High School 9–12 299; Total 981

Nationalities of student body US 286; UK 32; Jordanian 415; Other(s) (Canadian, Australian) 248
Tuition/fee currency US Dollar
Tuition range 2,922–8,415
Annual fees Insurance 170; Busing 830; Books 600
One time fees Registration 633
Graduates attending college 99%
Graduates have attended U of Toronto, Massachusetts Institute of Technology, Imperial Col of London, American U of Beirut

EDUCATIONAL PROGRAM

Curriculum US, UK, National, AP, IGCSE
Average class size Elementary 23; Secondary 22
Language(s) of instruction English
Language(s) taught Arabic, French
Staff specialists computer, counselor, ESL, librarian, nurse, physician
Special curricular programs art, instrumental music, computer/technology, physical education
Extra curricular programs computers, community service, dance, drama, environmental conservation, excursions/expeditions, newspaper, photography, yearbook
Sports badminton, basketball, football, gymnastics, martial arts, soccer, swimming, track and field, volleyball
Clubs environment, photography, Friends to the Library
Examinations A-level GCE, GCSE, IGCSE, Iowa, SAT, SAT II, TOEFL

CAMPUS FACILITIES

Location Urban
Campus 2 buildings, 4 computer labs, 25,000 library volumes, 1 auditorium, 2 cafeterias, 2 covered play areas, 1 gymnasium, 2 playing fields, 3 science labs, 1 pool

KAZAKHSTAN

KAZAKHSTAN

Area:	2,717,300 sq km
Population:	15,284,929
Capital:	Astana
Currency:	Tenge (KZT)
Languages:	Kazakh

ALMATY INTERNATIONAL SCHOOL

Phone	7 327 250-4561
Fax	7 327 250-4564
Email	almaty@qsi.org
Website	www.qsi.org/kaz
Address	185 Auezov St., Auezov District, Kalkaman Village, Almaty, 050006, Kazakhstan
Mailing address	c/o American Embassy, Almaty, Dept. of State, 7030 Almaty Place, Washington, DC 20521-7030, USA

STAFF

Director Daniel C. Bastien
Director of Instruction Russell S. Page
Elementary Coordinator Maura Martin
Counselor Gregory Collins
Director of Athletics and Activities Scott Roley

Business Manager Dang Garcia
IT Department Head James Martin
Librarian Kris Feller
Teaching staff Full time 42; Part time 4; Total 46
Nationalities of teaching staff US 41; Other(s) 5

INFORMATION

Grade levels PreK–12
School year August–June
School type coeducational, day, private non-profit
Year founded 1993
Governed by appointed Board of Directors
Accredited by Middle States
Regional organizations CEESA
Nationalities of student body US 37; UK 15; Kazakhstani 105; Other(s) (Korean, Indian) 218

Tuition/fee currency US Dollar
Tuition range 7,000–14,500
Annual fees Busing 1,500
One time fees Registration 100
Graduates attending college 100%
Graduates have attended Stanford U, U of Illinois, Georgetown U, U of Wisconsin, Texas A&M U

EDUCATIONAL PROGRAM

Curriculum US, AP
Average class size Elementary 16; Secondary 17
Language(s) of instruction English
Language(s) taught French, Russian, Spanish
Staff specialists computer, counselor, ESL, librarian, physician, reading resource
Special curricular programs art, instrumental music, vocal music, computer/technology, physical education

Extra curricular programs computers, community service, dance, drama, excursions/expeditions, newspaper, yearbook
Sports basketball, cross-country, soccer, softball, tennis, track and field, volleyball
Examinations AP, Iowa, PSAT, SAT

CAMPUS FACILITIES

Location Suburban
Campus 7 hectares, 2 buildings, 36 classrooms, 2 computer labs, 50 instructional computers,

18,500 library volumes, 1 cafeteria, 2 gymnasiums, 1 infirmary, 2 playing fields, 1 science lab, 3 tennis courts, air conditioning

QSI INTERNATIONAL SCHOOL OF ASTANA

Phone   7 3272 241 353
Fax   +7 3172 241 993
Email   astana@qsi.org
Website   www.qsi.org
Address   29/1 Arai St., Chubary District, Astana, 01000, Kazakhstan

STAFF

Director Barbara Reynolds, Ed.D.
Teaching staff Full time 11; Total 11

Nationalities of teaching staff US 4; Kazakhstani 7

INFORMATION

Grade levels PreK–8
School year August–June
School type day, private non-profit
Year founded 2005
Governed by appointed Advisory Board
Sponsored by Quality Schools International
Regional organizations CEESA

Enrollment PreK 10; Elementary K–5 20;
Middle School 6–8 5; Total 35
Nationalities of student body US 12; UK 1;
Kazakhstani 7; Other(s) (Japanese, Latvian) 15
Tuition/fee currency US Dollar
Tuition range 5,300–15,100
Annual fees Capital Levy 1,600
One time fees Registration 100

EDUCATIONAL PROGRAM

Curriculum US
Average class size Elementary 8
Language(s) of instruction English
Language(s) taught Russian

Special curricular programs art, vocal music,
computer/technology, physical education
Extra curricular programs computers, cooking,
arts and crafts
Examinations Iowa

CAMPUS FACILITIES

Location Urban
Campus 5 hectares, 1 building, 5 classrooms,
1 computer lab, 7 instructional computers,

200 library volumes, 1 cafeteria, 1 gymnasium,
1 playing field

DOSTYK AMERICAN INTERNATIONAL SCHOOL

Phone	7 3122 209203
Fax	7 3122 971345
Email	dais@daiskz.org
Website	www.daiskz.org
Address	Dostyk Village, Vladimirskaya Street, 37, Atyrau, 060011, Kazakhstan
Mailing address	Atyrau Pouch Mail, PO Box 6066, San Ramon, CA 94583, USA

STAFF

Head of School Charles Gregory
Technology Teacher Greg Person
Librarian, Head of Media and Information Resources Denise Gregory

Teaching staff Full time 8; Total 8
Nationalities of teaching staff US 4; UK 1; Kazakhstani 1; Other(s) (Canadian) 2

INFORMATION

Grade levels PreK–8
School year August–June
School type coeducational, company-sponsored, day, private non-profit
Year founded 2002
Governed by appointed Advisory Committee
Sponsored by ChevronTexaco; managed by International Schools Services, Inc.
Accredited by Middle States

Regional organizations NESA
Enrollment PreK 4; Elementary K–5 31; Middle School 6–8 5; Total 40
Nationalities of student body US 29; UK 4; Other(s) (Canadian, Australian) 7
Tuition/fee currency US Dollar
Tuition 16,400–16,400
Annual fees Registration 11,400
One time fees Capital Levy 5,000

EDUCATIONAL PROGRAM

Curriculum US
Average class size Elementary 8
Language(s) of instruction English
Language(s) taught Russian
Staff specialists computer, librarian

Special curricular programs art, vocal music, computer/technology, physical education
Extra curricular programs dance, excursions/expeditions, yearbook
Sports soccer, volleyball
Examinations Iowa

CAMPUS FACILITIES

Location Urban
Campus 2 hectares, 2 buildings, 10 classrooms, 1 computer lab, 35 instructional computers, 4,500 library volumes, 1 auditorium, 1 gymnasium, 1 infirmary, 1 playing field, 1 science lab, 2 pools, 2 tennis courts, air conditioning

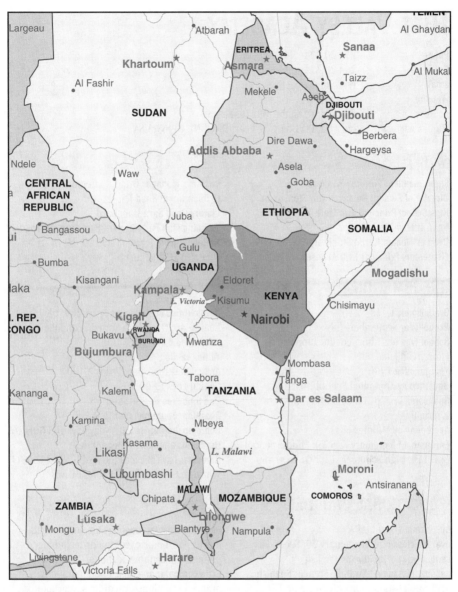

KENYA

Area:	582,650 sq km
Population:	36,913,721
Capital:	Nairobi
Currency:	Kenyan Shilling (KES)
Languages:	English

RIFT VALLEY ACADEMY

Phone	254 20 3246 249
Fax	254 20 3246 111
Email	rva@kijabe.net
Website	www.rva.org
Address	PO Box 80, Kijabe, 00220, Kenya
Mailing address	c/o AIM, PO Box 178, Pearl River, NY 10965, USA

STAFF

Superintendent Timothy W. Cook
Director of Student Guidance Jim Stenstrom
High School Principal Tim Hall
Dean of Men Mark Kinzer
Dean of Women Karen Stockton
Elementary Principal Kym Arensen

Business Manager Brian Richerson
IT Department Head Jeff Hazard
Library Head Sara Bouchard
Teaching staff Full time 40; Part time 12; Total 52
Nationalities of teaching staff US 45; UK 1;
Other(s) (Canadian) 6

INFORMATION

Grade levels K–12
School year September–July
School type boarding, coeducational,
church-affiliated
Year founded 1906
Governed by appointed School Board
Sponsored by Africa Inland Mission
International
Accredited by Middle States
Enrollment Elementary K–5 79; Middle School
6–8 119; High School 9–12 291; Total 489

Nationalities of student body US 269; UK 15;
Kenyan 40; Other(s) (Korean, Canadian) 165
Tuition/fee currency US Dollar
Tuition range 835–5,220
Annual fees Boarding, 7-day 2,100;
Capital Levy 1,800
One time fees Registration 50
Boarding program grades 2–12
Boarding program length 7-day **Boys** 165 **Girls** 162
Graduates attending college 95%
Graduates have attended Harvard U, Wake Forest U,
Wheaton Col, Stanford U, John Brown U

EDUCATIONAL PROGRAM

Curriculum US, UK, AP
Average class size Elementary 20; Secondary 25
Language(s) of instruction English
Language(s) taught Swahili, French, Spanish
Staff specialists computer, counselor, ESL,
learning disabilities, librarian, nurse,
psychologist, reading resource, speech/hearing

Special curricular programs art, instrumental
music, vocal music, computer/technology,
physical education, vocational
Extra curricular programs community service,
drama, excursions/expeditions, yearbook
Sports basketball, hockey, rugby, soccer, tennis,
volleyball
Examinations ACT, AP, GCSE, IGCSE, PSAT, SAT,
SAT II, Stanford, TOEFL

CAMPUS FACILITIES

Location Rural
Campus 30 hectares, 75 buildings, 24 classrooms,
4 computer labs, 92 instructional computers,
18,000 library volumes, 2 auditoriums,

1 cafeteria, 2 covered play areas, 1 gymnasium,
1 infirmary, 3 playing fields, 4 science labs,
4 tennis courts

INTERNATIONAL SCHOOL OF KENYA, LTD.

Phone	254 20 4183 622
Fax	254 20 4183 272
Email	isk_admin@isk.ac.ke
Website	www.isk.ac.ke
Address	Peponi Road, Nairobi, 00800, Kenya
Mailing address	PO Box 14103, Nairobi, 00800 Kenya

STAFF

Director Areta A. Williams
High School Principal Joseph Hollenbeck
Middle School Principal Terry Howard, Ph.D.
Elementary Principal Patricia Salleh Matta
Director of Human Resources and Administration
Sharon Wanyee
Curriculum Coordinator Jodi Lake

Business Manager David Gaitho
IT Head of Department William Smith
Library/Media Center Coordinator Sharon Brown
Teaching staff Full time 75; Part time 5; Total 80
Nationalities of teaching staff US 36; UK 8;
Kenyan 10; Other(s) 26

INFORMATION

Grade levels PreK–13
School year August–June
School type coeducational, day, private non-profit
Year founded 1976
Governed by appointed and elected Board of
Directors
Accredited by CIS, Middle States
Regional organizations AISA
Enrollment PreK 17; Elementary K–5 242;
Middle School 6–8 156;
High School 9–12 247; Total 662

Nationalities of student body US 225; UK 60;
Kenyan 54; Other(s) (Canadian, Israeli) 323
Tuition/fee currency US Dollar
Tuition range 4,390–14,400
Annual fees Busing 980
One time fees Registration 100; Capital Levy 4,000
Graduates attending college 98%
Graduates have attended McGill U, U of
Massachusetts, Amherst, London School of
Economics, Stanford U, Imperial Col of London

(Continued)

INTERNATIONAL SCHOOL OF KENYA, LTD. (Continued)

EDUCATIONAL PROGRAM

Curriculum US, IB Diploma
Average class size Elementary 18; Secondary 18
Language(s) of instruction English
Language(s) taught French, Spanish, Kiswahili
Staff specialists computer, counselor, ESL, learning disabilities, librarian, math resource, nurse, psychologist, reading resource
Special curricular programs art, instrumental music, vocal music, computer/technology, physical education

Extra curricular programs community service, drama, excursions/expeditions, literary magazine, newspaper, yearbook, Habitat for Humanity, Peer Helpers, student council
Sports basketball, football, hockey, soccer, swimming, tennis, track and field, volleyball
Clubs chess, environmental, Leo, drama,
Examinations AP, IB, Iowa, PSAT, SAT

CAMPUS FACILITIES

Location Suburban
Campus 20 hectares, 27 buildings, 60 classrooms, 3 computer labs, 75 instructional computers, 27,000 library volumes, 1 auditorium,

1 cafeteria, 1 covered play area, 1 gymnasium, 1 infirmary, 4 playing fields, 5 science labs, 1 pool, 3 tennis courts

ROSSLYN ACADEMY

Phone	254 020 7122407
Fax	254 020 7121306
Email	info@rosslynacademy.com
Website	www.rosslynacademy.com
Address	PO Box 14146, Nairobi, 00800, Kenya

STAFF

Superintendent Gary Nipper
High School Principal Don Mercer
Principal, K–8 Ralph Bressler
Accountant Simon Githinji
IT Coordinator Alan Davis

Media Department Head Donna Kranik
Teaching staff Full time 53; Part time 4; Total 57
Nationalities of teaching staff US 47; Kenyan 7;
Other(s) (Canadian) 3

INFORMATION

Grade levels K–12
School year August–May
School type coeducational, church-affiliated, day
Year founded 1948
Governed by appointed Board of Governors
Sponsored by Assemblies of God, International
Mission Board, Eastern Mennonite Missions
Accredited by Middle States
Regional organizations AISA
Enrollment Elementary K–5 157; Middle School
6–8 114; High School 9–12 195; Total 466

Nationalities of student body US 205; UK 5;
Kenyan 56; Other(s) (Korean, Canadian) 200
Tuition/fee currency US Dollar
Tuition range 3,912–10,100
Annual fees Capital Levy 300; Busing 675
One time fees Registration 40
Graduates attending college 98%
Graduates have attended Le Tourneau U,
U of California in Berkeley, Wheaton Col

EDUCATIONAL PROGRAM

Curriculum US, AP
Average class size Elementary 25; Secondary 26
Language(s) of instruction English
Language(s) taught Swahili, French, Spanish
Staff specialists computer, counselor, ESL,
learning disabilities, librarian, nurse, reading
resource

Special curricular programs art, instrumental
music, vocal music, computer/technology,
physical education
Extra curricular programs drama, yearbook
Sports baseball, basketball, hockey, rugby,
soccer, tennis, track and field
Examinations ACT, AP, PSAT, SAT, SAT II, PLAN

CAMPUS FACILITIES

Location Urban
Campus 16 hectares, 12 buildings, 38 classrooms,
4 computer labs, 140 instructional computers,

14,082 library volumes, 1 auditorium,
1 covered play area, 1 gymnasium, 4 playing
fields, 4 science labs, 1 pool, 1 tennis court

KUWAIT

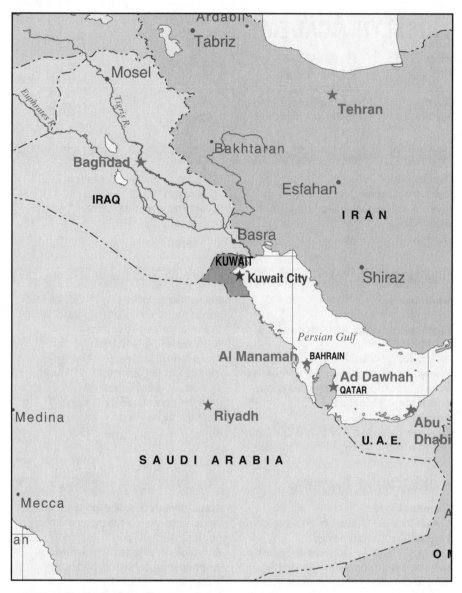

KUWAIT

Area:	17,820 sq km
Population:	2,505,559
Capital:	Kuwait
Currency:	Kuwaiti Dinar (KD)
Languages:	Arabic

AL-BAYAN INTERNATIONAL SCHOOL

Phone	965 263 2850
Fax	965 265 6423
Email	bbsjadm@bbs.edu.kw
Website	www.bbs.edu.kw
Address	Hawally, Beirut Street, Huda Sharawi Roundabout, Kuwait City, Kuwait
Mailing address	PO Box 24472, Safat 13105, Kuwait

STAFF

Director Brian L. McCauley, Ph.D.
Preschool Principal Maha Kaddoura
Elementary School Principal Mark Fox
Middle School Principal Debbie McIntosh
High School Principal Jihad Sadeddin
Assistant to Director Ghassan Al-Jilani
General Manager Dalia Al Falah

Head of Computer Science Amal Samarah
Media Center Specialists Ananda Padmanabhan and Gordana Dimitrijevic
Teaching staff Full time 190; Part time 6; Total 196
Nationalities of teaching staff US 50; UK 10; Kuwaiti 10; Other(s) (Canadian, Lebanese) 126

INFORMATION

Grade levels N–12
School year September–June
School type coeducational, day, private non-profit
Year founded 1977
Governed by appointed Board of Trustees
Accredited by CIS, New England
Regional organizations NESA
Enrollment Nursery 88; PreK 264; Elementary K–5 651; Middle School 6–8 385; High School 9–12 367; Total 1,755

Nationalities of student body US 25; UK 3; Kuwaiti 1,588; Other(s) (Lebanese, Jordanian) 139
Tuition/fee currency Kuwaiti Dinar
Tuition range 1,518–2,954
Annual fees Busing 250
One time fees Registration 100; Assessment 20
Graduates attending college 100%
Graduates have attended Massachusetts Institute of Technology, Georgetown U, U of Pennsylvania, U of South Carolina, Royal Col of Surgeons

EDUCATIONAL PROGRAM

Curriculum US, National, AP
Average class size Elementary 20; Secondary 20
Language(s) of instruction English, Arabic
Language(s) taught French
Special curricular programs art, instrumental music, computer/technology, physical education

Extra curricular programs computers, community service, drama, environmental conservation, newspaper, yearbook, Field Experiences
Sports badminton, basketball, football, soccer, tennis, track and field, volleyball
Clubs National Honor Society, bowling, ice skating, horseback riding, painting, table tennis, Spanish
Examinations AP, PSAT, SAT, SAT II, TOEFL

CAMPUS FACILITIES

Location Suburban
Campus 4 hectares, 6 buildings, 135 classrooms, 6 computer labs, 390 instructional computers, 38,000 library volumes, 3 auditoriums, 2 cafeterias, 4 covered play areas, 4 gymnasiums, 3 infirmaries, 2 playing fields, 12 science labs, air conditioning

AMERICAN ACADEMY FOR GIRLS

Phone	965 563 9612
Fax	965 563 9648
Email	aagkw@hotmail.com
Website	ajeducationalinstitute.com
Address	Box 6087, Hawalli, 32035, Kuwait

STAFF

Superintendent Betty Kummer-Koleilat, Ed.D.
High School Principal Caroline Flaherty
Middle School Principal Brenda MacCay
Elementary School Principal Tanya Sweeney
Early Childhood Principal Ilene Al Zaid

Curriculum and Staff Development Coordinator Jannette Autry
Teaching staff Full time 130; Total 130
Nationalities of teaching staff US 33; Kuwaiti 78; Other(s) (Canadian, Lebanese) 29

INFORMATION

Grade levels PreK–12
School year September–June
School type day, girls only, proprietary
Year founded 1995
Sponsored by Al-Jeel Al-Jadeeh Educational Inst.
Accredited by CIS, Middle States
Regional organizations ECIS, NESA
Enrollment PreK 30; Elementary K–5 400; Middle School 6–8 180; High School 9–12 240; Total 850

Nationalities of student body Kuwaiti 850
Tuition/fee currency Kuwaiti Dinar
Tuition range 900–2,500
One time fees Registration 100; Busing 210; Uniforms 9
Graduates attending college 75%
Graduates have attended Kuwait U

EDUCATIONAL PROGRAM

Curriculum US, AP
Average class size Elementary 18; Secondary 18
Language(s) of instruction English
Language(s) taught Arabic, French, Spanish
Staff specialists computer, counselor, ESL, librarian, nurse

Special curricular programs art, vocal music, computer/technology, physical education
Extra curricular programs newspaper, yearbook
Sports basketball, soccer, track and field, volleyball
Examinations Iowa, PSAT, SAT

CAMPUS FACILITIES

Location Urban
Campus 1 building, 60 classrooms, 3 computer labs, 80 instructional computers, 1 auditorium, 1 cafeteria, 3 covered play areas, 1 infirmary, 4 science labs, 1 tennis court, air conditioning

AMERICAN CREATIVITY ACADEMY

Phone	965 261 1711
Fax	965 263 2478
Email	ewvincent@yahoo.com
Website	www.aca.edu.kw
Address	Sharhabil Street-Block 9, PO Box 1740, Hawalli, Kuwait City, 32018, Kuwait

STAFF

Superintendent Eugene W. Vincent, Ed.D.
Middle/High School Principal Peter Visser
Elementary School Principal/Boys' Campus
Gertrude Gomez
Elementary School Principal/Girls' Campus
Jennifer Massicotte

Kindergarten Principal Sharon Meacham
Middle/High School Principal
Shaundale Letherberry
Business Manager Mohammed Jameel
Head of Technology Gulf Web
Library Head Sharon Thompson

INFORMATION

Grade levels PreK–12
School year September–June
School type day, proprietary
Year founded 1995
Accredited by Middle States
Regional organizations ECIS, NESA

Enrollment PreK 20; Elementary K–5 430;
Middle School 6–8 200; High School 9–12
200; Total 850
Tuition/fee currency US Dollar
Graduates attending college 75%
Graduates have attended Kuwait U

EDUCATIONAL PROGRAM

Curriculum US, AP
Average class size Elementary 18; Secondary 18
Language(s) of instruction English
Language(s) taught Arabic, French, Spanish
Staff specialists computer, counselor, ESL,
learning disabilities, librarian, nurse,
reading resource

Special curricular programs art, instrumental
music, computer/technology, physical education
Extra curricular programs newspaper, yearbook
Sports badminton, baseball, basketball,
gymnastics, soccer, swimming, tennis, track
and field, volleyball
Examinations AP, Iowa, SAT

CAMPUS FACILITIES

Location Urban
Campus 1 building, 60 classrooms, 3 computer
labs, 80 instructional computers, 1 auditorium,

1 cafeteria, 3 covered play areas, 1 infirmary,
4 science labs, 1 pool, 1 tennis court,
air conditioning

Data from 2006/07 school year.

THE AMERICAN INTERNATIONAL SCHOOL

Phone	965 225 5155
Fax	965 225 5155
Email	russ.mclean@aiskuwait.org
Website	www.aiskuwait.org
Address	Block 11, Humoud Al Nasser Street, Kuwait City, Salmiya, 22033, Kuwait
Mailing address	PO Box 3267, Salmiya 22033, Kuwait

STAFF

Superintendent Russ R. McLean
High School Principal Blair Lee
Middle School Principal Denise Walsh
Elementary Principal Robert Little
Business Manager Wafa'a Amarah

Coordinator of Educational Technology
Kevin McKeon
Librarian Tim Doran
Teaching staff Full time 142; Total 142
Nationalities of teaching staff US 32; UK 2;
Kuwaiti 4; Other(s) (Canadian, South African) 104

INFORMATION

Grade levels N–12
School year September–June
School type coeducational, day, proprietary
Year founded 1991
Governed by appointed Samera Al-Rayyes,
Director/Owner
Sponsored by Al-Rayyes Family
Accredited by Middle States
Regional organizations NESA

Enrollment Nursery 39; PreK 110;
Elementary K–5 615; Middle School 6–8 310;
High School 9–12 346; Total 1,420
Nationalities of student body US 140; UK 5;
Kuwaiti 720; Other(s) (Canadian, Korean) 555
Tuition/fee currency Kuwaiti Dinar
Tuition range 1,360–3,152
Graduates attending college 100%
Graduates have attended Johns Hopkins U,
Boston U, Columbia U, U of Southern
California, McGill U

EDUCATIONAL PROGRAM

Curriculum US, IB Diploma, IBPYP, IBMYP
Average class size Elementary 20; Secondary 21
Language(s) of instruction English
Language(s) taught Arabic, French, Spanish
Staff specialists computer, counselor, ESL,
librarian, math resource, reading resource
Special curricular programs art, instrumental
music, vocal music, computer/technology,
physical education

Extra curricular programs community service,
drama, environmental conservation,
excursions/expeditions, literary magazine,
newspaper, yearbook
Sports badminton, basketball, cross-country,
soccer, tennis, track and field, volleyball
Examinations IB, Iowa, PSAT, SAT

CAMPUS FACILITIES

Location Urban
Campus 3 hectares, 7 buildings, 104 classrooms,
4 computer labs, 300 instructional computers,
20,000 library volumes, 1 auditorium,

2 cafeterias, 4 covered play areas, 2 gymnasiums,
1 infirmary, 1 playing field, 10 science labs,
2 tennis courts, air conditioning

THE AMERICAN SCHOOL OF KUWAIT

Phone 965 266 4341
Fax 965 265 0438
Email ask@ask.edu.kw
Website www.ask.edu.kw
Address Al-Muthana St. & 4th Ring Rd., Block 7, Building 900017, Hawalli, Kuwait City, 32042, Kuwait
Mailing address PO Box 6735, Hawalli 32042, Kuwait

STAFF

Superintendent Bernard Mitchell, Ed.D.
Elementary School Principal Aisling Deehan
High School Principal Glenn Hooper
Middle School Principal Don Macmillan
Director of Student Services Rebecca Ness
Lower Elementary Principal Ted Mockrish

Business Manager Nael Attya
IT Department Chair Daniel Kilback
Librarian Carol Porter
Teaching staff Full time 146; Total 146
Nationalities of teaching staff US 64; UK 1; Kuwaiti 8; Other(s) (Australian, Canadian) 73

INFORMATION

Grade levels K–12
School year August–June
School type coeducational, day, private non-profit
Year founded 1964
Governed by appointed Advisory Board
Accredited by Middle States
Regional organizations NESA
Enrollment PreK 37; Elementary K–5 650; Middle School 6–8 331; High School 9–12 468; Total 1,486

Nationalities of student body US 417; UK 7; Kuwaiti 617; Other(s) (Canadian, Lebanese) 445
Tuition/fee currency Kuwaiti Dinar
Tuition range 705–3,475
Graduates attending college 98%
Graduates have attended Harvard U, Yale U, U of Pennsylvania, Columbia U, Massachusetts Institute of Technology

EDUCATIONAL PROGRAM

Curriculum US, AP
Average class size Elementary 18; Secondary 19
Language(s) of instruction English
Language(s) taught Arabic, French, Spanish
Staff specialists computer, counselor, ESL, librarian, math resource, nurse, physician, reading resource

Special curricular programs instrumental music, vocal music, computer/technology
Extra curricular programs newspaper, yearbook
Sports badminton, basketball, cross-country, soccer, softball, swimming, track and field, volleyball
Examinations AP, SAT

CAMPUS FACILITIES

Location Suburban
Campus 4 hectares, 8 buildings, 103 classrooms, 7 computer labs, 311 instructional computers, 26,500 library volumes, 1 auditorium,

1 cafeteria, 2 gymnasiums, 2 infirmaries, 3 playing fields, 9 science labs, 1 pool, air conditioning

CENTER FOR CHILD EVALUATION AND TEACHING

Phone	965 484 5221
Fax	617 489 0161
Email	dianecoulopoulos@aol.com
Address	P.O. Box 5453, Safat, Kuwait City, 13055, Kuwait
Mailing address	28 Glenn Road, Belmont, MA 02478, USA

STAFF

Director Faten Al-Bader

INFORMATION

Grade levels 2–8
School year September–June
School type coeducational, day, private non-profit

Year founded 1984
Tuition/fee currency US Dollar

EDUCATIONAL PROGRAM

Curriculum National
Language(s) of instruction Arabic
Language(s) taught Arabic, English

Staff specialists computer, counselor, learning disabilities, math resource, psychologist, reading resource
Special curricular programs art, instrumental music, physical education

CAMPUS FACILITIES

Location Urban

Campus air conditioning

Data from 2006/07 school year.

FAWZIA SULTAN INTERNATIONAL SCHOOL

Phone	965 2619725 ext. 212
Fax	965 2619724
Email	director@fsis.edu.kw
Website	www.fsis.edu.kw
Address	Beirut Street, Hawally, Across from Hawally Fire Station, Kuwait City, 13008, Kuwait
Mailing address	PO Box 719, Safat 13008, Kuwait

STAFF

Director Tania S. Woodburn
K–12 Principal Loa Midford
General Manager Ms. Dalia Al-Falah
Head Librarian Maudeane Taunton

Teaching staff Full time 42; Part time 1; Total 43
Nationalities of teaching staff US 16; Kuwaiti 1; Other(s) (Canadian, Egyptian) 26

INFORMATION

Grade levels K–12
School year September–June
School type coeducational, day, private non-profit
Year founded 1993
Governed by appointed Board of Trustees
Regional organizations ECIS, NESA
Enrollment Elementary K–5 36; Middle School 6–8 44; High School 9–12 57; Total 137

Nationalities of student body US 1; Kuwaiti 133; Other(s) (Swede, Indian) 3
Tuition/fee currency Kuwaiti Dinar
Tuition 7,000
Graduates attending college 95%
Graduates have attended Landmark Col, American U of Kuwait, Lynn U, Hogeschool Zeeland, Gulf U for Science and Technology
Curriculum US

EDUCATIONAL PROGRAM

Average class size Elementary 8; Secondary 8
Language(s) of instruction English
Language(s) taught Arabic
Staff specialists computer, counselor, ESL, learning disabilities, librarian, nurse, psychologist, reading resource, speech/hearing
Special curricular programs art, instrumental music, vocal music, computer/technology, physical education

Extra curricular programs computers, community service, drama, environmental conservation, excursions/expeditions, photography, yearbook
Sports basketball, football, gymnastics, soccer, squash, swimming, volleyball
Clubs chess, art, cooking, computer, model building, drama, ceramic
Examinations Iowa, PSAT, SAT, TOEFL

CAMPUS FACILITIES

Location Urban
Campus 1 building, 45 classrooms, 6 computer labs, 125 instructional computers, 6,000 library volumes, 1 auditorium, 1 cafeteria, 3 covered play areas, 1 gymnasium, 1 infirmary, 1 playing field, 3 science labs, 1 pool, air conditioning

UNIVERSAL AMERICAN SCHOOL

Phone	965 822 827
Fax	965 261-5007
Email	info@uas.edu.kw
Website	www.uas.edu.kw
Address	Hawalli 3rd Ring Road, Opposite Al-Qadsiya Area, Behind Al-Wazzan Mosque, Hawalli, Kuwait City, 17035, Kuwait
Mailing address	PO Box 17035 Khaldiya, 72451 Khaldiya, Kuwait

STAFF

Superintendent Michael Smith, Ed.D.
High School Principal Lance Zellmann
Middle School Principal Edmund Fitzgerland
Elementary Principal David Botbyl
Middle School Counselor Sussanne Isteero
Business Manager Mohammed Rashwan

Head of Technology Mohamed Wajid
Head of Library May AL-Hajjaj
Teaching staff Full time 102; Total 102
Nationalities of teaching staff US 42; UK 1; Other(s) (Australian, Jordanian) 59

INFORMATION

Grade levels N–12
School year August–June
School type coeducational, day, private non-profit
Year founded 1976
Governed by appointed Advisory Board
Accredited by CIS, New England
Regional organizations ECIS, NESA
Enrollment Nursery 39; PreK 92; Elementary K–5 506; Middle School 6–8 312; High School 9–12 400; Total 1,349

Nationalities of student body US 60; UK 6; Egyptian 770; Other(s) (Indian, Australian) 513
Tuition/fee currency Kuwaiti Dinar
Tuition range 1,067–2,644
Annual fees Busing 290
One time fees Registration 100; Library 50
Graduates attending college 90%
Graduates have attended Boston U, Carnegie U, Concordia U, Arizona State U, Bethany Col

EDUCATIONAL PROGRAM

Curriculum US, AP
Average class size Elementary 22; Secondary 25
Language(s) of instruction English
Language(s) taught French, Arabic, Spanish
Staff specialists computer, counselor, ESL, librarian, math resource, nurse, physician, reading resource
Special curricular programs art, instrumental music, vocal music, computer/technology, physical education

Extra curricular programs computers, community service, drama, environmental conservation, excursions/expeditions, literary magazine, newspaper, photography, yearbook
Sports basketball, football, soccer, swimming, track and field, volleyball
Clubs computer, chess, homework, horseback riding, skating, karate, painting, yoga, roller blading
Examinations ACT, AP, PSAT, SAT, SAT II, Stanford, TOEFL

CAMPUS FACILITIES

Location Suburban
Campus 2 hectares, 2 buildings, 88 classrooms, 3 computer labs, 200 instructional computers, 25,000 library volumes, 1 auditorium,

1 cafeteria, 1 covered play area, 1 gymnasium, 1 infirmary, 1 playing field, 4 science labs, 3 pools, 1 tennis court, air conditioning

KYRGYZSTAN

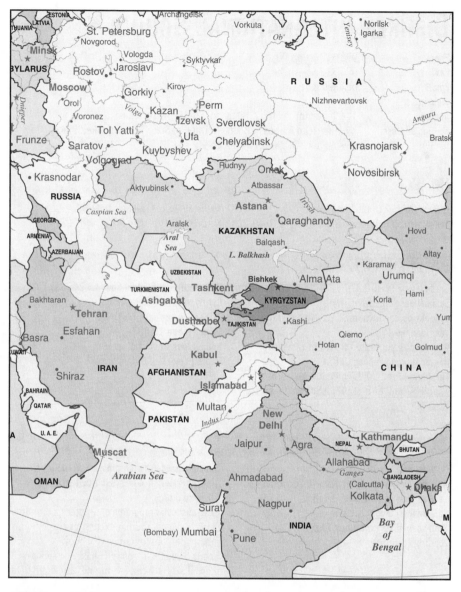

KYRGYZSTAN

Area:	198,500 sq km
Population:	5,284,149
Capital:	Bishkek
Currency:	Som (KGS)
Languages:	Kyrgyz

Bishkek International School

Phone	996 312 54 38 90
Fax	996 312 56-31-39
Email	bishkek@qsi.org
Website	www.qsi.org
Address	14A Tynystanova Street, Bishkek, 720055, Kyrgyzstan
Mailing address	c/o American Embassy, Bishkek, Dept. of State, 7040 Bishkek Place, Washington, DC 20521-7040, USA

STAFF

Director Arthur C. Barker, Ed.D.
Teaching staff Full time 18; Part time 4; Total 22

Nationalities of teaching staff US 6; Kyrgyzstani 10; Other(s) 6

INFORMATION

Grade levels PreK–12
School year September–June
School type coeducational, day, private non-profit
Year founded 1994
Governed by appointed Board of Directors
Regional organizations CEESA
Enrollment PreK 20; Elementary K–5 20; Middle School 6–8 10; High School 9–12 10; Total 60

Nationalities of student body US 20; Kyrgyzstani 5; Other(s) 35
Tuition/fee currency US Dollar
Tuition range 13,000–145,000
Annual fees Registration 100; Capital Levy 1,600; Lunch 600

EDUCATIONAL PROGRAM

Curriculum US
Average class size Elementary 9; Secondary 3
Language(s) of instruction English
Language(s) taught Russian
Staff specialists computer, ESL, librarian, reading resource

Special curricular programs art, vocal music, computer/technology, distance learning, physical education
Extra curricular programs computers, community service, dance, drama, excursions/expeditions, newspaper, photography, yearbook
Sports basketball, golf, gymnastics, hockey, martial arts, soccer, swimming, track and field

CAMPUS FACILITIES

Location Urban
Campus 1 hectare, 1 building, 15 classrooms, 1 computer lab, 20 instructional computers,

4,000 library volumes, 1 cafeteria, 1 covered play area, 1 playing field, air conditioning

LAOS

Area:	236,800 sq km
Population:	6,521,998
Capital:	Vientiane
Currency:	Kip (LAK)
Languages:	Lao

VIENTIANE INTERNATIONAL SCHOOL

Phone	856 21 313 606
Fax	856 21 315 008
Email	dragon@etllao.com
Website	www.vis.laopdr.com
Address	Ban Saphanthong Tai, Vientiane, Laos
Mailing address	PO Box 3180, Vientiane, Laos PDR

STAFF

Director Steve Alexander
Secondary School Coordinator Don Tingley
Primary School Coordinator Jodi Nielsen
College Counselor, Curriculum Coordinator
Don Tingley
Business Manager Stephan Aeschbach

IT Coordinator Bruce Knox
Head of Library/Media Center Laura Forgie
Teaching staff Full time 37; Part time 5; Total 42
Nationalities of teaching staff US 6; UK 2; Lao 10;
Other(s) (Canadian, Australian) 24

INFORMATION

Grade levels PreK–12
School year August–June
School type coeducational, day, private non-profit
Year founded 1991
Governed by elected School Board
Accredited by CIS, Western
Regional organizations EARCOS, ECIS
Enrollment PreK 25; Elementary K–5 145;
Middle School 6–8 65; High School 9–12 30;
Total 265

Nationalities of student body US 15; UK 8; Lao 30;
Other(s) (Australian, Dutch) 212
Tuition/fee currency US Dollar
Tuition range 4,100–10,250
Annual fees Capital Levy 1,500; School Bus 600;
Grade 6–12 Annual Trip 400
One time fees Registration 500
Graduates attending college 100%
Graduates have attended Wheaton Col,
Sorbonne U, U of Seattle, South Korean Science
and Techology U, U of Canterbury

EDUCATIONAL PROGRAM

Curriculum US, Intl, IB DYP and PYP Candidate
School
Average class size Elementary 19; Secondary 12
Language(s) of instruction English
Language(s) taught French
Staff specialists computer, counselor, ESL,
learning disabilities, librarian, nurse
Special curricular programs art, instrumental
music, vocal music, computer/technology,
physical education

Extra curricular programs computers, community
service, drama, environmental conservation,
excursions/expeditions, photography, yearbook
Sports basketball, martial arts, soccer, softball,
swimming, track and field, volleyball
Clubs cultural exchange, drama, student council
Examinations Iowa, PSAT, SAT, SAT II

CAMPUS FACILITIES

Location Suburban
Campus 1 hectare, 10 buildings, 25 classrooms,
2 computer labs, 50 instructional computers,

9,000 library volumes, 1 cafeteria, 1 covered
play area, 1 gymnasium, 1 infirmary, 2 playing
fields, 2 science labs, air conditioning

LATVIA

Area:	64,589 sq km
Population:	2,259,810
Capital:	Riga
Currency:	Latvian Lat (LVL)
Languages:	Latvian

INTERNATIONAL SCHOOL OF LATVIA

Phone	371 775 5146
Fax	371 775 5009
Email	isloffice@isl.edu.lv
Website	www.isl.edu.lv
Address	Viestura iela 6A, Jurmala, LV 2010, Latvia

STAFF

Director Michael P. Mack, Ph.D.
Deputy Director Kevin Reimer
Academic Dean and IB Diploma Coordinator
William Elman
MYP Coordinator Eleanor Surridge
PYP Coordinator Mark Case
Administrative Assistant Betsy Hanselmann

Finance Manager Elina Mocane
Technology Coordinator Chris Blessing
Library Head Dace Cernavska
Teaching staff Full time 29; Part time 2; Total 31
Nationalities of teaching staff US 18; UK 2;
Latvian 10; Other(s) (South African) 1

INFORMATION

Grade levels N–12
School year August–June
School type coeducational, day, private non-profit
Year founded 1994
Governed by elected Board of Directors
Accredited by CIS, New England
Regional organizations CEESA, ECIS
Enrollment Nursery 12; PreK 24;
Elementary K–5 52; Middle School 6–8 58;
High School 9–12 50; Total 196

Nationalities of student body US 31; UK 12;
Latvian 45; Other(s) (Dane, German) 108
Tuition/fee currency Euro
Tuition range 4,500–14,000
Annual fees Capital Levy 700; Busing 1,180
One time fees Registration 1,450
Graduates attending college 100%
Graduates have attended Oxford U,
U of San Diego, McGill U, U of Latvia,
U of Tel Aviv

EDUCATIONAL PROGRAM

Curriculum Intl, IB Diploma, IBPYP, IBMYP
Average class size Elementary 9; Secondary 14
Language(s) of instruction English
Language(s) taught German, French
Staff specialists computer, ESL, learning
disabilities, librarian, math resource, reading
resource

Special curricular programs art, instrumental
music, computer/technology
Extra curricular programs community service,
drama, excursions/expeditions, yearbook
Sports basketball, cross-country, soccer,
softball, swimming, tennis, track and field,
volleyball
Examinations IB, PSAT, SAT, SAT II

CAMPUS FACILITIES

Location Rural
Campus 1 building, 32 classrooms,
2 computer labs, 60 instructional computers,

9,750 library volumes, 1 auditorium,
1 cafeteria, 1 gymnasium, 1 infirmary,
1 playing field, 1 science lab, 1 pool

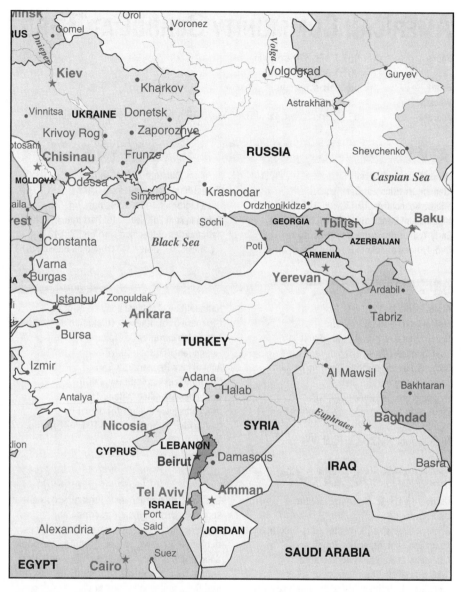

LEBANON

Area:	10,400 sq km
Population:	3,925,502
Capital:	Beirut
Currency:	Lebanese Pound (LBP)
Languages:	Arabic, French

AMERICAN COMMUNITY SCHOOL AT BEIRUT

Phone	961 1 374 370 ext. 105
Fax	961 1 366 050
Email	mbedeir@acs.edu.lb
Website	www.acs.edu.lb
Address	67 Nigeria Street, Jal al Bahr, Ras Beirut, Beirut, 2035-8003, Lebanon

STAFF

Head of School George H. Damon, Jr., Ph.D.
Elementary Principal Geri Branch
Middle School Principal Karim Abu Haydar
High School Principal Paul Raschke, Ph.D.
Early Years Principal Adele Hutchison
Deputy Head of School David Warren, Ph.D.

Business Manager Fadi A. Germanos
IT Coordinator Marie Jeanne Farris
Head Librarian Andrea Norman
Teaching staff Full time 146; Part time 6; Total 152
Nationalities of teaching staff US 32; UK 2;
Lebanese 103; Other(s) (Canadian, Bahamian) 15

INFORMATION

Grade levels N–12
School year September–June
School type day, private non-profit
Year founded 1905
Governed by appointed Board of Trustees
Accredited by Middle States
Regional organizations ECIS, NESA
Enrollment Nursery 153; Elementary K–5 319;
Middle School 6–8 204;
High School 9–12 317; Total 993

Nationalities of student body US 146; UK 35;
Lebanese 616; Other(s) (Canadian, Korean) 196
Tuition/fee currency US Dollar
Tuition range 7,258–10,477
Annual fees Registration 750
One time fees Capital Levy 2,000
Graduates attending college 100%
Graduates have attended Harvard U,
Cambridge U, Northeastern U, U of Toronto,
McGill U

EDUCATIONAL PROGRAM

Curriculum US, IB Diploma, Lebanese
Baccalaureate
Average class size Elementary 21; Secondary 15
Language(s) of instruction English
Language(s) taught French, Arabic
Staff specialists computer, counselor, ESL,
learning disabilities, librarian, math resource,
nurse, psychologist
Special curricular programs art, instrumental
music, vocal music, computer/technology,
physical education

Extra curricular programs computers, community
service, dance, drama, environmental
conservation, excursions/expeditions, literary
magazine, newspaper, photography, yearbook
Sports badminton, basketball, cross-country,
skiing, soccer, softball, swimming, tennis, track
and field, volleyball, floor hockey
Clubs movie club
Examinations IB, PSAT, SAT, SAT II, Stanford,
TOEFL, NNAT, WRAT

CAMPUS FACILITIES

Location Urban
Campus 16 hectares, 4 buildings, 65 classrooms,
3 computer labs, 156 instructional computers,
30,000 library volumes, 2 auditoriums,

1 cafeteria, 2 covered play areas, 1 gymnasium,
2 infirmaries, 3 playing fields, 4 science labs,
2 tennis courts, air conditioning

INTERNATIONAL COLLEGE

Phone	961 1 371 294
Fax	961 1 362 500
Email	proffice@cyberia.net.lb
Website	www.ic.edu.lb
Address	Bliss Street, PO Box 11-0236, Riad-El-Solh: 1107-2020, Beirut, Lebanon

STAFF

President John K. Johnson, Ph.D.
Senior Vice President Mishka M. Mourani
Vice President for Alumni and Development
Moufid Beydoun
Director of Secondary School Yusuf Korfali
Director of Middle School Wadad Hoss
Director of Elementary School Julia Kozak

Vice President for Administration Elie Kurban
IT Coordinator Mahmud Shihab
Librarian Randa Soubaih
Teaching staff Full time 290; Part time 23;
Total 313
Nationalities of teaching staff US 9; UK 3;
Lebanese 242; Other(s) 59

INFORMATION

Grade levels N–12
School year September–June
School type coeducational, day, private non-profit
Year founded 1891
Governed by elected Board of Trustees
Accredited by CIS, New England
Regional organizations ECIS, NESA
Enrollment Nursery 185; PreK 223;
Elementary K–5 1,306; Middle School 6–8 960;
High School 9–12 648; Total 3,322

Nationalities of student body US 509; UK 80;
Lebanese 2,012; Other(s) (Canadian, French) 721
Tuition/fee currency Lebanese Pound
Graduates attending college 100%
Graduates have attended American U of Beirut,
Harvard U, McGill U, Tufts U, Massachusetts
Institute of Technology

EDUCATIONAL PROGRAM

Curriculum US, National, IB Diploma, French
Baccalaureate
Average class size Elementary 25; Secondary 23
Language(s) of instruction English, French
Language(s) taught Arabic
Staff specialists counselor

Special curricular programs instrumental music,
vocal music
Extra curricular programs community service, drama
Sports basketball, soccer, swimming, tennis,
track and field, volleyball

CAMPUS FACILITIES

Location Urban
Campus 5 hectares, 6 buildings, 112 classrooms,
6 computer labs, 200 instructional computers,
76,521 library volumes, 4 auditoriums,

2 cafeterias, 4 covered play areas, 2 gymnasiums,
3 infirmaries, 6 playing fields, 6 science labs,
2 tennis courts

SAGESSE HIGH SCHOOL, MARY MOTHER OF WISDOM

Phone	961 1 872 145
Fax	961 1 872 149
Email	sagesse@sagesse.com
Website	www.sagessehs.edu.lb
Address	Aïn Saadeh, El Metn, Main Street, Aïn Saadeh, Lebanon

STAFF

President Reverend Edgard Madi, Ph.D.
High School Principal Edgard Chemali
Middle School Principal Kathleen Battah
Elementary School Principal Juhaina Abu Khalil

Preschool Principal Mireille Fortier
Auditor Charbel Maatouk
IT Manager Walid Geagea
Librarian Junella Berru

INFORMATION

Grade levels N–12
School year September–June
School type boarding, coeducational, church-affiliated, day
Year founded 1992
Governed by appointed Catholic Church
Sponsored by Mgr Paul Matar
Regional organizations ECIS
Enrollment Nursery 64; PreK 55; Elementary K–5 402; Middle School 6–8 272; High School 9–12 384; Total 1,177
Nationalities of student body US 206; UK 42; Lebanese 889; Other(s) (Canadian, Australian) 40

Tuition/fee currency Lebanese Pound
Tuition range 2,900,000–6,800,000
Annual fees Registration 150,000; Boarding, 7-day 15,000; Lunch 720,000; Costume 342,000; Home Internet Connection 180,000; Educational Material 560,000
Boarding program grades 1–12
Boarding program length 7-day **Boys** 22 **Girls** 3
Graduates attending college 100%
Graduates have attended American U of Beirut, Lebanese American U, McGill U, U of Michigan, Royal Col of Surgeons

EDUCATIONAL PROGRAM

Curriculum US, National, AP, IB Diploma
Average class size Elementary 22; Secondary 20
Language(s) of instruction English
Language(s) taught Arabic, French, Spanish
Staff specialists computer, counselor, ESL, learning disabilities, librarian, math resource, nurse, psychologist

Special curricular programs art, instrumental music, vocal music, computer/technology, physical education, vocational
Extra curricular programs computers, community service, dance, drama, excursions/expeditions, newspaper, yearbook
Sports basketball, football, skiing, swimming, track and field, volleyball, Tae Kwon Do, cheerleading
Examinations AP, IB, SAT, SAT II, TOEFL

CAMPUS FACILITIES

Location Rural
Campus 5 hectares, 2 buildings, 59 classrooms, 3 computer labs, 90 instructional computers, 12,100 library volumes, 2 auditoriums, 2 cafeterias, 2 covered play areas, 1 infirmary, 1 playing field, 3 science labs

Data from 2006/07 school year.

LESOTHO

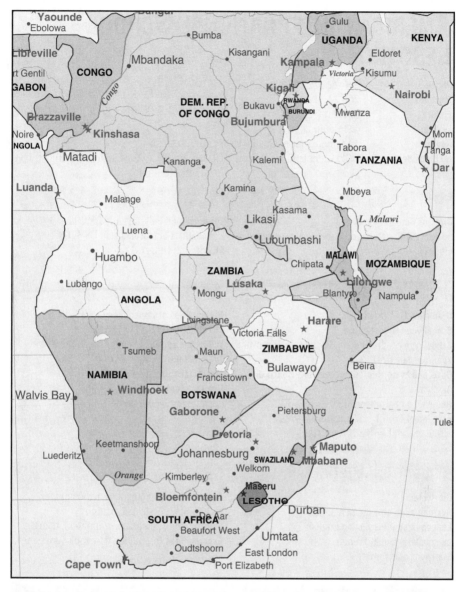

LESOTHO

Area:	30,355 sq km
Population:	2,125,262
Capital:	Maseru
Currency:	Loti (LSL); South African Rand (ZAR)
Languages:	Sesotho, English

AMERICAN INTERNATIONAL SCHOOL– LESOTHO

Phone	266 22 322 987
Fax	266 22 311 963
Email	director@aisl.co.ls
Website	aislesotho.com
Address	14 United Nations Road, Maseru, 100, Lesotho
Mailing address	DOS/Administrative Officer, 2340 Maseru Place, Washington, DC 20521, USA

STAFF

Director Benjamin P. Marsh
Business/Office Manager Mahlape Mosoeuyane
Librarian Rohini Pulyadath

Teaching staff Full time 12; Total 12
Nationalities of teaching staff US 3; UK 1; Mosotho 2; Other(s) 6

INFORMATION

Grade levels PreK–8
School year August–June
School type coeducational, day, private non-profit
Year founded 1991
Governed by appointed and elected Board of Advisors
Regional organizations AISA
Enrollment PreK 13; Elementary K–5 62; Middle School 6–8 25; Total 100

Nationalities of student body US 15; UK 5; Mosotho 40; Other(s) (Indian) 40
Tuition/fee currency South African Rand
Tuition range 16,500–33,000
Annual fees Busing 4,950
One time fees Registration 930; Capital Levy 2,300; Books 930

EDUCATIONAL PROGRAM

Curriculum US
Average class size Elementary 12
Language(s) of instruction English
Language(s) taught French
Staff specialists nurse

Special curricular programs art, computer/ technology, physical education
Extra curricular programs computers, dance
Examinations International Schools Assessment

CAMPUS FACILITIES

Location Urban
Campus 2 hectares, 7 buildings, 9 classrooms, 1 computer lab, 25 instructional computers,

6,000 library volumes, 1 covered play area, 1 infirmary, 1 playing field

MACHABENG COLLEGE, THE INTERNATIONAL SCHOOL OF LESOTHO

Phone	266 22 313 224
Fax	266 22 316 109
Email	machabhm@lesoff.co.za
Website	www.machcoll.co.ls
Address	Tonokolo Road, Maseru West, Maseru, 100, Lesotho
Mailing address	PO Box 1570, Maseru 100, Lesotho

STAFF

Head of School Christopher Philip
Deputy Head Academic N. Brook
Deputy Head Administration J. Humphreys
IB Coordinator M. Thompson
Middle School Coordinator J. Butterfield
Lower School Coordinator M. Makara

Bursar S. Setsomi
Head of Science K. Tomlinson, Ph.D.
Head of Library A. Tantuan
Teaching staff Full time 40; Total 40
Nationalities of teaching staff UK 15; Mosotho 9; Other(s) (Indian) 16

INFORMATION

Grade levels 6–12
School year August–June
School type boarding, coeducational, day, private non-profit
Year founded 1977
Governed by elected Board of Governors
Accredited by CIS, New England
Regional organizations AISA, ECIS
Enrollment Middle School 6–8 200; High School 9–12 300; Total 500
Nationalities of student body US 10; UK 4; Mosotho 380; Other(s) (Chinese, Indian) 106

Tuition/fee currency South African Rand
Tuition range 19,000–77,000
Annual fees Boarding, 5-day 23,160; Boarding, 7-day 23,160; Books 1,050; Computer 330
One time fees Registration 520; Capital Levy 2,580
Boarding program grades 6–12
Boarding program length 5-day and 7-day
Boys 45 **Girls** 45
Graduates attending college 98%
Graduates have attended U of Capetown, Medical U of Southern Africa, Rhodes U, U of KwaZulu-Natal

(Continued)

MACHABENG COLLEGE,
THE INTERNATIONAL SCHOOL OF LESOTHO (Continued)

EDUCATIONAL PROGRAM

Curriculum UK, IB Diploma, IGCSE
Average class size Secondary 20
Language(s) of instruction English
Language(s) taught Sesotho, French, Spanish
Staff specialists computer, counselor, librarian, nurse
Special curricular programs art, computer/technology, physical education

Extra curricular programs computers, community service, drama, excursions/expeditions, newspaper, yearbook
Sports badminton, basketball, cricket, cross-country, golf, hockey, martial arts, rugby, soccer, swimming, tennis, track and field, volleyball
Clubs chess, Scripture Union
Examinations GCSE, IB, IGCSE

CAMPUS FACILITIES

Location Suburban
Campus 4 hectares, 8 buildings, 23 classrooms, 2 computer labs, 35 instructional computers, 25,000 library volumes, 1 auditorium, 1 cafeteria, 1 infirmary, 1 playing field, 4 science labs

MASERU ENGLISH MEDIUM PREPARATORY SCHOOL

Phone	266 22312 276
Fax	266 22312 276
Email	headteacher@maseruprep.co.ls
Website	www.maseruprep.co.ls
Address	Calwell Road, Maseru West, Maseru, 100, Lesotho
Mailing address	PO Box 34, Maseru 100, Lesotho

STAFF

Head Teacher Ken Jarman
Deputy Headteacher Phaello Ntsonyane
Bursar Mapaseka Dube

Head of ICT Phaello Ntsonyane
Librarian Rosina Mphethi

INFORMATION

Grade levels N–6
School year August–July
School type coeducational, day, private non-profit
Year founded 1895
Governed by elected School Board of Governors
Accredited by CIS
Regional organizations AISA

Enrollment Nursery 20; PreK 40;
Elementary K–5 170; Middle School 6–8 40;
Total 270
Nationalities of student body UK 2; Mosotho 239;
Other(s) (Indian, Ghanaian) 29
Tuition/fee currency South African Rand
Tuition range 7,143–31,404
Annual fees Books 270; Computer Levy 300
One time fees Registration 373; Entrance 1,620

EDUCATIONAL PROGRAM

Curriculum Intl, IBPYP
Average class size Elementary 18
Language(s) of instruction English
Language(s) taught Sesotho, French
Staff specialists computer, ESL, librarian
Special curricular programs art, vocal music,
computer/technology, physical education, music

Extra curricular programs computers, dance,
drama, excursions/expeditions, newspaper,
yearbook
Sports basketball, cricket, cross-country,
gymnastics, martial arts, rugby, soccer, softball,
swimming, tennis, track and field, volleyball,
netball
Clubs arts and crafts, computer, French, board
games, library, sewing, cooking

CAMPUS FACILITIES

Location Urban
Campus 2 hectares, 8 buildings, 17 classrooms,
1 computer lab, 25 instructional computers,
5,000 library volumes, 1 auditorium,

1 covered play area, 1 gymnasium,
2 playing fields, 1 science lab, 1 pool,
2 tennis courts

Data from 2006/07 school year.

LIBYA

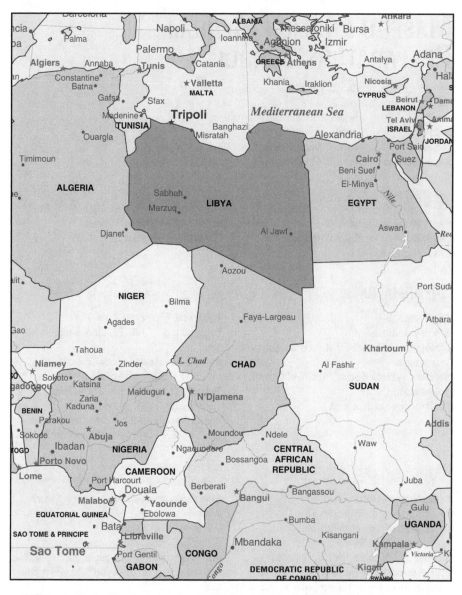

LIBYA

Area:	1,759,540 sq km
Population:	6,036,914
Capital:	Tripoli
Currency:	Libyan Dinar (LYD)
Languages:	Arabic, Italian

THE AMERICAN SCHOOL OF TRIPOLI

Phone	218 21 489 7059
Fax	218 21 489 7059
Email	astdirector@amschtripoli.org
Website	www.amschtripoli.org
Address	Seraj Road, Tripoli, Libya
Mailing address	Box 8850 Tripoli Place, Washington,DC 20521-8850, USA

STAFF

Director Judith Drotar
Media Center and IT Instructor
Janice Middleton, Ph.D.

Teaching staff Full time 12; Part time 4; Total 16
Nationalities of teaching staff US 14; Libyan 1;
Other(s) (Canadian) 1

INFORMATION

Grade levels PreK–10
School year September–June
School type day, private non-profit
Year founded 2005
Governed by appointed Board of Trustees
Sponsored by Several Oil Companies and The USG
Regional organizations NESA

Enrollment PreK 20; Elementary K–5 26; Middle
School 6–8 22; High School 9–12 10; Total 78
Nationalities of student body US 10; Other(s)
(Italian, Korean) 68
Tuition/fee currency US Dollar
Tuition range 5,000–14,500
Annual fees Capital Levy 2,000
One time fees Registration 200

EDUCATIONAL PROGRAM

Curriculum US
Average class size Elementary 12; Secondary 10
Language(s) of instruction English
Language(s) taught Arabic, Spanish
Staff specialists computer, ESL, librarian
Special curricular programs art, vocal music,
computer/technology, distance learning,

physical education
Extra curricular programs computers, drama,
newspaper, yearbook
Sports badminton, basketball, soccer, tennis,
volleyball

CAMPUS FACILITIES

Location Suburban
Campus 1 hectare, 2 buildings, 18 classrooms,
1 computer lab, 32 instructional computers,

5,000 library volumes, 1 covered play area,
1 playing field, 1 science lab, 1 tennis court,
air conditioning

LITHUANIA

LITHUANIA

Area:	65,200 sq km
Population:	3,575,439
Capital:	Vilnius
Currency:	Litas (LTL)
Languages:	Lithuanian

AMERICAN INTERNATIONAL SCHOOL OF VILNIUS

Phone	370 5 212 10 31
Fax	370 5 264 72 02
Email	office@aisvilnius.lt
Website	www.aisv.lt
Address	Subaciaus 41, Vilnius, LT-11350, Lithuania
Mailing address	c/o American Embassy Vilnius, Akmenu g.6, 03106 Vilnius, Lithuania

STAFF

Director Jeffrey Z. Haun
Activities Coordinator Jolita Norkunaite
Elementary Coordinator Sarah Haun
Admissions/Marketing Coordinator
Ieva Dovydeniene

Administrative Officer/Finance
Rasa Marija Sabaliauskiene
Computer Specialist/Coordinator Eric Olive
Librarian Diana Arya
Teaching staff Full time 16; Part time 15; Total 31
Nationalities of teaching staff US 8; Lithuanian 23

INFORMATION

Grade levels N–10
School year August–June
School type coeducational, day, private non-profit
Year founded 1993
Governed by elected Board of Directors
Regional organizations CEESA, ECIS

Enrollment Nursery 16; PreK 25; Elementary
K–5 55; Middle School 6–8 20; High School
9–12 10; Total 126
Nationalities of student body US 20; UK 2;
Lithuanian 60; Other(s) 44
Tuition/fee currency Euro
Tuition range 5,000-18,000

EDUCATIONAL PROGRAM

Curriculum US, National, Intl, IGCSE
Average class size Elementary 15; Secondary 5
Language(s) of instruction English
Language(s) taught German, French, Lithuanian
Staff specialists computer, ESL, librarian
Special curricular programs art, vocal music,
computer/technology, physical education

Extra curricular programs computers, community
service, drama, environmental conservation,
excursions/expeditions, literary magazine,
photography, yearbook
Examinations Iowa

CAMPUS FACILITIES

Location Urban
Campus 2 hectares, 1 building, 16 classrooms,
1 computer lab, 36 instructional computers,

8,500 library volumes, 1 cafeteria,
1 gymnasium, 1 playing field, 1 science lab,
1 tennis court

LUXEMBOURG

LUXEMBOURG

Area:	2,586 sq km
Population:	480,222
Capital:	Luxembourg
Currency:	Euro (EUR)
Languages:	Luxembourgish

INTERNATIONAL SCHOOL OF LUXEMBOURG

Phone	352 260 440
Fax	352 260 44704
Email	information@islux.lu
Website	www.islux.lu
Address	36 boulevard Pierre Dupong, Luxembourg, L-1430, Luxembourg

STAFF

Director Christopher Bowman
Upper School Principal Nicki Crush
Lower School Principal Jaime Roth
Financial Controller Ruth Smiley
Technology Manager David Perkins

Upper School Librarian Patricia Burn
Teaching staff Full time 83; Part time 11; Total 94
Nationalities of teaching staff US 40; UK 23; Luxembourger 2; Other(s) (Australian, Canadian) 29

INFORMATION

Grade levels N–12
School year August–June
School type coeducational, day, private non-profit
Year founded 1963
Governed by elected Board of Governors
Accredited by CIS, Middle States
Regional organizations ECIS
Enrollment Nursery 30; PreK 36; Elementary K–5 399; Middle School 6–8 192; High School 9–12 194; Total 851

Nationalities of student body US 139; UK 104; Luxembourger 54; Other(s) (Swede, Icelander) 554
Tuition/fee currency Euro
Tuition range 4,600–15,060
Annual fees Re-registration 400
One time fees Registration 900; Capital Levy 1,000
Graduates attending college 100%
Graduates have attended Cambridge U, Imperial Col, U of Reykjavik, Tokyo U, Georgetown U

EDUCATIONAL PROGRAM

Curriculum Intl, IB Diploma
Average class size Elementary 18; Secondary 17
Language(s) of instruction English
Language(s) taught French, German
Staff specialists computer, counselor, ESL, learning disabilities, librarian, math resource, nurse, psychologist, reading resource
Special curricular programs art, instrumental music, vocal music, computer/technology, physical education

Extra curricular programs community service, drama, environmental conservation, literary magazine, newspaper, photography, yearbook
Sports basketball, rugby, soccer, swimming, tennis, track and field, volleyball
Examinations ACT, AP, GCSE, IB, IGCSE, PSAT, SAT, SAT II, TOEFL

CAMPUS FACILITIES

Location Suburban
Campus 5 hectares, 3 buildings, 72 classrooms, 6 computer labs, 300 instructional computers, 20,000 library volumes, 1 auditorium,

3 cafeterias, 1 gymnasium, 2 infirmaries, 1 playing field, 4 science labs, 1 pool, air conditioning

MACEDONIA

MACEDONIA

Area:	25,333 sq km
Population:	2,055,915
Capital:	Skopje
Currency:	Macedonian Denar (MKD)
Languages:	Macedonian

AMERICAN SCHOOL, MACEDONIA

Phone	389 2 3063 265
Fax	389 2 3091 332
Email	contact@asm.edu.mk
Website	www.asm.edu.mk
Address	Nikola Parapunov BB, Makotex Complex, Karpos IV, Skopje, 1000, Macedonia
Mailing address	P.O. Box 125, La Canada, CA 91012, USA

STAFF

Superintendent Mike Bujko, Ed.D.
Assistant Superintendent Katerina Anguseva
Principal Jason Brown

Teaching staff Full time 4; Part time 6; Total 10
Nationalities of teaching staff US 1; UK 2; Macedonian 7

INFORMATION

Grade levels PreK–12
School year August–June
School type coeducational, day, private non-profit
Year founded 1994
Governed by elected Board of Directors
Regional organizations CEESA
Enrollment PreK 12; Elementary K–5 32; Middle School 6–8 11; High School 9–12 7; Total 62

Nationalities of student body US 2; UK 4; Macedonian 4; Other(s) (Greek, Croatian) 52
Tuition/fee currency ECU
Tuition range 3,000–3,500
Graduates attending college 100%
Graduates have attended U of Southern California, U of California in Los Angeles, New York U, Yale U, Stanford U

EDUCATIONAL PROGRAM

Curriculum US, AP, GenCSE
Average class size Elementary 8; Secondary 8
Language(s) of instruction English
Language(s) taught French, Macedonian
Staff specialists computer, counselor, librarian, physician

Special curricular programs art, computer/technology, distance learning, physical education
Extra curricular programs computers, community service, dance, drama, yearbook
Sports basketball, soccer, swimming, track and field, volleyball
Examinations AP, SAT, TOEFL

CAMPUS FACILITIES

Location Urban
Campus 2 hectares, 1 building, 10 classrooms, 1 computer lab, 20 instructional computers,

1,500 library volumes, 1 cafeteria, 1 gymnasium, 3 playing fields, 1 science lab, 1 pool, air conditioning

QSI INTERNATIONAL SCHOOL OF SKOPJE

Phone	389 2 306 7678
Fax	389 2 306 2250
Email	qsi-staff@qsi.edu.mk
Website	www.qsi.org/mcn
Address	Ilindenska BB, Reon 39, Skopje, 1000, Macedonia
Mailing address	Ilinden BB Reon 39, 1000 Skopje, Republic of Macedonia

STAFF

Director Eric Nelis
QSI Administrative Assistant Zaharija Tosanova
Administrative Coordinator Alex Kostadinovski
IT Specialist Vladimir Andovski

Librarian Stephanie Ciampini
Teaching staff Full time 22; Part time 3; Total 25
Nationalities of teaching staff US 6; Macedonian 14; Other(s) (Australian, French) 5

INFORMATION

Grade levels PreK–12
School year September–June
School type coeducational, day, private non-profit
Year founded 1996
Governed by appointed Board of Directors
Accredited by Middle States
Regional organizations CEESA
Enrollment PreK 10; Elementary K–5 54; Middle School 6–8 27; High School 9–12 18; Total 109

Nationalities of student body US 35; UK 8; Macedonian 18; Other(s) (Dutch, Hungarian) 48
Tuition/fee currency US Dollar
Tuition range 3,800–15,100
Annual fees Capital Levy 1,600; Busing 1,300; Lunch 550
One time fees Registration 100

EDUCATIONAL PROGRAM

Curriculum US
Average class size Elementary 9; Secondary 6
Language(s) of instruction English
Language(s) taught Macedonian, German, Spanish, French
Staff specialists computer, ESL, learning disabilities, math resource, reading resource

Special curricular programs art, instrumental music, computer/technology, physical education
Extra curricular programs computers, dance, drama, excursions/expeditions, newspaper, yearbook
Sports baseball, basketball, football, skiing, soccer, swimming, tennis, volleyball
Examinations AP, Iowa

CAMPUS FACILITIES

Location Urban
Campus 2 buildings, 13 classrooms, 1 computer lab, 35 instructional computers,

7,000 library volumes, 1 cafeteria, 1 gymnasium, 2 playing fields, 6 tennis courts, air conditioning

MADAGASCAR

MADAGASCAR

Area:	587,040 sq km
Population:	19,448,815
Capital:	Antananarivo
Currency:	Madagascar Ariary (MGA)
Languages:	French, Malagasy

AMERICAN SCHOOL OF ANTANANARIVO

Phone	261 20 22 42039
Fax	261 20 22 34539
Email	asamad@wanadoo.mg
Website	www.asamadagascar.org
Address	BP 1717, Antananarivo, 101, Madagascar
Mailing address	2040 Antananarivo Place, Dulles, VA 20189-2040, USA

STAFF

Director Steven J. Long
Registrar Chantal Razafindrakambana
Principal Pilar Starkey
Technology Coordinator Marco Alessio

Head of Library/Media Center
Lanto Rakotoarison
Teaching staff Full time 29; Part time 2; Total 31
Nationalities of teaching staff US 13; UK 1;
Malagasy 4; Other(s) (South African, Dutch) 13

INFORMATION

Grade levels N–12
School year August–June
School type coeducational, day, private non-profit
Year founded 1969
Governed by elected Board of Directors
Accredited by Middle States
Regional organizations AISA
Enrollment Nursery 25; PreK 12;
Elementary K–5 90; Middle School 6–8 45;
High School 9–12 40; Total 212

Nationalities of student body US 50; UK 3;
Malagasy 45; Other(s) (French, Indian) 114
Tuition/fee currency US Dollar
Tuition range 3,625–11,354
Annual fees Registration 250; Band 75
One time fees Capital Levy 2,000
Graduates attending college 100%

EDUCATIONAL PROGRAM

Curriculum US, AP
Average class size Elementary 12; Secondary 11
Language(s) of instruction English
Language(s) taught French, Spanish
Staff specialists computer, counselor, ESL,
librarian
Special curricular programs art, instrumental
music, computer/technology, distance learning,
physical education

Extra curricular programs computers, community
service, dance, environmental conservation,
excursions/expeditions, newspaper, yearbook
Sports basketball, soccer, tennis, volleyball
Clubs French
Examinations AP, PSAT, SAT, TOEFL, ISA (Int.
Schools Assessment)

CAMPUS FACILITIES

Location Suburban
Campus 1 hectare, 8 buildings, 17 classrooms,
2 computer labs, 55 instructional computers,

5,500 library volumes, 1 infirmary, 2 playing
fields, 1 science lab, air conditioning

MALAWI

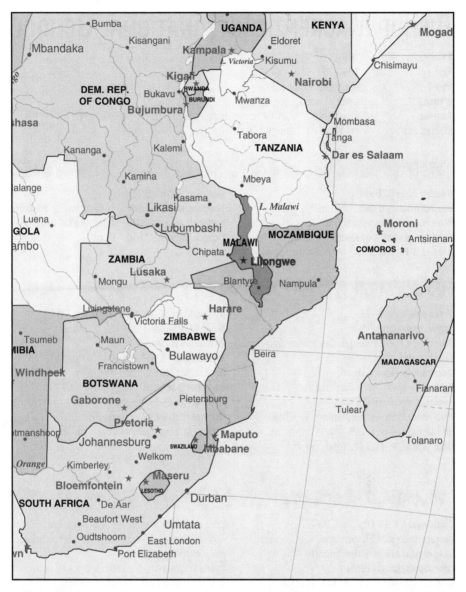

MALAWI

Area:	118,480 sq km
Population:	13,603,181
Capital:	Lilongwe
Currency:	Malawian Kwacha (MWK)
Languages:	Chichewa

BISHOP MACKENZIE INTERNATIONAL SCHOOL

Phone 265 1756 364
Fax 265 1751 374
Email info@bmismw.com
Website www.bmis.cois.org
Address Plot Number 3/3/019 Baron Avenue, Area 3, Lilongwe, Malawi
Mailing address PO Box 102, Lilongwe, Malawi

STAFF

Director Peter J. Todd
Head of Primary School Lee Chalkly
Head of Secondary School Bora Rancic
Chief Accountant Wily Horea
Head of IT Faculty Shane O'Loughlin

Librarian Veronica Mahari
Teaching staff Full time 55; Part time 1; Total 56
Nationalities of teaching staff US 6; UK 24;
Other(s) (South African) 26

INFORMATION

Grade levels PreK–12
School year August–June
School type coeducational, day, private non-profit
Year founded 1944
Governed by elected Board
Accredited by CIS, New England
Regional organizations AISA
Enrollment PreK 44; Elementary K–5 343;
Middle School 6–8 139;
High School 9–12 128; Total 654

Nationalities of student body US 44; UK 150;
South African 181; Other(s) (Zimbabwean) 279
Tuition/fee currency US Dollar
Tuition range 8,967–14,501
Annual fees Registration 65
One time fees Family Registration 2,125;
Refundable Book Deposit 50
Graduates attending college 95%
Graduates have attended Col of William and
Mary, California State U, British Columbia U,
U of Cambridge, Warwick U

EDUCATIONAL PROGRAM

Curriculum UK, IB Diploma, IGCSE
Average class size Elementary 21; Secondary 18
Language(s) of instruction English
Language(s) taught French
Staff specialists computer, ESL, learning
disabilities, librarian
Special curricular programs art, instrumental
music, vocal music, computer/technology,
physical education

Extra curricular programs computers, community
service, dance, drama, excursions/expeditions,
photography, yearbook
Sports badminton, basketball, cricket, golf,
hockey, martial arts, soccer, softball,
swimming, tennis, track and field, volleyball
Clubs chess, Mahjong, student council, Model
UN, cooking, music and dance performance,
computer
Examinations GCSE, IB, IGCSE, PSAT, SAT, SAT II

CAMPUS FACILITIES

Location Urban
Campus 12 hectares, 19 buildings, 40 classrooms,
2 computer labs, 65 instructional computers,

14,000 library volumes, 1 auditorium,
1 infirmary, 3 playing fields, 3 science labs,
2 pools, 2 tennis courts

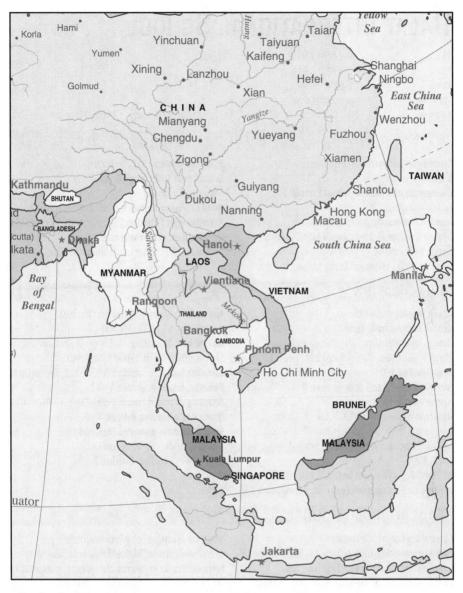

MALAYSIA

Area:	329,750 sq km
Population:	24,821,286
Capital:	Kuala Lumpur
Currency:	Ringgit (MYR)
Languages:	Bahasa Malaysia, English

DALAT INTERNATIONAL SCHOOL

Phone	60 4 899 2105
Fax	60 4 890 2141
Email	info@dalat.org
Website	www.dalat.org
Address	Dalat International School, Tanjung Bunga, Penang, 11200, Malaysia

STAFF

Director and High School Principal
Karl L. Steinkamp
Elementary and Middle School Principal
David Wilson
Head of Counseling Jacki Steinkamp
Deputy Director and Residence Life Supervisor
Brian Weidemann
Director of Development Larry Chinn

Business Comptroller Steve Koo
Educational Technology Coordinator
Nathanael Klassen
Head Librarian Kathaleen McClary
Teaching staff Full time 125; Part time 9; Total 134
Nationalities of teaching staff US 54;
Malaysian 60; Other(s) (Canadian) 20

INFORMATION

Grade levels PreK–12
School year August–June
School type boarding, coeducational,
church-affiliated, day, private non-profit
Year founded 1929
Governed by elected School Board
Accredited by Western
Regional organizations EARCOS
Enrollment PreK 12; Elementary K–5 118;
Middle School 6–8 111; High School 9–12 149;
Total 390
Nationalities of student body US 126; UK 2;
Malaysian 27; Other(s) (Korean, Taiwanese) 235

Tuition/fee currency Malaysian Ringgit
Tuition range 6,400–36,200
Annual fees Boarding, 7-day 26,800; Capital
Levy 4,500; Lunch 1,160; ESL 1,900
One time fees Registration 3,750; ESL Testing 200
Boarding program grades 1–12
Boarding program length 7-day **Boys** 40 **Girls** 40
Graduates attending college 95%
Graduates have attended Harvard U,
Johns Hopkins U, Wheaton Col,
Trinity Western Col, Purdue U

EDUCATIONAL PROGRAM

Curriculum US, AP, Christian
Average class size Elementary 15; Secondary 25
Language(s) of instruction English
Language(s) taught Mandarin, Malay, Spanish
Staff specialists computer, counselor, ESL,
learning disabilities, librarian, nurse, psychologist
Special curricular programs art, instrumental
music, vocal music, computer/technology,
distance learning, physical education,
vocational, virtual high school courses
Extra curricular programs computers, community
service, drama, excursions/expeditions,
newspaper, yearbook, Boy and Girl Scouts
Sports basketball, soccer, swimming, tennis,
track and field, volleyball
Clubs speech club (forensics), student council
Examinations ACT, Iowa, SAT, SAT II

CAMPUS FACILITIES

Location Suburban
Campus 4 hectares, 20 buildings, 43 classrooms,
3 computer labs, 240 instructional computers,
21,000 library volumes, 1 auditorium, 1 cafeteria,
1 covered play area, 1 gymnasium, 1 infirmary,
2 playing fields, 3 science labs, 1 pool,
1 tennis court, air conditioning

THE ALICE SMITH SCHOOL

Phone	60 3 2148 3674
Fax	60 3 2148 3418
Email	klass@alice-smith.edu.my
Website	www.alice-smith.edu.my
Address	2 Jalan Bellamy, Kuala Lumpur, 50460, Malaysia

STAFF

Chairman, Council of Governors Martin Sharp
Primary Principal Stephen Caulfield
Vice Principal Michael Welland
Vice Principal, Primary School Christine A. Boden
Secondary Principal Richard Dyer

Head of Finance and Administration Lim Chin Guan
Faculty Head, Design Technology Adam Philips
Teaching staff Full time 114; Part time 4; Total 118
Nationalities of teaching staff UK 86; Malaysian 8; Other(s) (Australian, French) 21

INFORMATION

Grade levels N–13
School year September–July
School type coeducational, day, private non-profit
Year founded 1946
Governed by appointed and elected Council
Regional organizations ECIS
Enrollment Nursery 23; PreK 80; Elementary K–5 529; Middle School 6–8 315; High School 9–12 323; Grade 13 30; Total 1,300

Nationalities of student body US 26; UK 494; Malaysian 364; Other(s) (Australian, Singaporean) 416
Tuition/fee currency Malaysian Ringgit
Tuition range 19,500–45,000
One time fees Registration 400; Capital Levy 2,000; Enrollment 16,000
Graduates attending college 99%
Graduates have attended Manchester U, Loughborough U, Purdue U, Monash U, Durham U

EDUCATIONAL PROGRAM

Curriculum UK
Average class size Elementary 22; Secondary 24
Language(s) of instruction English
Language(s) taught French, German, Malay, Mandarin
Staff specialists computer, counselor, ESL, learning disabilities, librarian, math resource, nurse, reading resource
Special curricular programs art, instrumental music, vocal music, computer/technology, physical education, vocational

Extra curricular programs computers, community service, dance, drama, environmental conservation, excursions/expeditions, yearbook
Sports basketball, cricket, gymnastics, hockey, martial arts, rugby, skiing, soccer, softball, swimming, tennis, track and field, volleyball, fencing, netball
Clubs Boy and Girl Scouts
Examinations A-level GCE, GCSE, IGCSE, SAT

CAMPUS FACILITIES

Location Suburban
Campus 14 hectares, 12 buildings, 89 classrooms, 4 computer labs, 150 instructional computers, 13,000 library volumes, 2 auditoriums, 2 cafeterias, 1 covered play area, 3 gymnasiums, 2 infirmaries, 2 playing fields, 7 science labs, 2 pools, 2 tennis courts

GARDEN INTERNATIONAL SCHOOL

Phone	60 3 6209 6888
Fax	60 3 6201 2468
Email	admissions@gardenschool.edu.my
Website	www.gardenschool.edu.my
Address	No 16 Jalan Kiara 3, Off Jalan Bukit Kiara, Kuala Lumpur, 50480, Malaysia

STAFF

Principal Raymond P. Davis, Ed.D.
Head of Secondary School Robert Lloyd
Head of Primary School Christopher FitzGerald
Head of Kuantan Campus Simon Jodrell

Finance and Administration Manager Jean Chang
IT Manager Michael Choong
Library and Learning Resource Manager
Annette Wilson

INFORMATION

Grade levels N–13
School year September–July
School type coeducational, day
Year founded 1951
Governed by appointed Board of Directors
Sponsored by Taylor's Education Group
Regional organizations ECIS
Enrollment Nursery 25; PreK 60;
Elementary K–5 675; Middle School 6–8 475;
High School 9–12 475; Grade 13 40; Total 1,750

Nationalities of student body US 25; UK 195;
Malaysian 620; Other(s) (Singaporean,
Australian) 910
Tuition/fee currency Malaysian Ringgit
Tuition range 18,660–33,990
Annual fees Busing 1,800; Technology 1,080
One time fees Registration 10,500; Deposit 11,330

EDUCATIONAL PROGRAM

Curriculum UK, IGCSE, GenCSE, IGCSE
Average class size Elementary 25; Secondary 25
Language(s) of instruction English
Language(s) taught French, Spanish, Malay,
Mandarin, English
Staff specialists computer, counselor, ESL,
learning disabilities, librarian, math resource,
nurse, reading resource
Special curricular programs art, instrumental
music, vocal music, computer/technology,
physical education, secondary school
leadership camps
Extra curricular programs computers, community
service, dance, drama, environmental
conservation, excursions/expeditions,
newspaper, photography, yearbook, fencing,
Tae Kwan Do, netball, mountain biking,
table tennis, ten-pin bowling
Sports badminton, basketball, cricket, football,
golf, hockey, martial arts, rugby, soccer,
softball, swimming, tennis, track and field,
volleyball
Clubs Model UN, Asia-Europe Classroom,
arts and crafts, science, Young Enterprise,
videography, chess, Karate, Mandarin
Examinations A-level GCE, GCSE, IGCSE, UK
National Tests

CAMPUS FACILITIES

Location Suburban
Campus 3 hectares, 9 buildings, 112 classrooms,
5 computer labs, 456 instructional computers,
25,000 library volumes, 1 auditorium,
2 cafeterias, 4 covered play areas, 2 gymnasiums,
2 infirmaries, 1 playing field, 7 science labs,
1 pool, 2 tennis courts, air conditioning

Data from 2006/07 school year.

The International School of Kuala Lumpur

Phone	60 3 4259 5600
Fax	60 3 4257 9044
Email	iskl@iskl.edu.my
Website	www.iskl.edu.my
Address	Jalan Kolam Air, Kuala Lumpur, Selangor Darul Ehsan, 68000, Malaysia
Mailing address	PO Box 12645, 50784 Kuala Lumpur, Malaysia

STAFF

Head of School Paul B. Chmelik
High School Principal Grant Millard
Middle School Principal Michael Callan
Elementary School Principal Anthony Harduar
Curriculum Coordinator Naomi Aleman
Director of Operations Robert Thompson

Director of Technology Chad Bates
Librarian Nancy Woodward
Teaching staff Full time 157; Part time 11;
Total 168
Nationalities of teaching staff US 82; UK 13;
Malaysian 15; Other(s) (Canadian, Australian) 58

INFORMATION

Grade levels N–12
School year August–June
School type coeducational, day, private non-profit
Year founded 1965
Governed by elected Board of Directors
Accredited by Western
Regional organizations EARCOS
Enrollment Nursery 13; PreK 43;
Elementary K–5 474; Middle School 6–8 341;
High School 9–12 567; Total 1,438

Nationalities of student body US 280; UK 87;
Malaysian 151; Other(s) (Korean, Japanese) 915
Tuition/fee currency US Dollar
Tuition range 8,372–15,535
Annual fees Re-enrollment 1,096
One time fees Registration 4,383;
Capital Levy 2,922
Graduates attending college 95%
Graduates have attended Harvard U, Stanford U,
London School of Economics, Yale U, Oxford U

(Continued)

THE INTERNATIONAL SCHOOL OF KUALA LUMPUR (Continued)

EDUCATIONAL PROGRAM

Curriculum US, AP, IB Diploma
Average class size Elementary 18; Secondary 20
Language(s) of instruction English
Language(s) taught Mandarin, Spanish, French, Bahasa Malaysia
Staff specialists computer, counselor, ESL, learning disabilities, librarian, math resource, nurse, psychologist, reading resource, speech/hearing
Special curricular programs art, instrumental music, vocal music, computer/technology, physical education

Extra curricular programs computers, community service, dance, drama, environmental conservation, excursions/expeditions, newspaper, photography, yearbook
Sports badminton, baseball, basketball, cross-country, football, rugby, soccer, swimming, tennis, track and field, volleyball
Clubs mural, dance, Homework Help, chess, Scrabble, 3-D Curiosity, climbing, drama and story telling, Model UN
Examinations AP, IB, Iowa, ERB, ISA

CAMPUS FACILITIES

Location Suburban
Campus 8 hectares, 2 buildings, 122 classrooms, 5 computer labs, 400 instructional computers, 50,000 library volumes, 2 auditoriums,

3 cafeterias, 2 covered play areas, 2 gymnasiums, 2 infirmaries, 4 playing fields, 13 science labs, 2 pools, 2 tennis courts, air conditioning

MONT'KIARA INTERNATIONAL SCHOOL

Phone   60 3 2093 8604
Fax   60 3 2093 6045
Email   info@mkis.edu.my
Website   www.mkis.edu.my
Address   22 Jalan Kiara, Mont'Kiara, Kuala Lumpur, 50480, Malaysia

STAFF

Head of School Walt Morris
Elementary Principal Paul Sicard
Middle/High School Principal
Robert B. Peterson, Ed.D.
Curriculum Coordinator Sharon Lee, Ph.D.

Business/Finance Manager KC Chua
Head of Library/Media Center Laurie Collins
Teaching staff Full time 99; Part time 2; Total 101
Nationalities of teaching staff US 49; UK 3;
Malaysian 7; Other(s) (Canadian, Australian) 42

INFORMATION

Grade levels PreK–12
School year August–June
School type coeducational, day, proprietary
Year founded 1994
Governed by appointed Board of Governors
Sponsored by M'KIS Sdn. Bhd.
Accredited by Western
Regional organizations EARCOS
Enrollment PreK 49; Elementary K–5 429;
Middle School 6–8 154;
High School 9–12 170; Total 802

Nationalities of student body US 118; UK 29;
Malaysian 121; Other(s) (Dutch, Korean) 534
Tuition/fee currency Malaysian Ringgit
Tuition range 31,247–60,593
Annual fees Re-enrollment 3,450
One time fees Registration 17,000; Application 600
Graduates attending college 99%
Graduates have attended Kings Col London,
California State U in Northridge, Baylor U,
U of Queensland, U of Alberta

EDUCATIONAL PROGRAM

Curriculum US, IB Diploma
Average class size Elementary 18; Secondary 15
Language(s) of instruction English
Language(s) taught French, Mandarin, Spanish,
Bahasa Malayu
Staff specialists computer, counselor, ESL,
learning disabilities, librarian, nurse

Special curricular programs art, instrumental
music, vocal music, computer/technology,
physical education
Extra curricular programs community service,
environmental conservation, newspaper, yearbook
Sports basketball, soccer, softball, swimming,
tennis, track and field, volleyball
Examinations IB, Iowa, PSAT, SAT

CAMPUS FACILITIES

Location Suburban
Campus 3 hectares, 4 buildings, 50 classrooms,
4 computer labs, 200 instructional computers,
16,000 library volumes, 1 auditorium,

1 cafeteria, 2 covered play areas, 1 gymnasium,
1 infirmary, 2 playing fields, 5 science labs,
1 pool, air conditioning

MELAKA INTERNATIONAL SCHOOL

Phone	6 06 286 2573
Fax	6 06 286 2575
Email	administrator@mis.edu.my
Website	www.mis.edu.my
Address	No 1, Jalan Kubu, Melaka, Melaka, 75300, Malaysia

STAFF

Administrator Shamsunnisa Ishak
Software Engineer Thanaletchumy
Teaching staff Full time 22; Total 22

Nationalities of teaching staff Malaysian 19;
Other(s) (Indian, Filipino) 3

INFORMATION

Grade levels PreK–13
School year September–August
School type coeducational, proprietary
Year founded 1993
Governed by appointed Mrs. Shamsunnisa Ishak
Enrollment PreK 25; Elementary K–5 150;
Middle School 6–8 75; High School 9–12 75;
Total 325
Nationalities of student body UK 10; Other(s)
(Indonesian, Finn) 315

Tuition/fee currency Malaysian Ringgit
Annual fees Capital Levy 1,000; Insurance 10;
Books 300
One time fees Registration 4,000
Graduates attending college 100%
Graduates have attended Monash U, Sunway Col,
Polytechnic Col in Singapore, U of Shanghai,
Aberdeen Col

EDUCATIONAL PROGRAM

Curriculum UK, IGCSE
Average class size Elementary 15; Secondary 15
Language(s) of instruction English
Language(s) taught Malay, Mandarin
Special curricular programs instrumental music

Sports badminton, hockey, track and field,
table tennis, netball
Clubs Boy and Girl Scouts, arts and crafts,
Examinations GCSE, IGCSE

CAMPUS FACILITIES

Location Urban
Campus 3 buildings, 35 classrooms, 1 computer
lab, 20 instructional computers, 5,000 library
volumes, 1 auditorium, 1 cafeteria,

1 covered play area, 1 gymnasium, 1 infirmary,
3 playing fields, 3 science labs, 1 pool,
1 tennis court, air conditioning

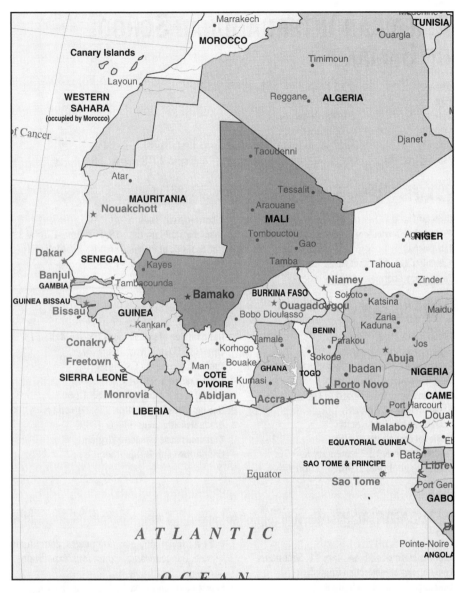

MALI

Area:	1.24 million sq km
Population:	11,995,402
Capital:	Bamako
Currency:	Communaute Financiere Africaine Franc (XOF)
Languages:	French, Bambara

AMERICAN INTERNATIONAL SCHOOL OF BAMAKO

Phone	223 222 47 38
Fax	223 222 08 53
Email	aisb@aisbmali.org
Website	www.aisbmali.org
Address	Porte 36, Rue 111, Badalabougou Ouest, Bamako, 34, Mali
Mailing address	DOS/AISB, 2050 Bamako Place, Dulles, VA 20189-2010, USA

STAFF

Director David G Henry
Principal of Curriculum & Instruction/Counselor Jan Derpak
Administrative Assistant Hoda Tamim
Technology Coordinator Bob Strozeski

Librarian Kelly Dalton
Teaching staff Full time 18; Part time 4; Total 22
Nationalities of teaching staff US 13; Malian 1; Other(s) (Canadian) 8

INFORMATION

Grade levels PreK–12
School year August–June
School type coeducational, day, private non-profit
Year founded 1977
Governed by elected Board of Directors
Sponsored by US Embassy
Accredited by Middle States
Regional organizations AISA
Enrollment PreK 12; Elementary K–5 76; Middle School 6–8 22; High School 9–12 16; Total 126

Nationalities of student body US 34; Malian 13; Other(s) (Dutch, Canadian) 79
Tuition/fee currency US Dollar
Tuition range 4,500–15,250
Annual fees Busing 1,600; ESL 1,600
One time fees Registration 275; Capital Levy 4,000
Graduates attending college 100%
Graduates have attended Virginia Commonwealth U, Richmond U

EDUCATIONAL PROGRAM

Curriculum US, AP
Average class size Elementary 11; Secondary 7
Language(s) of instruction English
Language(s) taught French (K–12)
Staff specialists computer, counselor, ESL, librarian
Special curricular programs art, instrumental music, vocal music, computer/technology, physical education, theater arts

Extra curricular programs computers, community service, dance, drama, excursions/expeditions, newspaper, yearbook
Sports badminton, basketball, gymnastics, martial arts, soccer, softball, swimming, track and field, volleyball
Clubs Model UN, student council
Examinations AP, Iowa, PSAT, SAT

CAMPUS FACILITIES

Location Suburban
Campus 2 hectares, 8 buildings, 22 classrooms, 2 computer labs, 40 instructional computers,

9,700 library volumes, 1 auditorium, 1 covered play area, 1 gymnasium, 1 playing field, 1 science lab, 1 pool, air conditioning

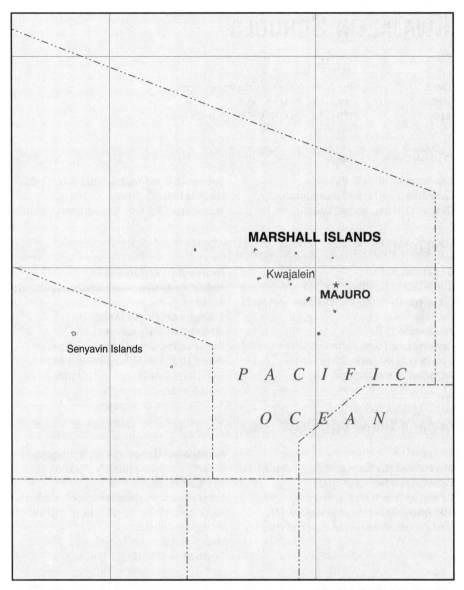

MARSHALL ISLANDS

Area:	11,854.3 sq km
Population:	61,815
Capital:	Majuro
Currency:	US Dollar (USD)
Languages:	Marshallese, English

KWAJALEIN SCHOOLS

Phone	805 355 3761
Fax	805 355 3584
Email	allan.robinson@kwajalein-school.com
Website	www.kwajalein-school.com
Address	PO Box 51, APO, AP, 96555, Marshall Islands

STAFF

Superintendent Allan W. Robinson
Elementary School Principal Deb Johnson
Director, Child Development Center Aimee Pang

Director, Child and Youth Services Jody Franke
Librarian Deborah Kirby
Teaching staff Full time 44; Part time 6; Total 50

INFORMATION

Grade levels K–12
School year August–June
School type coeducational, company-sponsored, day
Year founded 1956
Governed by appointed School Advisory Council
Sponsored by Kwajalein Range Services
Accredited by North Central

Enrollment Elementary K–5 180; Middle School 6–8 90; High School 9–12 101; Total 371
Tuition/fee currency US Dollar
Graduates attending college 94%
Graduates have attended Air Force Academy, Harvey Mudd Col, Massachusetts Institute of Technology, U of Texas, U of California in Santa Barbara

EDUCATIONAL PROGRAM

Curriculum US, AP
Average class size Elementary 14; Secondary 16
Language(s) of instruction English
Language(s) taught French, Spanish
Staff specialists computer, counselor, ESL, learning disabilities, librarian, speech/hearing

Special curricular programs art, instrumental music, vocal music, computer/technology, physical education
Extra curricular programs newspaper, yearbook
Sports baseball, basketball, soccer, softball, swimming, volleyball
Clubs National Honor Society
Examinations ACT, AP, SAT, TOEFL

CAMPUS FACILITIES

Location Rural
Campus 8 buildings, 36 classrooms, 3 computer labs, 150 instructional computers, 20,000 library volumes, 3 playing fields, 2 science labs, air conditioning

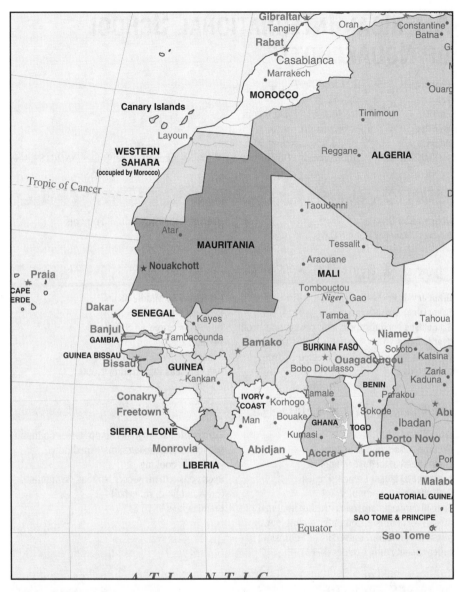

MAURITANIA

Area:	1,030,700 sq km
Population:	3,270,065
Capital:	Nouakchott
Currency:	Ouguiya (MRO)
Languages:	Arabic

AMERICAN INTERNATIONAL SCHOOL OF NOUAKCHOTT

Phone	222 52 52967
Fax	222 52 52967
Email	freetowanda@yahoo.com
Website	www.aisn.mr
Address	BP 222, Nouakchott, Mauritania
Mailing address	Administrative Officer (AISN), 2430 Nouakchott Place, Dulles, VA 20189, USA

STAFF

Director Ron Brown
Business Manager Debbie Davis

Head of Technology Sidi Ali Francois

INFORMATION

Grade levels PreK–9
School year August–June
School type coeducational, day, private non-profit
Year founded 1978
Governed by appointed and elected Board of Trustees

Accredited by Middle States
Regional organizations AISA
Tuition/fee currency US Dollar
Tuition 12,120
Annual fees PreK Tuition 4,747
One time fees Registration 1,000

EDUCATIONAL PROGRAM

Curriculum US
Average class size Elementary 8
Language(s) of instruction English
Language(s) taught French, English
Staff specialists computer
Special curricular programs art, instrumental music, vocal music, computer/technology, physical education, University of Nebraska Independent Study (grades 9–12)

Extra curricular programs computers, community service, drama, excursions/expeditions, yearbook, cooking
Sports basketball, soccer, softball, swimming, track and field, volleyball
Examinations PSAT, SAT

CAMPUS FACILITIES

Location Urban
Campus 1 hectare, 2 buildings, 6 classrooms, 1 computer lab, 11 instructional computers,

4,500 library volumes, 1 science lab, 1 pool, air conditioning

Data from 2006/07 school year.

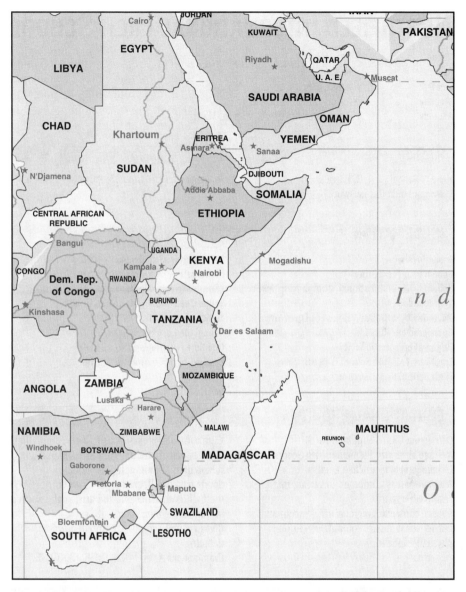

MAURITIUS

Area:	2,040 sq km
Population:	1,250,882
Capital:	Port Louis
Currency:	Mauritian Rupee (MUR)
Languages:	Creole

NORTHFIELD INTERNATIONAL HIGH SCHOOL

Phone	230 266 9448
Fax	230 266 9447
Email	northfields@intnet.mu
Website	www.northfieldsonline.com
Address	Labourdonnais Village, Mapou, Mauritius

STAFF

Head of School Clive R. Barnes
Librarian Linda Ramasawmy

Teaching staff Full time 33; Part time 2; Total 35

INFORMATION

Grade levels 6–13
School year September–July
School type coeducational, company-sponsored
Year founded 2002
Governed by appointed Board of Directors
Sponsored by NIHS Ltd.
Regional organizations AISA
Enrollment Middle School 6–8 86;
High School 9–12 36; Total 122

Nationalities of student body US 2; UK 15;
Mauritian 60; Other(s)
(South African, Zimbabwean) 45
Tuition/fee currency Mauritius Rupee
Tuition range 80,000–100,000
Annual fees Books 20,000
One time fees Registration 25,000;
Deposit of three months 24,000

EDUCATIONAL PROGRAM

Curriculum UK, IB Diploma, IGCSE
Average class size Elementary 18; Secondary 18
Language(s) of instruction English
Staff specialists computer, librarian, math
resource, nurse
Special curricular programs art, instrumental
music, vocal music, computer/technology,
physical education

Extra curricular programs computers, community
service, dance, drama, excursions/expeditions,
newspaper, photography, yearbook
Sports basketball, cricket, cross-country,
football, gymnastics, martial arts, rugby, soccer,
swimming, tennis, volleyball
Clubs reading, cooking, computer, drama,
debating
Examinations A-level GCE, GCSE, IB, IGCSE

CAMPUS FACILITIES

Location Rural
Campus 5 hectares, 5 buildings, 15 classrooms,
1 auditorium, 1 cafeteria, 1 infirmary,

3 playing fields, 3 science labs, 1 tennis court,
air conditioning

Data from 2006/07 school year.

LE BOCAGE INTERNATIONAL SCHOOL

Phone	230 433 0941
Fax	230 433 4914
Email	lbis@intnet.mu
Website	www.lebocage.net
Address	Mount Ory, Moka, Mauritius

STAFF

Head of School David Muddle
Principal of High School Shekar Dewoo
Principal of Middle School Robert Roopnaraine
IGCSE Coordinator Nadine Espiegle
IB Coordinator Rasika Khadun
Careers Guidance Officer Khatijah Ruhomutally

Business Manager Hemraz Gunesie
Head of IT Department Rechad Issack
Chief Librarian Angela de Robilliard
Teaching staff Full time 69; Part time 1; Total 70
Nationalities of teaching staff UK 2;
Mauritian 61; Other(s) (Australian, Guyanese) 6

INFORMATION

Grade levels 6–12
School year January–November
School type coeducational, day, private non-profit
Year founded 1990
Governed by appointed Board of Directors
Accredited by CIS
Regional organizations ECIS, NESA
Enrollment Middle School 6–8 209; High
School 9–12 378; Total 587

Nationalities of student body US 1; UK 19;
Mauritian 506; Other(s) (Indian, South African) 61
Tuition/fee currency Mauritius Rupee
Tuition range 109,000–209,000
Annual fees Books 2,500; PTA 300
One time fees Registration 40,000; PTA 200
Graduates attending college 95%
Graduates have attended Mercer U, U of
California in Berkeley, Imperial Col London,
U College London, U of Bath

EDUCATIONAL PROGRAM

Curriculum Intl, IB Diploma, IGCSE
Average class size Secondary 24
Language(s) of instruction English, French
Language(s) taught Spanish
Staff specialists computer, counselor, ESL,
librarian, math resource, nurse, reading resource
Special curricular programs art, physical
education, vocational

Extra curricular programs computers, community
service, drama, excursions/expeditions, literary
magazine, yearbook
Sports badminton, basketball, cricket,
cross-country, soccer, swimming, track and
field, volleyball
Clubs computer, games, outdoor, drums
Examinations GCSE, IB, IGCSE

CAMPUS FACILITIES

Location Rural
Campus 3 hectares, 4 buildings, 37 classrooms,
3 computer labs, 60 instructional computers,

9,000 library volumes, 1 auditorium, 1 cafeteria,
1 covered play area, 1 gymnasium, 1 infirmary,
2 playing fields, 3 science labs

MEXICO

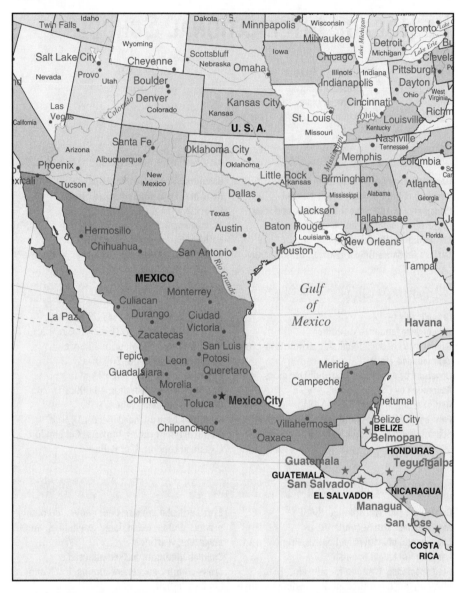

MEXICO

Area:	1,972,550 sq km
Population:	108,700,891
Capital:	Mexico (Distrito Federal)
Currency:	Mexican Peso (MXN)
Languages:	Spanish

CARDINAL SCHOOL, CAMPUS ALLENDE

Phone   82 6268 1870
Fax   82 6268 1872
Email   patricia_najera@prodigy.net.mx
Address   Carretera a La Colmena #888, La Colmena de Abajo, Allende,
               Nuevo Leon, 67350, Mexico

STAFF

Principals Robert and Leonor Arpee
Academic Director Mely Coronado
Elementry School Principal Reina Graciela Salazar
Preschool Principal Yolanda Lucio, Ph.D.
Admissions Patricia Najera

Comptroller Alejandro Fernandez
Technology Coordinator Edna Treviño
Teaching staff Full time 20; Part time 5; Total 25
Nationalities of teaching staff Mexican 25

INFORMATION

Grade levels N–5
School year August–July
School type coeducational, church-affiliated,
day, private non-profit
Year founded 2005
Enrollment Nursery 38; PreK 23;
Elementary K–5 106; Total 167

Nationalities of student body Mexican 167
Tuition/fee currency US Dollar
Tuition range 2,480–2,830
Annual fees Registration 445; Insurance 23;
Books 364; Personal Academic Supplies 46;
Uniform 175
Graduates attending college 100%

EDUCATIONAL PROGRAM

Curriculum US, National, College Board, Fourth R
Average class size Elementary 16
Language(s) of instruction English, Spanish
Staff specialists computer, counselor, ESL,
librarian, math resource, nurse, physician,
psychologist, reading resource

Special curricular programs art, instrumental
music, vocal music, computer/technology,
physical education, vocational, human values
Extra curricular programs computers, community
service, dance, environmental conservation,
excursions/expeditions, newspaper
Sports basketball, gymnastics, soccer, track and
field, volleyball

CAMPUS FACILITIES

Location Suburban
Campus 5 hectares, 2 buildings, 12 classrooms,

1 computer lab, 18 instructional computers,
200 library volumes, air conditioning

THE AMERICAN SCHOOL FOUNDATION OF GUADALAJARA A.C.

Phone	52 333 648 0299
Fax	52 333 817 3356
Email	asfg@asfg.mx
Website	www.asfg.mx
Address	Colomos 2100, APDO 6-280, Fracc. Italia Providencia, Guadalajara, Jalisco, 44630, Mexico

STAFF

Director General Janet L. Heinze
Early Childhood Principal
Tina Carstensen de Lopez
Elementary Principal Dawn Hernandez
Middle School Principal David Markman
High School Principal David McGrath
Academic Programs Director Sheree Nuncio

Administration and Finance Director Laura Jimenez
IT Manager Rafael De La Cruz
Information Technology and Literacy Director
Juliet Evans
Teaching staff Full time 125; Total 125
Nationalities of teaching staff US 49; UK 1;
Mexican 63; Other(s) (Canadian, Serb) 12

INFORMATION

Grade levels N–12
School year August–June
School type coeducational, day, private non-profit
Year founded 1956
Governed by appointed Board of Directors
Accredited by Southern
Regional organizations ASOMEX
Enrollment Nursery 30; PreK 68;
Elementary K–5 742; Middle School 6–8 275;
High School 9–12 337; Total 1,452

Nationalities of student body US 214; UK 1;
Mexican 1,116; Other(s) (Korean, Japanese) 121
Tuition/fee currency US Dollar
Tuition range 4,023–5,987
Annual fees Registration 2,636; Insurance 382
One time fees Admission 3,272
Graduates attending college 98%
Graduates have attended Massachusetts Institute
of Technology, U of Pennsylvania, U of Notre
Dame, U of Texas in Austin, Columbia U

EDUCATIONAL PROGRAM

Curriculum US, National, AP
Average class size Elementary 23; Secondary 25
Language(s) of instruction English, Spanish
Language(s) taught French, German
Staff specialists computer, counselor, ESL,
learning disabilities, librarian, math resource,
nurse, psychologist, reading resource
Special curricular programs art, instrumental
music, vocal music, computer/technology,
physical education, theater

Extra curricular programs computers, community
service, dance, drama, environmental
conservation, excursions/expeditions, literary
magazine, newspaper, photography, yearbook
Sports basketball, soccer, swimming, track and
field, volleyball
Clubs Model UN, National Junior Honor Society,
National Honor Society, Math Counts, ecology,
chess, cheerleading, Destination Imagination
Examinations ACT, AP, PSAT, SAT, SAT II,
Stanford, TOEFL, Enlace, MAP

CAMPUS FACILITIES

Location Urban
Campus 6 hectares, 7 buildings, 92 classrooms,
5 computer labs, 350 instructional computers,
30,000 library volumes, 1 auditorium,

2 cafeterias, 1 covered play area, 1 gymnasium,
1 infirmary, 2 playing fields, 6 science labs,
1 pool

THE AMERICAN SCHOOL FOUNDATION, A.C.

Phone	5255 5227 4900
Fax	5255 5273 9658
Email	tmiller@asf.edu.mx
Website	www.asf.edu.mx
Address	Bondojito 215, Col. Las Américas, Delegación Alvaro Obregón, Mexico City, DF, 01120, Mexico

STAFF

President and Executive Director Darío A. Cortés, Ph.D.
Associate Executive Director for Academic Affairs Paul Williams
Head of Upper School Rob Goodly
Head of Middle School David J. O'Connell
Head of Lower School Jon Fulk
Head of the Early Childhood Center Darlene Pugnali

Associate Executive Director of Finance and Administration Guillermo Turincio
Upper School Librarian Matthew Bosarge
Teaching staff Full time 255; Part time 3; Total 258
Nationalities of teaching staff US 105; UK 4; Mexican 118; Other(s) (Canadian, Argentine) 31

INFORMATION

Grade levels PreK–12
School year August–June
School type coeducational, day, private non-profit
Year founded 1888
Governed by elected Board of Trustees
Accredited by Southern
Regional organizations ASOMEX
Enrollment PreK 142; Elementary K–5 1,154; Middle School 6–8 511; High School 9–12 628; Total 2,435
Nationalities of student body US 649; UK 11; Mexican 1,451; Other(s) (Korean, Colombian) 324

Tuition/fee currency Mexican Peso
Tuition range 8,670–12,590
Annual fees Busing 1,340; LS Student Activity 410; MS Student Activity 585; US Student Activity 585
One time fees Registration 40,000
Graduates attending college 100%
Graduates have attended U Iberoamericana, Tecnologico de Monterrey, Instituto Tecnologico Autonomo de Mexico, U of British Columbia, Boston U

(Continued)

THE AMERICAN SCHOOL FOUNDATION, A.C. (Continued)

EDUCATIONAL PROGRAM

Curriculum US, National, Intl, AP, IB Diploma, IBPYP, IBMYP
Average class size Elementary 24; Secondary 22
Language(s) of instruction English, Spanish
Language(s) taught French
Staff specialists computer, counselor, ESL, learning disabilities, librarian, math resource, nurse, psychologist, reading resource
Special curricular programs art, instrumental music, vocal music, computer/technology, physical education

Extra curricular programs computers, community service, dance, drama, environmental conservation, excursions/expeditions, literary magazine, newspaper, photography, yearbook
Sports basketball, football, gymnastics, soccer, softball, swimming, tennis, track and field, volleyball
Clubs Asian Club, camping, ecology, Gamma, Habitat for Humanity, Model UN, Outreach, Risaterapia, Solidaridad, The Thespian Society
Examinations ACT, AP, IB, PSAT, SAT, SAT II, Stanford, TOEFL, NWEA

CAMPUS FACILITIES

Location Urban
Campus 17 hectares, 15 buildings, 168 classrooms, 5 computer labs, 800 instructional computers, 34,470 library volumes,

1 auditorium, 1 cafeteria, 2 covered play areas, 2 gymnasiums, 1 infirmary, 4 playing fields, 12 science labs, 1 pool, 4 tennis courts

WESTHILL INSTITUTE, S.C.

Phone	52 55 5292 6627
Fax	52 55 5292 6627 ext 105
Email	headmaster@westhill.edu.mx
Website	www.wi.edu.mx
Address	Domingo Garcia Ramos 56, Prados de la Montana I, Santa Fe Cuajimalpa, Mexico City, DF, 05610, Mexico

STAFF

Head of School Andrew N. Sherman
High School Assistant Principal Adriana San Millan
Middle School Assistant Principal Jason Clarke
Elementary Principal Sylvia Karam

Elementary Assistant Principal Tisa Rodríguez
Business/Finance Manager Luis Enrique Valdes
Head of Technology Hector Samperio
Head of Library/Media Center Norma Ramirez

INFORMATION

Grade levels N–12
School year August–June
School type coeducational, day, proprietary
Year founded 1992
Governed by appointed and elected Board of Directors
Sponsored by Owners and School Board
Accredited by Southern
Regional organizations ASOMEX
Enrollment Nursery 64; PreK 64; Elementary K–5 389; Middle School 6–8 162; High School 9–12 143; Total 822

Nationalities of student body US 304; UK 3; Mexican 328; Other(s) (Italian, Colombian) 187
Tuition/fee currency US Dollar
Tuition range 5,500–9,500
Annual fees Registration 500; Materials 800; Admission 2,500
Graduates attending college 96%
Graduates have attended U of British Columbia, Westhill U, American U, Le Rouche, Victoria Col

EDUCATIONAL PROGRAM

Curriculum US, National, AP
Average class size Elementary 16; Secondary 21
Language(s) of instruction English, Spanish
Language(s) taught Spanish, French
Staff specialists computer, counselor, ESL, learning disabilities, librarian, math resource, nurse, psychologist
Special curricular programs art, vocal music, computer/technology, physical education

Extra curricular programs computers, community service, drama, excursions/expeditions, newspaper, photography, yearbook, Model UN, debate, Math Counts
Sports basketball, soccer, swimming, volleyball
Examinations ACT, AP, PSAT, SAT, Stanford, TOEFL

CAMPUS FACILITIES

Location Urban
Campus 6 hectares, 4 buildings, 62 classrooms, 5 computer labs, 75 instructional computers, 14,000 library volumes, 2 auditoriums, 3 cafeterias, 2 covered play areas, 1 gymnasium, 3 infirmaries, 1 playing field, 5 science labs, 1 pool, 2 tennis courts

Data from 2006/07 school year.

AMERICAN INSTITUTE OF MONTERREY

Phone	52 81 81743700
Fax	52 81 81743701
Email	ehuergo@mail.aim-net.mx
Website	www.aim-net.mx
Address	Perseverancia No. 100, Col. Balcones del Valle, Monterrey, NL, 66220, Mexico

STAFF

General Director Elizabeth W. Huergo, Ed.D.
Santa Catarina Campus Assistant Director
David Arnold, Ed.D.
San Pedro Campus Director Margarita Romo, Ed.D.
Academic Coordinator Ivete Guerra, Ed.D.
Admissions Supervisor
María Teresa A. de Garcia-Gallo

Human Resources Coordinator
Amira Gonzalez, Ed.D.
Finance Coordinator Hilda Davila, Ph.D.
Technical Coordinator Guadalupe Gonzalez, Ph.D.
Educational Support Coordinator
Carmen Zeisler, Ed.D.

INFORMATION

Grade levels N–9
School year August–June
School type coeducational, day, proprietary
Year founded 1968
Governed by appointed Governing Board
Sponsored by Betty Wagner and Betina Elizondo
Accredited by CIS, New England
Regional organizations ASOMEX
Enrollment Nursery 100; PreK 105;
Elementary K–5 689; Middle School 6–8 242;
High School 9–12 71; Total 1,207

Nationalities of student body US 25; UK 3;
Mexican 1,143; Other(s)
(Korean, Venezuelan) 36
Tuition/fee currency US Dollar
Tuition range 420–682
Annual fees Registration 788; Insurance 51;
Busing 690; Lunch 500
One time fees Entrance 4,160

EDUCATIONAL PROGRAM

Curriculum US, National
Average class size Elementary 25; Secondary 25
Language(s) of instruction English
Language(s) taught Spanish/French/German
Staff specialists computer, counselor, ESL,
learning disabilities, librarian, math resource,
nurse, physician, psychologist, reading resource
Special curricular programs art, instrumental
music, computer/technology, physical education,
schoolwide enrichment model, student
aspirations, sustainable projects, citizen of the
world and human heritage
Extra curricular programs dance, drama,
French/German, visual arts, intrumental music,
cooking, handicrafts, science experiments
Sports basketball, soccer, track and field
Clubs student council
Examinations Iowa, TOEFL, PAA

CAMPUS FACILITIES

Location Urban
Campus 5.3 hectares, 2 buildings, 57 classrooms,
4 computer labs, 181 instructional computers,
24,701 library volumes, 1 auditorium,
2 cafeterias, 2 covered play areas,
1 gymnasium, 2 infirmaries, 8 playing fields,
2 science labs, air conditioning

Data from 2006/07 school year.

AMERICAN SCHOOL FOUNDATION OF MONTERREY

Phone	52 81 5000 4400
Fax	52 81 8378 2535
Email	jeff.keller@asfm.edu.mx
Website	www.asfm.edu.mx
Address	Rio Missouri 555 Ote., Colonia del Valle, Garza Garcia, Monterrey, Nuevo León, 66220, Mexico
Mailing address	AP 1762, Monterrey, N.L., Mexico 64000

STAFF

Superintendent D. Jeffrey Keller, Ed.D.
Elementary Principal Sonia Keller, Ed.D.
High School Principal Jeffrey Farrington
Business Manager Edilberto Martinez
Information Technology Director Jay Priebe

Head Librarian Beau Cain
Teaching staff Full time 209; Part time 7; Total 216
Nationalities of teaching staff US 51; UK 1; Mexican 112; Other(s) (Canadian) 52

INFORMATION

Grade levels N–12
School year August–June
School type coeducational, day, private non-profit
Year founded 1928
Governed by appointed Board of Directors
Accredited by Southern
Regional organizations ASOMEX
Enrollment Nursery 146; PreK 158; Elementary K–5 970; Middle School 6–8 482; High School 9–12 530; Total 2,286

Nationalities of student body US 139; Mexican 2,073; Other(s) 74
Tuition/fee currency US Dollar
Tuition range 6,972–10,624
Annual fees Registration 900; Busing 900; School Agenda 10
One time fees Capital Levy 6,000
Graduates attending college 100%
Graduates have attended Yale U, Massachusetts Institute of Technology, Princeton U, Harvard U, Stanford U

EDUCATIONAL PROGRAM

Curriculum US, National, AP
Average class size Elementary 22; Secondary 20
Language(s) of instruction English, Spanish
Language(s) taught French
Staff specialists computer, counselor, learning disabilities, librarian, math resource, nurse, psychologist, reading resource
Special curricular programs art, instrumental music, vocal music, computer/technology, physical education

Extra curricular programs computers, community service, drama, environmental conservation, photography
Sports basketball, gymnastics, soccer, track and field, volleyball
Clubs math counts, National Honor Society, Junior Honor Society, student council
Examinations AP, PSAT, SAT, NWEA

CAMPUS FACILITIES

Location Suburban
Campus 26 hectares, 3 buildings, 180 classrooms, 10 computer labs, 600 instructional computers, 300,000 library volumes, 2 auditoriums,
2 cafeterias, 3 gymnasiums, 2 infirmaries, 5 playing fields, 8 science labs, 2 tennis courts, air conditioning

PAN AMERICAN SCHOOL, MONTERREY CAMPUS

Phone	52 81 8342 0778
Fax	52 81 8340 2749
Email	dadmission@pas.edu.mx
Website	www.pas.edu.mx
Address	Hidalgo 656 pte., Monterrey, Nuevo Leon, 64000, Mexico
Mailing address	PO Box 474, Monterrey, Nuevo Leon, Mexico 64000

STAFF

Head of School and Co-Founder Leonor Arpee
Academic Director Hermelinda Coronado
Middle School Principal Nelly Granados
Elementary School Principal Delia Gonzalez
Preschool Principal Yolanda Vega
Sports Supervisor Ramiro Tovar

Comptroller Omar Garza
Technology Coordinator Edna Trevino
Head of Library and Media Resources Patricia Himes
Teaching staff Full time 67; Part time 6; Total 73
Nationalities of teaching staff Mexican 72;
Other(s) (Australian) 1

INFORMATION

Grade levels N–9
School year August–July
School type coeducational, day, private non-profit
Year founded 1952
Governed by appointed Board of Directors
Enrollment Nursery 72; PreK 55;
Elementary K–5 291; Middle School 6–8 132;
High School 9–12 48; Total 598
Nationalities of student body US 16;
Mexican 581; Other(s) (Indonesian) 1

Tuition/fee currency US Dollar
Tuition range 222–504
Annual fees Registration 595; Insurance 22;
Books 270; Personal Academic Supplies 90;
Physical Education Uniform 118
Graduates attending college 100%
Graduates have attended Tecnologico de
Monterrey, U de Monterrey,
U Autonoma de Nuevo Leon, Texas A&M U,
Trinity U

EDUCATIONAL PROGRAM

Curriculum US, National, Fourth R
Average class size Elementary 17; Secondary 25
Language(s) of instruction English, Spanish
Staff specialists computer, counselor, ESL,
librarian, math resource, nurse, psychologist,
reading resource
Special curricular programs art, instrumental music,
vocal music, computer/technology, physical
education, vocational, human values program

Extra curricular programs computers, community
service, dance, environmental conservation,
yearbook, social service
Sports basketball, soccer, volleyball
Clubs ecology, math, jazz
Examinations TOEFL, Admission Exam and
College Board

CAMPUS FACILITIES

Location Urban
Campus 1 building, 33 classrooms,
1 computer lab, 32 instructional computers,

4,338 library volumes, 1 auditorium, 1 cafeteria,
1 covered play area, 1 gymnasium, 1 infirmary,
1 playing field, 1 science lab, air conditioning

PAN AMERICAN SCHOOL, SAN PEDRO CAMPUS

Phone	52 8 363 5474
Fax	52 8 363 5602
Email	cadmission@pas.edu.mx
Website	www.pas.edu.mx
Address	Casolar 200, Villas de San Agustin, San Pedro Garza Garcia, Nuevo Leon, 66266, Mexico
Mailing address	PO Box 474, Centro Monterrey Nuevo Leon, Mexico 64000

STAFF

Head of School and Co-Founder Robert L. Arpee
Academic Director Hermelinda Coronado
Middle School Principal Sandra Fernandez
Elementary School Principal Lourdes Guerra
Preschool Principal Gabriela Aguilar
Sports Supervisor Gabriel Guzman
Comptroller Omar Garza

Technology Coordinator Edna Trevino
Head of Library and Media Resources Nancy Medeiros
Teaching staff Full time 63; Part time 7; Total 70
Nationalities of teaching staff UK 1; Mexican 67; Other(s) (Canadian, Costa Rican) 2

INFORMATION

Grade levels N–9
School year August–July
School type coeducational, day, private non-profit
Year founded 1952
Governed by appointed Board of Directors
Enrollment Nursery 89; PreK 64; Elementary K–5 293; Middle School 6–8 102; High School 9–12 45; Total 593
Nationalities of student body US 10; Mexican 579; Other(s) (Japanese, Venezuelan) 4

Tuition/fee currency US Dollar
Tuition range 331–614
Annual fees Registration 909; Insurance 22; Books 330; Academic Supplies 100; PE Uniform 130
Graduates attending college 100%
Graduates have attended Instituto Tecnologico de Monterrey, U de Monterrey, U Autonoma de Nuevo Leon, Texas A&M U, Trinity U

EDUCATIONAL PROGRAM

Curriculum US, National, Fourth R
Average class size Elementary 18; Secondary 21
Language(s) of instruction English, Spanish
Staff specialists computer, counselor, ESL, librarian, math resource, nurse, psychologist, reading resource
Special curricular programs art, instrumental music, vocal music, computer/technology, physical education, vocational, human values program

Extra curricular programs computers, community service, dance, drama, excursions/expeditions, newspaper, yearbook, social service
Sports basketball, gymnastics, hockey, soccer, track and field, volleyball
Clubs ecology
Examinations TOEFL, College Board

CAMPUS FACILITIES

Location Urban
Campus 4 hectares, 2 buildings, 35 classrooms, 1 computer lab, 32 instructional computers,

3,819 library volumes, 1 auditorium, 1 cafeteria, 1 covered play area, 1 gymnasium, 1 infirmary, 4 playing fields, 1 science lab, air conditioning

AMERICAN SCHOOL OF PUERTO VALLARTA

Phone	52 322 221 1525
Fax	52 322 226 7677
Email	gsel@aspv.edu.mx
Website	aspv.edu.mx
Address	Albatros 129, Marina Vallarta, Puerto Vallarta, Jalisco, 48354, Mexico
Mailing address	PO Box 2-280, Marina Vallarta, Puerto Vallarta, Jalisco 48354, Mexico

STAFF

General Director Gerald Selitzer
Junior and High School Principal
José Antonio Salgado
Primary Principal Kathleen Selitzer
Admission and Program Coordinator Elise Langley
School Counselor Robert Nation, Ph.D.

Comptroller Martha Vega
Technology Coordinator Christopher Davis
Librarian Renée Perez
Teaching staff Full time 36; Part time 4; Total 40
Nationalities of teaching staff US 17; Mexican 14;
Other(s) (Canadian, Italian) 9

INFORMATION

Grade levels N–12
School year September–June
School type coeducational, day, private non-profit
Year founded 1986
Governed by appointed School Board
Accredited by Southern
Regional organizations ASOMEX
Enrollment Nursery 16; PreK 18;
Elementary K–5 179; Middle School 6–8 75;
High School 9–12 74; Total 362

Nationalities of student body US 81; Mexican 242;
Other(s) (Canadian, New Zealander) 39
Tuition/fee currency US Dollar
Tuition range 5,110–8,423
Annual fees Registration 910
Graduates attending college 95%
Graduates have attended Beloit Col, Clark U,
Lawrence U, Mt. Holyoke Col, Brown U

EDUCATIONAL PROGRAM

Curriculum US, National, AP
Average class size Elementary 23; Secondary 25
Language(s) of instruction English, Spanish
Staff specialists computer, counselor, librarian,
math resource, nurse, psychologist, reading
resource

Special curricular programs art, vocal music,
computer/technology, physical education
Extra curricular programs community service,
dance, yearbook
Sports basketball, gymnastics, soccer, tennis,
volleyball
Examinations AP, PSAT, SAT, Stanford, TOEFL

CAMPUS FACILITIES

Location Suburban
Campus 3 hectares, 5 buildings, 23 classrooms,
2 computer labs, 100 instructional computers,

8,000 library volumes, 1 auditorium,
1 cafeteria, 1 infirmary, 3 playing fields,
2 science labs, air conditioning

JOHN F. KENNEDY SCHOOL

Phone	52 442 218 0075
Fax	52 442 218 1784
Email	mstappung@jfk.edu.mx
Website	www.jfk.edu.mx
Address	Av. Sabinos 272, Fracc. Jurica Campestre, Querétaro, Qro., 76100, Mexico

STAFF

General Director Mirtha Stappung, Ed.D.
Assistant Director Charles A. Weiss, Ed.D.
High School Principal Adrian Leece, Ed.D.
Middle School Principal Camille Shelfo, Ed.D.
Preschool Principal Denise Humphries, Ed.D.

Elementary School Principal Mark Dunn, Ed.D.
Business Manager Josefina Morgan, Ed.D.
Head of Systems Patricia Müller, Ed.D.
Head Librarian Carla Mendoza, Ed.D.

INFORMATION

Grade levels K–12
School year August–July
School type coeducational, day, private non-profit
Year founded 1964
Governed by elected Board of Directors
Accredited by Southern
Regional organizations ASOMEX
Tuition/fee currency US Dollar
Tuition range 3,279–5,550

Annual fees Registration 807; Insurance 28;
Books 363; Uniforms 350
One time fees Capital Levy 1,404
Graduates attending college 100%
Graduates have attended Florida Institute of
Technology, U of the Americas, Technólogico de
Monterrey, U del Valle de México,
U Autónoma de Querétaro

EDUCATIONAL PROGRAM

Curriculum US, National, IB Diploma
Average class size Elementary 25; Secondary 25
Language(s) of instruction English, Spanish
Language(s) taught Spanish, English
Staff specialists computer, counselor, ESL,
librarian, math resource, nurse, physician,
psychologist, speech/hearing
Special curricular programs art, instrumental
music, vocal music, computer/technology,
physical education, vocational

Extra curricular programs computers, community
service, dance, drama, environmental
conservation, excursions/expeditions, literary
magazine, photography, yearbook
Sports basketball, martial arts, soccer, softball,
track and field, volleyball
Examinations IB, PSAT, SAT, SAT II, TOEFL,
CTBS, Gates-MacGinitie, EXANI

CAMPUS FACILITIES

Location Suburban
Campus 6 hectares, 34 buildings, 67 classrooms,
4 computer labs, 175 instructional computers,

17,467 library volumes, 1 auditorium,
2 cafeterias, 1 gymnasium, 1 infirmary,
3 playing fields, 2 science labs

Data from 2006/07 school year.

THE AMERICAN SCHOOL OF TAMPICO

Phone	52 833 227 2081
Fax	52 833 227 208, ext 126
Email	avega@ats.edu.mx
Website	www.ats.edu.mx
Address	Calle Hidalgo No. 100, Col. Tancol, Tampico, Tamaulipas, 89320, Mexico
Mailing address	PO Box 407, Tampico, Tamaulipas 89000, Mexico

STAFF

Director Emma G. de Salazar
Early Childhood Coordinator
Ana Laura Luengas de Salazar
Elementary Principal Irelda Galván Garza
Upper School Principal Patricia Sánchez Sola

Public Relations and Admissions
Araceli Vega Paredes
Business Manager
Sandra Ma. Treviño de Alexandre
Director of Technology César Sánchez Rojas
Library Media Specialist Michael Ambrose

INFORMATION

Grade levels N–10
School year August–June
School type coeducational, day, private non-profit
Year founded 1917
Governed by appointed Board of Directors
Accredited by Southern
Regional organizations ASOMEX

Enrollment Nursery 88; PreK 97;
Elementary K–5 441; Middle School 6–8 214;
High School 9–12 133; Total 973
Nationalities of student body US 26;
Mexican 926; Other(s) (German, Chilean) 21
Tuition/fee currency Mexican Peso
Tuition range 2,060–5,410
Annual fees Registration 8,465; Books 2,000
One time fees Capital Levy 36,500
Graduates attending college 98%

EDUCATIONAL PROGRAM

Curriculum US
Average class size Elementary 22; Secondary 22
Language(s) of instruction English, Spanish
Language(s) taught English, Spanish
Staff specialists computer, counselor, ESL,
learning disabilities, librarian, math resource,
nurse, psychologist, reading resource
Special curricular programs art, instrumental
music, vocal music, computer/technology,
physical education, accelerated math & science

Extra curricular programs computers, community
service, dance, drama, environmental
conservation, excursions/expeditions, literary
magazine, newspaper, yearbook
Sports basketball, football, soccer, track and
field, volleyball
Examinations SAT, TOEFL, CTBS, ERB

CAMPUS FACILITIES

Location Urban
Campus 14 hectares, 8 buildings, 52 classrooms,
2 computer labs, 200 instructional computers,

13,000 library volumes, 1 cafeteria,
1 covered play area, 2 infirmaries, 4 playing
fields, 1 science lab, air conditioning

Data from 2006/07 school year.

COLEGIO AMERICANO DE TORREÓN, A.C.

Phone	52 871 222 51 00
Fax	52 871 733 26 68
Email	makhlouf.ouyed@cat.mx
Website	www.cat.mx
Address	Paseo del Algodón y Blvd. Carlos Lopez Sosa, Fraccionamiento Los Viñedos s/n, Torreón, Coahuila, 27019, Mexico
Mailing address	Colegio Americano of Torreon, 344 Rio Dulce, Suite 871-152, El Paso, Texas 79932

STAFF

Director General Makhlouf Ouyed, Ed.D.
Elementary Principal Shirley Hooper
Secondary Principal Craig Hoogendoorn
Mexican Secondary Program Director Jesus Cuellar
Mexican Elementary Program Director Alejandra Adriano

Business Manager Martha Martinez
Technology Coordinator Eros Muñoz
Head Librarian Ena Galindez
Teaching staff Full time 91; Part time 1; Total 92
Nationalities of teaching staff US 20; Host 61; Other(s) (Canadian) 11

INFORMATION

Grade levels K–12
School year August–June
School type coeducational, day, private non-profit
Year founded 1950
Governed by elected School Board
Accredited by Southern
Regional organizations ASOMEX
Enrollment Elementary K–5 632; Middle School 6–8 288; High School 9–12 295; Total 1,215

Nationalities of student body US 3; Mexican 1,212
Tuition/fee currency US Dollar
Tuition range 3,000–6,800
Annual fees Registration 682; Insurance 10; Books 228; Parents Association 20; Uniforms and Materials 200
One time fees Entrance 364
Graduates attending college 97%
Graduates have attended U of Pennsylvania, Michigan U, U of Texas, U of Florida

EDUCATIONAL PROGRAM

Curriculum US, National, AP
Average class size Elementary 20; Secondary 22
Language(s) of instruction English, Spanish
Language(s) taught French
Staff specialists computer, counselor, ESL, librarian, nurse, psychologist
Special curricular programs art, instrumental music, vocal music, computer/technology, physical education

Extra curricular programs computers, community service, drama, environmental conservation, excursions/expeditions, yearbook
Sports baseball, basketball, martial arts, soccer, softball, volleyball
Clubs National Honor Society, National Junior Honor Society, student council, chess, investigation
Examinations AP, PSAT, SAT, SAT II, Stanford

CAMPUS FACILITIES

Location Urban
Campus 5 hectares, 5 buildings, 61 classrooms, 4 computer labs, 96 instructional computers,

13,000 library volumes, 1 cafeteria, 1 covered play area, 2 gymnasiums, 1 infirmary, 4 playing fields, 4 science labs, air conditioning

MOLDOVA

MOLDOVA

Area:	33,843 sq km
Population:	4,320,490
Capital:	Chisinau (Kishinev)
Currency:	Moldovan Leu (MDL)
Languages:	Moldovan

QSI International School of Chisinau

Phone	373 22 240 822
Fax	373 22 240 822
Email	chisinau@qsi.org
Website	www.qsi.org
Address	18 Anton Crihan Street, 2009, Chisinau, Moldova
Mailing address	c/o American Embassy, Chisinau, Dept. of State, 7080 Chisinau Place, Washington, DC 20521-7080, USA

STAFF

Director Harold M. Strom, Ed.D.
Teaching staff Full time 8; Part time 4; Total 12

Nationalities of teaching staff US 5; Moldovan 7

INFORMATION

Grade levels N–8
School year August–June
School type coeducational, day, private non-profit
Year founded 1996
Governed by appointed Board of Directors
Regional organizations CEESA
Enrollment Nursery 5; PreK 5; Elementary K–5 28; Middle School 6–8 11; Total 49

Nationalities of student body US 18; Moldovan 5; Other(s) (German, Swede) 26
Tuition/fee currency US Dollar
Tuition range 5,000–14,500
Annual fees Capital Levy 1,600
One time fees Registration 100

EDUCATIONAL PROGRAM

Curriculum US
Average class size Elementary 8
Language(s) of instruction English
Language(s) taught Romanian, Russian

Extra curricular programs computers, dance, drama, Art, Music
Examinations Iowa

CAMPUS FACILITIES

Location Urban
Campus 1 building, 6 classrooms, 1 computer lab, 10 instructional computers,

2,000 library volumes, 1 cafeteria, 1 covered play area, 1 gymnasium, 1 playing field, air conditioning

MONGOLIA

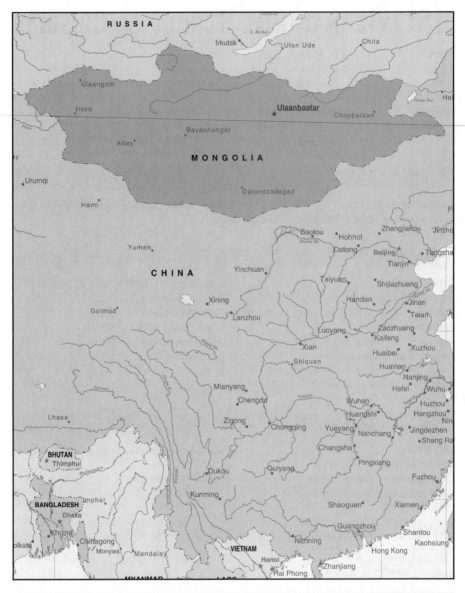

MONGOLIA

Area:	1,564,116 sq km
Population:	2,951,786
Capital:	Ulaanbaatar
Currency:	Togrog/Tugrik (MNT)
Languages:	Khalkha Mongol

INTERNATIONAL SCHOOL OF ULAANBAATAR

Phone	976 11 452 839
Fax	976 11 450 340
Email	int.school.ub@gmail.com
Website	www.isumongolia.edu.mn
Address	PO Box 49/564, Four Seasons Garden, Khanuul District, Khoroo District, Ulaanbaatar, 5, Mongolia

STAFF

Director Deidre Fischer
Deputy Director of Business Tuul Arildii
Head of Secondary and MYP Co-ordinator Paul Starr
IB DP Coordinator Andy Rossberg
Head of Primary School and PYP Coordinator Darren Arbour

Business/Finance Manager Tuul Arildii
Teaching staff Full time 39; Part time 7; Total 46
Nationalities of teaching staff US 11; UK 2; Mongolian 13; Other(s) 20

INFORMATION

Grade levels N–12
School year August–June
School type coeducational, day, private non-profit
Year founded 1992
Governed by elected School Board
Accredited by CIS, New England
Regional organizations EARCOS, ECIS
Enrollment Nursery 6; PreK 8; Elementary K–5 80; Middle School 6–8 43; High School 9–12 54; Total 191

Nationalities of student body US 34; UK 10; Mongolian 76; Other(s) (Korean, Australian) 71
Tuition/fee currency US Dollar
Tuition range 3,900–18,800
Annual fees Registration 100; Capital Levy 500; Busing 480
Graduates attending college 75%
Graduates have attended Rhodes U, U of British Columbia, U of Virginia, Duke U, Dartmouth Col

EDUCATIONAL PROGRAM

Curriculum IB Diploma, IBPYP, IBMYP
Average class size Elementary 17; Secondary 15
Language(s) of instruction English
Language(s) taught French, Mongolian, English, Chinese, Korean
Staff specialists counselor, ESL

Special curricular programs piano
Extra curricular programs computers, community service, drama, yearbook
Sports basketball, gymnastics, soccer, volleyball
Examinations PSAT, SAT, SAT II

CAMPUS FACILITIES

Location Suburban
Campus 2 hectares, 4 buildings, 25 classrooms, 2 computer labs, 75 instructional computers,

9,000 library volumes, 1 auditorium, 1 cafeteria, 1 gymnasium, 1 infirmary, 1 playing field, 2 science labs

MONTENEGRO

MONTENEGRO

Area:	14,026 sq km
Population:	684,736
Capital:	Podgorica
Currency:	Euro (EUR)
Languages:	Serbian

QSI INTERNATIONAL SCHOOL OF MONTENEGRO

Phone	381 81 643 235
Fax	381 81 643 235
Email	montenegro@qsi.org
Website	www.qsi.org
Address	ul. Vojislavljevica 36, Zabjelo, Podgorica, 81000, Montenegro

STAFF

Director Helen DeLamarter
Teaching staff Full time 4; Part time 2; Total 6

Nationalities of teaching staff US 1; UK 2; Montenegrin 3

INFORMATION

Grade levels K–8
School year September–June
School type coeducational, day, private non-profit
Year founded 2006
Regional organizations CEESA
Enrollment Elementary K–5 13; Middle School 6–8 7; Total 20

Nationalities of student body US 1; UK 3; Other(s) (Australian) 16
Tuition/fee currency US Dollar
Tuition range 9,800–12,500
Annual fees Capital Fund 1,600
One time fees Registration 100

EDUCATIONAL PROGRAM

Curriculum Intl
Average class size Elementary 7
Language(s) of instruction English
Language(s) taught Montenegrin, French

Special curricular programs art, instrumental music, vocal music, computer/technology, physical education
Examinations Iowa

CAMPUS FACILITIES

Location Suburban
Campus 1 building, 5 classrooms, 1 computer lab, 8 instructional computers, 750 library volumes, 1 playing field, air conditioning

MOROCCO

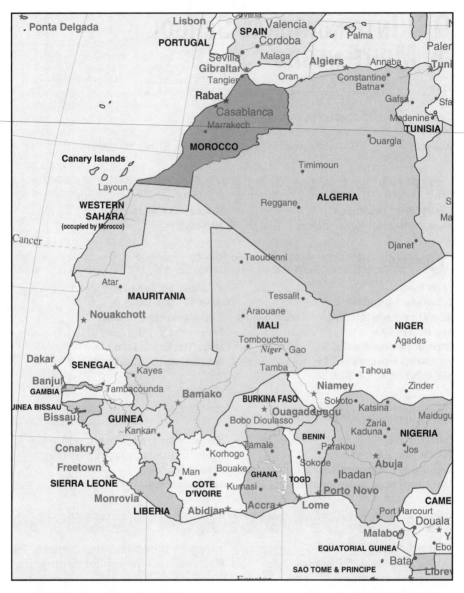

MOROCCO

Area:	446,550 sq km
Population:	33,757,175
Capital:	Rabat
Currency:	Moroccan Dirham (MAD)
Languages:	Arabic

CASABLANCA AMERICAN SCHOOL

Phone	212 (0)22 214 115
Fax	212 (0)22 212 488
Email	cas@cas.ac.ma
Website	www.cas.ac.ma
Address	Route de la Mecque, Lotissement Ougoug, Quartier Californie, Casablanca, 20150, Morocco

STAFF

Director Allen T Hughes, Ed.D.
Lower School Principal Tony Moniz
Upper School Principal Marcia Vitiello
Curriculum Coordinator Kim West Aba
Admissions Director Marti Fields Johnson
Registrar Atika Amani

Business Manager Saad Guessous
IT Coordinator Ali Sekkat
Head Librarian Nancy Hughes
Teaching staff Full time 65; Part time 10; Total 75
Nationalities of teaching staff US 65; UK 1; Moroccan 5; Other(s) (Canadian) 4

INFORMATION

Grade levels N–12
School year September–June
School type coeducational, day, private non-profit
Year founded 1973
Governed by elected Board of Directors
Accredited by New England
Regional organizations ECIS, MAIS
Enrollment Nursery 36; PreK 36; Elementary K–5 246; Middle School 6–8 108; High School 9–12 124; Total 550

Nationalities of student body US 10; UK 10; Moroccan 330; Other(s) (Korean, Dutch) 200
Tuition/fee currency US Dollar
Tuition range 4,728–11,515
Annual fees Registration 85; Capital Levy 560; PTA 22
One time fees Application 85; Admission 1,120
Graduates attending college 100%
Graduates have attended Yale U, Georgetown U, Brown U, Stanford U, California Institute of Technology

EDUCATIONAL PROGRAM

Curriculum US, AP, IB Diploma, IBMYP
Average class size Elementary 22; Secondary 22
Language(s) of instruction English
Language(s) taught Arabic, French, Spanish
Staff specialists computer, counselor, ESL, learning disabilities, librarian, nurse, psychologist, reading resource

Special curricular programs art, computer/technology, physical education
Extra curricular programs community service, drama, yearbook
Sports badminton, basketball, soccer, track and field, volleyball
Examinations ACT, AP, IB, PSAT, SAT, TOEFL, ERB-CPT 4

CAMPUS FACILITIES

Location Suburban
Campus 2 hectares, 5 buildings, 45 classrooms, 2 computer labs, 60 instructional computers,

16,000 library volumes, 1 auditorium, 1 cafeteria, 1 gymnasium, 1 infirmary, 1 playing field, 4 science labs

GEORGE WASHINGTON ACADEMY

Phone	212 22 95 30 00
Fax	212 22 95 30 01
Email	info@gwa.ac.ma
Website	www.gwa.ac.ma
Address	Km 5, 6 Route d'Azemmour, Dar Bouazza, Casablanca, 20220, Morocco

STAFF

Director Eric Crane
Elementary School Principal Marina DeBruyn
High School Principal Mark Luckey
Registrar Paula Davey
Director of Human Resources Ernest Lottman
Business Manager Youness Rouizem

Director of Information Technology Joe Canner
Teaching staff Full time 68; Part time 8; Total 76
Nationalities of teaching staff US 40; UK 2; Moroccan 24; Other(s) (French, South African) 10

INFORMATION

Grade levels PreK–12
School year September–June
School type coeducational, day, private non-profit
Year founded 1998
Governed by appointed Board of Directors
Sponsored by Global Education
Regional organizations AASSA, ECIS, MAIS
Enrollment PreK 46; Elementary K–5 274; Middle School 6–8 160; High School 9–12 142; Total 622

Nationalities of student body US 132; UK 34; Moroccan 387; Other(s) (Indian) 69
Tuition/fee currency Moroccan Dirham
Tuition range 38,000–66,200
Annual fees Registration 6,400; Busing 8,000; Lunch 7,300
One time fees Capital Levy 3,300
Graduates attending college 95%
Graduates have attended U of California in Berkeley, U College of London, American U of Paris, Seton Hall U, Pennylvania State U

EDUCATIONAL PROGRAM

Curriculum US, AP
Average class size Elementary 24; Secondary 18
Language(s) of instruction English, French, Arabic
Staff specialists computer, counselor, learning disabilities

Special curricular programs art, instrumental music, vocal music, computer/technology, physical education
Extra curricular programs photography, yearbook
Sports badminton, basketball, gymnastics, soccer, swimming, track and field, volleyball
Examinations ACT, AP, SAT

CAMPUS FACILITIES

Location Suburban
Campus 5 hectares, 2 buildings, 40 classrooms, 1 computer lab, 38 instructional computers,

30,000 library volumes, 1 auditorium, 1 cafeteria, 1 gymnasium, 1 infirmary, 1 playing field, 1 science lab, air conditioning

RABAT AMERICAN SCHOOL

Phone	212 3 767 1476
Fax	212 3 767 0963
Email	info@ras.ma
Website	www.ras.ma
Address	1 bis rue El Amir Abdelkader, Agdal, Rabat, 10102, Morocco
Mailing address	US Embassy, BP 120, Rabat, 10000 Morocco

STAFF

Director Paul W. Johnson, Ed.D.
Secondary Principal Dr. Lois Bishop
Elementary Principal Kathy Morabet
Admissions and Development Officer
Btissam Touijer
Accountant Elizabeth Skiredj

Technology Coordinator Tanya Ash
Librarian Gaylene Livingston
Teaching staff Full time 48; Part time 9; Total 57
Nationalities of teaching staff US 28; UK 5;
Moroccan 7; Other(s) (Canadian, German) 17

INFORMATION

Grade levels PreK–12
School year August–June
School type coeducational, day, private non-profit
Year founded 1962
Governed by elected Board of Trustees
Accredited by Middle States
Regional organizations MAIS
Enrollment PreK 20; Elementary K–5 150;
Middle School 6–8 80;
High School 9–12 128; Total 378

Nationalities of student body US 73; UK 19;
Moroccan 128; Other(s) (German, Canadian) 158
Tuition/fee currency US Dollar
Tuition range 3,983–15,361
Annual fees Busing 770
One time fees Registration 5,000
Graduates attending college 95%
Graduates have attended Boston U,
Georgetown U, McGill U, American U of Paris,
New York U

EDUCATIONAL PROGRAM

Curriculum US, Intl, IB Diploma
Average class size Elementary 18; Secondary 18
Language(s) of instruction English
Language(s) taught French, Arabic
Staff specialists computer, counselor, ESL,
librarian, nurse, psychologist
Special curricular programs art, instrumental
music, vocal music, computer/technology,
physical education

Extra curricular programs computers, community
service, drama, excursions/expeditions,
yearbook
Sports badminton, baseball, basketball, soccer,
softball, swimming, track and field, volleyball
Examinations ACT, IB, Iowa, PSAT, SAT, SAT II,
ERB, Terra Nova

CAMPUS FACILITIES

Location Suburban
Campus 4 hectares, 10 buildings, 41 classrooms,
4 computer labs, 183 instructional computers,
23,500 library volumes

MOZAMBIQUE

MOZAMBIQUE

Area:	801,590 sq km
Population:	20,905,585
Capital:	Maputo
Currency:	Metical (MZM)
Languages:	Emakhuwa, Portuguese

AMERICAN INTERNATIONAL SCHOOL OF MOZAMBIQUE

Phone	258 21 491 994
Fax	258 21 490 596
Email	aism@aism-moz.com
Website	www.aism-moz.com
Address	Rua 3753, No 266, Bairro da Costa do Sol, Maputo, Mozambique
Mailing address	American International School of Mozambique, PO Box 2026, Maputo, Mozambique

STAFF

Director Mary Jo Heatherington, Ph.D.
Deputy Director of Lower School Sandy Wilson
IB and High School Coordinator Lea-Carol Glennon
PYP and MYP Coodinator Jeni Arndt, Ph.D.
School Counselor Cherie Mobasnerie, Ph.D.
Activities Coordinator Melissa van Herksen
Director of Planning and Finance Mary Ann Przkikuart

Technology Coordinator Susana Fairley
Head Librarian John Kurtenbach
Teaching staff Full time 45; Part time 3; Total 48
Nationalities of teaching staff US 19; UK 3; Mozambican 5; Other(s) (South African, Canadian) 21

INFORMATION

Grade levels PreK–12
School year August–June
School type coeducational, day, private non-profit
Year founded 1990
Governed by elected Board of Directors
Accredited by Middle States
Regional organizations AISA
Enrollment PreK 17; Elementary K–5 183; Middle School 6–8 61; High School 9–12 65; Total 326

Nationalities of student body US 53; UK 16; Mozambican 39; Other(s) (South African, Dutch) 218
Tuition/fee currency US Dollar
Tuition range 8,000–13,200
Annual fees Busing 1,000
One time fees Capital Levy 3,000; Admissions and Testing 150
Graduates attending college 100%
Graduates have attended Purdue U, Illinois Wesleyan U, Vassar Col, U of Delhi, York U

EDUCATIONAL PROGRAM

Curriculum US, IB Diploma, IBPYP, IBMYP
Average class size Elementary 15; Secondary 15
Language(s) of instruction English
Language(s) taught Portuguese, French
Staff specialists computer, counselor, ESL, librarian, nurse, physician
Special curricular programs art, instrumental music, vocal music, computer/technology, drama

Extra curricular programs computers, community service, dance, drama, environmental conservation, excursions/expeditions, yearbook, martial arts
Sports baseball, basketball, cricket, football, hockey, soccer, swimming, tennis, track and field, volleyball
Clubs Model UN, chess, book, homework
Examinations IB, Iowa, PSAT, SAT, SAT II, TOEFL

CAMPUS FACILITIES

Location Suburban
Campus 5 hectares, 2 buildings, 36 classrooms, 3 computer labs, 100 instructional computers,

15,000 library volumes, 1 cafeteria, 1 covered play area, 1 infirmary, 3 playing fields, 2 science labs, 1 pool, 1 tennis court, air conditioning

MYANMAR (BURMA)

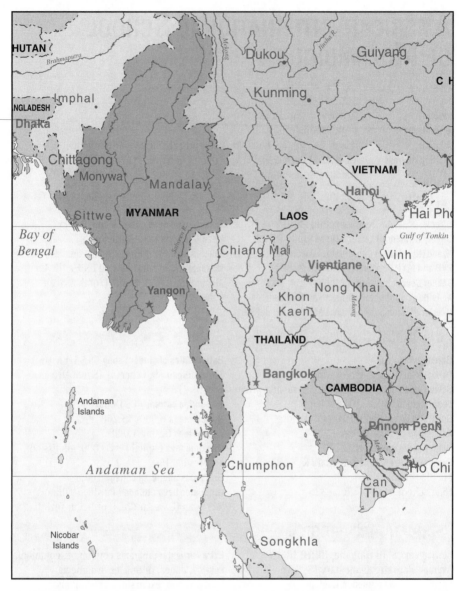

MYANMAR (BURMA)

Area:	678,500 sq km
Population:	47,373,958
Capital:	Yangon (Rangoon)
Currency:	Kyat (MMK)
Languages:	Burmese

INTERNATIONAL SCHOOL OF YANGON

Phone	95 1 512793
Fax	95 1 525020
Email	director@isy.net.mm
Website	www.isy.net.mm
Address	20 Shwe Taungyar, Bahan Township, Yangon, Myanmar
Mailing address	Dept. of State, 4250 Rangoon Place, Washington, DC 20521-4250, USA

STAFF

Director Dennis W. MacKinnon
Middle and High School Principal
David James Condon
Elementary School Principal Debra Baer
Middle and High School Counselor
Janet Susan Hallwood
Elementary Counselor Sarah Rooks Beesley

Business Manager Daw Khin Hla Khine
Technology Coordinator Susan Semmler
Librarian Melanie Tahan
Teaching staff Full time 50; Part time 1; Total 51
Nationalities of teaching staff US 36; UK 1;
Burmese 10; Other(s) (French) 4

INFORMATION

Grade levels PreK–12
School year August–June
School type coeducational, day, private non-profit
Year founded 1955
Governed by appointed and elected Board of
Management
Sponsored by American Embassy
Accredited by Western
Regional organizations EARCOS
Enrollment PreK 16; Elementary K–5 163;
Middle School 6–8 93; High School 9–12 136;
Total 408

Nationalities of student body US 43; UK 7;
Burmese 79; Other(s) (Indian) 279
Tuition/fee currency US Dollar
Tuition range 6,800–10,500
Annual fees Registration 1,000
One time fees Capital Levy 4,000
Graduates attending college 100%
Graduates have attended Stanford U, Brandeis U,
Rhode Island School of Design, Georgetown U,
U of California in Berkeley

EDUCATIONAL PROGRAM

Curriculum US, AP
Average class size Elementary 15; Secondary 13
Language(s) of instruction English
Language(s) taught French, Spanish, Burmese
Staff specialists computer, counselor, ESL,
librarian, physician
Special curricular programs art, instrumental
music, vocal music, computer/technology,
physical education

Extra curricular programs computers, community
service, dance, drama, environmental
conservation, excursions/expeditions, literary
magazine, photography, yearbook
Sports badminton, basketball, soccer, softball,
volleyball
Examinations AP, Iowa, PSAT, SAT, SAT II, TOEFL

CAMPUS FACILITIES

Location Suburban
Campus 4 hectares, 7 buildings, 40 classrooms,
4 computer labs, 100 instructional computers,

27,000 library volumes, 1 cafeteria, 2 covered
play areas, 1 infirmary, 1 playing field,
3 science labs, air conditioning

YANGON INTERNATIONAL EDUCARE CENTER

Phone 95 1 530 082
Fax 951 530 083
Email tjtravers@gmail.com
Website www.yiec.org
Address No. W-22, Mya Kan Thar Housing, 5th Quarter, Hlaing Township, Yangon, Myanmar

STAFF

Director Timothy J. Travers
Coordinator Daw Myint Myint Win
Executive Director Daw Hla Hnin Khine
Middle School Principal Richard Johnstone
Elementary Principal Don McCoy
Business Manager Khin Win Myint

Computer Coordinator Robert Widdicombe
Librarian Ni Ni Hla
Teaching staff Full time 50; Total 50
Nationalities of teaching staff US 35; UK 1;
Burmese 6; Other(s) (Canadian,
New Zealander) 8

INFORMATION

Grade levels PreK–12
School year August–May
School type coeducational, day, proprietary
Year founded 1998
Governed by appointed Board of Management
Sponsored by Myanmar Educare Co, Ltd
Enrollment PreK 40; Elementary K–5 400;
Middle School 6–8 210;
High School 9–12 200; Total 850

Nationalities of student body US 40; UK 10;
Burmese 550; Other(s) (Chinese, Korean) 250
Tuition/fee currency US Dollar
Tuition range 1,600–5,000
One time fees Registration 350
Graduates attending college 100%
Graduates have attended Wabash Col, Bucknell U,
Richmond U, Wilkes U, Providence Col

EDUCATIONAL PROGRAM

Curriculum US, Intl, AP
Average class size Elementary 23; Secondary 20
Language(s) of instruction English
Language(s) taught Chinese, Myanmar, French
Staff specialists computer, counselor, ESL,
librarian, math resource, nurse, reading resource
Special curricular programs art, instrumental
music, vocal music, computer/technology,
physical education, dance

Extra curricular programs computers, community
service, dance, drama, excursions/expeditions,
literary magazine, newspaper, photography,
yearbook
Sports badminton, basketball, football, soccer,
volleyball
Clubs community service, golf, badminton,
student council, cooking, yoga, guitar, French
Myanmar, computer
Examinations AP, PSAT, SAT, SAT II, TOEFL,
International Schools Assessment

CAMPUS FACILITIES

Location Suburban
Campus 2 hectares, 3 buildings, 80 classrooms,
3 computer labs, 100 instructional computers,
6,000 library volumes, 1 auditorium,

3 cafeterias, 1 covered play area,
2 gymnasiums, 1 infirmary, 2 playing fields,
3 science labs, air conditioning

YANGON INTERNATIONAL SCHOOL

Phone	95 1 578 171
Fax	95 1 578 604
Email	vonspreecken@yis.edu.mm
Address	117, Thumingalar Housing, Thingangyun Township, Yangon, Myanmar

STAFF

Director Greg L. Von Spreecken
Activities and Athletic Coordinator Devron Shephard
Technology Coordinator Russell Downs
Librarian Diana Dragonetti

Teaching staff Full time 24; Total 24
Nationalities of teaching staff US 14; UK 1; Burmese 2; Other(s) (Canadian, New Zealander) 7

INFORMATION

Grade levels K–11
School year August–May
School type private non-profit
Year founded 2004
Governed by Private
Enrollment Elementary K–5 66; Middle School 6–8 41; High School 9–12 30; Total 137

Nationalities of student body US 1; UK 3; Burmese 137
Tuition/fee currency Myanmar Kyat
Tuition range 7,000–8,800
One time fees Registration 1,000; Capital Levy 3,500

EDUCATIONAL PROGRAM

Average class size Elementary 15; Secondary 13
Language(s) of instruction English
Language(s) taught Chinese
Staff specialists computer, counselor, ESL, librarian
Special curricular programs art, vocal music, computer/technology, physical education, Myanmar Studies

Extra curricular programs computers, community service, drama, environmental conservation, excursions/expeditions, newspaper, yearbook, crafts
Sports badminton, basketball, soccer, swimming, volleyball
Clubs games, math, student council
Examinations Iowa

CAMPUS FACILITIES

Campus 13 classrooms, 2 computer labs, 50 instructional computers, 1 cafeteria, 1 covered play area, 1 gymnasium, 2 playing fields, 2 science labs, 1 pool, air conditioning

NAMIBIA

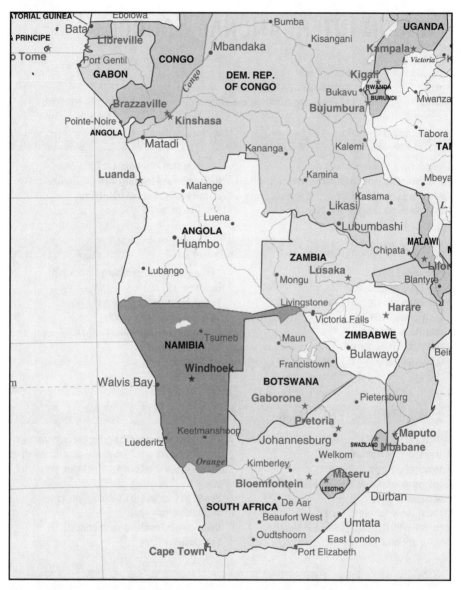

NAMIBIA

Area:	825,418 sq km
Population:	2,055,080
Capital:	Windhoek
Currency:	Namibian Dollar (NAD); South African Rand (ZAR)
Languages:	English, Afrikaans

WINDHOEK INTERNATIONAL SCHOOL

Phone	264 61 241 783
Fax	264 61 243 127
Email	cheimstadt@wis.edu.na
Website	www.wis.edu.na
Address	Scheppmann Street, Pionierspark extn. 1, Windhoek, 9000, Namibia
Mailing address	Private Bag 16007, Windhoek, Namibia

STAFF

Director Francis McGrath
Primary Principal Genie Albrecht
Secondary Principal Maureen Rainey
IB Coordinator David McMillan
IGCSE Coordinator Margarete Reiff

Accountant Marise du Plooy
Librarian Judith Henderson
Teaching staff Full time 32; Part time 9; Total 41
Nationalities of teaching staff US 4; UK 5;
Namibian 20; Other(s) (Irish, South African) 12

INFORMATION

Grade levels PreK–13
School year August–June
School type coeducational, day, private non-profit
Year founded 1991
Governed by appointed and elected Board of
Directors
Accredited by CIS, New England
Regional organizations ECIS
Enrollment Elementary K–5 149;
Middle School 6–8 80; High School 9–12 38;
Grade 13 29; Total 296

Nationalities of student body US 20; UK 6; South
African 146; Other(s) (Finn, Angolan) 124
Tuition/fee currency Namibia Dollar
Tuition range 19,360–125,730
One time fees Registration 21,000
Graduates attending college 66%
Graduates have attended Brandeis U, U of Port
Elizabeth, U of Cape Town, U of Columbia,
U of Namibia

EDUCATIONAL PROGRAM

Curriculum IB Diploma, IBPYP, IGCSE
Average class size Elementary 17; Secondary 18
Language(s) of instruction English
Language(s) taught French, German, Portuguese
Staff specialists computer, counselor, ESL,
learning disabilities, librarian, nurse

Extra curricular programs computers, dance,
drama, literary magazine, photography, yearbook
Sports basketball, cricket, soccer, track and
field, volleyball
Clubs voluntary work, chess, craft, ballet, band
Examinations GCSE, IB, IGCSE

CAMPUS FACILITIES

Location Urban
Campus 14 hectares, 41 buildings, 52 classrooms,
1 computer lab, 25 instructional computers,

10,100 library volumes, 1 auditorium,
1 gymnasium, 1 infirmary, 1 playing field,
3 science labs

NEPAL

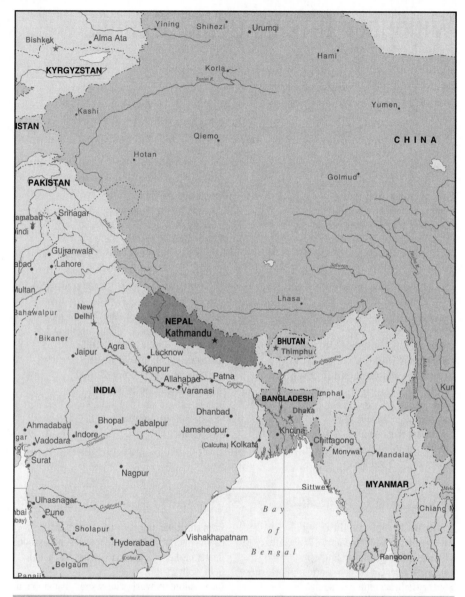

NEPAL

Area:	147,181 sq km
Population:	28,901,790
Capital:	Kathmandu
Currency:	Nepalese Rupee (NPR)
Languages:	Nepali

LINCOLN SCHOOL

Phone	977 1 4 270 482
Fax	977 1 4 272 685
Email	abredy@lsnepal.com.np
Website	www.lsnepal.com
Address	GPO 2673, Kathmandu, Nepal
Mailing address	Kathmandu (LS), Dept. of State, Washington, DC 20521-6190, USA

STAFF

Director and High School Principal Allan R. Bredy
Preschool–Grade 8 Principal Craig Baker
Guidance Counselor Tom Goetz
School Services Officer Dal Thapa
Transportation Director Rajendra Karmacharya
Business Manager Janne Shah

Director of Technology Robert Jenkinson
Librarian Peggy Keogh
Teaching staff Full time 27; Part time 5; Total 32
Nationalities of teaching staff US 19; UK 3; Nepalese 2; Other(s) (Canadian, French) 8

INFORMATION

Grade levels N–12
School year August–June
School type coeducational, day, private non-profit
Year founded 1954
Governed by elected Board of Directors
Accredited by New England
Regional organizations NESA
Enrollment Nursery 13; PreK 17; Elementary K–5 116; Middle School 6–8 51; High School 9–12 100; Total 297

Nationalities of student body US 98; UK 6; Nepalese 71; Other(s) (Dane, Korean) 122
Tuition/fee currency US Dollar
Tuition range 2,800–13,428
Annual fees Busing 750
One time fees Registration 3,000; Admission 450; Senior 120
Graduates attending college 100%
Graduates have attended U Penn, U of Chicago, Wesleyan U, Bryn Mawr Col, Brown U

EDUCATIONAL PROGRAM

Curriculum US, AP
Average class size Elementary 18; Secondary 16
Language(s) of instruction English
Language(s) taught French, Spanish, Nepali, German
Staff specialists computer, counselor, ESL, learning disabilities, librarian, math resource, nurse, reading resource
Special curricular programs art, instrumental music, vocal music, computer/technology, physical education

Extra curricular programs computers, community service, dance, drama, environmental conservation, excursions/expeditions, newspaper, photography, yearbook
Sports basketball, martial arts, soccer, swimming, tennis, track and field, volleyball
Clubs outdoor, National Honor Society, French Honor Society, environmental, Model UN
Examinations ACT, AP, Iowa, PSAT, SAT, SAT II

CAMPUS FACILITIES

Location Suburban
Campus 2 hectares, 4 buildings, 22 classrooms, 2 computer labs, 60 instructional computers, 23,000 library volumes, 1 auditorium, 1 covered play area, 1 gymnasium, 1 infirmary, 2 playing fields, 3 science labs, air conditioning

THE NETHERLANDS

THE NETHERLANDS

Area:	41,526 sq km
Population:	16,570,613
Capital:	Amsterdam
Currency:	Euro (EUR)
Languages:	Dutch

INTERNATIONAL SCHOOL OF AMSTERDAM

Phone	31 20 347 1111
Fax	31 20 347 1222
Email	info@isa.nl
Website	www.isa.nl
Address	Sportlaan 45, Amstelveen, 1185 TB, The Netherlands
Mailing address	PO Box 920, 1180 AX Amstelveen, The Netherlands

STAFF

Director Edward E. Greene, Jr., Ph.D.
Head of Lower School Bruce Ashton
Head of Upper School David Monk
Assistant Head, Upper School Chris Vincent
Assistant Head, Lower School Sarah Grace
Business Office Manager Harmen Veling

Library Media Center Director Donna Saxby
Teaching staff Full time 140; Part time 60;
Total 200
Nationalities of teaching staff US 35; UK 51;
Dutch 48; Other(s) (Australian, Canadian) 66

INFORMATION

Grade levels N–12
School year August–June
School type coeducational, day, private non-profit
Year founded 1964
Governed by elected Board of Governors
Accredited by CIS, New England
Regional organizations ECIS
Enrollment Nursery 60; PreK 61;
Elementary K–5 365; Middle School 6–8 161;
High School 9–12 196; Total 843

Nationalities of student body US 161; UK 92;
Dutch 121; Other(s) (Japanese, Korean) 469
Tuition/fee currency Euro
Tuition range 5,425–19,750
Annual fees Registration 250;
Administration 300; PTA 32
One time fees Enrollment 3,250
Graduates attending college 97%
Graduates have attended Cambridge U, Brown U,
U of Pennsylvania, Imperial Col London, Keio U

EDUCATIONAL PROGRAM

Curriculum Intl, IB Diploma, IBPYP, IBMYP
Average class size Elementary 20; Secondary 20
Language(s) of instruction English
Language(s) taught Dutch, French, Spanish,
German, Japanese
Staff specialists computer, counselor, ESL,
learning disabilities, librarian, math resource,
nurse, reading resource, speech/hearing

Special curricular programs art, instrumental
music, vocal music, computer/technology,
physical education
Extra curricular programs computers, community
service, dance, drama, yearbook
Sports badminton, baseball, basketball, cricket,
golf, gymnastics, hockey, martial arts, rugby,
soccer, softball, squash, swimming, tennis,
track and field, volleyball, flag football
Examinations IB, PSAT, SAT, SAT II

CAMPUS FACILITIES

Location Suburban
Campus 6 hectares, 2 buildings, 76 classrooms,
6 computer labs, 350 instructional computers,

18,000 library volumes, 1 auditorium,
1 cafeteria, 2 gymnasiums, 1 infirmary,
2 playing fields, 6 science labs, 2 tennis courts

AFNORTH INTERNATIONAL SCHOOL

Phone	31 45 527 8221
Fax	31 45 527 8233
Email	AIS.Directorate@eu.dodea.edu
Website	www.afnorth-is.com/index-1.html
Address	Ferd Bolstraat 1, Brunssum, 6445 EE, The Netherlands

STAFF

International Director H. Elsie Stresman
Assistant Director Gerhard Groblinghoff
US High School Section Head Carolyn Forbis
US Elementary Head Audrey Griffin
Canadian Elementary Heads
France Thibault and Robert Martin
UK Elementary Head Sheena Macleod

Assistant Business Manager Manfred Fritsch
Educational Technologist Jeff Black
Media Specialist Nancy Mitchell
Teaching staff Full time 127; Part time 5; Total 132
Nationalities of teaching staff US 70; UK 17;
Dutch 2; Other(s) (Canadian, German) 43

INFORMATION

Grade levels PreK–13
School year August–June
School type coeducational, day, private non-profit
Year founded 1967
Governed by appointed Board of Directors
Accredited by North Central
Regional organizations ECIS
Enrollment PreK 20; Elementary K–5 425;
Middle School 6–8 195; High School 9–12 450;
Grade 13 5; Total 1,095

Nationalities of student body US 605; UK 85;
Other(s) (Canadian, German) 405
Tuition/fee currency Euro
Tuition range 15,405–17,570
Graduates attending college 96%
Graduates have attended Queens Col,
Colorado School of Mines, U of Texas,
Auburn U, U of California

EDUCATIONAL PROGRAM

Curriculum US, AP, Allgemeine Hochschulreife,
Ontario HS Diploma
Average class size Elementary 22; Secondary 20
Language(s) of instruction English, German
Language(s) taught French, Spanish
Staff specialists computer, counselor, ESL,
learning disabilities, librarian, nurse,
psychologist, reading resource, speech/hearing

Special curricular programs art, instrumental
music, vocal music, computer/technology,
distance learning, physical education, vocational
Extra curricular programs computers, community
service, drama, excursions/expeditions, yearbook
Sports baseball, basketball, cross-country,
football, soccer, tennis, track and field, volleyball
Clubs International Club, National Honor
Society, Junior Honor Society
Examinations ACT, AP, SAT, SAT II, Tera Nova

CAMPUS FACILITIES

Location Suburban
Campus 1 auditorium, 1 cafeteria,

3 gymnasiums, 1 infirmary, 1 playing field,
3 science labs

REGIONAL INTERNATIONAL SCHOOL

Phone +31 40 251 9437
Fax +31 40 252 7675
Email info@riseindhoven.nl
Website www.riseindhoven.nl
Address Humperdincklaan, 4, Eindhoven, Noord-Brabant, 5654 PA, The Netherlands

STAFF

Director Thomas Gunneweg
Deputy Head Ab van de Haar
Head of International Department Jenny Muusze
Head of Dutch Department Carla Kemps

IT Manager W. Verwimp
Teacher/Librarian L. Starrenburg
Teaching staff Full time 29; Part time 31; Total 60

INFORMATION

Grade levels 1–8
School year August–June
School type coeducational, day
Year founded 1965

Governed by appointed School Board
Regional organizations ECIS
Tuition/fee currency Euro
Tuition range 2,230–3,200

EDUCATIONAL PROGRAM

Curriculum UK, Intl, IPC
Average class size Elementary 20, 22
Language(s) of instruction English, Dutch
Language(s) taught French

Staff specialists computer, counselor, ESL, librarian
Special curricular programs vocal music, computer/technology, physical education
Extra curricular programs drama

CAMPUS FACILITIES

Location Urban
Campus 1 building, 28 classrooms,

1 computer lab, 1 auditorium, 2 gymnasiums, 1 playing field

INTERNATIONAL SCHOOL GRONINGEN

Phone	31 50 534 0084
Fax	31 50 534 0056
Email	is@maartens.nl
Website	www.isgroningen.nl
Address	Postbus 6105, Groningen, 9702 HC, The Netherlands

STAFF

Head of School M. B. Weston
Deputy Head MYP J. Eschweiler

Deputy Head DP J. Jansma
Secretary Ms. C. Percival

INFORMATION

Grade levels 6–12
School year September–July
School type coeducational, day
Year founded 1984
Regional organizations ECIS

Tuition/fee currency Euro
Tuition 6,500
One time fees Registration 175
Graduates attending college 90%

EDUCATIONAL PROGRAM

Curriculum IB Diploma, IBMYP
Average class size Secondary 14
Language(s) of instruction English
Language(s) taught French, Dutch
Staff specialists computer, counselor, ESL, math resource

Special curricular programs art, computer/technology
Extra curricular programs community service
Examinations IB

CAMPUS FACILITIES

Location Rural

Data from 2006/07 school year.

INTERNATIONAL SCHOOL EERDE

Phone 31 529 451 452
Fax 31 529 456 377
Email info@eerde.nl
Website www.eerde.nl
Address Kasteellaan 1, Ommen, Overijssel, 7731 PJ, The Netherlands

STAFF

Principal H. G. Voogd
Deputy Principal E. Lock

Head of Library M. Plomp

INFORMATION

Grade levels PreK–12
School year August–July
School type boarding, coeducational, day, private non-profit
Year founded 1934
Governed by appointed Board, Landstede Education Group
Sponsored by Landstede Education Group
Accredited by CIS
Regional organizations ECIS

Enrollment PreK 2; Elementary K–5 28; Middle School 6–8 38; High School 9–12 62; Total 130
Tuition/fee currency Euro
Tuition range 11,820–15,735
Annual fees Boarding, 5-day 21,230; Boarding, 7-day 23,490; Books 500
One time fees Registration 2,500; Guarantee Deposit 1,000; Laptop (e-Learning) 1,500
Boarding program grades K–12

EDUCATIONAL PROGRAM

Curriculum UK, Intl, IB Diploma, IGCSE
Average class size Elementary 10; Secondary 12
Language(s) of instruction English
Language(s) taught Spanish, German, French, Dutch, Russian, Italian, Swedish, Finnish
Staff specialists computer, counselor, ESL, learning disabilities
Special curricular programs art, instrumental music, computer/technology, physical education, vocational

Extra curricular programs community service, dance, drama, excursions/expeditions, newspaper, photography, yearbook
Sports badminton, baseball, basketball, football, golf, hockey, soccer, softball, swimming, tennis, track and field, volleyball, fitness, horse riding
Examinations GCSE, IB, IGCSE, PSAT, SAT

CAMPUS FACILITIES

Location Rural
Campus 8 hectares, 7 buildings, 20 classrooms, 1 computer lab, 20 instructional computers,

5,000 library volumes, 1 auditorium, 1 cafeteria, 1 gymnasium, 1 playing field, 2 science labs, 1 pool, 1 tennis court

Data from 2006/07 school year.

AMERICAN INTERNATIONAL SCHOOL OF ROTTERDAM

Phone	31 10 422 5351
Fax	31 10 422 4075
Email	queries@aisr.nl
Website	www.aisr.nl
Address	Verhulstlaan 21, 3055 WJ, Rotterdam, 3055 WJ, The Netherlands

STAFF

Director Brian D. Atkins
Elementary Principal Anne Marie Blitz
Guidance Counselor Ruth Lopez
IB Coordinator Evelyn Armstrong
Public Relations Lesley Murphy
Finance Manager Maria Josey

IT Coordinator Phil Krumrei
Head of Library/Media Center Stewart Shipman
Teaching staff Full time 32; Part time 10; Total 42
Nationalities of teaching staff US 22; UK 6;
Dutch 3; Other(s) (Canadian, New Zealander) 11

INFORMATION

Grade levels PreK–12
School year August–June
School type coeducational, day, private non-profit
Year founded 1959
Governed by appointed Board of Directors
Accredited by CIS, New England
Regional organizations ECIS
Enrollment PreK 40; Elementary K–5 125;
Middle School 6–8 32; High School 9–12 45;
Total 242

Nationalities of student body US 55; UK 25;
Dutch 21; Other(s) (Japanese, Korean) 141
Tuition/fee currency Euro
Tuition range 11,300–16,400
Annual fees Registration 880; Busing 2,800
One time fees Capital Levy 3,000
Graduates attending college 98%
Graduates have attended U of Toronto,
Ithaca Col, Erasmus U, Cardiff U,
Berklee Col of Music

EDUCATIONAL PROGRAM

Curriculum US, IB Diploma
Average class size Elementary 18; Secondary 14
Language(s) of instruction English
Language(s) taught French, Spanish, Dutch
Staff specialists computer, counselor, ESL,
learning disabilities, librarian, nurse
Special curricular programs art, instrumental
music, computer/technology, physical education

Extra curricular programs computers, community
service, drama, environmental conservation,
excursions/expeditions, newspaper, photography,
yearbook, global issues
Sports basketball, soccer, softball, swimming,
tennis, track and field, volleyball
Examinations IB, ISA (international schools
assessment)

CAMPUS FACILITIES

Location Suburban
Campus 3 hectares, 1 building, 35 classrooms,
1 computer lab, 95 instructional computers,

11,000 library volumes, 1 auditorium,
1 cafeteria, 1 gymnasium, 4 playing fields,
3 science labs

AMERICAN SCHOOL OF THE HAGUE

Phone	31 70 512 1060
Fax	31 70 511 2400
Email	admissions@ash.nl
Website	www.ash.nl
Address	Rijksstraatweg 200, Wassenaar, 2241 BX, The Netherlands

STAFF

Superintendent Richard L. Spradling, Ph.D.
High School Principal Robin Appleby
Middle School Principal Mary Russman
Elementary School Principal Tim Messick
Business Manager Ton Ravensbergen
Technology Coordinator Lal Abraham

Head Librarian Kim Tyo-Dickerson
Teaching staff Full time 110; Part time 30;
Total 140
Nationalities of teaching staff US 80; UK 15;
Dutch 15; Other(s) (Canadian, Australian) 30

INFORMATION

Grade levels PreK–12
School year August–June
School type coeducational, day, private non-profit
Year founded 1953
Governed by elected Board of Trustees
Accredited by CIS, Middle States
Regional organizations ECIS
Enrollment PreK 50; Elementary K–5 350;
Middle School 6–8 300; High School 9–12 350;
Total 1,050

Nationalities of student body US 400; UK 50;
Dutch 100; Other(s) (Swede, Canadian) 500
Tuition/fee currency Euro
Tuition range 13,000–15,800
Annual fees Capital Levy 2,200; Busing 2,000
One time fees Registration 3,100
Graduates attending college 98%
Graduates have attended Cornell U,
Pennsylvania State U, Rice U, Stanford U,
Tulane U

EDUCATIONAL PROGRAM

Curriculum US, AP, IB Diploma
Average class size Elementary 18; Secondary 18
Language(s) of instruction English
Language(s) taught French, Spanish, Dutch, German
Staff specialists computer, counselor, ESL,
librarian, math resource, nurse, reading
resource, speech/hearing
Special curricular programs art, instrumental
music, vocal music, computer/technology,
physical education, theatre, newspaper, yearbook,
Literary Magazine, Movement, Service Learning

Extra curricular programs community service,
dance, drama, excursions/expeditions,
newspaper, photography, yearbook, speech and
debate, student senate, Odyssey of the Mind,
Math Counts, Model UN, chess
Sports baseball, basketball, cross-country, golf,
soccer, softball, swimming, tennis, track and
field, volleyball
Examinations ACT, AP, IB, PSAT, SAT, SAT II, TOEFL

CAMPUS FACILITIES

Location Suburban
Campus 15 hectares, 1 building, 100 classrooms,
15 computer labs, 500 instructional computers,

50,000 library volumes, 2 auditoriums,
2 cafeterias, 5 gymnasiums, 1 infirmary,
3 playing fields, 10 science labs, 2 tennis courts

THE BRITISH SCHOOL IN THE NETHERLANDS

Phone	31 070 315 4077
Fax	31 070 315 4078
Email	info@britishschool.nl
Website	www.britishschool.nl
Address	Tarwekamp 3, Den Haag, 2592 XG, The Netherlands

STAFF

Principal Trevor Rowell, Ph.D.
Head of Senior School Steffen Sommer
Head of Junior School Vlaskamp Neil Hendriksen
Head of Junior School Diamanthorst Paul Ellis
Head of Junior School Assen Tim Unsworth
Head of Foundation School Sally Gray

Finance Director Wouter Hoobroeckx
Teaching staff Full time 235; Part time 181;
Total 416
Nationalities of teaching staff US 7; UK 275;
Dutch 68; Other(s) (Irish) 66

INFORMATION

Grade levels N–13
School year September–July
School type coeducational, day, private non-profit
Year founded 1931
Enrollment Nursery 124; PreK 141;
Elementary K–5 830; Middle School 6–8 413;
High School 9–12 446; Grade 13 104; Total 2,058
Nationalities of student body US 62; UK 900;
Dutch 88; Other(s) 1,004

Tuition/fee currency Euro
Tuition range 5,490–14,820
Annual fees Busing 1,932
One time fees Registration 580
Graduates attending college 98%
Graduates have attended Oxford U, Cambridge U,
London U, U of East Anglia, Edinburgh U

EDUCATIONAL PROGRAM

Curriculum UK, GenCSE
Average class size Elementary 22; Secondary 20
Language(s) of instruction English
Language(s) taught French, German, Dutch,
Spanish, Latin, Chinese Mandarin, Italian
Staff specialists computer, ESL, learning
disabilities, librarian, nurse

Special curricular programs art, instrumental
music, computer/technology, physical education
Sports badminton, basketball, cross-country,
golf, gymnastics, hockey, rugby, skiing, soccer,
swimming
Examinations A-level GCE, GCSE

CAMPUS FACILITIES

Location Urban
Campus 4 buildings, 105 classrooms, 5
computer labs, 350 instructional computers,

28,000 library volumes, 3 auditoriums,
1 cafeteria, 4 gymnasiums, 5 infirmaries,
4 playing fields, 8 science labs, 5 tennis courts

NICARAGUA

Area:	129,494 sq km
Population:	5,675,356
Capital:	Managua
Currency:	Gold Cordoba (NIO)
Languages:	Spanish

AMERICAN-NICARAGUAN SCHOOL

Phone	505 278 0029
Fax	505 278 2565
Email	director@ans.edu.ni
Website	www.ans.edu.ni
Address	INCEG 800 varas al oeste, Lomas de Montserrat, Managua, Nicaragua
Mailing address	PO Box 2670, Managua, Nicaragua

STAFF

Director General Elsa C. Lamb
Secondary Principal Joseph Azmeh
Middle School Coordinator Rodolfo Narvaez
Elementary Principal Fredy Ramirez
Athletic Director Oswaldo Ortiz
Director of Finance and Support Services
Roberto Cardenal

Technology and Media Coordinator
Roberta Arguello
Teaching staff Full time 103; Part time 3; Total 106
Nationalities of teaching staff US 51; UK 1;
Nicaraguan 43; Other(s) (Canadian,
Honduran) 11

INFORMATION

Grade levels N–12
School year August–June
School type coeducational, day, private non-profit
Year founded 1944
Governed by elected Board of Directors
Accredited by Southern
Regional organizations AASCA, AASSA
Enrollment Nursery 19; PreK 34;
Elementary K–5 377; Middle School 6–8 222;
High School 9–12 340; Total 992

Nationalities of student body US 338; UK 5;
Nicaraguan 482; Other(s) (Korean, Costa
Rican) 167
Tuition/fee currency US Dollar
Tuition range 4,125–5,445
Annual fees Registration 150
One time fees construction K3–12 1,500;
entrance K3–5 2,800; entrance 6–12 3,500
Graduates attending college 95%
Graduates have attended Harvard U, Georgetown
U, Brown U, U of Pennsylvania, North Western U

EDUCATIONAL PROGRAM

Curriculum US, AP
Average class size Elementary 20; Secondary 22
Language(s) of instruction English
Language(s) taught Spanish, French
Staff specialists computer, counselor, ESL,
learning disabilities, librarian, nurse,
psychologist, reading resource
Special curricular programs art, instrumental
music, vocal music, computer/technology,
physical education
Extra curricular programs computers, community
service, dance, drama, environmental

conservation, excursions/expeditions, literary
magazine, newspaper, photography, yearbook
Sports badminton, baseball, basketball, football,
gymnastics, soccer, softball, swimming, tennis,
track and field, volleyball, water polo, ping pong
Clubs National Honor Society, National Junior
Honor Society, Hacia Democracy, Operation
Smile, Green Project, drama, multicultural, ANS
Magazine
Examinations ACT, AP, PSAT, SAT, SAT II,
Stanford, TOEFL, GBE, GRE Subject, GMAT

CAMPUS FACILITIES

Location Suburban
Campus 12 hectares, 22 buildings, 75 classrooms,
4 computer labs, 210 instructional computers,

19,315 library volumes, 1 cafeteria, 1 covered
play area, 1 infirmary, 5 playing fields,
4 science labs, 1 pool, 1 tennis court

NIGER

Area:	1.267 million sq km
Population:	12,894,865
Capital:	Niamey
Currency:	Communaute Financiere Africaine Franc (XOF)
Languages:	French

AMERICAN INTERNATIONAL SCHOOL OF NIAMEY

Phone	227 20723 942
Fax	227 20723 457
Email	asniger@intnet.ne
Website	www.geocities.com/asniamey
Address	c/o American Embassy, BP 11201, Rue des Ambassades, Niamey, Niger
Mailing address	MO/Director (ASN), 2420 Niamey Place, Dulles, VA 20189-2420, USA

STAFF

Director Frank O. Walsh
Business Manager Fidele Dassi
Teaching staff Full time 9; Part time 3; Total 12

Nationalities of teaching staff US 4; Nigerien 4; Other(s) (Russian, French) 4

INFORMATION

Grade levels PreK–12
School year August–June
School type coeducational, day, private non-profit
Year founded 1982
Governed by appointed and elected Board of Directors
Accredited by Middle States
Regional organizations AISA
Enrollment PreK 12; Elementary K–5 35; Middle School 6–8 22; High School 9–12 3; Total 72

Nationalities of student body US 21; UK 2; Nigerien 21; Other(s) (Nigerian, French) 28
Tuition/fee currency US Dollar
Tuition range 11,250–13,500
Annual fees Busing 1,840; ESL 2,000; Special needs 2,000
One time fees Registration 3,000
Graduates attending college 100%
Graduates have attended California State U

EDUCATIONAL PROGRAM

Curriculum US
Average class size Elementary 12; Secondary 10
Language(s) of instruction English
Language(s) taught French
Special curricular programs art, vocal music, distance learning, physical education

Extra curricular programs computers, community service, dance, yearbook
Sports basketball, soccer, softball
Examinations Iowa, PSAT, SAT

CAMPUS FACILITIES

Location Suburban
Campus 3 hectares, 5 buildings, 12 classrooms, 1 computer lab, 22 instructional computers,

12,000 library volumes, 1 auditorium, 1 cafeteria, 4 playing fields, 1 science lab, 1 pool, 1 tennis court, air conditioning

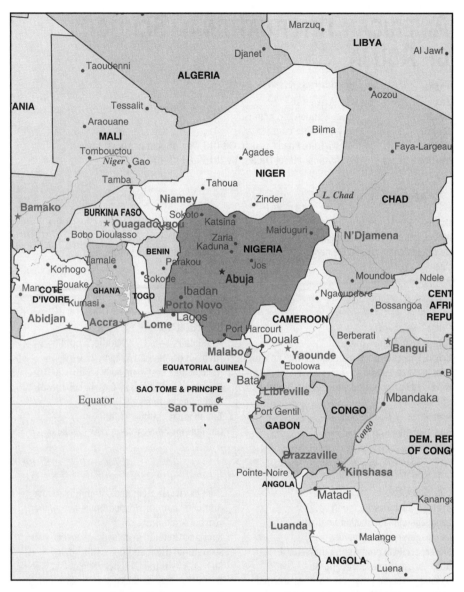

NIGERIA

Area:	923,768 sq km
Population:	135,031,164
Capital:	Abuja
Currency:	Naira (NGN)
Languages:	English

AMERICAN INTERNATIONAL SCHOOL OF ABUJA

Phone	234 9 413 4464
Fax	234 9 413 4464
Email	auzoewulu@yahoo.com
Website	www.aisabuja.com
Address	No. 61 Lake Chad Cresent, Off IBB Way, Maitama, Abuja, Nigeria
Mailing address	8320 Abuja Place, Dulles, VA 20189-8320, USA

STAFF

Director Amy Uzoewulu, Ed.D.
Middle and High School Principal Debra Giles
Guidance Counselor and Elementary Principal Rachel LecoQ

Finance Officer Emmanuella Obiejemba
IT Director Debra Giles
Librarian Funke Abegunde, Ed.D.

INFORMATION

Grade levels N–10
School year August–June
School type coeducational, day, private non-profit
Year founded 1993
Governed by appointed and elected Board of Directors
Accredited by Middle States
Regional organizations AISA, ECIS

Enrollment Nursery 14; PreK 51; Elementary K–5 139; Middle School 6–8 48; High School 9–12 13; Total 265
Nationalities of student body US 66; UK 10; Nigerian 66; Other(s) (Israeli, Lebanese) 123
Tuition/fee currency US Dollar
Tuition range 3,000–12,000
One time fees Registration 200; Capital Levy 4,500

EDUCATIONAL PROGRAM

Curriculum US
Average class size Elementary 20
Language(s) of instruction English
Language(s) taught French
Staff specialists computer, counselor, ESL, librarian, math resource, nurse
Special curricular programs art, instrumental music, computer/technology, distance learning, physical education, University of Nebraska Independent Study for grades 10–12

Extra curricular programs computers, dance, drama, excursions/expeditions, newspaper, yearbook, cooking
Sports basketball, gymnastics, soccer, swimming, track and field, volleyball
Clubs Crafty Hands, French, Speak Out, Tae Kwon Do, drama, chess, soccer, swimming
Examinations Iowa

CAMPUS FACILITIES

Location Suburban
Campus 3 hectares, 3 buildings, 15 classrooms, 1 computer lab, 20 instructional computers, 6,000 library volumes, 1 covered play area, 1 playing field, 1 science lab, 1 pool, 1 tennis court, air conditioning

Data from 2006/07 school year.

HILLCREST SCHOOL

Phone	234 73 465410
Fax	234 73 465410
Email	hillcrestschool@yahoo.com
Website	www.hillcrestschool.net
Address	13 Old Bukuru Road, Jos, Plateau, 930001, Nigeria
Mailing address	c/o Nigerian Courier, 3901 E. Paris Ave S.E., Grand Rapids, MI 49512-3906 USA

STAFF

Superintendent Dick A. Seinen
High School and Middle School Principal Brian Huff, Ph.D.
Elementary School Principal Jennifer Bhide
Finance Officer Vikram Bhide
Head of Computer Department Dele Alabi
Librarian Aisha Garba
Teaching staff Full time 20; Part time 10; Total 30
Nationalities of teaching staff US 18; UK 2; Nigerian 5; Other(s) 5

INFORMATION

Grade levels 1–12
School year August–May
School type boarding, coeducational, church-affiliated, day, private non-profit
Year founded 1942
Governed by appointed Cooperating Body
Accredited by Middle States
Regional organizations AISA
Enrollment Elementary K–5 87; Middle School 6–8 91; High School 9–12 90; Total 268
Nationalities of student body US 58; UK 3; Nigerian 161; Other(s) 46
Tuition/fee currency US Dollar
Tuition range 1,700–7,600
Annual fees Boarding, 7-day 4,462
One time fees Registration 1,915
Boarding program length 7-day **Boys** 28 **Girls** 15
Graduates attending college 92%
Graduates have attended American U, American U of Beirut, Calvin Col, George Washington U, Texas A&M U

EDUCATIONAL PROGRAM

Curriculum US, AP
Average class size Elementary 18; Secondary 22
Language(s) of instruction English
Language(s) taught French, Spanish, Hausa
Staff specialists computer, learning disabilities, librarian, nurse
Special curricular programs art, instrumental music, vocal music, computer/technology, physical education, vocational
Extra curricular programs computers, community service, dance, excursions/expeditions, literary magazine, newspaper, photography, yearbook
Sports badminton, baseball, basketball, cross-country, golf, gymnastics, soccer, tennis, track and field, volleyball
Examinations ACT, AP, Iowa, PSAT, SAT

CAMPUS FACILITIES

Location Urban
Campus 16 hectares, 9 buildings, 23 classrooms, 3 computer labs, 45 instructional computers, 1 auditorium, 1 gymnasium, 1 infirmary, 2 playing fields, 3 science labs, 5 tennis courts

AMERICAN INTERNATIONAL SCHOOL OF LAGOS

Phone	234 1 261 7793
Fax	234 1 261 7794
Email	information@aislagos.com
Website	www.aislagos.com
Address	Behind 1004 Estates, Victoria Island, Lagos, Nigeria
Mailing address	c/o TPS-AIS Lagos, PO Box 1357, Tacoma, WA 98401-1357, USA

STAFF

Superintendent Thomas P Shearer, Ed.D.
Secondary Principal Sharon Schauss, Ed.D.
Elementary Principal and Director of Admissions Terry Burns, Ed.D.
Curriculum Coordinator Carla Massoud
Counselor Barry Phipps
Business Manager Trudy Mafe

Technology Teacher and IB Coordinator John Stewart, Ed.D.
Librarian Amanda Mecca, Ed.D.
Teaching staff Full time 54; Part time 1; Total 55
Nationalities of teaching staff US 40; UK 1; Nigerian 6; Other(s) (Australian, Indian) 8

INFORMATION

Grade levels PreK–10
School year August–June
School type coeducational, day, private non-profit
Year founded 1964
Governed by elected Board of Directors
Accredited by Middle States
Regional organizations AISA
Enrollment PreK 48; Elementary K–5 355; Middle School 6–8 160; High School 9–12 40; Total 603

Nationalities of student body US 278; UK 63; Nigerian 113; Other(s) (Chinese, Dutch) 149
Tuition/fee currency US Dollar
Tuition range 7,700–17,600
One time fees Registration 6,000; Application 300
Graduates attending college 95%
Graduates have attended U of Chicago, Stanford U, Harvard U, U of Southern California, U of Virginia

EDUCATIONAL PROGRAM

Curriculum US
Average class size Elementary 18; Secondary 22
Language(s) of instruction English
Language(s) taught French, Spanish
Staff specialists computer, counselor, ESL, librarian, nurse, reading resource
Special curricular programs art, instrumental music, vocal music, computer/technology, physical education

Extra curricular programs computers, community service, dance, drama, environmental conservation, excursions/expeditions, newspaper, yearbook
Sports badminton, baseball, basketball, football, golf, gymnastics, martial arts, soccer, softball, swimming, tennis, track and field, volleyball
Clubs National Honor Society, Model UN
Examinations PSAT, SAT

CAMPUS FACILITIES

Location Suburban
Campus 4 hectares, 4 buildings, 45 classrooms, 6 computer labs, 240 instructional computers, 23,000 library volumes, 1 auditorium, 1 covered play area, 1 gymnasium, 1 infirmary, 1 playing field, 3 science labs, 1 pool, 3 tennis courts, air conditioning

NORWAY

Area:	323,802 sq km
Population:	4,627,926
Capital:	Oslo
Currency:	Norwegian Krone (NOK)
Languages:	Bokmal Norwegian

INTERNATIONAL SCHOOL OF BERGEN

Phone	47 55 306 330
Fax	47 55 306 331
Email	june@isob.no
Website	www.isb.gs.hl.no or www.isob.no
Address	Vilhelm Bjerknesvei 15, Bergen, 5081, Norway

STAFF

Director June Murison
Deputy Director of Upper School Julia Watson
MYP Coordinator Gillian Boniface
PYP Coordinator Christina Raynor
Business Coordinator Anne Helen Austgulen

Library Coordinator Juliet Crossley-Nilsen
Teaching staff Full time 20; Part time 8; Total 28
Nationalities of teaching staff US 3; UK 13;
Norwegian 6; Other(s) (French) 6

INFORMATION

Grade levels PreK–10
School year August–June
School type coeducational, day, private non-profit
Year founded 1975
Governed by elected Board of Trustees
Accredited by CIS, New England
Regional organizations ECIS

Enrollment PreK 36; Elementary K–5 108;
Middle School 6–8 46; High School 9–12 30;
Total 220
Nationalities of student body US 20; UK 30;
Norwegian 120; Other(s) (German, Swede) 50
Tuition/fee currency Norwegian Kroner
Tuition range 23,000–140,000

EDUCATIONAL PROGRAM

Curriculum National, Intl, IBPYP, IBMYP
Average class size Elementary 18; Secondary 15
Language(s) of instruction English, Norwegian
Language(s) taught French

Staff specialists computer, counselor, ESL,
learning disabilities, librarian
Examinations ISA

CAMPUS FACILITIES

Location Suburban
Campus 2 hectares, 2 buildings, 13 classrooms,
2 computer labs, 50 instructional computers,

8,000 library volumes, 2 covered play areas,
2 gymnasiums, 1 infirmary, 1 science lab

INTERNATIONAL SCHOOL OF STAVANGER

Phone	47 51 554300
Fax	47 51 554301
Email	Lduevel@isstavanger.no
Website	www.isstavanger.no
Address	Treskeveien 3, Hafrsfjord, 4043, Norway

STAFF

Director Linda M. Duevel, Ph.D.
Middle School and High School Principal
T. A. Hennard
Primary Principal and Curriculum Coordinator
Len Duevel, Ph.D.
Business Manager Brynhild Asheim

Technology Manager Allen Smith
Librarian Jill Egan
Teaching staff Full time 68; Part time 8; Total 76
Nationalities of teaching staff US 30; UK 20;
Norwegian 7; Other(s) (Australian) 19

INFORMATION

Grade levels PreK–12
School year August–June
School type coeducational, day, private non-profit
Year founded 1966
Governed by appointed Board of Trustees
Accredited by CIS, New England
Regional organizations CEESA, ECIS
Enrollment PreK 32; Elementary K–5 278;
Middle School 6–8 130;
High School 9–12 160; Total 600

Nationalities of student body US 95; UK 95;
Norwegian 80; Other(s) (Canadian, German) 330
Tuition/fee currency Norwegian Kroner
Tuition 136,000
Graduates attending college 95%
Graduates have attended London School of
Economics, McGill U, St. Andrews U,
U of Sydney, Texas A&M U

EDUCATIONAL PROGRAM

Curriculum US, UK, Intl, IB Diploma, IGCSE
Average class size Elementary 18; Secondary 18
Language(s) of instruction English
Language(s) taught Norwegian, French, Spanish,
German, Dutch
Staff specialists computer, counselor, ESL,
learning disabilities, librarian, nurse
Special curricular programs art, instrumental
music, vocal music, computer/technology,
physical education

Extra curricular programs computers, community
service, drama, environmental conservation,
excursions/expeditions, yearbook
Sports basketball, rugby, skiing, soccer,
softball, swimming, track and field, volleyball
Clubs Model UN, skating, Girl and Boy Scouts,
environmental
Examinations ACT, GCSE, IB, IGCSE, PSAT, SAT,
SAT II, TOEFL

CAMPUS FACILITIES

Location Suburban
Campus 7 hectares, 1 building, 70 classrooms,
2 computer labs, 250 instructional computers,
30,000 library volumes, 1 auditorium,

1 cafeteria, 3 covered play areas,
3 gymnasiums, 1 infirmary, 3 playing fields,
6 science labs

OMAN

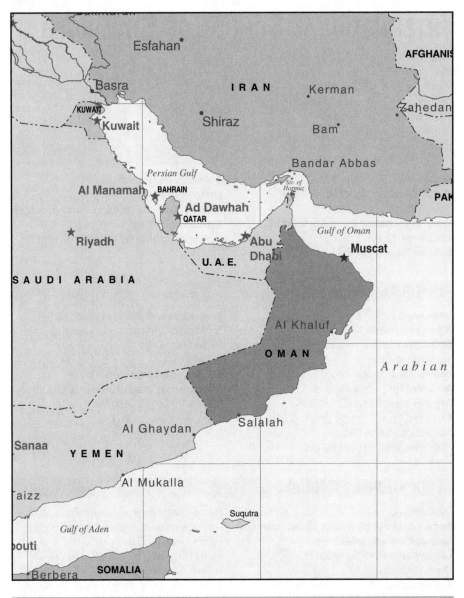

OMAN

Area:	212,460 sq km
Population:	3,204,897
Capital:	Muscat
Currency:	Omani Rial (OMR)
Languages:	Arabic, English

ABA–An IB World School

Phone	968 24603 646
Fax	968 24603 544
Email	abaad@omantel.net.om
Website	www.abaoman.edu.om
Address	PO Box 372, Medinat Al Sultan Qaboos, Muscat, 115, Oman

STAFF

Superintendent Mona Nashman-Smith
Elementary School Principal Rod Harding
Director of Student Services Tony Salt
Secondary School Principal Larry McIlvain
Asst Elementary School Principal Steven Madden
Asst Secondary School Principal Elsbeth Lang

Business Manager Bahul S. Pillai
Head of Information Technology Shahji Prabhakar
Librarian Fiona Mulvaney
Teaching staff Full time 74; Part time 2; Total 76
Nationalities of teaching staff US 13; UK 16;
Other(s) (Canadian, Australian) 47

INFORMATION

Grade levels N–12
School year August–June
School type coeducational, day, private non-profit
Year founded 1987
Governed by elected Board of Directors
Accredited by CIS, Middle States
Regional organizations MAIS, NESA
Enrollment Nursery 40; PreK 40;
Elementary K–5 289; Middle School 6–8 199;
High School 9–12 237; Total 805

Nationalities of student body US 60; UK 115;
Omani 18; Other(s) (Indian, Nigerian) 612
Tuition/fee currency US Dollar
Tuition range 5,285–12,900
Annual fees Re-registration 258
One time fees Registration 388; Capital Levy 1,943
Graduates attending college 98%
Graduates have attended Brown U, U of Virginia,
Waterloo U, Duke U, London U

EDUCATIONAL PROGRAM

Curriculum Intl, IB Diploma, IBPYP, IBMYP, IGCSE
Average class size Elementary 22; Secondary 22
Language(s) of instruction English
Language(s) taught French, Spanish, Arabic
Staff specialists computer, counselor, ESL,
librarian, nurse
Special curricular programs art, instrumental
music, vocal music, computer/technology,
physical education, design and technology, text
and performance

Extra curricular programs computers, community
service, dance, drama, environmental
conservation, excursions/expeditions,
photography, yearbook
Sports badminton, basketball, football,
gymnastics, hockey, rugby, soccer, softball,
swimming, tennis, track and field, volleyball,
ultimate frisbee, netball, fitness, dance
Examinations GCSE, IB, IGCSE, PSAT, SAT, SAT II,
TOEFL

CAMPUS FACILITIES

Location Suburban
Campus 3 hectares, 8 buildings, 60 classrooms,
3 computer labs, 180 instructional computers,
25,483 library volumes, 1 auditorium,

1 cafeteria, 3 covered play areas,
2 gymnasiums, 1 infirmary, 2 playing fields,
6 science labs, 1 pool, 3 tennis courts,
air conditioning

THE AMERICAN INTERNATIONAL SCHOOL OF MUSCAT

Phone	968 2459 5180
Fax	968 2450 3815
Email	taism@omantel.net.om
Website	www.taism.com
Address	Way 6305, Building 86, Ghala Street, Muscat, 130, Oman
Mailing address	PO Box 584, Azaiba, PC 130, Muscat, Oman

STAFF

Director Kevin D. Schafer
High School Principal Nelson File
Middle School Principal Keith Boniface
Elementary School Principal Daniel Hovland
Business Manager Hemant Dutia

IT Network Manager Gokul Krishnan
Librarian Martha Langille
Teaching staff Full time 63; Part time 4; Total 67
Nationalities of teaching staff US 46; UK 1;
Other(s) (Canadian, Lebanese) 20

INFORMATION

Grade levels PreK–12
School year August–June
School type coeducational, day, private non-profit
Year founded 1998
Governed by appointed and elected Board of Directors
Sponsored by U.S. Embassy
Accredited by CIS, New England
Regional organizations CEESA, ECIS, NESA
Enrollment PreK 40; Elementary K–5 260; Middle School 6–8 142; High School 9–12

153; Total 595
Nationalities of student body US 190; UK 12; Omani 12; Other(s) (Dane, Lebanese) 381
Tuition/fee currency Omani Rial
Tuition range 2,545–5,990
Annual fees Busing 350
One time fees Registration 50; Capital Levy 3,250
Graduates attending college 100%
Graduates have attended Stanford U, Hampshire Col, Northwestern U, Southern Methodist U, U of British Columbia

EDUCATIONAL PROGRAM

Curriculum US, AP
Average class size Elementary 20; Secondary 20
Language(s) of instruction English
Language(s) taught French, Arabic, Spanish
Staff specialists computer, counselor, ESL, learning disabilities, librarian, nurse, reading resource, speech/hearing
Special curricular programs art, instrumental music, vocal music, computer/technology, physical education

Extra curricular programs computers, community service, dance, drama, excursions/expeditions, literary magazine, newspaper, yearbook, crafts, study assistance
Sports basketball, gymnastics, soccer, softball, swimming, track and field, volleyball
Clubs Model UN, speech, chess, student council, poetry
Examinations AP, Iowa, PSAT, SAT, SAT II, TOEFL, MAP

CAMPUS FACILITIES

Location Suburban
Campus 6 hectares, 1 building, 52 classrooms, 2 computer labs, 200 instructional computers, 15,000 library volumes, 1 auditorium,

1 cafeteria, 3 covered play areas, 1 gymnasium, 1 infirmary, 3 playing fields, 4 science labs, 1 pool, air conditioning

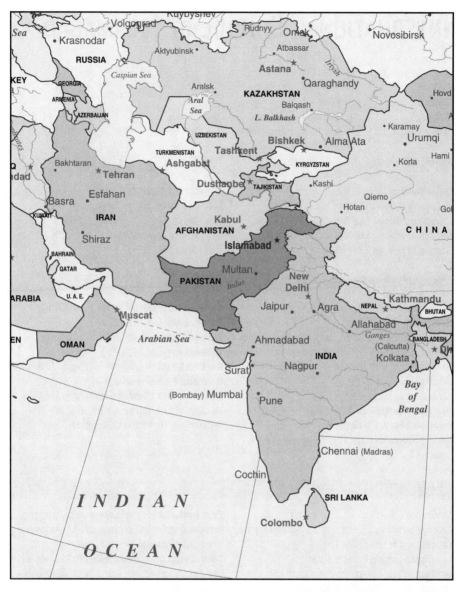

PAKISTAN

Area:	803,940 sq km
Population:	164,741,924
Capital:	Islamabad
Currency:	Pakistani Rupee (PKR)
Languages:	Punjabi

INTERNATIONAL SCHOOL OF ISLAMABAD

Phone	92 51 443 4950
Fax	92 51 444 0193
Email	school@isoi.edu.pk
Website	www.isoi.edu.pk
Address	Sector H-9/1, Islamabad, 44000, Pakistan
Mailing address	PO Box 1124, Islamabad - 44000, Pakistan

STAFF

Superintendent Rose C. Puffer
Secondary School Principal Daniel Polta
Elementary School Principal Constance Turner
Director of Student Services Victor Godden
Director of Finance Sibte Hassan

Manager M.I.S. Saqib Baloch
School Librarian Tahira Shahid
Teaching staff Full time 45; Part time 5; Total 50
Nationalities of teaching staff US 23; UK 2;
Pakistani 12; Other(s) 13

INFORMATION

Grade levels PreK–12
School year August–June
School type coeducational, day, private non-profit
Year founded 1965
Governed by appointed and elected Board of
Directors
Accredited by Middle States
Regional organizations NESA
Enrollment PreK 13; Elementary K–5 206;
Middle School 6–8 69; High School 9–12 93;
Total 381

Nationalities of student body US 50; UK 12;
Pakistani 90; Other(s) 229
Tuition/fee currency US Dollar
Tuition range 4,680–14,765
One time fees Registration 150; Capital Levy 3,750
Graduates attending college 95%
Graduates have attended Georgetown U,
Macalester Col, Rochester Institute of
Technology, U of Sussex, McGill U

EDUCATIONAL PROGRAM

Curriculum US, AP
Average class size Elementary 16; Secondary 14
Language(s) of instruction English
Language(s) taught French, Urdu
Staff specialists computer, counselor, ESL,
learning disabilities, librarian, nurse
Special curricular programs art, instrumental
music, vocal music, computer/technology,
distance learning, physical education,
Model UN, Host Nation

Extra curricular programs computers, community
service, drama, literary magazine, newspaper,
yearbook, National Honor Society
Sports badminton, basketball, cricket, soccer,
swimming, tennis, track and field, volleyball,
table tennis
Examinations ACT, AP, PSAT, SAT, SAT II, TOEFL,
SAT 10

CAMPUS FACILITIES

Location Suburban
Campus 9 hectares, 14 buildings, 54 classrooms,
4 computer labs, 225 instructional computers,
35,000 library volumes, 1 auditorium,

1 cafeteria, 1 covered play area, 1 gymnasium,
1 infirmary, 3 playing fields, 4 science labs,
1 pool, 2 tennis courts, air conditioning

KARACHI AMERICAN SCHOOL

Phone	92 21 453 9096
Fax	92 21 454 7305
Email	pelosipeter@kas.edu.pk
Website	www.kas.edu.pk
Address	Amir Khusro Road, KDA Scheme No. I, Karachi, 75350, Pakistan

STAFF

Superintendent Peter L. Pelosi, Ph.D.
Elementary Principal Lois Schaper, Ph.D.
Assistant Principal Bonnie Maddalone
Business Manager Erna Faruqui
Director of Technology Toby Youngs

Head Librarian Terri Smith
Teaching staff Full time 41; Part time 2; Total 43
Nationalities of teaching staff US 23;
Pakistani 16; Other(s) 4

INFORMATION

Grade levels PreK–12
School year August–May
School type coeducational, day, private non-profit
Year founded 1953
Governed by elected Board of Directors
Accredited by Middle States
Regional organizations NESA
Enrollment PreK 10; Elementary K–5 120;
Middle School 6–8 79; High School 9–12 127;
Total 336

Nationalities of student body US 68; UK 16;
Pakistani 174; Other(s) 78
Tuition/fee currency US Dollar
Tuition range 7,580–11,660
One time fees Registration 4,000; Application
100
Graduates attending college 100%
Graduates have attended Cornell U, U of
Pennsylvania, Johns Hopkins U, Smith Col,
Tufts U

EDUCATIONAL PROGRAM

Curriculum US, AP
Average class size Elementary 20; Secondary 20
Language(s) of instruction English
Language(s) taught Urdu, Spanish, French
Staff specialists computer, counselor, ESL,
librarian, physician
Special curricular programs art, instrumental
music, vocal music, computer/technology,
physical education

Extra curricular programs computers, community
service, drama, environmental conservation,
excursions/expeditions, literary magazine,
newspaper, photography, yearbook, Girl Guides
Sports badminton, basketball, cricket, golf,
martial arts, soccer, squash, swimming, tennis,
track and field, volleyball
Clubs cricket, Tae Kwon Do, table tennis,
computers, camping, Proud Pakistan, language, board games, art, puppet
Examinations ACT, AP, Iowa, PSAT, SAT, SAT II,
Stanford, TOEFL

CAMPUS FACILITIES

Location Urban
Campus 5 hectares, 11 buildings, 40 classrooms,
3 computer labs, 90 instructional computers,
35,500 library volumes, 1 auditorium,
1 cafeteria, 1 covered play area, 1 gymnasium,
1 infirmary, 2 playing fields, 3 science labs,
1 pool, 2 tennis courts, air conditioning

LAHORE AMERICAN SCHOOL

Phone 92 42 576 2406
Fax 92 42 571 1901
Email las@las.edu.pk
Website www.las.edu.pk
Address 15 Upper Mall, Canal Bank, Lahore, 54000, Pakistan

STAFF

Superintendent Ron Dowty
Elementary and Middle School Principal
Kathryn D. Cochran
Elementary and Middle School Assistant Principal
Nadine Savage
High School Principal Dennis Tangeman
Athletic Director Louise Lodge

Curriculum Director Kathy Khan
Business and Accounts Manager Ali Yousaf Sheikh
IT Coordinator Tariq Khokhar
Librarian Sabrina Kamal Khan
Teaching staff Full time 55; Part time 6; Total 61
Nationalities of teaching staff US 19; UK 2;
Host 27; Other(s) 13

INFORMATION

Grade levels N–12
School year August–June
School type coeducational, day, private non-profit
Year founded 1956
Governed by elected Board of Directors
Accredited by Middle States
Regional organizations NESA
Enrollment Nursery 7; PreK 15;
Elementary K–5 163; Middle School 6–8 86;
High School 9–12 172; Total 443

Nationalities of student body US 68; UK 27;
Pakistani 291; Other(s) (Korean, Canadian) 57
Tuition/fee currency US Dollar
Tuition range 2,544–7,990
Annual fees activity 150; English as a Foreign
Language 500
One time fees Registration 2,000
Graduates attending college 100%
Graduates have attended Brown U, Columbia U,
Johns Hopkins U, U of Pennsylvania,
Dartmouth Col

EDUCATIONAL PROGRAM

Curriculum US, AP
Average class size Elementary 14; Secondary 12
Language(s) of instruction English
Language(s) taught French, Urdu
Staff specialists computer, counselor, ESL,
librarian, math resource, physician, reading
resource
Special curricular programs art, instrumental
music, computer/technology, physical education

Extra curricular programs computers, community
service, drama, literary magazine, yearbook
Sports baseball, basketball, cricket, soccer,
swimming, tennis, track and field, volleyball
Clubs puppet making, book cooks, arts and
crafts, board games, community service, yoga,
dance, bowling
Examinations ACT, AP, Iowa, PSAT, SAT, SAT II,
TOEFL

CAMPUS FACILITIES

Location Suburban
Campus 1 hectare, 6 buildings, 47 classrooms,
3 computer labs, 110 instructional computers,
20,000 library volumes, 1 auditorium,

1 cafeteria, 1 covered play area, 1 gymnasium,
1 infirmary, 2 playing fields, 4 science labs,
1 pool, air conditioning

PANAMA

Area:	78,200 sq km
Population:	3,242,173
Capital:	Panama
Currency:	Balboa (PAB); US Dollar (USD)
Languages:	Spanish

THE INTERNATIONAL SCHOOL OF PANAMA

Phone	507 266 7037
Fax	507 266 7808
Email	isp@isp.edu.pa
Website	www.isp.edu.pa
Address	New Golf Club Road, Cerro Viento Rural, Distrito San Miguelito, Panama City, El Dorado, 6-7589, Panama

STAFF

Director Alexander Bennett
High School Principal Dennis Dunn
Elementary and Middle School Principal

Diane Guevara
Curriculum Coordinator
Alida de Garcia de Paredes

INFORMATION

Business Manager Jania Jacob
Grade levels PreK–12
School year August–June
School type coeducational, day, private non-profit
Year founded 1982
Governed by elected Board of Directors
Accredited by Southern
Regional organizations AASCA
Enrollment Nursery 15; PreK 15;
Elementary K–5 240; Middle School 6–8 135;
High School 9–12 180; Total 585

Nationalities of student body US 100; UK 10;
Panamanian 175; Other(s) (Colombian,
Korean) 300
Tuition/fee currency US Dollar
Tuition range 3,020–8,360
Annual fees Registration 460; Busing 875;
Yearbook 40
One time fees Capital Levy 6,000
Graduates attending college 95%
Graduates have attended U of Pennsylvania,
Georgetown U, Duke U, U of Toronto,
U of British Colombia

EDUCATIONAL PROGRAM

Curriculum US, National, IB Diploma
Average class size Elementary 23; Secondary 25
Language(s) of instruction English
Language(s) taught Spanish, French
Staff specialists computer, counselor, ESL,
learning disabilities, librarian, nurse,
psychologist
Special curricular programs art, instrumental
music, vocal music, computer/technology,
physical education

Extra curricular programs community service,
dance, drama, excursions/expeditions, literary
magazine, newspaper, yearbook
Sports basketball, football
Clubs drama, science, photography,
Spanish, film and photo, cooking, dance,
advanced calculus
Examinations IB, Iowa, PSAT, SAT, SAT II

CAMPUS FACILITIES

Location Suburban
Campus 8 hectares, 6 buildings, 44 classrooms,
4 computer labs, 210 instructional computers,
16,000 library volumes, 1 cafeteria,

2 covered play areas, 1 gymnasium,
1 infirmary, 2 playing fields, 2 science labs,
air conditioning

Data from 2006/07 school year.

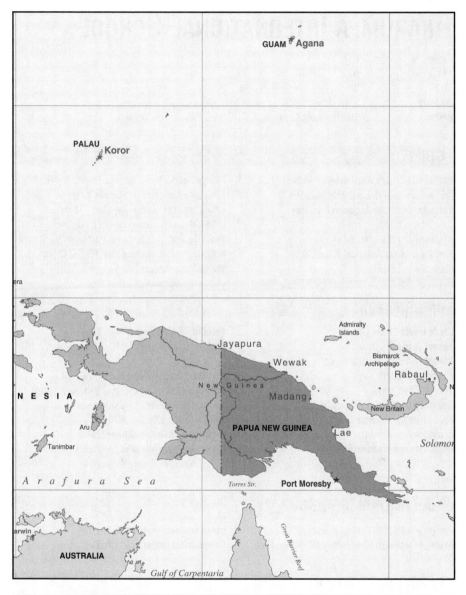

PAPUA NEW GUINEA

Area:	462,840 sq km
Population:	5,795,887
Capital:	Port Moresby
Currency:	Kina (PGK)
Languages:	Melanesian Pidgin

UKARUMPA INTERNATIONAL SCHOOL

Phone	675 737 4575
Fax	675 737 3532
Email	uissc-principal@sil.org.pg
Website	www.UkarumpaInternationalSchool.org
Address	SIL Box 406, Ukarumpa, EHP 444, Papua New Guinea

STAFF

Education Division Administrator Robert Musum
Primary School Principal Max Sahl, Ed.D.
Secondary Campus Assistant Principal
John Price, Ed.D.
Registrar Jan Hanson, Ed.D.
Primary Campus Assistant Principal
Clare Koens, Ed.D.

Middle School Head Teacher Donna Smith, Ed.D.
Director's Assistant for Finance Craig Swanson
UISSC Head of Technology Barry Moeckel
UISSC Head Librarian Glenda Holliday
Teaching staff Full time 40; Part time 20; Total 60
Nationalities of teaching staff US 35; Other(s)
(Canadian, Australian) 5

INFORMATION

Grade levels PreK–12
School year July–June
School type coeducational, company-sponsored,
church-affiliated, day
Year founded 1962
Governed by elected School Board
Sponsored by Summer Institute of Linguistics
Accredited by Western
Regional organizations EARCOS

Enrollment Elementary K–5 139;
Middle School 6–8 79; High School 9–12 136;
Total 354
Nationalities of student body US 194; UK 14;
Guinean 21; Other(s) (Canadian, Australian) 125
Tuition/fee currency US Dollar
Tuition range 1,065–4,800
Graduates attending college 95%
Graduates have attended Messiah Col,
Houghton Col, Trinity Western U

EDUCATIONAL PROGRAM

Curriculum US, UK, National, Intl, AP
Average class size Elementary 18; Secondary 15

Language(s) of instruction English
Language(s) taught Spanish, French

CAMPUS FACILITIES

Location Rural
Campus 10 buildings, 26 classrooms,
3 computer labs, 30 instructional computers,

12,000 library volumes, 2 auditoriums,
1 covered play area, 2 gymnasiums, 2 playing
fields, 3 science labs, 6 tennis courts

PARAGUAY

Area:	406,750 sq km
Population:	6,669,086
Capital:	Asuncion
Currency:	Guarani (PYG)
Languages:	Spanish

THE AMERICAN SCHOOL OF ASUNCIÓN

Phone	595 21 600 479
Fax	595 21 603 518
Email	director@asa.edu.py
Website	www.asa.edu.py
Address	Av. España 1175 esq. Sgto. Marecos, Asunción, Paraguay
Mailing address	7331 NW 35th Street, Suite MC 30020, Miami, FL 33122, USA

STAFF

Director General Eric H. Habegger, Ed.D.
Elementary Principal Brian Donaldson
Secondary Principal Alex Kremer
Curriculum Coordinator Megan Maher
Paraguayan Studies Coordinator Rodrigo Colman
Athletic Director Pablo Arsenault

Business Manager Norman Stark
Technology Coordinator Mark Page-Botelho
Librarian Lisa Habegger
Teaching staff Full time 66; Part time 4; Total 70
Nationalities of teaching staff US 29; Paraguayan 26;
Other(s) (Canadian, Argentine) 15

INFORMATION

Grade levels PreK–12
School year August–June
School type coeducational, day, private non-profit
Year founded 1954
Governed by elected Board of Directors
Accredited by Southern
Regional organizations AASSA
Enrollment PreK 45; Elementary K–5 260;
Middle School 6–8 135; High School 9–12 165;
Total 605

Nationalities of student body US 76; UK 4;
Paraguayan 378; Other(s) (Argentine,
Brazilian) 147
Tuition/fee currency US Dollar
Tuition range 3,192–5,220
Annual fees Registration 550
One time fees Entrance 5,500
Graduates attending college 98%
Graduates have attended Brown U, Boston Col,
Williams Col, Rollins Col, Ringling School of Art
and Design

EDUCATIONAL PROGRAM

Curriculum US, National, AP
Average class size Elementary 23; Secondary 20
Language(s) of instruction English, Spanish
Language(s) taught Guarani, French, Portuguese
Staff specialists computer, counselor, ESL,
librarian, nurse, psychologist, reading resource
Special curricular programs art, instrumental
music, vocal music, computer/technology,
physical education

Extra curricular programs community service,
dance, environmental conservation,
excursions/expeditions, literary magazine,
newspaper, yearbook
Sports basketball, soccer, track and field,
volleyball, handball
Clubs chess, Destination Imagination, computer
games, comprehensive reading, Girls Club,
Story Tales, recycling, National Honor Society,
Knowledge Bowl, Operation Smile, Model UN
Examinations AP, Iowa, MAT, PSAT, SAT, SAT II,
Stanford, TOEFL

CAMPUS FACILITIES

Location Urban
Campus 8 hectares, 12 buildings, 46 classrooms,
3 computer labs, 133 instructional computers,

25,000 library volumes, 1 cafeteria, 1 covered
play area, 1 gymnasium, 1 infirmary, 3 playing
fields, 2 science labs, air conditioning

PERU

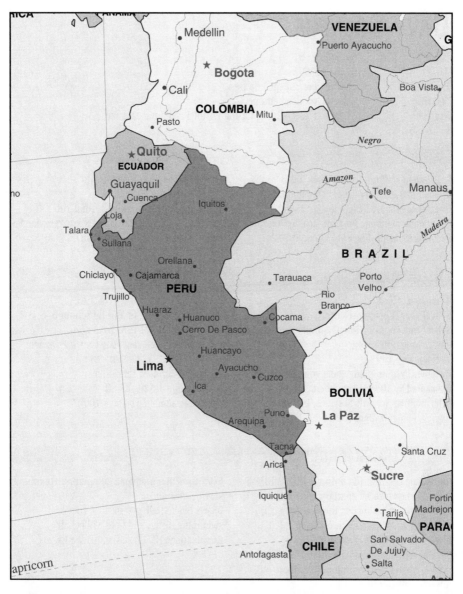

PERU

Area:	1,285,220 sq km
Population:	28,674,757
Capital:	Lima
Currency:	Nuevo Sol (PEN)
Languges:	Spanish

DAVY COLLEGE

Phone	51 76 367501
Fax	51 76 367502
Email	ohara@davycollege.edu.pe
Website	www.davycollege.edu.pe
Address	Av. Hoyos Rubio 2684, Casilla Postal 1, Cajamarca, Peru

STAFF

Superintendent James M. O'Hara, Ed.D.
Director of Secondary School Luis Requna
Director of Primary School Robert Hagenbucher
Coordinator of Infants Program Arlette Rondon
Business Manager Marisabel Abanto

Head of Technology Jose Cerruto
Librarian Liliana Baldini
Teaching staff Full time 100; Total 100
Nationalities of teaching staff US 10; Peruvian 85; Other(s) (Argentine, Romanian) 5

INFORMATION

Grade levels N–11
School year February–December
School type coeducational, company-sponsored, day, private non-profit
Year founded 1995
Governed by appointed Asociación Educativa Davy
Sponsored by Minera Yanacocha; Managed by International Schools Services, Inc.
Regional organizations AASSA

Enrollment Nursery 34; PreK 126; Elementary K–5 296; Middle School 6–8 102; High School 9–12 105; Total 663
Nationalities of student body US 15; Peruvian 639; Other(s) (Canadian) 10
Tuition/fee currency US Dollar
Tuition range 2,520–2,760
Graduates attending college 100%

EDUCATIONAL PROGRAM

Curriculum US, Intl, IB Diploma, IBPYP, IBMYP
Average class size Elementary 14; Secondary 16
Language(s) of instruction English, Spanish
Staff specialists computer, counselor, ESL, librarian, nurse, psychologist
Special curricular programs art, instrumental music, vocal music, computer/technology, physical education

Extra curricular programs computers, community service, drama
Sports basketball, gymnastics, soccer, swimming, track and field, volleyball
Examinations IB, Iowa, Cambridge Exams

CAMPUS FACILITIES

Location Suburban
Campus 8 hectares, 8 buildings, 58 classrooms, 4 computer labs, 240 instructional computers,

12,000 library volumes, 2 cafeterias, 1 gymnasium, 2 infirmaries, 2 playing fields, 4 science labs

HUASCARÁN INTERNATIONAL SCHOOL

Phone	51 43 45 2126
Fax	51 43 45 2216
Email	his@hisperu.edu.pe
Website	www.hisperu.edu.pe
Address	Calle Los Quenuales 215, Condominio El Pinar - Huanchac, Huaráz, Ancash, Peru
Mailing address	Casilla Postal 347, Huaráz, Ancash, Peru

STAFF

Director Peter Gubbe
Media Center Coordinator Isabel Meza
Teaching staff Full time 5; Part time 1; Total 6

Nationalities of teaching staff US 3; Peruvian 1; Other(s) (Canadia

INFORMATION

Grade levels K–8
School year August–June
School type coeducational, company-sponsored, day
Year founded 2000
Governed by Company

Sponsored by Compañía Minera Antamina; Managed by International Schools Services, Inc.
Enrollment Elementary K–5 30; Middle School 6–8 2; Total 32
Nationalities of student body US 2; Peruvian 28; Other(s) (Canadian) 2
Tuition/fee currency US Dollar

EDUCATIONAL PROGRAM

Curriculum Intl
Average class size Elementary 8
Language(s) of instruction English
Language(s) taught Spanish, English
Staff specialists computer, ESL
Special curricular programs art, computer/technology, physical education

Extra curricular programs computers, dance, drama, excursions/expeditions, newspaper, yearbook
Sports basketball, cricket, soccer, softball
Examinations Iowa

CAMPUS FACILITIES

Location Suburban
Campus 2 buildings, 6 classrooms, 1 computer lab, 40 instructional computers,

4,500 library volumes, 1 auditorium, 1 cafeteria, 1 infirmary, 3 playing fields, 1 science lab, 1 pool, 1 tennis court

Data from 2006/07 school year.

COLEGIO FRANKLIN DELANO ROOSEVELT

Phone	51 1 435 0890
Fax	51 1 702-4500
Email	fdr@amersol.edu.pe
Website	www.amersol.edu.pe
Address	Las Palmeras 325, Camacho, La Molina, Lima, Peru
Mailing address	Apartado 18-0977, Lima 18, Peru

STAFF

Superintendent Carol Kluznik, Ph.D.
Director Guadalupe Méndez, Ph.D.
High School Principal Philip Bradley
Middle School Principal Marilyn Holladay
Elementary Principal Linda Paz Soldán
Director of Curriculum and Planning Kristy Krahl

Business Manager Maria Isabel Payet
Technology Director John Lakatos
Media Center Director Catherine Corum
Teaching staff Full time 128; Part time 4; Total 132
Nationalities of teaching staff US 46; UK 2;
Peruvian 72; Other(s) (Canadian, Chinese) 12

INFORMATION

Grade levels PreK–12
School year August–June
School type coeducational, day, private non-profit
Year founded 1946
Governed by appointed Board of Directors
Accredited by Southern
Regional organizations AASSA
Enrollment PreK 118; Elementary K–5 570;
Middle School 6–8 252; High School 9–12 328;
Total 1,268

Nationalities of student body US 275; UK 11;
Peruvian 721; Other(s) (Korean, Brazilian) 261
Tuition/fee currency US Dollar
Tuition range 7,800–8,850
Annual fees Technology 200
One time fees Registration 200; Capital Levy 6,800
Graduates attending college 95%
Graduates have attended Georgetown U,
Columbia U, U of Pennsylvania, Purdue U,
Boston Col

EDUCATIONAL PROGRAM

Curriculum US, National, Intl, AP, IB Diploma,
IBPYP, IBMYP
Average class size Elementary 17; Secondary 17
Language(s) of instruction English, Spanish
Language(s) taught French
Staff specialists computer, counselor, ESL,
learning disabilities, librarian, speech/hearing
Special curricular programs art, instrumental
music, computer/technology, physical education

Extra curricular programs community service,
drama, newspaper, photography, yearbook
Sports basketball, gymnastics, hockey, martial
arts, rugby, soccer, softball, swimming, tennis,
track and field, volleyball, aquatics, rollerhockey
Clubs Operation Smile, debate, photography,
jazz band, drama, Korean Culture, Model UN
Examinations ACT, IB, PSAT, SAT, SAT II

CAMPUS FACILITIES

Location Urban
Campus 9 hectares, 11 buildings, 105 classrooms,
3 computer labs, 280 instructional computers,

55,000 library volumes, 1 auditorium,
2 gymnasiums, 1 infirmary, 4 playing fields,
7 science labs, 4 tennis courts

INTERNATIONAL CHRISTIAN SCHOOL OF LIMA

Phone	51 1 442 6149
Fax	51 1 440 3134
Email	icslimaperu@gmail.com
Website	www.icslima.org
Address	Av. Angamos Oeste 1155, Lima, Miraflores, 18, Peru

STAFF

Director John D. Havill
Head of Technology James Korsmo
Head of Library/Media Center Cindy Korsmo

Teaching staff Full time 18; Part time 6; Total 24
Nationalities of teaching staff US 20; Peruvian 4

INFORMATION

Grade levels K–12
School year August–June
School type private non-profit
Year founded 2001
Governed by appointed School Board
Sponsored by Network of International Christian Schools
Enrollment Elementary K–5 50; Middle School 6–8 30; High School 9–12 40; Total 120

Nationalities of student body US 65; Host 10; Other(s) (Canadian, Korean) 45
Tuition/fee currency US Dollar
Tuition range 3,300–6,000
Annual fees Registration 1,200
One time fees Capital Levy 4,000
Graduates attending college 100%
Graduates have attended Pace U, John Brown U, Mt. Vernon Nazarene U, Gordon Col

EDUCATIONAL PROGRAM

Curriculum US, AP
Average class size Elementary 8; Secondary 10
Language(s) of instruction English
Language(s) taught Spanish
Staff specialists ESL, learning disabilities, librarian

Special curricular programs art, vocal music, computer/technology, distance learning, physical education
Extra curricular programs computers, community service, dance, drama, newspaper, yearbook
Sports badminton, basketball, martial arts, soccer, softball, swimming, volleyball

CAMPUS FACILITIES

Location Urban
Campus 1 hectare, 1 building, 15 classrooms, 1 computer lab, 24 instructional computers, 9,000 library volumes, 1 auditorium, 1 science lab

PHILIPPINES

PHILIPPINES

Area:	300,000 sq km
Population:	91,077,287
Capital:	Manila
Currency:	Philippine Peso (PHP)
Languages:	Filipino

BRENT INTERNATIONAL SCHOOL BAGUIO

Phone	63 74 442 4050
Fax	63 74 442 3638
Email	brent@brentschoolbaguio.com
Website	www.brentschoolbaguio.com
Address	Brent Road, Baguio City, 2600, Philippines
Mailing address	PO Box 35, Baguio City 2600, Philippines

STAFF

Head of School Dick B. Robbins
Deputy Head Ursula Daoey
Academic Director and IB Coordinator Les Pickett
Lower School Principal Katharine Flores
Registrar and Admission Contact Lourdes Balanza
Executive Secretary Marissa Narvaez

Chief Administrative Officer Marissa Caluya
Information Technology Manager Mike Maclean
Librarian Vivien Torres
Teaching staff Full time 38; Part time 6; Total 44
Nationalities of teaching staff US 6; UK 2;
Filipino 30; Other(s) (Canadian) 6

INFORMATION

Grade levels N–12
School year August–May
School type boarding, coeducational, day,
private non-profit
Year founded 1909
Governed by appointed Board of Trustees
Accredited by Western
Regional organizations EARCOS
Enrollment Nursery 12; Elementary K–5 85;
Middle School 6–8 90; High School 9–12 110;
Total 297

Nationalities of student body US 35; UK 10;
Filipino 85; Other(s) (Korean, German) 167
Tuition/fee currency US Dollar
Tuition range 1,860–9,950
Annual fees Boarding, 7-day 7,250
One time fees Capital Levy 1,000
Boarding program grades 9–12
Boarding program length 7-day **Boys** 9 **Girls** 3
Graduates attending college 86%
Graduates have attended McGill U, U of British
Columbia, U of Victoria, Pennsylvania State U,
U of Miami

EDUCATIONAL PROGRAM

Curriculum US, UK, National, Intl, IB Diploma
Average class size Elementary 20; Secondary 22
Language(s) of instruction English
Language(s) taught French, Spanish, Filipino,
Korean
Staff specialists computer, counselor, ESL,
librarian, nurse
Extra curricular programs computers, community
service, drama, excursions/expeditions, literary
magazine, newspaper, yearbook

Sports badminton, basketball, cross-country,
football, soccer, track and field, volleyball
Clubs photography, sports, dance, community
service, computer, music, art, personality
development, scrapbooking
Examinations ACT, AP, IB, Iowa, MAT, PSAT, SAT,
SAT II, Stanford

CAMPUS FACILITIES

Location Suburban
Campus 13 hectares, 19 buildings, 32 classrooms,
2 computer labs, 42 instructional computers,
17,210 library volumes, 2 auditoriums,

2 cafeterias, 1 covered play area, 1 gymnasium,
1 infirmary, 1 playing field, 4 science labs,
1 tennis court

CEBU INTERNATIONAL SCHOOL

Phone	0063 32 417 6390 to 93
Fax	0063 32 417 6394
Email	Superintendent@cis.edu.ph
Website	www.cis.edu.ph
Address	Pit-os Road, Pit-os, Talamban, Cebu City, Cebu, 6000, Philippines
Mailing address	PO Box 735, Pit-os, Talamban, 6000 Cebu City, Philippines

STAFF

Superintendent Mark Bretherton
Elementary School Principal Clarissa Sayson
Middle and High School Principal Kurt Mecklem
Registrar Emma Peligro
IB Coordinator Brian Deichmeister
Curriculum and Accreditation Coordinator
Ma Luisa Villano

Business Manager Steve Sanchez
System Administrator Roel Cayme
Educational Media Center Head Alfredo Papaseit
Teaching staff Full time 52; Part time 5; Total 57
Nationalities of teaching staff US 5; UK 1;
Filipino 41; Other(s) (Peruvian, Canadian) 10

INFORMATION

Grade levels N–12
School year August–June
School type coeducational, day, private non-profit
Year founded 1924
Governed by elected Board of Trustees
Accredited by Western
Regional organizations EARCOS, ECIS
Enrollment Nursery 8; PreK 16;
Elementary K–5 185; Middle School 6–8 108;
High School 9–12 154; Total 471

Nationalities of student body US 85; UK 17;
Filipino 94; Other(s) (Korean, Japanese) 275
Tuition/fee currency US Dollar
Tuition range 1,111–3,806
Annual fees Capital Levy 935; IB 154;
Miscellaneous 1,419
One time fees Registration 2,000
Graduates attending college 98%
Graduates have attended Nottingham U, U of the Philippines, Boston U, La Salle U, Adelaide U

EDUCATIONAL PROGRAM

Curriculum Intl, IB Diploma
Average class size Elementary 20; Secondary 20
Language(s) of instruction English
Language(s) taught Spanish, Filipino, Chinese
Staff specialists computer, counselor, ESL, librarian, nurse
Special curricular programs art, instrumental music, vocal music, computer/technology, physical education

Extra curricular programs computers, community service, drama, environmental conservation, excursions/expeditions, literary magazine, yearbook
Sports basketball, hockey, soccer, swimming, volleyball, lacrosse, rollerblading
Clubs cooking, wall climbing, swimming, Model UN, Hapkido, horseback riding, yoga
Examinations IB

CAMPUS FACILITIES

Location Suburban
Campus 4 hectares, 3 buildings, 51 classrooms,

2 computer labs, 120 instructional computers, 18,000 library volumes, air conditioning

BRENT INTERNATIONAL SCHOOL, MANILA

Phone	63 2 631 1265
Fax	63 2 633 8420
Email	bism@brentmanila.edu.ph
Website	www.brentmanila.edu.ph
Address	University of Life Complex, Meralco Avenue, Pasig City, 1603, Philippines

STAFF

Head of School Dick B. Robbins
Lower and Middle School Principal (Pasig Campus) Robert Hartleip
Director for Finance Edna Ballesteros

Head of Media Center Kurt Kamb
Teaching staff Full time 23; Part time 2; Total 25
Nationalities of teaching staff US 4; UK 1; Canadian 11; Other(s) (Australian, German) 9

INFORMATION

Grade levels PreK–8
School year August–May
School type coeducational, church-affiliated, day, private non-profit
Year founded 1984
Governed by appointed Board of Trustees
Accredited by Western
Regional organizations EARCOS, ECIS

Enrollment Elementary K–5 80; Middle School 6–8 52; Total 132
Nationalities of student body US 14; UK 7; Filipino 30; Other(s) (Korean, Indian) 81
Tuition/fee currency US Dollar
Tuition range 4,988–9,792
Annual fees Capital Levy 1,575; ESL 1,100
One time fees Matriculation 2,888; Application/Testing 100

EDUCATIONAL PROGRAM

Curriculum US, IB Diploma
Average class size Elementary 13; Secondary 13
Language(s) of instruction English

Language(s) taught French, Spanish, Chinese, Korean, Filipino

CAMPUS FACILITIES

Location Urban
Campus 10 hectares, 4 buildings, 42 classrooms, 2 computer labs, 54 instructional computers,

18,577 library volumes, 1 cafeteria, 1 covered play area, 1 gymnasium, 1 infirmary, 1 playing field, 2 science labs, 1 pool, air conditioning

BRENT INTERNATIONAL SCHOOL, MANILA (SOUTH CAMPUS)

Phone	63 2 600 10300
Fax	63 49 511 4343
Email	bism@brent.edu.ph
Website	www.brent.edu.ph
Address	Brentville Subdivision, Brgy. Mamplasan, Biñan, Laguna, 4024, Philippines
Mailing address	University of Life Complex, Meralco Avenue, 1603 Pasig City, Philippines

STAFF

Head of School Dick B. Robbins
Upper School Principal Jeffrey Hammett
Middle School Principal Thomas Egerton
Lower School Principal
Maureen O'Shaughnessy, Ph.D.
Director for Admissions & Administrative Services
Ronald Knapp

Director for Student Activities Charles Bates
Director for Finance Edna Ballesteros
Head of Library/Media Center Kurt Lamb
Teaching staff Full time 150; Part time 2; Total 152
Nationalities of teaching staff US 35; UK 2;
Filipino 93; Other(s) (Australian, Canadian) 22

INFORMATION

Grade levels N–12
School year August–May
School type boarding, coeducational, church-affiliated, day, private non-profit
Year founded 1984
Governed by appointed Board of Trustees
Accredited by Western
Regional organizations EARCOS
Enrollment Nursery 73; Elementary K–5 499;
Middle School 6–8 342;
High School 9–12 485; Total 1,399
Nationalities of student body US 215; UK 59;
Filipino 260; Other(s) 865

Tuition/fee currency US Dollar
Tuition range 5,240–11,900
Annual fees Boarding, 5-day 3,000;
Capital Levy 1,575; Busing 936; ESL 1,100
One time fees Matriculation 2,888;
Application/Testing 110
Boarding program grades 7–12
Boarding program length 5-day
Graduates attending college 96%
Graduates have attended Stanford U, Harvard U,
Yale U, U of British Columbia, Simon Fraser U

EDUCATIONAL PROGRAM

Curriculum US, IB Diploma
Average class size Elementary 20; Secondary 22
Language(s) of instruction English

Language(s) taught French, Chinese, Korean,
Spanish, Filipino, Japanese
Examinations IB, PSAT, SAT, SAT II, Stanford

CAMPUS FACILITIES

Location Urban
Campus 6 hectares, 6 buildings, 85 classrooms,
5 computer labs, 196 instructional computers,
31,741 library volumes, 1 auditorium,

3 cafeterias, 3 covered play areas, 3 gymnasiums,
2 infirmaries, 3 playing fields, 7 science labs,
1 pool, 3 tennis courts, air conditioning

FAITH ACADEMY, INC.

Phone	63 2 658 0048
Fax	63 2 658 0026
Email	vanguard@faith.edu.ph
Website	www.faith.edu.ph
Address	Penny Lane, off Valley Golf Road, Victoria Valley, Cainta, Rizal, 1900, Philippines
Mailing address	MCPO BOX 2016, 0706 Makati City, Philippines

STAFF

Superintendent Thomas D. Hardeman
Deputy Superintendent Mike Hause
Elementary Principal Steve Taylor
Middle School Principal Peter Winslade
High School Principal Brian Foutz
Boarding Administrator Steve Anderson
Business Administrator David Williams

Computer Services Director Tony Book
Learning Resource Center Director Sharon Tully
Teaching staff Full time 110; Part time 31; Total 141
Nationalities of teaching staff US 100; UK 1; Filipino 2; Other(s) (Canadian) 38

INFORMATION

Grade levels K–12
School year August–May
School type boarding, coeducational, day, private non-profit
Year founded 1956
Governed by elected Board of Trustees
Accredited by Western
Regional organizations EARCOS
Enrollment Elementary K–5 147; Middle School 6–8 150; High School 9–12 266; Total 563
Nationalities of student body US 316; UK 7; Filipino 18; Other(s) (Korean, Canadian) 240

Tuition/fee currency US Dollar
Tuition range 1,753–5,089
Annual fees Registration 60; Boarding, 5-day 90; Capital Levy 5,056; Busing 1,176; Room and Board, All Girls 3,498; Room and Board, Middle School and Secondary School 3,731
Boarding program grades 6–12
Boarding program length 5-day **Boys** 39 **Girls** 26
Graduates attending college 85%
Graduates have attended Stanford U, US Air Force Academy, Wheaton Col, U of Southern California

EDUCATIONAL PROGRAM

Curriculum US, UK, Intl, AP, IGCSE
Average class size Elementary 20; Secondary 25
Language(s) of instruction English
Language(s) taught French, Spanish, Tagalog, Korean
Staff specialists computer, counselor, ESL, learning disabilities, librarian, nurse

Special curricular programs art, instrumental music, vocal music, computer/technology, physical education
Extra curricular programs drama, photography
Sports baseball, basketball, cross-country, football, soccer, softball, swimming, tennis, track and field, volleyball
Examinations A-level GCE, AP, GCSE, IGCSE, Iowa, PSAT, SAT, Stanford, TOEFL

CAMPUS FACILITIES

Location Suburban
Campus 5 hectares, 12 buildings, 60 classrooms, 5 computer labs, 210 instructional computers, 22,000 library volumes, 1 auditorium,

1 cafeteria, 2 covered play areas, 1 gymnasium, 1 infirmary, 2 playing fields, 5 science labs, 2 pools, 2 tennis courts, air conditioning

INTERNATIONAL SCHOOL MANILA

Phone	63 2 840 8400
Fax	63 2 840 8441
Email	super@ismanila.org
Website	www.ismanila.org
Address	University Parkway, Fort Bonifacio Global City, Taguig, Manila, 1634, Philippines
Mailing address	PO Box 1526, MCPO 1255, Makati City, Philippines

STAFF

Superintendent David E. Toze
Assistant Superintendent Stephen Dare
High School Principal William Brown
Middle School Principal Paul Passamonte
Elementary School Principal Jacquie Pender
Director of Finance and Administration Juris Lallana
IT Network Director Aurel Dimaculangan

Director of Media Services David Birchenall
Teaching staff Full time 170; Part time 18;
Total 188
Nationalities of teaching staff US 48; UK 32;
Filipino 30; Other(s) (Australian, Canadian) 78

INFORMATION

Grade levels PreK–12
School year August–June
School type coeducational, day, private non-profit
Year founded 1920
Governed by elected Board of Trustees
Accredited by Western
Regional organizations EARCOS
Enrollment PreK 62; Elementary K–5 581;
Middle School 6–8 466;
High School 9–12 647; Total 1,756

Nationalities of student body US 380; UK 37;
Filipino 312; Other(s) (Korean, Japanese) 1,027
Tuition/fee currency US Dollar
Tuition range 6,180–17,000
One time fees Registration 2,800;
Refundable Deposit 5,000
Graduates attending college 99%
Graduates have attended Harvard U, Yale U,
Stanford U, Princeton U, Dartmouth U

(Continued)

INTERNATIONAL SCHOOL MANILA (Continued)

EDUCATIONAL PROGRAM

Curriculum Intl, AP, IB Diploma
Average class size Elementary 20; Secondary 18
Language(s) of instruction English
Language(s) taught Spanish, French, Chinese, Japanese, Korean, Filipino
Staff specialists computer, counselor, ESL, learning disabilities, librarian, math resource, nurse, physician, psychologist, reading resource
Special curricular programs art, instrumental music, vocal music, computer/technology, physical education

Extra curricular programs computers, community service, dance, drama, environmental conservation, excursions/expeditions, literary magazine, newspaper, photography, yearbook
Sports badminton, basketball, cross-country, football, golf, gymnastics, martial arts, rugby, soccer, softball, squash, swimming, tennis, track and field, volleyball
Clubs scouting, environmental, cultural, outreach, Scholia, publications, debate, math, charity, IT
Examinations AP, IB, PSAT, SAT, SAT II, TOEFL, ERB; ISA

CAMPUS FACILITIES

Location Urban
Campus 7 hectares, 1 building, 149 classrooms, 9 computer labs, 1000 instructional computers, 87,000 library volumes, 2 auditoriums,

2 cafeterias, 2 covered play areas, 4 gymnasiums, 1 infirmary, 3 playing fields, 16 science labs, 3 pools, 8 tennis courts, air conditioning

BRENT INTERNATIONAL SCHOOL SUBIC, INC.

Phone	63 47 252 6871
Fax	63 47 252 3240
Email	info@brentsubic.edu.ph
Website	www.brentsubic.edu.ph
Address	Bldg 6601, Binictican Drive, Subic Bay Freeport Zone, Olongapo City, 2200, Philippines
Mailing address	PO Box 078, Olongapo City Post Office, Olongapo City 2200, Philippines

STAFF

Head of School Dick B. Robbins
Principal Garth Wyncoll
Director of Admissions Maricar Peralta
Guidance Counselor Sarah Borgerding
Director of Student Activities Stephen Davis
Treasury Officer Norma Lingad

Head of Library Gemma Afable
Teaching staff Full time 32; Part time 1; Total 33
Nationalities of teaching staff US 11; UK 1; Filipino 18; Other(s) (New Zealander, British Virgin Islander) 3

INFORMATION

Grade levels PreK–12
School year August–May
School type coeducational, church-affiliated, day, private non-profit
Year founded 1994
Governed by appointed Board of Trustees
Accredited by Western
Regional organizations EARCOS
Enrollment PreK 24; Elementary K–5 161; Middle School 6–8 39; High School 9–12 100; Total 324

Nationalities of student body US 39; UK 11; Filipino 54; Other(s) (Korean, Taiwanese) 220
Tuition/fee currency US Dollar
Tuition range 4,450–10,600
Annual fees ESL 1,150; Matriculation for New Students 1,500; Application and Testing for New Students 100
Graduates attending college 100%
Graduates have attended Ateneo de Manila U, Oberlin U, Emory U, Glion U, Marymont Col

EDUCATIONAL PROGRAM

Curriculum US, AP
Average class size Elementary 22; Secondary 24
Language(s) of instruction English
Language(s) taught Mandarin, Spanish
Staff specialists computer, counselor, ESL, librarian, nurse
Special curricular programs art, instrumental music, computer/technology, physical education

Extra curricular programs computers, drama, excursions/expeditions, newspaper, yearbook
Sports badminton, basketball, cross-country, football, soccer, swimming, tennis, track and field, volleyball, kickboxing
Clubs arts and crafts, gym, MiniBacks, movie, production crew, scuba, violin, yoga, pilates, Spanish
Examinations AP, Stanford

CAMPUS FACILITIES

Location Suburban
Campus 5 hectares, 15 buildings, 27 classrooms, 2 computer labs, 61 instructional computers, 22,422 library volumes, 2 auditoriums,

1 cafeteria, 1 covered play area, 1 gymnasium, 1 infirmary, 2 playing fields, 1 science lab, 1 pool, air conditioning

POLAND

POLAND

Area:	312,685 sq km
Population:	38,518,241
Capital:	Warsaw
Currency:	Zloty (PLN)
Languages:	Polish

INTERNATIONAL SCHOOL OF KRAKOW

Phone	48 12 270 14 09
Fax	48 12 270 14 09
Email	admin@iskonline.org
Website	www.iskonline.org
Address	ul. Sw. Floriana 57, Krakow - Lusina, 30-698, Poland

STAFF

Director Erica T. Mazzeo, Ed.D.
Head of Middle School Erik Lutley
Head of Secondary Anna Filipiuk
Head of Early Years and Elementary Susan Mleczko
Special and Exceptional Needs Coordinator Jean-Pierre Zink
Special and Exceptional Needs Coordinator Lilianna Lutley

Legal Advisor/Accountant Rafal Kaminski
Head of IT Szymon Bobek
Librarian Agata Mlodynia-Zink
Teaching staff Full time 19; Part time 7; Total 26
Nationalities of teaching staff US 6; UK 1; Pole 13; Other(s) (Jamaican, Icelander) 6

INFORMATION

Grade levels N–12
School year September–June
School type coeducational, day, private non-profit
Year founded 1992
Governed by appointed School Board
Sponsored by US Department of State
Regional organizations CEESA, ECIS
Enrollment Nursery 10; PreK 9; Elementary K–5 58; Middle School 6–8 21; High School 9–12 21; Total 119

Nationalities of student body US 25; UK 12; Pole 19; Other(s) (French, Dutch) 63
Tuition/fee currency Euro
Tuition range 4,500–10,000
Annual fees Capital Levy 700
One time fees Registration 200
Graduates attending college 100%
Graduates have attended Jagiellonian U, U of Toronto, U College of London

EDUCATIONAL PROGRAM

Curriculum Intl, AP
Average class size Elementary 12; Secondary 10
Language(s) of instruction English
Language(s) taught Polish, Dutch, French, German, Spanish
Staff specialists computer, counselor, ESL, learning disabilities, librarian
Special curricular programs art, instrumental music, vocal music, computer/technology, distance learning, physical education

Extra curricular programs computers, community service, dance, drama, excursions/expeditions, newspaper, photography, yearbook
Sports baseball, skiing, soccer, swimming, archery
Clubs languages, science, yoga, math, After School of Rock, gardening, Book Worms, guitar, chess, Snow Riders
Examinations ACT, AP, PSAT, SAT, SAT II, ISA/OPI

CAMPUS FACILITIES

Location Suburban
Campus 2 hectares, 2 buildings, 19 classrooms, 1 computer lab, 30 instructional computers,

10,000 library volumes, 1 auditorium, 1 cafeteria, 1 covered play area, 1 infirmary, 3 playing fields, 1 science lab, air conditioning

THE AMERICAN SCHOOL OF WARSAW

Phone 48 22 702 85 00
Fax 48 22 702 85 99
Email director@asw.waw.pl
Website www.asw.waw.pl
Address Bielawa, Ul. Warszawska 202, Konstancin-Jeziorna, 05-520, Poland

STAFF

Director Charles P. Barder, Ph.D.
High School Principal Jane McGee
Middle School Principal Leanne Dunlap
Elementary School Principal Donna Swagers, Ed.D.
Elementary School Assistant Principal Kristen DiMatteo

Director of Finance and Operations Rebecca Brown
Director of Technology Brett DiMatteo
Librarians Matthew Kollasch and Susan Matter
Teaching staff Full time 126; Part time 12; Total 138
Nationalities of teaching staff US 73; UK 3; Pole 49; Other(s) (Canadian, Dutch) 13

INFORMATION

Grade levels PreK–12
School year August–June
School type coeducational, day, private non-profit
Year founded 1953
Governed by appointed and elected Board of Trustees
Accredited by CIS, New England
Regional organizations CEESA, ECIS
Enrollment PreK 30; Elementary K–5 402; Middle School 6–8 176; High School 9–12 223; Total 831

Nationalities of student body US 215; UK 26; Pole 177; Other(s) (Korean, Dane) 413
Tuition/fee currency US Dollar
Tuition range 9,688–17,736
Annual fees Capital Levy 2750 New/2250 Returning
One time fees Registration 750
Graduates attending college 100%
Graduates have attended New York U, Emory U, Oxford U, U College London, U of Toronto

EDUCATIONAL PROGRAM

Curriculum Intl, IB Diploma
Average class size Elementary 18; Secondary 18
Language(s) of instruction English
Language(s) taught French, German, Spanish, Polish, Dutch, Swedish
Staff specialists computer, counselor, ESL, learning disabilities, librarian, math resource, nurse, reading resource, speech/hearing
Special curricular programs art, instrumental music, vocal music, computer/technology, physical education

Extra curricular programs computers, community service, dance, drama, environmental conservation, excursions/expeditions, photography, yearbook
Sports basketball, cross-country, football, soccer, softball, swimming, tennis, track and field, volleyball, flag football
Clubs mask-making, cultural arts, jazz ensemble, sign language, chess, Math Olympiads, card making, Fun with Fabrics
Examinations IB, Iowa, PSAT, SAT

CAMPUS FACILITIES

Location Suburban
Campus 10 hectares, 1 building, 56 classrooms, 3 computer labs, 486 instructional computers, 25,000 library volumes, 1 auditorium, 1 cafeteria, 2 gymnasiums, 1 infirmary, 4 playing fields, 7 science labs, 1 pool, 4 tennis courts

PORTUGAL

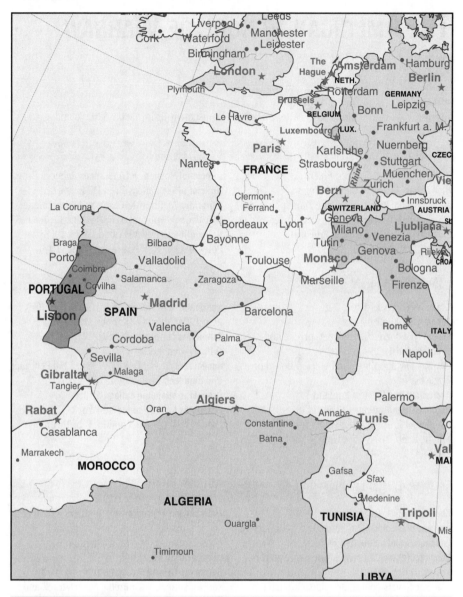

PORTUGAL

Area:	10,642,836
Population:	10,605,870
Capital:	Lisbon
Currency:	Euro (EUR)
Languages:	Portuguese

St. Julian's School

Phone	351 21 458 5300
Fax	351 21 458 5312
Email	mail@stjulians.com
Website	www.stjulians.com
Address	2776-601 Carcavelos, Carcavelos, Lisbon, 2776-601, Portugal

STAFF

Head of School David Smith, Ed.D.
Secondary School Principal Nicholas Connolly
Primary School Principal Robert Bienkowski
Business/Finance Manager Ormond Fannon
Director of Design and Technology David Pendlebury

Head of Careers and Library Resources
Christine Sousa e Sá
Teaching staff Full time 163; Part time 11;
Total 174

INFORMATION

Grade levels N–13
School year September–June
School type coeducational, day, private non-profit
Year founded 1932
Governed by elected Governors
Accredited by CIS, New England
Regional organizations ECIS
Enrollment Nursery 40; PreK 50; Elementary
K–5 353; Middle School 6–8 268;
High School 9–12 278; Grade 13 56; Total 1,045

Nationalities of student body US 21; UK 195;
Portuguese 627; Other(s) (Brazilian,
Spaniard) 202
Tuition/fee currency Euro
Tuition range 6,651–16,293
Annual fees Insurance 50; Lunch 964
One time fees Registration 470; Capital Levy
1,935; Returnable Deposit 150
Graduates attending college 100%
Graduates have attended Cambridge U, Imperial
Col, U Catolica, St. Andrew's Col, U of Bath

EDUCATIONAL PROGRAM

Curriculum UK, National, IB Diploma, IGCSE
Average class size Elementary 18; Secondary 18
Language(s) of instruction English, Portuguese
Language(s) taught French
Staff specialists computer, ESL, learning
disabilities, librarian, nurse, physician
Special curricular programs art, instrumental
music, vocal music, computer/technology,
physical education

Extra curricular programs community service,
drama, environmental conservation,
excursions/expeditions
Sports badminton, basketball, cricket,
cross-country, hockey, rugby, soccer, tennis,
track and field, volleyball
Examinations GCSE, IB, IGCSE, PSAT, SAT

CAMPUS FACILITIES

Location Suburban
Campus 8 hectares, 7 buildings, 55 classrooms,
4 computer labs, 248 instructional computers,

18,000 library volumes, 2 auditoriums,
2 cafeterias, 3 gymnasiums, 2 infirmaries,
4 playing fields, 7 science labs, 4 tennis courts

CARLUCCI AMERICAN INTERNATIONAL SCHOOL–LISBON

Phone	351 21 923 9800
Fax	351 21 923 9899
Email	info@caislisbon.org
Website	www.caislisbon.org
Address	Rua Antonio dos Reis, 95, Linhó, Sintra, 2710-301, Portugal

STAFF

Director Blannie M. Curtis
Secondary School Principal Nathan Chapman
Elementary School Principal Katie Morris
Director of Marketing/Admissions Cindy Ferrell
Business Manager António Vilhena

IT Coordinator Vera Tamen
Library/Media Specialist Margaret Guiton
Teaching staff Full time 59; Part time 1; Total 60
Nationalities of teaching staff US 38; UK 6; Portuguese 11; Other(s) (Canadian) 5

INFORMATION

Grade levels N–12
School year September–June
School type coeducational, day, private non-profit
Year founded 1956
Governed by appointed Board of Trustees
Accredited by CIS, New England
Regional organizations ECIS, MAIS
Enrollment Nursery 19; PreK 19; Elementary K–5 237; Middle School 6–8 120; High School 9–12 140; Total 535

Nationalities of student body US 112; UK 6; Portuguese 276; Other(s) (Brazilian, Spaniard) 141
Tuition/fee currency Euro
Tuition range 6,468–15,084
Annual fees Capital Levy 1,608; Busing 2,080; Lunch 592
One time fees Registration 470
Graduates attending college 95%
Graduates have attended Yale U, Georgetown U, Massachusetts Institute of Technology, California Institute of Technology, Edinburgh U

EDUCATIONAL PROGRAM

Curriculum US, National, AP, IB Diploma
Average class size Elementary 17; Secondary 15
Language(s) of instruction English
Language(s) taught Portuguese, French, Spanish
Staff specialists computer, counselor, ESL, learning disabilities, librarian, nurse, psychologist
Special curricular programs art, instrumental music, vocal music, computer/technology, physical education

Extra curricular programs computers, community service, dance, drama, environmental conservation, excursions/expeditions, literary magazine, yearbook, Model UN, handbells
Sports basketball, cross-country, golf, soccer, swimming, track and field, volleyball
Clubs debate, National Honor Society, student council, drama, community service
Examinations AP, IB, Iowa, PSAT, SAT, SAT II, TOEFL

CAMPUS FACILITIES

Location Suburban
Campus 4 hectares, 4 buildings, 32 classrooms, 2 computer labs, 118 instructional computers,

30,000 library volumes, 2 cafeterias, 1 covered play area, 1 infirmary, 2 playing fields, 3 science labs, 1 tennis court

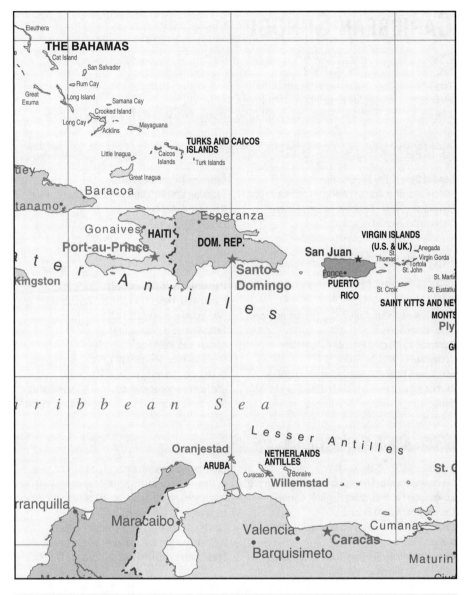

PUERTO RICO

Area:	13,790 sq km
Population:	3,944,259
Capital:	San Juan
Currency:	US Dollar (USD)
Languages:	Spanish, English

CARIBBEAN SCHOOL

Phone 787 843 2048
Fax 787 844 5626
Email discovercs@gmail.com
Website www.caribbeanschool.org
Address Urb. La Rambla, 1689 Calle Navarra, Ponce, 00731-4043, Puerto Rico

STAFF

Head of School Jim DiSebastian
Middle and High School Principal Claudia Procko
Elementary School Principal Ginny Martelle
Comptroller Israel Gonzalez

Librarian Belinda Cabassa
Teaching staff Full time 50; Part time 2; Total 52
Nationalities of teaching staff US 8;
Puerto Rican 44

INFORMATION

Grade levels PreK–12
School year August–May
School type coeducational, day, private non-profit
Year founded 1954
Governed by elected Board of Directors
Accredited by Middle States
Enrollment PreK 40; Elementary K–5 260;
Middle School 6–8 95; High School 9–12 120;
Total 515

Nationalities of student body US 15; Puerto
Rican 490; Other(s) (Indian, Ecuadorian) 10
Tuition/fee currency US Dollar
Tuition range 3,300–4,600
Annual fees Registration 1,120
One time fees New family 1,000
Graduates attending college 100%
Graduates have attended Yale U, Pennsylvania
State U, Brown U, U of North Carolina, Miami U

EDUCATIONAL PROGRAM

Curriculum US, AP, Puerto Rican
Average class size Elementary 20; Secondary 20
Language(s) of instruction English, Spanish
Language(s) taught French
Staff specialists computer, counselor, librarian,
nurse
Special curricular programs art, computer/
technology, physical education

Extra curricular programs community service,
drama, excursions/expeditions, literary
magazine, photography, yearbook, math bowl,
spelling bee, geography bee
Sports basketball, cross-country, soccer,
softball, tennis, track and field, volleyball
Examinations ACT, AP, Iowa, PSAT, SAT, TOEFL

CAMPUS FACILITIES

Location Urban
Campus 10 hectares, 4 buildings, 44 classrooms,
2 computer labs, 50 instructional computers,

10,000 library volumes, 1 cafeteria, 2 covered
play areas, 1 gymnasium, 1 infirmary, 3 playing
fields, 4 science labs, 2 tennis courts

CARIBBEAN PREPARATORY SCHOOL

Phone	787 765 4411
Fax	787 764 3809
Email	rmarracino@cpspr.org
Website	www.cpspr.org
Address	Urb Roosevelt, 100 Castillo Street, San Juan, 00918, Puerto Rico
Mailing address	PO Box 70177, San Juan, Puerto Rico 00936-8177

STAFF

Head of School Richard Marracino
Director of Lower Elementary School Noemí Ramírez
Director of Upper Elementary School Judith Rivera
Director of Middle and High School Maeve Hitzenbuhler

Dean of Students of Elementary School Gloria Cuevas
Dean of Students of High School Edmundo Báez
Business Manager Diana de Jesús
Librarian Magali Sánchez
Teaching staff Full time 91; Total 91
Nationalities of teaching staff US 91

INFORMATION

Grade levels N–12
School year August–May
School type coeducational, day, private non-profit
Year founded 1952
Governed by appointed and elected Board of Directors
Accredited by Middle States
Enrollment Nursery 15; PreK 40; Elementary K–5 370; Middle School 6–8 118; High School 9–12 151; Total 694

Nationalities of student body US 684; Other(s) (Colombian, Mexican) 10
Tuition/fee currency US Dollar
Tuition range 3,950–10,950
Annual fees Capital Levy 975; Re-enrollment 375; Technology 150
One time fees Registration 1,500; Graduation fee 160
Graduates attending college 100%
Graduates have attended Brown U, Syracuse U, Amherst Col, Emory U, U of Puerto Rico

EDUCATIONAL PROGRAM

Curriculum US, AP
Average class size Elementary 25; Secondary 20
Language(s) of instruction English
Language(s) taught Spanish
Staff specialists computer, counselor, learning disabilities, librarian, nurse, psychologist
Special curricular programs art, instrumental music, vocal music, computer/technology, physical education

Extra curricular programs computers, community service, dance, drama, environmental conservation, excursions/expeditions, literary magazine, newspaper, photography, yearbook
Sports baseball, basketball, football, soccer, softball, tennis, track and field, volleyball, indoor soccer
Clubs National Honor Society, Junior National Honor Society, forensics, drama, interact spelling bee, Spanish oratory, science, mathematics, recycling
Examinations ACT, AP, PSAT, SAT, SAT II, TOEFL

CAMPUS FACILITIES

Location Urban
Campus 2 hectares, 4 buildings, 70 classrooms, 4 computer labs, 124 instructional computers,

41,000 library volumes, 2 auditoriums, 2 cafeterias, 1 covered play area, 1 infirmary, 2 playing fields, 5 science labs, air conditioning

ROBINSON SCHOOL

Phone	787 999 4600
Fax	787 727 7736
Email	admissions@robinsonschool.org
Website	www.RobinsonSchool.org
Address	5 Nairn Street, Condado, San Juan, 00907, Puerto Rico

STAFF

Headmaster Robert E. Graves
Elementary School Principal Patricia Lopez
Secondary School Principal Carmen Morales
Admissions and Registration Officer Angie Fromnic
Learning Center Principal Maria Burset

Preschool Coordinator Cindy Ogg
Business Manager Jannette Santiago
IT Manager Juan Ayala
Secondary School Librarian Linda Ramos

INFORMATION

Grade levels 1–12
School year August–May
School type coeducational, church-affiliated, day, private non-profit
Year founded 1902
Governed by elected Board of Directors
Sponsored by General Board of Global Ministries
Accredited by Middle States
Tuition/fee currency US Dollar

Tuition range 5,000–7,560
Annual fees Registration 600; New Millennium Building Fund 500
One time fees Entrance, PPK-K 550; Entrance, 1st–12th 1,000
Graduates attending college 100%
Graduates have attended Villanova U, Florida Institute of Technology, U of Central Florida, New York U, Pennsylvania State U

EDUCATIONAL PROGRAM

Curriculum US, AP
Average class size Elementary 20; Secondary 20
Language(s) of instruction English
Language(s) taught English, Spanish, French
Staff specialists computer, counselor, ESL, learning disabilities, librarian, math resource, nurse, psychologist
Special curricular programs art, vocal music, computer/technology, physical education, journalism
Extra curricular programs computers, community service, dance, drama, environmental conservation, excursions/expeditions, newspaper, photography, yearbook, Model UN, Mu Alpha Theta
Sports baseball, basketball, cross-country, gymnastics, soccer, swimming, tennis, track and field, volleyball
Clubs travel, science, Spanish, Investors in Training, personal enhancement
Examinations ACT, AP, Iowa, PSAT, SAT, SAT II, Stanford, TOEFL, Learn-Aid, Key Math, TAP, The Border Test of Reading-Spelling Patterns, Riverside Performance Assessment Test

CAMPUS FACILITIES

Location Urban
Campus 5 hectares, 5 buildings, 70 classrooms, 3 computer labs, 140 instructional computers, 6,000 library volumes, 1 auditorium, 1 cafeteria, 1 gymnasium, 1 infirmary, 2 playing fields, 5 science labs, air conditioning

Data from 2006/07 school year.

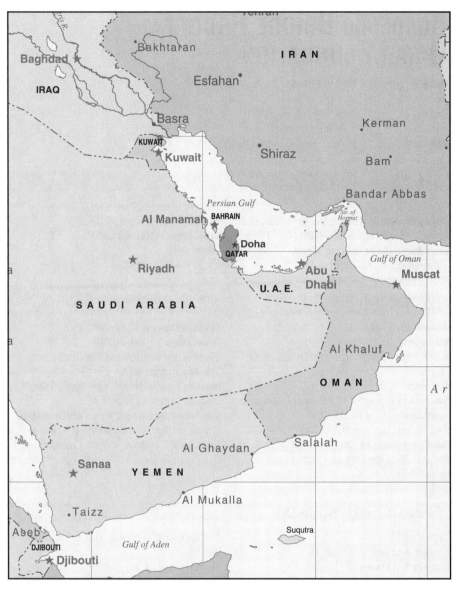

QATAR

Area:	11,437 sq km
Population:	907,229
Capital:	Doha
Currency:	Qatari Rial (QAR)
Languages:	Arabic, English

ACADEMIC BRIDGE PROGRAM– QATAR FOUNDATION

Phone	974 492 7300
Fax	974 481 9928
Email	info-ABP@qf.org.qa
Website	www.qf.org.qa
Address	PO Box 24404, Doha, Qatar

STAFF

Director Miles Lovelace, Ph.D.
Student Services Coordinator Shetha Numan, Ph.D.
Admissions and Records Coordinator Bob Lamb
Office Administrator Deborah Hogue
IT Coordinator Flurin Waelti

Library Department Chair Michel Ogilvie
Teaching staff Full time 35; Total 35
Nationalities of teaching staff US 20; UK 3; Other(s) 12

INFORMATION

Grade levels 13–13
School year August–May
School type coeducational, private non-profit, proprietary
Year founded 2001
Governed by appointed ABP Board of Governors
Sponsored by Qatar Foundation
Regional organizations ECIS, NESA
Enrollment Grade 13 180; Total 180
Nationalities of student body Qatari 145; Other(s) 35

Tuition/fee currency Qatari Rial
Tuition range 50,000–60,000
One time fees Registration 2,300
Boarding program grades 13–13
Boarding program length 7-day **Boys** 20 **Girls** 15
Graduates attending college 85%
Graduates have attended Weill Cornell Medical School in Qatar, Carnegie-Mellon U in Qatar, Texas A&M U in Qatar, Virginia Commonwealth U in Qatar, Georgetown School Foreign Service

EDUCATIONAL PROGRAM

Curriculum US
Average class size Secondary 15
Language(s) of instruction English

Staff specialists computer, counselor, ESL, librarian
Examinations ACT, SAT, TOEFL

CAMPUS FACILITIES

Location Urban
Campus 300 hectares, 1 building, 20 classrooms, 6 computer labs, 200 instructional computers, 7,000 library volumes, 2 auditoriums,

1 cafeteria, 1 gymnasium, 1 infirmary, 3 playing fields, 4 science labs, 2 pools, 8 tennis courts, air conditioning

AMERICAN SCHOOL OF DOHA

Phone	974 442 1377
Fax	974 442 0885
Email	info@asd.edu.qa
Website	www.asd.edu.qa
Address	PO Box 22090, E Ring Road, Al Waab/South Al Soudan District, Doha, Qatar
Mailing address	American School of Doha, PO Box 22090, Doha, Qatar

STAFF

Director Edwin V. Ladd
High School Principal Michael Shahen
Elementary Principal Donald LeBlanc
Middle School Principal Brad Latzke
Curriculum Coordinator Gail Seay
Elementary Associate Principal Lana Al Aghbar

Business Manager Muna Kelly
Coordinator of Technology David Beaty
Head of MS/HS Library Kathy Patterson
Teaching staff Full time 149; Part time 2; Total 151
Nationalities of teaching staff US 83; UK 5;
Other(s) (Canadian, South African) 63

INFORMATION

Grade levels PreK–12
School year August–June
School type coeducational, day, private non-profit
Year founded 1988
Governed by appointed and elected Board of
Directors
Accredited by New England
Regional organizations NESA
Enrollment PreK 90; Elementary K–5 697;
Middle School 6–8 327;
High School 9–12 371; Total 1,485

Nationalities of student body US 682; UK 16;
Qatari 118; Other(s) (Canadian, Dutch) 669
Tuition/fee currency US Dollar
Tuition range 5,300–12,474
Annual fees Busing 1,233; Capital 3,500
One time fees Registration 1,000
Graduates attending college 98%
Graduates have attended Johns Hopkins U,
Stanford U, Duke U, Carnegie Mellon U,
Texas A&M U

EDUCATIONAL PROGRAM

Curriculum US, AP
Average class size Elementary 15–20;
Secondary 22
Language(s) of instruction English
Language(s) taught Arabic, French, Spanish
Staff specialists computer, counselor, ESL,
librarian, math resource, nurse, reading resource
Special curricular programs art, instrumental
music, vocal music, computer/technology,
physical education

Extra curricular programs computers, community
service, drama, environmental conservation,
excursions/expeditions, newspaper, yearbook
Sports baseball, basketball, cross-country, gymnastics, soccer, swimming, tennis, track and
field, volleyball
Clubs Boy and Girl Scouts, chamber orchestra,
soccer league, baseball, Booster Club,
Tae Kwon Do, Doha Debates
Examinations ACT, AP, Iowa, PSAT, SAT, SAT II, TOEFL

CAMPUS FACILITIES

Location Suburban
Campus 26 hectares, 23 buildings, 128 classrooms,
4 computer labs, 420 instructional computers,
27,000 library volumes, 1 auditorium, 2 cafeterias,

2 covered play areas, 2 gymnasiums,
2 infirmaries, 4 playing fields, 8 science labs,
2 pools, 2 tennis courts, air conditioning

INTERNATIONAL SCHOOL OF CHOUEIFAT

Phone	974 4933110
Fax	974 4835874
Email	iscdoha@sabis.net
Website	www.iscdoha-sabis.net
Address	West Bay Area No. 66, Al Onaizah Street No. 825, Doha, 22085, Qatar

STAFF

Regional Director Ramzi Germanos, Ph.D.
Director Joseph Salemeh
Head of Infants Department Fiona Fraser
Head of Primary Department Louise Salemeh
Finance Manager Oussama Loubani

IT Manager Shinu Varughese
Head of Library Mona Hamza
Teaching staff Full time 58; Total 58
Nationalities of teaching staff UK 7; Other(s) (Lebanese, Jordanian) 51

INFORMATION

Grade levels PreK–13
School year September–June
School type coeducational, day, proprietary
Year founded 1886
Sponsored by SABIS School Network
Enrollment PreK 61; Elementary K–5 867;
Middle School 6–8 192; High School 9–12 112;
Total 1,232

Nationalities of student body US 105; UK 19;
Qatari 284; Other(s) (Jordanian, Egyptian) 824
Tuition/fee currency Qatari Rial
Tuition range 11,400–24,000
Annual fees Busing 3,000; Books 1,000
One time fees Registration 1,000
Graduates attending college 100%
Graduates have attended Cornell U, Carnegie
Mellon U, Texas A&M U, Georgetown U,
American U of Beirut

EDUCATIONAL PROGRAM

Curriculum US, UK, Intl, AP, IGCSE, GenCSE
Average class size Elementary 32; Secondary 36
Language(s) of instruction English
Language(s) taught French, Arabic
Staff specialists computer, nurse, reading resource
Special curricular programs art, instrumental
music, physical education

Extra curricular programs community service,
dance, excursions/expeditions, yearbook,
ballet, gymnastics, Tae Kwan Do
Sports basketball, gymnastics, hockey, soccer,
swimming, track and field, volleyball
Examinations A-level GCE, AP, GCSE, IGCSE, SAT,
SAT II, TOEFL

CAMPUS FACILITIES

Location Suburban
Campus 5 hectares, 4 buildings, 50 classrooms,
1 computer lab, 20 instructional computers,
1 auditorium, 1 cafeteria, 4 covered play areas,

1 gymnasium, 1 infirmary, 4 playing fields,
3 science labs, 2 pools, 2 tennis courts,
air conditioning

QATAR ACADEMY

Phone	974 482 6666
Fax	974 480 2769
Email	qataracademy@qf.org.qa
Website	www.qataracademy.edu.qa
Address	PO Box 1129, Al Luqta Street, Doha, Qatar

STAFF

Director Gregory A. Hedger, Ed.D.
Head of Senior School Michael Hitchman
Head of Primary School Sandy Sheppard
Assistant Head of Senior School Ronald Smith
Assistant Head of Primary School Kirsten Holland
Curriculum Coordinator Diana Knox-Wolfe

Administrative Coordinator Reem Abu Harb
IT Coordinator Julie Lindsay
Teaching staff Full time 169; Part time 4; Total 173
Nationalities of teaching staff US 26; UK 29;
Qatari 5; Other(s) (Canadian, New Zealander) 113

INFORMATION

Grade levels PreK–12
School year September–June
School type coeducational, day, private non-profit
Year founded 1996
Governed by appointed Board of Governors
Sponsored by Qatar Foundation for Education,
Science and Community Development
Accredited by CIS, New England
Regional organizations ECIS, NESA
Enrollment PreK 180; Elementary K–5 650;
Middle School 6–8 298; High School 9–12 236;
Total 1,364

Nationalities of student body US 151; UK 48;
Qatari 621; Other(s) (Canadian, Jordanian) 544
Tuition/fee currency Qatari Rial
Tuition range 13,004–33,793
One time fees Registration 2,000; Testing 250
Graduates attending college 99%
Graduates have attended Georgetown U, Texas
A&M U, American U of Beirut, McGill U,
London School of Economics

EDUCATIONAL PROGRAM

Curriculum Intl, IB Diploma, IBPYP, IBMYP
Average class size Elementary 15–18;
Secondary 16–22
Language(s) of instruction English
Language(s) taught Arabic, French, Spanish
Staff specialists computer, counselor, ESL,
librarian, nurse, reading resource
Special curricular programs art, computer/
technology, physical education, music, drama

Extra curricular programs community service,
drama, environmental conservation,
excursions/expeditions, yearbook, student
council, Model UN, art, guitar, beginners band,
choir, ice hockey
Sports badminton, basketball, rugby, soccer,
swimming, track and field, volleyball, netball,
table tennis
Examinations IB, PSAT, SAT, ACER

CAMPUS FACILITIES

Location Suburban
Campus 300 hectares, 2 buildings, 97 classrooms,
8 computer labs, 690 instructional computers,
58,000 library volumes, 1 auditorium,

1 cafeteria, 3 covered play areas, 6 gymnasiums,
2 infirmaries, 5 playing fields, 12 science labs,
2 pools, 2 tennis courts, air conditioning

ROMANIA

ROMANIA

Area:	237,500 sq km
Population:	22,276,056
Capital:	Bucharest
Currency:	"New" Leu (RON)
Languages:	Romanian

AMERICAN INTERNATIONAL SCHOOL OF BUCHAREST

Phone	40 21 204 4300
Fax	40 21 204 4306
Email	office@aisb.ro
Website	www.aisb.ro
Address	Sos. Pipera-Tunari 196, Comuna Voluntari-Pipera, Jud. Ilfov, 077190, Romania

STAFF

Director Arnold B. Bieber, Ed.D.
Elementary Principal Tamara Shreve
Secondary Principal Brian Roach
Admission and Advancement Director Lynn Wells
Elementary School Vice Principal Jimena Zalba
Secondary School Vice Principal Lorne Bird

Director of Finance and Operations
William Scarborough
IT Director Johnson Jacob
Head Librarian John Cecil
Teaching staff Full time 84; Part time 9; Total 93
Nationalities of teaching staff US 35; UK 12;
Romanian 26; Other(s) (Canadian, Australian) 20

INFORMATION

Grade levels PreK–12
School year August–June
School type coeducational, day, private non-profit
Year founded 1962
Governed by appointed Ten Member Board of
Directors
Accredited by CIS, New England
Regional organizations CEESA, ECIS
Enrollment PreK 58; Elementary K–5 239;
Middle School 6–8 139; High School 9–12 179;
Total 615

Nationalities of student body US 100; UK 34;
Romanian 132; Other(s) (Israeli, Dutch) 349
Tuition/fee currency Euro
Tuition range 7,000–18,150
Annual fees Capital Levy 3,000
One time fees Registration 800
Graduates attending college 100%
Graduates have attended Carleton Col, Vassar
Col, Wesleyan U, U of Pennylvania, New York U

EDUCATIONAL PROGRAM

Curriculum US, Intl, IB Diploma, IBPYP, IBMYP
Average class size Elementary 18; Secondary 18
Language(s) of instruction English
Language(s) taught French, Spanish, Romanian
Staff specialists computer, counselor, ESL,
learning disabilities, librarian, physician
Special curricular programs art, instrumental
music, vocal music, computer/technology,
physical education

Extra curricular programs community service,
dance, drama, excursions/expeditions,
yearbook
Sports basketball, cross-country, football,
martial arts, soccer, softball, swimming, tennis,
volleyball
Examinations IB, PSAT, SAT, SAT II, ISA

CAMPUS FACILITIES

Location Suburban
Campus 10 hectares, 3 buildings, 50 classrooms,
4 computer labs, 180 instructional computers,
24,000 library volumes, 1 auditorium,

1 cafeteria, 2 gymnasiums, 1 infirmary,
3 playing fields, 4 science labs, 4 tennis courts,
air conditioning

RUSSIA

RUSSIA

Area:	17,075,200 sq km
Population:	141,377,752
Capital:	Moscow
Currency:	Russian Ruble (RUR)
Languages:	Russian

ANGLO-AMERICAN SCHOOL OF MOSCOW

Phone	7 495 231 4488
Fax	7 495 231 4475
Email	director@aas.ru
Website	www.aas.ru
Address	Beregovaya 1, Moscow, 125367, Russia
Mailing address	c/o American Embassy, Box M 00140, Helsinki, Finland

STAFF

Director Drew N. Alexander
High School Principal Ronald Gleason
Middle School Principal Christophe Henry
Elementary School Principal Tony Simone
St. Petersburg Campus Principal Jill Wheatley

Director of Technology Ilya Pekshev
Librarian Ann Symons
Teaching staff Full time 131; Part time 5; Total 136
Nationalities of teaching staff US 66; UK 20;
Russian 11; Other(s) (Canadian, French) 39

INFORMATION

Grade levels PreK–12
School year August–June
School type coeducational, day, private non-profit
Year founded 1949
Governed by appointed School Board
Sponsored by US, UK and Canadian Embassies in
Moscow
Accredited by CIS, New England
Regional organizations CEESA, ECIS
Enrollment PreK 64; Elementary K–5 576;
Middle School 6–8 270;
High School 9–12 358; Total 1,268

Nationalities of student body US 469; UK 139;
Russian 115; Other(s) (Korean, Canadian) 545
Tuition/fee currency US Dollar
Tuition range 12,340–19,100
Annual fees Capital Levy 6,000;
ESL (Gr.1–10) 2,000
One time fees Registration 500
Graduates attending college 100%
Graduates have attended Cornell U, Queen's U,
London School of Economics,
U of Southern California, Duke U

EDUCATIONAL PROGRAM

Curriculum US, UK, Intl, IB Diploma, IBPYP
Average class size Elementary 18; Secondary 18
Language(s) of instruction English
Language(s) taught French, Russian, Spanish
Staff specialists computer, counselor, ESL,
learning disabilities, librarian, nurse,
psychologist, reading resource, speech/hearing
Special curricular programs art, instrumental
music, vocal music, computer/technology,
physical education, performing arts

Extra curricular programs community service,
dance, drama, environmental conservation,
excursions/expeditions, yearbook
Sports basketball, cross-country, skiing, soccer,
softball, swimming, tennis, volleyball
Clubs cooking, fitness, business, crafts, board
games, active games, painting, Gymnastics Fun,
Reading Fun, ballet
Examinations IB, PSAT, SAT, ERB

CAMPUS FACILITIES

Location Urban
Campus 6 hectares, 1 building, 75 classrooms,
4 computer labs, 360 instructional computers,
30,000 library volumes, 1 auditorium,

2 cafeterias, 3 gymnasiums, 1 infirmary,
3 playing fields, 8 science labs, 1 pool, 3 tennis
courts, air conditioning

ANGLO-AMERICAN SCHOOL OF ST. PETERSBURG

Phone	7 812 320 8925
Fax	7 812 320 8926
Email	aas-sp@aas.ru
Address	5 Penkovaya, St. Petersburg, 197046, Russia
Mailing address	US Consulate, Box L, 00140 Helsinki, Finland

STAFF

Director Drew Alexander
Principal Jill Wheatley

Director of Finance and Operations Chuck Tennes
IT Consultant Alexey Sheglov

INFORMATION

Grade levels K–12
School year August–June
School type coeducational, day
Year founded 1993
Governed by appointed Anglo-American School of Moscow School Board
Regional organizations CEESA, ECIS
Enrollment Elementary K–5 75; Middle School 6–8 13; High School 9–12 23; Total 111

Nationalities of student body US 7; UK 7; Other(s) (Canadian, Swede) 97
Tuition/fee currency US Dollar
Tuition range 16,700–17,500
Annual fees Busing 2,000
One time fees Registration 400
Graduates attending college 100%
Graduates have attended New York U, Webster U, State U of St. Petersburg, Brown U, U of Virginia

EDUCATIONAL PROGRAM

Curriculum US, UK
Average class size Elementary 18; Secondary 14
Language(s) of instruction English
Language(s) taught French, Russian
Staff specialists computer, ESL
Special curricular programs art, computer/technology, physical education

Extra curricular programs computers, community service, drama, excursions/expeditions, yearbook
Sports basketball, cross-country, soccer
Clubs Russian, recreation activities, crafts, music, drama, board games, magic
Examinations SAT, ERB

CAMPUS FACILITIES

Location Urban
Campus 1 hectare, 1 building, 9 classrooms, 30 instructional computers,

5,200 library volumes, 1 gymnasium, 1 playing field, 1 science lab

Data from 2006/07 school year.

SAUDI ARABIA

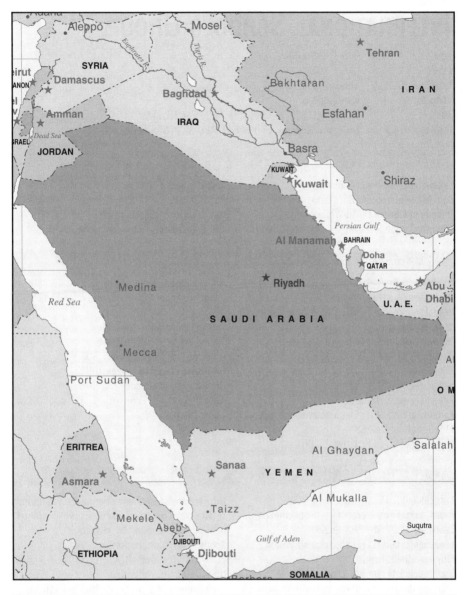

SAUDI ARABIA

Area:	2,149,690 sq km
Population:	27,601,038
Capital:	Riyadh
Currency:	Saudi Riyal (SAR)
Languages:	Arabic

INTERNATIONAL SCHOOLS GROUP

Phone	966 3 330 0555
Fax	966 3 330 3270
Email	nhudson@isgdh.org
Website	www.isgdh.org
Address	P.O. Box 31677, Al-Khobar, 31952, Saudi Arabia
Mailing address	Dhahran Academy, Unit 66804, APO AE 09858-6804, USA

STAFF

Superintendent Norma Hudson
Deputy Superintendent Bill Stapp
Director of Finance David Whitaker
Librarian Vargie Johnson

Teaching staff Full time 217; Part time 35; Total 252
Nationalities of teaching staff US 51; UK 37; Saudi 1; Other(s) (Indian, Canadian) 163

INFORMATION

Grade levels PreK–12
School year August–June
School type coeducational, day, private non-profit
Year founded 1962
Governed by elected Board of Trustees
Sponsored by Saudi Arabian Ministry of Education
Accredited by Middle States
Regional organizations ECIS, NESA
Enrollment PreK 291; Elementary K–5 1,181; Middle School 6–8 688; High School 9–12 801; Total 2,961

Nationalities of student body US 230; UK 210; Saudi 30; Other(s) (Lebanese, Canadian) 2,491
Tuition/fee currency Saudi Riyal
Tuition range 18,620–47,680
One time fees Registration 7,500
Graduates attending college 100%
Graduates have attended Stanford U, New York U, U of Pennsylvania, Dartmouth Col, Columbia U

EDUCATIONAL PROGRAM

Curriculum US, UK, AP, IGCSE, GenCSE
Average class size Elementary 18; Secondary 22
Language(s) of instruction English
Language(s) taught French, Spanish, Arabic, Filipino, Hindi, Urdu
Staff specialists computer, counselor, ESL, learning disabilities, librarian, math resource, nurse, reading resource
Special curricular programs art, instrumental music, vocal music, computer/technology, physical education, Arab Culture

Extra curricular programs computers, community service, dance, drama, excursions/expeditions, newspaper, photography, yearbook
Sports badminton, basketball, cricket, cross-country, football, soccer, softball, tennis, track and field, volleyball
Examinations ACT, AP, GCSE, IGCSE, PSAT, SAT, SAT II, Stanford

CAMPUS FACILITIES

Location Rural
Campus 20 hectares, 16 buildings, 60 classrooms, 7 computer labs, 300 instructional computers, 100,000 library volumes, 1 auditorium, 1 cafeteria, 6 covered play areas, 2 gymnasiums, 1 infirmary, 2 playing fields, 4 science labs, air conditioning

SAUDI ARAMCO SCHOOLS

Phone	966 3 877 1676
Fax	966 3 872 0783
Email	timothy.hansen@aramco.com
Address	c/o Saudi Aramco, Box 73, Dhahran, 31311, Saudi Arabia

STAFF

Superintendent of Schools Timothy T. Hansen, Ph.D.
Associate Superintendent John A. Carey
Curriculum Coordinator Ellen G. Alquist
Curriculum Coordinator Brian R. Bahr
Director of Pupil Personnel/Special Services
Nathan H. Taylor, Ph.D.

Business Office Manager David M. Jackson
Technology Coordinator Benjamin L. Jacobs
Teaching staff Full time 167; Part time 42;
Total 209
Nationalities of teaching staff US 183; Saudi 4;
Other(s) (Canadian) 22

INFORMATION

Grade levels K–9
School year September–June
School type company-sponsored, day
Year founded 1945
Governed by Saudi Arabian Oil Company
Sponsored by Saudi Arabian Oil Company
Accredited by Middle States

Regional organizations NESA
Enrollment Elementary K–5 828;
Middle School 6–8 468; High School 9–12
146; Total 1,442
Nationalities of student body US 745; Saudi 41;
Other(s) (Canadian, Jordanian) 656
Tuition/fee currency US Dollar

EDUCATIONAL PROGRAM

Curriculum US
Average class size Elementary 14; Secondary 14
Language(s) of instruction English
Language(s) taught Spanish, French, Arabic
Staff specialists computer, counselor, ESL,
learning disabilities, librarian, nurse,
psychologist, reading resource, speech/hearing
Special curricular programs art, instrumental
music, vocal music, computer/technology,
physical education

Extra curricular programs computers, drama,
excursions/expeditions, newspaper, yearbook
Sports basketball, cross-country, golf,
gymnastics, track and field, volleyball,
community programs for ballet, baseball,
soccer, softball, swimming, tennis
Clubs Student Council, Knowledge Bowl, jazz
band, Math Olympiads, climbing, photography,
media
Examinations Iowa, SSAT, ERB WrAP

CAMPUS FACILITIES

Location Rural
Campus 10 buildings, 133 classrooms,
20 computer labs, 500 instructional computers,
105,000 library volumes, 16 covered play

areas, 6 gymnasiums, 5 playing fields,
10 science labs, 5 pools, 50 tennis courts,
air conditioning

AMERICAN INTERNATIONAL SCHOOL OF JEDDAH

Phone	966 2 662 0051
Fax	966 2 691 2402
Email	aisj@aisjed.net
Website	www.aisjed.net
Address	Abdullah ibn Saydan Street, 41, Al-Zahra District 4, PO Box 127328, Jeddah, 21352, Saudi Arabia
Mailing address	PO Box 127328, Jeddah, Saudi Arabia 21352

STAFF

Director Paul S Pescatore
Curriculum Coordinator Margaret Pescatore
Elementary Principal Susan Clark
High School Principal Daniel Gordon

Middle School Principal Paul Sibley
IT Coordinator Chandra Kumar Sinnappah
Librarian Laura Gordon

INFORMATION

Grade levels N–12
School year August–June
School type coeducational, day, private non-profit
Year founded 1952
Governed by elected Board of Trustees
Accredited by Middle States
Regional organizations ECIS, NESA
Enrollment Nursery 14; PreK 54;
Elementary K–5 193; Middle School 6–8 141;
High School 9–12 240; Total 642

Nationalities of student body US 161; UK 2;
Saudi 78; Other(s) (Egyptian, Lebanese) 401
Tuition/fee currency Saudi Riyal
Tuition range 14,000–36,000
Annual fees ESL K–10 3,000; Resource 3,000
One time fees Registration 3,500; Testing 500
Graduates attending college 94%
Graduates have attended U of Melbourne,
Concordia U, U of Toronto, Sharjah U,
American U of Beirut

EDUCATIONAL PROGRAM

Curriculum US, AP
Average class size Elementary 18; Secondary 24
Language(s) of instruction English
Language(s) taught French, Spanish, Arabic
Staff specialists computer, counselor, ESL,
learning disabilities, librarian, math resource,
nurse, psychologist, reading resource
Special curricular programs art, instrumental
music, vocal music, computer/technology,
physical education, Islamic studies, industrial arts

Extra curricular programs computers, community
service, drama, excursions/expeditions,
newspaper, photography, yearbook
Sports badminton, baseball, basketball, tennis,
volleyball
Clubs National Junior Honor Society, National
Honor Society, student council, Knowledge
Bowl, Model UN
Examinations ACT, AP, PSAT, SAT, SAT II,
Stanford, TOEFL, PLAN

CAMPUS FACILITIES

Location Urban
Campus 9 buildings, 85 classrooms, 5 computer
labs, 300 instructional computers,

12,000 library volumes, 2 auditoriums, 1 cafeteria,
3 covered play areas, 2 gymnasiums, 1 infirmary,
3 playing fields, 2 science labs, air conditioning

Data from 2006/07 school year.

THE BRITISH INTERNATIONAL SCHOOL OF JEDDAH (THE CONTINENTAL SCHOOL)

Phone	966 2 699 0019
Fax	966 2 699 1943
Email	conti@conti.sch.sa
Website	www.continentalschool.com
Address	West of Al Amir Sultan St., Mohammadiyah District, Al Basateen Development, North Jeddah and South Obhur, Jeddah, Makkah Region, 21442, Saudi Arabia
Mailing address	PO Box 6453, Jeddah 21442, Saudi Arabia

STAFF

Director Bruce Gamwell
Head Teacher of Lower School Paul Guy-Byrne
Head Teacher of Middle School Neil Hugo
Head Teacher of Upper School Helen Mack
Business Manager Dammes Ledeboer

IT Manager Jacques Gouws
Upper School Librarian Avan Kazzaz
Teaching staff Full time 131; Part time 8; Total 139
Nationalities of teaching staff US 4; UK 68; Saudi 4; Other(s) (Lebanese, Canadian) 63

INFORMATION

Grade levels N–13
School year September–June
School type coeducational, day, private non-profit
Year founded 1977
Governed by elected Board of Trustees
Accredited by CIS, New England
Enrollment Nursery 35; PreK 141; Elementary K–5 710; Middle School 6–8 310; High School 9–12 245; Grade 13 70; Total 1,511

Nationalities of student body US 122; UK 144; Saudi 236; Other(s) (Egyptian, Lebanese) 1,009
Tuition/fee currency Saudi Riyal
Tuition range 14,700–53,400
One time fees Registration 650; Entrance 4,900
Graduates attending college 99%
Graduates have attended London School of Economics, Pennsylvania State U, McGill U, King's Col, American U of Beirut

EDUCATIONAL PROGRAM

Curriculum UK, Intl, IB Diploma, IGCSE
Average class size Elementary 21; Secondary 21
Language(s) of instruction English, Arabic
Language(s) taught French, Spanish
Staff specialists computer, counselor, ESL, learning disabilities, librarian, nurse
Special curricular programs art, instrumental music, vocal music, physical education

Extra curricular programs community service, drama, yearbook
Sports badminton, basketball, cricket, gymnastics, hockey, soccer, swimming, tennis, track and field, volleyball
Examinations GCSE, IB, IGCSE

CAMPUS FACILITIES

Location Suburban
Campus 3 hectares, 10 buildings, 100 classrooms, 5 computer labs, 228 instructional computers, 35,500 library volumes, 1 auditorium,

1 cafeteria, 3 covered play areas, 2 gymnasiums, 1 infirmary, 1 playing field, 8 science labs, 3 pools, 3 tennis courts, air conditioning

ADVANCED LEARNING SCHOOLS

Phone	0096612070926
Fax	009614700754
Email	admin@alsschools.com
Website	www.als-schools.net
Address	PO Box 221985, Riyadh, 11311, Saudi Arabia

STAFF

Superintendent Iain Stirling
Girls' Principal Lina Lews, Ph.D.
Boys' Principal Neil Tomalin
Human Resources Manager Elham Barghouty
Marketing and Administration Manager Anoud Anani
Facilities Manager Shaji Mathew

Business Manager Essam El-Soubky
ICT Systems Manager Imran Mahmood
Librarian Nenita Hermann
Teaching staff Full time 52; Total 52
Nationalities of teaching staff US 11; UK 6; Other(s) (Jordanian, Lebanese) 35

INFORMATION

Grade levels K–11
School year September–June
School type boys only, coeducational, day, girls only, private non-profit
Year founded 2005
Governed by appointed Board of Trustees
Regional organizations NESA

Enrollment Elementary K–5 173; Middle School 6–8 79; High School 9–12 103; Total 355
Nationalities of student body US 2; UK 1; Saudi 345; Other(s) (Canadian, Qatari) 7
Tuition/fee currency Saudi Riyal
Tuition 55,000
Annual fees Registration 5,000

EDUCATIONAL PROGRAM

Curriculum Intl
Average class size Elementary 16–18; Secondary 16–18
Language(s) of instruction English
Language(s) taught Arabic, French
Staff specialists computer, counselor, ESL, learning disabilities, librarian, physician
Special curricular programs art, instrumental music, vocal music, computer/technology, physical education

Extra curricular programs computers, community service, dance, excursions/expeditions, newspaper, photography, yearbook
Sports badminton, basketball, football, martial arts, soccer, volleyball
Clubs Model UN, Debating Society, student council
Examinations PSAT, SAT

CAMPUS FACILITIES

Location Suburban
Campus 32 buildings, 48 classrooms, 2 computer labs, 36 instructional computers,

400 library volumes, 2 cafeterias, 2 covered play areas, 2 infirmaries, 3 playing fields, 2 science labs, air conditioning

Data from 2005/06 school year.

AMERICAN INTERNATIONAL SCHOOL–RIYADH

Phone	966 1 491 4270
Fax	966 1 491 7101
Email	superintendent@ais-r.edu.sa
Website	www.aisr.org
Address	PO Box 990, Riyadh, 11421, Saudi Arabia
Mailing address	Unit 61320, APO AE 09803-1320, USA

STAFF

Superintendent Til Fullerton, Ph.D.
High School Principal Daniel Gordon, Ed.D.
Middle School Principal John Higgs, Ed.D.
Elementary School Principal Jan Young
IB Program Coordinator Cristina Pennington
Finance Manager Leila Giansiracusa

Head of Technology Michael Pelletier
Head of K–12 Library/Media Patricia McNair
Teaching staff Full time 120; Total 120
Nationalities of teaching staff US 95; UK 5; Saudi 5; Other(s) (Canadian) 15

INFORMATION

Grade levels PreK–12
School year August–June
School type coeducational, day, private non-profit
Year founded 1963
Governed by elected Board of Trustees
Accredited by CIS, New England
Regional organizations ECIS, NESA
Enrollment PreK 30; Elementary K–5 304; Middle School 6–8 197; High School 9–12 285; Total 816

Nationalities of student body US 500; UK 6; Saudi 50; Other(s) (Pakistani, Lebanese) 260
Tuition/fee currency Saudi Riyal
Tuition range 27,700–1,665
One time fees Registration 7,000
Graduates attending college 95%
Graduates have attended American U of Beirut, Brown U, Harvard U, Stanford U, U of Michigan in Ann Arbor

(Continued)

AMERICAN INTERNATIONAL SCHOOL–RIYADH (Continued)

EDUCATIONAL PROGRAM

Curriculum US, IB Diploma
Average class size Elementary 20; Secondary 18
Language(s) of instruction English
Language(s) taught French, Spanish, Arabic
Staff specialists computer, counselor, ESL, librarian, nurse
Special curricular programs art, instrumental music, computer/technology, physical education

Extra curricular programs community service, drama, excursions/expeditions, literary magazine, yearbook
Sports badminton, baseball, basketball, cricket, football, gymnastics, soccer, softball, tennis, track and field, volleyball
Examinations IB, PSAT, SAT, SAT II, Stanford

CAMPUS FACILITIES

Location Suburban
Campus 10 hectares, 10 buildings, 131 classrooms, 9 computer labs, 220 instructional computers, 50,000 library volumes, 2 auditoriums, 2 cafeterias, 4 covered play areas, 1 gymnasium, 1 infirmary, 6 playing fields, 6 science labs, 2 tennis courts, air conditioning

SENEGAL

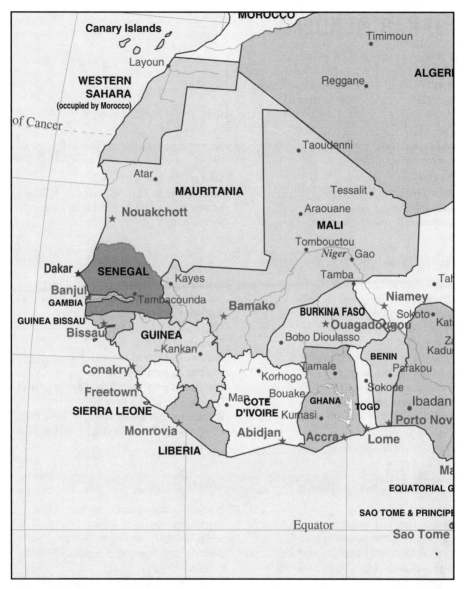

SENEGAL

Area:	196,190 sq km
Population:	12,521,851
Capital:	Dakar
Currency:	Communaute Financiere Africaine Franc (XOF)
Languages:	French

DAKAR ACADEMY

Phone	221 832 0682
Fax	221 832 1721
Email	Office@Dakar-Academy.org
Website	www.dakar-academy.org
Address	BP 3189, 69 Rue des Peres Maristes, Hann II, Dakar, Senegal

STAFF

Director Ann M. Marklund, Ed.D.
Assistant Director Dan Mulay
Counselor Deborah Aisenbrey
Curriculum Coordinator Barb Van Straten

Business Manager Murray Sitte
Teaching staff Full time 45; Part time 5; Total 50
Nationalities of teaching staff US 45; UK 2;
Singaporean 3

INFORMATION

Grade levels K–12
School year August–June
School type boarding, coeducational,
church-affiliated, day
Year founded 1961
Governed by appointed Owning Missions
Accredited by Middle States
Regional organizations AISA
Enrollment Elementary K–5 70;
Middle School 6–8 70; High School 9–12 120;
Total 260

Nationalities of student body US 144; UK 1;
Senegalese 3; Other(s) (Canadian, Korean) 112
Tuition/fee currency US Dollar
Tuition range 2,420–8,800
Annual fees Registration 300
One time fees Capital Levy 3,000
Boarding program grades 6–12
Boarding program length 7-day **Boys** 29 **Girls** 18
Graduates attending college 96%
Graduates have attended Carson-Newman Col,
Houghton Col, Col of the Ozarks, Wheaton Col,
Covenant Col

EDUCATIONAL PROGRAM

Curriculum US, AP, ACSI
Average class size Elementary 11; Secondary 23
Language(s) of instruction English
Language(s) taught French, Spanish
Staff specialists computer, counselor, ESL,
learning disabilities, librarian
Special curricular programs art, vocal music,
physical education

Extra curricular programs community service,
drama, newspaper, yearbook
Sports basketball, soccer, softball, volleyball
Clubs National Honor Society, Association of
Christian Athletes
Examinations ACT, AP, PSAT, SAT, SAT II,
Stanford

CAMPUS FACILITIES

Location Urban
Campus 2 hectares, 8 buildings, 25 classrooms,
2 computer labs, 25 instructional computers,

30,000 library volumes, 1 auditorium,
2 playing fields, 1 science lab, 1 tennis court,
air conditioning

INTERNATIONAL SCHOOL OF DAKAR

Phone	(221) 825 0871 or 860 2332
Fax	(221) 825 5030
Email	admin_isd@orange.sn
Website	www.isd.sn
Address	Route de Ouakam, á coté de l'ENEA, BP 5136-Fann, Dakar, Senegal
Mailing address	International School of Dakar, c/o Admin. Officer, Department of State, 2130 Dakar Place, Washington, DC 20521-2130

STAFF

Director Wayne Rutherford
Principal Eric Klauda
High School Counselor Olatokunbo Fashoyin
Finance Manager Adams Ndoye
Technology Coordinator Jonathan Smith

Librarian Roxann Siegel
Teaching staff Full time 28; Part time 4; Total 32
Nationalities of teaching staff US 17;
Senegalese 1; Other(s) (French, Canadian) 14

INFORMATION

Grade levels PreK–12
School year August–June
School type coeducational, day, private non-profit
Year founded 1983
Governed by elected Seven Member Board
Accredited by Middle States
Regional organizations AISA
Enrollment PreK 20; Elementary K–5 124;
Middle School 6–8 59; High School 9–12 51;
Total 254

Nationalities of student body US 65; UK 9;
Senegalese 6; Other(s) (Dutch, French) 174
Tuition/fee currency US Dollar
Tuition range 3,560–15,310
Annual fees Registration 100; Technology 150;
Special Education 1,415; Re-registration 35
One time fees Capital Levy 3,500
Graduates attending college 100%
Graduates have attended McGill U,
Col of William and Mary, U of North Carolina,
U of Pennsylvania, Webster U

EDUCATIONAL PROGRAM

Curriculum US, AP
Average class size Elementary 17; Secondary 11
Language(s) of instruction English
Language(s) taught French, Spanish
Staff specialists computer, counselor, ESL,
learning disabilities, librarian, nurse
Special curricular programs art, vocal music,
computer/technology, physical education

Extra curricular programs computers, community
service, dance, drama, newspaper, yearbook
Sports badminton, basketball, martial arts,
rugby, soccer, softball, swimming, track and
field, volleyball, floorball
Examinations ACT, AP, Iowa, PSAT, SAT, SAT II

CAMPUS FACILITIES

Location Suburban
Campus 2 hectares, 7 buildings, 25 classrooms,
2 computer labs, 67 instructional computers,
13,700 library volumes, 1 auditorium,

1 gymnasium, 1 infirmary, 1 playing field,
2 science labs, 1 pool, 2 tennis courts,
air conditioning

SERBIA

SERBIA

Area:	88,361 sq km
Population:	10,150,265
Capital:	Belgrade
Currency:	Serbian Dinar (RSD)
Languages:	Serbian

INTERNATIONAL SCHOOL OF BELGRADE

Phone	381 11 206 9999
Fax	381 11 206 9940
Email	isb@isb.co.yu
Website	www.isb.co.yu
Address	Temisvarska 19, Belgrade, 11040, Serbia

STAFF

Director Eric W. Sands, Ph.D.
Lower School Principal and Curriculum Coordinator Wendy McArthur
High School and Middle School Principal Clinton Calzini
Middle School Vice Principal Eric Lyman
High School and Middle School Counselor Aleka Noviski

Lower School Counselor Jill Maloney
Business Manager Snezana Hasanovic
IT Coordinator Melissa Enderle
Librarian Kathryn Calzini
Teaching staff Full time 55; Part time 6; Total 61
Nationalities of teaching staff US 26; UK 4; Serb 23; Other(s) (Canadian, Australian) 8

INFORMATION

Grade levels PreK–12
School year September–June
School type coeducational, day, private non-profit
Year founded 1948
Governed by appointed and elected Board of Directors
Accredited by CIS, New England
Regional organizations CEESA, ECIS

Enrollment PreK 46; Elementary K–5 178; Middle School 6–8 95; High School 9–12 81; Total 400
Nationalities of student body US 80; UK 32; Serb 112; Other(s) (Hungarian, French) 176
Tuition/fee currency US Dollar
Tuition range 7,500–17,500
Annual fees Capital Levy 1,700; Busing 2,000
Graduates attending college 100%
Graduates have attended Union U, U of San Diego

EDUCATIONAL PROGRAM

Curriculum US, IB Diploma, IBPYP, IBMYP
Average class size Elementary 13; Secondary 12
Language(s) of instruction English
Language(s) taught French, Serbian, Spanish
Staff specialists computer, counselor, ESL, librarian, physician
Special curricular programs art, instrumental music, vocal music, computer/technology, physical education

Extra curricular programs computers, community service, dance, drama, excursions/expeditions, literary magazine, yearbook, instrumental music
Sports baseball, basketball, gymnastics, soccer, track and field, volleyball
Examinations PSAT, SAT, SAT II, TOEFL, ISA

CAMPUS FACILITIES

Location Suburban
Campus 5 hectares, 7 buildings, 30 classrooms, 2 computer labs, 80 instructional computers,

12,000 library volumes, 2 gymnasiums, 1 infirmary, 2 playing fields, 2 science labs, 1 tennis court, air conditioning

QSI INTERNATIONAL SCHOOL OF PRISTINA

Phone	381 038 231 333
Fax	381 038 235 102
Email	pristina@qsi.org
Website	www.qsi.org
Address	15 Ismail Qemali Street, Pristina, Kosovo, UNMIK, Serbia
Mailing address	Box 17, Pristina, Kosovo, Serbia

STAFF

Director Melissa R. Newman, Ph.D.
Administrative Assistant Lindita Kadriu
Teaching staff Full time 3; Part time 3; Total 6

Nationalities of teaching staff US 2; UK 1; Albanian 3

INFORMATION

Grade levels PreK–8
School year August–June
School type coeducational, day, private non-profit
Year founded 2003
Governed by appointed Board of Directors
Enrollment PreK 11; Elementary K–5 14; Total 25

Nationalities of student body US 5; UK 3; Albanian 3; Other(s) (German, Italian) 14
Tuition/fee currency US Dollar
Tuition range 5,300–12,500
Annual fees Capital Levy 1,600
One time fees Registration 100

EDUCATIONAL PROGRAM

Curriculum US, Intl
Average class size Elementary 8
Language(s) of instruction English
Staff specialists learning disabilities

Special curricular programs art, instrumental music, vocal music, computer/technology, physical education, intensive English
Extra curricular programs computers, environmental conservation, excursions/ expeditions, yearbook

CAMPUS FACILITIES

Location Urban
Campus 1 building, 5 classrooms,

3 instructional computers, 600 library volumes, 1 covered play area, 1 playing field

SINGAPORE

Area:	692.7 sq km
Population:	4,553,009
Capital:	Singapore
Currency:	Singapore Dollar (SGD)
Languages:	Mandarin

CANADIAN INTERNATIONAL SCHOOL

Phone	65 6467 1732
Fax	65 6467 1729
Email	admissions@cis.edu.sg
Website	www.cis.edu.sg
Address	5 Toh Tuck Road, Singapore, 596679, Singapore

STAFF

Head Principal and CEO Glenn D. Odland
Elementary Principal Sharon Gibson
Elementary Vice Principal Katy Morrison
Middle School Principal Keith Bland
Middle School Vice Principal Rebecca Caverly
Principal Ted Cowan

Accountant Chua Ping
ICT Coordinator Martin Laidlaw
Teacher Librarian Lisa Patton
Teaching staff Full time 140; Part time 3; Total 143
Nationalities of teaching staff US 2; UK 2;
Singaporean 4; Other(s) (Canadian) 135

INFORMATION

Grade levels N–12
School year August–June
School type coeducational, day, proprietary
Year founded 1990
Governed by appointed Board of Directors
Regional organizations ECIS
Enrollment Nursery 45; PreK 153;
Elementary K–5 844; Middle School 6–8 220;
High School 9–12 220; Total 1,482

Nationalities of student body US 145; UK 75;
Singaporean 40; Other(s) (Korean,
Canadian) 1,222
Tuition/fee currency Singapore Dollar
Tuition range 7,444–10,403
Annual fees Building Fund 2,200
One time fees Registration 1,000
Graduates attending college 96%
Graduates have attended U of Toronto,
U of Sydney, Penn State U, Tsing Hua U,
Kwansei-Gakuin U

EDUCATIONAL PROGRAM

Curriculum National, IB Diploma, IBPYP, IBMYP
Average class size Elementary 20; Secondary 15
Language(s) of instruction English
Language(s) taught French, Mandarin
Staff specialists computer, ESL, librarian, nurse
Special curricular programs art, instrumental
music, vocal music, computer/technology,
physical education

Extra curricular programs computers, drama,
environmental conservation, excursions/
expeditions, yearbook
Sports basketball, cross-country, football, golf,
gymnastics, martial arts, soccer, swimming,
tennis, volleyball
Examinations IB

CAMPUS FACILITIES

Location Urban
Campus 10 hectares, 5 buildings, 106
classrooms, 6 computer labs, 400 instructional
computers, 8,000 library volumes,

1 auditorium, 3 cafeterias, 2 covered play
areas, 3 gymnasiums, 3 infirmaries,
2 playing fields, 5 science labs,
air conditioning

INTERNATIONAL COMMUNITY SCHOOL

Phone	65 6776 7435
Fax	65 6776 7436
Email	ftan@ics.edu.sg
Website	www.ics.edu.sg
Address	27A Jubilee Road, Singapore, 128575, Singapore

STAFF

Director Joseph W. Beeson, Ed.D.
Elementary and Middle School Principal Knute Reierson
Admissions Director Florence Tan
High School Principal Matt Eiler
School Counselor Sam Fleischmann

Business/Finance Manager Peter Cowles
IT Director Robert Brosius
Librarian Cynthia Peck
Teaching staff Full time 36; Part time 10; Total 46
Nationalities of teaching staff US 43; Host 1; Other(s) (Canadian, Australian) 2

INFORMATION

Grade levels PreK–12
School year August–June
School type coeducational, day, private non-profit
Year founded 1993
Governed by appointed Board of Directors
Sponsored by Network of International Christian Schools
Accredited by Western
Regional organizations EARCOS
Enrollment PreK 20; Elementary K–5 130; Middle School 6–8 90; High School 9–12 100; Total 340

Nationalities of student body US 170; UK 2; Korean 61; Other(s) (Australian, Chinese) 107
Tuition/fee currency Singapore Dollar
Tuition range 17,000–20,000
Annual fees Registration 1,200
Graduates attending college 100%
Graduates have attended Virginia Military Institute, Purdue U, Massachusetts Institute of Technology, U of Virginia, U of California in Berkeley

EDUCATIONAL PROGRAM

Curriculum US, AP, A Beka Publications, ACSI
Average class size Elementary 12; Secondary 17
Language(s) of instruction English
Language(s) taught Mandarin, Spanish
Staff specialists counselor, ESL, librarian, nurse
Special curricular programs art, physical education

Extra curricular programs computers, community service, dance, newspaper
Sports basketball, soccer, track and field, volleyball
Examinations ACT, SAT, Stanford

CAMPUS FACILITIES

Location Urban
Campus 1 hectare, 3 buildings, 30 classrooms, 1 computer lab, 45 instructional computers,

10,000 library volumes, 1 auditorium, 1 cafeteria, 1 gymnasium, 1 infirmary, 1 playing field, 2 science labs, air conditioning

INTERNATIONAL SCHOOL SINGAPORE

Phone	65 6475 4188
Fax	65 6273 7065
Email	hm@iss.edu.sg
Website	www.iss.edu.sg
Address	21 Preston Road, Singapore, 109355, Singapore

STAFF

Head Teacher Anthony Race
Head of Elementary School George Piacentini
Middle School Coordinator Mel Hughes
Head of High School Mark McCallum
CEO Chan Ching Oi
IT Instructional Leader Les Casey

Librarian Judith McManus
Teaching staff Full time 69; Part time 8; Total 77
Nationalities of teaching staff US 11; UK 16; Singaporean 8; Other(s) (Australian, Canadian) 42

INFORMATION

Grade levels PreK–12
School year August–June
School type coeducational, day, private non-profit, proprietary
Year founded 1981
Governed by appointed Committee of Management
Accredited by Western
Regional organizations EARCOS, ECIS
Enrollment PreK 15; Elementary K–5 243; Middle School 6–8 96; High School 9–12 205; Total 559

Nationalities of student body US 40; UK 60; Singaporean 25; Other(s) (Korean, Japanese) 434
Tuition/fee currency Singapore Dollar
Tuition range 10,000–21,000
Annual fees Registration 1,605
Graduates attending college 97%
Graduates have attended Suffolk U, Michigan State U, State U of New York, Cesar Ritz U, Monash U

EDUCATIONAL PROGRAM

Curriculum Intl, IB Diploma, IBPYP, IBMYP, IGCSE
Average class size Elementary 20; Secondary 16
Language(s) of instruction English
Language(s) taught French, Japanese, Mandarin, Spanish
Staff specialists computer, counselor, ESL, learning disabilities, librarian, nurse
Special curricular programs art, instrumental music, computer/technology, physical education

Extra curricular programs computers, community service, dance, drama, environmental conservation, excursions/expeditions, photography, yearbook
Sports basketball, rugby, soccer, swimming, track and field
Examinations GCSE, IB, IGCSE

CAMPUS FACILITIES

Location Urban
Campus 5 buildings, 60 classrooms, 5 computer labs, 150 instructional computers, 22,000 library volumes, 3 auditoriums, 2 cafeterias, 2 covered play areas, 1 playing field, 5 science labs, air conditioning

Overseas Family School

Phone	65 6738 0211
Fax	65 6733 8825
Email	executive_director@ofs.edu.sg
Website	www.ofs.edu.sg
Address	25F Paterson Road, Singapore, 238515, Singapore

STAFF

Chairman David A. Perry
Kindergarten Principal Rani Suppiah
Elementary School Principal Pat Keenan
Middle School Principal Wayne Holden
High School Principal Sue Bentin

Dean of the College Jeffrey Twitchell-Waas, Ph.D.
Executive Director Irene Chee
Technology Development Consultant James Clark
Library Manager Florence Solomon

INFORMATION

Grade levels PreK–13
School year August–June
School type coeducational, day, proprietary
Year founded 1991
Governed by appointed Executive Board
Accredited by Western

Enrollment PreK 100; Elementary K–5 1,600;
Middle School 6–8 700; High School 9–12 700;
Total 3,100
Tuition/fee currency Singapore Dollar
Tuition range 12,000–25,000
Graduates attending college 98%

EDUCATIONAL PROGRAM

Curriculum Intl, IB Diploma, IBPYP, IBMYP, IGCSE
Average class size Elementary 25; Secondary 20
Language(s) of instruction English
Language(s) taught French, German, Japanese,
Mandarin, Spanish
Staff specialists computer, ESL, math resource,
nurse, physician, reading resource
Special curricular programs art, instrumental
music, vocal music, computer/technology,
physical education

Extra curricular programs computers, community
service, dance, drama, environmental
conservation, excursions/expeditions, literary
magazine, newspaper, photography, yearbook
Sports basketball, cricket, cross-country, gymnastics, martial arts, rugby, soccer, swimming,
tennis, track and field, volleyball
Examinations GCSE, IB, IGCSE, SAT, TOEFL

CAMPUS FACILITIES

Location Urban
Campus 7 hectares, 12 buildings, 170 classrooms,
8 computer labs, 1200 instructional computers,
82,000 library volumes, 1 auditorium,

1 cafeteria, 4 covered play areas, 1 gymnasium,
1 infirmary, 2 playing fields, 11 science labs,
2 pools, 1 tennis court, air conditioning

SINGAPORE AMERICAN SCHOOL

Phone	65 6363 3403
Fax	65 6363 3408
Email	ann@sas.edu.sg
Website	www.sas.edu.sg
Address	40 Woodlands Street 41, Singapore, 738547, Singapore

STAFF

Superintendent Brent A. Mutsch, Ed.D.
High School Principal David Norcott
Intermediate School Principal Marian DeGroot
Assistant Superintendent for Curriculum and Instruction Mark Boyer
Middle School Principal Robert Godley
Primary School Principal David Hoss

Assistant Superintendent for Business Rhonda Norris
Director of Instructional Technology Ed Gilbreath
Teaching staff Full time 309; Part time 14; Total 323
Nationalities of teaching staff US 215; UK 4; Singaporean 12; Other(s) (Canadian, Australian) 92

INFORMATION

Grade levels N–12
School year August–June
School type coeducational, day, private non-profit
Year founded 1956
Governed by elected Board of Governors
Accredited by Western
Regional organizations EARCOS, NESA
Enrollment Nursery 64; PreK 96; Elementary K–5 1,650; Middle School 6–8 924; High School 9–12 1,144; Total 3,878

Nationalities of student body US 2,252; UK 89; Singaporean 210; Other(s) (Korean, Indian) 1,327
Tuition/fee currency Singapore Dollar
Tuition range 9,725–23,600
Annual fees Capital Levy 2,500; ESL 3,000
One time fees Registration 7,000
Graduates attending college 99%
Graduates have attended Brown U, Duke U, U of Penn, Stanford U, Johns Hopkins U

(Continued)

SINGAPORE AMERICAN SCHOOL (Continued)

EDUCATIONAL PROGRAM

Curriculum US, AP
Average class size Elementary 21; Secondary 21
Language(s) of instruction English
Language(s) taught French, Spanish, Japanese, Mandarin
Staff specialists computer, counselor, ESL, learning disabilities, librarian, math resource, nurse, psychologist, reading resource, speech/hearing
Special curricular programs art, instrumental music, vocal music, computer/technology, physical education, vocational

Extra curricular programs computers, community service, dance, drama, environmental conservation, excursions/expeditions, literary magazine, newspaper, photography, yearbook
Sports badminton, baseball, basketball, cross-country, football, golf, hockey, rugby, soccer, softball, swimming, tennis, track and field, volleyball
Clubs chess, wrestling
Examinations AP, Iowa, SAT

CAMPUS FACILITIES

Location Suburban
Campus 14 hectares, 14 buildings, 289 classrooms, 26 computer labs, 1690 instructional computers, 116,852 library volumes,

3 auditoriums, 3 cafeterias, 3 covered play areas, 5 gymnasiums, 2 infirmaries, 6 playing fields, 23 science labs, 3 pools, 5 tennis courts, air conditioning

TANGLIN TRUST SCHOOL

Phone	65 6778 0771
Fax	65 6777 5862
Email	marketg@tts.edu.sg
Website	www.tts.edu.sg
Address	Portsdown Road, Singapore, 139299, Singapore

STAFF

Chief Executive Officer Steven Andrews
Head of Senior School David Woods
Head of Junior School David Porritt
Head of Infant School Geraldine Chandran

Director of Curriculum David Clegg
Chief Operating Officer Diren Dorai Raj
Director of Finance and Administration Violet Lee

INFORMATION

Grade levels N–13
School year September–August
School type coeducational, day, private non-profit
Year founded 1925
Governed by appointed Board of Governors
Tuition/fee currency Singapore Dollar

Tuition range 14,775–25,275
Annual fees Capital Levy 2,100
One time fees Registration 2,500;
Enrollment 1,500; Application Deposit 1,000
Graduates attending college 100%

EDUCATIONAL PROGRAM

Curriculum UK
Average class size Elementary 24; Secondary 24
Language(s) of instruction English
Language(s) taught French, German, Mandarin,
Bahasa, Spanish
Staff specialists counselor, ESL, learning
disabilities, math resource, nurse, reading
resource
Special curricular programs art, instrumental
music, vocal music, computer/technology,
physical education, vocational

Extra curricular programs computers, community
service, dance, environmental conservation,
excursions/expeditions, newspaper, speech and
debate
Sports cricket, cross-country, football, golf,
hockey, rugby, soccer, swimming, tennis,
Karate, fencing, scuba diving, Judo, netball,
dodgeball, rock climbing
Clubs Boy and Girl Scouts, cooking, fired
ceramics, scrap booking, chess, yoga, Lego,
sewing
Examinations A-level GCE, GCSE

CAMPUS FACILITIES

Location Suburban
Campus 4 hectares, 3 buildings, 96 classrooms,
8 computer labs, 550 instructional computers,
40,029 library volumes, 3 auditoriums,

3 cafeterias, 1 covered play area, 1 gymnasium,
3 infirmaries, 3 playing fields, 6 science labs,
1 pool, 4 tennis courts, air conditioning

UNITED WORLD COLLEGE OF SOUTHEAST ASIA

Phone	65 6775 5344
Fax	65 6778 5846
Email	admissions@uwcsea.edu.sg
Website	www.uwcsea.edu.sg
Address	1207 Dover Road, Singapore, 139654, Singapore

STAFF

Head of College Julian P. Whiteley
Deputy Head Mike Price, Ph.D.
Assistant Head (External Relations) David Shepherd
Assistant Head (Personnel and Logistics) Geraint Jones
High and Upper School Principal Di Smart
Middle School Principal James Dalziel
Director of Administration Chegne How Poon

Director of ITC Ben Morgan
Librarian Yvonne Krishnan
Teaching staff Full time 215; Part time 50; Total 265
Nationalities of teaching staff US 9; UK 114; Singaporean 4; Other(s) (Australian, Canadian) 138

INFORMATION

Grade levels K–12
School year August–June
School type boarding, coeducational, day, private non-profit
Year founded 1971
Governed by appointed Board of Governors
Regional organizations EARCOS, ECIS
Enrollment PreK 154; Elementary K–5 767; Middle School 6–8 740; High School 9–12 1,157; Total 2,818
Nationalities of student body US 221; UK 564; Singaporean 173; Other(s) (Indian, Australian) 1,860

Tuition/fee currency Singapore Dollar
Tuition range 19,482–24,315
Annual fees Boarding, 7-day 22,935; Capital Levy 5,352; Busing 1,200; Lunch 900
One time fees Registration 2,140
Boarding program grades 7–12
Boarding program length 7-day **Boys** 93 **Girls** 86
Graduates attending college 98%
Graduates have attended Oxford U, Cambridge U, Stanford U, Princeton U, U of Pennsylvania

(Continued)

UNITED WORLD COLLEGE OF SOUTHEAST ASIA (Continued)

EDUCATIONAL PROGRAM

Curriculum Intl, IB Diploma, IBPYP, IGCSE, GenCSE
Average class size Elementary 22; Secondary 20
Language(s) of instruction English
Language(s) taught Mandarin, French, Spanish, Japanese, Dutch, German
Staff specialists computer, counselor, librarian, math resource, nurse, physician, reading resource

Extra curricular programs computers, community service, drama, environmental conservation, excursions/expeditions, literary magazine, newspaper, photography, yearbook
Sports badminton, basketball, cricket, cross-country, golf, gymnastics, hockey, rugby, soccer, swimming, tennis, track and field, volleyball
Examinations GCSE, IB, IGCSE

CAMPUS FACILITIES

Location Suburban
Campus 11 hectares, 20 buildings, 145 classrooms, 10 computer labs, 445 instructional computers, 40,100 library volumes, 4 auditoriums, 2 cafeterias, 1 covered play area, 3 gymnasiums, 1 infirmary, 6 playing fields, 18 science labs, 1 pool, 6 tennis courts, air conditioning

SLOVAKIA

SLOVAKIA

Area:	48,845 sq km
Population:	5,447,502
Capital:	Bratislava
Currency:	Slovak Koruna (SKK)
Languages:	Slovak

BRITISH INTERNATIONAL SCHOOL

Phone	421 2 6930 7081 (2)
Fax	421 2 6930 7083
Email	info@bisb.sk
Website	www.bis.sk
Address	Dolinskeho 1 (Infant School), Peknikova 6 (Primary & Secondary School), Bratislava, 841 02, Slovakia

STAFF

Acting Head of School and Head of Secondary School Gareth Pugh, Ed.D.
Head of Primary Paul Rogers
Admissions Officer Milina Bires
Administration and Business Manager Barbara Kanclirova

Teaching staff Full time 80; Part time 10; Total 90
Nationalities of teaching staff US 3; UK 50; Slovak 33; Other(s) (French, German) 4

INFORMATION

Grade levels N–13
School year September–July
School type coeducational, day, proprietary
Year founded 1997
Sponsored by Nord Anglia Education Group
Regional organizations ECIS

Enrollment Nursery 40; PreK 20;
Elementary K–5 260; Middle School 6–8 120;
High School 9–12 100; Grade 13 15; Total 555
Nationalities of student body US 45; UK 55;
Slovak 120; Other(s) (French, Korean) 335
Tuition/fee currency British Pound
Tuition range 4,160–8,450
One time fees Registration 300

EDUCATIONAL PROGRAM

Curriculum UK, Intl, IB Diploma, IGCSE, AS and A Levels
Average class size Elementary 18; Secondary 15
Language(s) of instruction English
Language(s) taught German, Slovak, French
Staff specialists computer, counselor, ESL, learning disabilities, librarian, physician, psychologist
Special curricular programs art, computer/technology, physical education

Extra curricular programs computers, community service, drama, environmental conservation, excursions/expeditions, photography, yearbook
Sports badminton, basketball, cricket, football, gymnastics, skiing, soccer, swimming, volleyball, floorball, netball, athletics
Clubs choir, design and technology, jewelery, cookery, ICT games, nature, sewing, chess, Young Enterprise, arts and crafts, rounders, guitar, Scrabble, sign language
Examinations A-level GCE, GCSE, IB, IGCSE, CIPP

CAMPUS FACILITIES

Location Suburban
Campus 6 hectares, 2 buildings, 30 classrooms, 2 computer labs, 70 instructional computers,

5,000 library volumes, 1 cafeteria, 4 gymnasiums, 1 playing field, 3 science labs, 3 tennis courts

QSI INTERNATIONAL SCHOOL OF BRATISLAVA

Phone 421 2 6542 2844
Fax 421 2 6541 1646
Email office@qsi.sk
Website www.qsi.sk
Address Iuventa Building, Karloveska 64, Karlova Ves, Bratislava, 842 20, Slovakia
Mailing address Karloveska 64, 842 20 Bratislava, Slovak Republic, Europe

STAFF

Director Matthew R. Lake
Director of Instruction Kevin Hall
IB Coordinator and Student Services Michelle Lake
Finance Manager Jana Mezovska
Technology Coordinator Kevin Frederick

Librarian Gail Fike
Teaching staff Full time 40; Total 40
Nationalities of teaching staff US 23; Host 10;
Other(s) (Canadian, French) 7

INFORMATION

Grade levels N–12
School year August–June
School type coeducational, day, private non-profit
Year founded 1994
Governed by appointed Board of Directors
Accredited by Middle States
Regional organizations CEESA
Enrollment Nursery 10; PreK 10;
Elementary K–5 100; Middle School 6–8 30;
High School 9–12 100; Total 250

Nationalities of student body US 20; UK 5; Slovak
75; Other(s) (Korean, German) 150
Tuition/fee currency US Dollar
Tuition range 11,800–14,500
Annual fees Registration 100; Capital Levy 1,600;
Busing 1,800
Graduates attending college 100%
Graduates have attended Purdue U, Boston Col,
Becconi U, Otawa U, Pennsylvania State U

EDUCATIONAL PROGRAM

Curriculum US, AP, IB Diploma
Average class size Elementary 15; Secondary 20
Language(s) of instruction English
Language(s) taught Slovak, German, French
Staff specialists computer, counselor, ESL
Special curricular programs art, computer/
technology, distance learning

Extra curricular programs computers, community
service, dance, drama, excursions/expeditions,
yearbook
Sports basketball, cross-country, soccer,
swimming, tennis, volleyball
Examinations AP, IB, Iowa, PSAT, SAT, SAT II

CAMPUS FACILITIES

Location Suburban
Campus 4 hectares, 1 building, 73 classrooms,
3 computer labs, 65 instructional computers,
9,000 library volumes, 1 auditorium,

1 cafeteria, 1 covered play area, 1 gymnasium,
1 infirmary, 1 playing field, 2 science labs,
1 pool, 1 tennis court

QSI International School of Kosice

Phone	421 55 6250040
Fax	421 55 7294157
Email	kosice@qsi.org
Website	www.qsi.org/ksc
Address	Nam. L. Novomeskeho 2, Kosice, 04001, Slovakia

STAFF

Director Sam Thomas, Ed.D.
Office Manager Maria Skriabova
Computer Coordinator Peter Harcar

Head of Library/Media Center Alina Novakova
Teaching staff Full time 14; Total 14
Nationalities of teaching staff US 10; Slovak 4

INFORMATION

Grade levels PreK–12
School year August–June
School type coeducational, company-sponsored, day, private non-profit
Year founded 2001
Governed by appointed Board of Directors
Sponsored by U.S. Steel–Kosice
Accredited by Middle States
Regional organizations CEESA

Enrollment PreK 5; Elementary K–5 25; Middle School 6–8 11; High School 9–12 7; Total 48
Nationalities of student body US 23; UK 3; Slovene 3; Other(s) (German) 14
Tuition/fee currency US Dollar
Tuition 5,000
One time fees Capital Levy 16,000
Graduates attending college 100%
Graduates have attended American U of Prague, Webster U Vienna

EDUCATIONAL PROGRAM

Curriculum US, AP
Average class size Elementary 6; Secondary 2
Language(s) of instruction English
Language(s) taught Slovak, Spanish
Staff specialists computer, librarian

Special curricular programs art, instrumental music, vocal music, computer/technology, physical education
Extra curricular programs drama, excursions/expeditions, yearbook
Examinations AP, Iowa, PSAT, SAT, TOEFL

CAMPUS FACILITIES

Location Urban
Campus 3 hectares, 1 building, 8 classrooms, 1 computer lab, 14 instructional computers,

3,000 library volumes, 1 cafeteria, 2 gymnasiums, 1 playing field, 1 science lab

SLOVENIA

SLOVENIA

Area:	20,273 sq km
Population:	2,009,245
Capital:	Ljubljana
Currency:	Euro (EUR)
Languages:	Slovenian

QSI INTERNATIONAL SCHOOL OF LJUBLJANA

Phone	386 1 256 6069
Fax	386 1 256 6068
Email	steveminer@qsi.org
Website	www.qsi.org
Address	Dolgi most 6a, 1000 Ljubljana, Ljubljana, Slovenia
Mailing address	c/o US Embassy, Ljubljana, Dept. of State, 7140 Ljubljana Place, Washington, DC 20521-7140, USA

STAFF

Director Steve Miner
Teaching staff Full time 6; Part time 7; Total 13

Nationalities of teaching staff US 6; Slovene 7

INFORMATION

Grade levels PreK–12
School year September–June
School type coeducational, day, private non-profit
Year founded 1995
Governed by appointed Board of Directors
Sponsored by Quality Schools International
Accredited by Middle States
Regional organizations CEESA

Enrollment PreK 12; Elementary K–5 19; Middle School 6–8 6; High School 9–12 8; Total 45
Nationalities of student body US 5; UK 3; Slovene 6; Other(s) (Norwegian) 31
Tuition/fee currency US Dollar
Tuition range 5,000–14,500
Annual fees Capital Levy 1,600
One time fees Registration 100

EDUCATIONAL PROGRAM

Curriculum US, Intl, AP, QSI Certificate
Average class size Elementary 7; Secondary 3
Language(s) of instruction English
Language(s) taught German, Spanish, Slovene
Staff specialists computer, speech/hearing
Special curricular programs art, vocal music, computer/technology, distance learning, physical education

Extra curricular programs community service, drama, environmental conservation, newspaper
Sports badminton, basketball, cross-country, soccer, softball, swimming, tennis, track and field, volleyball
Clubs Boy and Girl Scouts, cooking, drama, study group, instrumental music, sports
Examinations Iowa, SAT, SAT II

CAMPUS FACILITIES

Location Urban
Campus 1 hectare, 1 building, 6 classrooms, 3 computer labs, 30 instructional computers,

4,000 library volumes, 1 covered play area, 1 gymnasium, 1 playing field, 1 science lab, 2 tennis courts

SOUTH AFRICA

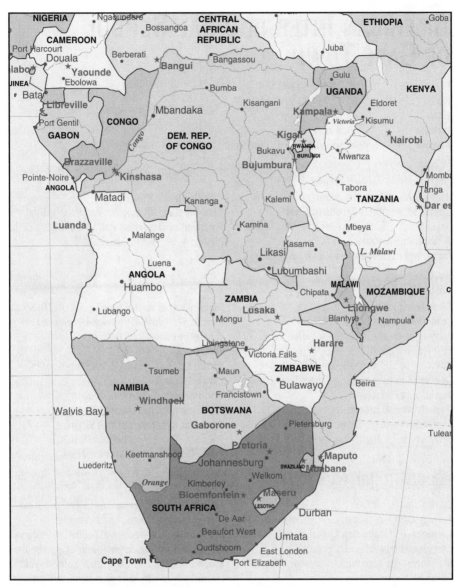

SOUTH AFRICA

Area:	1,219,912 sq km
Population:	43,997,828
Capital:	Pretoria
Currency:	Rand (ZAR)
Languages:	IsiZulu

AMERICAN INTERNATIONAL SCHOOL OF CAPE TOWN

Phone	27 21 713 2220
Fax	27 21 713 2240
Email	info@aisct.org.za
Website	www.aisct.org.za
Address	42 Soetvlei Avenue, Constantia, Cape Town, 7806, South Africa

STAFF

Head of School Ryan P. Blanton
Administrative Officer Brenda Roberts
Upper School Coordinator Alison van der Merwe
Accounts Administrator Cecille Collins
Technology Department Head Rick Briggs

Librarian Heidi Mouret
Teaching staff Full time 20; Part time 3; Total 23
Nationalities of teaching staff US 12; UK 2; South African 4; Other(s) (Canadian) 5

INFORMATION

Grade levels PreK–12
School year August–June
School type coeducational, day, private non-profit
Year founded 2001
Governed by appointed Board of Governors
Sponsored by International School Foundation
Accredited by Western
Regional organizations AISA
Enrollment PreK 15; Elementary K–5 75; Middle School 6–8 35; High School 9–12 75; Total 200

Nationalities of student body US 50; UK 20; South African 50; Other(s) (Norwegian, Swede) 80
Tuition/fee currency US Dollar
Tuition range 3,000–9,000
Annual fees Capital Levy 1,500; Busing 500; Lunch 1,000
One time fees Registration 100
Graduates attending college 90%
Graduates have attended U of Virginia, Fordham U, U of Southern California, U of Edinburgh, Pennsylvania State U

EDUCATIONAL PROGRAM

Curriculum US, Intl, AP
Average class size Elementary 16; Secondary 14
Language(s) of instruction English
Language(s) taught French, Spanish
Staff specialists computer, counselor, ESL, librarian, nurse
Special curricular programs art, instrumental music, vocal music, computer/technology, distance learning, physical education

Extra curricular programs computers, community service, dance, drama, environmental conservation, excursions/expeditions, literary magazine, newspaper, photography, yearbook
Sports basketball, cricket, cross-country, golf, martial arts, rugby, soccer, softball, swimming, tennis, volleyball
Clubs student council, art, culture, Play Dough, Model UN, surfing, games
Examinations AP, PSAT, SAT, SAT II, TOEFL, International Schools Assessment

CAMPUS FACILITIES

Location Suburban
Campus 10 hectares, 4 buildings, 20 classrooms, 1 computer lab, 60 instructional computers, 5,000 library volumes, 2 auditoriums,

1 cafeteria, 1 covered play area, 1 infirmary, 2 playing fields, 1 science lab, 2 pools, 2 tennis courts

THE AMERICAN INTERNATIONAL SCHOOL OF JOHANNESBURG

Phone	27 11 464 1505
Fax	27 11 464 1327
Email	rbeck@aisj-jhb.com
Website	www.aisj-jhb.com
Address	Private Bag X4, Bryanston, 2021, Johannesburg, Gauteng, South Africa

STAFF

Director Rob Beck, Ed.D.
Elementary Principal Lory Thiessen
High School Principal Maddy Hewitt
Middle School Principal Dick Moore
Finance Manager Chris Pretorius

Technology Manager Barry Locker
High School Librarian Shannon Coyne
Teaching staff Full time 78; Total 78
Nationalities of teaching staff US 35; UK 2; South African 25; Other(s) (Canadian) 16

INFORMATION

Grade levels PreK–12
School year August–June
School type coeducational, day, private non-profit
Year founded 1982
Governed by elected Board
Accredited by Middle States
Regional organizations AISA, ECIS
Enrollment PreK 24; Elementary K–5 232; Middle School 6–8 147; High School 9–12 155; Total 558

Nationalities of student body US 207; UK 30; South African 41; Other(s) (Indian, Swede) 280
Tuition/fee currency US Dollar
Tuition range 7,424–19,295
Annual fees Busing 2,583
One time fees Registration 200; Capital Levy 3,467
Graduates attending college 100%
Graduates have attended Corcoran School of Art and Design, Amherst Col, Morehouse Col, Macalester Col, Cambridge U

EDUCATIONAL PROGRAM

Curriculum US, IB Diploma
Average class size Elementary 15; Secondary 15
Language(s) of instruction English
Language(s) taught French, Spanish
Staff specialists computer, counselor, ESL, librarian, nurse, psychologist, reading resource, speech/hearing
Special curricular programs art, instrumental music, vocal music, computer/technology, physical education

Extra curricular programs computers, community service, dance, drama, environmental conservation, excursions/expeditions, newspaper, yearbook, Model UN, Mount Kilimanjaro Climb
Sports baseball, basketball, cricket, golf, martial arts, rugby, soccer, softball, swimming, tennis, volleyball, horseback riding
Examinations IB, PSAT, SAT, Stanford, TOEFL

CAMPUS FACILITIES

Location Rural
Campus 35 hectares, 17 buildings, 66 classrooms, 3 computer labs, 285 instructional computers,

30,000 library volumes, 1 gymnasium, 1 infirmary, 2 playing fields, 6 science labs, 1 pool, 3 tennis courts, air conditioning

THE AMERICAN INTERNATIONAL SCHOOL OF JOHANNESBURG AT PRETORIA

Phone	27 12 344 6242
Fax	27 12 344 2502
Email	bweinberg@aisj-jhb.com
Website	www.aisj-jhb.com
Address	PO Box 20817, Arcadia, Pretoria, 0007, South Africa

STAFF

Site Administrator and Principal Ben Weinberg
Director Rob Beck, Ed.D.
Elementary Principal Lory Thiessen
High School Principal Madeleine Hewitt
Middle School Principal Dick Moore

Finance Manager Chris Pretorius
Technology Manager Barry Locker
High School Librarian Shannon Coyne
Teaching staff Full time 11; Part time 3; Total 14
Nationalities of teaching staff US 5; South African 9

INFORMATION

Grade levels PreK–6
School year August–June
School type coeducational, day, private non-profit
Year founded 2001
Governed by elected Board of Education
Accredited by Middle States
Regional organizations AISA

Enrollment PreK 5; Elementary K–5 70; Middle School 6–8 8; Total 83
Nationalities of student body US 30; UK 10; South African 1; Other(s) (Swede, Indian) 44
Tuition/fee currency US Dollar
Tuition 14,000–14,000
Annual fees Registration 200; Busing 2,700
One time fees Capital Levy 4,000

EDUCATIONAL PROGRAM

Curriculum US, Intl, IB Diploma
Average class size Elementary 12
Language(s) of instruction English
Language(s) taught Spanish
Staff specialists computer, learning disabilities, reading resource, speech/hearing
Special curricular programs art, instrumental music, vocal music, computer/technology, physical education

Extra curricular programs computers, community service, dance, drama, environmental conservation
Sports baseball, martial arts, soccer, swimming, tennis
Examinations Stanford

CAMPUS FACILITIES

Location Urban
Campus 5 buildings, 10 classrooms, 3 computer labs, 47 instructional computers,

5,000 library volumes, 1 cafeteria, 1 infirmary, 2 playing fields, 1 science lab, air conditioning

SOUTH KOREA

Area:	98,480 sq km
Population:	49,044,790
Capital:	Seoul
Currency:	South Korean Won (KRW)
Languages:	Korean, English

KOREA INTERNATIONAL SCHOOL

Phone	82 31 789 0509
Fax	82 31 748 0509
Email	aclapper@kis.or.kr
Website	www.kis.or.kr
Address	373-6 Baekhyun-dong, Bundang-gu, Sungnam-si, 436-420, South Korea

STAFF

Director Ann T. Clapper, Ed.D.
Elementary Principal Shane Kells
Middle School Principal Patrick Seymour
High School Principal Richard Boerner
Director of Business Operations Daniel Choi
Computer Specialist Kenny Park

Library Media Specialists Donna Seymour and Colleen Boerner
Teaching staff Full time 99; Part time 5; Total 104
Nationalities of teaching staff US 72; UK 3; Korean 7; Other(s) (Canadian, Australian) 22

INFORMATION

Grade levels K–12
School year August–June
School type coeducational, day, proprietary
Year founded 2000
Governed by appointed Founder Chung, Soon II and Board of Directors
Sponsored by YBM Si-sa
Accredited by Western
Enrollment Elementary K–5 301; Middle School 6–8 216; High School 9–12 194; Total 711

Nationalities of student body US 312; UK 3; Korean 338; Other(s) (Canadian, Australian) 58
Tuition/fee currency US Dollar
Tuition range 17,160–23,880
Annual fees Busing 1,900; Books 200
One time fees Registration 800
Graduates attending college 100%
Graduates have attended Stanford U, Wellesley Col, U of California in Los Angeles, U of Illinois, Bowdoin Col

EDUCATIONAL PROGRAM

Curriculum US, AP
Average class size Elementary 20; Secondary 20
Language(s) of instruction English
Language(s) taught Korean, Chinese, Spanish, French
Staff specialists counselor, librarian, nurse
Special curricular programs art, instrumental music, vocal music, computer/technology, physical education

Extra curricular programs community service, drama, excursions/expeditions, newspaper, yearbook
Sports basketball, cross-country, soccer, swimming, tennis, volleyball
Clubs Model UN, Habitat for Humanity, National Honor Society, Quiz Bowl, student council, speech and debate, Visual Impact Club, Style and Design Club
Examinations AP, PSAT, SAT, SAT II, Stanford

CAMPUS FACILITIES

Location Suburban
Campus 1 hectare, 6 buildings, 56 classrooms, 4 computer labs, 500 instructional computers, 7,500 library volumes, 2 auditoriums,

1 cafeteria, 1 covered play area, 2 gymnasiums, 1 infirmary, 1 playing field, 6 science labs, 1 pool, air conditioning

INTERNATIONAL SCHOOL OF BUSAN

Phone	82 51 742 3332
Fax	82 51 742 3375
Email	ispusan@ispusan.co.kr
Website	www.ispusan.co.kr
Address	1492-12, Jung-2-Dong, Haeundae-gu, Busan, 612-849, South Korea

STAFF

Principal Stephen J. Palmer
Head of Early Learning Center Karen Norris
Head of Middle or High School Michael Reeve
Head of Elementary School Kevin Smith
Finance Manager Jan Benggaard
Head of ICT Dawn Skarset

Head of Library John Jugenheimer
Teaching staff Full time 22; Part time 2; Total 24
Nationalities of teaching staff US 4; UK 8;
Korean 3; Other(s) (Australian, Canadian) 9

INFORMATION

Grade levels N–10
School year August–June
School type coeducational, day, private non-profit
Year founded 1983
Governed by elected Board of Governors
Accredited by CIS
Regional organizations EARCOS, ECIS
Enrollment Nursery 10; PreK 28;
Elementary K–5 90; Middle School 6–8 35;
High School 9–12 15; Total 178

Nationalities of student body US 53; UK 16;
Korean 21; Other(s) (Norwegian, Dane) 88
Tuition/fee currency South-Korean Won
Tuition range 4,080,000–16,640,000
Annual fees Busing 1,400,000; Lunch 950,000
One time fees Registration 800,000;
Capital Levy 750,000

EDUCATIONAL PROGRAM

Curriculum Intl, IBPYP, IGCSE
Average class size Elementary 15; Secondary 8
Language(s) of instruction English
Language(s) taught Korean, Spanish
Staff specialists computer, ESL, librarian, math resource, reading resource
Special curricular programs art, instrumental music, vocal music, computer/technology, physical education

Extra curricular programs computers, dance, drama, photography, yearbook
Sports basketball, cross-country, football, gymnastics, martial arts, rugby, skiing, soccer, swimming, track and field
Clubs ceramics, orchestra, string group, choir, calligraphy, folk dance, crafts, debating
Examinations GCSE, IGCSE, ACER - ISA Tests

CAMPUS FACILITIES

Location Suburban
Campus 2 buildings, 24 classrooms, 2 computer labs, 60 instructional computers,

17,000 library volumes, 1 auditorium, 1 cafeteria, 1 playing field, 1 science lab

INTERNATIONAL CHRISTIAN SCHOOL–PYONGTAEK

Phone	82 31 651 1376
Fax	82 31 653 1375
Email	johnpeterson@nics.org
Website	www.icsptk.org
Address	Shin-Dae Dong 367-3, Pyongtaek-Si, Kyunggi Do, Pyongtaek, 450-820, South Korea
Mailing address	PO Box 24, Pyongtaek 450-600, Korea

STAFF

Director John L. Peterson
Assistant Principal Grace Maxwell
Athletic Director Aaron Harring
Business Manager Mylene Haselman
Computer Teacher Jacob Maier

Librarian Crystal Boysen
Teaching staff Full time 22; Part time 1; Total 23
Nationalities of teaching staff US 21; Canadian 1; Other(s) 1

INFORMATION

Grade levels K–12
School year August–June
School type coeducational, day, private non-profit
Year founded 1990
Governed by appointed Administration
Sponsored by Network of International Christian Schools
Accredited by Western
Regional organizations EARCOS
Enrollment Elementary K–5 100; Middle School 6–8 60; High School 9–12 40; Total 200

Nationalities of student body US 90; Korean 90; Other(s) 20
Tuition/fee currency South-Korean Won
Tuition range 7,380,000–8,010,000
Annual fees Registration 300,000
One time fees Capital Levy 500,000
Graduates attending college 90%
Graduates have attended U of Maryland, Indiana State U, U of Illinois, Liberty U, U of Washington

EDUCATIONAL PROGRAM

Curriculum US
Average class size Elementary 20; Secondary 20
Language(s) of instruction English
Language(s) taught Spanish, Korean
Staff specialists computer, ESL, librarian

Special curricular programs art, vocal music, computer/technology, physical education
Sports basketball, soccer, volleyball, Cheerleading
Examinations PSAT, SAT, Stanford

CAMPUS FACILITIES

Location Suburban
Campus 1 building, 18 classrooms, 1 computer lab, 40 instructional computers,

7,000 library volumes, 1 cafeteria, 1 science lab, air conditioning

SEOUL FOREIGN SCHOOL

Phone	82 2 330 3100
Fax	82 2 335 1857
Email	sfsoffice@seoulforeign.org
Website	www.sfs.or.kr
Address	55 Yonhi Dong, Seoul, 120-113, South Korea

STAFF

Head of School Harlan E. Lyso, Ph.D.
High School Principal Kevin C. Baker, Ed.D.
Middle School Principal Shirley M. Droese
Elementary School Principal John E. Gaylord
British School Headteacher Timothy J. Gray
Director of Business Operations Langston K. Rogde
Head of Technology Three Technology Specialists

Head of Library/Media Center Four Librarians in three locations
Teaching staff Full time 128; Part time 21; Total 149
Nationalities of teaching staff US 73; UK 22; Korean 6; Other(s) (Canadian, Australian) 48

INFORMATION

Grade levels N–12
School year August–June
School type coeducational, day, private non-profit
Year founded 1912
Governed by elected School Board
Accredited by Western
Regional organizations EARCOS, ECIS
Enrollment Nursery 37; PreK 50; Elementary K–5 621; Middle School 6–8 371; High School 9–12 373; Total 1,452
Nationalities of student body US 813; UK 105; Other(s) (Canadian, Australian) 534

Tuition/fee currency US Dollar
Tuition range 9,578–24,857
Annual fees Busing 1,900; IB– Junior Year 600; IB–Senior Year 1,200
One time fees Registration 450; Capital Levy 2,000; Application 250
Graduates attending college 100%
Graduates have attended Brown U, Johns Hopkins U, Columbia U, Northwestern U, New York U

EDUCATIONAL PROGRAM

Curriculum US, UK, AP, IB Diploma
Average class size Elementary 20; Secondary 14
Language(s) of instruction English
Language(s) taught French, Spanish, Korean
Staff specialists computer, counselor, ESL, learning disabilities, librarian, math resource, nurse, psychologist, reading resource
Special curricular programs art, instrumental music, vocal music, computer/technology, physical education

Extra curricular programs computers, community service, drama, environmental conservation, excursions/expeditions, literary magazine, newspaper, photography, yearbook
Sports baseball, basketball, cross-country, gymnastics, soccer, swimming, tennis, volleyball
Clubs National Honor Society, student council, Fellowship of Christian Students
Examinations ACT, AP, IB, PSAT, SAT, SAT II

CAMPUS FACILITIES

Location Urban
Campus 10 hectares, 10 buildings, 99 classrooms, 4 computer labs, 140 instructional computers, 60,000 library volumes, 3 auditoriums, 1 cafeteria, 2 gymnasiums, 1 infirmary, 1 playing field, 4 science labs, 1 pool, 4 tennis courts, air conditioning

SEOUL INTERNATIONAL SCHOOL

Phone	82 31 750 1325
Fax	82 31 759 5133
Email	roekyung@siskorea.or.kr
Website	www.siskorea.or.kr
Address	San 32-16, Bokjeong-dong, Sujeong-gu, Seongnam-si, Gyeonggi-do, 461-200, South Korea
Mailing address	Songpa P.O. Box 47, Seoul 138-600, Korea

STAFF

Head of School Hyung Shik Kim
Deputy Headmaster Gary Conley
High School Principal Gary Lilley
Middle School Principal Andy Valadka
Elementary School Principal Joseph Moore
Elementary Vice Principal Liset Palmitessa
Secretary to the Head of School Mrs. Young Ok Chi

Technology Coordinator Jason Kaiser
Secondary Librarian/Elementary Librarian Chris Fazenbaker/Heather Purcell
Teaching staff Full time 101; Total 101
Nationalities of teaching staff US 58; UK 2; Korean 4; Other(s) (Canadian, New Zealander) 37

INFORMATION

Grade levels PreK–12
School year August–June
School type coeducational, day, proprietary
Year founded 1973
Governed by appointed Foundation Board
Sponsored by Hyung Shik Kim
Accredited by Western
Regional organizations EARCOS
Enrollment PreK 35; Elementary K–5 465; Middle School 6–8 265; High School 9–12 335; Total 1,100

Nationalities of student body US 900; Other(s) 200
Tuition/fee currency US Dollar
Tuition range 16,000–21,000
Annual fees Busing 1,700
One time fees Registration 350; Application 175; Testing 125
Graduates attending college 100%
Graduates have attended Columbia U, Duke U, U of Chicago, U of Pennsylvania, Yale U

EDUCATIONAL PROGRAM

Curriculum US, AP
Average class size Elementary 20; Secondary 19
Language(s) of instruction English
Language(s) taught Spanish, Chinese
Staff specialists computer, counselor, ESL, librarian, nurse, reading resource
Special curricular programs art, instrumental music, vocal music, computer/technology, physical education

Extra curricular programs computers, community service, drama, environmental conservation, excursions/expeditions, literary magazine, newspaper, yearbook
Sports basketball, cross-country, soccer, swimming, tennis, volleyball, cheerleading
Clubs creative writing, forensics, Model UN, mathematics, National Honor Society, drama, student council, Habitat for Humanity
Examinations AP, PSAT, SAT, TOEFL, Terra Nova, LPTS

CAMPUS FACILITIES

Location Suburban
Campus 3 hectares, 2 buildings, 77 classrooms, 5 computer labs, 300 instructional computers,

30,000 library volumes, 1 auditorium, 1 cafeteria, 2 gymnasiums, 1 infirmary, 1 playing field, 4 science labs, 1 pool, air conditioning

YONGSAN INTERNATIONAL SCHOOL OF SEOUL

Phone	82 2 797 5104
Fax	82 2 797 5224
Email	admissions@yisseoul.org
Website	www.yisseoul.org
Address	San 10-213, Hannam 2 Dong, Yongsan Ku, Seoul, 140-210, South Korea
Mailing address	YSPO Box 62, Seoul, Korea 140-600

STAFF

Head of School Jeff Pinnow
Director of Admissions Benjamin Hale
Elementary Principal Gretchen Schlie
High School Principal Seth Parish
Guidance Counselor Wilson Lee
Middle School Principal Susan Sevey

Business Manager Stephen Bouch, Ph.D.
Lead Librarian Gabe Johnson
Teaching staff Full time 60; Part time 5; Total 65
Nationalities of teaching staff US 55; UK 2; Korean 6; Other(s) (Canadian) 2

INFORMATION

Grade levels K–12
School year August–June
School type coeducational, day, private non-profit
Year founded 1990
Governed by appointed Board Members
Sponsored by NICS/OASIS
Accredited by Western
Enrollment Elementary K–5 280; Middle School 6–8 150; High School 9–12 195; Total 625
Nationalities of student body US 285; UK 15; Korean 80; Other(s) (Nigerian, Indian) 245

Tuition/fee currency South-Korean Won
Tuition range 11,928,000–13,543,000
Annual fees Registration 200,000; Busing 1,500,000; Capital Development (Returning Student) 1,000,000
One time fees Application 300,000; Capital Development (New Student) 5,000,000
Graduates attending college 100%
Graduates have attended Northwestern U, Brown U, U of California in Berkeley, New York U, U of Michigan

EDUCATIONAL PROGRAM

Curriculum US, AP
Average class size Elementary 20; Secondary 22
Language(s) of instruction English
Language(s) taught Spanish, French, Russian
Staff specialists computer, counselor, ESL, learning disabilities, librarian, nurse, reading resource
Special curricular programs art, instrumental music, vocal music, computer/technology, physical education

Extra curricular programs computers, community service, dance, drama, environmental conservation, excursions/expeditions, literary magazine, yearbook
Sports basketball, cross-country, martial arts, rugby, soccer, swimming, tennis, volleyball, lacrosse
Examinations AP, PSAT, SAT, SAT II, Stanford, Star Reading, Star Math

CAMPUS FACILITIES

Location Urban
Campus 3 hectares, 5 buildings, 50 classrooms, 2 computer labs, 83 instructional computers, 14,000 library volumes, 1 auditorium, 2 cafeterias,

1 covered play area, 2 gymnasiums, 1 infirmary, 1 playing field, 4 science labs, 1 pool, air conditioning

TAEJON CHRISTIAN INTERNATIONAL SCHOOL

Phone 82 42 633 3663
Fax 82 42 631 5732
Email hdmst@tcis.or.kr
Website www.tcis.or.kr
Address 210-1 O Jung Dong, Daeduk-gu, Taejon, 306 010, South Korea
Mailing address 210-1 Ojung Dong, Taeduk-ku, Taejon, 300-603 Korea

STAFF

Head of School Thomas J Penland, Ed.D.
High School Principal Ron Wilder, Ed.D.
Middle School Principal Mike Moimoi
Elementary Principal George Zickefoose
Residence Program Director Brent Frazier
Secondary School Asst Principal Ryan Roberts
Business Administrator Jackie Lee

Information Technology Coordinator Cynthia Dhinaharan
Media Center Director Kyunghae Lee
Teaching staff Full time 100; Part time 10; Total 110
Nationalities of teaching staff US 80; Korean 10; Other(s) (South African, Canadian) 10

INFORMATION

Grade levels PreK–12
School year August–June
School type boarding, coeducational, church-affiliated, private non-profit
Year founded 1958
Governed by appointed Board of Trustees
Accredited by Western
Regional organizations EARCOS
Enrollment PreK 8; Elementary K–5 125; Middle School 6–8 145; High School 9–12 350; Total 628

Nationalities of student body US 438; Korean 60; Other(s) (Chinese, Japanese) 127
Tuition/fee currency US Dollar
Tuition range 11,000–17,000
Annual fees Boarding, 7-day 10,000; Busing 1,000; Lunch 950
One time fees Registration 200; Application 200; Capital 3,500
Boarding program grades 6–12
Boarding program length 7-day **Boys** 145 **Girls** 85
Graduates attending college 100%
Graduates have attended Harvard U, Stanford U, Yale U, Massachusetts Institute of Techology, Duke U

(Continued)

TAEJON CHRISTIAN INTERNATIONAL SCHOOL (Continued)

EDUCATIONAL PROGRAM

Curriculum US, IB Diploma, IBPYP
Average class size Elementary 14; Secondary 18
Language(s) of instruction English
Language(s) taught Korean, French
Staff specialists computer, counselor, ESL, learning disabilities, librarian, math resource, nurse, reading resource
Special curricular programs art, instrumental music, vocal music, computer/technology, physical education, vocational

Extra curricular programs computers, community service, dance, drama, environmental conservation, excursions/expeditions, literary magazine, newspaper, photography, yearbook
Sports basketball, cross-country, soccer, swimming, tennis, volleyball
Clubs Spanish, Mandarin, French, international, Key, National Honor Society, forensics, Korean, cooking, Knowledge Bowl
Examinations ACT, IB, PSAT, SAT, SAT II, Stanford, TOEFL

CAMPUS FACILITIES

Location Urban
Campus 7 hectares, 9 buildings, 25 classrooms, 3 computer labs, 185 instructional computers, 10,000 library volumes, 1 auditorium, 3 cafeterias, 1 gymnasium, 2 infirmaries, 1 playing field, 4 science labs, 3 tennis courts, air conditioning

Data from 2006/07 school year.

INDIANHEAD INTERNATIONAL SCHOOL

Phone	(82)31-8703475
Fax	(82)31-8263476
Email	es@iis.or.kr
Website	www.iis.or.kr
Address	#233-3 Howon-1 Dong, Uijeongbu City, Gyeonggi-Do, 480701, South Korea

STAFF

Principal Edmund P. Fitzgerald
Teaching staff Full time 29; Part time 1; Total 30

Nationalities of teaching staff US 13; Korean 4; Other(s) (Canadian, Australian) 13

INFORMATION

Grade levels PreK–12
School year August–June
School type coeducational, day, private non-profit, proprietary
Year founded 1979
Governed by appointed Board
Accredited by Western
Regional organizations EARCOS, ECIS
Enrollment PreK 1; Elementary K–5 33; Middle School 6–8 61; High School 9–12 77; Total 172

Nationalities of student body US 116; Korean 32; Other(s) (Japanese, Filipino) 24
Tuition/fee currency South-Korean Won
Tuition range 9,000,000–15,750,000
Annual fees Registration 600,000; Busing 1,380,000; Lunch 920,000; Books 200,000; Senior 300,000
Graduates attending college 100%
Graduates have attended Stanford U, U of Virginia, Fashion Institute of Technology, Oberlin U, U of Illinois

EDUCATIONAL PROGRAM

Curriculum US, Intl, AP
Average class size Elementary 8; Secondary 13
Language(s) of instruction English
Language(s) taught Spanish, Korean, Mandarin
Staff specialists counselor, ESL, librarian
Special curricular programs art, instrumental music, vocal music, physical education

Extra curricular programs community service, drama, literary magazine, yearbook
Sports basketball, soccer, swimming, tennis, volleyball
Clubs chess
Examinations AP, PSAT, SAT, SAT II, Stanford

CAMPUS FACILITIES

Location Suburban
Campus 1000 hectares, 3 buildings, 25 classrooms, 3 computer labs, 48 instructional computers, 10,000 library volumes, 1 auditorium,

1 cafeteria, 1 covered play area, 1 infirmary, 1 playing field, 2 science labs, 1 tennis court, air conditioning

INTERNATIONAL CHRISTIAN SCHOOL– UIJONGBU

Phone	82 031 855 1277
Fax	82 031 855 1278
Email	RexFreel@nics.org
Website	www.ics-ujb.org
Address	PO Box 23, Nok yang Dong 375-2, Uijongbu, 480-120, South Korea
Mailing address	CTC Unit 15707, APO AP 96258, USA

STAFF

Director Rex A. Freel
High School Principal Randy Lounds
Guidance Counselor Jennifer Scudder
Head of Technology David Richardson

Head of Library/Media Center Kelli Patchin
Teaching staff Full time 30; Part time 1; Total 31
Nationalities of teaching staff US 30; Canadian 1; Other(s) 1

INFORMATION

Grade levels K–12
School year August–June
School type coeducational, day, private non-profit
Year founded 1983
Governed by appointed School Board and NICS International
Accredited by Western
Regional organizations EARCOS
Enrollment Elementary K–5 100; Middle School 6–8 60; High School 9–12 100; Total 260

Nationalities of student body US 208; UK 6; Korean 20; Other(s) (Filipino, Japanese) 26
Tuition/fee currency South-Korean Won
Tuition range 11,000,000–12,500,000
Annual fees Registration 500,000; Busing 1,575,000; Lunch 480,000; ESL 837,000
Graduates attending college 100%
Graduates have attended Harvard U, Wheaton Col, Liberty U, U of California in Los Angeles, West Point

EDUCATIONAL PROGRAM

Curriculum US, AP
Average class size Elementary 15; Secondary 20
Language(s) of instruction English
Language(s) taught German, Spanish, French, Korean
Staff specialists computer, counselor, ESL, librarian

Special curricular programs art, vocal music, computer/technology, physical education
Extra curricular programs drama, yearbook
Sports basketball, cross-country, soccer, swimming, volleyball
Examinations AP, PSAT, SAT, Stanford

CAMPUS FACILITIES

Location Suburban
Campus 1 building, 21 classrooms, 1 computer lab, 50 instructional computers,

12,000 library volumes, 1 cafeteria, 2 gymnasiums, 2 playing fields, 1 science lab, 1 pool, air conditioning

SPAIN

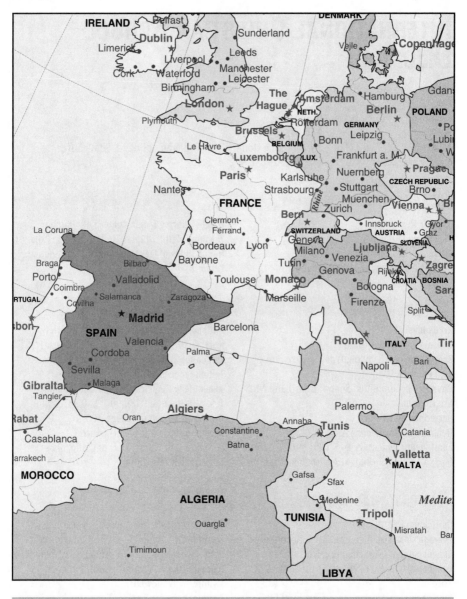

SPAIN

Area:	504,782 sq km
Population:	40,448,191
Capital:	Madrid
Currency:	Euro (EUR)
Languages:	Castilian Spanish

AMERICAN SCHOOL OF BARCELONA

Phone	34 93 371 4016
Fax	34 93 473 4787
Email	info@a-s-b.com
Website	www.a-s-b.com
Address	C/Jaume Balmes, 7, Esplugues de Llobregat, Barcelona, 08950, Spain

STAFF

Director Lee Fertig
Elementary Principal Nancy Boyd
Secondary Principal William Volchok
Early Childhood Coordinator Christine Crandall
Middle School Coordinator Deborah Ralenbeck
Business/Finance Manager Luis Manzano

Technology Coordinator Ros Greehy
Librarian Lorena Ferreira
Teaching staff Full time 85; Part time 5; Total 90
Nationalities of teaching staff US 38; UK 10;
Spaniard 25; Other(s) (Canadian, Colombian) 17

INFORMATION

Grade levels PreK–12
School year September–June
School type coeducational, day, private non-profit
Year founded 1962
Governed by elected Parent-Board of Governors
Sponsored by Parents' Association
Accredited by Middle States
Regional organizations ECIS, MAIS
Enrollment PreK 77; Elementary K–5 290;
Middle School 6–8 112; High School 9–12 151;
Total 630

Nationalities of student body US 82; UK 15;
Spaniard 308; Other(s) (Swede) 225
Tuition/fee currency Euro
Tuition range 5,300–10,560
Annual fees Registration 900; Insurance 425;
Busing 1,330; Lunch 1,400
One time fees Capital Levy 3,250
Graduates attending college 99%
Graduates have attended Rice U, U of Texas,
Georgetown U, Brown U, Texas A&M U

EDUCATIONAL PROGRAM

Curriculum US, National, IB Diploma
Average class size Elementary 17; Secondary 18
Language(s) of instruction English
Language(s) taught Spanish, Catalan
Staff specialists computer, counselor, ESL,
learning disabilities, librarian, nurse

Special curricular programs art, vocal music,
computer/technology, physical education
Extra curricular programs community service,
dance, drama, excursions/expeditions, literary
magazine, yearbook, languages
Sports basketball, soccer, volleyball
Examinations IB, Iowa, PSAT, SAT

CAMPUS FACILITIES

Location Suburban
Campus 2 hectares, 2 buildings, 35 classrooms,
3 computer labs, 100 instructional computers,

17,000 library volumes, 1 cafeteria, 2 covered
play areas, 1 infirmary, 3 playing fields,
3 science labs

THE BENJAMIN FRANKLIN INTERNATIONAL SCHOOL

Phone	34 93 434 2380
Fax	34 93 417 3633
Email	bfranklin@bfischool.org
Website	www.bfischool.org
Address	Martorell i Peña, 9, Barcelona, 08017, Spain

STAFF

Director David Penberg, Ph.D.
Middle and High School Principal Daniel McKee
Preschool and Elementary School Principal
James Duval
Elementary School Counselor Kathryn Manu
College/Guidance Counselor (grades 6–12)
Monna McDiarmid
Optimal Match Program (grades 3–8)
Jessica Noe and Angelene Hanna

Business Managers
Imma Sánchez and Thomas Park
Computer Coordinator Bryan Scholes
Librarian David Cevoli
Teaching staff Full time 47; Part time 6; Total 53
Nationalities of teaching staff US 32; UK 3;
Spaniard 15; Other(s) (Canadian, Mexican) 3

INFORMATION

Grade levels N–12
School year September–June
School type coeducational, day, private non-profit
Year founded 1986
Governed by appointed Foundation Board
Accredited by Middle States
Regional organizations ECIS, MAIS
Enrollment Nursery 30; PreK 19;
Elementary K–5 183; Middle School 6–8 85;
High School 9–12 109; Total 426

Nationalities of student body US 120; UK 18;
Spaniard 141; Other(s) (Dutch, Japanese) 147
Tuition/fee currency Euro
Tuition range 7,310–11,090
Annual fees Registration 745; Busing 1,410;
Lunch 1,110
One time fees Capital Levy 3,125
Graduates attending college 99%
Graduates have attended John Carroll U,
British American U, New York U, U of Toronto,
San Francisco State U

EDUCATIONAL PROGRAM

Curriculum US, National, AP
Average class size Elementary 17; Secondary 15
Language(s) of instruction English
Language(s) taught Spanish, French, Catalan
Staff specialists computer, counselor, ESL,
learning disabilities, librarian, reading resource
Special curricular programs art, vocal music,
computer/technology, distance learning,
physical education, Young Authors Festival

Extra curricular programs computers, community
service, dance, drama, excursions/expeditions,
yearbook, Model UN, National Honor Society,
National Junior Honor Society
Sports basketball, football, soccer, swimming
Examinations AP, Iowa, SAT, SAT II, ERB, PSAT

CAMPUS FACILITIES

Location Urban
Campus 6 buildings, 38 classrooms,
2 computer labs, 102 instructional computers,

11,200 library volumes, 1 cafeteria, 3 playing
fields, 2 science labs, air conditioning

AMERICAN SCHOOL OF MADRID

Phone	34 91 740 1900
Fax	34 91 357 2678
Email	admissions@asmadrid.org
Website	www.asmadrid.org
Address	Carretera de Aravaca a Humera, km 2, Madrid, 28023, Spain
Mailing address	Apartado 80, 28080 Madrid, Spain

STAFF

Head of School William D. O'Hale
Upper School and Middle School Director Joanne Reykdal
Lower School Director Karen Dunmire
Admissions Head Sholeh Farpour
Development Head Veronica Rossi
Head of Spanish Program Juan Ortíz

Director of Administrative Services Jesús Hortal
Technology Coordinator Fernando Montalban
Librarian Diantha McBride
Teaching staff Full time 84; Part time 10; Total 94
Nationalities of teaching staff US 76; Spaniard 15; Other(s) (French) 3

INFORMATION

Grade levels N–12
School year September–June
School type coeducational, day, private non-profit
Year founded 1961
Governed by appointed Board of Trustees
Accredited by Middle States
Regional organizations ECIS, MAIS, NESA
Enrollment Nursery 25; PreK 41; Elementary K–5 342; Middle School 6–8 200; High School 9–12 260; Total 868

Nationalities of student body US 286; Spaniard 226; Other(s) 356
Tuition/fee currency Euro
Tuition range 3,127–14,713
Annual fees Busing 1,800
One time fees Registration 2,350; Preliminary Application 125; Application 650
Graduates attending college 99%
Graduates have attended Barnard Col, Cornell U, New York U, Pratt Institute of Art & Design, U College of London

EDUCATIONAL PROGRAM

Curriculum US, National, IB Diploma, Spanish
Average class size Elementary 17; Secondary 23
Language(s) of instruction English
Language(s) taught Spanish, French
Staff specialists computer, counselor, ESL, librarian, math resource, nurse, reading resource

Special curricular programs art, instrumental music, vocal music, computer/technology, physical education
Extra curricular programs community service, dance, drama, literary magazine, yearbook
Sports basketball, golf, gymnastics, soccer, tennis, volleyball
Examinations AP, IB, PSAT, SAT

CAMPUS FACILITIES

Location Suburban
Campus 4 hectares, 4 buildings, 60 classrooms, 3 computer labs, 150 instructional computers, 32,000 library volumes, 1 auditorium, 2 cafeterias, 1 covered play area, 1 gymnasium, 1 infirmary, 2 playing fields, 4 science labs, 2 tennis courts

EVANGELICAL CHRISTIAN ACADEMY

Phone	34 91 886 5003
Fax	34 91 886 6419
Email	info@ecaspain.com
Website	http://ecaspain.com
Address	Calle la Manda, 47, Camarma de Esteruelas, Madrid, 28816, Spain

STAFF

Head of School Scot A. Musser
Guidance Stephanie Kellum
Principal Eric DeHaan
Business Manager Brian Calderwood

Webmaster Paul Madsen
Librarian Jill DeHaan
Teaching staff Full time 12; Part time 8; Total 20
Nationalities of teaching staff US 18; Spaniard 2

INFORMATION

Grade levels K–12
School year August–June
School type coeducational, day, private non-profit
Year founded 1973
Governed by elected Board of Trustees
Enrollment Elementary K–5 25; Middle School 6–8 25; High School 9–12 35; Total 85
Nationalities of student body US 65; UK 2; Spaniard 10; Other(s) (Korean) 8
Tuition/fee currency Euro
Tuition range 1,650–4,329

Annual fees Registration 50; Instumental Lessons 225; High School Activity 100
One time fees Boarding, 5-day 275; Boarding, 7-day 275
Boarding program grades 9–12
Boarding program length 5-day and 7-day **Girls** 4
Graduates attending college 98%
Graduates have attended Wheaton Col, Asbury Col, U of North Carolina, Moody Bible Institute, King's Col

EDUCATIONAL PROGRAM

Curriculum US, AP
Average class size Elementary 8; Secondary 12
Language(s) of instruction English
Language(s) taught Spanish
Staff specialists learning disabilities

Special curricular programs art, instrumental music, vocal music, physical education
Extra curricular programs community service, yearbook
Clubs soccer, basketball
Examinations AP, PSAT, SAT, Stanford

CAMPUS FACILITIES

Location Rural
Campus 1 building, 15 classrooms, 1 computer lab, 14 instructional computers,

12,500 library volumes, 1 auditorium, 1 playing field, 1 science lab

INTERNATIONAL COLLEGE SPAIN

Phone	34 91 650 2398
Fax	34 91 650 1035
Email	info@icsmadrid.org
Website	www.icsmadrid.com
Address	Calle Vereda Norte 3, La Moraleja, Madrid, 28109, Spain
Mailing address	Apartado 1271, 28108 Alcobendas, Madrid, Spain

STAFF

Director David Gatley
Deputy Director/Head of Secondary School
Derek Gaudet
Deputy Director/Head of Primary School
Christina Barlow

Librarian Ursula Garcia
Teaching staff Full time 98; Part time 26; Total 124
Nationalities of teaching staff US 14; UK 25;
Spaniard 22; Other(s) (Irish, Dutch) 63

INFORMATION

Grade levels N–12
School year September–June
School type coeducational, day, proprietary
Year founded 1980
Governed by appointed Board of Trustees
Sponsored by International College Spain SA
Accredited by CIS, New England
Regional organizations ECIS, MAIS
Enrollment Nursery 25; PreK 38;
Elementary K–5 256; Middle School 6–8 147;
High School 9–12 188; Total 654

Nationalities of student body US 42; UK 63;
Spaniard 221; Other(s) (Dutch, Israeli) 328
Tuition/fee currency Euro
Tuition range 7,230–13,560
Annual fees Books 450
One time fees Registration 500; Capital Levy
1,800; Deposit 600
Graduates attending college 95%
Graduates have attended Boston U, Duke U,
Yale U, Cambridge U, Imperial Col

EDUCATIONAL PROGRAM

Curriculum Intl, IB Diploma, IBPYP, IBMYP
Average class size Elementary 20; Secondary 17
Language(s) of instruction English
Language(s) taught Spanish, French, Dutch
Staff specialists computer, counselor, ESL,
learning disabilities, librarian, math resource,
nurse, psychologist, reading resource

Extra curricular programs computers, community
service, dance, drama, environmental
conservation, excursions/expeditions,
newspaper, yearbook, orchestra
Sports badminton, basketball, golf, hockey,
martial arts, skiing, soccer, softball, tennis,
track and field, volleyball
Clubs Model UN
Examinations IB, PSAT, SAT, TOEFL

CAMPUS FACILITIES

Location Suburban
Campus 3 hectares, 2 buildings, 54 classrooms,
3 computer labs, 60 instructional computers,

34,000 library volumes, 1 auditorium,
1 cafeteria, 1 gymnasium, 1 infirmary,
3 playing fields, 5 science labs, 1 tennis court

RUNNYMEDE COLLEGE

Phone	34 91 650 8302
Fax	34 91 650 8236
Email	mail@runnymede-college.com
Website	www.runnymede-college.com
Address	Salvia 30, La Moraleja, Madrid, 28109, Spain

STAFF

Head of School Frank M. Powell, Ed.D.
Head of Junior School Christopher Say, Ed.D.
Deputy Head Francis Murphy, Ed.D.

Bursar Juan Antonio Llorente
Head of IT Luis de Avendaño
Librarian Natalia Ciordia

INFORMATION

Grade levels N–12
School year September–June
School type coeducational, day
Year founded 1967
Tuition/fee currency Euro
Tuition range 5,226–10,389

Annual fees Insurance 19; Busing 1,650;
Lunch 1,145
One time fees Registration 1,355
Graduates attending college 90%
Graduates have attended Oxford U, Imperial Col,
Queen Mary U of London, U Pontificia Comillas,
U of Sussex

EDUCATIONAL PROGRAM

Curriculum UK, IGCSE, GCE Advanced Levels
Average class size Elementary 25; Secondary 22
Language(s) of instruction English
Language(s) taught Spanish, French
Staff specialists computer, counselor, ESL,
learning disabilities, librarian, math resource,
psychologist

Special curricular programs art, instrumental
music, vocal music, computer/technology,
physical education
Extra curricular programs computers, dance,
drama, excursions/expeditions, newspaper,
photography, yearbook
Sports basketball, football, golf, hockey, martial
arts, rugby, soccer, swimming, tennis, track and
field, volleyball
Examinations A-level GCE, GCSE, IGCSE, PSAT, SAT

CAMPUS FACILITIES

Location Urban
Campus 1 hectare, 2 buildings, 34 classrooms,
1 computer lab, 51 instructional computers,

19,000 library volumes, 1 auditorium,
1 cafeteria, 1 gymnasium, 1 infirmary,
2 playing fields, 2 science labs

Data from 2006/07 school year.

BELLVER INTERNATIONAL COLLEGE

Phone	34 971 401679
Fax	34 971 401762
Email	info@bellvercollege.com
Website	bellvercollege.com
Address	Jose Costa Ferrer 5, Marivent, Cala Mayor, Palma de Mallorca, Baleares, 07015, Spain

STAFF

Head Teacher Larry J. Longhurst, Ed.D.
Secondary Coordinator David Anderson

Primary Coordinator Gillian Amengual
Business/Finance Manager Mark Muirhead

INFORMATION

Grade levels N–13
School year September–June
School type coeducational, day, proprietary
Year founded 1950
Enrollment Nursery 24; PreK 24;
Elementary K–5 144; Middle School 6–8 70;
High School 9–12 60; Grade 13 10; Total 332
Nationalities of student body US 5; UK 92;
Spaniard 181; Other(s) (German) 54

Tuition/fee currency Euro
Tuition range 4,530–7,560
Annual fees Insurance 15; Lunch 1,360
One time fees Registration 1,200
Graduates attending college 100%
Graduates have attended Cambridge U,
Imperial Col London, King's Col, Durham U

EDUCATIONAL PROGRAM

Curriculum UK, GCE Advanced Level
Average class size Elementary 24; Secondary 22
Language(s) of instruction English
Language(s) taught French, Spanish, Catalan, German
Staff specialists computer, counselor, librarian
Special curricular programs art, vocal music, computer/technology, physical education, drama

Extra curricular programs computers, excursions/expeditions, choir, recorder, German, Karate
Sports basketball, football, hockey, soccer, swimming, tennis, track and field, volleyball
Examinations A-level GCE, GCSE, IGCSE

CAMPUS FACILITIES

Location Urban
Campus 1 hectare, 2 buildings, 25 classrooms, 1 computer lab, 40 instructional computers,

1 auditorium, 2 covered play areas, 1 gymnasium, 2 science labs, air conditioning

Data from 2006/07 school year.

AMERICAN SCHOOL OF VALENCIA (COLEGIO HISPANO-NORTEAMERICANO)

Phone	34 96 140 5412
Fax	34 96 140 5039
Email	saaratatem@asvalencia.org
Website	www.asvalencia.org
Address	Avenida Sierra Calderona 29, Urb. Los Monasterios, Puzol, Valencia, 46530, Spain
Mailing address	Apartado de Correos No. 9, 46530 Puzol, Valencia, Spain

STAFF

Director Saara Tatem
High School Principal Robyn Chapel
Elementary and Preschool Principal Kym Brown
High School Guidance Counselor Emily Thomsen
Elementary Counselor Felicitas Berazay
IB Diploma Coordinator Marc Boyer

Finance Manager Ildefonso Segura
Librarian Alex Caamaño
Teaching staff Full time 57; Part time 5; Total 62
Nationalities of teaching staff US 24; UK 14;
Spaniard 19; Other(s) (Canadian) 5

INFORMATION

Grade levels N–12
School year September–June
School type coeducational, day, private non-profit
Year founded 1980
Governed by elected Board of Directors
Accredited by Middle States
Regional organizations ECIS, MAIS
Enrollment Nursery 18; PreK 103;
Elementary K–5 301; Middle School 6–8 143;
High School 9–12 170; Total 735

Nationalities of student body US 45; UK 3;
Spaniard 648; Other(s) (Dane, Japanese) 39
Tuition/fee currency Euro
Tuition range 3,850–4,800
Annual fees Registration 160; Busing 1,170;
Lunch 870; Books 190
Graduates attending college 100%
Graduates have attended Tufts U, Oxford U,
U de Navarra, U Pontificia Comillas

EDUCATIONAL PROGRAM

Curriculum US, National, IB Diploma
Average class size Elementary 24; Secondary 22
Language(s) of instruction English, Spanish
Language(s) taught French, Valenciano, German
Staff specialists computer, counselor, ESL, learning
disabilities, librarian, nurse, psychologist
Special curricular programs art, instrumental
music, computer/technology, physical education

Extra curricular programs dance, excursions/
expeditions, yearbook, art and crafts
Sports basketball, martial arts, soccer,
swimming, volleyball
Clubs soccer, basketball, volleyball, Judo, art
and crafts, ballet, Model UN, FCE preparation,
PET preparation, Europrojects
Examinations IB, PSAT, SAT, FCE, PET

CAMPUS FACILITIES

Location Suburban
Campus 3 buildings, 57 classrooms,
2 computer labs, 50 instructional computers,
8,500 library volumes, 1 auditorium,

2 cafeterias, 1 gymnasium, 1 infirmary,
5 playing fields, 4 science labs, 1 pool,
air conditioning

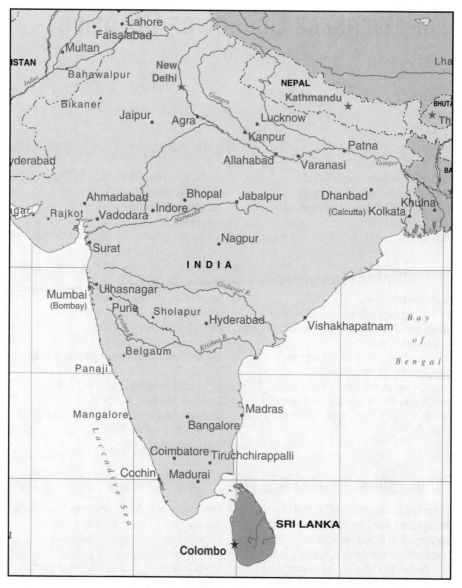

SRI LANKA

Area:	65,610 sq km
Population:	20,926,315
Capital:	Colombo
Currency:	Sri Lankan Rupee (LKR)
Languages:	Sinhala

THE OVERSEAS SCHOOL OF COLOMBO

Phone	94 11 2 784 920
Fax	94 11 2784 999
Email	admin@osc.lk
Website	www.osc.lk
Address	Pelawatte, PO Box 9, Battaramulla, Colombo, Sri Lanka

STAFF

Head of School Laurie McLellan
Primary Principal Adam Campbell
Assistant Head and Secondary Principal
Oli Tooher-Hancock
Business Manager H. A. P. Wanigasekera

Head of Information Technology Toni Nash
Library Coordinator Cathy Hunt
Teaching staff Full time 65; Total 65
Nationalities of teaching staff US 7; UK 15; Sri
Lankan 27; Other(s) (Australian, Canadian) 16

INFORMATION

Grade levels PreK–12
School year August–June
School type coeducational, day, private non-profit
Year founded 1957
Governed by elected Board of Directors
Accredited by CIS, Middle States
Regional organizations ECIS, NESA
Enrollment PreK 34; Elementary K–5 173;
Middle School 6–8 94; High School 9–12 113;
Total 414

Nationalities of student body US 39; UK 48; Sri
Lankan 42; Other(s) (Dutch, Indian) 285
Tuition/fee currency US Dollar
Tuition range 6,628–14,732
One time fees Registration 2,875; Refundable
Deposit–Preschool to Grade 5: 228;
Refundable Deposit–Grades 6–12: 455
Graduates attending college 95%
Graduates have attended London School of
Economics, Stanford U, Monash U,
U of Pennsylvania, McGill U

EDUCATIONAL PROGRAM

Curriculum IB Diploma, IBPYP, IBMYP
Average class size Elementary 20; Secondary 15
Language(s) of instruction English
Language(s) taught French, Spanish, Japanese
Staff specialists computer, counselor, ESL,
learning disabilities, librarian, physician
Special curricular programs art, vocal music,
computer/technology, physical education

Extra curricular programs computers, community
service, dance, drama, environmental
conservation, excursions/expeditions,
photography, yearbook
Sports basketball, cricket, football, soccer,
swimming, track and field
Examinations IB, PSAT, SAT, SAT II, TOEFL

CAMPUS FACILITIES

Location Suburban
Campus 2 hectares, 6 buildings, 42 classrooms,
3 computer labs, 100 instructional computers,
23,000 library volumes, 1 auditorium,

1 cafeteria, 1 covered play area, 1 gymnasium,
1 infirmary, 2 playing fields, 3 science labs,
1 pool, 1 tennis court, air conditioning

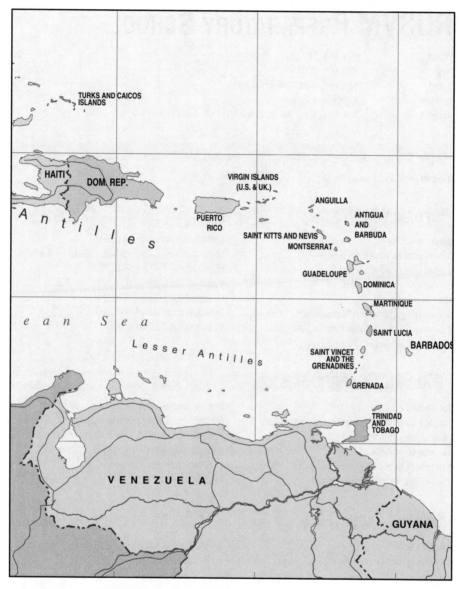

ST. KITTS, WEST INDIES

Area:	168 sq km
Population:	39,349
Capital:	Basseterre
Currency:	East Caribbean Dollar (XCD)
Languages:	English

RUSVM PREPARATORY SCHOOL

Phone	869 465 2405
Fax	869 465 1203
Email	jsandquist@rossvet.edu.kn
Website	www.rossu.edu
Address	Box 334, West Farm, Basseterre, St. Kitts

STAFF

Director Jane Sandquist, Ph.D.

INFORMATION

Grade levels N–12
School year September–June
School type coeducational,
company-sponsored, day
Year founded 2001
Governed by appointed Management Team
Sponsored by Ross University School of
Veterinary Medicine

Enrollment Nursery 5; PreK 9;
Elementary K–5 20; Middle School 6–8 10;
High School 9–12 9; Total 53
Nationalities of student body US 41; UK 4;
Other(s) (Argentine, Thai) 8
Tuition/fee currency US Dollar
Tuition range 1,050–6,000

EDUCATIONAL PROGRAM

Curriculum US
Average class size Elementary 6; Secondary 2
Language(s) of instruction English
Language(s) taught Spanish
Staff specialists computer, counselor, learning
disabilities, nurse, psychologist

Special curricular programs art, computer/
technology, distance learning, physical education
Extra curricular programs computers, community
service, dance, environmental conservation,
excursions/expeditions, newspaper
Examinations Iowa

CAMPUS FACILITIES

Location Rural
Campus 40 hectares, 1 building, 7 classrooms,
1 computer lab, 24 instructional computers,

2,000 library volumes, 1 cafeteria, 1 infirmary,
air conditioning

Data from 2006/07 school year.

SUDAN

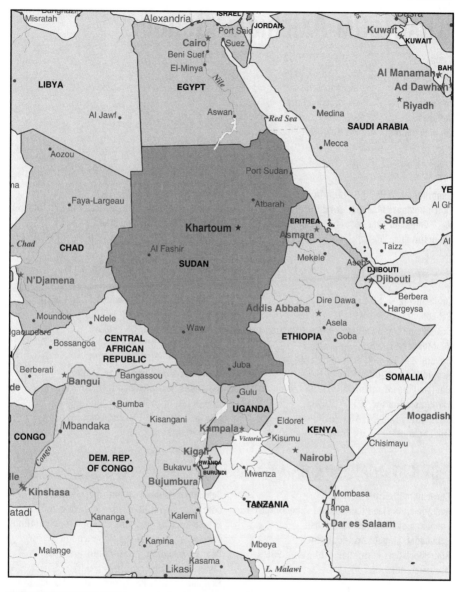

SUDAN

Area:	2,505,810 sq km
Population:	39,379,358
Capital:	Khartoum
Currency:	Sudanese Dinar (SDD)
Languages:	Arabic

KHARTOUM AMERICAN SCHOOL

Phone	249 183 512042
Fax	249 183 512044
Email	kas@krtams.org
Website	www.krtams.org
Address	Street 69 and Cemetery Road, Khartoum, 11111, Sudan
Mailing address	PO Box 699, Khartoum, Sudan

STAFF

Superintendent Philip L. Clinton
Office/Business Manager Anna Garcia
K–12 Computer Teacher/Network Administrator
Damianne President

Librarian Sara Stubbins
Teaching staff Full time 32; Part time 2; Total 34
Nationalities of teaching staff US 15; UK 2;
Sudanese 4; Other(s) (Australian, Filipino) 13

INFORMATION

Grade levels N–12
School year August–May
School type coeducational, day, private non-profit
Year founded 1957
Governed by elected School Board
Accredited by Middle States
Regional organizations AISA, ECIS
Enrollment Nursery 10; PreK 30;
Elementary K–5 95; Middle School 6–8 50;
High School 9–12 50; Total 235

Nationalities of student body US 28; UK 10;
Sudanese 25; Other(s) 172
Tuition/fee currency US Dollar
Tuition range 5,000–13,800
Annual fees Capital Levy 1,200
Graduates attending college 100%
Graduates have attended U of Colorado in
Boulder, U of Indiana in Bloomington,
U of Toledo, Col of William and Mary,
U of Virginia

EDUCATIONAL PROGRAM

Curriculum US, Intl, AP
Average class size Elementary 15; Secondary 12
Language(s) of instruction English
Language(s) taught Arabic, French
Staff specialists computer, counselor, ESL,
librarian, nurse

Special curricular programs art, vocal music,
computer/technology, physical education
Extra curricular programs computers, community
service, literary magazine, yearbook
Sports basketball, cross-country, soccer
Clubs Model UN
Examinations AP, PSAT, SAT, SAT II, TOEFL, ISA

CAMPUS FACILITIES

Location Suburban
Campus 3 hectares, 10 buildings, 23 classrooms,
1 computer lab, 70 instructional computers,

8,500 library volumes, 4 covered play areas,
1 infirmary, 2 playing fields, 1 science lab,
air conditioning

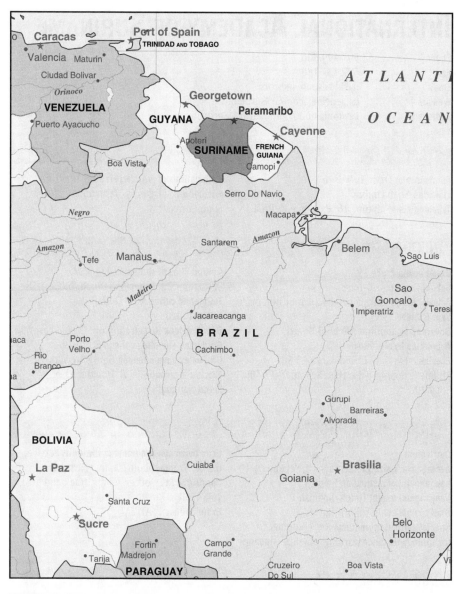

SURINAME

Area:	163,270 sq km
Population:	470,784
Capital:	Paramaribo
Currency:	Surinam Dollar (SRD)
Languages:	Dutch, English

INTERNATIONAL ACADEMY OF SURINAME

Phone   597 499 806
Fax   597 427 188
Email   davidwilson@nics.org
Website   ca.geocities.com/acssuriname/
Address   Lawtonlaan 20, Paramaribo, Suriname

STAFF

Administrator David L. Wilson
Librarian Noah Lindsay
Teaching staff Full time 16; Part time 2; Total 18

Nationalities of teaching staff US 12;
Surinamer 3; Other(s) (Canadian,
South African) 3

INFORMATION

Grade levels PreK–12
School year August–June
School type coeducational, day, private non-profit
Year founded 1985
Governed by appointed School Board
Accredited by Southern
Enrollment PreK 6; Elementary K–5 50;
Middle School 6–8 14; High School 9–12 30;
Total 100

Nationalities of student body US 22;
Surinamer 20; Other(s) (Dutch, Indian) 58
Tuition/fee currency US Dollar
Tuition 6,000
One time fees Registration 60; Capital Levy 600
Graduates attending college 88%
Graduates have attended Georgetown U,
Florida International U, Houghton Col,
Seoul National U

EDUCATIONAL PROGRAM

Curriculum US
Average class size Elementary 10; Secondary 10
Language(s) of instruction English
Language(s) taught Dutch, Spanish
Staff specialists ESL, librarian
Special curricular programs art, computer/
technology, distance learning, physical education

Extra curricular programs community service,
dance, drama, photography, yearbook
Sports cricket, soccer, tennis, track and field,
volleyball
Examinations PSAT, SAT

CAMPUS FACILITIES

Location Suburban
Campus 2 hectares, 3 buildings, 15 classrooms,
1 computer lab, 15 instructional computers,

9,000 library volumes, 1 auditorium,
1 cafeteria, 1 gymnasium, 1 playing field,
1 science lab, air conditioning

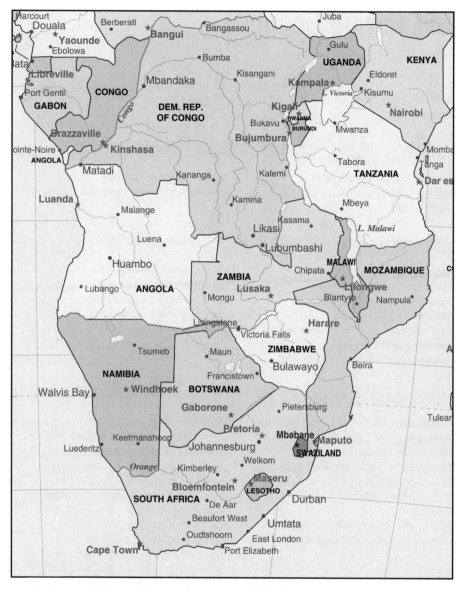

SWAZILAND

Area:	17,363 sq km
Population:	1,133,066
Capital:	Mbabane
Currency:	Lilangeni (SZL)
Languages:	English, siSwati

Sifundzani School

Phone	268 404 2465
Fax	268 404 0320
Email	sifundzani@realnet.co.sz
Address	Riverside Drive, Ridge Street, Mbabane, Hhohho, H100, Swaziland
Mailing address	PO Box A286, Swazi Plaza, Mbabane, Swaziland

STAFF

Principal Ella M Magongo, Ed.D.
Principal, grades 8–12 P. R. Magongo
Deputy Principal Anna Simelane

School Secretary Z. Hatton
Head of Library/Media Center Margaret Briar

INFORMATION

Grade levels 1–12
School year January–December
School type coeducational, day
Year founded 1981
Governed by appointed and elected School Board
Regional organizations AISA
Tuition/fee currency Swaziland Lilangeni

Tuition range 5,400–14,400
Annual fees Capital Levy 100
One time fees Registration 100
Graduates attending college 100%
Graduates have attended Stellenbosch U, Rhodes U, Witwatersrand U, Durban U

EDUCATIONAL PROGRAM

Curriculum US, UK, National, Intl, IGCSE, HIGSE
Average class size Elementary 30; Secondary 20
Language(s) of instruction English
Language(s) taught English, French, Siswati, Portuguese, Afrikaans
Staff specialists computer, librarian, math resource
Special curricular programs art, vocal music, computer/technology, physical education

Extra curricular programs computers, community service, dance, drama, environmental conservation, excursions/expeditions, yearbook, hand crafts, cooking, pottery
Sports badminton, basketball, cricket, cross-country, football, golf, gymnastics, hockey, rugby, soccer, squash, swimming, tennis, track and field, volleyball
Clubs chess, sewing, painting, craft, drama, home industries, knitting
Examinations GCSE, IGCSE, SPC, HIGCSE

CAMPUS FACILITIES

Location Urban
Campus 20 hectares, 12 buildings, 36 classrooms, 2 computer labs, 50 instructional computers,

9,000 library volumes, 2 auditoriums, 2 cafeterias, 4 covered play areas, 3 playing fields, 2 science labs, 1 pool, 2 tennis courts

Data from 2006/07 school year.

SWEDEN

Area:	449,964 sq km
Population:	9,031,088
Capital:	Stockholm
Currency:	Swedish Krona (SEK)
Languages:	Swedish

INTERNATIONAL SCHOOL OF THE GOTHENBURG REGION

Phone	46 31 3672900
Fax	46 31 3672901
Email	kakf@isgr.se
Website	www.isgr.se
Address	Molinsgatan 6, Gothenburg, 411 33, Sweden
Mailing address	Molinsgatan 6, S-411 33 Göteborg, Sweden

STAFF

Managing Director Tage Y. Gumaelius, Ed.D.
Principal, International Section
Kathy Khayatt Farajallah
Principal, Swedish Section AnnChristin Rothstein
Principal, High School Ann Malmberg
Business Manager Imre Tomasits

ICT Manager Magnus Hall
Librarian Rouhia Lotfkhah
Teaching staff Full time 74; Part time 4; Total 78
Nationalities of teaching staff US 9; UK 8;
Swede 42; Other(s) (Australian, Canadian) 19

INFORMATION

Grade levels K–10
School year December–June
School type coeducational, day, private
non-profit, proprietary
Year founded 1997
Governed by appointed Gothenburg Region
Sponsored by Gothenburg Regional Municipalities

Regional organizations ECIS
Enrollment Elementary K–5 416;
Middle School 6–8 442; Total 858
Nationalities of student body US 27; UK 21;
Swede 327; Other(s) (Dutch, French) 483
Tuition/fee currency Swedish Krona
Tuition range 5,100–25,100

EDUCATIONAL PROGRAM

Curriculum National, Intl, IBPYP, IBMYP
Average class size Elementary 20; Secondary 25
Language(s) of instruction English, Swedish
Language(s) taught French, Spanish

Staff specialists computer, counselor, ESL,
learning disabilities, librarian, math resource,
nurse, physician, psychologist, reading resource
Special curricular programs art, computer/
technology, physical education
Sports basketball, soccer, track and field

CAMPUS FACILITIES

Location Urban
Campus 4 buildings, 40 classrooms,
2 computer labs, 60 instructional computers,

6,000 library volumes, 1 auditorium,
1 cafeteria, 2 gymnasiums, 2 infirmaries,
2 playing fields, 4 science labs

INTERNATIONAL SCHOOL OF HELSINGBORG

Phone 46 42 10 57 05
Fax 46 42 13 41 90
Email ish@helsingborg.se
Website www.helsingborg.se/internationalschool
Address Västra Allén 7, Helsingborg, S 25451, Sweden

STAFF

Head of School Anders Nilsson
MYP Coordinator Roseanne McCormack
PYP Coordinator Carla Johansson
IB Diploma Coordinator Gideon Boulton
Guidance Counselor Gabrielle Mastmeier

Head of Technology John Noonan
Librarians Margareta Carlquist and Annelie Kharadi
Teaching staff Full time 38; Total 38
Nationalities of teaching staff US 9; UK 10;
Swede 14; Other(s) (Canadian, Irish) 5

INFORMATION

Grade levels PreK–12
School year August–June
School type coeducational, day
Year founded 1995
Governed by The City of Helsingborg
Regional organizations ECIS

Enrollment PreK 21; Elementary K–5 143;
Middle School 6–8 101;
High School 9–12 111; Total 376
Nationalities of student body US 42; UK 57;
Swede 79; Other(s) (French, Dutch) 198
Graduates attending college 50%

EDUCATIONAL PROGRAM

Curriculum National, IB Diploma, IBPYP, IBMYP
Average class size Elementary 17; Secondary 18
Language(s) of instruction English
Language(s) taught French, German, Spanish,
Swedish
Staff specialists computer, counselor, ESL,
learning disabilities, librarian, math resource,
nurse, psychologist, reading resource,
speech/hearing

Special curricular programs art, instrumental
music, vocal music, computer/technology,
physical education
Extra curricular programs computers, community
service, drama
Sports badminton, baseball, basketball,
cross-country, football, rugby, soccer, swimming
Clubs homework, art, language
Examinations IB

CAMPUS FACILITIES

Location Urban
Campus 2 hectares, 1 building, 36 classrooms,
2 computer labs, 80 instructional computers,

7,000 library volumes, 1 auditorium,
1 cafeteria, 1 gymnasium, 1 infirmary,
1 playing field, 2 science labs

SIGTUNASKOLAN HUMANISTISKA LÄROVERKET

Phone	46 8 592 57100
Fax	46 8 592 57250
Email	info@sshl.se
Website	www.sshl.se
Address	Manfred Björkquists allé 6-8, PO Box 508, Sigtuna, Stockholm, SE-193 28, Sweden

STAFF

Principal Rune E.S. Svaninger, Ed.D.
Deputy Principal Conny Lindberg
Deputy Principal/MYP Coordinator
Lena Månsson, Ed.D.

Manager Jan-Peter Grundström
Technology Coordinator Anna-Märta Stolt-Eidman
Librarian Malin Bucht

INFORMATION

Grade levels 7–12
School year August–June
School type boarding, coeducational, day, private non-profit
Year founded 1926
Governed by appointed Board

Regional organizations ECIS
Tuition/fee currency Swedish Krona
Tuition range 132,500–261,100
Annual fees Boarding, 7–day 261,100
One time fees Registration 5,000
Graduates attending college 90%

EDUCATIONAL PROGRAM

Curriculum National, IB Diploma, IBMYP
Average class size Elementary 22; Secondary 20
Language(s) of instruction English, Swedish
Language(s) taught German, French, Spanish, Latin
Staff specialists computer, counselor, learning disabilities, librarian, math resource, nurse, physician, psychologist, reading resource, speech/hearing
Special curricular programs art, instrumental music, vocal music, computer/technology, physical education, vocational

Extra curricular programs computers, community service, dance, drama, environmental conservation, excursions/expeditions, literary magazine, newspaper, photography, yearbook
Sports badminton, basketball, golf, gymnastics, hockey, skiing, soccer, softball, swimming, tennis, track and field, volleyball, rowing, fencing, shooting
Clubs political, literary, theater, environmental systems
Examinations IB, SAT, TOEFL

CAMPUS FACILITIES

Location Rural
Campus 175 hectares, 42 buildings, 38 classrooms, 3 computer labs, 150 instructional computers,

6,000 library volumes, 3 auditoriums, 1 cafeteria, 1 gymnasium, 1 infirmary, 3 playing fields, 4 science labs, 1 tennis court

Data from 2006/07 school year.

THE STOCKHOLM INTERNATIONAL SCHOOL

Phone	46 8 412 4000
Fax	46 8 412 4001
Email	admin@intsch.se
Website	www.intsch.se
Address	Johannesgatan 18, Stockholm, SE-111 38, Sweden

STAFF

Director Richard E. Mast
Director Chris Mockrish
Registrar Erik Bennett
Business Manager Cecilia Frygner

Teaching staff Full time 56; Part time 14; Total 70
Nationalities of teaching staff US 15; UK 13; Swede 42

INFORMATION

Grade levels PreK–12
School year August–June
School type coeducational, day, private non-profit
Year founded 1951
Governed by appointed and elected Board of Directors
Accredited by CIS, Middle States
Regional organizations ECIS
Enrollment PreK 15; Elementary K–5 151; Middle School 6–8 107; High School 9–12 126; Total 399

Nationalities of student body US 55; UK 37; Swede 68; Other(s) (Korean, Finn) 239
Tuition/fee currency Swedish Krona
Tuition range 73,000–151,000
One time fees Registration 22,000; Building Fund 7,000
Graduates attending college 68%
Graduates have attended U of Tokyo, U of Stockholm, U of Antwerp, U of Budapest, American U of Vienna

EDUCATIONAL PROGRAM

Curriculum Intl, IB Diploma, IBMYP
Average class size Elementary 18; Secondary 18
Language(s) of instruction English

Language(s) taught French, Swedish, German, Spanish

CAMPUS FACILITIES

Location Urban
Campus 1 building, 28 classrooms, 1 computer lab, 100 instructional computers,

15,000 library volumes, 1 auditorium, 1 cafeteria, 1 covered play area, 1 gymnasium, 1 infirmary, 1 playing field, 2 science labs

SWITZERLAND

SWITZERLAND

Area:	41,290 sq km
Population:	7,554,661
Capital:	Bern
Currency:	Swiss Franc (CHF)
Languages:	German

THE INTERNATIONAL SCHOOL OF THE BASEL REGION AG

Phone	41 61 715 3333
Fax	41 61 715 3375
Email	info@isbasel.ch
Website	www.isbasel.ch
Address	Fleischbachstrasse 2, Reinach, 4153, Switzerland

STAFF

Director Lesley M. Barron
Junior School Principal Brenda Christopherson
Middle School Principal Brian Weinrich
High School Principal Kevin Skeoch
Finance Officer Judith Thorsteinsson
IT Services Manager Claude Sanford

Librarian Robyn Stewart
Teaching staff Full time 160; Part time 10; Total 170
Nationalities of teaching staff US 25; UK 55; Swiss 25; Other(s) (Canadian, New Zealander) 65

INFORMATION

Grade levels PreK–12
School year August–June
School type coeducational, day, private non-profit
Year founded 1979
Governed by elected Board
Accredited by CIS, New England
Regional organizations ECIS, SGIS
Enrollment PreK 80; Elementary K–5 400; Middle School 6–8 260; High School 9–12 310; Total 1,050

Nationalities of student body US 160; UK 220; Swiss 90; Other(s) (Canadian, German) 580
Tuition/fee currency Swiss Franc
Tuition range 17,136–29,500
One time fees Registration 4,500
Graduates attending college 95%
Graduates have attended Cambridge U, Columbia U, Harvard U, Oxford U, Stanford U

EDUCATIONAL PROGRAM

Curriculum Intl, IB Diploma, IBPYP, IBMYP, ISB Academic Diploma
Average class size Elementary 20; Secondary 18
Language(s) of instruction English
Language(s) taught German, French, English
Staff specialists computer, ESL, learning disabilities, librarian, nurse
Special curricular programs art, instrumental music, vocal music, computer/technology, physical education

Extra curricular programs computers, community service, dance, drama, environmental conservation, excursions/expeditions, newspaper, photography, yearbook
Sports baseball, basketball, cross-country, rugby, skiing, soccer, softball, swimming, track and field, volleyball
Examinations IB, PSAT, SAT, SAT II

CAMPUS FACILITIES

Location Suburban
Campus 24000 hectares, 2 buildings, 100 classrooms, 5 computer labs, 200 instructional computers, 25,000 library volumes, 2 auditoriums, 2 cafeterias, 2 covered play areas, 6 gymnasiums, 2 infirmaries, 2 playing fields, 6 science labs

INTERNATIONAL SCHOOL OF BERNE

Phone	41 31 951 2358
Fax	41 31 951 1710
Email	office@isberne.ch
Website	www.isberne.ch
Address	Mattenstrasse 3, Gümligen, 3073, Switzerland

STAFF

Director Kevin T. Page
Secondary School Principal Barry Mansfield
Elementary School Principal Jason Barton
Early Learning Center Coordinator Patricia Drechsel
Guidance and Pastoral Care Coordinator Christopher Warren

Business Manager Fiona Meins
Head of IT Alain Levy
Head of Media Center Jill Pennington
Teaching staff Full time 39; Part time 4; Total 43
Nationalities of teaching staff US 9; UK 11; Swiss 3; Other(s) (New Zealander) 20

INFORMATION

Grade levels N–12
School year August–June
School type coeducational, day, private non-profit
Year founded 1961
Governed by elected Nine Member Board of Directors
Accredited by CIS, New England
Regional organizations ECIS, SGIS
Enrollment Nursery 12; PreK 15; Elementary K–5 113; Middle School 6–8 60; High School 9–12 80; Total 280

Nationalities of student body US 36; UK 26; Swiss 32; Other(s) (German, Indian) 186
Tuition/fee currency Swiss Franc
Tuition range 7,458–27,030
Annual fees Registration 250; Books 250; Re-Enrollment 250
One time fees Capital 3,500
Graduates attending college 95%
Graduates have attended Stanford U, Southhampton U, McGill U, U of British Columbia, George Washington U

EDUCATIONAL PROGRAM

Curriculum Intl, IB Diploma, IBPYP, IBMYP
Average class size Elementary 20; Secondary 18
Language(s) of instruction English
Language(s) taught French, German
Staff specialists computer, ESL, learning disabilities, librarian
Special curricular programs art, instrumental music, vocal music, computer/technology, physical education

Extra curricular programs community service, drama, environmental conservation, newspaper, yearbook
Sports basketball, cross-country, football, rugby, skiing, soccer, swimming, track and field, volleyball
Examinations IB, PSAT, SAT, SAT II

CAMPUS FACILITIES

Location Suburban
Campus 5 hectares, 5 buildings, 25 classrooms, 2 computer labs, 100 instructional computers, 10,000 library volumes, 1 auditorium, 1 cafeteria, 1 gymnasium, 1 infirmary, 1 playing field, 3 science labs

Geneva   **SWITZERLAND**

COLLÈGE DU LÉMAN INTERNATIONAL SCHOOL

Phone	41 22 775 5555
Fax	41 22 775 5559
Email	info@cdl.ch
Website	www.cdl.ch
Address	74 Route de Sauverny, Versoix/Geneva, CH-1290, Switzerland

STAFF

Director General DeHaven Fleming
Head of School Terence B. Gale
High School Principal James Bearblock
Middle School Principal Ian Menzies
Primary School Principal Alain Delaune
Principal of French Programme Giao Fehr

Financial Director Françoise Bommensatt
Head of Library/Media Center Elizabeth Brown
Teaching staff Full time 209; Total 209
Nationalities of teaching staff US 30; UK 42; Swiss 75; Other(s) 62

INFORMATION

Grade levels PreK–13
School year September–June
School type boarding, coeducational, day
Year founded 1960
Governed by appointed Advisory Board
Accredited by CIS, New England
Regional organizations ECIS, SGIS
Enrollment PreK 225; Elementary K–5 540; Middle School 6–8 331; High School 9–12 659; Total 1,755
Nationalities of student body US 333; UK 333; Swiss 562; Other(s) 527

Tuition/fee currency Swiss Franc
Tuition range 53,500–56,200
Annual fees Busing 3,500; Lunch 2,750
One time fees Registration 1,000; Capital Levy 3,000
Boarding program grades 6–13
Boarding program length 5-day and 7-day
Boys 120 **Girls** 100
Graduates attending college 98%
Graduates have attended Cornell U, Georgetown U, Oxford U, Ecole Polytechnique Federale de Lausanne, London School of Economics

(Continued)

COLLÈGE DU LÉMAN INTERNATIONAL SCHOOL (Continued)

EDUCATIONAL PROGRAM

Curriculum US, UK, National, AP, IB Diploma, IBPYP, IBMYP, IGCSE, Swiss Maturite, French Baccalaureat
Average class size Elementary 20; Secondary 20

Language(s) of instruction English, French
Language(s) taught German, Spanish, Italian, Russian, Arabic

CAMPUS FACILITIES

Location Suburban
Campus 8 hectares, 18 buildings, 90 classrooms, 3 computer labs, 66 instructional computers, 20,000 library volumes, 2 auditoriums, 2 cafeterias, 2 covered play areas, 1 gymnasium, 1 infirmary, 5 playing fields, 6 science labs, 1 pool, 3 tennis courts

FOUNDATION OF THE INTERNATIONAL SCHOOL OF GENEVA

Phone	41 22 787 24 00
Fax	41 22 787 24 10
Email	admissions@ecolint.ch
Website	www.ecolint.ch
Address	62, route de Chene, 1208 Genève (La Grande Boissière Campus), 1297 Founex (La Châtaigneraie Campus), 11 route des Morillons, 1218 Grand Saconnex (Campus des Nations), Geneva, 1208, Switzerland
Mailing address	62 Route de Chêne, 1208 Genève, Switzerland

STAFF

Director General Nicholas Tate, Ph.D.
Campus Principal La Ch,taigneriae Michel Chinal
Campus Principal La Grande Boissière
Jean-Guy Carpentier
Campus Principal Campus des Nations
Andrew Hand

Director of Finance Francois Collini
IT Director Eric Domenig
Teaching staff Full time 243; Part time 150; Total 393
Nationalities of teaching staff US 23; UK 130; Swiss 90; Other(s) (French, Canadian) 150

INFORMATION

Grade levels N–13
School year September–June
School type coeducational, day, private non-profit
Year founded 1924
Governed by elected Governing Board
Accredited by Middle States
Regional organizations ECIS, SGIS
Enrollment Nursery 75; PreK 145; Elementary K–5 1,450; Middle School 6–8 870; High School 9–12 1,035; Grade 13 300; Total 3,875

Nationalities of student body US 765; UK 790; Swiss 670; Other(s) (French) 1,650
Tuition/fee currency Swiss Franc
Tuition range 15,320–26,030
One time fees Registration 2,000; Capital Levy 2,500
Graduates attending college 95%
Graduates have attended McGill U, Oxbridge U, London School of Economics, Georgetown U, Princeton U

(Continued)

FOUNDATION OF THE INTERNATIONAL SCHOOL OF GENEVA
(Continued)

EDUCATIONAL PROGRAM

Curriculum UK, National, IB Diploma, IBPYP, IBMYP, IGCSE
Average class size Elementary 22; Secondary 18
Language(s) of instruction English, French
Language(s) taught German, Spanish, Italian
Staff specialists computer, counselor, ESL, learning disabilities, librarian, nurse, psychologist

Extra curricular programs community service, drama, excursions/expeditions, yearbook
Sports basketball, cross-country, rugby, skiing, soccer, track and field, volleyball
Examinations GCSE, IB, IGCSE, Maturité Suisse

CAMPUS FACILITIES

Location Suburban
Campus 11 hectares, 13 buildings, 6 computer labs, 100,000 library volumes, 2 tennis courts

GSTAAD INTERNATIONAL SCHOOL

Phone 41 33 744 2373
Fax 41 33 744 3578
Email gis@gstaad.ch
Website www.gstaadschool.ch
Address Ahorn, Gstaad, 3780, Switzerland

STAFF

Director Alain G. Souperbiet

INFORMATION

Grade levels 9–12
School year September–June
School type boarding, coeducational, proprietary
Year founded 1963
Governed by Private School
Sponsored by Limited Liability Company
Enrollment High School 9–12 23; Total 23
Nationalities of student body US 4; Host 19

Tuition/fee currency Swiss Franc
Tuition range 45,000–67,800
Boarding program grades 9–12
Boarding program length 7-day **Boys** 17 **Girls** 5
Graduates attending college 100%
Graduates have attended Suffolk U, Madrid, George Washington U, Business School of Lausanne, Brown U, Diplomacy School of Geneva

EDUCATIONAL PROGRAM

Curriculum US, UK, AP, IGCSE
Average class size Secondary 5
Language(s) of instruction English
Language(s) taught French, German, Spanish
Staff specialists computer, counselor, ESL, learning disabilities, math resource, reading resource
Special curricular programs computer/technology, physical education, special education

Extra curricular programs computers, excursions/expeditions
Sports basketball, football, golf, soccer, squash, swimming, tennis, track and field, rock climbing, mountain biking
Examinations A-level GCE, AP, GCSE, IGCSE, SAT, SAT II, TOEFL

CAMPUS FACILITIES

Location Rural
Campus 1 hectare, 1 building, 5 classrooms,
1 computer lab, 9 instructional computers, 2,000 library volumes

Data from 2006/07 school year.

AIGLON COLLEGE

Phone	41 24 496 6161
Fax	41 24 496 6162
Email	info@aiglon.ch
Website	www.aiglon.ch
Address	Rue Centrale, Chesières-Villars, Chesières, Vaud, 1885, Switzerland

STAFF

College Principal Rick Harwood, Ph.D.
Head of Junior School Didier Boutroux
Deputy Principal (Pastoral) Frank Thomson
Deputy Principal (Academic)
Richard Harwood, Ph.D.

Chief Operating Officer David Harris
Computer Services Manager Andre Jordaan
Library Services Manager Alison Jeffery

INFORMATION

Grade levels 5–13
School year September–July
School type boarding, coeducational, day, private non-profit
Year founded 1949
Governed by appointed Board of Governors
Accredited by New England
Regional organizations ECIS, SGIS
Enrollment Elementary K–5 11; Middle School 6–8 72; High School 9–12 204; Grade 13 68; Total 355
Nationalities of student body US 23; UK 41; Swiss 24; Other(s) (Saudi, Russian) 267

Tuition/fee currency Swiss Franc
Tuition range 17,000–64,400
Annual fees Insurance 2,200; Ski Pass 435
One time fees Registration 300; Alumni Association 1,250; Clothing (max) 3,700
Boarding program grades 5–13
Boarding program length 7-day
Boys 152 **Girls** 137
Graduates attending college 100%
Graduates have attended Stanford U, Oxford U, Yale U, Brown U, Tufts U

EDUCATIONAL PROGRAM

Curriculum UK, IGCSE
Average class size Elementary 15; Secondary 12
Language(s) of instruction English, French (Prep Form)
Language(s) taught English, French, Spanish, German, Italian, Russian
Staff specialists computer, counselor, ESL, learning disabilities, librarian, math resource, nurse, psychologist, reading resource, speech/hearing
Special curricular programs art, computer/technology, physical education, outdoor

Extra curricular programs computers, community service, dance, drama, environmental conservation, excursions/expeditions, literary magazine, newspaper, photography, yearbook, art, sports
Sports badminton, basketball, cross-country, football, golf, gymnastics, hockey, rugby, skiing, soccer, squash, swimming, tennis, track and field, volleyball
Examinations A-level GCE, GCSE, IGCSE, PSAT, SAT, SAT II, TOEFL

CAMPUS FACILITIES

Location Rural
Campus 5 hectares, 16 buildings, 29 classrooms, 4 computer labs, 125 instructional computers,

15,000 library volumes, 1 auditorium, 1 infirmary, 2 playing fields, 8 science labs, 2 tennis courts

Data from 2006/07 school year.

BRILLANTMONT INTERNATIONAL COLLEGE

Phone   41 21 310 0400
Fax   41 21 320 8417
Email   info@brillantmont.ch
Website   www.brillantmont.ch
Address   Avenue Secrétan 16, Lausanne, Vaud, 1005, Switzerland

STAFF

Director Philippe Pasche
Academic Head and Deputy Director
Geraldine Boland

Webmaster Christophe Guignard
Librarian John Maxwell

INFORMATION

Grade levels 8–12
School year September–June
School type boarding, coeducational, day,
proprietary
Year founded 1882
Accredited by CIS, New England
Regional organizations ECIS, SGIS
Nationalities of student body US 30; UK 30;
Swiss 10; Other(s) 70
Tuition/fee currency Swiss Franc

Tuition range 54,000–56,000
Annual fees Registration 500
Boarding program grades 8–12
Boarding program length 5-day and 7-day
Boys 30 **Girls** 60
Graduates attending college 95%
Graduates have attended U of New York, U of
Pittsburgh, Tufts U, George Washington U,
U of Sussex

EDUCATIONAL PROGRAM

Curriculum US, UK, AP, IGCSE, A Level
Average class size Secondary 15
Language(s) of instruction English
Language(s) taught French, German, Italian,
Spanish, Russian, English, Chinese
Staff specialists computer, counselor, ESL,
librarian, math resource
Special curricular programs art, computer/
technology, physical education

Extra curricular programs computers, community
service, dance, drama, environmental conservation,
excursions/expeditions, literary magazine,
photography, yearbook, Model UN, film and
media, cooking, aerobics, hip hop, salsa
Sports badminton, basketball, cross-country,
football, hockey, skiing, soccer, swimming,
tennis, track and field, volleyball, mountain
biking, ice-skating
Examinations A-level GCE, AP, GCSE, IGCSE,
PSAT, SAT, SAT II, TOEFL, AS level & A Level
(Cambridge Board), AICE

CAMPUS FACILITIES

Location Urban
Campus 4 hectares, 7 buildings, 12 classrooms,
2 computer labs, 20 instructional computers,

4,400 library volumes, 1 cafeteria, 1 gymnasium,
1 playing field, 2 science labs, 2 tennis courts

Data from 2006/07 school year.

INTERNATIONAL SCHOOL OF LAUSANNE

Phone	41 21 5600202
Fax	41 21 5600203
Email	info@isl.ch
Website	www.isl.ch
Address	Chemin de la Grangette 2, Le Mont sur Lausanne, 1052, Switzerland

STAFF

Director Simon G. Taylor
Asstistant Director and Secondary Principal John Ivett
Primary Principal Edward McBride
Middle School Principal Anthony Coles
High School Principal Yvonne Secker

Operations Manager Patricia Girardbille
Technology Coordinator Matt Plummer
Head of Library Janet Gereige
Teaching staff Full time 70; Part time 25; Total 95
Nationalities of teaching staff US 15; UK 25; Swiss 25; Other(s) (Australian) 30

INFORMATION

Grade levels PreK–12
School year September–June
School type coeducational, day, private non-profit
Year founded 1962
Governed by appointed Board
Accredited by CIS, New England
Regional organizations ECIS, SGIS
Enrollment Nursery 24; PreK 36; Elementary K–5 228; Middle School 6–8 132; High School 9–12 197; Total 617

Nationalities of student body US 144; UK 110; Swiss 81; Other(s) (German, Dutch) 282
Tuition/fee currency Swiss Franc
Tuition range 12,000–29,600
One time fees Registration 2,500
Graduates attending college 99%
Graduates have attended McGill U, Harvard U, Brown U, London School of Economics, Ecole Polytechnique Federale de Lausanne

EDUCATIONAL PROGRAM

Curriculum Intl, IB Diploma, IBPYP, IBMYP, IGCSE
Average class size Elementary 18; Secondary 20
Language(s) of instruction English
Language(s) taught French, Spanish, German, Swedish
Staff specialists computer, counselor, learning disabilities, librarian, nurse
Special curricular programs art, computer/ technology, physical education

Extra curricular programs community service, drama, yearbook
Sports badminton, basketball, cross-country, skiing, soccer, swimming, tennis, track and field, volleyball
Clubs student council, excursions
Examinations IB, SAT

CAMPUS FACILITIES

Location Suburban
Campus 1 building, 45 classrooms, 2 computer labs, 120 instructional computers, 15,000 library volumes, 1 auditorium,

1 cafeteria, 1 covered play area, 1 gymnasium, 1 infirmary, 1 playing field, 3 science labs, 4 tennis courts

KUMON LEYSIN ACADEMY OF SWITZERLAND

Phone	41 24 493 5335
Fax	41 24 493 5300
Email	klas@klas.ch
Website	www.kumon.ac.jp/klas
Address	Ave. Secretan, Leysin, Vaud, 1854, Switzerland
Mailing address	CH-1854, Leysin, Switzerland

STAFF

Principal Hiroshi Watanabe
Academic Dean Masahiro Zaita
Dean of Students William Mangan
Head of DFL John Southworth
General Manager Akemi Takayama

IT Coordinator/Campus Network Administrator
Michael Stowers
Teaching staff Full time 33; Part time 1; Total 34
Nationalities of teaching staff US 3; UK 8;
Other(s) (Japanese) 23

INFORMATION

Grade levels 10–12
School year July–May
School type boarding, coeducational
Year founded 1990
Governed by appointed Board of KLAS S.A.
Regional organizations ECIS, SGIS
Enrollment High School 9–12 177; Total 177
Nationalities of student body Other(s) 177

Tuition/fee currency Swiss Franc
Tuition 47,552
One time fees Registration 6,000; Insurance 300
Boarding program grades 10–12
Boarding program length 7-day **Boys** 87 **Girls** 90
Graduates attending college 99%
Graduates have attended U of Pennsylvania,
Tufts U, Hitotsubashi U, Waseda U, Keio U

EDUCATIONAL PROGRAM

Curriculum National, Japanese
Average class size Secondary 15
Language(s) of instruction English, Japanese
Language(s) taught French
Staff specialists computer, ESL, nurse
Special curricular programs art, computer/
technology

Extra curricular programs drama, yearbook, music
Sports badminton, basketball, cross-country,
football, skiing, soccer, squash, swimming,
tennis, track and field, volleyball
Examinations AP, PSAT, SAT, SAT II, TOEFL

CAMPUS FACILITIES

Location Rural
Campus 4 buildings, 21 classrooms,
2 computer labs, 45 instructional computers,

9,000 library volumes, 1 auditorium,
1 cafeteria, 1 infirmary, 1 science lab

Leysin American School

Phone	41 24 493 3777
Fax	41 24 494 1585
Email	vkuskovski@las.ch
Website	www.las.ch
Address	Batiment Beau Site, Leysin, CH 1854, Switzerland
Mailing address	CH 1854, Leysin, Switzerland

STAFF

Head of School Vladimir D. Kuskovski
Executive Director Steven Ott, Ph.D.
Administrative Director Doris Ott
Dean of Students Tim Stefanishyn
Academic Dean Brent McAvoy
IB Coordinator Tina Juurlink

Business Manager Maurice Felli
Director of Technology John Squier
Librarian Jeanne Hatch
Teaching staff Full time 55; Part time 9; Total 64
Nationalities of teaching staff US 46; UK 6;
Swiss 2; Other(s) (Canadian, French) 10

INFORMATION

Grade levels 9–13
School year September–June
School type boarding, coeducational, proprietary
Year founded 1960
Governed by appointed Board of Directors
Sponsored by Doris and Steven Ott
Accredited by CIS, Middle States
Regional organizations ECIS, SGIS
Enrollment High School 9–12 340;
Grade 13 15; Total 355

Nationalities of student body US 110; UK 3;
Swiss 4; Other(s) (Russian, Korean) 243
Tuition/fee currency Euro
Tuition 34,500
Boarding program grades 9–12
Boarding program length 7-day **Boys** 170 **Girls** 185
Graduates attending college 98%
Graduates have attended US Air Force Academy,
Harvard U, Boston U, Dartmouth Col,
Hamilton Col

EDUCATIONAL PROGRAM

Curriculum US, AP, IB Diploma
Average class size Secondary 13
Language(s) of instruction English
Language(s) taught French, Spanish, German
Staff specialists computer, counselor, ESL,
learning disabilities, librarian, nurse,
psychologist
Special curricular programs art, instrumental
music, vocal music, computer/technology,
physical education

Extra curricular programs community service,
dance, drama, excursions/expeditions, literary
magazine, newspaper, photography, yearbook
Sports basketball, cross-country, golf, hockey,
skiing, soccer, squash, swimming, tennis, track
and field, volleyball
Examinations IB, SAT, SAT II, TOEFL

CAMPUS FACILITIES

Location Rural
Campus 5 hectares, 12 buildings, 50 classrooms,
3 computer labs, 100 instructional computers,
19,000 library volumes, 2 auditoriums,

1 cafeteria, 1 covered play area, 2 gymnasiums,
1 infirmary, 2 playing fields, 4 science labs,
1 pool, 6 tennis courts

SWITZERLAND

ECOLE D'HUMANITÉ

Phone	41 33 972 9292
Fax	41 33 972 9211
Email	us.office@ecole.ch
Website	www.ecole.ch
Address	CH-6085, Hasliberg-Goldern, Switzerland

STAFF

Co-Director Kathleen Hennessy
Business/Finance Manager Hans Willi
Head of Technology Jim Lowry
Head of Library/Media Center Natalie Lüthi

Teaching staff Full time 38; Total 38
Nationalities of teaching staff US 7; UK 2; Swiss 15; Other(s) (German) 14

INFORMATION

Grade levels 1–13
School year September–June
School type boarding, coeducational, private non-profit
Year founded 1934
Governed by Genossenschaft der Ecole d'Humanité
Regional organizations ECIS, SGIS
Enrollment Elementary K–5 4; Middle School 6–8 44; High School 9–12 100; Total 148
Nationalities of student body US 20; UK 5; Swiss 78; Other(s) (German) 45

Tuition/fee currency Swiss Franc
Tuition range 38,000–42,000
One time fees Deposit for those residing outside of Switzerland 3,000; Deposit for those residing in Switzerland 2,000
Boarding program grades 5–13
Boarding program length 7-day **Boys** 74 **Girls** 70
Graduates attending college 95%
Graduates have attended U of Chicago, McGill U, Middlebury Col, Bard Col, Vassar Col

EDUCATIONAL PROGRAM

Curriculum US, UK, National, AP, Swiss Matura
Average class size Elementary 5; Secondary 8
Language(s) of instruction English, German
Language(s) taught French
Staff specialists counselor, psychologist

Extra curricular programs community service, drama, excursions/expeditions
Sports basketball, gymnastics, martial arts, skiing, soccer, tennis, volleyball
Examinations AP, PSAT, SAT, SAT II, TOEFL, LTE

CAMPUS FACILITIES

Location Rural
Campus 5 hectares, 20 buildings, 32 classrooms, 1 computer lab, 10 instructional computers,

22,000 library volumes, 1 auditorium, 1 cafeteria, 2 covered play areas, 1 gymnasium, 3 playing fields, 3 science labs, 1 tennis court

TASIS, THE AMERICAN SCHOOL IN SWITZERLAND

Phone	41 91 960 5151
Fax	41 91 993 2979
Email	admissions@tasis.ch
Website	www.tasis.com
Address	Via Collina D'Oro, Montagnola-Lugano, 6926, Switzerland

STAFF

Chairman of the Board of Directors Lynn F. Aeschliman
Head of School Jeffrey C. Bradley
Director of Admissions William E. Eichner
Director of Development Hans Figi

Dean of Student Affairs Thomas Bendel
Academic Dean John Nelson
Business Manager Massimo Gygax
Director of Information Technology Fulvio Galli
Librarian Thomas Mauro, Ph.D.

INFORMATION

Grade levels PreK–13
School year September–June
School type boarding, coeducational, day, private non-profit
Year founded 1956
Governed by elected TASIS Foundation Board
Accredited by CIS, New England
Regional organizations ECIS, SGIS
Enrollment PreK 6; Elementary K–5 85; Middle School 6–8 38; High School 9–12 300; Grade 13 6; Total 435

Nationalities of student body US 113; UK 9; Swede 13; Other(s) (Italian, German) 300
Tuition/fee currency Swiss Franc
Tuition 63,000
Annual fees Boarding, 7-day 63,000; Refundable Enrollment Deposit 3,500
One time fees Registration 300; Capital Levy 3,000
Boarding program length 7-day **Graduates attending college** 100%
Graduates have attended U of Virginia, Geroge Washington U, Boston U, Tufts U, New York U

(Continued)

TASIS, THE AMERICAN SCHOOL IN SWITZERLAND (Continued)

EDUCATIONAL PROGRAM

Curriculum US, AP, IB Diploma, Core Knowledge Curriculum for the Elementary School
Average class size Elementary 12; Secondary 13
Language(s) of instruction English
Language(s) taught French, German, Italian, Spanish
Staff specialists counselor, ESL, librarian, nurse
Special curricular programs art
Extra curricular programs community service, drama, environmental conservation, excursions/expeditions, newspaper, photography, yearbook

Sports baseball, basketball, cross-country, golf, martial arts, rugby, skiing, soccer, softball, squash, swimming, tennis, track and field, volleyball, ultimate frisbee, lacrosse, aerobics, horseback riding, hiking, mountain biking, rafting
Clubs Amnesty International, chess, environmental, Habitat for Humanity, Model UN, peer counseling, peer tutoring, student government
Examinations AP, IB, PSAT, SAT, SAT II, TOEFL

CAMPUS FACILITIES

Location Suburban
Campus 15 hectares, 19 buildings, 29 classrooms, 4 computer labs, 45 instructional computers, 20,000 library volumes, 1 auditorium,

2 cafeterias, 1 covered play area, 1 gymnasium, 1 infirmary, 1 playing field, 4 science labs, 1 pool

INSTITUT LE ROSEY

Phone	41 21 822 5500
Fax	41 21 822 5555
Email	rosey@rosey.ch
Website	www.rosey.ch
Address	Ch,teau du Rosey, Rolle, Vaud, 1180, Switzerland

STAFF

Directeur Général
Philippe A. Gudin de la Sablonnière
Head of School Michael Gray, Ph.D.
Head of Studies Henri-François Vellut, Ph.D.
IB Coordinator Steven Cranville
Counselor Malcolm Higgins

Secrétaire Général Danielle Llewellyn
IT Director Jean-Jacques Pioget
Librarian Pierre Bérubé
Teaching staff Full time 92; Part time 25; Total 117
Nationalities of teaching staff US 10; UK 25;
Swiss 30; Other(s) (French, Italian) 52

INFORMATION

Grade levels 1–12
School year September–July
School type boarding, coeducational, proprietary
Year founded 1880
Sponsored by Philippe Gudin
Accredited by CIS, New England
Regional organizations ECIS, SGIS
Enrollment Elementary K–5 40; Middle School
6–8 100; High School 9–12 240; Total 380
Nationalities of student body US 38; UK 38;
Swiss 38; Other(s) (French, Spaniard) 266

Tuition/fee currency Swiss Franc
Tuition range 70,000–81,000
Annual fees Boarding, 7-day 81,000
One time fees Registration 2,000
Boarding program grades 1–12
Boarding program length 7-day **Boys** 180 **Girls** 180
Graduates attending college 100%
Graduates have attended Chicago U, Princeton U,
Tufts U, Ecole Polytechnique de Lausanne,
London School of Economics

(Continued)

INSTITUT LE ROSEY (Continued)

EDUCATIONAL PROGRAM

Curriculum UK, National, Intl, IB Diploma, IGCSE, French Baccalauréat
Average class size Elementary 12; Secondary 12
Language(s) of instruction English, French
Language(s) taught German, Italian, Spanish
Staff specialists computer, counselor, ESL, librarian, math resource, nurse
Special curricular programs art, instrumental music, vocal music, computer/technology, physical education

Extra curricular programs computers, community service, dance, drama, environmental conservation, excursions/expeditions, literary magazine, photography, yearbook
Sports badminton, baseball, basketball, cross-country, football, golf, gymnastics, hockey, martial arts, rugby, skiing, soccer, squash, swimming, tennis, track and field, volleyball
Examinations GCSE, IGCSE, SAT, SAT II, TOEFL

CAMPUS FACILITIES

Location Rural
Campus 40 hectares, 24 buildings, 80 classrooms, 3 computer labs, 300 instructional computers, 26,500 library volumes, 2 auditoriums,

3 cafeterias, 8 covered play areas, 2 gymnasiums, 4 infirmaries, 5 playing fields, 8 science labs, 2 pools, 11 tennis courts

JOHN F. KENNEDY INTERNATIONAL SCHOOL

Phone	+41 (0)33 744 1372
Fax	+41 (0)33 744 8982
Email	info@jfk.ch
Website	www.jfk.ch
Address	Kirchgasse, Saanen, BE, 3792, Switzerland

STAFF

Director William M. Lovell
Director of Studies Sandra Lovell
Director of Administration Catherine Lovell

Teaching staff Full time 8; Part time 4; Total 12
Nationalities of teaching staff US 2; UK 2;
Canadian 2; Other(s) (Australian) 6

INFORMATION

Grade levels PreK–8
School year September–June
School type boarding, coeducational, day,
proprietary
Year founded 1950
Governed by appointed Owners and Co-directors
Regional organizations ECIS, SGIS
Enrollment Elementary K–5 40;
Middle School 6–8 35; Total 75

Nationalities of student body US 17; UK 7;
Spaniard 9; Other(s) (Italian) 42
Tuition/fee currency Swiss Franc
Tuition range 22,200–46,400
Annual fees Insurance 1,000; Ski School 1,500;
Trips and Excursion 1,500; Uniform 1,000
Boarding program grades 3–8
Boarding program length 7-day **Boys** 16 **Girls** 12

EDUCATIONAL PROGRAM

Curriculum US, UK, Intl, Canadian and
International Primary Curriculum
Average class size Elementary 10
Language(s) of instruction English
Language(s) taught French
Staff specialists computer, ESL, learning
disabilities, librarian, nurse

Special curricular programs art, vocal music,
computer/technology, physical education
Extra curricular programs dance, environmental
conservation, excursions/expeditions, yearbook
Sports cross-country, hockey, martial arts,
skiing, soccer, swimming, tennis, track and field
Examinations ERB CTP IV

CAMPUS FACILITIES

Location Rural
Campus 3 hectares, 5 buildings, 10 classrooms,
1 computer lab, 30 instructional computers,

10,000 library volumes, 1 cafeteria,
2 playing fields

THE RIVERSIDE SCHOOL

Phone	41 41 726 0450
Fax	41 41 726 0452
Email	info@riverside.ch
Website	www.riverside.ch
Address	Artherstrasse 55, Zug, 6300, Switzerland

STAFF

Director Dominic Currer
Dean of Students Colin Walker
Director of Studies Tony Jones
Business Manager Jelena Vasak

Head of Library Susan Glausen
Teaching staff Full time 20; Part time 5; Total 25
Nationalities of teaching staff US 3; UK 8;
Swiss 3; Other(s) (Australian, Canadian) 11

INFORMATION

Grade levels 7–13
School year August–June
School type coeducational, day
Year founded 1990
Governed by appointed Board of Governors
Regional organizations ECIS, SGIS
Enrollment Middle School 6–8 35;
High School 9–12 100; Grade 13 5; Total 140
Nationalities of student body US 15; UK 15;
Swiss 10; Other(s) (Dutch) 100

Tuition/fee currency Swiss Franc
Tuition range 26,000–30,000
One time fees Registration 2,000;
Development 2,000
Graduates attending college 90%
Graduates have attended Yale U, Villanova U,
Valparaiso U, Wimbledon Col of Art,
Manchester U

EDUCATIONAL PROGRAM

Curriculum US, Intl, AP, IB Diploma, IBMYP
Average class size Secondary 14
Language(s) of instruction English
Language(s) taught German, French
Staff specialists computer, ESL, learning
disabilities, librarian

Extra curricular programs community service,
dance, drama, excursions/expeditions,
newspaper, yearbook
Sports basketball, cross-country, skiing, soccer,
tennis, track and field
Examinations AP, IB, PSAT, SAT

CAMPUS FACILITIES

Location Rural
Campus 1 hectare, 2 buildings, 12 classrooms,
2 computer labs, 50 instructional computers,

4,000 library volumes, 1 cafeteria,
1 playing field, 3 science labs, 2 tennis courts

THE INTER-COMMUNITY SCHOOL ZURICH

Phone 41 44 919 8300
Fax 41 44 919 8320
Email admin@icsz.ch
Website www.icsz.ch
Address Strubenacher 3, CH-8126 Zumikon, Zumikon, Switzerland

STAFF

Head of School Michael Matthews
Primary Principal Brett Penny
Secondary Principal Martin Hall
Business Manager Liliane Malenchini

Teaching staff Full time 83; Part time 33; Total 116
Nationalities of teaching staff US 18; UK 39; Swiss 10; Other(s) (Canadian) 49

INFORMATION

Grade levels N–12
School year August–June
School type coeducational, day, private non-profit
Year founded 1960
Governed by appointed Board of Trustees
Accredited by CIS, New England
Regional organizations ECIS, SGIS
Enrollment Nursery 17; PreK 38; Elementary K–5 323; Middle School 6–8 176; High School 9–12 231; Total 785

Nationalities of student body US 162; UK 157; Swiss 77; Other(s) (German) 389
Tuition/fee currency Swiss Franc
Tuition range 14,000–31,000
Annual fees Busing 2,500
One time fees Registration 500; Capital Levy 4,000
Graduates attending college 90%
Graduates have attended Harvard U, McGill U, Oxford U, London U, Zurich U

EDUCATIONAL PROGRAM

Curriculum Intl, IB Diploma, IBPYP, IBMYP
Average class size Elementary 18; Secondary 18
Language(s) of instruction English
Language(s) taught German, French, Italian, Spanish
Staff specialists computer, counselor, ESL, learning disabilities, librarian, math resource, nurse, psychologist, reading resource, speech/hearing

Special curricular programs art, instrumental music, vocal music, computer/technology, physical education
Extra curricular programs community service, dance, excursions/expeditions, yearbook
Sports badminton, basketball, cricket, cross-country, golf, hockey, skiing, soccer, softball, swimming, tennis, track and field, volleyball
Examinations IB

CAMPUS FACILITIES

Location Suburban
Campus 20 hectares, 6 buildings, 46 classrooms, 4 computer labs, 300 instructional computers,

1 auditorium, 1 cafeteria, 1 covered play area, 2 gymnasiums, 1 infirmary, 1 playing field, 5 science labs, 2 tennis courts

ZURICH INTERNATIONAL SCHOOL

Phone	41 43 833 22 22
Fax	41 43 833 22 23
Email	zis@zis.ch
Website	www.zis.ch
Address	Steinacherstrasse 140, Wädenswil, CH-8820, Switzerland

STAFF

Director Peter C. Mott
Upper School Principal Jon McLeod
Middle School Principal Mark Hemphill
Lower School Principal Viki Stiebert
Early Childhood Assistant Principal Laurel Sutcliffe
Finance Manager Edgar Suppiger

IT Curriculum Coordinator Jason Cone
Upper School Librarian Edel Sturcke
Teaching staff Full time 133; Part time 39; Total 172
Nationalities of teaching staff US 45; UK 31; Swiss 39; Other(s) (Dutch, German) 57

INFORMATION

Grade levels N–13
School year August–June
School type coeducational, day, private non-profit
Year founded 2001
Governed by elected Board of Trustees
Accredited by CIS, New England
Regional organizations ECIS, SGIS
Enrollment Nursery 28; PreK 61; Elementary K–5 412; Middle School 6–8 271; High School 9–12 399; Grade 13 2; Total 1,173

Nationalities of student body US 286; UK 188; Swiss 145; Other(s) (German, Dutch) 554
Tuition/fee currency Swiss Franc
Tuition range 22,000–31,000
Annual fees Busing 4,500; Lunch 750
One time fees Registration 500; Capital Levy 4,000
Graduates attending college 97%
Graduates have attended Columbia U, London School of Economics, Georgetown U, U of Edinburgh, U of Zurich

EDUCATIONAL PROGRAM

Curriculum Intl, AP, IB Diploma, IBPYP
Average class size Elementary 16; Secondary 14
Language(s) of instruction English
Language(s) taught German, French, Swedish
Staff specialists computer, counselor, ESL, learning disabilities, librarian, nurse, psychologist
Special curricular programs art, instrumental music, vocal music, computer/technology, distance learning, physical education, Theater

Extra curricular programs computers, community service, drama, excursions/expeditions, literary magazine, newspaper, photography, yearbook, National Honor Society
Sports basketball, cross-country, golf, rugby, skiing, soccer, softball, swimming, tennis, track and field, volleyball
Clubs Model UN, student council, Junior Achievement, Young Enterprise Switzerland, Harvard Model Congress, Amnesty International, climbing
Examinations AP, IB, PSAT, SAT, SAT II, TOEFL

CAMPUS FACILITIES

Location Suburban
Campus 10 hectares, 6 buildings, 6 computer labs, 325 instructional computers,

25,000 library volumes, 2 auditoriums, 2 cafeterias, 1 gymnasium, 3 infirmaries, 1 playing field, 6 science labs, 3 tennis courts

SYRIA

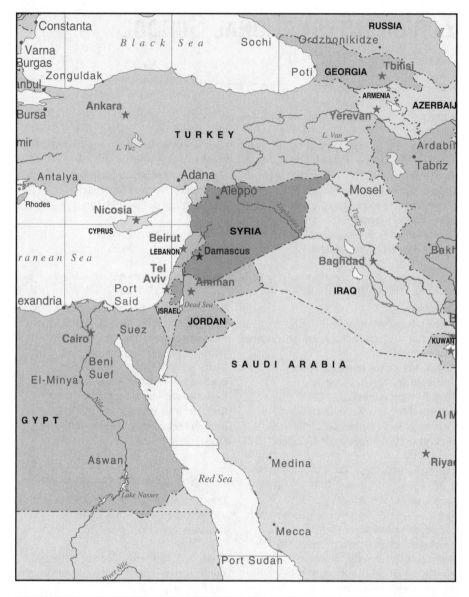

SYRIA

Area:	185,180 sq km
Population:	19,314,747
Capital:	Damascus
Currency:	Syrian Pound (SYP)
Languages:	Arabic

ICARDA INTERNATIONAL SCHOOL OF ALEPPO

Phone	963 21 574 3104
Fax	963 21 576 3936
Email	rettga@yahoo.com
Website	www.icarda.org
Address	PO Box 5466, Aleppo, Syria

STAFF

Head of School Robert E. Thompson
Elementary Principal Jeanne Korstange
Secondary Principal Martin Mai
Counselor Teresa Gaeta-Arejola
IB Coordinator Peter Krader
Assistant Principal Middle School Ryan Kopf

School Accountant Munzer Kastaly
Teacher of Information Technology Michael White
Librarian Jane Krader
Teaching staff Full time 42; Part time 6; Total 48
Nationalities of teaching staff US 12; UK 3;
Syrian 21; Other(s) (Canadian, Australian) 11

INFORMATION

Grade levels N–12
School year August–June
School type coeducational, company-sponsored, day
Year founded 1977
Governed by appointed Committee
Sponsored by ICARDA
Accredited by Middle States
Regional organizations ECIS, MAIS, NESA
Enrollment Nursery 12; PreK 15;
Elementary K–5 125; Middle School 6–8 70;
High School 9–12 80; Total 302

Nationalities of student body US 33; UK 18;
Syrian 139; Other(s) (Canadian, German) 112
Tuition/fee currency US Dollar
Tuition range 2,483–8,519
Annual fees Registration 200; Busing 185
One time fees Capital Levy 915;
Admissions Testing 200
Graduates attending college 98%
Graduates have attended Massachusetts Institute
of Technology, Harvard U, U of California in
Los Angeles, American U of Beirut, McGill U

EDUCATIONAL PROGRAM

Curriculum US, Intl, IB Diploma, IBPYP, IGCSE
Average class size Elementary 18; Secondary 20
Language(s) of instruction English

Language(s) taught French, Arabic, Spanish
Staff specialists computer

CAMPUS FACILITIES

Location Urban
Campus 2 hectares, 5 buildings, 24 classrooms,
2 computer labs, 85 instructional computers,
13,000 library volumes, 1 auditorium,
1 covered play area, 1 infirmary, 2 playing
fields, 3 science labs, 2 tennis courts,
air conditioning

DAMASCUS COMMUNITY SCHOOL

Phone	963 11 333 7737
Fax	963 11 332 1457
Email	dcs@dcssyria.org
Website	www.dcssyria.org
Address	Al Mahdi Bin Baraka Street, Damascus, Syria
Mailing address	DCS Director, 6110 Damascus Place, Dulles, VA 20189-6110, USA

STAFF

Director John E. Gates
Elementary School Principal and Curriculum Director Mark Baker
Middle and High School Principal Sheena Nabholz
Business Manager Diana Yazigi

Computer Coordinator Susan Hiba
Librarian Trina Roth
Teaching staff Full time 41; Part time 3; Total 44
Nationalities of teaching staff US 29; Syrian 4; Other(s) (Canadian, New Zealander) 11

INFORMATION

Grade levels PreK–12
School year August–June
School type coeducational, day, private non-profit
Year founded 1957
Governed by appointed Board of Directors
Accredited by Middle States
Regional organizations ECIS, NESA
Enrollment PreK 19; Elementary K–5 152; Middle School 6–8 78; High School 9–12 104; Total 353

Nationalities of student body US 79; UK 2; Syrian 63; Other(s) (Canadian, Japanese) 209
Tuition/fee currency US Dollar
Tuition range 4,400–13,100
Annual fees Registration 300; Capital Levy 1,500
One time fees Testing 200; Entrance 600
Graduates attending college 100%
Graduates have attended McGill U, U of Virginia, Col of William and Mary, American U of Beirut, Parsons School of Design

EDUCATIONAL PROGRAM

Curriculum US, AP
Average class size Elementary 15; Secondary 15
Language(s) of instruction English
Language(s) taught Arabic, French
Staff specialists computer, counselor, ESL, librarian, nurse
Special curricular programs art, vocal music, computer/technology, physical education

Extra curricular programs community service, drama, excursions/expeditions, literary magazine, newspaper, yearbook
Sports basketball, soccer, volleyball
Clubs Model UN, student council, National Honor Society
Examinations AP, Iowa, PSAT, SAT, SAT II, TOEFL, ERB

CAMPUS FACILITIES

Location Urban
Campus 5 hectares, 9 buildings, 39 classrooms, 2 computer labs, 80 instructional computers,

14,000 library volumes, 1 cafeteria, 1 infirmary, 1 playing field, 3 science labs, 1 tennis court, air conditioning

TAIWAN

Area:	35,980 sq km
Population:	22,858,872
Capital:	Taipei
Currency:	New Taiwan Dollar (TWD)
Languages:	Mandarin Chinese

NATIONAL EXPERIMENTAL HIGH SCHOOL

Phone	886 3 5777011 ext 280
Fax	886 3 578 5565
Email	chuang06@ms17.hinet.net
Website	bilingual.nehs.hc.edu.tw
Address	300 Jieshou Road, Hsinchu, 300, Taiwan

STAFF

Principal Rong-Feng Wu, Ph.D.
Dean of the Bilingual Department Christine Huang
Academic Affairs Coordinator Ray Chin, Ph.D.
Student Affairs Coordinator Jean Tien
Registrar Yi-chi
Foreign Teachers Liaison Jess Cheng

Dean of General Affairs Office Gary Cheng
Director of Computer Center Shih-Jen Lee
Director Felicia Lo
Teaching staff Full time 61; Part time 20; Total 81
Nationalities of teaching staff US 19; Taiwanese 58; Other(s) (Canadian) 4

INFORMATION

Grade levels 1–12
School year August–July
School type boarding, coeducational, day
Year founded 1983
Governed by Taiwan Ministry of Education
Sponsored by National Science Council
Enrollment Elementary K–5 230; Middle School 6–8 150; High School 9–12 220; Total 600
Nationalities of student body US 390; Taiwanese 160; Other(s) (Korean, Singaporean) 50

Tuition/fee currency Taiwan Dollar
Tuition range 35,000–43,000
Annual fees Boarding, 5-day 9,000;
Insurance 300; Books 15,000
Boarding program grades 1012
Boarding program length 5-day **Boys** 7 **Girls** 4
Graduates attending college 100%
Graduates have attended Yale U, Harvard U, Stanford U, Princeton U, U of California in Los Angeles

EDUCATIONAL PROGRAM

Curriculum US, National, AP
Average class size Elementary 28; Secondary 28
Language(s) of instruction English, Mandarin Chinese
Language(s) taught Chinese, Japanese, French
Staff specialists computer, counselor, ESL, learning disabilities, librarian, math resource, nurse, physician, reading resource, speech/hearing
Special curricular programs art, instrumental music, vocal music, computer/technology, distance learning, physical education

Extra curricular programs computers, community service, drama, environmental conservation, excursions/expeditions, literary magazine, newspaper, photography, yearbook
Sports badminton, basketball, cross-country, golf, martial arts, soccer, softball, tennis, track and field, volleyball, table tennis
Clubs student council, HOPE (Environment), Interact, Key, Humane Society, Chinese chess, drama, computer
Examinations ACT, AP, Iowa, PSAT, SAT, SAT II, TOEFL, CTP IV

CAMPUS FACILITIES

Location Urban
Campus 9 hectares, 11 buildings, 113 classrooms, 5 computer labs, 200 instructional computers, 60,000 library volumes, 2 auditoriums,

2 cafeterias, 1 covered play area, 1 gymnasium, 1 infirmary, 4 playing fields, 5 science labs, 2 pools, 4 tennis courts, air conditioning

PACIFIC AMERICAN SCHOOL

Phone	886 35717070
Fax	886 3 5429293
Email	pchu@pacificamerican.org
Website	www.pacificamerican.org
Address	3F, No. 151, Section 2, Kuang-Fu Road, Hsinchu, 30013, Taiwan
Mailing address	7F, No.83, Kuan-Hwa North Street, Hsinchu, Taiwan 30053, ROC

STAFF

Head of School Pamela Chu, Ed.D.
Vice Principal and Acting Principal Darin Murphy
Executive Assistant Tiffany Wu
Technology Coordinator/Technology Instructor
Ben Hayes

Teaching staff Full time 21; Part time 4; Total 25
Nationalities of teaching staff US 15; UK 1;
Taiwanese 4; Other(s) (Canadian, Indian) 5

INFORMATION

Grade levels PreK–12
School year September–June
School type boarding, coeducational, day,
proprietary
Year founded 2005
Governed by appointed Board of Directors
Sponsored by Proprietary
Regional organizations EARCOS
Enrollment PreK 15; Elementary K–5 75; Middle
School 6–8 35; High School 9–12 35; Total 160
Nationalities of student body US 120; Other(s)
(Australian, Singaporean) 40

Tuition/fee currency Taiwan Dollar
Tuition range 260,000–350,000
Annual fees Insurance 700; Busing 40,000;
Lunch 150,000; Books 15,000
One time fees Registration 30,000
Boarding program grades 712
Boarding program length 5-day **Boys** 7 **Girls** 8
Graduates attending college 100%
Graduates have attended Northwestern U, U of
Michigan in Ann Arbor, U of Illinois in
Urbana-Champaign, U of California in
San Diego, Purdue U

EDUCATIONAL PROGRAM

Curriculum US, AP
Average class size Elementary 20; Secondary 20
Language(s) of instruction English
Language(s) taught Mandarin, French, Spanish
Staff specialists computer, counselor, ESL, math
resource, reading resource
Special curricular programs art, instrumental
music, computer/technology, distance learning,
physical education

Extra curricular programs computers, community
service, dance, drama, newspaper, photography,
yearbook
Sports badminton, basketball, hockey, soccer,
swimming, tennis, track and field
Clubs horseback riding, robotics, chess, reading
fan, current issues, hip-hop, choir, school band
Examinations AP, Iowa, PSAT, SAT, SAT II, TOEFL

CAMPUS FACILITIES

Location Urban
Campus 2 hectares, 2 buildings, 15 classrooms,
1 computer lab, 50 instructional computers,
170,000 library volumes, 3 auditoriums,

1 cafeteria, 1 gymnasium, 1 infirmary, 3 playing
fields, 2 science labs, 1 pool, 1 tennis court,
air conditioning

Kaohsiung American School

Phone	886 7 5830112
Fax	886 7 5824536
Email	dchang@kas.kh.edu.tw
Website	www.kas.kh.edu.tw
Address	35 Sheng Li Road, Tzuo-Ying Dist., Kaohsiung, 81351, Taiwan

STAFF

Director Peter Nanos, Ed.D.
Assistant Director and Elementary Principal
Deborah Taylor, Ed.D.
Secondary School Coordinator Michael DeNeef
Curriculum Coordinator Rose White
Executive Secretary and Operations Manager
Daisy Chang

Accountant Leah Chao
Technology Coordinator Peter Lacroix
Librarian and Curriculum Coordinator Rose White
Teaching staff Full time 34; Part time 8; Total 42
Nationalities of teaching staff US 17; UK 1;
Taiwanese 8; Other(s) (Canadian) 16

INFORMATION

Grade levels PreK–12
School year August–June
School type coeducational, day, private non-profit
Year founded 1989
Governed by appointed and elected Board of
Directors
Accredited by Western
Regional organizations EARCOS
Enrollment PreK 8; Elementary K–5 86; Middle
School 6–8 65; High School 9–12 92; Total 251

Nationalities of student body US 115; UK 7;
Other(s) (Canadian) 129
Tuition/fee currency Taiwan Dollar
Tuition range 180,000–301,000
Annual fees Registration 25,000;
Capital Levy 45,000; Insurance 1,400
Graduates attending college 99%
Graduates have attended Northwestern U,
Brown U, Macalester Col, U of California in
Berkeley, Washington U in St. Louis

EDUCATIONAL PROGRAM

Curriculum US, AP
Average class size Elementary 18; Secondary 15
Language(s) of instruction English
Language(s) taught Mandarin, Spanish, Japanese
Staff specialists computer, counselor, ESL,
librarian, nurse
Special curricular programs art, instrumental
music, vocal music, computer/technology,
physical education

Extra curricular programs community service,
dance, drama, environmental conservation,
yearbook
Sports basketball, football, soccer, softball,
swimming, volleyball
Clubs Model UN, National Honor Society, global
issues, science, yearbook, Shakespeare for
Kids, drama
Examinations AP, Iowa, PSAT, SAT

CAMPUS FACILITIES

Location Urban
Campus 4 hectares, 3 buildings, 43 classrooms,
2 computer labs, 88 instructional computers,

13,000 library volumes, 1 auditorium,
1 cafeteria, 1 covered play area, 1 playing field,
2 science labs, air conditioning

AMERICAN SCHOOL IN TAICHUNG

Phone	886 4 2239 7532
Fax	886 4 2239 7520
Email	istein2@lycos.com
Website	www.ast.tc.edu.tw
Address	21-1 Chu Yuan Lane, Pei-Tun, Taichung, 406, Taiwan

STAFF

Director Irwin M. Stein
Counselor Tina Oelke
Business Manager Anna Lee
Technology Coordinator Alex Marcon
Librarian Debra Chen

Teaching staff Full time 21; Total 21
Nationalities of teaching staff US 15; UK 1; Taiwanese 1; Other(s) (Canadian, South African) 4

INFORMATION

Grade levels K–12
School year August–June
School type boarding, coeducational, day, private non-profit
Year founded 1989
Governed by appointed Board
Sponsored by International Schools Services, Inc. Consultant
Accredited by Western
Regional organizations EARCOS
Enrollment Elementary K–5 35; Middle School 6–8 58; High School 9–12 80; Total 173
Nationalities of student body US 50; UK 4; Taiwanese 90; Other(s) (Canadian, Japanese) 29

Tuition/fee currency Taiwan Dollar
Tuition range 270,000–320,000
Annual fees Registration 40,000; Boarding, 5-day 180,000; Capital Levy 80,000; Busing 35,000; Lunch 20,000; ESOL Intensive 84,000; ESOL Regular 62,000
Boarding program grades 912
Boarding program length 5-day **Boys** 4 **Girls** 2
Graduates attending college 99%
Graduates have attended U of Pennsylvania, Tufts U, Brandeis U, Washington U, Parsons School of Design

EDUCATIONAL PROGRAM

Curriculum US, AP
Average class size Elementary 15; Secondary 18
Language(s) of instruction English
Language(s) taught Spanish, Chinese
Staff specialists computer, ESL
Special curricular programs art, instrumental music, vocal music, computer/technology, physical education

Extra curricular programs community service, drama, excursions/expeditions, newspaper, yearbook
Sports basketball, cross-country, soccer, softball, volleyball
Clubs Model UN
Examinations AP, PSAT, SAT, SAT II, Stanford, TOEFL

CAMPUS FACILITIES

Location Suburban
Campus 10 buildings, 24 classrooms, 2 computer labs, 45 instructional computers,
9,000 library volumes, 1 auditorium, 2 cafeterias, 1 infirmary, 2 playing fields, 3 science labs, air conditioning

MORRISON CHRISTIAN ACADEMY

Phone	886 4 2297 3927
Fax	886 4 2292 1174
Email	morrison@mca.org.tw
Website	www.MorrisonAcademy.org
Address	136-1 Shui Nan Road, Taichung, 406, Taiwan

STAFF

Superintendent Timothy C. McGill
Assistant Superintendent for Educational Services Jeff Sheppard
Taichung Campus Principal Dan Robinson
Bethany Campus Principal Uwe Maurer
Kaohsiung Campus Principal Gabe Choi
Director of Human Services Bonnie McGill, Ph.D.

Assistant Superintendent for Financial Services Michele Law
Director of Information Technology Services Larry Dilley
System Library Coordinator Ginann Franklin
Teaching staff Full time 92; Part time 18; Total 110
Nationalities of teaching staff US 71; Chinese 13; Other(s) (Canadian) 26

INFORMATION

Grade levels K–12
School year August–June
School type boarding, coeducational, church-affiliated, day, private non-profit
Year founded 1952
Governed by appointed Board of Trustees
Accredited by Western
Regional organizations EARCOS
Enrollment Elementary K–5 369; Middle School 6–8 223; High School 9–12 272; Total 864
Nationalities of student body US 530; UK 9; Other(s) (Canadian, Korean) 325

Tuition/fee currency US Dollar
Tuition range 8,945–10,733
Annual fees Registration 758; Boarding, 7-day 9,846; Lunch 606
Boarding program grades 1012
Boarding program length 7-day **Boys** 33 **Girls** 44
Graduates attending college 97%
Graduates have attended U of South California, U of Washington, Santa Monica Col, U of Illinois, U of Michigan

EDUCATIONAL PROGRAM

Curriculum US, AP
Average class size Elementary 22; Secondary 25
Language(s) of instruction English
Language(s) taught Mandarin, Spanish
Staff specialists computer, counselor, ESL, librarian, nurse

Special curricular programs art, instrumental music, vocal music, computer/technology, physical education
Extra curricular programs drama, yearbook
Sports basketball, soccer, softball, swimming, track and field, volleyball
Examinations ACT, AP, Iowa, PSAT, SAT, SAT II, Stanford

CAMPUS FACILITIES

Location Urban
Campus 9 hectares, 8 buildings, 3 computer labs, 120 instructional computers, 20,000 library volumes, 1 auditorium, 1 cafeteria, 1 covered play area, 2 gymnasiums, 1 infirmary, 3 playing fields, 4 science labs, 1 pool, 2 tennis courts, air conditioning

TAIPEI ADVENTIST AMERICAN SCHOOL

Phone	886 2 2861 6400
Fax	886 2 2861 5121
Email	ymscsprin@gmail.com
Website	www.taas-taiwan.com
Address	64 Ln. 80 Zhwang Ding Rd., Shihlin 111, Taipei, 111, Taiwan

STAFF

Principal JoAnne W. Lafever

Nationalities of teaching staff US 12; Taiwanese 4; Other(s) (Filipino) 2

INFORMATION

Grade levels K–8
School year August–June
School type coeducational, church-affiliated, day, private non-profit
Year founded 1950
Governed by appointed JoAnne Lafever
Sponsored by Seventh-day Adventist Church

Enrollment Elementary K–5 65; Middle School 6–8 54; Total 119
Nationalities of student body US 40; Other(s) (Filipino, Japanese) 79
Tuition/fee currency Taiwan Dollar
Tuition range 230,000–270,000
Annual fees Registration 26,000; Busing 54,000; ESL 60,000

EDUCATIONAL PROGRAM

Curriculum US
Average class size Elementary 15
Language(s) of instruction English
Language(s) taught Chinese
Staff specialists computer, ESL
Special curricular programs instrumental music, vocal music, computer/technology, physical education

Extra curricular programs community service, excursions/expeditions, yearbook
Sports badminton, basketball, football, soccer, softball, track and field, volleyball
Examinations Iowa

CAMPUS FACILITIES

Location Rural
Campus 5 hectares, 1 building, 8 classrooms, 1 computer lab, 25 instructional computers,

5,000 library volumes, 1 covered play area, 2 playing fields, 1 science lab, air conditioning

TAIPEI AMERICAN SCHOOL

Phone	886 2 2873 9900
Fax	886 2 2873 1641
Email	mainadmn@tas.edu.tw
Website	www.tas.edu.tw
Address	800 Chung Shan North Road, Section 6, Shih Lin, Taipei, 11152, Taiwan

STAFF

Superintendent Sharon D. Hennessy, Ed.D.
Assistant Superintendent Ira B. Weislow
Upper School Principal Richard Hartzel, Ph.D.
Middle School Principal Cathy Funk
Lower School Principal Catriona Moran, Ph.D.
Human Resources Director Emily Yang
Controller Gloria Shuang

Information Technology Director David Sinclair
Library Coordinator Glenn Wolfe
Teaching staff Full time 217; Part time 17; Total 234
Nationalities of teaching staff US 143; UK 3; Taiwanese 22; Other(s) (Canadian, New Zealander) 66

INFORMATION

Grade levels PreK–12
School year August–June
School type coeducational, day, private non-profit
Year founded 1949
Governed by elected Board of Directors
Accredited by Western
Regional organizations EARCOS, ECIS
Enrollment PreK 32; Elementary K–5 745; Middle School 6–8 572; High School 9–12 840; Total 2,189
Nationalities of student body US 1,490; UK 14; Other(s) (Canadian, Korean) 685

Tuition/fee currency Taiwan Dollar
Tuition range 392,400–435,400
Annual fees Registration 25,000; Busing 18,600; Lunch 8,000; ESL 210,000; Middle School Alternative Education 8,000; Lower School Alternative Education 5,300
One time fees Capital Levy 150,000
Graduates attending college 52%
Graduates have attended Stanford U, Duke U, Cornell U, Johns Hopkins U, University of California in Berkeley

EDUCATIONAL PROGRAM

Curriculum US, AP, IB Diploma
Average class size Elementary 20; Secondary 24
Language(s) of instruction English
Language(s) taught Mandarin, French, Spanish, Japanese
Staff specialists computer, counselor, ESL, learning disabilities, librarian, math resource, nurse, psychologist, reading resource, speech/hearing

Special curricular programs art, instrumental music, vocal music, computer/technology, physical education, vocational
Sports badminton, basketball, cross-country, golf, rugby, soccer, softball, swimming, tennis, track and field, volleyball
Examinations ACT, AP, IB, PSAT, SAT, SAT II

CAMPUS FACILITIES

Location Urban
Campus 7 hectares, 3 buildings, 142 classrooms, 9 computer labs, 625 instructional computers, 91,690 library volumes, 2 auditoriums,

1 cafeteria, 1 covered play area, 3 gymnasiums, 1 infirmary, 2 playing fields, 12 science labs, 1 pool, 4 tennis courts, air conditioning

TAIPEI EUROPEAN SCHOOL

Phone	886 2 2862 2920
Fax	886 2 2862 1458
Email	Registrar@tes.tp.edu.tw
Website	www.taipeieuropeanschool.com
Address	Swire European Campus, 31, Chien Yeh Road, Yang Ming Shan, Shihlin District, Taipei, 111, Taiwan

STAFF

Chief Executive Officer John Nixon
Head of TES High School Section Roger Schultz
Head of British Infant School Section Ruth Martin
Head of British Junior School Section Chris Pritchard
Head of French School Section Annie Guillotin
Head of German School Emmanuel Fritzen

Director of Finance Joyce Tsao
ICT Coordinator Jonathan Marshall
LRC Manager Barbara Coughlan
Teaching staff Full time 145; Part time 34; Total 179
Nationalities of teaching staff US 8; UK 38; Taiwanese 25; Other(s) (French, German) 108

INFORMATION

Grade levels N–12
School year August–June
School type coeducational, day, private non-profit
Year founded 1990
Governed by elected Board of Governors
Regional organizations ECIS
Enrollment Nursery 68; PreK 139; Elementary K–5 384; Middle School 6–8 216; High School 9–12 164; Total 971

Nationalities of student body US 200; UK 92; Other(s) (French, German) 679
Tuition/fee currency Taiwan Dollar
Tuition range 120,000–400,000
Annual fees Capital Levy 60,000; Busing 61,000
One time fees Registration 21,000
Graduates attending college 96%
Graduates have attended Cambridge U, Boston U, Melbourne U, Bristol U, The Sorbonne in Paris

EDUCATIONAL PROGRAM

Curriculum UK, IB Diploma, IGCSE, GenCSE, French and German National Curricula
Average class size Elementary 20; Secondary 20
Language(s) of instruction English, French, German
Language(s) taught Mandarin, Dutch, Spanish
Staff specialists computer, counselor, ESL, learning disabilities, librarian, math resource, nurse, reading resource
Special curricular programs art, instrumental music, vocal music, computer/technology, physical education

Extra curricular programs computers, community service, dance, drama, environmental conservation, excursions/expeditions, literary magazine, newspaper, yearbook, choir, debating
Sports badminton, basketball, martial arts, soccer, softball, swimming, track and field, volleyball
Clubs International Award, Model UN
Examinations GCSE, IB, IGCSE

CAMPUS FACILITIES

Location Suburban
Campus 4 hectares, 5 buildings, 70 classrooms, 7 computer labs, 250 instructional computers,

30,000 library volumes, 1 auditorium, 2 cafeterias, 1 covered play area, 2 gymnasiums, 2 playing fields, 5 science labs, air conditioning

TAJIKISTAN

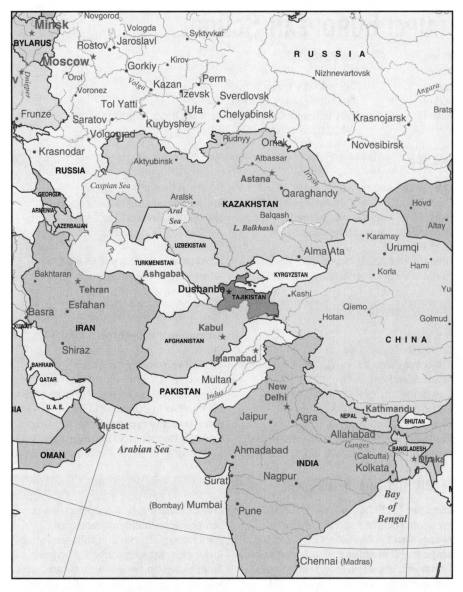

TAJIKISTAN

Area:	143,100 sq km
Population:	7,076,598
Capital:	Dushanbe
Currency:	Somoni (TJS)
Languages:	Tajik, Russian

QSI International School of Dushanbe

Phone	992 372 224 44 93
Fax	992 372 221 98 44
Email	dushanbe@qsi.org
Website	www.qsi.org
Address	2 Osipenko Street, Dushanbe, Tajikistan

STAFF

Director Richard Meier
Teaching staff Full time 4; Part time 4; Total 8

Nationalities of teaching staff US 3; Tajikistani 3; Other(s) (Indian, Swiss) 2

INFORMATION

Grade levels K–8
School year August–June
School type coeducational, day, private non-profit
Year founded 2004
Governed by appointed Advisory Board
Sponsored by Quality Schools International, QSI
Regional organizations CEESA

Enrollment PreK 20; Elementary K–5 12; Middle School 6–8 4; Total 36
Nationalities of student body US 5; Tajikistani 5; Other(s) (French, Indian) 26
Tuition/fee currency US Dollar
Tuition range 3,500–13,500
Annual fees Capital Levy 1,600
One time fees Registration 100

EDUCATIONAL PROGRAM

Curriculum US
Average class size Elementary 2
Language(s) of instruction English

Language(s) taught Russian, French
Examinations Iowa

CAMPUS FACILITIES

Location Urban
Campus 1 building, 9 classrooms, 1 computer lab,

3 instructional computers, 500 library volumes, air conditioning

TANZANIA

TANZANIA

Area:	945,087 sq km
Population:	39,384,223
Capital:	Dar es Salaam
Currency:	Tanzanian Shilling (TZS)
Languages:	Kiswahili, Swahili

INTERNATIONAL SCHOOL OF TANGANYIKA LTD.

Phone	255 22 2151 817
Fax	255 22 2152 077
Email	director@istafrica.com
Website	www.istafrica.com
Address	United Nations Road, Upanga, Dar es Salaam, Tanzania
Mailing address	PO Box 2651, Dar es Salaam, Tanzania, East Africa

STAFF

Director David Shawver, Ph.D.
Elementary School Principal Susan Peacock, Ph.D.
Secondary School Principal Justin Alexander
General Manager of Finance and Administration Nazir Thawer

Secondary School Librarian Veronica Aflredsson
Teaching staff Full time 92; Part time 5; Total 97
Nationalities of teaching staff US 26; UK 28; Tanzanian 5; Other(s) (Canadian, Australian) 38

INFORMATION

Grade levels N–12
School year August–June
School type coeducational, day, private non-profit
Year founded 1963
Governed by elected Board of Directors
Accredited by CIS, Middle States
Regional organizations AISA, ECIS
Enrollment Nursery 18; PreK 24; Elementary K–5 370; Middle School 6–8 208; High School 9–12 251; Total 871

Nationalities of student body US 73; UK 119; Tanzanian 217; Other(s) (South African, Dutch) 462
Tuition/fee currency US Dollar
Tuition range 8,600–16,800
Annual fees Registration 500; Alumni 100; Maintenance 1,000
One time fees Capital Levy 4,000; Application 500
Graduates attending college 95%
Graduates have attended Cambridge U, London School of Economics, Yale U, Princeton U, Harvard U

EDUCATIONAL PROGRAM

Curriculum Intl, IB Diploma, IBPYP, IBMYP
Average class size Elementary 22; Secondary 20
Language(s) of instruction English
Language(s) taught French, Kiswahili, Spanish
Staff specialists computer, counselor, ESL, learning disabilities, librarian, nurse
Special curricular programs art, instrumental music, computer/technology, physical education

Extra curricular programs computers, community service, drama, excursions/expeditions, newspaper, yearbook
Sports basketball, cricket, rugby, soccer, swimming, volleyball, netball
Clubs community service, Model UN
Examinations IB, PSAT, SAT, SAT II

CAMPUS FACILITIES

Location Suburban
Campus 8 hectares, 59 buildings, 70 classrooms,

5 computer labs, 300 instructional computers, 26,000 library volumes, air conditioning

INTERNATIONAL SCHOOL MOSHI

Phone	255 27 275 5004
Fax	255 27 275 2877
Email	school@ismoshi.org
Website	www.ismoshi.org
Address	Lema Road, PO Box 733, Moshi, Kilimanjaro, Tanzania

STAFF

Chief Executive Officer Barry Sutherland
Head of Moshi Campus Keiron White
Head of Secondary, Moshi Campus Colin Beveridge
Head of Boarding Richard Eaton
Head of Arusha Campus Adrian Moody
Head of Secondary, Arusha Campus John Iglar

Finance Manager Mustafa Madan
Information Technology Teacher Simon Mainwaring
Head Librarian Catriona Sutherland
Teaching staff Full time 60; Part time 5; Total 65
Nationalities of teaching staff US 16; UK 30;
Tanzanian 6; Other(s) (Canadian) 13

INFORMATION

Grade levels PreK–12
School year August–June
School type boarding, day, private non-profit
Year founded 1969
Governed by appointed Governing Board
Accredited by CIS, Middle States
Regional organizations AISA
Nationalities of student body US 10; UK 10;
Tanzanian 30; Other(s) (Dutch, German) 50
Tuition/fee currency US Dollar

Tuition range 3,800–14,400
One time fees Capital Levy 2,150;
Refundable Deposit 600; IGCSE 660; IB 720
Boarding program grades 312
Boarding program length 5-day and 7-day
Boys 30 **Girls** 30
Graduates attending college 95%
Graduates have attended Yale U, Duke U,
U of Manchester, McGill U, Harvard U

EDUCATIONAL PROGRAM

Curriculum Intl, IB Diploma, IBPYP, IBMYP, IGCSE
Average class size Elementary 22; Secondary 20
Language(s) of instruction English
Language(s) taught French, Kiswahili
Staff specialists counselor, ESL, learning
disabilities, math resource, reading resource
Special curricular programs art, instrumental
music, physical education

Extra curricular programs computers, community
service, dance, drama, environmental
conservation, excursions/expeditions
Sports basketball, football, rugby, swimming,
tennis, netball
Clubs Model UN, Amnesty International

CAMPUS FACILITIES

Location Suburban
Campus 40 hectares, 25 buildings, 30 classrooms,
3 computer labs, 50 instructional computers,
15,000 library volumes, 1 auditorium,

2 cafeterias, 1 gymnasium, 1 infirmary,
3 playing fields, 6 science labs, 2 pools,
4 tennis courts

THAILAND

THAILAND

Area:	514,000 sq km
Population:	65,068,149
Capital:	Bangkok
Currency:	Baht (THB)
Languages:	Thai, English

BANGKOK PATANA SCHOOL

Phone	66 2 398 0200
Fax	66 2 399 3179
Email	reception@patana.ac.th
Website	www.patana.ac.th
Address	643 Lasalle Road, Sukhumvit 105, Bangna, Bangkok, 10260, Thailand

STAFF

Head of School Andrew Homden
Principal of Secondary School Mick Smith
Principal of Primary School David Knott
Director to the Office of the Foundation Board
Kulvadee Siribhadra
Business Director Andrew Gordon

**Assistant Principal for Campus Curriculum
Technology** John Tranter
Head of Resource Centre Gerald Moore
Teaching staff Full time 205; Part time 3; Total 208
Nationalities of teaching staff US 5; UK 156;
Thai 18; Other(s) (Australian, New Zealander) 29

INFORMATION

Grade levels N–13
School year August–July
School type coeducational, day, private non-profit
Year founded 1957
Governed by Nominated Board of Trustees
Accredited by CIS, New England
Regional organizations EARCOS, ECIS
Enrollment Nursery 30; PreK 168; Elementary
K–5 955; Middle School 6–8 476; High School
9–12 417; Grade 13 104; Total 2,150
Nationalities of student body US 174; UK 457;
Thai 422; Other(s) (Australian, Indian) 1,097

Tuition/fee currency Thai Baht
Tuition range 310,410–603,510
Annual fees Busing 56,700; Lunch 10,000;
residential trip 10,000; ESL 105,000
One time fees Registration 2,000,000;
Capital Levy 400,000
Graduates attending college 95%
Graduates have attended Cambridge U,
U of Bristol, U of Bath, U of Melbourne,
Imperial Col

(Continued)

BANGKOK PATANA SCHOOL (Continued)

EDUCATIONAL PROGRAM

Curriculum UK, IB Diploma, IGCSE, GenCSE
Average class size Elementary 22; Secondary 20
Language(s) of instruction English
Language(s) taught Thai, French, Spanish, Mandarin, Japanese, German
Staff specialists computer, counselor, ESL, learning disabilities, librarian, math resource, nurse, physician, psychologist, reading resource, speech/hearing
Special curricular programs art, instrumental music, vocal music, computer/technology, physical education

Extra curricular programs computers, community service, dance, drama, environmental conservation, excursions/expeditions, literary magazine, photography, yearbook
Sports badminton, basketball, cricket, football, gymnastics, rugby, soccer, swimming, tennis, track and field, volleyball, outdoor education
Clubs youth, International Award for Young People
Examinations GCSE, IB, IGCSE, SAT, SAT II

CAMPUS FACILITIES

Location Suburban
Campus 20 hectares, 18 buildings, 107 classrooms, 9 computer labs, 782 instructional computers, 90,000 library volumes, 3 auditoriums,

2 cafeterias, 3 covered play areas, 2 gymnasiums, 2 infirmaries, 5 playing fields, 10 science labs, 2 pools, 11 tennis courts, air conditioning

CONCORDIAN INTERNATIONAL SCHOOL

Phone	66 2 706 9000
Fax	66 2 706 9001
Email	enquiries@concordian.ac.th
Website	www.concordian.ac.th
Address	918 Moo 8 Tambon Bangkaew, Amphur Pangplee, Bangplee, Samutprakarn, 10540 Thailand, Bangkok, 10540, Thailand

STAFF

Director Tarek B. Razik, Ed.D.
Principal Ian Russell, Ed.D.
PYP Coordinator Chris Frost
MYP Coordinator Gregory Mellor
Diploma Coordinator James Leung, Ph.D.
Administrative Manager Mimi Rakamnuaykit

Technology Coordinator Laurent Goetschmann
Head Librarian Jen Russell
Teaching staff Full time 45; Part time 20; Total 65
Nationalities of teaching staff US 15; UK 2; Thai 6; Other(s) (Canadian, Chinese) 42

INFORMATION

Grade levels N–10
School year August–June
School type coeducational, day
Year founded 2001
Governed by appointed Ministry of Education
Accredited by CIS, New England
Regional organizations EARCOS, ECIS

Enrollment Nursery 20; Elementary K–5 200; Middle School 6–8 45; High School 9–12 25; Total 290
Nationalities of student body US 5; Thai 270; Other(s) (Chinese) 15
Tuition/fee currency Thai Baht
Tuition range 275,500–400,000
Annual fees Lunch 7,500
One time fees Registration 2,000

EDUCATIONAL PROGRAM

Curriculum Intl, IBPYP, IBMYP
Average class size Elementary 18; Secondary 12
Language(s) of instruction English, Chinese, Thai
Staff specialists computer, counselor, ESL, librarian, nurse

Special curricular programs art, instrumental music, vocal music, computer/technology, physical education
Extra curricular programs community service, excursions/expeditions, yearbook
Sports basketball, golf, soccer, swimming, tennis
Examinations PSAT, SAT, ACER

CAMPUS FACILITIES

Location Suburban
Campus 5 hectares, 6 buildings, 18 classrooms, 2 computer labs, 200 instructional computers, 30,000 library volumes, 1 auditorium,

1 cafeteria, 2 covered play areas, 1 gymnasium, 1 infirmary, 2 playing fields, 2 science labs, 2 pools, 2 tennis courts, air conditioning

INTERNATIONAL COMMUNITY SCHOOL

Phone	662 338 0777
Fax	662 338 0778
Email	info@icsbangkok.com
Website	www.icsbangkok.com
Address	1225 The Parkland Rd., Khwaeng Bangna, Khet Bangna, Bangkok, 10260, Thailand

STAFF

Head of School Darren Gentry
High School Principal Rebel Houston
Elementary Principal Elsie Poosawtsee
Middle School Principal Shawnna Patterson
Thai Principal Aungsana Kinghirunwatana
Financial Manager Junya Thanathanya

Head of Technology Anchalee Tanabodeeumpon
Librarian Sujimon Supphaophas
Teaching staff Full time 83; Part time 2; Total 85
Nationalities of teaching staff US 60; Thai 12; Other(s) (Canadian, New Zealander) 13

INFORMATION

Grade levels PreK–12
School year August–June
School type coeducational, day, private non-profit
Year founded 1993
Governed by appointed ICS Local School Board
Accredited by Western
Enrollment PreK 15; Elementary K–5 290; Middle School 6–8 240; High School 9–12 265; Total 810
Nationalities of student body US 130; Thai 420; Other(s) (Korean, Indian) 260

Tuition/fee currency Thai Baht
Tuition range 178,600–302,200
Annual fees Capital Levy 30,000; Lunch 14,400; ESL 72,100
One time fees Registration 200,000
Graduates attending college 100%
Graduates have attended New York U, U of Michigan, Northeastern U, Hawaii Pacific U, Mahidol U

EDUCATIONAL PROGRAM

Curriculum US, AP
Average class size Elementary 20; Secondary 27
Language(s) of instruction English
Language(s) taught Thai, Spanish, Mandarin
Staff specialists computer, counselor, ESL, librarian, nurse
Special curricular programs art, instrumental music, vocal music, computer/technology

Extra curricular programs community service, drama, excursions/expeditions, yearbook
Sports badminton, basketball, martial arts, soccer, swimming, volleyball
Clubs chess, Bible, student council
Examinations AP, PSAT, SAT, Stanford

CAMPUS FACILITIES

Location Urban
Campus 16 hectares, 7 buildings, 60 classrooms, 3 computer labs, 230 instructional computers, 14,600 library volumes, 1 auditorium,

2 cafeterias, 1 covered play area, 1 gymnasium, 1 infirmary, 1 playing field, 4 science labs, 1 pool, 1 tennis court, air conditioning

INTERNATIONAL SCHOOL BANGKOK

Phone	66 2 963 5800
Fax	66 2 583 5431
Email	daladk@isb.ac.th
Website	www.isb.ac.th
Address	39/7 Soi Nichada Thani, Samakee Road, Pakkret, Nonthaburi, 11120, Thailand
Mailing address	PO Box 20-1015, Ha Yaek Pakkret, Nonthaburi 11121 , Thailand

STAFF

Head of School William H. Gerritz, Ph.D.
Headmistress Usa Somboon
High School Principal Andrew Davies
Middle School Principal James Souza
Elementary School Principal Annelies Hoogland
Deputy Head of School for Learning Tom Baker
Deputy Head of School/Chief Financial Officer Ugo Costessi

Director of Information Technology Stephen Lehmann
Librarian Robert Rubis
Teaching staff Full time 185; Part time 24; Total 209
Nationalities of teaching staff US 123; UK 11; Thai 16; Other(s) (Australian, Canadian) 59

INFORMATION

Grade levels PreK–12
School year August–June
School type coeducational, day, private non-profit
Year founded 1951
Governed by elected Board of Trustees
Accredited by Western
Regional organizations EARCOS, ECIS
Enrollment PreK 36; Elementary K–5 662; Middle School 6–8 497; High School 9–12 727; Total 1,922

Nationalities of student body US 615; UK 34; Thai 351; Other(s) (Australian, Canadian) 922
Tuition/fee currency Thai Baht
Tuition range 365,000–648,000
Annual fees Busing 57000–91300; Deposit 20,000; Membership 10
One time fees Registration 220,000
Graduates attending college 99%
Graduates have attended Yale U, Stanford U, Brown U, Columbia U, Massachusetts Institute of Technology

(Continued)

INTERNATIONAL SCHOOL BANGKOK (Continued)

EDUCATIONAL PROGRAM

Curriculum US, Intl, AP, IB Diploma
Average class size Elementary 19; Secondary 20
Language(s) of instruction English
Language(s) taught French, Spanish, Japanese, Mandarin, Thai
Staff specialists computer, counselor, ESL, learning disabilities, librarian, nurse, psychologist, speech/hearing
Special curricular programs art, instrumental music, vocal music, computer/technology, physical education

Extra curricular programs computers, community service, dance, drama, environmental conservation, excursions/expeditions, literary magazine, newspaper, photography, yearbook
Sports badminton, basketball, cross-country, golf, gymnastics, rugby, soccer, softball, swimming, tennis, track and field, volleyball
Examinations ACT, AP, IB, Iowa, PSAT, SAT, SAT II

CAMPUS FACILITIES

Location Suburban
Campus 13 hectares, 8 buildings, 152 classrooms, 10 computer labs, 700 instructional computers, 65,000 library volumes, 5 auditoriums,

2 cafeterias, 2 covered play areas, 2 gymnasiums, 1 infirmary, 5 playing fields, 7 science labs, 1 pool, 7 tennis courts, air conditioning

KIS INTERNATIONAL SCHOOL

Phone 66 2 274 3444
Fax 66 2 274 3452
Email info@kis.ac.th
Website www.kis.ac.th
Address 999/124 Kesinee Ville, Pracha-Utit Rd., Huay-Kwang, Bangkok, 10320, Thailand

STAFF

Head of School Sally L. Holloway
Primary School Principal June van den Bos
Secondary School Principal Michael Embley
Grade School Coordinator John Sullivan
IB MYP Coordinator Michael Hirsch

IB PYP Coordinator Gerry Campbell
Business Director Suraphong Thunyatada
Head of Technology Piyarat Khanthap, Ph.D.
Head of Library/Media Center Sally Embley, Ed.D.

INFORMATION

Grade levels PreK–10
School year August–June
School type coeducational, day
Year founded 1998
Governed by appointed and elected School Board
Accredited by CIS

Tuition/fee currency Thai Baht
Tuition range 297,000–365,000
Annual fees Lunch 19,500
One time fees Registration 120,000;
Capital Levy 150,000

EDUCATIONAL PROGRAM

Curriculum Intl, IBPYP, IBMYP
Average class size Elementary 18; Secondary 15
Language(s) of instruction English
Language(s) taught Thai, Spanish, Japanese
Staff specialists computer, counselor, ESL, librarian, nurse
Special curricular programs art, instrumental music, computer/technology, physical education

Extra curricular programs computers, community service, dance, drama, environmental conservation, newspaper
Sports badminton, basketball, soccer, swimming, tennis, volleyball
Examinations IB

CAMPUS FACILITIES

Location Urban
Campus 16 hectares, 4 buildings, 30 classrooms, 3 computer labs, 60 instructional computers, 13,000 library volumes, 1 auditorium,

1 cafeteria, 2 covered play areas, 2 gymnasiums, 1 infirmary, 1 playing field, 3 science labs, 1 pool, 2 tennis courts, air conditioning

NEW INTERNATIONAL SCHOOL OF THAILAND

Phone   66 02 651 2065
Fax   66 02 253 3800
Email   nist@nist.ac.th
Website   www.nist.ac.th
Address   36, Sukhumvit Soi 15, Sukhumvit Road, Bangkok, 10110, Thailand

STAFF

Head of School Simon Leslie
Deputy Head & Director of Academic Studies
Jan Gould
Secondary School Principal Adrian Watts
Elementary School Principal Paul Hamlyn
Director of Development Jaemi Hodgson

Director of IT Paul White
Librarians Stephanie Wallis and Suzanne McCluskey
Teaching staff Full time 134; Part time 12;
Total 146
Nationalities of teaching staff US 20; UK 46;
Thai 7; Other(s) (Australian) 73

INFORMATION

Grade levels PreK–13
School year August–June
School type coeducational, day, private non-profit
Year founded 1992
Governed by appointed and elected Foundation
for International Education
Accredited by CIS, New England
Regional organizations AASCA, EARCOS, ECIS
Enrollment PreK 86; Elementary K–5 530;
Middle School 6–8 297; High School 9–12 379;
Grade 13 88; Total 1,380

Nationalities of student body US 148; UK 78;
Thai 350; Other(s) (Indian) 804
Tuition/fee currency Thai Baht
Tuition range 154,000–299,000
Annual fees Busing 56,070
One time fees Registration 260,000
Graduates attending college 100%
Graduates have attended Oxford U,
Massachusetts Institute of Technology,
U of Melbourne, U of British Columbia,
U of Otago

EDUCATIONAL PROGRAM

Curriculum Intl, IB Diploma, IBPYP, IBMYP
Average class size Elementary 25; Secondary 22
Language(s) of instruction English
Language(s) taught Thai, Mandarin, Spanish,
French, Japanese, Hindi, Korean, German,
Finnish
Staff specialists computer, counselor, ESL,
learning disabilities, librarian, math resource,
nurse, psychologist, reading resource
Special curricular programs art, instrumental
music, vocal music, computer/technology,

distance learning, physical education,
vocational, SEASAC sport
Extra curricular programs computers, community
service, dance, drama, environmental
conservation, excursions/expeditions, literary
magazine, newspaper, photography, yearbook
Sports badminton, basketball, cricket, football,
golf, rugby, soccer, softball, swimming, tennis,
track and field, volleyball
Clubs environmental, Amnesty International
Examinations GCSE, IB, IGCSE, PSAT, SAT, SAT II,
TOEFL

CAMPUS FACILITIES

Location Urban
Campus 4 hectares, 9 buildings, 87 classrooms,
4 computer labs, 350 instructional computers,
36,000 library volumes, 1 auditorium,

1 cafeteria, 1 covered play area, 4 gymnasiums,
1 infirmary, 2 playing fields, 5 science labs,
1 pool, 2 tennis courts, air conditioning

REDEEMER INTERNATIONAL SCHOOL THAILAND

Phone	66 2 916 6257
Fax	66 2 916 6279
Email	wirach@rism.ac.th
Website	www.rist.ac.th
Address	6/2 Moo 4, Ramkhamhaeng 164, Minburi, Bangkok, 10510, Thailand

STAFF

Head of School Fr. Wirach Amonpattana, C.Ss.R.
Headmaster Fr. Apisit Kritsaralam, C.Ss.R.
Principal Penny Lorwatanapongsa, Ph.D.
Assistant Principal Michael Booton
School Counselor Sarah Charles
Deputy Head of School Resources and Director of Technology Fr. Sukhum Thanasingha, C.Ss.R.
Teaching staff Full time 29; Part time 3; Total 32
Nationalities of teaching staff US 19; UK 1; Thai 5; Other(s) (Japanese, Filipino) 7

INFORMATION

Grade levels 1–12
School year August–June
School type coeducational, church-affiliated, day, private non-profit
Year founded 2003
Governed by appointed School Board
Sponsored by The Redemptorist Foundation of Thailand
Accredited by Western
Regional organizations EARCOS
Enrollment Elementary K–5 40; Middle School 6–8 59; High School 9–12 83; Total 182
Nationalities of student body Thai 85; Other(s) (Japanese, Korean) 97
Tuition/fee currency Thai Baht
Tuition range 436,000–523,000
One time fees Registration 150,000; Capital Levy 200,000; Books 30,000
Graduates attending college 100%

EDUCATIONAL PROGRAM

Curriculum US
Average class size Elementary 12; Secondary 12
Language(s) of instruction English
Language(s) taught Thai
Staff specialists computer, counselor, ESL, librarian, nurse, psychologist
Special curricular programs art, vocal music, physical education, business studies
Extra curricular programs community service, dance, drama, environmental conservation, excursions/expeditions, yearbook, extended day program
Sports badminton, baseball, basketball, golf, soccer, softball, swimming, tennis, volleyball
Examinations PSAT, SAT, Stanford, TOEFL

CAMPUS FACILITIES

Location Suburban
Campus 3 hectares, 2 buildings, 23 classrooms, 2 computer labs, 110 instructional computers, 10,000 library volumes, 2 auditoriums, 1 cafeteria, 2 gymnasiums, 1 infirmary, 1 playing field, 2 science labs, 2 pools, 2 tennis courts, air conditioning

RUAMRUDEE INTERNATIONAL SCHOOL

Phone	66 2 518 0320
Fax	66 2 518 0334
Email	director@rism.ac.th
Website	www.rism.ac.th
Address	6 Ramkhamhaeng 184 Road, Minburi, Bangkok, 10510, Thailand

STAFF

Head of School Fr. Wirach Amonpattana, C.Ss.R. **Deputy Head of School Academics and Director of Technology** Fr. Davidjieng Ketsurin, C.Ss.R. **Elementary School Principal** Jeannie Haugh **Middle School Principal** Sudha Augustine Ratnasamy **High School Principal** David Miller

Director of Curriculum and Professional Development Susan Misner **Deputy Head of School Resources** Fr. Sukhum Thanasingha, C.Ss.R. **MS/HS Library and Media Specialist** Katherine Revelle, Ph.D.

INFORMATION

Grade levels PreK–12 **School year** August–June **School type** coeducational, church-affiliated, day, private non-profit **Year founded** 1957 **Governed by** appointed School Board **Sponsored by** The Redemptorist Foundation of Thailand **Accredited by** Western **Regional organizations** EARCOS, ECIS

Enrollment PreK 16; Elementary K–5 450; Middle School 6–8 484; High School 9–12 710; Total 1,660 **Nationalities of student body** US 62; UK 9; Thai 1,070; Other(s) (Indian, Chinese) 519 **Tuition/fee currency** Thai Baht **Tuition range** 314,000–429,000 **One time fees** Registration 150,000; Capital Levy 200,000; Books 30,000 **Graduates attending college** 98% **Graduates have attended** Cornell U, Boston U, Stanford U, Brandeis U, Columbia U

(Continued)

RUAMRUDEE INTERNATIONAL SCHOOL (Continued)

EDUCATIONAL PROGRAM

Curriculum US, AP, IB Diploma
Average class size Elementary 20; Secondary 20
Language(s) of instruction English
Language(s) taught Thai, Mandarin, Japanese, French, Spanish
Staff specialists computer, counselor, ESL, learning disabilities, librarian, nurse, psychologist, reading resource, speech/hearing
Special curricular programs art, instrumental music, vocal music, computer/technology, physical education

Extra curricular programs computers, community service, dance, drama, environmental conservation, excursions/expeditions, literary magazine, newspaper, photography, yearbook, chorus
Sports badminton, baseball, basketball, football, golf, rugby, soccer, softball, squash, swimming, tennis, track and field, volleyball, table tennis, scuba diving, Tae Kwon Do, running/jogging
Clubs forensics, Model UN, math, chess, Interact (Rotary), Amnesty International, Keys, French, drama, astronomy
Examinations AP, IB, Iowa, PSAT, SAT, Stanford, TOEFL, ISA (International Schools Assessment)

CAMPUS FACILITIES

Location Suburban
Campus 15 hectares, 10 buildings, 125 classrooms, 9 computer labs, 950 instructional computers, 45,000 library volumes, 2 auditoriums,

4 cafeterias, 3 covered play areas, 5 gymnasiums, 1 infirmary, 3 playing fields, 13 science labs, 2 pools, 2 tennis courts, air conditioning

Data from 2006/07 school year.

ST. STEPHEN'S INTERNATIONAL SCHOOL

Phone 66 2 513 0270
Fax 66 2 930 3307
Email info@sis.edu
Website www.sis.edu
Address 998 Viphavadi Rangsit Road, Lad Yao, Chatuchak, Bangkok, 10900, Thailand

STAFF

School Director Richard A. Ralphs
Assistant School Director Christine Larke
Assistant Principal, Bangkok Campus Kevin McGee
School Manager Supatra Angkawinijwong

IT Manager Collin Anderson
Teaching staff Full time 41; Part time 1; Total 42
Nationalities of teaching staff UK 17; Thai 8;
Other(s) (Australian, Canadian) 16

INFORMATION

Grade levels PreK–13
School year August–July
School type boarding, coeducational, day,
proprietary
Year founded 1998
Governed by appointed School Board
Sponsored by Ocean Group
Accredited by CIS, New England, World-Wide
Education Service

Enrollment PreK 41; Elementary K–5 225;
Middle School 6–8 85; High School 9–12 25;
Total 376
Nationalities of student body US 18; UK 18;
Thai 320; Other(s) 20
Tuition/fee currency Thai Baht
Tuition range 210,000–346,500
Graduates attending college 100%

EDUCATIONAL PROGRAM

Curriculum UK, National, Intl, IGCSE, GenCSE
Average class size Elementary 20; Secondary 20
Language(s) of instruction English
Language(s) taught Thai, Mandarin, Spanish
Staff specialists computer, ESL, learning
disabilities, librarian, math resource, nurse
Special curricular programs art, instrumental
music, vocal music, computer/technology,
physical education

Extra curricular programs computers, community
service, dance, drama, environmental
conservation, excursions/expeditions
Sports badminton, basketball, football, golf,
gymnastics, martial arts, softball, swimming,
track and field, volleyball
Clubs art, dance, Italian, French, origamy,
face painting, UNESCO, table tennis, bowling,
Tae Kwon Do
Examinations GCSE, IGCSE

CAMPUS FACILITIES

Location Urban
Campus 42 hectares, 4 buildings, 78 classrooms,

3 computer labs, 64 instructional computers,
20,000 library volumes, air conditioning

THAI-CHINESE INTERNATIONAL SCHOOL

Phone	66 2 751 1201
Fax	66 2 751 1210
Email	dr_lalima@tcis.ac.th
Website	www.tcis.ac.th
Address	101/177 Moo 7, Prasertsin Road, Bangplee Yai, Bangplee, Samutprakarn, 10540, Thailand

STAFF

Superintendent Lalima Jenckes, Ed.D.
Academic Director, Middle and High School Principal John Jenckes, Ed.D.
Assistant Academic Director and Elementary Principal Susan Clark
Thai Principal Krongchanok T. Hsieh
Curriculum Coordinator Jane Blazek

Business Manager Sheng-Fang Pao
IT Coordinator Oscar Sala
School Librarian Courtney Morgan
Teaching staff Full time 94; Total 94
Nationalities of teaching staff US 46; UK 2; Thai 9; Other(s) (Canadian, Chinese) 37

INFORMATION

Grade levels PreK–12
School year August–June
School type coeducational, day, private non-profit
Year founded 1995
Governed by elected School Board
Accredited by Western
Regional organizations EARCOS
Enrollment Elementary K–5 415; Middle School 6–8 265; High School 9–12 255; Total 935
Nationalities of student body US 10; UK 15; Thai 440; Other(s) (Chinese, Korean) 470
Tuition/fee currency Thai Baht

Tuition range 186,156–248,194
Annual fees Insurance 926; Lunch 10,836; Books 11,576; ESL 50,000; English Intensive Program 70,000; Chinese as a Foreign Language 30,000
One time fees Registration 100,000; Capital Levy 100,000
Graduates attending college 100%
Graduates have attended McGill U, Georgia Institute of Technology, U of Wisconsin in Madison, U of British Columbia, U of Pittsburg

(Continued)

THAI-CHINESE INTERNATIONAL SCHOOL (Continued)

EDUCATIONAL PROGRAM

Curriculum US, National, Intl, AP, Mandarin, Thai
Average class size Elementary 22; Secondary 23
Language(s) of instruction English
Language(s) taught Thai, Mandarin, Spanish, French, Japanese
Staff specialists computer, counselor, ESL, learning disabilities, librarian, nurse, psychologist, reading resource
Special curricular programs art, instrumental music, vocal music, computer/technology, physical education

Extra curricular programs community service, drama, environmental conservation, excursions/expeditions, literary magazine, yearbook
Sports badminton, baseball, basketball, football, golf, martial arts, soccer, softball, swimming, tennis, volleyball
Clubs chess, math, junior council, student council, environmental, jazz ensemble
Examinations ACT, AP, PSAT, SAT, SAT II, Stanford, TOEFL

CAMPUS FACILITIES

Location Suburban
Campus 1 hectare, 4 buildings, 82 classrooms, 5 computer labs, 239 instructional computers, 45,000 library volumes, 2 auditoriums, 2 cafeterias, 2 covered play areas, 2 gymnasiums, 1 infirmary, 1 playing field, 3 science labs, 2 pools, air conditioning

AMERICAN PACIFIC INTERNATIONAL SCHOOL

Phone	66 53 365 303
Fax	66 53 365 304
Email	admissions@apis.ac.th
Website	www.apis.ac.th
Address	158/1 Moo 3 Hangdong-Samoeng Road, Banpong, Hangdong, Chiang Mai, 50230, Thailand

STAFF

Head of School Keith B. Wecker
Deputy Head Holly Gardner
Thai Head of School Panthip Kolyanee

Thai Head of School Ladda Ahmad-Mahidi
Admissions and Marketing Director Kathyrn Phillips
Principal (Nursery–Grade 5) Patsy Wecker

INFORMATION

Grade levels N–12
School year August–June
School type boarding, coeducational, day, proprietary
Year founded 1997
Governed by appointed Board of Trustees
Sponsored by Kritsanant Palarit
Accredited by Western
Regional organizations EARCOS
Enrollment Nursery 25; PreK 50; Elementary K–5 100; Middle School 6–8 45; High School 9–12 55; Total 275
Nationalities of student body US 25; UK 10; Thai 135; Other(s) (Korean, Japanese) 100

Tuition/fee currency Thai Baht
Tuition range 120,000–480,000
Annual fees Boarding, 5-day 393,000; Boarding, 7-day 525,000; Busing 9,000; Lunch 18,000; Laundry (Optional) 9,000; Misc. 30,000
One time fees Registration 80,000; Application 2,000
Boarding program grades 1–12
Boarding program length 7-day **Boys** 65 **Girls** 35
Graduates attending college 90%
Graduates have attended Allegheny Col, Boston U, Monash U, Richmond U, Trent U

EDUCATIONAL PROGRAM

Curriculum US, Intl, AP, IBPYP
Average class size Elementary 15; Secondary 15
Language(s) of instruction English
Language(s) taught Mandarin, Japanese, Thai
Staff specialists computer, counselor, ESL, librarian, math resource, nurse
Special curricular programs art, instrumental music, vocal music, computer/technology, physical education, drama

Extra curricular programs computers, community service, dance, drama, environmental conservation, excursions/expeditions, literary magazine, newspaper, photography, yearbook
Sports badminton, basketball, football, martial arts, soccer, softball, swimming, tennis, track and field, volleyball
Clubs Tae Kwon Do, swimming
Examinations AP, PSAT, SAT, SAT II, TOEFL

CAMPUS FACILITIES

Location Rural
Campus 4 hectares, 8 buildings, 28 classrooms, 1 computer lab, 30 instructional computers, 10,000 library volumes, 1 auditorium,

1 cafeteria, 2 covered play areas, 1 gymnasium, 1 infirmary, 1 playing field, 2 science labs, 2 pools, 3 tennis courts, air conditioning

Data from 2006/07 school year.

CHIANG MAI INTERNATIONAL SCHOOL

Phone	66 53 242 027
Fax	66 53 242 255
Email	info@cmis.ac.th
Website	www.cmis.ac.th
Address	13 Chetupon Road, Tumbon Watket, Muang, Chiang Mai, 50000, Thailand
Mailing address	PO Box 38, 13 Chetupon Road, Chiang Mai, Thailand 50000

STAFF

Director Supaporn Yanasarn
Principal Terry Gamble
High School Curriculum Coordinator Nathen Rhead
Elementary Curriculum Coordinator Catherine Erpen

Librarian Ruth Erickson
Teaching staff Full time 53; Total 53
Nationalities of teaching staff US 23; UK 4;
Thai 10; Other(s) (Canadian, Australian) 16

INFORMATION

Grade levels K–12
School year August–June
School type coeducational, church-affiliated,
day, private non-profit
Year founded 1954
Governed by appointed School Board
Sponsored by Foundation of the Church of
Christ in Thailand
Accredited by Western
Regional organizations EARCOS
Enrollment Elementary K–5 169; Middle School
6–8 117; High School 9–12 153; Total 439

Nationalities of student body US 120; UK 20;
Thai 116; Other(s) (Korean, Japanese) 183
Tuition/fee currency Thai Baht
Tuition range 121,000–164,000
Annual fees ESL 44,000
One time fees Registration 65,000
Graduates attending college 90%
Graduates have attended Massachusetts Institute
of Technology, The U of Southern California,
Australian National U, Bucknell U, Trent U

EDUCATIONAL PROGRAM

Curriculum US, Intl, AP
Average class size Elementary 18; Secondary 20
Language(s) of instruction English
Language(s) taught Thai, French, Mandarin,
Spanish
Staff specialists computer, counselor, ESL,
librarian, nurse
Special curricular programs art, computer/
technology, physical education

Extra curricular programs community service,
dance, drama, environmental conservation,
excursions/expeditions, yearbook
Sports badminton, basketball, gymnastics,
martial arts, soccer, swimming, track and field,
volleyball, futsal, street hockey
Clubs Boy Scouts, Kendo, gymnastics, Tae Kwon
Do, Thai music and dance, strength training,
ROTC
Examinations AP, PSAT, SAT, SAT II, Stanford

CAMPUS FACILITIES

Location Urban
Campus 5 buildings, 19 classrooms,
2 computer labs, 48 instructional computers,
12,000 library volumes, 1 auditorium,

1 cafeteria, 2 covered play areas, 1 gymnasium,
1 infirmary, 1 playing field, 1 science lab,
air conditioning

LANNA INTERNATIONAL SCHOOL THAILAND

Phone	66 53 806 231
Fax	66 53 271 159
Email	lannaist@loxinfo.co.th
Website	www.lannaist.ac.th
Address	300 Grandview Moo 1, Chiang-Mai to Hang Dong Road, Chiang Mai, 50100, Thailand

STAFF

Head of School Roy Lewis
Thai Head of School Diane Willems
Elementary Principal Randall Jones
Secondary Principal Ingrid Simons
Business/Finance Manager Surin De Muth
ICT Teacher Kevin Pugh

INFORMATION

Grade levels PreK–12
School year August–June
School type coeducational, day, proprietary
Year founded 1993
Governed by appointed and elected Board of Investors/Advisory Board
Sponsored by High Standard International Consultant Co. Ltd

Accredited by Western
Regional organizations EARCOS
Tuition/fee currency Thai Baht
Tuition range 63,500–118,450
Annual fees Insurance 200; Busing 12,000; Lunch 6,000
One time fees Registration 10,000; Capital Levy 15,000

EDUCATIONAL PROGRAM

Curriculum US, UK, National, Intl, IGCSE
Average class size Elementary 16; Secondary 10
Language(s) of instruction English
Language(s) taught Thai, Chinese, French
Staff specialists computer, counselor, ESL, learning disabilities, librarian, math resource, nurse, reading resource
Special curricular programs art, vocal music, computer/technology, physical education

Extra curricular programs computers, community service, dance, drama, environmental conservation, excursions/expeditions, literary magazine, newspaper, photography, yearbook, student council
Sports badminton, basketball, football, golf, martial arts, soccer, softball, swimming, track and field, volleyball
Examinations GCSE, IGCSE, PSAT, SAT, SAT II

CAMPUS FACILITIES

Location Suburban
Campus 3 buildings, 25 classrooms, 1 computer lab, 35 instructional computers,

5,000 library volumes, 1 cafeteria, 1 covered play area, 1 infirmary, 1 playing field, 1 science lab, 1 pool, air conditioning

Data from 2006/07 school year.

INTERNATIONAL SCHOOL
EASTERN SEABOARD

Phone	66 3 837 2591
Fax	66 3 837 2590
Email	ise@ise.ac.th
Website	www.ise.ac.th
Address	282 Moo 5, Tambon Bo vin, Amphur Sriracha, Sriracha, Chonburi, 20230, Thailand
Mailing address	PO Box 6, Banglamung, Chonburi, 20150 Thailand

STAFF

Superintendent and Secondary Principal Robert W. Brewitt, Ed.D.
Guidance Counselor and Psychologist Joan Fedoruk
Elementary Principal Heather Naro
Purchasing Director Jenny Kerdlappol
IB Coordinator Tim Overacker

Chief Financial Officer Charlie Chuvapituck
Technology Coordinator Megan Eastlake
Librarian Carol Fifield
Teaching staff Full time 44; Part time 6; Total 50
Nationalities of teaching staff US 30; UK 4; Thai 3; Other(s) (Canadian, Australian) 13

INFORMATION

Grade levels PreK–12
School year August–June
School type coeducational, day, proprietary
Year founded 1994
Governed by appointed Board of Directors
Sponsored by Investors
Accredited by Western
Regional organizations EARCOS
Enrollment PreK 47; Elementary K–5 198; Middle School 6–8 82; High School 9–12 80; Total 407

Nationalities of student body US 50; UK 16; Thai 88; Other(s) (Japanese, Korean) 253
Tuition/fee currency Thai Baht
Tuition range 197,600–406,000
Annual fees Busing 48,000; Lunch 16,000
One time fees Registration 83,000; Capital Levy 155,000
Graduates attending college 90%
Graduates have attended Cornell U, U of Washington, U of British Columbia, Tokyo U, Carnegie Mellon U

(Continued)

INTERNATIONAL SCHOOL EASTERN SEABOARD (Continued)

EDUCATIONAL PROGRAM

Curriculum US, IB Diploma
Average class size Elementary 16; Secondary 17
Language(s) of instruction English
Language(s) taught Thai, Spanish, Japanese, French
Staff specialists computer, counselor, ESL, librarian, nurse, psychologist
Special curricular programs art, instrumental music, computer/technology, physical education

Extra curricular programs computers, community service, drama, environmental conservation, excursions/expeditions, newspaper, yearbook
Sports basketball, cricket, cross-country, golf, rugby, soccer, softball, swimming, tennis, volleyball
Clubs Model UN, honor society, CAS Program, drama society, student council, forensics
Examinations ACT, IB, Iowa, PSAT, SAT, SAT II, Stanford, TOEFL

CAMPUS FACILITIES

Location Rural
Campus 8 hectares, 12 buildings, 32 classrooms, 3 computer labs, 75 instructional computers, 10,000 library volumes, 1 auditorium, 1 cafeteria, 2 covered play areas, 2 gymnasiums, 1 infirmary, 1 playing field, 4 science labs, 1 pool, 2 tennis courts, air conditioning

QSI INTERNATIONAL SCHOOL OF PHUKET

Phone	66 076 354 077
Fax	66 076 354 076
Email	qsi@phuketinternet.co.th
Website	www.qsi.org
Address	8 1/4 Moo 1, Chalemprakiat R.9, Soi Teepaksong Samkong, T. Kathu A. Kathu, Phuket, Phuket, 83120, Thailand

STAFF

Director Alan J. Siporin
Head of School Jantira Nobnorb
Office Manager Angelika Langner
Technology Coordinator Mike Tipton

Library Coordinator Marivic Maxwell
Teaching staff Full time 23; Part time 2; Total 25
Nationalities of teaching staff US 14; Thai 7; Other(s) (Australian) 4

INFORMATION

Grade levels PreK–12
School year August–June
School type coeducational, day, private non-profit
Year founded 2000
Governed by appointed Board of Directors
Enrollment PreK 7; Elementary K–5 39; Middle School 6–8 27; High School 9–12 43; Total 116
Nationalities of student body US 21; UK 10; Thai 20; Other(s) (Korean, French) 65

Tuition/fee currency US Dollar
Tuition range 4,200–7,500
Annual fees Capital Levy 1,600; Insurance 10; Busing 500; Lunch 360; Uniform Shirt 10; Extra Activities 20
One time fees Registration 100
Graduates attending college 100%
Graduates have attended Prince of Songkla U, Western Canada Technical Col

EDUCATIONAL PROGRAM

Curriculum US, AP
Average class size Elementary 11; Secondary 11
Language(s) of instruction English
Language(s) taught Thai
Staff specialists computer, counselor, ESL, librarian

Special curricular programs art, instrumental music, vocal music, computer/technology, physical education
Extra curricular programs computers, excursions/ expeditions, newspaper, yearbook, Thai dancing
Sports badminton, basketball, golf, soccer, swimming, volleyball, chair ball
Examinations Iowa, PSAT, SAT

CAMPUS FACILITIES

Location Suburban
Campus 5 hectares, 3 buildings, 19 classrooms, 1 computer lab, 17 instructional computers,

2,500 library volumes, 1 cafeteria, 1 covered play area, 1 infirmary, 3 playing fields, 1 science lab, air conditioning

TOGO

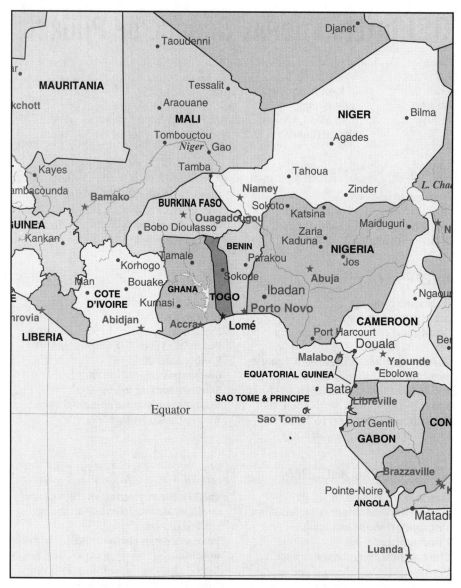

TOGO

Area:	56,785 sq km
Population:	5,701,579
Capital:	Lome
Currency:	Communaute Financiere Africaine Franc (XOF)
Languages:	French, Ewe, Mina

AMERICAN INTERNATIONAL SCHOOL OF LOMÉ

Phone	228 221 30 00
Fax	228 222 7358
Email	aisl@laposte.tg
Website	www.multimania.com/aisl
Address	35 Rue Kayigan Lawson, Avenue Duisburg, Kodjoviakope, BP 852, Lomé, Togo
Mailing address	2300 Lome Place, Dulles, VA 20189-2300, USA

STAFF

Director Ruth L. Kramer-Sackett, Ph.D.

INFORMATION

Grade levels N–12
School year August–June
School type coeducational, day, private non-profit
Year founded 1967
Governed by elected Board of Directors
Accredited by Middle States
Regional organizations AISA
Enrollment PreK 3; Elementary K–5 15;
Middle School 6–8 10; High School 9–12 15;
Total 43

Nationalities of student body US 5; Togolese 13;
Other(s) (Belgian, Lebanese) 25
Tuition/fee currency US Dollar
Tuition range 1,500–9,450
Annual fees Books 1500 (grades 9–12 only)
One time fees Registration 700
Graduates attending college 100%
Graduates have attended U of Washington,
Hunter Col, Los Angeles Community Col,
U of Nebraska, Edmonds Community Col

EDUCATIONAL PROGRAM

Curriculum US, UK
Average class size Elementary 10; Secondary 10
Language(s) of instruction English
Language(s) taught French, English
Special curricular programs art, vocal music,
physical education, UNL Correspondence

Extra curricular programs community service,
yearbook, general music
Sports badminton, basketball, hockey, soccer,
swimming, volleyball, yoga
Examinations Iowa, PSAT, SAT

CAMPUS FACILITIES

Location Urban
Campus 1 building, 13 classrooms,
1 computer lab, 5 instructional computers,

4,000 library volumes, 1 covered play area,
1 playing field, air conditioning

Data from 2006/07 school year.

TRINIDAD AND TOBAGO

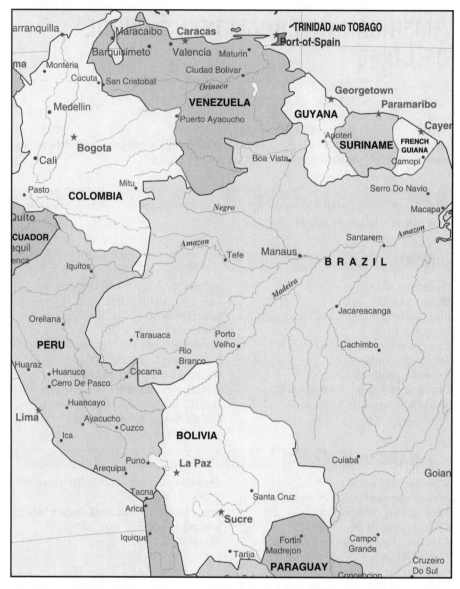

TRINIDAD AND TOBAGO

Area:	5,128 sq km
Population:	1,056,608
Capital:	Port-of-Spain
Currency:	Trinidad and Tobago Dollar (TTD)
Languages:	English, Caribbean Hindustani, French

THE INTERNATIONAL SCHOOL OF PORT OF SPAIN

Phone	868 633 4777
Fax	868 632 4595
Email	blatham@isps.edu.tt
Website	www.isps.edu.tt
Address	1 International Drive, Westmoorings, Trinidad and Tobago
Mailing address	#POS 1369, 1601 NW 97th Avenue, PO Box 025307, Miami, FL 33102-5307, USA

STAFF

Director J. Barney Latham
High School Principal John Horsfall
Middle School Principal Alicia Solozano
Elementary School Principal Suzette Julien
Admissions Director Jackie Fung-Kee-Fung
Business/Finance Manager Nadine Perreira

Head of Technology Arnold Thomas
Head of Library/Media Center Debbie Jacob
Teaching staff Full time 77; Part time 2; Total 79
Nationalities of teaching staff US 12; UK 6;
Trinidadian 50; Other(s) 9

INFORMATION

Grade levels PreK–12
School year August–June
School type coeducational, day
Year founded 1994
Governed by appointed and elected Board of Directors
Sponsored by US Embassy, EOG Resources, bpTT, British Gas
Accredited by Southern
Regional organizations AASSA

Enrollment PreK 16; Elementary K–5 173;
Middle School 6–8 115; High School 9–12 136;
Total 440
Nationalities of student body US 127; UK 67;
Trinidadian 135; Other(s) 121
Tuition/fee currency US Dollar
Tuition range 9,000–13,000
One time fees Registration 100; Capital Levy 6,000
Graduates attending college 95%
Graduates have attended Cornell U, Boston Col,
Yale U, Princeton U, Stanford U

(Continued)

THE INTERNATIONAL SCHOOL OF PORT OF SPAIN (Continued)

EDUCATIONAL PROGRAM

Curriculum US, Intl, AP
Average class size Elementary 16; Secondary 16
Language(s) of instruction English
Language(s) taught Spanish, French
Staff specialists computer, counselor, ESL, learning disabilities, librarian, nurse
Special curricular programs art, instrumental music, vocal music, computer/technology, distance learning, physical education

Extra curricular programs computers, community service, dance, drama, environmental conservation, excursions/expeditions, newspaper, yearbook
Sports badminton, basketball, cricket, gymnastics, martial arts, rugby, soccer, swimming, volleyball
Examinations ACT, AP, Iowa, PSAT, SAT, SAT II

CAMPUS FACILITIES

Location Suburban
Campus 3 hectares, 1 building, 30 classrooms, 5 computer labs, 150 instructional computers, 20,000 library volumes, 1 auditorium, 1 cafeteria, 1 covered play area, 1 gymnasium, 1 infirmary, 2 playing fields, 5 science labs, air conditioning

TUNISIA

Area:	163,610 sq km
Population:	10,276,158
Capital:	Tunis
Currency:	Tunisian Dinar (TND)
Languages:	Arabic

AMERICAN COOPERATIVE SCHOOL OF TUNIS

Phone	216 71 760 905
Fax	216 71 761 412
Email	american.school@acst.intl.tn
Website	www.acst.net
Address	c/o US Embassy (ACST), Zone Nord-Est des Berges du Lac, La Goulette, Tunis, 2045, Tunisia
Mailing address	6360 Tunis Place, Dulles, VA 20189-6360, USA

STAFF

Director Patrick M. Meyer
Secondary Principal Daphne Neal
Elementary Principal Michael Adams
Secondary Guidance Kathryn Bogie
Elementary Guidance Janice King
Curriculum Coordinator Joyce Meyer
Business Manager / Finance Manager
Faouzi Ben Sedrine / Paul Murray

Director of Technology Rick Park
Elementary and Upper School Librarians
Muriel Curtis and Mary Alice Osborne
Teaching staff Full time 59; Part time 2; Total 61
Nationalities of teaching staff US 46; UK 4;
Tunisian 8; Other(s) 3

INFORMATION

Grade levels PreK–12
School year August–June
School type coeducational, day, private non-profit
Year founded 1959
Governed by elected Board of Governors
Accredited by Middle States
Regional organizations ECIS, MAIS, NESA
Enrollment PreK 34; Elementary K–5 226;
Middle School 6–8 120; High School 9–12 120;
Total 500

Nationalities of student body US 100; UK 40;
Tunisian 25; Other(s) (German, Nigerian) 335
Tuition/fee currency US Dollar
Tuition range 6,742–15,235
Annual fees Capital Levy 820; Busing 1,400;
Lunch 540; ESL 2,600; Special Needs 2,600
One time fees Registration 5,500; Testing 120
Graduates attending college 98%
Graduates have attended Oxford U, McGill U,
U of Virginia, St. Mary's Col, Oberlin Col

(Continued)

AMERICAN COOPERATIVE SCHOOL OF TUNIS (Continued)

EDUCATIONAL PROGRAM

Curriculum US, Intl, IB Diploma
Average class size Elementary 20; Secondary 18
Language(s) of instruction English
Language(s) taught French, Arabic, German
Staff specialists computer, counselor, ESL, learning disabilities, librarian, nurse, reading resource
Special curricular programs art, instrumental music, vocal music, computer/technology, physical education

Extra curricular programs computers, community service, dance, drama, excursions/expeditions, literary magazine, newspaper, yearbook
Sports baseball, basketball, cross-country, martial arts, soccer, swimming, track and field, volleyball
Clubs National Honor Society, student council, community service,
Examinations ACT, AP, IB, Iowa, PSAT, SAT, SAT II, TOEFL, Gates MacGinitie Reading Test

CAMPUS FACILITIES

Location Suburban
Campus 3 hectares, 18 buildings, 54 classrooms, 3 computer labs, 140 instructional computers, 25,000 library volumes, 1 auditorium,

1 cafeteria, 3 covered play areas, 2 gymnasiums, 1 infirmary, 1 playing field, 3 science labs, 1 pool, air conditioning

TURKEY

TURKEY

Area:	780,580 sq km
Population:	71,158,647
Capital:	Ankara
Currency:	Turkish Lira (TRY)
Languages:	Turkish

BILKENT UNIVERSITY PREPARATORY SCHOOL/BILKENT INTERNATIONAL SCHOOL

Phone	90 312 266 4961
Fax	90 312 266 4963
Email	school@bups.bilkent.edu.tr
Website	www.bupsbis.bilkent.edu.tr
Address	East Campus, Bilkent, Ankara, 06533, Turkey

STAFF

Director Gary R. Crippin, Ph.D.
High School/Middle School Principal Eric Sturm
Elementary School Principal Daniel Keller, Ed.D.

Administrative Manager Gulcan Ataman
Technician Denis Connely
Head Librarian Josephine Howard

INFORMATION

Grade levels PreK–12
School year September–June
School type coeducational, day, private non-profit
Year founded 1993
Governed by appointed Board of Directors
Accredited by CIS, New England
Regional organizations ECIS
Enrollment PreK 32; Elementary K–5 226; Middle School 6–8 150; High School 9–12 180; Total 588

Nationalities of student body US 15; UK 7; Host 468; Other(s) 98
Tuition/fee currency US Dollar
Tuition range 10,000–16,000
Annual fees Busing 700; Lunch 700; Books 300
One time fees Registration 15
Graduates attending college 100%
Graduates have attended Massachusetts Institute of Technology, Stanford U, Cornell U, Cambridge U, Johns Hopkins U

EDUCATIONAL PROGRAM

Curriculum US, UK, National, Intl, IB Diploma, IGCSE
Average class size Elementary 20; Secondary 12
Language(s) of instruction English, Turkish
Language(s) taught French, German, Spanish
Staff specialists computer, counselor, ESL, learning disabilities, librarian, nurse
Special curricular programs art, instrumental music, vocal music, computer/technology, physical education, drama

Extra curricular programs computers, community service, dance, drama, environmental conservation, excursions/expeditions, literary magazine, newspaper, photography, yearbook
Sports badminton, basketball, hockey, soccer, softball, track and field, volleyball
Clubs student council, roller blading
Examinations GCSE, IB, IGCSE, PSAT, SAT, SAT II, TOEFL

CAMPUS FACILITIES

Location Suburban
Campus 1 hectare, 8 buildings, 70 classrooms, 2 computer labs, 55 instructional computers,

25,000 library volumes, 1 auditorium, 3 cafeterias, 2 gymnasiums, 3 infirmaries, 6 playing fields, 5 science labs

Data from 2006/07 school year.

OASIS INTERNATIONAL SCHOOL

Phone	90 312 285 7524
Fax	90 312 286 0560
Email	info@icsankara.org
Website	www.icsankara.org
Address	362 Sokak No 5, Cigdem Mah., Ankara, 06530, Turkey

STAFF

Director Ross Campbell
Assistant Principal Eric Lawrence
Business Administrator Troy Lundy

Teaching staff Full time 26; Part time 3; Total 29
Nationalities of teaching staff US 22; Turk 4; Other(s) (Canadian) 3

INFORMATION

Grade levels PreK–12
School year September–June
School type coeducational, day
Year founded 2004
Sponsored by Oasis Int'l Schools (a division of Network of Int'l Christian Schools)
Accredited by Middle States
Enrollment PreK 10; Elementary K–5 87; Middle School 6–8 37; High School 9–12 51; Total 185

Nationalities of student body US 67; UK 6; Other(s) (Korean, Nigerien) 112
Tuition/fee currency US Dollar
Tuition range 5,800–8,200
Annual fees Capital Levy 500; Busing 1,000
Graduates attending college 98%
Graduates have attended Northwestern U, Wheaton Col, Texas A&M U

EDUCATIONAL PROGRAM

Curriculum US, Intl
Average class size Elementary 14; Secondary 14
Language(s) of instruction English
Language(s) taught Spanish, Turkish
Staff specialists computer, counselor, ESL, learning disabilities

Special curricular programs art, instrumental music, computer/technology, physical education
Extra curricular programs drama, yearbook
Sports basketball, soccer, volleyball
Examinations AP, PSAT, SAT, Stanford

CAMPUS FACILITIES

Location Urban
Campus 1 building, 20 classrooms, 2 computer labs, 40 instructional computers,

7,000 library volumes, 1 cafeteria, 1 infirmary, 1 playing field, 4 science labs

ENKA OKULLARI-ENKA SCHOOLS

Phone	90 212 276 0545
Fax	90 212 276 8294
Email	mailbox@enkaschools.com
Website	www.enkaschools.com
Address	Sadi Gulcelik Spor Sitesi, Istinye, Istanbul, 34460, Turkey

STAFF

Director Darlene J. Fisher
Primary School Principal Filiz Aktepe
High School Principal Mustafa Balkas
Preschool Principal Ayten Yilmaz
Primary Assistant Principal Zerrin Özsoy
Lise Assistant Principal Erkan Gultekin

Business Manager Cumhur Göksoy
Technology Coordinator Cetin Artan
Librarian Cara Keyman
Teaching staff Full time 160; Part time 3; Total 163
Nationalities of teaching staff US 10; UK 5;
Turk 123; Other(s) (Australian, Canadian) 25

INFORMATION

Grade levels PreK–12
School year September–June
School type coeducational, company-sponsored, day, private non-profit
Year founded 1995
Governed by appointed Board of Trustees
Sponsored by Enka Holdings
Regional organizations ECIS

Enrollment PreK 72; Elementary K–5 528;
Middle School 6–8 297; High School 9–12 278;
Total 1,175
Nationalities of student body Turk 1,173;
Other(s) (Russian, Azerbaijani) 2
Tuition/fee currency Turkish Lira
Tuition range 11,452–18,111
Annual fees Busing 2,500; Lunch 1,656;
Books 350; Clothing 300

EDUCATIONAL PROGRAM

Curriculum National, Intl, IB Diploma, IBPYP
Average class size Elementary 22; Secondary 18
Language(s) of instruction English, Turkish
Language(s) taught French, German
Staff specialists computer, counselor, ESL, learning disabilities, librarian, nurse, physician, reading resource
Special curricular programs art, instrumental music, vocal music, computer/technology, physical education

Extra curricular programs computers, community service, dance, drama, environmental conservation, excursions/expeditions, literary magazine, newspaper, yearbook
Sports basketball, football, gymnastics, martial arts, skiing, soccer, swimming, tennis, track and field
Examinations IB, Turkish National

CAMPUS FACILITIES

Location Suburban
Campus 10 hectares, 2 buildings, 105 classrooms, 5 computer labs, 150 instructional computers, 35,000 library volumes, 1 auditorium, 3 cafeterias, 2 gymnasiums, 2 infirmaries, 1 playing field, 3 science labs, 2 pools, 10 tennis courts

ISTANBUL INTERNATIONAL COMMUNITY SCHOOL

Phone	90 212 857 8264
Fax	90 212 857 8270
Email	headmast@iics.k12.tr
Website	www.iics.k12.tr
Address	Karaagac Koyu, Hadimkoy, Istanbul, 34866, Turkey

STAFF

Head of School Jeremy A. Lewis
Primary Principal Sean Murphy
Secondary Principal Paul Sebastian
Primary Vice Principal Jonathan Twigg
University Counselor Lane Ceylan
Business Manager Nalan Yalcin

Head of Technology Ash Esmail
Librarian Rebecca Boardman
Teaching staff Full time 60; Total 60
Nationalities of teaching staff US 12; UK 12; Turk 5; Other(s) (Australian, Canadian) 31

INFORMATION

Grade levels PreK–12
School year August–June
School type coeducational, day, private non-profit
Year founded 1911
Governed by appointed and elected Volunteer Board
Accredited by CIS, New England
Regional organizations CEESA, ECIS
Enrollment PreK 45; Elementary K–5 191; Middle School 6–8 101; High School 9–12 133; Total 470

Nationalities of student body US 111; UK 43; Other(s) (German, Korean) 316
Tuition/fee currency US Dollar
Tuition range 11,450–22,950
Annual fees Registration 350
One time fees Capital Levy 2,500
Graduates attending college 98%
Graduates have attended Harvard U, U of Warwick, Princeton U, Bryn Mawr Col, Swarthmore U

EDUCATIONAL PROGRAM

Curriculum Intl, IB Diploma, IBPYP, IBMYP
Average class size Elementary 16; Secondary 19
Language(s) of instruction English
Language(s) taught French, German, Spanish, Turkish (Turkish Culture)
Staff specialists computer, counselor, ESL, learning disabilities, librarian, nurse, psychologist

Special curricular programs art, instrumental music, vocal music, computer/technology, physical education, design technology, theater arts
Extra curricular programs computers, community service, dance, drama, Model UN, Math Counts, Knowledge Bowl, Student Leadership
Sports basketball, cross-country, soccer, softball, tennis, volleyball, table tennis, ballet, karate, swimming, field hockey, Tae Kwon Do
Examinations IB

CAMPUS FACILITIES

Location Suburban
Campus 13 hectares, 2 buildings, 40 classrooms, 4 computer labs, 94 instructional computers, 16,000 library volumes, 1 auditorium, 1 cafeteria, 2 covered play areas, 1 gymnasium, 1 infirmary, 3 playing fields, 4 science labs, 2 tennis courts, air conditioning

Koç School

Phone	90 216 585 6282
Fax	90 216 304 1048
Email	info@kocschool.k12.tr
Website	www.kocschool.k12.tr
Address	PK 60-Tuzla, Istanbul, 34941, Turkey

STAFF

General Director John A. Paulus, II
Assistant General Director Jale Onur
Elementary School Director Mesrure Tekay
High School Director M. Ilkin Ozyurt
Chief Financial Officer Aynur Demirayak

Chair, Computer Department Erdem Tursen
Librarian Sebnem Yalcin
Teaching staff Full time 285; Part time 6; Total 291
Nationalities of teaching staff US 27; UK 8;
Turk 218; Other(s) (Canadian, Australian) 38

INFORMATION

Grade levels K–12
School year September–June
School type boarding, coeducational, day,
private non-profit
Year founded 1988
Governed by appointed Board of Directors
Regional organizations ECIS, NESA
Enrollment PreK 48; Elementary K–5 745;
Middle School 6–8 420; High School 9–12 865;
Total 2,078

Nationalities of student body US 1; UK 2; Turk
2,072; Other(s) (German, Italian) 3
Tuition/fee currency US Dollar
Tuition range 15,053–27,773
Boarding program grades 812
Boarding program length 5-day and 7-day
Boys 81 **Girls** 54
Graduates attending college 100%
Graduates have attended Yale U, Harvard U,
Princeton U, Dartmouth Col, Columbia U

EDUCATIONAL PROGRAM

Curriculum National, Intl, IB Diploma
Average class size Elementary 24; Secondary 22
Language(s) of instruction English, Turkish
Language(s) taught French, German
Staff specialists computer, counselor, ESL,
librarian, nurse

Extra curricular programs community service,
dance, drama, environmental conservation,
excursions/expeditions, literary magazine,
photography
Sports basketball, football, gymnastics, skiing,
tennis, volleyball
Examinations IB, SAT, National

CAMPUS FACILITIES

Location Suburban
Campus 81 hectares, 118 classrooms,
6 computer labs, 202 instructional computers,
55,000 library volumes, 2 auditoriums,
2 cafeterias, 2 gymnasiums, 2 infirmaries,
4 playing fields, 8 science labs, 2 tennis courts

ROBERT COLLEGE

Phone	90 212 359 2211
Fax	90 212 287 0117
Email	jchandler@robcol.k12.tr
Website	www.robcol.k12.tr
Address	Kurucesme Cad. No. 87, Arnavutkoy, Istanbul, 34345, Turkey

STAFF

Head of School John R. Chandler
Turkish Assistant Head Guler Erdur
Academic Director Maria Orhon
Dean of Student Affairs Margaret Halicioglu
Dean of Student Activities Joseph Welch
Director of Business and Finance Ümranüngün

Director of Technical Computing Metin Ferhatoglu
Director of Library John Royce
Teaching staff Full time 102; Part time 5; Total 107
Nationalities of teaching staff US 30; UK 10; Turk 58; Other(s) (Australian) 9

INFORMATION

Grade levels 9–12
School year September–June
School type boarding, coeducational, day, private non-profit
Year founded 1863
Governed by Board of Trustees and Ministry of Education
Regional organizations ECIS, NESA
Enrollment High School 9–12 998; Total 998
Nationalities of student body Turk 998
Tuition/fee currency Turkish Lira

Tuition 20,000–20,000
Annual fees Boarding, 5-day 8,500; Boarding, 7-day 12,000; Lunch 2,500
Boarding program grades 912
Boarding program length 5-day and 7-day
Boys 100 **Girls** 70
Graduates attending college 100%
Graduates have attended Harvard U, Yale U, Princeton U, Massachusetts Institute of Technology, Cambridge U

EDUCATIONAL PROGRAM

Curriculum US, National, AP
Average class size Secondary 22
Language(s) of instruction English, Turkish
Language(s) taught German, French
Staff specialists computer, counselor, ESL, librarian, nurse, physician, psychologist
Special curricular programs art, instrumental music, vocal music, computer/technology, physical education
Extra curricular programs computers, community service, dance, drama, environmental

conservation, excursions/expeditions, literary magazine, newspaper, photography, yearbook
Sports badminton, basketball, cross-country, golf, skiing, soccer, softball, tennis, track and field, volleyball
Clubs Model UN, European Youth Parliament, drama, music, intermural sports, community service, art, student publications, Destination Imagination, subject area clubs (Math, Science, IT).
Examinations ACT, AP, PSAT, SAT, SAT II, TOEFL

CAMPUS FACILITIES

Location Urban
Campus 60 hectares, 8 buildings, 50 classrooms, 3 computer labs, 130 instructional computers, 45,000 library volumes, 2 auditoriums,

1 cafeteria, 2 covered play areas, 1 gymnasium, 1 infirmary, 2 playing fields, 11 science labs, 4 tennis courts

Istanbul   **TURKEY**

ÜSKÜDAR AMERICAN ACADEMY AND SEV ELEMENTARY SCHOOL

Phone	90 216 310 6823
Fax	90 216 553 1818
Email	WShepard@uaa.k12.tr
Website	www.uaa.k12.tr
Address	Vakif Sokak No. 1, Baglarbasi, Istanbul, 34664, Turkey

STAFF

Director Whitman O. Shepard
Primary Principal Dilek Yakar
Secondary Principal Melike Ates
Business Manager Simay Barim
IT Coordinator Birkan Kilic

Head Librarian Ruth Briddock
Teaching staff Full time 188; Part time 10; Total 198
Nationalities of teaching staff US 24; UK 13; Turk 152; Other(s) (Canadian, French) 9

INFORMATION

Grade levels K–12
School year September–June
School type coeducational, day, private non-profit
Year founded 1876
Governed by elected Board
Regional organizations ECIS
Enrollment Elementary K–5 673; Middle School 6–8 324; High School 9–12 623; Total 1,620

Nationalities of student body Turk 1,620
Tuition/fee currency US Dollar
Tuition 15,000–15,000
Annual fees Busing 1,500; Lunch 1,000; Books 300
Graduates attending college 100%
Graduates have attended Harvard U, Brown U, Princeton U, Cornell U, Yale U

EDUCATIONAL PROGRAM

Curriculum US, National, Turkish
Average class size Elementary 28; Secondary 24
Language(s) of instruction English, Turkish
Language(s) taught French, German
Staff specialists computer, counselor, ESL, librarian, nurse, physician, psychologist
Special curricular programs art, instrumental music, vocal music, computer/technology, physical education

Extra curricular programs community service, dance, drama, environmental conservation, excursions/expeditions, literary magazine, photography, yearbook
Sports badminton, basketball, rugby, skiing, soccer, swimming, tennis, volleyball, Floor Hockey, Snowboarding
Clubs student association, Model UN, art, hiking, chess, juggling, Destination Imagination, Esperanto
Examinations AP, PSAT, SAT, SAT II, TOEFL

CAMPUS FACILITIES

Location Urban
Campus 6 hectares, 10 buildings, 66 classrooms, 5 computer labs, 120 instructional computers, 29,050 library volumes, 2 auditoriums,

3 cafeterias, 1 covered play area, 3 gymnasiums, 3 infirmaries, 2 playing fields, 7 science labs, 1 tennis court

ACI High School and SEV Elementary School

Phone	90 232 285 3401
Fax	90 232 246 1674
Email	school@aci.k12.tr
Website	www.aci.k12.tr OR www.sevizmir.k12.tr
Address	Inonu Cad. No: 476, Goztepe, Izmir, 35290, Turkey

STAFF

Campus Director Charles Hanna
Turkish High School Principal Anet Gomel
SEV Elementary Principal Nilhan Cubuk
Overseas University Counselor Steve Gustin
Marketing and Development Coordinator Aydan Yakin
Business Manager Canturk Candan, Ed.D.

Campus IT Coordinator Serpil Kilic
Director of Library and Media Center Services Judy March
Teaching staff Full time 80; Part time 30; Total 110
Nationalities of teaching staff US 10; UK 10; Turk 80; Other(s) (Canadian, South African) 10

INFORMATION

Grade levels K–12
School year September–June
School type coeducational, day, private non-profit
Year founded 1878
Governed by elected Board of Directors
Accredited by CIS
Regional organizations ECIS
Enrollment Elementary K–5 350; Middle School 6–8 300; High School 9–12 500; Total 1,150

Nationalities of student body Turk 1,150
Tuition/fee currency Turkish Lira
Tuition range 15,180–15,478
Graduates attending college 96%
Graduates have attended Georgetown U, Yale U, U of California in Berkeley, London School of Economics, Cornell Col

EDUCATIONAL PROGRAM

Curriculum National, AP, IB Diploma, Turkish National Curriculum
Average class size Elementary 26; Secondary 24
Language(s) of instruction English, Turkish
Language(s) taught German, French
Staff specialists computer, counselor, ESL, librarian, nurse, physician, psychologist
Special curricular programs art, instrumental music, vocal music, computer/technology, physical education

Extra curricular programs computers, community service, dance, drama, environmental conservation, excursions/expeditions, literary magazine, newspaper, photography, yearbook
Sports badminton, basketball, cross-country, soccer, tennis, volleyball
Examinations AP, IB, PSAT, SAT, SAT II, TOEFL

CAMPUS FACILITIES

Location Suburban
Campus 14 hectares, 8 buildings, 86 classrooms, 8 computer labs, 250 instructional computers, 55,000 library volumes, 2 auditoriums, 3 cafeterias, 2 covered play areas, 2 gymnasiums, 3 infirmaries, 3 playing fields, 8 science labs, 1 tennis court, air conditioning

TARSUS AMERICAN SCHOOL

Phone	90 324 613 5402
Fax	90 324 624 6347
Email	info@tac.k12.tr
Website	www.tac.k12.tr
Address	Caminur Mahallesi, Cengiz Topel Caddesi, No. 44, Tarsus, Mersin, 33444, Turkey
Mailing address	PK 6, 33444, Tarsus, Turkey

STAFF

Director Robert Mallett
Elementary School Principal Sýdýka Albayrak
Turkish First Vice Principal Can Ýstif
Assistant Principal Francis van der Hoeven
Assistant Principal Taner Uslu
Academic Dean Esma Çalýk, Ph.D.

Business Manager Ayse Apa Dildar
Network Manager Mehmet Ozdemir
Librarian Sezin Ozkan
Teaching staff Full time 71; Part time 7; Total 78
Nationalities of teaching staff US 3; UK 1;
Turk 66; Other(s) (Canadian, Australian) 8

INFORMATION

Grade levels K–12
School year September–June
School type boarding, coeducational, day, private non-profit
Year founded 1888
Governed by appointed Board of Directors
Sponsored by UCBWM
Regional organizations ECIS
Enrollment Elementary K–5 232; Middle School 6–8 139; High School 9–12 250; Total 621

Nationalities of student body Host 621
Tuition/fee currency US Dollar
Annual fees Registration 10,903; Boarding, 5-day 3,846; Boarding, 7-day 5,769; Busing 1,390; Lunch 889; Books 230
Boarding program grades 912
Boarding program length 5-day **Boys** 25
Graduates attending college 100%
Graduates have attended Harvard U, Georgetown U, Yale U, Princeton U, Stanford U

EDUCATIONAL PROGRAM

Curriculum National, IB Diploma
Average class size Elementary 20; Secondary 20
Language(s) of instruction English, Turkish
Language(s) taught German, French
Staff specialists computer, counselor, librarian, nurse, physician

Special curricular programs art, computer/technology, physical education
Extra curricular programs community service, drama, excursions/expeditions, literary magazine, yearbook
Sports basketball, tennis, volleyball, Handball
Examinations IB, PSAT, SAT, SAT II, TOEFL

CAMPUS FACILITIES

Location Urban
Campus 25 hectares, 14 buildings, 47 classrooms, 2 computer labs, 62 instructional computers, 25,000 library volumes, 1 auditorium,
2 cafeterias, 1 covered play area, 1 gymnasium, 2 infirmaries, 7 playing fields, 6 science labs, 1 tennis court, air conditioning

TURKMENISTAN

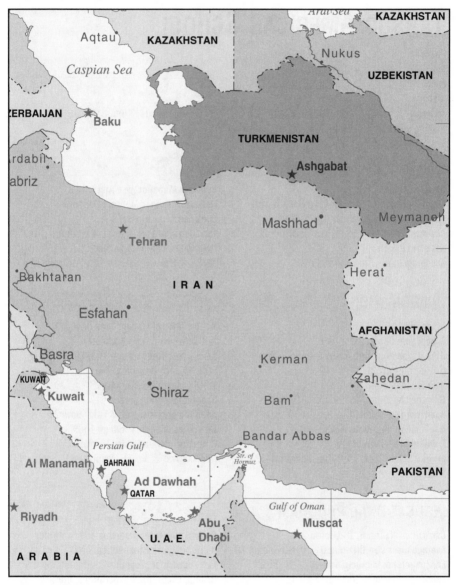

TURKMENISTAN

Area:	488,100 sq km
Population:	5,097,028
Capital:	Ashgabat (Ashkhabad)
Currency:	Turkmen Manat (TMM)
Languages:	Turkmen

ASHGABAT INTERNATIONAL SCHOOL

Phone	993 12 489 027
Fax	993 12 489 028
Email	paulbateman@qsi.org
Website	www.qsi.org
Address	Berzengi, Ataturk Street, Ashgabat, Turkmenistan
Mailing address	c/o American Embassy, Ashgabat, Dept. of State, 7070 Ashgabat Place, Washington, DC 20521-7070, USA

STAFF

Director Brad Goth
Teaching staff Full time 10; Total 10

Nationalities of teaching staff US 5; UK 2; Other(s) (Canadian) 3

INFORMATION

Grade levels PreK–12
School year August–June
School type day, private non-profit
Year founded 1994
Governed by appointed Board of Directors
Sponsored by Quality Schools International
Accredited by Middle States
Regional organizations CEESA
Enrollment PreK 11; Elementary K–5 39; Middle School 6–8 20; High School 9–12 15; Total 85

Nationalities of student body US 8; UK 2; Turkmen 32; Other(s) (Malaysian, Indian) 43
Tuition/fee currency US Dollar
Tuition 12,500
Annual fees Registration 100; Capital Levy 1,600; Busing 600
Graduates attending college 100%
Graduates have attended Wheaton Col, American U of Bishkek

EDUCATIONAL PROGRAM

Curriculum US
Average class size Elementary 11; Secondary 8
Language(s) of instruction English

Language(s) taught Russian, Turkmen, German, French
Examinations PSAT, SAT

CAMPUS FACILITIES

Location Suburban
Campus 5 hectares, 1 building, 8 classrooms, 1 computer lab, 14 instructional computers,

6,000 library volumes, 1 playing field, air conditioning

UGANDA

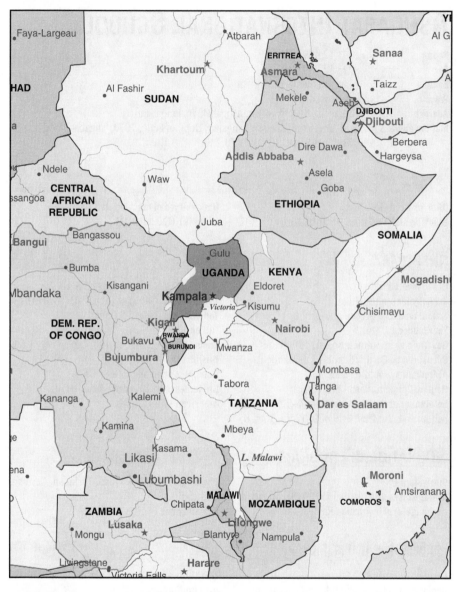

UGANDA

Area:	236,040 sq km
Population:	30,262,610
Capital:	Kampala
Currency:	Ugandan Shilling (UGX)
Languages:	English

THE INTERNATIONAL SCHOOL OF UGANDA

Phone	256 41 200374/8/9
Fax	256 41 200303
Email	gmail@isu.ac.ug
Website	www.isu.ac.ug
Address	Plot 272 Lubowa, Entebbe Rd, Kampala, Uganda
Mailing address	PO Box 4200, Kampala, Uganda

STAFF

Head of School Donald S. Groves, Ph.D.
Junior School Principal Corine van den Wildenberg
Secondary School Principal Jennifer Lees
Dean of Studies Jan Coyle Groves

Operations and Business Manager Pieter Visser
ICT Coordinator Daniel Todd
Librarian Cathy Kreutter

INFORMATION

Grade levels PreK–12
School year August–June
School type coeducational, day, private non-profit
Year founded 1963
Governed by elected Board of Trustees
Accredited by CIS, Middle States
Regional organizations AISA
Enrollment PreK 34; Elementary K–5 175;
Middle School 6–8 127;
High School 9–12 145; Total 481

Nationalities of student body US 112; UK 77;
Ugandan 35; Other(s) 257
Tuition/fee currency US Dollar
Tuition range 2,592–14,676
Annual fees Busing 870
One time fees Registration 2,000;
Capital Levy 2,000
Graduates attending college 95%
Graduates have attended Brown U, McGill U,
Mt Holyoke Col, Emory U, Bristol U

EDUCATIONAL PROGRAM

Curriculum Intl, IB Diploma, IBPYP, IBMYP
Average class size Elementary 20; Secondary 20
Language(s) of instruction English
Language(s) taught French, German, Spanish
Staff specialists computer, counselor, ESL,
learning disabilities, librarian, nurse
Special curricular programs art, instrumental
music, vocal music, computer/technology,
physical education, Ugandan culture

Extra curricular programs community service,
drama, excursions/expeditions, newspaper,
yearbook
Sports badminton, baseball, basketball, cricket,
football, golf, hockey, martial arts, soccer,
softball, swimming, tennis, track and field,
volleyball
Clubs student council, Model UN, Roots and
Shoots, papermaking, math
Examinations IB, Iowa, PSAT, SAT, SAT II

CAMPUS FACILITIES

Location Rural
Campus 13 hectares, 26 buildings, 45 classrooms,
2 computer labs, 44 instructional computers,

16,000 library volumes, 1 cafeteria, 1 covered
play area, 1 gymnasium, 1 infirmary, 3 playing
fields, 4 science labs, 1 pool, 4 tennis courts

Data from 2006/07 school year.

KAMPALA INTERNATIONAL SCHOOL, UGANDA

Phone	256 41 530 472
Fax	256 41 543 444
Email	office@kisu.com
Website	www.kisu.com
Address	Old Kira Road, Bukoto, Kampala, Uganda
Mailing address	PO Box 2020, Kampala, Uganda

STAFF

Principal Graham Pheby
Secondary Coordinator Catherine Meyer

Head of Primary Kurtis Peterson
Bursar Peer Abu Bakar

INFORMATION

Grade levels N–11
School year September–July
School type coeducational, day, proprietary
Year founded 1993
Governed by appointed and elected Board of Management
Sponsored by Ruparelia Companies
Accredited by CIS, New England
Regional organizations ECIS

Enrollment Nursery 30; PreK 35; Elementary K–5 120; Middle School 6–8 55; High School 9–12 18; Total 258
Nationalities of student body US 21; UK 53; Ugandan 27; Other(s) (South African, French) 157
Tuition/fee currency US Dollar
Tuition range 2,835–11,970
Annual fees Busing 600
One time fees Registration 160

EDUCATIONAL PROGRAM

Curriculum UK, Intl, IB Diploma, IBMYP, GenCSE
Average class size Elementary 20; Secondary 15
Language(s) of instruction English
Language(s) taught French
Staff specialists computer, counselor, ESL, learning disabilities, librarian, nurse, psychologist, reading resource
Special curricular programs art, instrumental music, vocal music, computer/technology, physical education, outdoor education, science fair, equestrian
Extra curricular programs computers, community service, dance, drama, environmental conservation, excursions/expeditions, newspaper, photography, yearbook, Dutch, Kiswahili, Arabic
Sports baseball, basketball, cricket, cross-country, football, golf, gymnastics, hockey, rugby, skiing, soccer, softball, squash, swimming, tennis, track and field, volleyball, sailing, horseriding
Clubs Model UN, drama, choir, Samba band, hockey, Cub Scouts, crafts,ceramics, world art
Examinations GCSE, IGCSE, QCA (UK) Standard Attainment Tests (years 7, 11)

CAMPUS FACILITIES

Location Suburban
Campus 13 buildings, 29 classrooms, 1 computer lab, 55 instructional computers, 15,000 library volumes, 1 auditorium, 1 cafeteria, 1 covered play area, 1 infirmary, 3 playing fields, 1 science lab, 2 pools, 4 tennis courts

Data from 2006/07 school year.

UKRAINE

UKRAINE

Area:	603,700 sq km
Population:	46,299,862
Capital:	Kiev
Currency:	Hryvnia (UAH)
Languages:	Ukrainian

KIEV INTERNATIONAL SCHOOL

Phone	380 44 452 2792
Fax	380 44 452 2998
Email	kiev@qsi.org
Website	www.qsi.org/ukr
Address	3A Svyatoshinskiy Provulok, Kyiv, 03115, Ukraine
Mailing address	Administrative Officer, Kiev Int'l School, 5850 Kiev Place, Dulles, VA 20189-5850, USA

STAFF

Director Michael J. Seefried
Director of Instruction Andrew Melnyk
Guidance Counselor David Lewis
Elementary Coordinator Brian Garner
Athletic/Activities Coordinator Jeremy Tinsley
Business Office Manager Yulia Usikova

Information Technologist Victor Datsyyuk
Librarian Claire Ansell
Teaching staff Full time 86; Total 86
Nationalities of teaching staff US 42; UK 1; Ukrainian 36; Other(s) (Canadian, Irish) 7

INFORMATION

Grade levels PreK–12
School year August–June
School type coeducational, day, private non-profit
Year founded 1992
Governed by appointed Board of Directors
Accredited by Middle States
Regional organizations CEESA
Enrollment PreK 75; Elementary K–5 230; Middle School 6–8 91; High School 9–12 82; Total 478

Nationalities of student body US 93; UK 10; Ukrainian 120; Other(s) (Israeli, Korean) 255
Tuition/fee currency US Dollar
Tuition range 4,700–12,500
Annual fees Capital Levy 1,600; Busing 1,500; Lunch 750
One time fees Registration 100
Graduates attending college 100%
Graduates have attended Boston U, U of Chicago, Pennsylvania State U, George Washington U, Indiana U

EDUCATIONAL PROGRAM

Curriculum US, AP, IB Diploma
Average class size Elementary 14; Secondary 14
Language(s) of instruction English
Language(s) taught Russian, French, Ukrainian, German, Spanish, Dutch, Hindi
Staff specialists computer, counselor, ESL, librarian, physician, reading resource

Extra curricular programs computers, community service, dance, drama, excursions/expeditions, newspaper, yearbook
Sports basketball, cross-country, skiing, soccer, softball, swimming, tennis, track and field, volleyball
Examinations AP, IB, Iowa, PSAT, SAT, Stanford

CAMPUS FACILITIES

Location Suburban
Campus 4 hectares, 1 building, 30 classrooms, 2 computer labs, 130 instructional computers,

18,000 library volumes, 1 auditorium, 1 cafeteria, 1 gymnasium, 1 infirmary, 2 playing fields, 2 science labs, 1 pool, 3 tennis courts

PECHERSK SCHOOL INTERNATIONAL

Phone 380 44 455 9585
Fax 380 44 455 9580
Email communication@psi.kiev.ua
Website www.psi.kiev.ua
Address Victor Zabila 7a, Kiev, 03039, Ukraine

STAFF

Director John Young
Primary Principal Sharon Ingerson
Secondary Principal Ian Williams
Counselor Louis Murillo
PA to the Director Anne Glover

Librarian Graham Grant
Teaching staff Full time 59; Part time 3; Total 62
Nationalities of teaching staff US 12; UK 10;
Ukrainian 15; Other(s) (Canadian) 25

INFORMATION

Grade levels N–12
School year August–June
School type coeducational, day, private non-profit
Year founded 1995
Governed by elected Board of Governors
Accredited by CIS, New England
Regional organizations CEESA, ECIS
Enrollment Nursery 16; PreK 30;
Elementary K–5 160; Middle School 6–8 90;
High School 9–12 140; Total 436

Nationalities of student body US 50; UK 25;
Ukrainian 60; Other(s) 301
Tuition/fee currency US Dollar
Tuition range 6,300–1,600
Annual fees Capital Levy 1,500; Busing 1,500
One time fees Registration 500
Graduates attending college 90%
Graduates have attended Cambridge U,
British Columbia U, Boston U, Kiev U

EDUCATIONAL PROGRAM

Curriculum IB Diploma, IBPYP, IBMYP
Average class size Elementary 15; Secondary 15
Language(s) of instruction English
Language(s) taught Ukrainian, Russian, French,
German, Spanish
Staff specialists computer, counselor, ESL,
librarian
Special curricular programs art, instrumental
music, vocal music, computer/technology,
physical education

Extra curricular programs community service,
drama, environmental conservation, excursions/
expeditions, literary magazine, newspaper,
yearbook
Sports basketball, cross-country, gymnastics,
martial arts, soccer, softball, swimming, tennis,
track and field
Examinations IB, PSAT, SAT

CAMPUS FACILITIES

Campus 1 hectare, 4 buildings, 28 classrooms,
2 computer labs, 70 instructional computers,

5,000 library volumes, 1 cafeteria, 1 gymnasium,
2 science labs

UNITED ARAB EMIRATES

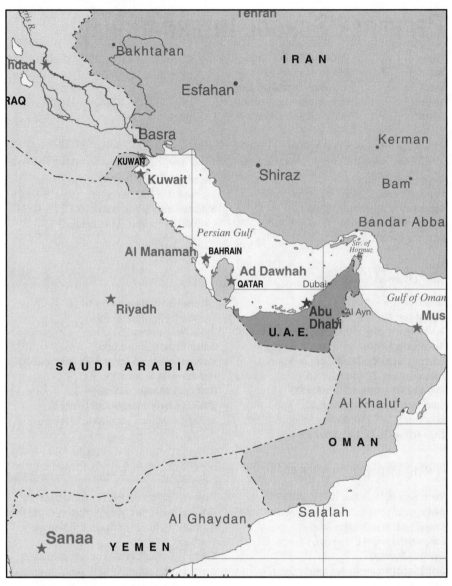

UNITED ARAB EMIRATES

Area:	83,600 sq km
Population:	4,444,011
Capital:	Abu Dhabi
Currency:	Emirati Dirham (AED)
Languages:	Arabic

AL-WOROOD SCHOOL

Phone	971 2 444 7655
Fax	971 2 444 9732
Email	alworood@emirates.net.ae
Website	www.alworood.sch.ae
Address	Off Airport Road, after 29th Street, Opposite old Municipal Garage site, Abu Dhabi, United Arab Emirates
Mailing address	PO Box 46673, Abu Dhabi, United Arab Emirates

STAFF

President Abdulla Al Nowais, Ph.D.
Academic Controller
Ahmed Osman Mohamed, Ph.D.
Academic Controller, grades 1 to 3 Nadia Loutfi
Examinations Officer Habibullah A. Salam
College Counselor Robert Sivers

Administrative and Financial Controller Yasmin Edah
IT Manager Kamaludheen Abdul Jabber
Deputy Head Robert Sivers
Teaching staff Full time 144; Total 144
Nationalities of teaching staff US 2; UK 2;
Emirati 2; Other(s) (Jordanian, Egyptian) 138

INFORMATION

Grade levels N–12
School year September–June
School type coeducational, day, proprietary
Year founded 1982
Governed by School President
Sponsored by Dr. Abdulla Al Nowais
Accredited by Middle States
Regional organizations ECIS, NESA
Enrollment Nursery 29; PreK 188;
Elementary K–5 1,166; Middle School 6–8 496;
High School 9–12 551; Total 2,430

Nationalities of student body US 43; UK 9;
Emirati 1,774; Other(s) (Jordanian, Egyptian) 604
Tuition/fee currency Utd. Arab Emir. Dirham
Tuition range 11,220–24,860
Annual fees Busing 3,500; Books 2,500
One time fees Entrance Exam 250
Graduates attending college 99%
Graduates have attended American U of Sharjah,
American U of Beirut, Zayed U, Manchester U,
Birmingham U

EDUCATIONAL PROGRAM

Curriculum Intl, IGCSE, A-Level GCE
Average class size Elementary 27; Secondary 25
Language(s) of instruction English, Arabic
Language(s) taught Arabic, French
Staff specialists computer, nurse, physician

Special curricular programs computer/technology
Sports basketball, soccer
Examinations A-level GCE, GCSE, IGCSE, PSAT,
SAT, TOEFL

CAMPUS FACILITIES

Location Suburban
Campus 2 hectares, 2 buildings, 102 classrooms,
3 computer labs, 120 instructional computers,
55,000 library volumes, 1 auditorium,

2 cafeterias, 2 covered play areas, 1 gymnasium,
1 infirmary, 6 science labs, 1 pool,
air conditioning

AMERICAN COMMUNITY SCHOOL OF ABU DHABI

Phone	971 2 681 5115
Fax	971 2 681 6006
Email	acs@acs.sch.ae
Website	www.acs.sch.ae
Address	Sheikh Sultan Bin Zayed Street, Street No. 32, PO Box 42114, Abu Dhabi, United Arab Emirates

STAFF

Superintendent George H. Robinson, Ed.D.
High School Principal Michelle Remington, Ph.D.
Middle School Principal Mark Hardeman
Elementary School Principal Jane Shartzer
Curriculum Coordinator Fred Schafer
Director of Finance Jan Al Hafi

Technology/Media Specialist, K–12 Bill Willis
School Librarian Steve Crandell
Teaching staff Full time 74; Part time 6; Total 80
Nationalities of teaching staff US 54; UK 6; Other(s) (Canadian) 20

INFORMATION

Grade levels PreK–12
School year August–June
School type coeducational, day, private non-profit
Year founded 1973
Governed by elected Board of Trustees
Accredited by Middle States
Regional organizations NESA
Enrollment PreK 40; Elementary K–5 367; Middle School 6–8 207; High School 9–12 257; Total 871

Nationalities of student body US 411; UK 24; Emirati 31; Other(s) (Canadian) 405
Tuition/fee currency US Dollar
Tuition range 5,520–14,134
One time fees Registration 70; Capital Levy 2,860
Graduates attending college 97%
Graduates have attended Stanford U, U of Pennsylvania, Wellesley Col, Notre Dame U, Vanderbilt U

EDUCATIONAL PROGRAM

Curriculum US, IB Diploma
Average class size Elementary 20; Secondary 22
Language(s) of instruction English
Language(s) taught French, Spanish, Arabic
Staff specialists computer, counselor, ESL, learning disabilities, librarian, nurse, psychologist
Special curricular programs art, instrumental music, vocal music, computer/technology, distance learning, physical education

Extra curricular programs community service, drama, excursions/expeditions, literary magazine, newspaper, yearbook
Sports badminton, basketball, cross-country, soccer, softball, swimming, track and field, volleyball
Clubs Habitat for Humanity, Medicins sans Frontieres, National Honor Society, student council, film, robotics
Examinations ACT, IB, PSAT, SAT, ERB-CTP4 & WrAP

CAMPUS FACILITIES

Location Suburban
Campus 3 hectares, 3 buildings, 58 classrooms, 4 computer labs, 245 instructional computers, 25,000 library volumes, 1 auditorium, 1 cafeteria, 2 covered play areas, 2 gymnasiums, 1 infirmary, 2 playing fields, 4 science labs, 1 pool, air conditioning

656

AMERICAN INTERNATIONAL SCHOOL IN ABU DHABI

Phone	971 2 444 4333
Fax	971 2 444 4005
Email	aisa@emirates.net.ae
Website	www.aisa.sch.ae
Address	Airport Road, 29th Street, Maroor, Abu Dhabi, United Arab Emirates
Mailing address	P O Box 5992, Abu Dhabi, United Arab Emirates

STAFF

Superintendent Walid K. Abushakra
Director Walther Hetzer, Ph.D.
Elementary Principal Robert Evans, Ed.D.
Middle and High School Principal Félim Bolster
Middle and High School Vice Principal Jim Rehburg
Elementary Vice Principal Elizabeth Naidis

Head of Finance Abdul Kader Salim Rayammarakkarveettil
Librarian Elaine Fortune
Teaching staff Full time 127; Total 127
Nationalities of teaching staff US 25; UK 6; Other(s) (Australian, Jordanian) 96

INFORMATION

Grade levels PreK–12
School year September–June
School type day, proprietary
Year founded 1995
Governed by appointed ESOL
Sponsored by ESOL
Accredited by Middle States
Regional organizations MAIS
Enrollment PreK 17; Elementary K–5 650; Middle School 6–8 180; High School 9–12 200; Total 1,047

Nationalities of student body US 25; UK 6; Emirati 467; Other(s) (South African, Jordanian) 549
Tuition/fee currency US Dollar
Tuition range 4,350–10,060
Annual fees Registration 135; Busing 1,090
Graduates attending college 95%
Graduates have attended Duke U, Boston U, U of Toronto, Bentley U, Queen's U

(Continued)

AMERICAN INTERNATIONAL SCHOOL IN ABU DHABI (Continued)

EDUCATIONAL PROGRAM

Curriculum US, Intl, IB Diploma, IBPYP
Average class size Elementary 19; Secondary 19
Language(s) of instruction English
Language(s) taught Arabic, French, Spanish
Staff specialists computer, counselor, ESL, librarian, nurse, physician
Special curricular programs art, computer/technology, physical education, drama

Extra curricular programs community service, drama, excursions/expeditions, literary magazine, yearbook, Model UN, Global Village
Sports badminton, basketball, hockey, soccer, track and field, volleyball
Examinations IB, PSAT, SAT

CAMPUS FACILITIES

Location Urban
Campus 3 hectares, 7 buildings, 79 classrooms, 4 computer labs, 125 instructional computers, 11,500 library volumes, 2 cafeterias, 6 covered play areas, 1 gymnasium, 2 infirmaries, 3 playing fields, 4 science labs, air conditioning

Abu Dhabi   **UNITED ARAB EMIRATES**

INTERNATIONAL SCHOOL OF CHOUEIFAT

Phone	971 2 446 1444
Fax	971 2 446 1048
Email	iscad@sabis.net
Website	www.iscad-sabis.net
Address	Mohamed Bin Khalifa Street, PO Box 7212, Abu Dhabi, 7212, United Arab Emirates

STAFF

Director John Ormerod

INFORMATION

Grade levels PreK–13
School year September–June
School type coeducational, day

Year founded 1886
Sponsored by SABIS
Tuition/fee currency Utd. Arab Emir. Dirham

EDUCATIONAL PROGRAM

Tuition range 14,400–26,400
Annual fees Busing 3,850; Lunch 4,600
Curriculum US, UK, Intl, AP, IGCSE, GenCSE, SABIS
Average class size Elementary 25; Secondary 32
Language(s) of instruction English
Language(s) taught English, French, Italian, Arabic (for native speakers)
Staff specialists computer, counselor, librarian, math resource, nurse, physician, reading resource

Special curricular programs art, vocal music, computer/technology, distance learning, physical education, learning through video conferencing
Extra curricular programs computers, dance, drama, environmental conservation, excursions/expeditions, newspaper, photography, yearbook, student government
Sports badminton, baseball, basketball, cricket

CAMPUS FACILITIES

Location Urban
Campus 5 hectares, 15 buildings, 110 classrooms, 4 computer labs, 300 instructional computers, 18,000 library volumes, 1 auditorium,

2 cafeterias, 8 covered play areas, 1 gymnasium, 2 infirmaries, 4 playing fields, 4 science labs, 2 pools, 3 tennis courts, air conditioning

Data from 2006/07 school year.

AMERICAN SCHOOL OF DUBAI

Phone	971 4 344 0824
Fax	971 4 344 1510
Email	asdadmin@emirates.net.ae
Website	www.asdubai.org
Address	332/53b Street, Bldg #30, Jumairah, Dubai, United Arab Emirates
Mailing address	PO Box 71188, Dubai, United Arab Emirates

STAFF

Superintendent Harold S. Fleetham, Ed.D.
High School Principal Keith W. Cincotta, Ed.D.
Middle School Principal Mary J. Harty
Elementary School Principal
Monica Medina-Olds, Ed.D.

Computer Coordinator Robert Ackerman
Teaching staff Full time 78; Part time 11; Total 89
Nationalities of teaching staff US 61; UK 2;
Emirati 1; Other(s) (Canadian) 25

INFORMATION

Grade levels PreK–12
School year August–June
School type coeducational, day, private non-profit
Year founded 1966
Governed by appointed Board of Trustees
Sponsored by Cultural Foundation
Accredited by Middle States
Regional organizations NESA
Enrollment PreK 60; Elementary K–5 398;
Middle School 6–8 210; High School 9–12 280;
Total 948

Nationalities of student body US 567; UK 29;
Emirati 4; Other(s) (Canadian, Indian) 348
Tuition/fee currency US Dollar
Tuition range 3,072–12,965
Annual fees Seat Rental Non User Companies
3,000; Seat Rental User Companies 1,500
One time fees Registration 136; Books 136
Graduates attending college 100%
Graduates have attended McGill U, Stanford U,
U of Pennsylvania, California Institute of
Technology, Tufts U

EDUCATIONAL PROGRAM

Curriculum US, AP
Average class size Elementary 23; Secondary 25
Language(s) of instruction English
Language(s) taught French, Spanish
Staff specialists computer, counselor, learning
disabilities, librarian, nurse
Special curricular programs art, instrumental
music, vocal music, computer/technology,
physical education
Extra curricular programs computers, community
service, dance, drama, excursions/expeditions,
literary magazine, newspaper, photography,
yearbook, debate, forensics, sailing, scuba diving
Sports basketball, cross-country, skiing, soccer,
softball, swimming, tennis, track and field,
volleyball, wrestling
Clubs National Honor Society, National Junior
Honor Society, Thespians, Medicins Sans
Frontiers, student council, backgammon,
chess, Scouts
Examinations ACT, AP, Iowa, PSAT, SAT, SAT II

CAMPUS FACILITIES

Location Urban
Campus 3 hectares, 4 buildings, 67 classrooms,
4 computer labs, 325 instructional computers,
50,000 library volumes, 1 cafeteria, 1 covered
play area, 2 gymnasiums, 1 infirmary, 1 playing
field, 4 science labs, 1 pool, 2 tennis courts,
air conditioning

DUBAI AMERICAN ACADEMY

Phone	971 4 347 9222
Fax	971 4 347 6070
Email	dacademy@emirates.net.ae
Website	www.gemsaa-dubai.com
Address	PO Box 32762, Al Barsha, Sheik Zayed Road, Dubai, United Arab Emirates

STAFF

Superintendent Dan E. Young
Assistant Superintendent Brian Matthews, Ed.D.
High School Principal Anthony Mock
Middle School Principal Andrew Ball
Elementary Principal Jeffery Wornstaff
Accounts Manager Nitin Vasudeo

IT Director Amy Smith
MS/HS Librarian Maggie Travis
Teaching staff Full time 150; Total 150
Nationalities of teaching staff US 75; UK 10;
Other(s) (Canadian, Australian) 65

INFORMATION

Grade levels PreK–12
School year August–June
School type coeducational, proprietary
Year founded 1997
Governed by appointed Board of Directors
Sponsored by Varkey Group/GEMS
Accredited by CIS, New England
Regional organizations ECIS, NESA
Enrollment PreK 50; Elementary K–5 990;
Middle School 6–8 375; High School 9–12 485;
Total 1,900

Nationalities of student body US 450; UK 75;
Emirati 15; Other(s) (Swede, Dutch) 1,900
Tuition/fee currency Utd. Arab Emir. Dirham
Tuition range 40,000–56,000
One time fees Registration 350
Graduates attending college 97%
Graduates have attended University of California
in Los Angeles, U of Toronto, Syracuse U,
U of Michigan, U College of London

EDUCATIONAL PROGRAM

Curriculum US, IB Diploma
Average class size Elementary 23; Secondary 20
Language(s) of instruction English
Language(s) taught French, Spanish, Arabic
Staff specialists computer, counselor, ESL,
librarian, math resource, nurse, physician,
reading resource
Special curricular programs art, instrumental
music, vocal music, computer/technology,
distance learning, physical education

Extra curricular programs computers, community
service, dance, drama, environmental
conservation, excursions/expeditions, literary
magazine, newspaper, photography, yearbook
Sports badminton, basketball, cross-country,
golf, hockey, martial arts, rugby, skiing, soccer,
softball, swimming, tennis, track and field,
volleyball
Clubs Student Senate, student council,
community service, foreign language, art,
environmental
Examinations IB, Iowa, PSAT, SAT

CAMPUS FACILITIES

Location Suburban
Campus 5 hectares, 5 buildings, 116 classrooms,
9 computer labs, 450 instructional computers,
15,000 library volumes, 1 auditorium,

2 cafeterias, 4 covered play areas, 2 gymnasiums,
2 infirmaries, 4 playing fields, 6 science labs,
2 pools, 4 tennis courts, air conditioning

JUMEIRAH ENGLISH SPEAKING SCHOOL

Phone 971 4 3945515
Fax 971 4 3943531
Email jess@jess.sch.ae
Address PO Box 24942, Dubai, United Arab Emirates

STAFF

Director Robert D. Stokoe
Head of Primary School, Arabian Ranches Ann Jones
Head of Secondary School, Arabian Ranches M. Biggs, Ph.D.

Head of Primary School, Jumeirah Carole Denny
Bursar Avril Southwell
Director of E Learning Catherine Convery
Librarian Yvette Judge

INFORMATION

Grade levels PreK–6
School year September–June
School type coeducational, day, private non-profit
Year founded 1975
Governed by appointed Board

Regional organizations ECIS
Tuition/fee currency Utd. Arab Emir. Dirham
Tuition range 24,500–43,000
One time fees Registration 100

EDUCATIONAL PROGRAM

Curriculum UK
Average class size Elementary 22
Language(s) of instruction English
Language(s) taught French, Arabic
Staff specialists computer, librarian, math resource, nurse, reading resource
Special curricular programs art, instrumental music, vocal music, computer/technology, physical education

Extra curricular programs computers, dance, drama, excursions/expeditions, newspaper, yearbook
Sports basketball, cricket, football, gymnastics, rugby, soccer, swimming, tennis, track and field
Clubs golf, horse riding, sailing, badminton, arts & crafts, drama, table tennis, cookery, rock climbing
Examinations SAT, SAT II

CAMPUS FACILITIES

Location Suburban
Campus 14 buildings, 84 classrooms, 3 computer labs, 140 instructional computers, 12,000 library volumes, 1 auditorium,

1 cafeteria, 1 covered play area, 2 gymnasiums, 1 infirmary, 2 playing fields, 8 science labs, 2 pools, 4 tennis courts, air conditioning

Data from 2006/07 school year.

UNITED KINGDOM

Area:	244,820 sq km
Population:	60,776,238
Capital:	London
Currency:	British Pound (GBP)
Languages:	English

INTERNATIONAL SCHOOL OF ABERDEEN

Phone 44 1224 732267
Fax 44 1224 735648
Email admin@isa.aberdeen.sch.uk
Website www.isa.aberdeen.sch.uk
Address 296 North Deeside Road, Milltimber, Aberdeen, Scotland, AB13 0AB, United Kingdom

STAFF

Director Dan Hovde, Ph.D.
Middle School and High School Principal Robert Evans
Elementary School Principal Don Newbury
Business Manager Cyria Scott

IT Coordinator Stan Richards
Library Media Teacher Sarah Isaac
Teaching staff Full time 61; Part time 5; Total 66
Nationalities of teaching staff US 24; UK 23; Other(s) (Canadian, Australian) 19

INFORMATION

Grade levels PreK–12
School year August–June
School type coeducational, company-sponsored, day
Year founded 1972
Governed by appointed and elected Board of Directors
Sponsored by Petroleum and Multinational Companies
Accredited by CIS, Middle States
Regional organizations ECIS

Enrollment PreK 32; Elementary K–5 178; Middle School 6–8 89; High School 9–12 99; Total 398
Nationalities of student body US 161; UK 42; Other(s) (Dutch, Nigerian) 195
Tuition/fee currency British Pound
Tuition range 13,800–15,435
Annual fees Registration 250; Capital Levy 2,000
Graduates attending college 99%
Graduates have attended Duke U, Boston U, Texas A&M U, Oxford U, Cambridge U

EDUCATIONAL PROGRAM

Curriculum US, UK, Intl, IB Diploma
Average class size Elementary 14; Secondary 18
Language(s) of instruction English
Language(s) taught French, Spanish, Dutch
Staff specialists computer, counselor, ESL, learning disabilities, librarian, math resource, nurse, reading resource
Special curricular programs art, instrumental music, vocal music, computer/technology, physical education
Extra curricular programs computers, community service, drama, environmental conservation, excursions/expeditions, photography, yearbook
Sports badminton, baseball, basketball, cross-country, golf, gymnastics, hockey, martial arts, soccer, softball, swimming, tennis, volleyball
Clubs Girl and Boy Scouts, National Honor Society, Model UN, English as an additional language, Spanish, chess, pottery
Examinations ACT, IB, Iowa, PSAT, SAT, International Schools Assessment

CAMPUS FACILITIES

Location Suburban
Campus 4 hectares, 3 buildings, 56 classrooms, 2 computer labs, 200 instructional computers, 23,000 library volumes, 1 auditorium, 1 cafeteria, 2 gymnasiums, 1 infirmary, 2 playing fields, 3 science labs, air conditioning

Kingston upon Thames, Surrey, England   **UNITED KINGDOM**

Marymount International School

Phone	0044 20 8949 0571
Fax	0044 20 8336 2485
Email	admissions@marymountlondon.com
Website	www.marymountlondon.com
Address	George Road, Kingston upon Thames, Surrey, KT2 7PE, United Kingdom

STAFF

Head of School Sister Kathleen Fagan, RSHM
Academic Dean Brian Johnson, Ph.D.
MYP and Curriculum Coordinator Nick Marcou
Bursar Caroline Churchman

Librarian Jennifer Beeftink
Teaching staff Full time 28; Part time 6; Total 34
Nationalities of teaching staff US 6; UK 18;
Other(s) (South African, Spaniard) 10

INFORMATION

Grade levels 6–12
School year September–June
School type boarding, church-affiliated, day, girls only
Year founded 1955
Governed by appointed Board of Governors
Accredited by CIS
Regional organizations ECIS
Enrollment Middle School 6–8 60;
High School 9–12 180; Total 240
Nationalities of student body US 20; UK 50;
Other(s) (Japanese, Chinese) 170

Tuition/fee currency British Pound
Tuition range 14,450–16,050
Annual fees Boarding, 5-day 10,000; Boarding, 7-day 11,150
One time fees Registration 100
Boarding program grades 6–12
Boarding program length 5-day and 7-day **Girls** 100
Graduates attending college 98%
Graduates have attended Boston Col, Tufts U, Stanford U, Col of William and Mary, U of California

EDUCATIONAL PROGRAM

Curriculum US, Intl, IB Diploma, IBMYP
Average class size Secondary 11
Language(s) of instruction English
Language(s) taught French, Spanish, Japanese, Arabic, German, Italian
Staff specialists computer, counselor, ESL, librarian, math resource, nurse, reading resource
Special curricular programs instrumental music, vocal music, computer/technology, physical education

Extra curricular programs computers, community service, dance, drama, excursions/expeditions, photography, yearbook
Sports badminton, basketball, cross-country, football, golf, gymnastics, hockey, martial arts, skiing, soccer, softball, swimming, tennis, track and field, volleyball
Examinations IB, PSAT, SAT

CAMPUS FACILITIES

Location Suburban
Campus 2 hectares, 10 buildings, 24 classrooms, 2 computer labs, 50 instructional computers, 10,000 library volumes, 1 auditorium,

1 cafeteria, 1 gymnasium, 1 infirmary, 1 playing field, 3 science labs, 2 tennis courts, air conditioning

ACS COBHAM INTERNATIONAL SCHOOL

Phone	44 1932 867 251
Fax	44 1932 869 789
Email	CobhamAdmissions@acs-england.co.uk
Website	www.acs-england.co.uk
Address	Heywood, Portsmouth Road, Cobham, Surrey, KT11 1BL, United Kingdom

STAFF

Head of School Thomas J. Lehman
High School Principal Steve Baker
Middle School Principal Diane Hren
Lower School Principal Lacy Chapman
Academic Dean Craig Worthington
Chief Accountant Clive Abbott

IT Coordinator Peter Tilghman, Ph.D.
High School Librarian Dacel Casey
Teaching staff Full time 127; Part time 13;
Total 140
Nationalities of teaching staff US 57; UK 50;
Other(s) (Canadian, French) 33

INFORMATION

Grade levels N–12
School year August–June
School type boarding, coeducational, day,
proprietary
Year founded 1967
Governed by appointed Board of Directors
Sponsored by Chairman of Board of Directors
Accredited by New England
Regional organizations ECIS
Enrollment Nursery 68; PreK 64;
Elementary K–5 548; Middle School 6–8 300;
High School 9–12 430; Total 1,410

Nationalities of student body US 705; UK 141;
Other(s) (Canadian, Norwegian) 564
Tuition/fee currency British Pound
Tuition range 5,380–17,410
Annual fees Boarding, 5-day 9,570; Boarding,
7-day 13,100; Busing 2,080
One time fees Registration 125; Debenture 500
Boarding program grades 7–12
Boarding program length 5-day and 7-day
Boys 60 **Girls** 40
Graduates attending college 100%
Graduates have attended Harvard U, London
School of Economics, Oxford U, Pennsylvania
State U, Imperial Col London

(Continued)

ACS COBHAM INTERNATIONAL SCHOOL (Continued)

EDUCATIONAL PROGRAM

Curriculum US, Intl, AP, IB Diploma
Average class size Elementary 20; Secondary 20
Language(s) of instruction English
Language(s) taught French, Spanish, German, Danish, Dutch, Japanese, Swedish, Norwegian
Staff specialists computer, counselor, ESL, learning disabilities, librarian, math resource, nurse, reading resource, speech/hearing
Special curricular programs art, instrumental music, vocal music, computer/technology, physical education

Extra curricular programs computers, community service, dance, drama, environmental conservation, excursions/expeditions, literary magazine, newspaper, photography, yearbook
Sports badminton, baseball, basketball, cross-country, golf, gymnastics, hockey, rugby, soccer, softball, swimming, tennis, track and field, volleyball
Clubs student council, honor society, drama, art, Habitat for Humanity, Model UN, peer supporters, animation and science, junior and senior math teams
Examinations AP, IB, PSAT, SAT

CAMPUS FACILITIES

Location Suburban
Campus 52 hectares, 11 buildings, 91 classrooms, 5 computer labs, 258 instructional computers, 26,500 library volumes, 3 gymnasiums, 1 infirmary, 6 playing fields, 9 science labs, 1 pool, 6 tennis courts

ACS Egham International School

Phone	44 1784 430 800
Fax	44 1784 742 146
Email	EghamAdmissions@acs-england.co.uk
Website	www.acs-england.co.uk
Address	Woodlee, London Road (A30), Egham, Surrey, TW20 0HS, United Kingdom

STAFF

Head of School Moyra Hadley
High School Principal Virginia McKniff
Middle School Principal Peter Hosier
Lower School Principal Sandra Hite
PYP Coordinator and Assistant to Lower School Principal Colin Sercombe
High School Academic Dean and Counselor Keith Ord

Chief Accountant Clive Abbott
Head of Computer Technology Department Donna Ellery
Upper School Librarian Sandra Houston
Teaching staff Full time 65; Part time 6; Total 71
Nationalities of teaching staff US 17; UK 38; Other(s) (Canadian, Australian) 16

INFORMATION

Grade levels N–12
School year August–June
School type coeducational, day
Year founded 1967
Governed by appointed Board of Directors
Sponsored by Chairman of Board of Directors
Accredited by New England
Regional organizations ECIS
Enrollment Nursery 24; PreK 32; Elementary K–5 240; Middle School 6–8 144; High School 9–12 144; Total 584

Nationalities of student body US 251; UK 82; Other(s) (Dutch, German) 251
Tuition/fee currency British Pound
Tuition range 5,380–17,130
Annual fees Busing 2,080
One time fees Registration 125; Debenture 500
Graduates attending college 100%
Graduates have attended King's Col London, University Col London, Oxford U, London School of Economics, New York U

EDUCATIONAL PROGRAM

Curriculum US, Intl, IB Diploma, IBPYP, IBMYP
Average class size Elementary 16; Secondary 16
Language(s) of instruction English
Language(s) taught French, Spanish
Staff specialists computer, counselor, ESL, learning disabilities, librarian, math resource, nurse, reading resource, speech/hearing
Special curricular programs art, instrumental music, vocal music, computer/technology, physical education, information and design technology

Extra curricular programs computers, community service, dance, drama, environmental conservation, excursions/expeditions, literary magazine, newspaper, photography, yearbook
Sports badminton, baseball, basketball, cross-country, golf, gymnastics, rugby, soccer, softball, tennis, track and field, volleyball
Clubs student council, Model UN, chess, Duke of Edinburgh Award, horseback riding, math, homework, creative writing, arts and crafts, Boy and Girl Scouts
Examinations IB, PSAT, SAT, ISA

CAMPUS FACILITIES

Location Suburban
Campus 8 hectares, 10 buildings, 50 classrooms, 2 computer labs, 168 instructional computers,

20,000 library volumes, 1 cafeteria, 2 gymnasiums, 1 infirmary, 2 playing fields, 3 science labs, 2 tennis courts

ACS HILLINGDON INTERNATIONAL SCHOOL

Phone	44 1895 259771
Fax	44 1895 818404
Email	HillingdonAdmissions@acs-england.co.uk
Website	www.acs-england.co.uk
Address	Hillingdon Court, 108 Vine Lane, Hillingdon, Middlesex, UB10 0BE, United Kingdom

STAFF

Head of School Ginger G. Apple
Lower School Principal Michelle Eriksen
Middle School Principal Alan Phan
High School Principal Joseph F. McDonald
Assistant High School Principal and IB Coordinator
David Wynne-Jones

Chief Accountant Clive Abbott
IT Coordinator Michael Parr
High School Librarian Ruth Ross
Teaching staff Full time 66; Part time 2; Total 68
Nationalities of teaching staff US 17; UK 18;
Other(s) (Australian, Canadian) 33

INFORMATION

Grade levels PreK–12
School year August–June
School type coeducational, day, proprietary
Year founded 1967
Governed by appointed Board of Directors
Sponsored by Chairman of Board of Directors
Accredited by New England
Regional organizations ECIS
Enrollment PreK 13; Elementary K–5 193;
Middle School 6–8 163; High School 9–12 246;
Total 615

Nationalities of student body US 279; UK 46;
Other(s) (Japanese, Canadian) 290
Tuition/fee currency British Pound
Tuition range 7,950–16,520
Annual fees Busing 2,080
One time fees Registration 125; Debenture 500
Graduates attending college 100%
Graduates have attended Oxford U, U College
London, Imperial Col, Baylor U, Bowdoin Col

EDUCATIONAL PROGRAM

Curriculum US, Intl, AP, IB Diploma, MYP
Average class size Elementary 20; Secondary 20
Language(s) of instruction English
Language(s) taught French, Spanish, Japanese,
Dutch, Mandarin
Staff specialists computer, counselor, ESL,
learning disabilities, librarian, nurse
Special curricular programs art, instrumental
music, vocal music, computer/technology,
physical education, drama, individual musical
instrument lessons

Extra curricular programs community service,
drama, excursions/expeditions, newspaper,
yearbook
Sports badminton, baseball, basketball,
cross-country, golf, gymnastics, hockey, rugby,
soccer, softball, swimming, tennis, track and
field, volleyball
Clubs student council, honor society, homework,
drama, jazz music, Boy and Girl Scouts
Examinations AP, IB, PSAT, SAT

CAMPUS FACILITIES

Location Suburban
Campus 5 hectares, 3 buildings, 72 classrooms,
4 computer labs, 100 instructional computers,

23,000 library volumes, 1 auditorium, 1 cafeteria,
1 gymnasium, 1 infirmary, 2 playing fields,
7 science labs, 3 tennis courts, air conditioning

London, England

The American School in London

Phone 44 207 449 1200
Fax 44 207 449 1350
Email admissions@asl.org
Website www.asl.org
Address One Waverley Place, St Johns Wood, London, NW8 0NP, United Kingdom

STAFF

Head of School Coreen R. Hester
Interim High School Principal Gary Gruber, Ph.D.
Middle School Principal Michael Ehrhardt
Lower School Principal Julie Ryan
Director of Finance and Operations Chris Almond
Director of Technology Jim Heynderickx

Head of Library Cathy Yount
Teaching staff Full time 146; Part time 19; Total 165
Nationalities of teaching staff US 112; UK 35; Other(s) (Australian, New Zealander) 18

INFORMATION

Grade levels PreK–12
School year September–June
School type coeducational, day, private non-profit
Year founded 1951
Governed by elected Board of Trustees
Accredited by CIS, Middle States
Regional organizations ECIS
Enrollment PreK 36; Elementary K–5 480; Middle School 6–8 360; High School 9–12 460; Total 1,336

Nationalities of student body US 1,092; UK 72; Other(s) (Indian, Canadian) 172
Tuition/fee currency British Pound
Tuition range 16,340–20,020
Annual fees Busing 2,250
One time fees Registration 75
Graduates attending college 99%
Graduates have attended Harvard U, Yale U, New York U, Wellesley Col, London School of Economics

EDUCATIONAL PROGRAM

Curriculum US, AP
Average class size Elementary 20; Secondary 16
Language(s) of instruction English
Language(s) taught French, Spanish, German, Italian, Chinese, Arabic, Russian
Staff specialists computer, counselor, ESL, learning disabilities, librarian, math resource, nurse, psychologist, reading resource, speech/hearing

Special curricular programs art, instrumental music, vocal music, computer/technology, physical education, yearbook, newspaper, photography
Extra curricular programs computers, community service, dance, drama, excursions/expeditions, literary magazine, yearbook
Sports baseball, basketball, golf, hockey, rugby, soccer, softball, swimming, tennis, track and field, volleyball, crew
Examinations AP, PSAT, SAT, ERB

CAMPUS FACILITIES

Location Urban
Campus 1 hectare, 1 building, 80 classrooms, 4 computer labs, 600 instructional computers, 42,000 library volumes, 1 auditorium, 1 cafeteria, 3 gymnasiums, 1 infirmary, 1 playing field, 10 science labs, 2 tennis courts, air conditioning

London, England

INTERNATIONAL SCHOOL OF LONDON

Phone	44 0 20 8992 5823
Fax	44 0 20 8993 7012
Email	mail@islondon.com
Website	www.islondon.com
Address	139 Gunnersbury Avenue, London, W3 8LG, United Kingdom

STAFF

Director Amin Makarem
Deputy Head–Pastoral Huw Davies
Deputy Head–Curriculum Sergio Pawel, Ph.D.
MYP Coordinator Paul Morris
PYP Coordinator Hala Fadda
Business Officer Sesil Costandi

Systems Administrator Jay Kelly
Librarian Farideh Urrestarazu
Teaching staff Full time 40; Part time 20; Total 60
Nationalities of teaching staff US 8; UK 10; Host 10; Other(s) (French, Italian) 32

INFORMATION

Grade levels N–12
School year September–June
School type coeducational, day, proprietary
Year founded 1972
Accredited by CIS
Regional organizations ECIS
Enrollment Nursery 10; PreK 10;
Elementary K–5 120; Middle School 6–8 90;
High School 9–12 80; Total 310

Nationalities of student body US 20; UK 15;
Other(s) (Italian, French) 275
Tuition/fee currency British Pound
Tuition range 12,400–17,000
Annual fees Busing 2,150; Lunch 1,300
One time fees Registration 100; Capital Levy 1,000
Graduates attending college 100%
Graduates have attended U of Chicago,
U of Oxford, U of London, Keio U, Bocconi U

EDUCATIONAL PROGRAM

Curriculum IB Diploma, IBPYP, IBMYP
Average class size Elementary 20; Secondary 20
Language(s) of instruction English
Language(s) taught over 20
Staff specialists computer, ESL, librarian
Extra curricular programs computers, community service, dance, drama, newspaper, photography, yearbook

Sports badminton, basketball, cross-country, football, gymnastics, hockey, martial arts, rugby, soccer, softball, squash, swimming, tennis, track and field, volleyball
Examinations IB

CAMPUS FACILITIES

Location Urban
Campus 2 buildings, 45 classrooms, 3 computer labs, 40 instructional computers,

1 auditorium, 1 cafeteria, 1 covered play area, 1 gymnasium, 1 playing field, 3 science labs, 1 pool

TASIS, THE AMERICAN SCHOOL IN ENGLAND

Phone	44 1932 565 252
Fax	44 1932 564 644
Email	ukadmissions@tasis.com
Website	www.tasis.com
Address	Coldharbour Lane, Thorpe, Surrey, TW20 8TE, United Kingdom

STAFF

Head of School James A. Doran, Ed.D.
Head of Upper School Claudia Werner
Head of Middle School Debi Cross
Head of Lower School Susan Porter
Director of Finance Adrian Bowcher

Director of Information Technology John Arcay
Librarian Victoria Doran
Teaching staff Full time 105; Part time 5; Total 110
Nationalities of teaching staff US 77; UK 28; Other(s) 5

INFORMATION

Grade levels N–12
School year September–June
School type boarding, coeducational, day, private non-profit
Year founded 1976
Governed by appointed TASIS Board of Directors
Accredited by CIS, New England
Regional organizations ECIS
Enrollment Nursery 10; PreK 15; Elementary K–5 250; Middle School 6–8 155; High School 9–12 340; Total 770

Nationalities of student body US 530; UK 40; Other(s) (Spaniard, Korean) 200
Tuition/fee currency British Pound
Tuition range 5,000–25,700
Annual fees Boarding, 7-day 25,700; Busing 2,600
One time fees Registration 1,500; Capital Levy 750
Boarding program grades 9–12
Boarding program length 7-day **Boys** 80 **Girls** 80
Graduates attending college 99%
Graduates have attended U of Pennsylvania, Stanford U, Cornell U, U of Cambridge, Oxford U

EDUCATIONAL PROGRAM

Curriculum US, Intl, AP, IB Diploma
Average class size Elementary 12; Secondary 15
Language(s) of instruction English
Language(s) taught French, Spanish, Latin
Staff specialists computer, counselor, ESL, librarian, math resource, nurse, psychologist, reading resource
Special curricular programs art, instrumental music, vocal music, computer/technology, physical education, photography

Extra curricular programs computers, community service, dance, drama, excursions/expeditions, literary magazine, newspaper, photography, yearbook, Model UN, Duke of Edinburgh Award
Sports baseball, basketball, cross-country, football, golf, rugby, soccer, softball, squash, tennis, volleyball
Examinations ACT, AP, IB, PSAT, SAT, TOEFL

CAMPUS FACILITIES

Location Rural
Campus 20 hectares, 23 buildings, 3 computer labs, 12,000 library volumes, 1 auditorium,

2 cafeterias, 2 gymnasiums, 1 infirmary, 3 playing fields, 4 science labs, 6 tennis courts

UNITED STATES OF AMERICA

Area:	9,826,630 sq km
Population:	301,139,947
Capital:	Washington, DC
Currency:	US Dollar (USD)
Languages:	English

ATLANTA INTERNATIONAL SCHOOL

Phone	404 841 3840
Fax	404 841 3873
Email	info@aischool.org
Website	www.aischool.org
Address	2890 North Fulton Drive, Atlanta, GA, 30305, United States of America

STAFF

Head of School Robert K. Brindley, Ph.D.
Head of Upper School Suzanna Jemsby, Ed.D.
Head of Middle School Marsha Huitt

Head of Primary School Daljit Sohi
Director of Finance and Operations Ken Wilkins
Head Librarian Elena Barrio

INFORMATION

Grade levels PreK–12
School year August–June
School type coeducational, day, private non-profit
Year founded 1985
Governed by appointed Board of Trustees
Accredited by CIS, Southern
Regional organizations ECIS

Tuition/fee currency US Dollar
Tuition range 13,500–15,375
One time fees Registration 3,000
Graduates attending college 100%
Graduates have attended Yale U, Princeton U, Standford U, UC Berkeley, Georgetown U

EDUCATIONAL PROGRAM

Curriculum US, IB Diploma, IBPYP, IGCSE
Average class size Elementary 15; Secondary 15
Language(s) of instruction English, German, French, Spanish
Language(s) taught Hebrew, Latin, German, French, Spanish, Mandarin
Staff specialists computer, counselor, ESL, learning disabilities, librarian, math resource, nurse, reading resource
Special curricular programs art, instrumental music, vocal music, computer/technology, physical education

Extra curricular programs computers, community service, dance, drama, environmental conservation, excursions/expeditions, literary magazine, newspaper, photography, yearbook
Sports baseball, basketball, cross-country, soccer, softball, swimming, tennis, track and field, volleyball, fencing
Clubs robotics
Examinations ACT, GCSE, IB, IGCSE, PSAT, SAT, TOEFL

CAMPUS FACILITIES

Location Urban
Campus 1 hectare, 4 buildings, 83 classrooms, 4 computer labs, 250 instructional computers, 32,000 library volumes, 2 auditoriums,

2 cafeterias, 1 covered play area, 1 gymnasium, 1 infirmary, 1 playing field, 6 science labs, 1 tennis court, air conditioning

Data from 2006/07 school year.

INTERNATIONAL ACADEMY

Phone	248 341 5900
Fax	248 341 5959
Email	bokma@bloomfield.org
Website	www.iatoday.org
Address	1020 E. Square Lake Rd., Bloomfield Hills, MI, 48304, United States of America

STAFF

Principal Lambert Okma
Associate Principal Lynne Nagy
Counselor, grades 9–12 Jane Dittus
Business Manager Carol Arola
Head of Technology Mary Miner

Head of Library Klaudia Janek
Teaching staff Full time 30; Part time 3; Total 33
Nationalities of teaching staff US 30; UK 1;
Other(s) (Spaniard, Dutch) 2

INFORMATION

Grade levels 9–12
School year August–June
School type coeducational, day
Year founded 1996
Governed by Local Public School Districts
Accredited by North Central
Enrollment High School 9–12 667; Total 667
Nationalities of student body US 200; UK 8;
Other(s) (Indian, Chinese) 459

Tuition/fee currency US Dollar
Annual fees lab 145
One time fees Books 150
Graduates attending college 100%
Graduates have attended Brown U, Harvard U,
Massachusetts Institute of Technology,
Stanford U, U of Michigan

EDUCATIONAL PROGRAM

Curriculum IB Diploma
Average class size Secondary 25
Language(s) of instruction English
Language(s) taught French, German, Spanish
Staff specialists computer, counselor, ESL,
librarian, psychologist
Special curricular programs art, instrumental
music, vocal music, physical education

Extra curricular programs community service,
drama, literary magazine, newspaper, yearbook,
Enrichment Program
Clubs Key, National Honor Society, Building
with Books, Indian American Student
Association, German Honor Society, French
Honor Society, Spanish Honor Society, Model
UN, robotics, Science Olympiad
Examinations ACT, AP, IB, PSAT, SAT, SAT II

CAMPUS FACILITIES

Location Suburban
Campus 1 building, 23 classrooms,
2 computer labs, 80 instructional computers,

10,000 library volumes, 1 cafeteria,
1 playing field, 5 science labs, air conditioning

HAWAII PREPARATORY ACADEMY

Phone	808 881 4054
Fax	808 881 4045
Email	bdawson@hpa.edu
Website	www.hpa.edu
Address	65-1692 Kohala Mtn. Road, Kamuela, Hawaii, 96743, United States of America

STAFF

Head of School Olaf Jorgenson, Ed.D.
Assistant Head of School Dee Priester, Ed.D.
Upper School Principal Mark Noetzel
Elementary Principal Terry Factor
Business Manager Karen Yamasato

Director of Information Technology Steve Bernstein
Teaching staff Full time 65; Part time 7; Total 72
Nationalities of teaching staff US 69; UK 1;
Other(s) (New Zealander, Australian) 2

INFORMATION

Grade levels K–12
School year August–May
School type boarding, coeducational, private non-profit
Year founded 1949
Governed by appointed Board of Governors
Accredited by Western
Enrollment Elementary K–5 120;
Middle School 6–8 130; High School 9–12 350;
Total 600

Nationalities of student body US 520; Other(s) (Chinese, Japanese) 80
Tuition/fee currency US Dollar
Tuition range 12,500–38,000
Boarding program grades 6–12
Boarding program length 5-day and 7-day
Boys 95 **Girls** 95
Graduates attending college 100%
Graduates have attended Massachusetts Institute of Technology, Stanford U, Yale U, Cornell U, U.S. Naval Academy

EDUCATIONAL PROGRAM

Curriculum US, AP
Average class size Elementary 20; Secondary 14
Language(s) of instruction English
Language(s) taught French, Spanish, Japanese
Staff specialists computer, counselor, ESL, librarian, nurse
Special curricular programs art, instrumental music, vocal music, computer/technology, physical education, vocational

Extra curricular programs computers, community service, dance, drama, environmental conservation, excursions/expeditions, literary magazine, yearbook, engineering, Turtle Research Project
Sports baseball, basketball, cross-country, football, golf, rugby, soccer, softball, swimming, tennis, track and field, volleyball, wrestling, outrigger canoe paddling
Clubs Red Cross, Model UN, environmental, robotics, recycling, ultimate frisbee, SCUBA
Examinations AP, SAT, TOEFL

CAMPUS FACILITIES

Location Rural
Campus 50 hectares, 25 buildings, 30 classrooms, 5 computer labs, 150 instructional computers,

20,000 library volumes, 1 auditorium, 2 cafeterias, 1 gymnasium, 2 infirmaries, 5 playing fields, 4 science labs, 1 pool, 4 tennis courts

Honolulu, Hawaii   **UNITED STATES OF AMERICA**

PUNAHOU SCHOOL

Phone   808 944 5711
Fax   808 944 5779
Email   hr@punahou.edu
Website   www.punahou.edu
Address   1601 Punahou Street, Honolulu, HI, 96822, United States of America

STAFF

President James K. Scott, Ph.D.
Academy Principal Kevin Conway, Ed.D.
Junior School Principal Michael Walker
Director of Instruction Diane Anderson
Director of Human Resources Pauline Bailey
Director of Admissions Betsy Hata

Vice President and Treasurer, Finance and Administration John Field
Director of Technology Wendi Takemoto
Academy Head Librarian Deb Peterson
Teaching staff Full time 260; Part time 45; Total 305
Nationalities of teaching staff US 290; Other(s) 15

INFORMATION

Grade levels K–12
School year August–June
School type coeducational, church-affiliated, day, private non-profit
Year founded 1841
Governed by appointed Board of Trustees
Accredited by Western
Enrollment Elementary K–5 960; Middle School 6–8 1,050; High School 9–12 1,730; Total 3,740

Nationalities of student body US 3,740
Tuition/fee currency US Dollar
Tuition 15,725–15,725
Graduates attending college 99%
Graduates have attended Stanford U, Princeton U, Harvard U, U of South Carolina, U of Washington

EDUCATIONAL PROGRAM

Curriculum US, AP
Average class size Elementary 22; Secondary 22
Language(s) of instruction English
Language(s) taught Japanese, Chinese, Spanish, French, Hawaiian
Staff specialists computer, counselor, librarian, nurse, psychologist
Special curricular programs art, instrumental music, vocal music, computer/technology, physical education

Extra curricular programs community service, dance, drama, environmental conservation, excursions/expeditions, literary magazine, photography, yearbook
Sports baseball, basketball, cross-country, football, golf, gymnastics, soccer, softball, swimming, tennis, track and field, volleyball, water polo, paddling
Clubs National Honor Society, Key, Model UN, SADD, ROTC, Young Life, Amnesty International, Math Counts
Examinations AP, PSAT, SAT, SAT II, ERB

CAMPUS FACILITIES

Location Suburban
Campus 30 hectares, 43 buildings, 190 classrooms, 7 computer labs, 1900 instructional computers, 95,000 library volumes, 1 auditorium,

1 cafeteria, 1 covered play area, 2 gymnasiums, 1 infirmary, 3 playing fields, 20 science labs, 1 pool, 9 tennis courts, air conditioning

AWTY INTERNATIONAL SCHOOL

Phone	713 686 4850
Fax	713 686 4956
Email	admissions@awty.org
Website	www.awty.org
Address	7455 Awty School Lane, Houston, TX, 77055, United States of America

STAFF

Head of School David J. Watson, Ph.D.
Head of Upper School Sam Waugh
Head of Middle School Tom Beuscher
Head of Lower School Chantal Vessali

Deputy Head and Proviseur Jean Stephan
Business/Finance Manager Teresa La Bonte
Director of Technology Willie Roberts
Librarian Diana Armentor

INFORMATION

Grade levels PreK–12
School year August–June
School type coeducational, day, private non-profit
Year founded 1956
Governed by appointed and elected Board of Trustees
Accredited by CIS
Enrollment PreK 90; Elementary K–5 480; Middle School 6–8 260; High School 9–12 350; Total 1,180

Nationalities of student body US 450; UK 100; Other(s) (French) 630
Tuition/fee currency US Dollar
Tuition range 10,835–14,845
Annual fees Registration 250; Capital Levy 750
Graduates attending college 100%
Graduates have attended Harvard U, Princeton U, Stanford U, Cornell U, Rice U

EDUCATIONAL PROGRAM

Curriculum US, Intl, IB Diploma, French Baccalaureate
Average class size Elementary 18; Secondary 18
Language(s) of instruction English, French
Language(s) taught French, Spanish, Arabic, Dutch, German, Mandarin
Staff specialists computer, counselor, ESL, librarian, nurse, speech/hearing
Special curricular programs art, instrumental music, vocal music, computer/technology, physical education
Extra curricular programs computers, community service, dance, drama, excursions/expeditions, literary magazine, newspaper, photography, yearbook, Model UN, Academic Challenge, student council
Sports basketball, cross-country, golf, soccer, tennis, track and field, volleyball
Clubs National Honor Society, French Honor Society, Tri-M Music Honor Society, Amnesty International, foreign language clubs, Lion's Leo Club, Model UN, Red Cross, student council
Examinations IB, PSAT, SAT, SAT II, Stanford, French Baccalaureate

CAMPUS FACILITIES

Location Urban
Campus 15 hectares, 14 buildings, 111 classrooms, 6 computer labs, 170 instructional computers, 36,000 library volumes, 1 auditorium, 1 cafeteria, 1 covered play area, 2 gymnasiums, 1 infirmary, 2 playing fields, 6 science labs, air conditioning

Data from 2006/07 school year.

Indianapolis, Indiana   **UNITED STATES OF AMERICA**

INTERNATIONAL SCHOOL OF INDIANA

Phone   317 923 1951
Fax   312 923 1910
Email   info@isind.org
Website   www.isind.org
Address   4330 North Michigan Road, Indianapolis, IN, 46208, United States of America

STAFF

Head of School David Garner
High School Director Gerald Buhaly
Assistant Head of School Anita Tychsen
Preschool Coordinator Annick Bernard
Middle School Coordinator Donna Albrecht

Elementary School Coordinator Eric Peschard
Director of Finance and Operations Lynn Greggs
Associate Director of Technology Rick Seifert
Librarian Deirdre McDaniel
Teaching staff Full time 80; Part time 5; Total 85

INFORMATION

Grade levels PreK–12
School year August–June
School type coeducational, day, private non-profit
Year founded 1994
Governed by appointed Board of Directors
Enrollment PreK 125; Elementary K–5 245;
Middle School 6–8 115; High School 9–12 125;
Total 610

Nationalities of student body US 427; Other(s)
(French, Mexican) 183
Tuition/fee currency US Dollar
Tuition range 11,350–12,000
Graduates attending college 100%
Graduates have attended Harvard U, Brandies U,
New York U, Washington U, U of Tours

EDUCATIONAL PROGRAM

Curriculum US, National, Intl, IB Diploma,
French, Spanish
Average class size Elementary 16; Secondary 14
Language(s) of instruction English, Spanish, French
Staff specialists computer, counselor, librarian,
nurse, reading resource
Special curricular programs art, vocal music,
computer/technology, physical education

Extra curricular programs community service,
dance, drama, literary magazine, yearbook,
exchange programs
Sports basketball, cross-country, soccer,
swimming, tennis, track and field, volleyball,
lacrosse, crew
Examinations ACT, IB, SAT

CAMPUS FACILITIES

Location Urban
Campus 63 hectares, 3 buildings, 70 classrooms,
3 computer labs, 100 instructional computers,

17,000 library volumes, 2 cafeterias,
2 gymnasiums, 2 infirmaries, 1 playing field,
2 science labs, air conditioning

INTERNATIONAL SCHOOL OF MONTEREY

Phone	831 583 2165
Fax	831 899 7653
Email	info@ismonterey.org
Website	www.ismonterey.org
Address	1720 Yosemite Street, Seaside, CA, 93955, United States of America
Mailing address	PO Box 711, Monterey, CA 93942-0711, USA

STAFF

Executive Director Chrissie P. Jahn
Counselor Neli Volante, Ph.D.
Director of Advancement Lorraine Williby
Business Administrator Lisa G. Burns

Teaching staff Full time 20; Part time 4; Total 24
Nationalities of teaching staff US 20; Other(s) (Bolivian, Chilean) 4

INFORMATION

Grade levels K–8
School year August–June
School type coeducational, day
Year founded 2001
Governed by appointed Board of Directors
Regional organizations ECIS

Enrollment Elementary K–5 260; Middle School 6–8 100; Total 360
Nationalities of student body US 350; Other(s) (Korean) 10
Tuition/fee currency US Dollar

EDUCATIONAL PROGRAM

Curriculum US, National, Intl, International Primary Curriculum (IPC)
Average class size Elementary 20; Secondary 25
Language(s) of instruction English
Language(s) taught Spanish
Staff specialists counselor, ESL, learning disabilities, math resource, reading resource, speech/hearing

Special curricular programs art, instrumental music, vocal music, physical education, drama
Extra curricular programs community service, newspaper
Clubs taiko drumming, chess, Chinese jewelry making, ROV explorers, Tae Kwon Do
Examinations ISA, STAR

CAMPUS FACILITIES

Location Suburban
Campus 4 buildings, 18 classrooms, 2 computer labs, 25 instructional computers, 1 auditorium, 1 cafeteria, 1 infirmary, 1 playing field

New York City, New York   **UNITED STATES OF AMERICA**

THE DWIGHT SCHOOL

Phone	212 724 6360
Fax	212 724 2539
Email	admissions@dwight.edu
Website	www.dwight.edu
Address	291 Central Park West, New York, New York, 10024, United States of America

STAFF

Chancellor Stephen Spahn
Associate Head of School Blake Spahn, Ph.D.
Director of Admissions Alicia P. Janiak
Director of Admissions Marina Bernstein

Business/Finance Manager Rose LaMorte
Head of Technology Basel Kolnai
Head of Library/Media Center Susan Lissim
Teaching staff Full time 125; Total 125

INFORMATION

Grade levels PreK–12
School year September–June
School type coeducational, day
Year founded 1880
Governed by elected Trustees
Accredited by CIS, Middle States
Regional organizations ECIS

Enrollment PreK 40; Elementary K–5 130;
Middle School 6–8 80; High School 9–12 260;
Total 510
Tuition/fee currency US Dollar
Tuition range 28,200–30,300
Annual fees Registration 750; Books 800
Graduates attending college 100%
Graduates have attended Harvard U, Brown U,
Dartmouth U, Columbia U, Middlebury Col

EDUCATIONAL PROGRAM

Curriculum Intl, AP, IB Diploma, IBPYP, IBMYP
Average class size Elementary 15; Secondary 15
Language(s) of instruction English
Language(s) taught Dutch, French, Spanish,
Latin, German, Italian, Japanese, Hebrew,
Chinese, Arabic, Russian
Staff specialists computer, counselor, ESL,
librarian
Special curricular programs art, instrumental
music, vocal music, computer/technology,
physical education

Extra curricular programs computers, community
service, dance, drama, environmental
conservation, excursions/expeditions, literary
magazine, newspaper, photography, yearbook
Sports badminton, baseball, basketball, cross-
country, soccer, softball, swimming, tennis,
track and field, volleyball, fencing
Examinations ACT, AP, IB, PSAT, SAT, SAT II,
TOEFL, ERB

CAMPUS FACILITIES

Location Urban
Campus 2 buildings, 48 classrooms, 2 computer
labs, 200 instructional computers, 15,000

library volumes, 1 auditorium, 1 cafeteria,
1 covered play area, 3 gymnasiums, 1 infirmary,
3 science labs, air conditioning

New York City, New York

UNITED NATIONS INTERNATIONAL SCHOOL

Phone	212 684 7400
Fax	212 779 2259
Email	administration@unis.org
Website	www.unis.org
Address	24-50 FDR Drive, New York, NY, 10010, United States of America

STAFF

Executive Director Kenneth J. Wrye, Ed.D.
Assistant Executive Director George B. Dymond
High School Principal Radha Rajan
Junior School Principal Deborah Karmozyn
Middle School Principal Anthony Brown
Queens School Principal Judith Honor
Director of Business Operations Stephen Roache

Director of Technology Dominique Lap
Head of Library Jerome Dutilloy
Teaching staff Full time 177; Part time 35; Total 212
Nationalities of teaching staff US 80; UK 17; Other(s) (French, Spaniard) 115

INFORMATION

Grade levels K–12
School year September–June
School type coeducational, day, private non-profit
Year founded 1947
Governed by appointed Board of Trustees
Accredited by CIS
Regional organizations ECIS
Enrollment Elementary K–5 675; Middle School 6–8 390; High School 9–12 435; Total 1,500

Nationalities of student body US 705; UK 54; Other(s) (French, Japanese) 741
Tuition/fee currency US Dollar
Tuition range 20,250–22,500
Annual fees Lunch 740; Parents Association 150; Construction Levy 300
One time fees Registration 150; Capital Levy 1,500; JA Snack Program 215
Graduates attending college 100%
Graduates have attended Harvard U, Princeton U, Yale U, U of Oxford, U of Bath

(Continued)

UNITED NATIONS INTERNATIONAL SCHOOL (Continued)

EDUCATIONAL PROGRAM

Curriculum Intl, IB Diploma
Average class size Elementary 20; Secondary 22
Language(s) of instruction English
Language(s) taught Arabic, Chinese, French, German, Italian, Japanese, Russian, Spanish
Staff specialists computer, counselor, ESL, learning disabilities, librarian, nurse, psychologist, reading resource
Special curricular programs art, instrumental music, vocal music, computer/technology, physical education

Extra curricular programs computers, community service, dance, drama, environmental conservation, excursions/expeditions, literary magazine, newspaper, photography, yearbook, UNIS/UN Annual Conference
Sports baseball, basketball, cross-country, gymnastics, soccer, softball, swimming, tennis, track and field, volleyball
Clubs Amnesty International, Solutions To Environmental Problems, Prevent Violence Against Women, Student Against Landmines, Neel Bagh Committee
Examinations ACT, IB, PSAT, SAT, SAT II, TOEFL

CAMPUS FACILITIES

Location Urban
Campus 2 hectares, 2 buildings, 140 classrooms, 6 computer labs, 850 instructional computers, 75,000 library volumes, 1 auditorium,

1 cafeteria, 2 covered play areas, 5 gymnasiums, 1 infirmary, 1 playing field, 7 science labs, 3 tennis courts, air conditioning

KAMEHAMEHA SCHOOLS MAUI CAMPUS

Phone	808 572 3100
Fax	808 573 7062
Email	ledelima@ksbe.edu
Website	maui.ksbe.edu
Address	270 'A' Apueo Parkway, Pukalani, Hawaii, 96768, United States of America

STAFF

Head of School Lee Ann L. DeLima
High School Principal Warren Hitz, Ph.D.
Interim Middle School Principal and Campus Outreach Director Lois Nishikawa

Elementary School Principal Paul Prevenas, Ph.D.
Director of Campus Operations Carl Alexander
Teaching staff Full time 83; Part time 6; Total 89
Nationalities of teaching staff US 89

INFORMATION

Grade levels K–12
School year August–May
School type coeducational, day, private non-profit
Year founded 1996
Governed by appointed Board of Trustees
Accredited by Western
Enrollment Elementary K–5 256; Middle School 6–8 324; High School 9–12 504; Total 1,084

Nationalities of student body US 1,084
Tuition/fee currency US Dollar
Tuition range 2,566–3,237
Annual fees Busing 1,100
Graduates attending college 95%
Graduates have attended Brigham Young U, Oregon State U, San Diego State U, Stanford U, U of Hawaii in Manoa

EDUCATIONAL PROGRAM

Curriculum US
Average class size Elementary 22; Secondary 22
Language(s) of instruction English
Language(s) taught Hawaiian, Japanese, Spanish
Staff specialists computer, counselor, librarian, math resource, nurse, reading resource
Special curricular programs art, instrumental music, vocal music, computer/technology, physical education, Hawaiian chant and dance
Extra curricular programs community service, drama, environmental conservation, excursions/expeditions, newspaper, photography, yearbook, student council

Sports baseball, basketball, cross-country, football, golf, martial arts, soccer, softball, swimming, tennis, track and field, volleyball, wrestling, cheerleading, water polo, paddling (canoe)
Clubs National Honor Society, astronomy, chess, fishing, Hawaiian Ensemble, Math League, mock trial
Examinations ACT, PSAT, SAT, SAT II, PPVT-IV

CAMPUS FACILITIES

Location Rural
Campus 73 hectares, 23 buildings, 110 classrooms, 4 computer labs, 1100 instructional computers, 2 gymnasiums, 3 infirmaries, 3 playing fields, 8 science labs, 1 pool, 6 tennis courts, air conditioning

San Francisco, California **UNITED STATES OF AMERICA**

CHINESE AMERICAN INTERNATIONAL SCHOOL

Phone	415 865 6000
Fax	415 865 6089
Email	j_leiner@cais.org
Website	www.cais.org
Address	150 Oak Street, San Francisco, CA, 94102, United States of America

STAFF

Head of School Andrew W. Corcoran
PreK–K Director Susan Martin
Middle School Director Josee Mayette
Lower School Director Kevin Chang
Chinese Program Coordinator Jiun Chou Young

Director of Admission John Leiner
Assistant Head for Institutional Advancement and Finance Betty Shon
IT Director Lam Loi
Library Media Specialist Warren Wright

INFORMATION

Grade levels PreK–8
School year August–June
School type coeducational, day, private non-profit
Year founded 1981
Governed by elected Board of Trustees
Accredited by Western
Enrollment PreK 50; Elementary K–5 231; Middle School 6–8 82; Total 363

Nationalities of student body US 363
Tuition/fee currency US Dollar
Tuition range 17,200–18,000
One time fees Registration 75
Graduates have attended U of California in Berkeley, U of Southern California, Boston Col, Georgetown U, George Washington U

EDUCATIONAL PROGRAM

Curriculum US
Average class size Elementary 20; Secondary 15
Language(s) of instruction English, Mandarin
Staff specialists computer, counselor, ESL, learning disabilities, librarian, math resource, nurse, psychologist, reading resource
Special curricular programs art, instrumental music, vocal music, computer/technology, physical education, Orff-Schulwerk Music Program

Extra curricular programs computers, community service, dance, drama, environmental conservation, excursions/expeditions, literary magazine, photography, yearbook, team sports, MathCounts, martial arts, Chinese music, Chinese dance, Chinese calligraphy, Chinese brushpainting
Sports basketball, cross-country, golf, martial arts, soccer, swimming, track and field, volleyball, fencing, futsal
Examinations SAT, ERB

CAMPUS FACILITIES

Location Urban
Campus 2 hectares, 2 buildings, 25 classrooms, 2 computer labs, 37 instructional computers,

50,000 library volumes, 5 cafeterias, 1 covered play area, 1 gymnasium, 1 infirmary, 1 science lab

Data from 2006/07 school year.

FRENCH-AMERICAN INTERNATIONAL SCHOOL

Phone	415 558 2000
Fax	415 558 2024
Email	janec@frenchamericaninternational.org
Website	www.frenchamericansf.org
Address	150 Oak Street, San Francisco, CA, 94102, United States of America

STAFF

Head of School Jane A. Camblin
Lower School Principal Raymond Hinz
Assistant Head and International High School Principal Russell Jones
Middle School Principal Edouard Mayoral
Director of Admissions K–8 Andrew Brown
Director of Admissions 9–12 Betsy Brody

CFO Aaron Levine
Head Librarian Catherine Sullivan
Teaching staff Full time 108; Part time 16; Total 124
Nationalities of teaching staff US 38; UK 4; Other(s) (French, Canadian) 82

INFORMATION

Grade levels PreK–12
School year August–June
School type coeducational, day, private non-profit
Year founded 1962
Governed by elected Board of Directors
Accredited by CIS, Western
Regional organizations ECIS
Enrollment PreK 55; Elementary K–5 389; Middle School 6–8 156; High School 9–12 320; Total 920

Nationalities of student body US 750; UK 25; Other(s) (French, Canadian) 145
Tuition/fee currency US Dollar
Tuition range 18,150–26,290
Annual fees Registration/Applied to Tuition 1,000
One time fees new student 2,000
Graduates attending college 99%
Graduates have attended U of California in Berkeley, Columbia U, McGill U, U of Paris in Sorbonne, Yale U

EDUCATIONAL PROGRAM

Curriculum US, Intl, AP, IB Diploma, French National
Average class size Elementary 20; Secondary 20
Language(s) of instruction English, French
Language(s) taught Spanish, German, Mandarin, Italian
Staff specialists computer, counselor, learning disabilities, librarian
Special curricular programs art, instrumental music, vocal music, computer/technology, physical education

Extra curricular programs community service, drama, excursions/expeditions, yearbook
Sports badminton, baseball, basketball, cross-country, golf, soccer, swimming, tennis, track and field, volleyball
Clubs jazz, Multicultural Students' Association, improv, Amnesty International, film, international chorus, The Exposer, bicycle, Casa Para Amigo
Examinations AP, IB, PSAT, SAT, SAT II

CAMPUS FACILITIES

Location Urban
Campus 3 buildings, 60 classrooms, 3 computer labs, 50 instructional computers,

39,500 library volumes, 2 auditoriums, 1 covered play area, 1 gymnasium, 1 infirmary, 5 science labs

WASHINGTON INTERNATIONAL SCHOOL

Phone	202 243 1800
Fax	202 243 1802
Email	admissions@wis.edu
Website	www.wis.edu
Address	3100 Macomb Street NW, Washington, DC, 20008, United States of America

STAFF

Head of School Clayton Lewis
Deputy Head of School David Merkel
Upper School Head Gareth Vaughan
Middle School Head Sandra Bourne
Primary School Head Naomi Woolsey
Director of Business Operations Tom Alexander

Director of Technology Steve Hoare
Head Librarian Patricia Kyle
Teaching staff Full time 97; Part time 12; Total 109
Nationalities of teaching staff US 28; UK 15;
Other(s) (French, Argentine) 66

INFORMATION

Grade levels PreK–12
School year September–June
School type coeducational, day, private non-profit
Year founded 1966
Governed by appointed Trustees
Accredited by CIS, Middle States
Regional organizations ECIS
Enrollment PreK 59; Elementary K–5 388;
Middle School 6–8 196; High School 9–12 254;
Total 897

Nationalities of student body US 478; UK 49;
Other(s) (Dutch, French) 363
Tuition/fee currency US Dollar
Tuition range 12,675–27,585
One time fees Capital Levy 2,000
Graduates attending college 100%
Graduates have attended Yale U, Stanford U,
Columbia U, U of Virginia, Georgetown U

EDUCATIONAL PROGRAM

Curriculum Intl, IB Diploma, IBPYP, IBMYP
Average class size Elementary 16; Secondary 16
Language(s) of instruction English, French,
Spanish, Dutch
Language(s) taught Japanese, Chinese, Italian
Staff specialists computer, counselor, ESL,
librarian, nurse, reading resource
Special curricular programs art, instrumental
music, vocal music, computer/technology,
physical education

Extra curricular programs community service,
drama, environmental conservation,
excursions/expeditions, literary magazine,
newspaper, photography, yearbook
Sports baseball, basketball, cross-country, golf,
soccer, softball, swimming, tennis, track and
field, volleyball
Examinations IB, SAT, ERB

CAMPUS FACILITIES

Location Urban
Campus 4 hectares, 8 buildings, 77 classrooms,
3 computer labs, 240 instructional computers,
32,000 library volumes, 1 auditorium,

1 cafeteria, 2 covered play areas,
2 gymnasiums, 1 infirmary, 2 playing fields,
7 science labs, air conditioning

URUGUAY

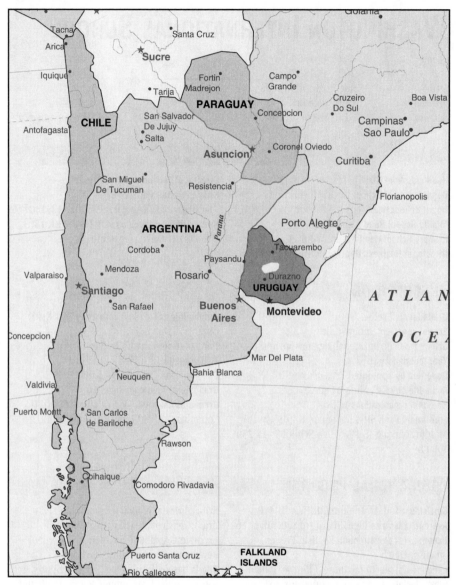

URUGUAY

Area:	176,220 sq km
Population:	3,460,607
Capital:	Montevideo
Currency:	Uruguayan Peso (UYU)
Languages:	Spanish, Portunol

URUGUAYAN AMERICAN SCHOOL

Phone	598 2 600 7681
Fax	598 2 606 1935
Email	toden@uas.edu.uy
Website	www.uas.edu.uy
Address	Saldun de Rodriguez 2375, CP 11500, Montevideo, Uruguay

STAFF

Director Thomas E. Oden
Elementary Principal Sue Bonenfant
High School Counselor Trudy Harder
Middle School Coordinator Sara Kaste
Business Manager Ian Babirecki

IT Coordinator Alejandro Amado
Librarian Rocio Ravera
Teaching staff Full time 33; Part time 15; Total 48
Nationalities of teaching staff US 10; Uruguayan 35; Other(s) 3

INFORMATION

Grade levels N–12
School year August–June
School type coeducational, day, private non-profit
Year founded 1958
Governed by elected Board
Accredited by Southern
Regional organizations AASSA
Enrollment Nursery 10; PreK 15; Elementary K–5 85; Middle School 6–8 60; High School 9–12 50; Total 220

Nationalities of student body US 68; Uruguayan 78; Other(s) (Brazilian, Argentine) 116
Tuition/fee currency US Dollar
Tuition range 4,025–11,160
One time fees Registration 4,000
Graduates attending college 99%
Graduates have attended Col of William and Mary, U of Virginia, Stanford U, Colby Col, Yale U

EDUCATIONAL PROGRAM

Curriculum US, National, AP
Average class size Elementary 20; Secondary 16
Language(s) of instruction English, Spanish
Language(s) taught Portuguese, French
Staff specialists computer, counselor, ESL, learning disabilities, librarian, nurse
Special curricular programs art, instrumental music, computer/technology, distance learning, physical education

Extra curricular programs computers, community service, dance, drama, environmental conservation, excursions/expeditions, literary magazine, newspaper, yearbook
Sports baseball, basketball, gymnastics, soccer, swimming, track and field, volleyball
Examinations AP, Iowa, PSAT, SAT, SAT II

CAMPUS FACILITIES

Location Suburban
Campus 3 hectares, 3 buildings, 31 classrooms, 2 computer labs, 65 instructional computers, 12,400 library volumes, 1 auditorium,

1 cafeteria, 1 covered play area, 1 gymnasium, 1 infirmary, 2 playing fields, 2 science labs, air conditioning

689

US VIRGIN ISLANDS

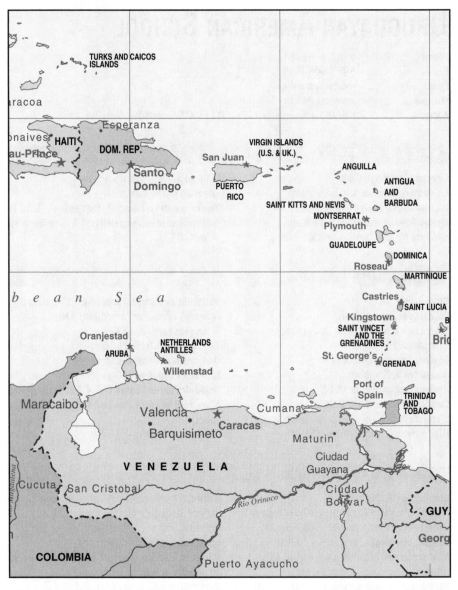

US VIRGIN ISLANDS

Area:	1,910 sq km
Population:	108,448
Capital:	Charlotte Amalie
Currency:	US Dollar (USD)
Languages:	English

ANTILLES SCHOOL

Phone	340 776 1600
Fax	340 776 1019
Email	lwoodbury@antilles.vi
Website	www.antilles.vi
Address	Frenchman's Bay 16-1, St. Thomas, 00802, US Virgin Islands

STAFF

Head of School Ted Morse
Head of Upper School Marva Wiklund
Head of Middle School Michael Harrigan
Head of Lower School Jean Barrows
Assistant Head Chris Teare

Admissions Director Barbara Birt
Chief Financial Officer Joycelyn Phillips
Director of Technology Joyce McKenzie
Head of Library/Media Center Carol Wax

INFORMATION

Grade levels PreK–12
School year August–May
School type coeducational, day, private non-profit
Year founded 1950
Governed by elected Board of Trustees
Accredited by Middle States

Tuition/fee currency US Dollar
Tuition range 10,850–13,625
One time fees Registration 75; Capital Levy 1,000
Graduates attending college 100%
Graduates have attended Harvard U, Columbia U, Stanford U, Dartmouth U, Wellesley Col

EDUCATIONAL PROGRAM

Curriculum US, AP
Average class size Elementary 17; Secondary 20
Language(s) of instruction English
Language(s) taught Spanish, French
Staff specialists computer, counselor, learning disabilities, librarian, math resource, nurse, psychologist, reading resource
Special curricular programs art, instrumental music, vocal music, computer/technology, physical education

Extra curricular programs computers, community service, dance, drama, environmental conservation, yearbook
Sports baseball, basketball, football, golf, martial arts, soccer, softball, swimming, tennis, volleyball, cross-country, wrestling
Examinations ACT, AP, PSAT, SAT, SAT II

CAMPUS FACILITIES

Location Suburban
Campus 27 hectares, 10 buildings, 40 classrooms,
2 computer labs, 150 instructional computers, 2 tennis courts, air conditioning

Data from 2006/07 school year.

THE GOOD HOPE SCHOOL

Phone	340 772 0022
Fax	340 772 0951
Email	mail.ghs@gmail.com
Website	www.ghsvi.org
Address	170 Estate Whim, Frederiksted, 00840, US Virgin Islands

STAFF

Head of School Michael E. Mongeau
Director of the Lower and Middle Schools
Raquel Boucher Cedano
Director of Upper School and College Counseling
Patricia Swan

Director of Admissions Richard Carter
Director of Finance Kalila Quow
Technology Director Robert Freiburghouse
Librarian Wanda Bishop

INFORMATION

Grade levels PreK–12
School year August–June
School type coeducational, day, private non-profit
Year founded 1967
Governed by elected Board of Trustees
Accredited by Middle States
Enrollment PreK 15; Elementary K–5 115;
Middle School 6–8 70; High School 9–12 80;
Total 280

Tuition/fee currency US Dollar
Tuition range 6,700–10,000
Annual fees Books 265
One time fees Application 50
Graduates attending college 100%
Graduates have attended Yale U, Princeton U,
Harvard U, Massachusetts Institute of
Technology, U of Chicago

EDUCATIONAL PROGRAM

Curriculum US, AP, Honors
Average class size Elementary 15; Secondary 12
Language(s) of instruction English
Language(s) taught Spanish, French
Staff specialists computer, counselor, learning
disabilities, librarian, math resource, reading
resource, speech/hearing

Special curricular programs instrumental music,
vocal music, computer/technology
Extra curricular programs computers, drama
Sports baseball, basketball, golf, soccer, softball,
swimming, tennis, volleyball, dodge ball

CAMPUS FACILITIES

Location Suburban
Campus 32 hectares, 12 buildings, 33 classrooms,
3 computer labs, 100 instructional computers,
15,000 library volumes, 1 auditorium,

2 covered play areas, 1 gymnasium,
1 infirmary, 3 playing fields, 3 science labs,
1 pool

UZBEKISTAN

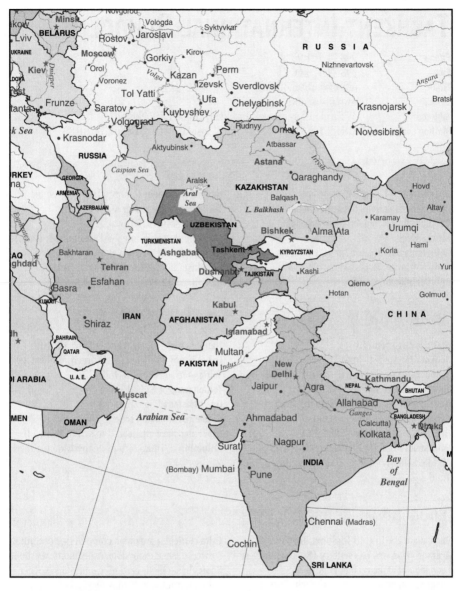

Area:	447,400 sq km
Population:	27,780,059
Capital:	Tashkent (Toshkent)
Currency:	Uzbekistani Soum (UZS)
Languages:	Uzbek

TASHKENT INTERNATIONAL SCHOOL

Phone	998 71 191 96 67
Fax	998 71 120 66 21
Email	office@tashschool.org
Website	www.tashschool.org
Address	38 Sarakulskaya Street, Tashkent, 100005, Uzbekistan
Mailing address	ADM/2 TIS, Dept. of State, 7110 Tashkent Place, Dulles, VA 20189-7110, USA

STAFF

Director Kevin J. Glass
Principal and College Counselor Mamie Heard
PYP Coordinator and Assistant Principal
Elyane Ruel
IB Diploma Coordinator Timothy Getter
Athletic Director Brian Kratz
CAS Coordinator Alex Ross

Business Manager Geoffroy De Vaulgrenant
Technology Coordinator Mark Brookes
Librarian Sayyora Tairova
Teaching staff Full time 24; Part time 14; Total 38
Nationalities of teaching staff US 9; UK 3;
Uzbekistani 14; Other(s) (Australian,
Canadian) 12

INFORMATION

Grade levels PreK–12
School year August–June
School type coeducational, day, private non-profit
Year founded 1994
Governed by elected School Board
Accredited by CIS, New England
Regional organizations CEESA, ECIS
Enrollment PreK 40; Elementary K–5 108;
Middle School 6–8 54; High School 9–12 72;
Total 274

Nationalities of student body US 27; UK 10;
Uzbekistani 40; Other(s) (Korean, Indian) 197
Tuition/fee currency US Dollar
Tuition range 1,800–15,654
One time fees Registration 500
Graduates attending college 100%
Graduates have attended Harvard U, Brown U,
Columbia U, Duke U, U of Pennsylvania

EDUCATIONAL PROGRAM

Curriculum US, Intl, IB Diploma, IBPYP
Average class size Elementary 18; Secondary 18
Language(s) of instruction English
Language(s) taught Russian, French, Korean
Staff specialists computer, ESL, librarian
Special curricular programs art, instrumental
music, vocal music, computer/technology,
physical education, CAS Program

Extra curricular programs computers, community
service, drama, excursions/expeditions, yearbook
Sports basketball, cricket, gymnastics, soccer,
softball, track and field, volleyball
Clubs Model UN, student council, cooking,
board games, chess, multimedia, martial arts,
art and crafts
Examinations ACT, IB, PSAT, SAT, SAT II, TOEFL,
ISA

CAMPUS FACILITIES

Location Suburban
Campus 6 hectares, 7 buildings, 35 classrooms,
2 computer labs, 50 instructional computers,

25,000 library volumes, 1 auditorium,
1 gymnasium, 1 infirmary, 2 playing fields,
3 science labs, air conditioning

VENEZUELA

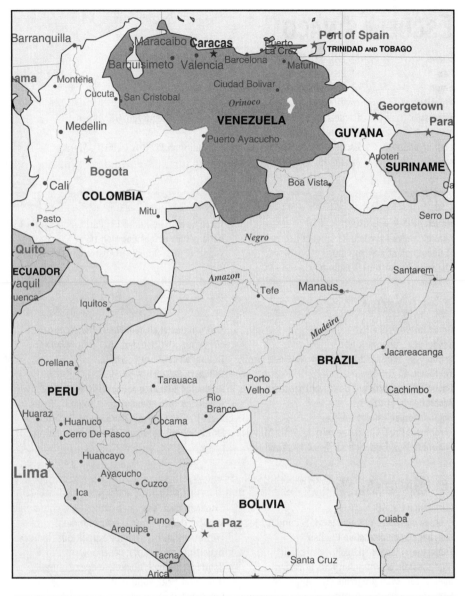

VENEZUELA

Area:	912,050 sq km
Population:	26,023,528
Capital:	Caracas
Currency:	Bolivar (VEB)
Languages:	Spanish

Escuela Anaco

Phone	58 28 2422 2683
Fax	58 28 2422 2683
Email	director@escuelaanaco.com
Website	www.escuelaanaco.com
Address	Escuela Anaco, Avenida Jose Antonio Anzoategui Km. 98, Anaco, Anzoategui, Venezuela
Mailing address	Escuela Anaco, c/o Jet Cargo International, PO Box 020010, M-42, Miami, FL 33102-0010, USA

STAFF

Director Bill R. Kralovec
Administrative Assistant Rosangela Uriarte
IT Coordinator Gary Donahue
Librarian Maryestehl Donahue

Teaching staff Full time 13; Part time 2; Total 15
Nationalities of teaching staff US 5; Venezuelan 5; Other(s) (Australian, Canadian) 5

INFORMATION

Grade levels PreK–12
School year August–June
School type coeducational, day, private non-profit
Year founded 1956
Governed by appointed Board of Directors
Accredited by Southern
Regional organizations AASSA
Enrollment PreK 10; Elementary K–5 37; Middle School 6–8 5; High School 9–12 10; Total 62

Nationalities of student body US 6; Venezuelan 47; Other(s) (Trinidadian, Ecuadorian) 9
Tuition/fee currency US Dollar
Tuition range 2,800–31,500
Graduates attending college 100%
Graduates have attended Oklahoma U, Texas A&M U, U of Central Queensland, McNally Smith School of Music, Florida International U

EDUCATIONAL PROGRAM

Curriculum US, AP
Average class size Elementary 8; Secondary 5
Language(s) of instruction English
Language(s) taught Spanish, Norwegian
Staff specialists computer, ESL, librarian
Special curricular programs computer/technology, distance learning, physical education

Extra curricular programs computers, community service, dance, drama, environmental conservation, excursions/expeditions, literary magazine, newspaper, yearbook
Sports basketball, hockey, soccer, softball, track and field, volleyball
Clubs board game, chess
Examinations ACT, Iowa, PSAT, SAT

CAMPUS FACILITIES

Location Suburban
Campus 6 hectares, 4 buildings, 13 classrooms, 2 computer labs, 25 instructional computers,

8,000 library volumes, 1 cafeteria, 1 gymnasium, 4 playing fields, 1 science lab, 1 tennis court, air conditioning

Barcelona   **VENEZUELA**

COLEGIO INTERNACIONAL PUERTO LA CRUZ

Phone   58 281 277 6051
Fax   58 281 274 1134
Email   superintendent@ciplc.net
Website   www.ciplc.net
Address   Avenida Country Club c/c Calle Ricaurte, Barcelona, Anzoategui, 6023, Venezuela
Mailing address MUN 6111, 11010 NW 30th Street, Suite 104, Miami, FL 33172-5032, USA

STAFF

Superintendent Michael Martell
Assistant Principal Robert Imholt
Counselor Heather Villaparedes
Business Manager Rafael Rincon
Technology Coordinator Robert Cowie

Library/Media Center Coordinator Teresa Thomas
Teaching staff Full time 24; Total 24
Nationalities of teaching staff US 14;
Venezuelan 8; Other(s) (Canadian) 2

INFORMATION

Grade levels N–12
School year August–June
School type coeducational, company-sponsored,
day, private non-profit
Year founded 1997
Governed by appointed Board of Directors
Accredited by Southern
Regional organizations AASSA
Enrollment Nursery 7; PreK 8;
Elementary K–5 55; Middle School 6–8 18;
High School 9–12 22; Total 110

Nationalities of student body US 30; UK 4;
Venezuelan 64; Other(s) (Argentine) 12
Tuition/fee currency US Dollar
Tuition range 6,500–35,500
Annual fees Busing 3,200
One time fees Capital Levy 8,000
Graduates attending college 99%
Graduates have attended U of Chicago, Texas
A&M U, Vanderbilt U, U of Texas in Austin,
U of California in Davis

EDUCATIONAL PROGRAM

Curriculum US, AP
Average class size Elementary 10; Secondary 8
Language(s) of instruction English
Language(s) taught Spanish
Staff specialists computer, counselor, librarian,
physician
Special curricular programs art, instrumental
music, vocal music, computer/technology,
distance learning, physical education, Virtual
High School

Extra curricular programs computers, community
service, drama, environmental conservation,
excursions/expeditions, yearbook
Sports basketball, soccer, softball, volleyball,
roller hockey
Clubs scuba diving, chess, National Honor
Society, Junior National Honor Society, student
council
Examinations ACT, AP, PSAT, SAT, SAT II,
Stanford, TOEFL

CAMPUS FACILITIES

Location Suburban
Campus 2 hectares, 4 buildings, 30 classrooms,
2 computer labs, 120 instructional computers,

9,000 library volumes, 1 auditorium, 1 cafeteria,
2 covered play areas, 2 gymnasiums,
1 infirmary, 2 science labs, air conditioning

Colegio Internacional de Caracas

Phone	58 212 945 0444
Fax	58 212 945 0533
Email	Bensona@ciccaracas.com.ve
Website	www.cic-caracas.org
Address	Calle Colegio Americano, entre Las Minas y Los Samanes, Baruta, Caracas, 1080, Venezuela
Mailing address	PAKMAIL 6030, PO Box 025304, Miami, FL 33102-5304, USA

STAFF

Superintendent Robert A. Benson, Ph.D.
Assistant Superintendent Carmen Sweeting
Assistant Principal Secondary School Brian Lettinga
Assistant Principal Elementary Rachel Harrington
Business Manager Robert A. Benson

Head of Technology James Pojman
Director of Media Services Ilana Locker
Teaching staff Full time 48; Total 48
Nationalities of teaching staff US 16; UK 6; Venezuelan 23; Other(s) (Canadian) 3

INFORMATION

Grade levels N–12
School year August–June
School type coeducational, day, private non-profit
Year founded 1958
Governed by elected School Board
Accredited by Southern
Regional organizations AASSA, ECIS
Enrollment Nursery 17; PreK 7; Elementary K–5 72; Middle School 6–8 40; High School 9–12 70; Total 206

Nationalities of student body US 24; UK 6; Venezuelan 74; Other(s) (Brazilian) 102
Tuition/fee currency Venezuelan Bolivar
Tuition range 37,000,000–73,000,000
One time fees Busing 2,365,000
Graduates attending college 100%
Graduates have attended Dartmouth Col, Boston U, Northeastern U, Notre Dame U, Middlebury U

EDUCATIONAL PROGRAM

Curriculum US, Intl, IB Diploma, IBMYP
Average class size Elementary 14; Secondary 15
Language(s) of instruction English
Language(s) taught Spanish, French
Staff specialists computer, counselor, ESL, librarian, math resource, nurse, psychologist, reading resource

Special curricular programs art, instrumental music, vocal music, computer/technology, physical education
Extra curricular programs computers, community service, dance, drama, literary magazine, photography
Sports basketball, hockey, soccer, track and field, volleyball
Examinations IB, MAT, SAT, SAT II, TOEFL

CAMPUS FACILITIES

Location Urban
Campus 4 hectares, 8 buildings, 45 classrooms, 4 computer labs, 245 instructional computers,

18,000 library volumes, 1 auditorium, 1 cafeteria, 1 covered play area, 1 infirmary, 1 playing field, 4 science labs, 1 tennis court

ESCUELA CAMPO ALEGRE

Phone	58 212 993 3922
Fax	58 212 993 0219
Email	admissions@eca.com.ve
Website	www.eca.com.ve
Address	Final Calle La Cinta, Las Mercedes, Caracas, 1060A, Venezuela
Mailing address	8424 NW 56th Street, Suite CCS 00007, Miami, FL 33166, USA

STAFF

Superintendent Jean K. Vahey
High School Principal Jeff Paulson
Middle School Principal Alicia Brown
Elementary School Principal Kurt Nordness
Director of Admissions Joan Bastianini
Academic Dean Win Lowman

Director of Support Services Erik Do Valle
I.T. Coordinator Aland Russell
Director of Library Media Center Patricia Sonnet
Teaching staff Full time 91; Part time 5; Total 96
Nationalities of teaching staff US 44; UK 8;
Venezuelan 31; Other(s) 13

INFORMATION

Grade levels N–12
School year August–June
School type coeducational, company-sponsored, day, private non-profit
Year founded 1937
Governed by appointed Board of Directors
Sponsored by Multinational Corporations & Parents
Accredited by CIS, Southern
Regional organizations ACCAS, AASSA, ECIS
Enrollment Nursery 19; PreK 30;
Elementary K–5 248; Middle School 6–8 145;
High School 9–12 199; Total 641

Nationalities of student body US 164; UK 13;
Venezuelan 92; Other(s) (Brazilian, Argentine) 372
Tuition/fee currency US Dollar
Tuition range 7,430–19,350
Annual fees Registration 640
One time fees Capital Levy 7,000
Graduates attending college 100%
Graduates have attended Boston U, U of Miami, McGill U, Colombia U, Duke U

EDUCATIONAL PROGRAM

Curriculum US, Intl, IB Diploma
Average class size Elementary 17; Secondary 16
Language(s) of instruction English
Language(s) taught Spanish, French
Staff specialists computer, counselor, ESL, learning disabilities, librarian, math resource, nurse
Special curricular programs art, instrumental music, vocal music, computer/technology, physical education, excursions
Extra curricular programs computers, community service, dance, drama, environmental

conservation, excursions/expeditions, literary magazine, newspaper, yearbook
Sports baseball, basketball, martial arts, soccer, softball, swimming, tennis, volleyball, Ultimate Frisbee
Clubs Model UN, chess, Hope, dance, fitness, conservation
Examinations ACT, AP, IB, PSAT, SAT, SAT II, TOEFL, ERB, ITBS, Developmental Assets, Exploration, Strengths Quest, ACER

CAMPUS FACILITIES

Location Urban
Campus 3 hectares, 9 buildings, 77 classrooms, 5 computer labs, 350 instructional computers, 55,000 library volumes, 3 auditoriums,

1 cafeteria, 1 covered play area, 3 gymnasiums, 1 infirmary, 1 playing field, 9 science labs, 1 pool, 3 tennis courts, air conditioning

VENEZUELA   El Tigre

QSI International School of El Tigre

Phone	58 283 2412005
Fax	58 283 2412467
Email	ronaldsalazar@qsi.org
Website	www.qsi.org
Address	Avenida Intercomunal detras de C.C. El Roble, El Tigre, Anzoategui, Venezuela
Mailing address	Mun 5018, PO Box 02-5352, Miami, Florida 33102-5352, USA

STAFF

Director Ronald Salazar, Ed.D.
Finance Manager Bonita Van Veen
Head of Library/Media Center Juline Thomley

Teaching staff Full time 9; Part time 2; Total 11
Nationalities of teaching staff US 5; Other(s)
(Canadian, Mexican) 6

INFORMATION

Grade levels PreK–12
School year August–June
School type coeducational, day, private non-profit
Year founded 1994
Sponsored by Quality Schools International
Accredited by Southern
Enrollment PreK 7; Elementary K–5 33; Middle
School 6–8 15; High School 9–12 14; Total 69

Nationalities of student body US 6; Venezuelan 58;
Other(s) (Argentine, Peruvian) 5
Tuition/fee currency US Dollar
Tuition range 5,500–22,100
One time fees Registration 100
Graduates attending college 100%
Graduates have attended U of Buenos Aires,
U of Kentucky, York U, Oklahoma State U,
Technological Institute in Argentina

EDUCATIONAL PROGRAM

Curriculum US, National
Average class size Elementary 10; Secondary 5
Language(s) of instruction English
Language(s) taught Spanish
Staff specialists computer, ESL, librarian
Special curricular programs computer/
technology, physical education

Extra curricular programs community service, drama,
excursions/expeditions, newspaper, yearbook
Sports baseball, basketball, soccer, softball,
track and field, volleyball
Clubs sports, Girl Scouts, cheerleaders, student
council, drama, forensics
Examinations AP, Iowa, SAT

CAMPUS FACILITIES

Location Urban
Campus 1 hectare, 1 building, 13 classrooms,
1 computer lab, 15 instructional computers,

6,000 library volumes, 1 cafeteria, 2 covered
play areas, 1 gymnasium, 1 playing field,
1 science lab, air conditioning

Maracaibo   **VENEZUELA**

Escuela Bella Vista

Phone	58 261 794 0000
Fax	58 261 794 0099
Email	sibleys@ebv.org.ve
Website	www.ebv.org.ve
Address	Calle 67 entre Avs. 3D y 3E, Sector La Lago, Maracaibo, Zulia, 4001, Venezuela
Mailing address	C-MAR-P 1815, PO BOX 02-8537, Miami, FL 33102-8537, USA

STAFF

Superintendent Stephen E. Sibley
Elementary Principal Mary Jane Flores
Secondary Principal Todd Zukewich
IB Coordinator Padmini Sankaran
Counselor Laura Cobo
Business Manager Cira Rincon

Technology Coordinator Alejandro Chacon
Library/Media Center Head Fiona Romero
Teaching staff Full time 48; Total 48
Nationalities of teaching staff US 24;
Venezuelan 18; Other(s) (Canadian) 6

INFORMATION

Grade levels PreK–12
School year August–June
School type coeducational, day, private non-profit
Year founded 1948
Governed by elected Board of Directors
Accredited by Southern
Regional organizations AASSA
Enrollment PreK 15; Elementary K–5 206;
Middle School 6–8 84; High School 9–12 75;
Total 380

Nationalities of student body US 31; UK 3;
Venezuelan 243; Other(s) (Brazilian) 103
Tuition/fee currency Venezuelan Bolivar
Tuition range 16,555–20,284
Annual fees Registration 6,980
Graduates attending college 100%
Graduates have attended Massachusetts Institute
of Technology, U of California, U of Florida,
Purdue U, Pennsylvania State U

EDUCATIONAL PROGRAM

Curriculum US, Intl, IB Diploma
Average class size Elementary 15; Secondary 17
Language(s) of instruction English
Language(s) taught Spanish, French
Staff specialists computer, counselor, ESL,
learning disabilities, librarian, math resource,
physician, psychologist, reading resource

Special curricular programs art, instrumental
music, vocal music, computer/technology,
distance learning, physical education
Extra curricular programs community service,
drama, excursions/expeditions, yearbook
Sports basketball, gymnastics, soccer, softball,
tennis, volleyball
Examinations ACT, IB, Iowa, PSAT, SAT, TOEFL

CAMPUS FACILITIES

Location Urban
Campus 7 hectares, 7 buildings, 37 classrooms,
2 computer labs, 175 instructional computers,
20,000 library volumes, 1 auditorium,

1 cafeteria, 2 covered play areas, 2 gymnasiums,
1 infirmary, 1 playing field, 2 science labs,
2 tennis courts, air conditioning

INTERNATIONAL SCHOOL OF MONAGAS

Phone	58 291 315 0011
Fax	58 414 992 1392
Email	ejspin@hotmail.com
Website	www.ismonagas.com
Address	Km.1, Carretera via a La Toscana, Sector Costo Abajo, Maturin, Monagas, 6201, Venezuela
Mailing address	MUN 39, PO Box 02-5352, Miami, FL 33102-5352, USA

STAFF

Head of School Eric J. Spindler, Ed.D.
Business Manager Rafael Lopez
Head of Technology/Media Center Juan Facendo

Teaching staff Full time 20; Total 20
Nationalities of teaching staff US 10; Host 10

INFORMATION

Grade levels N–12
School year August–June
School type coeducational, company-sponsored, day, private non-profit
Year founded 1997
Governed by elected Board of Directors
Sponsored by Shareholding Companies (Oil Business)
Accredited by Southern
Regional organizations AASSA

Enrollment Nursery 12; PreK 12; Elementary K–5 78; Middle School 6–8 33; High School 9–12 16; Total 151
Nationalities of student body US 10; UK 3; Venezuelan 100; Other(s) 38
Tuition/fee currency US Dollar
Tuition range 8,000–22,800
One time fees Capital Levy 5,000
Graduates attending college 100%
Graduates have attended Georgia Intitute of Technology, Oklahoma Baptist U, U of Tampa, Louisiana State U, U of Tulsa

EDUCATIONAL PROGRAM

Curriculum US, Intl
Average class size Elementary 13; Secondary 8
Language(s) of instruction English
Language(s) taught Spanish
Staff specialists computer, counselor, ESL
Special curricular programs art, vocal music, computer/technology, distance learning, physical education

Extra curricular programs computers, community service, dance, drama, environmental conservation, excursions/expeditions, newspaper, yearbook
Sports basketball, soccer, softball, volleyball
Examinations AP, Iowa, PSAT, SAT, ERB WrAP

CAMPUS FACILITIES

Location Suburban
Campus 14 hectares, 6 buildings, 32 classrooms, 1 computer lab, 64 instructional computers,

8,000 library volumes, 2 cafeterias, 1 gymnasium, 1 infirmary, 3 playing fields, 2 science labs, air conditioning

Ojeda VENEZUELA

ESCUELA LAS MOROCHAS

Phone	58 265 631 5539
Fax	58 265 631 5539
Email	abriggs@escuelalasmorochas.com
Website	www.escuelalasmorochas.com
Address	Avenida Intercomunal,Via Terminales Maracaibo, Diagonal a Baker Hughes, Sector Las Morochas, Ciudad Ojeda, Zulia, Venezuela
Mailing address	Bamco Mar 01900, PO 522237, Miami, FL 33152, USA

STAFF

Director Austin E. Briggs Jr.
Elementary Coordinator Donna Valentino
Administrative Secretary Maria de Arrieta

Math/Computer Coordinator Tim Post
Librarian Neilin Dookie

INFORMATION

Grade levels PreK–12
School year August–June
School type coeducational, day, private non-profit
Year founded 1971
Governed by appointed School Board
Sponsored by Corporate Shareholders
Accredited by Southern
Regional organizations AASSA

Enrollment PreK 9; Elementary K–5 38; Middle School 6–8 10; High School 9–12 2; Total 59
Nationalities of student body US 3; UK 1; Venezuelan 34; Other(s) (Colombian, Mexican) 21
Tuition/fee currency US Dollar
Tuition range 8,000–25,000
Annual fees Busing 10 weekly; Lunch 10 weekly
Graduates attending college 100%

EDUCATIONAL PROGRAM

Curriculum US, AP
Average class size Elementary 6; Secondary 3
Language(s) of instruction English
Language(s) taught Spanish
Staff specialists computer, counselor, ESL, librarian
Special curricular programs art, computer/ technology, distance learning, physical education, music

Extra curricular programs computers, community service, dance, drama, yearbook, gymnastics, arts and crafts, studio arts, Venezuelan studies
Sports basketball, soccer, softball, tennis, volleyball
Examinations AP, Iowa, PSAT, SAT, SAT II

CAMPUS FACILITIES

Location Suburban
Campus 3 hectares, 3 buildings, 14 classrooms, 1 computer lab, 21 instructional computers, 6,000 library volumes, 1 auditorium, 1 cafeteria,

1 covered play area, 1 gymnasium, 1 playing field, 1 science lab, 1 tennis court, air conditioning

Data from 2006/07 school year.

QSI INTERNATIONAL SCHOOL OF PUERTO LA CRUZ

Phone	58 281 281 9954
Fax	58 281 281 6293
Email	puertolacruz@qsi.org
Website	www.qsi.org
Address	Avenida Piritu cruce con Calle Sucre, Lecheria, Anzoategui, 6016, Venezuela
Mailing address	Escuelamer, C.A., QSI International School of PLC, BLA 0693, P.O.Box 02-8537, Miami, FL 33102-8537, USA

STAFF

Director Sally O. Hefley
Director of Instruction Kenneth B. Hall
Head of Technology Daniel Hefley

Head of Library MariPuri de Madariaga
Teaching staff Full time 9; Part time 1; Total 10
Nationalities of teaching staff US 7; Host 3

INFORMATION

Grade levels PreK–12
School year September–June
School type coeducational, day, private non-profit
Year founded 1996
Governed by appointed Board of Directors
Sponsored by Quality Schools International
Accredited by Southern
Enrollment PreK 5; Elementary K–5 32; Middle School 6–8 10; High School 9–12 15; Total 62

Nationalities of student body US 10; Venezuelan 42; Other(s) (Argentine, Colombian) 10
Tuition/fee currency US Dollar
Tuition range 3,000–12,200
One time fees Registration 100
Graduates attending college 100%
Graduates have attended U of Alabama, U de Carabobo, Venezuela, Florida International U, Sam Houston U

EDUCATIONAL PROGRAM

Curriculum US, Intl
Average class size Elementary 15; Secondary 10
Language(s) of instruction English
Language(s) taught Spanish, French
Staff specialists computer, ESL, librarian
Special curricular programs art, computer/technology, physical education

Extra curricular programs computers, community service, dance, drama, excursions/expeditions, newspaper, photography, yearbook
Sports basketball, gymnastics, soccer, softball, track and field, volleyball
Clubs sailing, computer, chess, library, sports
Examinations Iowa, PSAT, SAT, SAT II

CAMPUS FACILITIES

Location Suburban
Campus 1 hectare, 1 building, 15 classrooms, 2 computer labs, 15 instructional computers,

7,000 library volumes, 1 cafeteria, 1 covered play area, 1 science lab, air conditioning

Valencia **VENEZUELA**

COLEGIO INTERNACIONAL DE CARABOBO

Phone 58 241 842 6551
Fax 58 241 842 6510
Email admin@cic-valencia.org.ve
Website www.cic-valencia.org.ve
Address Final Avenida Alejo Zuloaga, c/c Calle Colegio, Urb. Trigal Centro, Valencia, Carabobo, 2001, Venezuela
Mailing address VLN 1010, PO Box 025685, Miami, FL 33102-5685, USA

STAFF

Director Joe H. Walker
Secondary School Principal James Daniel Marcum
Elementary Principal Judith Tostenrud
Early Childhood Coordinator Mary Jane Mikolji
School Psychologist Ana Cristina Perez-Mena
Business Manager and Administrative Assistant Belkis Monks

Administrative Coordinator in Charge of Technology and Special Projects Michael Waters
Library/Media Center Specialist Carolyn Standerfer
Teaching staff Full time 58; Part time 8; Total 66
Nationalities of teaching staff US 23; Venezuelan 33; Other(s) (Canadian, Colombian) 10

INFORMATION

Grade levels N–12
School year August–May
School type coeducational, company-sponsored, day, private non-profit
Year founded 1955
Governed by elected Board of Directors
Sponsored by Corporate/Private Sectors
Accredited by Southern
Regional organizations AASSA
Enrollment Nursery 10; PreK 22; Elementary K–5 153; Middle School 6–8 103; High School 9–12 92; Total 380

Nationalities of student body US 44; Venezuelan 217; Other(s) (Italian, Brazilian) 119
Tuition/fee currency US Dollar
Tuition range 4,600–18,913
Annual fees Registration 1,500; Busing 820
One time fees Capital Levy 5,000
Graduates attending college 100%
Graduates have attended Ohio Wesleyan U, Georgetown U, St. Olaf Col, Boston Col, Babson Col

(Continued)

COLEGIO INTERNACIONAL DE CARABOBO (Continued)

EDUCATIONAL PROGRAM

Curriculum US, Intl, AP
Average class size Elementary 15; Secondary 18
Language(s) of instruction English, Spanish
Language(s) taught French
Staff specialists computer, counselor, ESL, learning disabilities, librarian, psychologist
Special curricular programs art, computer/technology, physical education

Extra curricular programs computers, community service, drama, excursions/expeditions, literary magazine, newspaper, yearbook
Sports baseball, basketball, football, soccer, softball, volleyball
Examinations ACT, AP, Iowa, PSAT, SAT, SAT II

CAMPUS FACILITIES

Location Suburban
Campus 17 hectares, 12 buildings, 46 classrooms, 3 computer labs, 180 instructional computers, 12,500 library volumes, 1 auditorium, 1 cafeteria, 1 covered play area, 1 gymnasium, 2 playing fields, 2 science labs

VIETNAM

Area:	329,560 sq km
Population:	85,262,356
Capital:	Hanoi
Currency:	Dong (VND)
Languages:	Vietnamese

QSI INTERNATIONAL SCHOOL OF HAIPHONG

Phone	0084 912 083 198
Fax	0084-31-389 2614
Email	huong@qsi.org
Website	www.qsi.org
Address	Unit 106-104, Sunflower International Village, 1 Van Cao St., Haiphong, Vietnam

STAFF

Directory Sidney Rodnunsky
Business/Finance Manager Bonita Vanveen
Head of Technology Kevin Gilson

Teaching staff Full time 2; Part time 2; Total 4
Nationalities of teaching staff Other(s)
(Canadian, Vietnamese) 4

INFORMATION

Grade levels PreK–8
School year August–June
School type proprietary
Year founded 2005
Governed by appointed Advisory Board
Sponsored by Quality Schools International
Regional organizations AISA

Enrollment PreK 10; Elementary K-5 10;
Middle School 6-8 10; Total 30
Nationalities of student body US 10; Host 10;
Other(s) (Korean, Australian) 10
Tuition/fee currency US Dollar
Tuition range 10,800-13,500
Annual fees Capital Fund 1,600
One time fees Registration 100

EDUCATIONAL PROGRAM

Curriculum US
Average class size Elementary 10; Secondary 10
Language(s) of instruction English, Vietnamese
Language(s) taught Vietnamese
Staff specialists computer, ESL, math resource,
reading resource

Special curricular programs instrumental music,
computer/technology, distance learning
Extra curricular programs yearbook,
cultural/historical trips
Sports golf, swimming, tennis, volleyball
Examinations ITBS

CAMPUS FACILITIES

Location Urban
Campus 1 building, 7 classrooms,
1 computer lab, 5 instructional computers,

2,500 library volumes, 1 covered play area,
1 gymnasium, 1 pool, 3 tennis courts,
air conditioning

UNITED NATIONS INTERNATIONAL SCHOOL OF HANOI

Phone	84 4 758 1551
Fax	84 4 758 1542
Email	postmaster@unishanoi.org
Website	www.unishanoi.org
Address	Phu Thuong Ward, Tay Ho District, Hanoi, Vietnam
Mailing address	U.S. Mail: PO Box 1608 GRNL, New York, NY 10163-1608, USA, International Postal Address: GPO Box 313, Hanoi, Vietnam

STAFF

Head of School Alun Cooper
Middle and High School Principal Lesley Peacock
Elementary School Principal Conal Atkins
Elementary School Guidance Counselor Jane Kilpatrick
Middle School Counselor Amanda Abel
High School Guidance Counselor Christina Powers

Business Manager David King
Director of Technology Harry Bennett, Ph.D.
Librarian Lois Coulthart
Teaching staff Full time 84; Part time 10; Total 94
Nationalities of teaching staff US 11; UK 16; Vietnamese 3; Other(s) (Australian, Canadian) 64

INFORMATION

Grade levels N–12
School year August–June
School type coeducational, day, private non-profit
Year founded 1988
Governed by appointed and elected Board of Directors
Accredited by CIS, New England
Regional organizations EARCOS, ECIS
Enrollment Nursery 12; PreK 22; Elementary K–5 295; Middle School 6–8 192; High School 9–12 193; Total 714

Nationalities of student body US 73; UK 52; Vietnamese 124; Other(s) (Korean, Australian) 465
Tuition/fee currency US Dollar
Tuition range 5,358–13,156
Graduates attending college 98%
Graduates have attended Oxford U, London School of Economics, U of Pennsylvania, Georgetown U, McGill U

(Continued)

United Nations International School of Hanoi (Continued)

EDUCATIONAL PROGRAM

Curriculum Intl, IB Diploma, IBPYP, IBMYP
Average class size Elementary 18; Secondary 22
Language(s) of instruction English
Language(s) taught French, Vietnamese, Swedish, Korean, Mandarin
Staff specialists computer, counselor, ESL, learning disabilities, librarian, math resource, nurse, psychologist, reading resource
Special curricular programs art, instrumental music, vocal music, computer/technology, physical education, vocational

Extra curricular programs computers, community service, dance, drama, environmental conservation, excursions/expeditions, literary magazine, newspaper, photography, yearbook
Sports badminton, basketball, gymnastics, hockey, martial arts, rugby, soccer, softball, swimming, tennis, track and field, volleyball
Clubs cooking, guitar, school musical and plays, painting, school band, arts and crafts
Examinations IB, PSAT, SAT, TOEFL

CAMPUS FACILITIES

Location Suburban
Campus 10 hectares, 9 buildings, 60 classrooms, 3 computer labs, 200 instructional computers,

25,000 library volumes, 1 cafeteria, 1 covered play area, 1 infirmary, 2 playing fields, 3 science labs, 1 pool, air conditioning

Ho Chi Minh City   **VIETNAM**

INTERNATIONAL SCHOOL HO CHI MINH CITY

Phone	84 8 898 9100
Fax	84 8 887 4022
Email	ishcmc@hcm.vnn.vn
Website	www.ishcmc.com
Address	649A Vo Truong Toan, An Phu, District 2, Ho Chi Minh City, Vietnam

STAFF

Head of School Sean P. O'Maonaigh
Head of High School Martin Gough
Head of Middle School Robyn Blenkiron
Head of Elementary School Claire McLeod
Business Manager Tony Shadwell

Director of Technology Derek Rutt
Librarian Kimbra Weeks
Teaching staff Full time 73; Part time 3; Total 76
Nationalities of teaching staff US 5; UK 15;
Vietnamese 3; Other(s) (Australian, Canadian) 53

INFORMATION

Grade levels N–12
School year August–June
School type coeducational, day
Year founded 1993
Governed by appointed Board of Management
Accredited by CIS
Regional organizations EARCOS, ECIS
Enrollment Nursery 36; PreK 36;
Elementary K–5 343; Middle School 6–8 211;
High School 9–12 236; Total 862

Nationalities of student body US 71; UK 30;
Vietnamese 180; Other(s) (Korean,
Taiwanese) 581
Tuition/fee currency US Dollar
Tuition range 3,750–14,850
Annual fees Annual Development 2,000
One time fees Registration 500; Certificates of
Entitlement 12,000
Graduates attending college 90%
Graduates have attended Stanford U, U of
Melbourne, McGill U, U of Michigan, Les
Roches Hotel Management School

EDUCATIONAL PROGRAM

Curriculum Intl, IB Diploma, IBPYP, IBMYP, IGCSE
Average class size Elementary 20; Secondary 22
Language(s) of instruction English
Language(s) taught Korean, French, Vietnamese,
Chinese
Staff specialists computer, counselor, ESL,
librarian, nurse
Special curricular programs art, instrumental
music, vocal music, computer/technology,
physical education

Extra curricular programs computers, community
service, dance, drama, excursions/expeditions,
literary magazine, newspaper, yearbook
Sports badminton, baseball, basketball, cricket,
cross-country, football, golf, gymnastics,
martial arts, rugby, soccer, softball, swimming,
tennis, track and field, volleyball
Examinations IB, PSAT, SAT, SAT II, TOEFL

CAMPUS FACILITIES

Location Suburban
Campus 1 hectare, 3 buildings, 42 classrooms,
5 computer labs, 200 instructional computers,
23,000 library volumes, 1 auditorium, 1 cafeteria,

1 covered play area, 1 gymnasium, 1 infirmary,
1 playing field, 4 science labs, 1 pool,
air conditioning

SAIGON SOUTH INTERNATIONAL SCHOOL

Phone	84 8 413 0901
Fax	84 8 413 0902
Email	info@ssischool.org
Website	www.ssischool.org
Address	Nguyen Van Linh Parkway, Tan Phong Ward, District 7, Ho Chi Minh City, Vietnam

STAFF

Head of School Charles S. Barton
Elementary Principal Mary Lower
Secondary Principal Jim Scorgie
Director of Admissions Brie Goolbis
Curriculum Director/Coordinator
Theresa Flaspohler
Secondary Assistant Principal Rhonda Isley

Business Manager Fong Wai Mun
IT Coordinator Santha Kumar
Library/Media Specialist Anton Pav
Teaching staff Full time 55; Part time 2; Total 57
Nationalities of teaching staff US 42; UK 1;
Vietnamese 2; Other(s) (Canadian, Australian) 12

INFORMATION

Grade levels PreK–12
School year August–June
School type coeducational, company-sponsored,
day, private non-profit
Year founded 1996
Governed by appointed Board
Sponsored by Phu My Hung Corporation
Accredited by Western
Regional organizations EARCOS
Enrollment PreK 32; Elementary K–5 260;
Middle School 6–8 116; High School 9–12 155;
Total 563

Nationalities of student body US 125; UK 10;
Vietnamese 80; Other(s) (Korean,
Taiwanese) 343
Tuition/fee currency US Dollar
Tuition range 7,150–14,250
Annual fees Busing 450; Lunch 400; PTA 40
One time fees Registration 200; Uniforms 100
Graduates attending college 100%
Graduates have attended Cornell U,
Singapore National U, Wake Forest U,
Boston Col, Bentley Col

EDUCATIONAL PROGRAM

Curriculum US, AP
Average class size Elementary 18; Secondary 20
Language(s) of instruction English
Language(s) taught Vietnamese, Spanish, Mandarin
Staff specialists computer, counselor, ESL,
librarian, nurse
Special curricular programs art, instrumental
music, vocal music, computer/technology,
physical education, dance, swimming

Extra curricular programs computers, community
service, dance, drama, excursions/expeditions,
literary magazine, newspaper, photography,
yearbook
Sports basketball, soccer, softball, swimming,
volleyball
Examinations AP, PSAT, SAT, SAT II, TOEFL,
ISA-ACER

CAMPUS FACILITIES

Location Suburban
Campus 8 hectares, 2 buildings, 32 classrooms,
4 computer labs, 90 instructional computers,
10,000 library volumes, 1 cafeteria,

2 covered play areas, 1 gymnasium,
1 infirmary, 2 playing fields, 2 science labs,
1 pool, 1 tennis court, air conditioning

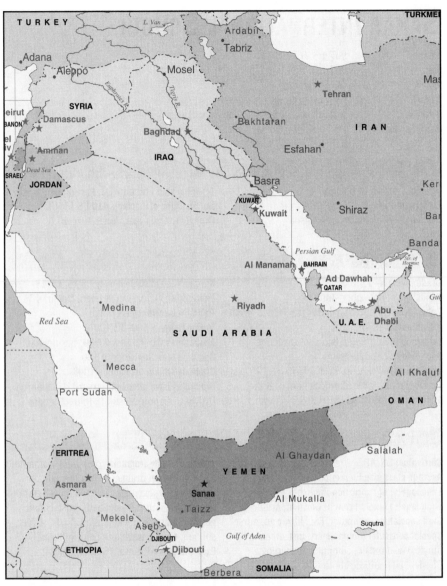

YEMEN

Area:	527,970 sq km
Population:	22,230,531
Capital:	Sanaa
Currency:	Yemeni Rial (YER)
Languages:	Arabic

SANAA INTERNATIONAL SCHOOL

Phone	967 1 370 191
Fax	967 1 370 193
Email	sanaa@qsi.org
Website	www.qsi.org/yem
Address	Wadi Dahar Street, Shamlan Area, Sanaa, Yemen
Mailing address	PO Box 2002, Sanaa, Yemen

STAFF

Director Gordon B. Blackie
Director of Instruction Cary Hauth
Systems Administrator Kevin Gilson

Teaching staff Full time 22; Part time 3; Total 25
Nationalities of teaching staff US 15; UK 4;
Other(s) (Canadian, South African) 6

INFORMATION

Grade levels N–12
School year September–June
School type coeducational, day, private non-profit
Year founded 1971
Governed by appointed Board of Directors
Accredited by Middle States
Enrollment Nursery 60; PreK 15;
Elementary K–5 85; Middle School 6–8 25;
High School 9–12 50; Total 235

Nationalities of student body US 25; UK 15;
Yemeni 60; Other(s) (German, Dutch) 135
Tuition/fee currency US Dollar
Tuition range 3,300–12,400
Annual fees Capital Levy 1,600; Busing 900
One time fees Registration 100
Graduates attending college 100%
Graduates have attended Harvard U, Stanford U,
Brown U, George Mason U, Johns Hopkins U

EDUCATIONAL PROGRAM

Curriculum US, AP
Average class size Elementary 8; Secondary 8
Language(s) of instruction English
Language(s) taught French, German, Arabic
Staff specialists computer, ESL, librarian, nurse
Special curricular programs art, instrumental
music, vocal music, computer/technology,
physical education, robotics

Extra curricular programs computers, community
service, dance, drama, environmental
conservation, excursions/expeditions, yearbook
Sports badminton, basketball, cross-country,
golf, gymnastics, hockey, martial arts, soccer,
softball, tennis, track and field, volleyball
Examinations AP, Iowa, PSAT, SAT, SAT II

CAMPUS FACILITIES

Location Rural
Campus 5 hectares, 3 buildings, 21 classrooms,
2 computer labs, 75 instructional computers,

15,000 library volumes, 1 auditorium,
1 gymnasium, 3 playing fields, 2 science labs,
2 tennis courts

ZAMBIA

Area:	752,614 sq km
Population:	11,477,447
Capital:	Lusaka
Currency:	Zambian Kwacha (ZMK)
Languages:	English

AMERICAN INTERNATIONAL SCHOOL OF LUSAKA

Phone	260 1 260 509
Fax	260 1 260 538
Email	cmuller@aislusaka.org
Website	www.aislusaka.org
Address	487A Leopard's Hill Road, Lusaka, Zambia
Mailing address	PO Box 31617, Lusaka, Zambia

STAFF

Director Chris Muller, Ed.D.
Secondary Principal James Anderson
Primary Principal Sean Areais
Business Manager Shirley Mee
IT Coordinator Michael Ortman
Librarian Kelly Kraft

Teaching staff Full time 70; Part time 8; Total 78
Nationalities of teaching staff US 28; UK 11; Zambian 20; Other(s) (Australian, New Zealander) 19

INFORMATION

Grade levels N–12
School year August–June
School type coeducational, day, private non-profit
Year founded 1986
Governed by appointed and elected US Embassy and Board of Directors
Accredited by CIS, Middle States
Regional organizations AISA, ECIS
Enrollment Nursery 48; PreK 36; Elementary K–5 218; Middle School 6–8 100; High School 9–12 99; Total 501

Nationalities of student body US 126; UK 66; Zambian 53; Other(s) (South African, Dutch) 256
Tuition/fee currency US Dollar
Tuition range 3,600–12,850
Annual fees Busing 1,070
One time fees Registration 2,500; Capital Levy 2,000
Graduates attending college 98%
Graduates have attended Stanford U, U of Edinburgh, Loyola U, Aquinas Col, Calvin Col

EDUCATIONAL PROGRAM

Curriculum US, Intl, IB Diploma, IBPYP, IBMYP
Average class size Elementary 17; Secondary 15
Language(s) of instruction English
Language(s) taught French, Spanish
Staff specialists computer, counselor, ESL, learning disabilities, librarian
Special curricular programs art, computer/technology, physical education, performing arts

Extra curricular programs computers, community service, dance, drama
Sports baseball, basketball, cross-country, golf, hockey, rugby, soccer, tennis
Clubs Model UN, Monkeynastixs, chess, entomology, climbing, musical theatre, Zambian Cultural Activity, knitting, Student Council
Examinations IB, SAT, SAT II

CAMPUS FACILITIES

Location Suburban
Campus 22 hectares, 16 buildings, 39 classrooms, 2 computer labs, 130 instructional computers, 10,000 library volumes, 2 cafeterias, 1 covered play area, 1 infirmary, 3 playing fields, 3 science labs, 2 pools, 2 tennis courts

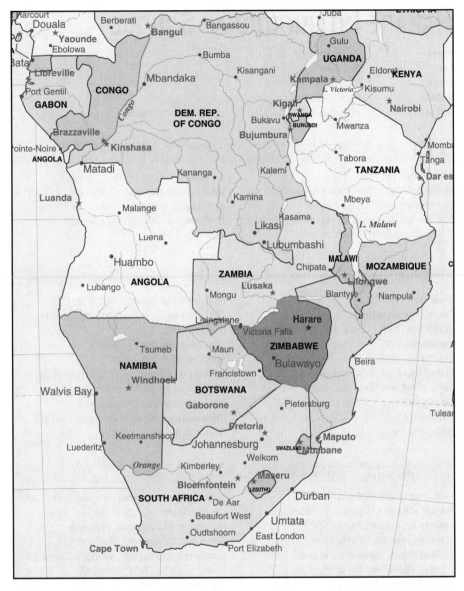

ZIMBABWE

Area:	390,580 sq km
Population:	12,311,143
Capital:	Harare
Currency:	Zimbabwean Dollar (ZWD)
Languages:	English

HARARE INTERNATIONAL SCHOOL

Phone 263 4 870514
Fax 263 4 883 371
Email his@his.ac.zw
Website www.his-zim.com
Address 66 Pendennis Road, Mt. Pleasant, Harare, Zimbabwe

STAFF

Director Paul Olson
Middle and High School Principal Russell Menard
Elementary Principal Angus Ogilvy
Business and Operations Manager Vivien Brelsford
IT Coordinator Kathy Chromicz

Librarian Rae Anne Kelley
Teaching staff Full time 52; Part time 2; Total 54
Nationalities of teaching staff US 18; UK 8; Zimbabwean 16; Other(s) (Canadian, Australian) 12

INFORMATION

Grade levels N–12
School year August–June
School type coeducational, day, private non-profit
Year founded 1992
Governed by elected 7 member Board
Accredited by CIS, New England
Regional organizations AISA, ECIS
Enrollment Nursery 14; PreK 16; Elementary K–5 189; Middle School 6–8 99; High School 9–12 117; Total 435

Nationalities of student body US 78; UK 43; Zimbabwean 53; Other(s) (South African, Chadian) 261
Tuition/fee currency US Dollar
Tuition range 4,500–16,200
One time fees Registration 500; Elementary Capital Levy 3,500; Secondary Capital Levy 4,500
Graduates attending college 100%
Graduates have attended Columbia U, Yale U, Oxford U, Tufts U, Harvard U

EDUCATIONAL PROGRAM

Curriculum US, IB Diploma, IBPYP
Average class size Elementary 16; Secondary 18
Language(s) of instruction English
Language(s) taught French, Spanish
Staff specialists computer, counselor, ESL, learning disabilities, librarian, nurse
Special curricular programs art, instrumental music, vocal music, computer/technology, physical education

Extra curricular programs computers, community service, drama, excursions/expeditions, newspaper, photography, yearbook
Sports badminton, basketball, cricket, gymnastics, martial arts, soccer, swimming, tennis, track and field, volleyball
Examinations IB, PSAT, SAT, ACER/ISA

CAMPUS FACILITIES

Location Suburban
Campus 9 hectares, 12 buildings, 42 classrooms, 3 computer labs, 150 instructional computers, 20,000 library volumes, 1 auditorium, 1 cafeteria, 1 gymnasium, 1 infirmary, 2 playing fields, 4 science labs, 4 tennis courts

MAPS

AND
ADDITIONAL INFORMATION

TIME ZONES

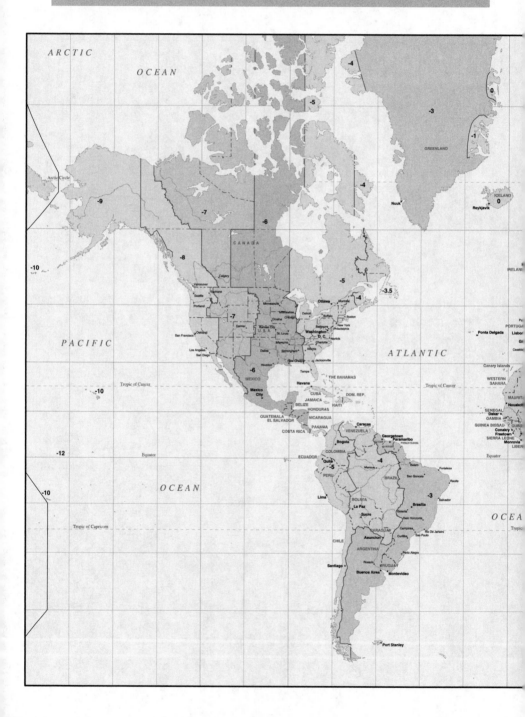

TIME ZONES

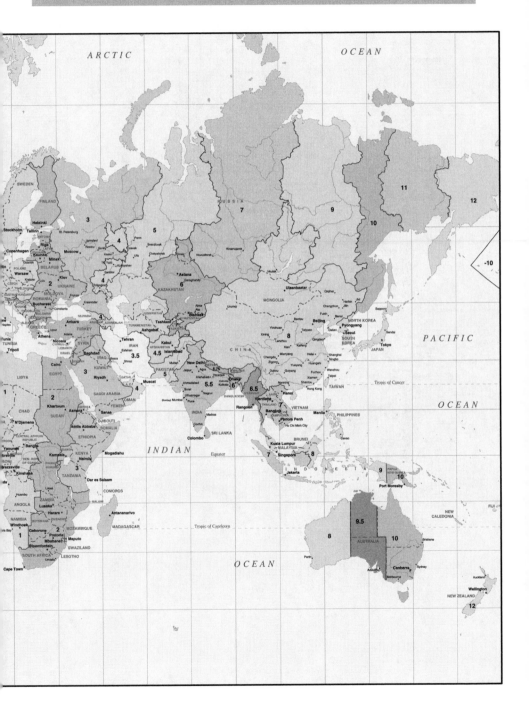

EUROPE

AFRICA

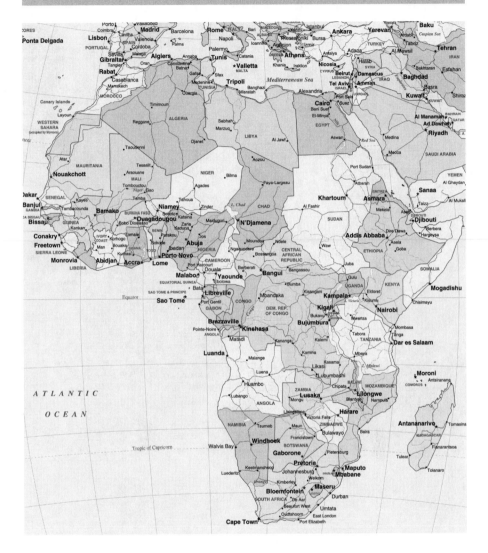

MIDDLE EAST

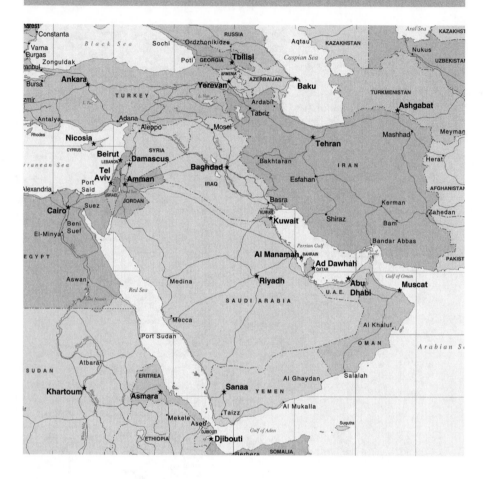

SOUTHEAST ASIA

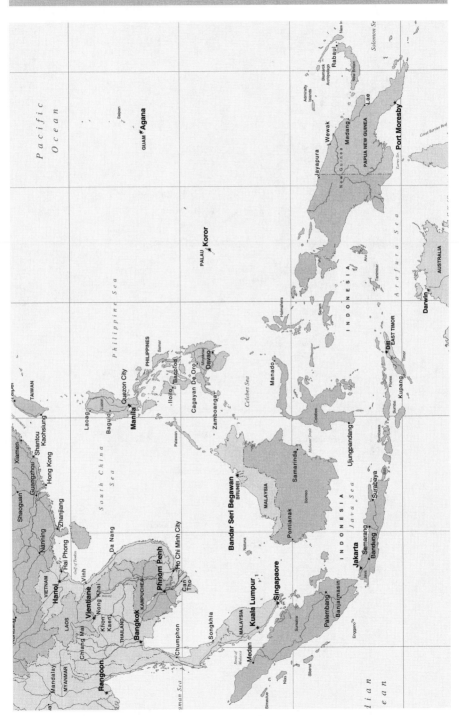

SOUTH ASIA

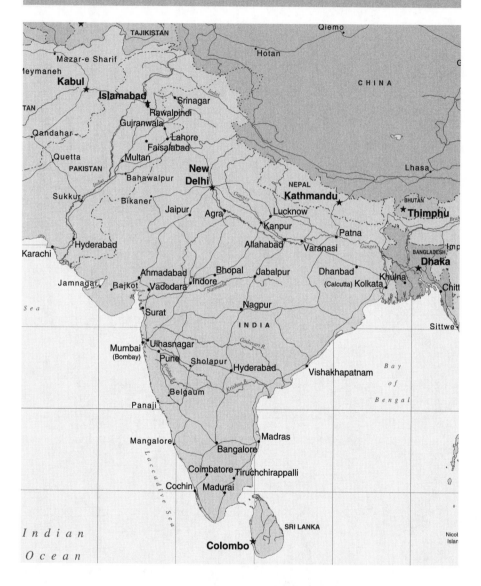

EAST ASIA – JAPAN

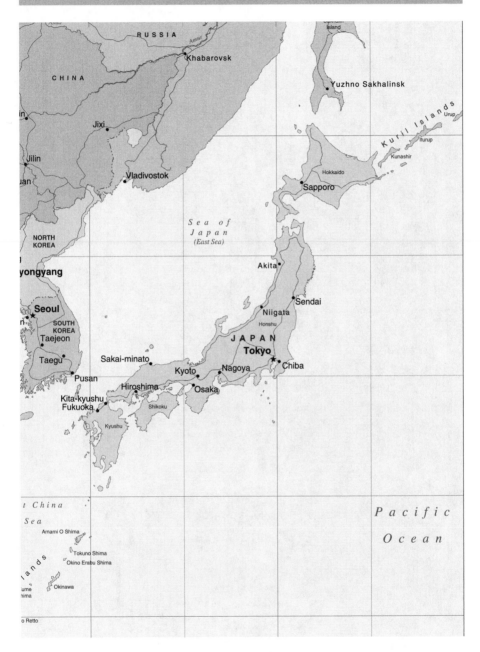

RUSSIA

Khabarovsk

CHINA

Yuzhno Sakhalinsk

Jixi

Kuril Islands

Urup

Iturup

Jilin

Kunashir

Vladivostok

Hokkaido

Sapporo

Sea of Japan
(East Sea)

NORTH KOREA

Akita

yongyang

Sendai

Seoul

Niigata

SOUTH KOREA

Honshu

Taejeon

JAPAN

Tokyo

Taegu

Sakai-minato

Kyoto

Nagoya

Chiba

Pusan

Hiroshima

Osaka

Kita-kyushu
Fukuoka

Shikoku

Kyushu

t China Sea

Amami O Shima

Pacific

Ocean

Tokuno Shima

Okino Erabu Shima

lands

ume
hima

Okinawa

o Retto

EAST ASIA – CHINA

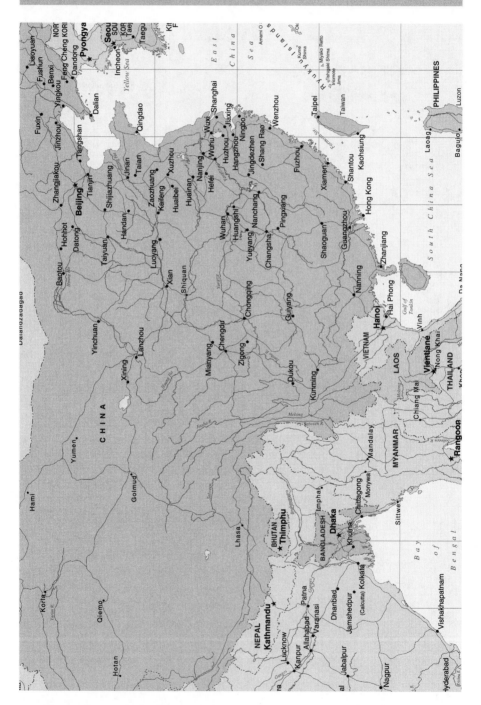

CENTRAL AMERICA AND CARIBBEAN

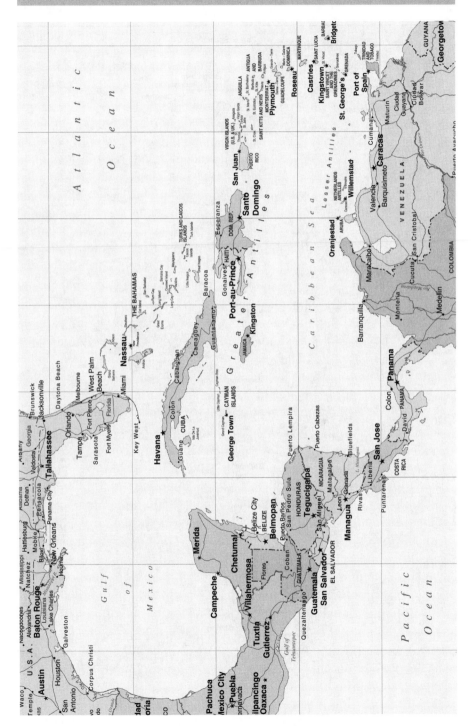

SOUTH AMERICA

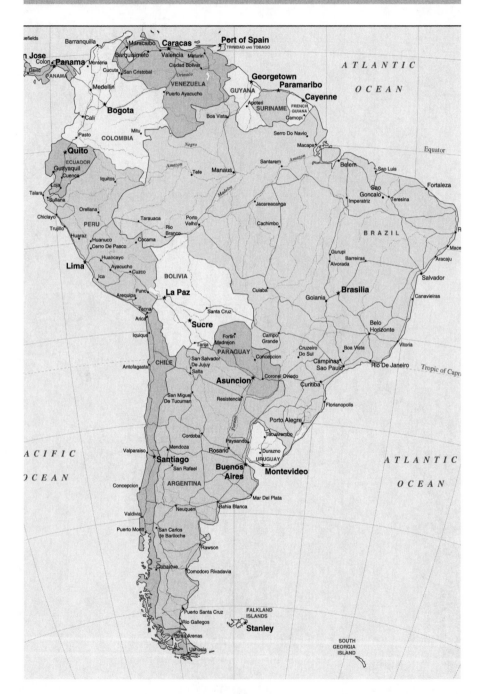

NORTH AMERICA

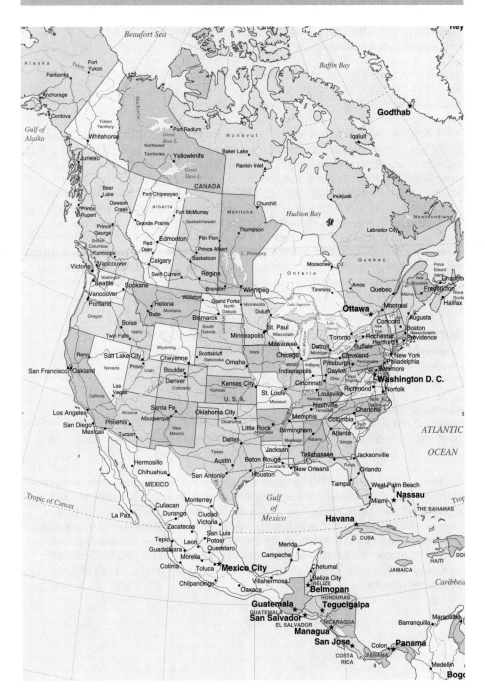

ACCREDITING ORGANIZATIONS

COUNCIL OF INTERNATIONAL SCHOOLS (ACCREDITATION SERVICE): CIS
Director of Accreditation Services Gerry Percy, Ph.D.

Address C/Almirante 3/10 izda., Madrid, 28004, Spain
Phone 34 91 522 6395   **Fax**   34 91 521 4068
Email cismadrid@cois.org   **Website** www.cois.org

The Accreditation Service operated from 1970 by the European Council of International Schools (ECIS) became part of the Council of International Schools (CIS) in July 2003. CIS is a membership organization serving approximately 500 international schools around the world. The CIS Accreditation Process is recognized in the United States under the Recognition Program of the National Association of Independent Schools (NAIS), and CIS is a member of the NAIS Commission on Accreditation.The main purpose of the CIS programme of Evaluation and Accreditation is to support international schools in their pursuit of excellence by providing a system for periodic self examination combined with external appraisal. The award of Accreditation also assures both a school's own constituency and the community at large that the institution so recognized has achieved high standards of professional performance and has a continuing commitment to their maintenance and to institutional improvement.

MIDDLE STATES ASSOCIATION OF COLLEGES AND SCHOOLS: MSA
Associate Director, Committee on Institution-Wide Accreditation Steven C. Heft
President/Executive Director Dr. Henry G. Cram
President/Executive Director Dr. F. Laird Evans

Address 3624 Market Street, Philadelphia, PA, 19104, USA
Phone 267 284 5042   **Fax**   215 662 0957
Email sheft@css-msa.org   **Website** www.ces-msa.org; www.css-msa.org;
                                                                www.ciwa-msa.org

The Middle States Association (MSA) provides accreditation and school improvement services for American international schools overseas and in the Caribbean, as well as those in the Middle Atlantic region of the United States. MSA believes schools should be granted a choice of accreditation processes that best meets their developmental needs and so offers strategic planning, traditional, and content area standards protocols. Middle States enjoys the support of an International Schools Advisory Committee (ISAC) composed of the heads of representative international schools. ISAC meets twice yearly to make accreditation recommendations and to provide MSA with guidance on policies and procedures.

New England Association of Schools and Colleges: NEASC
Executive Director, NEASC Jacob Ludes, III
Director, CAISA/NEASC Rev. Brinton W. Woodward, Jr.

Address 209 Burlington Road, Bedford, MA, 01730-1433, USA
Phone 781 271 0022   **Fax** 781 271 0950
Email bwwjr@worldpath.net   **Website** www.neasc.org

The Commission on American and International Schools Abroad (CAISA) of the New England Association of Schools and Colleges (NEASC) provides accreditation services, peer review, and an institutional improvement process to schools in 65 countries. CAISA often collaborates in its work with the Council of International Schools (CIS). NEASC has 1,900 member institutions and is the oldest regional accrediting agency, founded in 1885.

North Central Association Commission on Accreditation and School Improvement: NCA CASI
Executive Director Kenneth F. Gose, Ed.D.

Address Commission on Accreditation and School Improvement, Arizona State University,
Box 871008, Tempe, AZ, 85287-1008, USA
Phone 480 773 6900; 1 800 525 9517   **Fax** 480 773 6901
Email nca@ncacasi.org   **Website** www.ncacasi.org

The North Central Association Commission on Accreditation and School Improvement evaluates and accredits schools including the Department of Defense Schools overseas.

Northwest Association of Accredited Schools: NAAS
Executive Secretary/Treasurer David G. Steadman
Associate Director Leonard Paul
Manager Shelli D. Clemens
Secretary/Accountant Norene Rice

Address Boise State University, 1910 University Drive, Boise, ID, 83725-1060, USA
Phone 208 426 5727   **Fax** 208 334 3228
Email sclemens@boisestate.edu   **Website** www.boisestate.edu/naas

NAAS currently accredits 1,800 schools in the seven northwest states of Alaska, Idaho, Montana, Oregon, Nevada, Utah and Washington as well as through out the world. Our commission accredits elementary, middle level schools, high schools, distance education schools, supplementary education schools, and travel study schools. Schools must file an annual report and go through self study. On-site evaluations are performed at least every six years. In order to be accredited, all schools must be in substantial compliance with the standards for accreditation.

Accrediting Organizations

SOUTHERN ASSOCIATION OF COLLEGES AND SCHOOLS, COUNCIL ON ACCREDITATION AND SCHOOL IMPROVEMENT: ADVANCEED/SACS CASI

President/CEO, Council on Accreditation and School Improvement Mark A. Elgart, Ed.D.

Address 1866 Southern Lane, Decatur, GA, 30033-4097, USA
Phone 404 679 4500   **Fax** 404 679 4541
Email melgart@advance-ed.org   **Website** www.advance-ed.org

AdvancED is the unified organization of the North Central Association Commission on Accreditation and School Improvement (NCA CASI), Southern Association of Colleges and Schools Council on Accreditation and School Improvement (SACS CASI), and National Study of School Evaluation (NSSE). AdvancED is dedicated to advancing excellence in education through accreditation, research, and professional services.

This unified organization creates the world's largest education community, representing 23,000 public and private schools and districts in 30 states and 65 countries and serving nearly 15 million students. The inclusion of NSSE brings to schools and districts greater access to NSSE's products, services, and strong research base on the factors that impact student learning.

The creation of AdvancED is the beginning of a new journey in the century-long histories of NCA CASI, SACS CASI, and NSSE. Through AdvancED, NCA CASI and SACS CASI will transition from setting standards for their respective regions to establishing unified quality standards for education in a global society. In essence, the transformation is from regional accreditation to a global system of accreditation, continuous improvement, and research.

NCA CASI and SACS CASI schools also will share a unified, clear and powerful accreditation process designed to help schools continuously improve. The new standards and accreditation process will go into effect in 2007–08.

WESTERN ASSOCIATION OF SCHOOLS AND COLLEGES ACCREDITING COMMISSION FOR SCHOOLS: WASC

Executive Director David E. Brown, Ph.D.
Associate Executive Director Marilyn S. George, Ed. D
Associate Executive Director, Operations George Bronson, Ed. D

Address 533 Airport Boulevard, Suite 200, Burlingame, CA, 94010-2009, USA
Phone 1 650 696 1060   **Fax** 1 650 696 1867
Email mail@acswasc.org   **Website** www.acswasc.org

The Western Association of Schools and Colleges Accrediting Commission for Schools (WASC) was formed in 1962 and is one of six regional accrediting bodies in the United States. WASC is a nonprofit, voluntary, nongovernmental association that accredits nearly 3,400 public and private schools in California, Hawaii, Fiji, Guam, American Samoa, Commonwealth of the Northern Mariana Islands, and American/international schools in Asia. WASC's mission is to foster excellence in member schools through a process of continuing evaluation and to recognize schools that meet an acceptable level of quality.

ORGANIZATIONS SUPPORTING INTERNATIONAL EDUCATION

ACADEMY FOR INTERNATIONAL SCHOOL HEADS: AISH
Chief Executive Officer Clark M. Kirkpatrick, Ph.D.

Address 1156 Bay Drive Southeast, Forest Lake, MN, 55025, USA
Phone 651 464 8895   **Fax** 651 464 6469
Email info@academyish.org   **Website** www.AcademyISH.org

AMERICAN ASSOCIATION OF SCHOOL ADMINISTRATORS: AASA
Executive Director Paul D. Houston, Ed.D.

Address 801 N. Quincy Street, Suite 700, Arlington, VA, 22203-1730, USA
Phone 703 528 0700   **Fax**   703 841 1543
Email info@aasa.org   **Website**   www.aasa.org

AASA, founded in 1865, is the professional organization for over 14,000 educational leaders across America and in many other countries. AASA's mission is to support and develop effective school system leaders who are dedicated to the highest quality public education for all children.

AMERICAN SCHOOLS ASSOCIATION OF CENTRAL AMERICA, COLOMBIA-CARIBBEAN AND MEXICO: LATIN AMERICAN TRI-ASSOCIATION
Executive Director Mary Virginia Sanchez

Address Executive Director (ASQ), c/o US Embassy Quito, Unit 5372 Box 004, APO AA 34039
Phone 593 2 2242 996; 2449 141; 2477 534 ext. 3; 2474 795 ext. 3; 2472 975 ext. 3
Fax 593 2 2434 985; 2472 972
Email marsanc@uio.satnet.net   **Website** www.tri-association.org

The American Schools Association of Central America, Colombia-Caribbean and Mexico is a service organization with a special relationship to three regional organizations, The Association of American Schools in Central America, The Association of Colombian-Caribbean American Schools, and The Association of the American Schools of Mexico. The Association works with 61 schools in order to explore ways to achieve better understanding through international education, improve the quality of teaching and learning in the member schools, provide an avenue for communication and cooperation among member institutes, and to facilitate cooperation with national, state, local, and non-governmental agencies in the field of international education.

Supporting Organizations

ASSOCIATION FOR THE ADVANCEMENT OF INTERNATIONAL EDUCATION: AAIE
Inter-Executive Director Everett McGlothlin
Co-Executive Director Dr. Elsa Lamb
Administrative Assistant Michele Fritz
Administrative Assistant Heidi Davidson

Address c/o Sheridan College, PO Box 1500, Sheridan, WY, 82801, USA
Phone 1 307 674 6446 ext 5202   **Fax**   1 307 674 7205
Email aaie@sheridan.edu   **Website** www.aaie.org

AAIE is a dynamic global community providing a forum for the exchange of ideas and research concerning development in the field of international education and school leadership and to advance international education through partnerships with educational institutions and associations worldwide.

ASSOCIATION OF AMERICAN SCHOOLS IN CENTRAL AMERICA: AASCA
President Charles Skipper, Ph.D.
Vice President/Treasurer Linda Niehaus
Secretary Scott MacLaughlan

Address Escuela Americana, PO Box 025364, VIPSAL #1352, Miami, FL, 33102-5364, USA
Phone 503 2257 8411   **Fax**   503 2257 8303
Email skipper.charles@amschool.edu.sv **Website** www.aasca.net

The Association of American Schools in Central America was founded to provide a collective means of serving the needs and interests of the member schools through sharing ideas, programs, facilities and experiences. The goals of the Association through the sharing of resources and information are to assist member schools in establishing and maintaining high standards, to enhance the multicultural/bilingual aspects of member schools, to provide qualified consultants for inservice to teachers and administrators, to help orient new personnel to the schools, to assist in the selection and procurement of educational materials and equipment, and to develop communications and relations among students and staffs of member schools. The Association currently has 18 member schools.

ASSOCIATION OF AMERICAN SCHOOLS IN SOUTH AMERICA: AASSA
Executive Director Paul Poore

Address 12333 NW 18th St., Pembroke Pines, FL, 33026, USA
Phone 1 305 821 0345   **Fax** 1 305 821 4244
Email aassa@bellsouth.net   **Website** www.aassa.com

Established in 1961, AASSA is a nonprofit membership association currently serving 41 American/international schools throughout South America and offshore islands. AASSA is administered by an executive director who employs a professional staff to assist with publications, inservice programs, grant management, purchasing, shipping, and accounting. The association serves as a structure through which personnel in member schools can plan cooperatively to attain common goals and to solve mutual problems. AASSA seeks to broaden the dimensions of education and to enhance the quality of teaching and learning in member schools.

ASSOCIATION OF AMERICAN SCHOOLS OF MEXICO: **ASOMEX**
President Janet Heinze
Vice President/Treasurer Mirtha Stappung
Secretary Hortensia Preito

Address The American School Foundation of Guadalajara, A.C., Colomos 2100, Fracc. Italia Providencia, Guadalajara, Jalisco, 44630, Mexico
Phone 52 333 648 0299 ext. 1001　　**Fax** 52 833 227 2080
Email janet.heinze@asfg.mx　　**Website** www.asfg.mx

ASOMEX is the oldest of the regional associations and has a long history of promoting an American type of education in the Mexican Republic. Its focus is school improvement and the organization of staff in-service and student interaction within its member schools. Currently, there are eighteen active members. New members must be either accredited U.S. institutions or candidates for accrediation.

ASSOCIATION OF CHRISTIAN SCHOOLS INTERNATIONAL: **ACSI**
President Ken Smitherman
Vice President, International Ministries Daniel J. Egeler, Ed.D.
International Director, Latin America/Asia David K. Wilcox, Ph.D.
International Director, Africa, CIS/Baltics, Europe, Mid East Michael Epp, MEd

Address PO Box 65130, Colorado Springs, CO, 80962-5130, USA
Phone 1 719 528 6906　　**Fax** 1 719 531 0631
Email intlmin@acsi.org　　**Website** www.acsi.org

The Association of Christian Schools International (ACSI) is a service organization for Protestant Christian schools in over 100 countries. The association assists its international member schools in recruiting new staff, organizing international conferences, providing accreditation services, offering a transcript depository, and developing educational resource materials, texts, and other publications.

ASSOCIATION OF COLOMBIAN-CARIBBEAN AMERICAN SCHOOLS: **ACCAS**
President Jack Delman
Vice President Michael Adams

Address Avda. Sarasota, esq Nunez de Caceres, Bella Vista, Santo Domingo, Dominican Republic
Phone 809 947 1005　　**Fax** 809 533 9222
Email jdelman@cms.edu.do　　**Website** www.accas.org

The Association of Colombian-Caribbean American Schools is one of the three regional associations affiliated with the Tri-Association. Our membership of 21 schools supports the continuation of an American education in our part of the world. Our focus is on school improvement, encouraging an ongoing program of staff development and teacher and student interactions. New members must be either U.S. accredited institutions or candidates for accreditation.

Supporting Organizations

ASSOCIATION OF INTERNATIONAL SCHOOLS IN AFRICA: AISA

Executive Director Mary (Miffie) Greer

Address c/o International School of Kenya, Peponi Road, PO Box 14103, Nairobi, 00800, Kenya
Phone 254 20 4182 578; 254 20 4183 622   **Fax** 254 20 4180 596; 254 20 4183 272
Email miffie@pop.isk.ac.ke   **Website** www.aisa.or.ke

The Association of International Schools in Africa is a support organization for over 95 international schools in sub-Saharan Africa. In addition, we have 47 school related business associate members. Our services include providing two regional teachers' conferences and one administrators' conference each October/November, regular newsletters, consultants for professional development in schools, institutes on current professional topics, various statistical surveys, a yearly membership directory, and several scholarships to professional courses. We also have a website which is updated on a regular basis and from which information on our organization can be obtained. In addition, we serve as a central office where schools and teachers can request information and maintain contact.

CANADIAN ASSOCIATION OF INDEPENDENT SCHOOLS: CAIS

Executive Director Susan Both

Address 202-12 Bannockburn Ave, Toronto, ON, M5M 2M8, Canada
Phone 416 780 1779   **Fax** 416 780 9301
Email admin@cais.ca   **Website** www.cais.ca

The Canadian Association of Independent Schools is a membership association representing 79 schools with founding dates from 1788 to 2005. Member schools, all "nonprofit," are committed to excellence and provide outstanding academic preparation for higher education. CAIS schools also provide a wide spectrum of co-curricular activities related to arts, athletics, leadership development, and community service. Our member schools offer a range of choices for students and teachers including various combinations of co-education, single-gender environments, boarding and day programs.

CENTRAL AND EASTERN EUROPEAN SCHOOLS ASSOCIATION: CEESA

Executive Director David M. Cobb

Address Vocarska 106, Zagreb, 10000, Croatia
Phone 385 1 460 9935   **Fax** 385 1 460 9936
Email office@ceesa.org   **Website** www.ceesa.org

The Central and Eastern European Schools Association facilitates communication among schools in the region as well as with service providers and other regional organizations. It promotes professional development for teachers, administrators and board members while also promoting activities for students and providing services to members as needed.

COLLEGE BOARD, THE
Vice President for Higher Education James M. Montoya

Address 1233 20th Street, NW, Suite 600, Washington, DC, 20036, USA
Phone 202 741 4700   **Fax** 202 822 5234
Email Internatl@collegeboard.org   **Website** www.collegeboard.com

The College Board is a not-for-profit membership association whose mission is to connect students to college success and opportunity. Founded in 1900, the association is composed of more than 5,000 schools, colleges, universities, and other educational organizations. Each year, the College Board serves seven million students and their parents, 23,000 high schools, and 3,500 colleges through major programs and services in college admissions, guidance, assessment, financial aid, enrollment, and teaching and learning. Among its best-known programs are the SAT®, the PSAT/NMSQT®, and the Advanced Placement Program® (AP®). The College Board is committed to the principles of excellence and equity, and that commitment is embodied in all of its programs, services, activities, and concerns.

COLLEGE BOARD, THE (ADVANCE PLACEMENT (AP) PROGRAM AND PSAT/NMSQT PROGRAM)
Associate Director, International Services Clay T. Hensley

Address 45 Columbus Avenue, New York, NY, 10023, USA
Phone 212 373 8723   Fax 212 262 0946
Email chensley@collegeboard.org   Website apcentral.collegeboard.com

The International Services unit of the College Board is dedicatedto our mission to connect students to college success and opportunities.The College Board is a not-for-profit membership organization committedto excellence and equity in education. The International Services unit supports schools outside of the United States who participate in CollegeBoard programs, such as AP® and PSAT/NMSQT®. InternationalServices also promotes AP recognition at universities outside the UnitedStates, and supports other College Board programs and services including SAT®, MyRoad™, CollegeEd™, and Springboard™. The College Board places a strong emphasis on access and equity for all itsprograms, including AP® and PSAT/NMSQT®. The goal of the International Services team is to provide exemplary service to international schools and to their students, teachers, administrators, and parents.

Supporting Organizations

COUNCIL OF BRITISH INDEPENDENT SCHOOLS IN THE EUROPEAN COMMUNITIES: COBISEC

Chairman Roger Fry, CBE
General Secretary Albert Hudspeth

Address 14 Fernham Road, Faringdon, Oxfordshire, SN7 7JY, United Kingdom
Phone 44 1367 242655   **Fax** 44 1367 242655
Email general.secretary@cobisec.org   **Website** www.cobisec.org

COBISEC is an association of British international schools situated mainly in Europe but also in many other countries worldwide. All member schools offer an educational program based on the British national curriculum taught by British trained teachers. Schools are expected to undertake an approved inspection arranged by the Independent Schools Inspectorate, which is authorized by the British Department of Education and Science, on a regular basis. COBISEC works in association with the Council of British Independent Schools (BISW) which incorporates COBISEC (Europe), FOBISSEA (Asia), BSME (Middle East), LAHC (South America), and BSNA (U.S.A.)

COUNCIL OF INTERNATIONAL SCHOOLS: CIS

Executive Director Richard S. Tangye

Address 21A Lavant Street, Petersfield, Hampshire, GU32 3EL, United Kingdom
Phone 44 1730 263131   **Fax** 44 1730 268913
Email cois@cois.org   **Website** www.cois.org

The Council of International Schools (CIS) is a not-for-profit association of schools and post-secondary institutions working collaboratively for the continuous improvement of international education.

COUNCIL OF INTERNATIONAL SCHOOLS (OFFICE OF HIGHER EDUCATION–ITHACA, NEW YORK): CIS

Director Paula J. Mitchell

Address 401 East State Street, Suite 405, Ithaca, NY, 14850, USA
Phone 1 607 272 5758   **Fax** 1 607 272 5051
Email paulamitchell@cois.org   **Website** www.cois.org

Through a portfolio of services, the CIS Office of Higher Education links our higher education and secondary school members, and supports their efforts to assist prospective undergraduate students at schools worldwide to matriculate at CIS higher education member institutions.

Council of International Schools
(Office of Higher Education–San Diego, California): CIS
Associate Director Thomas C. LePere

Address 2722 Ariane Drive #38, San Diego, CA, 92117, USA
Phone 858 483 1673   **Fax** 858 581 1585
Email tomlepere@cois.org   **Website** www.cois.org

East Asia Regional Council of Overseas Schools: EARCOS
Executive Director Robert A. Sills, Ph.D.
Associate Director Linda C. Sills

Address Brentville Subdivision, Barangay Mamplasan, Biñan, Laguna, 4024, Philippines
Phone 63 49 511 5993 or 5994   **Fax** 63 49 511 4694
Email info@earcos.org   **Website** www.earcos.org

EARCOS (East Asia Regional Council of Overseas Schools) is a nonprofit 501(C)3, incorporated in the state of Delaware, USA, with a regional office in Biñan, Laguna, Philippines. Membership in EARCOS is open to elementary and secondary schools in East Asia which offer an educational program using English as the primary language of instruction, and to other organizations, institutions, and individuals interested in the mission and vision of the Council. Objectives and purposes are to promote intercultural understanding and international friendship through the activities of Member Schools, to broaden the dimensions of education of all schools involved in the Council in the interest of a total program of education, to advance the professional growth and welfare of individuals belonging to the educational staff of member schools, to facilitate communication and cooperative action between and among all associated schools, and to cooperate with other organizations and individuals pursuing the same objectives as the Council.

European Council of International Schools: ECIS
Executive Director/CEO Dixie A. McKay

Address 21B Lavant Street, Petersfield, Hampshire, GU32 3EL, United Kingdom
Phone 44 1730 268 244   **Fax** 44 1730 267 914
Email ecis@ecis.org   **Website** www.ecis.org

ECIS is a nonprofit membership organization dedicated to the advancement of internationalism through education by the provision of a comprehensive range of services to its members. Nearly 400 international schools around the globe, both primary and secondary, are members of ECIS. Full details of all services offered can be found on the Council's website.

European Council of International Schools/
Council of International Schools (Australian Office): ECIS/CIS
Regional Representative Allan J. Wilcox
Administrative Assistant Mavis Wilcox

Address Cumburri I.E.C., PO Box 367, Kilmore 3764, Victoria, Australia
Phone 61 3 578 113 51   **Fax** 61 3 578 111 51
Email intedcon@hyperlink.net.au

Supporting Organizations

INTER-REGIONAL CENTER, INC.: IRC
Director Burton Fox, Ed.D.

Address PO Box 020470, Tuscaloosa, AL, 35402, USA
Phone 1 205 391 0727   **Fax** 1 205 391 0927

The Inter-Regional Center, Inc., established in 1969, provides seminars and workshops for international school board members, chief administrators, and educational specialists on an annual basis. Additionally, the IRC provides consultative services to international schools on site.

INTERNATIONAL BACCALAUREATE NORTH AMERICA: IBNA
Regional Director Bradley Richardson

Address 475 Riverside Drive, Suite 1600, New York, NY, 10115, USA
Phone 1 212 696 4464   **Fax** 1 212 889 9242
Email ibna@ibo.org   **Website** www.ibo.org

The International Baccalaureate (IB) offers high quality programmes of international education to a worldwide community of schools. Our three programmes for students aged 3 to 19 help develop the intellectual, personal, emotional and social skills to live, learn and work in a rapidly globalizing world. There are more than 541,000 IB students at 2,061 schools in 125 countries.

INTERNATIONAL BACCALAUREATE ORGANIZATION: IBO
Director General Jeffrey Beard
Deputy Director General Ian Hill

Address Route des Morillons 15, 1218 Grand-Saconnex, Geneva, Switzerland
Phone 41 22 791 7740   Fax 41 22 791 0277
Email ibhq@ibo.org   Website www.ibo.org

The International Baccalaureate Organization (IBO) is a nonprofit, Swiss educational foundation that was established in 1968. The Diploma Program for which it is best known was developed by a group of schools seeking to establish a common curriculum and a university entry credential for geographically mobile students. They believed that an education emphasizing critical thinking and exposure to a variety of points of view would encourage intercultural understanding and acceptance of others by young people. They designed a comprehensive curriculum for the last two years of secondary school that could be administered in any country and that would be recognized by universities worldwide. Grants from UNESCO, the Century Fund, the Ford Foundation, and other groups made it possible to further develop the Diploma Program which is now offered by a wide variety of schools and is accepted by universities around the world. Today the IBO offers three programs to schools. The Diploma Program is for students in the final two years of secondary school. The Middle Years Program (MYP), adopted in 1994, is for students aged 11 to 16, and the Primary Years Program, adopted in 1997, is for students aged 3 to 12. All programs are available in English,

French, and Spanish. The MYP is also available in Chinese. The IBO in May of 2006 had 1,779 authorized schools in 122 countries. The number is nearly evenly divided between state schools and private, including international, schools. The IBO provides a wide range of services to the schools that are authorized to administer its programs. These include curriculum and assessment development, professional development activities for teachers, and research on issues related to international education. The IBO's website provides information about the organization and its programs.

INTERNATIONAL SCHOOLS SERVICES: ISS
President Daniel L. Scinto

Address 15 Roszel Road, PO Box 5910, Princeton, NJ, 08543-5910, USA
Phone 1 609 452 0990   **Fax** 1 609 452 2690
Email iss@iss.edu   **Website** www.iss.edu

A nonprofit corporation dedicated to educational excellence for children attending international schools worldwide since 1955, International Schools Services is the world leader in providing a comprehensive range of quality educational services for schools, educators, families and corporations. Headquartered in Princeton, New Jersey, International Schools Services is led by a team of professionals, each with decades of overseas educational experience. We pride ourselves in offering individualized assistance to international schools facing the many challenges unique to the overseas community.

MEDITERRANEAN ASSOCIATION OF INTERNATIONAL SCHOOLS: MAIS
Executive Director Reina L. O'Hale

Address c/o American School of Madrid, Apartado 80, Madrid, 28080, Spain
Phone 34 91 740 1900   **Fax** 34 91 357 2678
Email rohale@mais-web.org   **Website** www.mais-web.org

The Mediterranean Association of International Schools is a professional organization that strives to improve the quality of education in its member schools through several venues. It promotes the professional development of faculty, administrators and school board members, effects communication and interchange, and creates international understanding. MAIS serves as a liaison between its 26 member schools, host country schools, associate member organizations and other regional, professional and in-service organizations. At present, MAIS is composed of schools located in Spain, Portugal, Morocco, Tunisia, Italy, Egypt, France and Cyprus. In addition, several associate members, such as schools outside the Mediterranean region, colleges, businesses, and interested individuals support MAIS' endeavors and have joined the organization.

Supporting Organizations

NATIONAL ASSOCIATION OF BRITISH SCHOOLS IN SPAIN: NABSS
President Anne Farré

Address British School of Barcelona, c/Giuesta 26, Apartado 172, 08860 Castelldefels, Barcelona,
Phone 34 93 665 1584 **Fax** 34 93 664 1444
Website www.NABSS.org

NABSS is an organization comprising over 40 British schools in Spain. In order to become members, schools have to be fully authorized via a rigorous inspection system. The association represents schools' interests, for example in educational issues involving the British or Spanish authorities, and offers advice and high-level training. In these ways we try to ensure that the schools stay up-to-date and offer a quality education. Although there are some curricular differences between schools-and, of course, each school has its own particular personality and style-they all follow the British curriculum in English and usually teach a few obligatory subjects in Spanish. All in all, the British schools, with the support of the association, provide a broad and bicultural education for students.

NATIONAL ASSOCIATION OF ELEMENTARY SCHOOL PRINCIPALS: NAESP
Executive Director Gail Connelly

Address 1615 Duke Street, Alexandria, VA, 22314-3483, USA
Phone 1 703 684 3345 **Fax** 1 703 518 6285
Email gconnelly@naesp.org **Website** www.naesp.org

Established in 1921, the National Association of Elementary School Principals serves 29,000 Elementary and Middle School Principals in the United States, Canada and overseas.

NATIONAL ASSOCIATION OF INDEPENDENT SCHOOLS: NAIS
President Patrick F. Bassett

Address 1620 L Street, NW, Suite 1100, Washington, DC, 20036-5605, USA
Phone 1 202 973 9700 **Fax** 1 202 973 9790
Website www.nais.org

NAIS, representing over 1,200 schools nationally and internationally, has as its mission to be the national voice of independent schools and the center for collective action. Visitors to its website, www.nais.org, will find a cornucopia of information, statistics, monographs, and other resources on topics related to precollegiate education.

Supporting Organizations

NATIONAL ASSOCIATION OF SECONDARY SCHOOL PRINCIPALS: NASSP
Executive Director Gerald N. Tirozzi, Ph.D.

Address 1904 Association Drive, Reston, VA, 20191, USA
Phone 1 703 860 7205   **Fax** 1 703 476 9214
Email tirozzig@principals.org   **Website** www.principals.org

The National Association of Secondary School Principals-the preeminent organization and the national voice for middle level and high school principals, assistant principals, and aspiring school leaders-provides its members the professional resources to serve as visionary leaders. NASSP promotes the intellectual growth, academic achievement, character development, leadership development, and physical well-being of youth through its programs and student leadership services. NASSP sponsors the National Honor Society™, the National Junior Honor Society™, and the National Association of Student Councils™.

NEAR EAST SOUTH ASIA COUNCIL OF OVERSEAS SCHOOLS: NESA
Executive Director David Chojnacki
Executive Assistant/Business Manager Jill Kalamaris

Address The NESA Center, American College of Greece, PO Box 60018,
     #6 Gravias Street, Aghia Paraskevi, 15342, Greece
Phone 30 210 600 9821   **Fax** 30 210 600 9928
Email nesa@nesacenter.org   **Website** www.nesacenter.org

NESA is a nonprofit, voluntary association of more than 75 American/international schools in the Middle East and the Asian subcontinent, stretching from Libya and Greece in the west to India, Bangladesh, India and Sri Lanka in the east. A "community of schools", we strive to create a sense of belonging and identity, diminish feelings of professional isolation and foster a culture of mutual support and professional engagement. Our vision is to create dynamic, collaborative professional relationships which transcend current barriers and boundaries in order to maximize student learning in our member schools.

OFFICE OF OVERSEAS SCHOOLS: A/OS
Director Keith D. Miller, Ph.D.

Address Room H328, SA-1, Department of State, Washington, DC, 20522-0132, USA
Phone 1 202 261 8200   **Fax** 1 202 261 8224
Email OverseasSchools@state.gov   **Website** www.state.gov/m/a/os

Supporting Organizations

OVERSEAS ASSOCIATION FOR COLLEGE ADMISSION COUNSELING: OACAC

President Andrew Whyte
President-Elect Lisa Ball
Past President David Zutautas
Administrative Assistant Doug Thompson

Address 36 Reservoir Road, Marlboro, NY, 12542, USA
Phone 1 845 236 3074   **Fax** 1 845 236 2626
Email thompson@oacac.com   **Website** www.oacac.com

The mission of the Overseas Association for College Admission Counseling (OACAC) is to facilitate global interaction among counselors and institutions in support of students in their transition from secondary to higher education. OACAC is a chartered regional organization affiliated with the U.S.-based National Association for College Admission Counseling.

SOUTH ASIA INTER SCHOOL ASSOCIATION: SAISA

Executive Secretary Laurie S. McLellan

Address The Overseas School of Colombo, PO Box 9, Palewatte, Battaramulla, Sri Lanka
Phone 94 11 2784920   **Fax** 94 11 2784999
Email lmclellan@osc.lk

SAISA (South Asia Inter School Association) is a ten member organization of international schools located in the South Asia region. The purpose of SAISA is to "promote and coordinate regional professional development activities, academic and cultural festivals, athletic tournaments, and other events deemed appropriate by the member schools." The member schools are the American Embassy School in New Delhi, American School of Bombay, American International School–Chennai, American International School/Dhaka, International School of Islamabad, Karachi American School, Lahore American School, Lincoln School in Kathmandu, Murree Christian School in Murree, Pakistan, and the Overseas School of Colombo. This last year SAISA sponsored regional athletic events in volleyball, basketball, soccer, swimming, and track and field as well as a music festival, an art festival and a math competition.

SWISS GROUP OF INTERNATIONAL SCHOOLS: SGIS

Chair Richard McDonald
Secretary Jacqueline Chan-Kam

Address 66, chemin de la Caracole, Genthod Parc, Genthod 1294, Geneva, Switzerland
Phone 00 41 22 7791606
Email info@sgischools.com   **Website** www.sgischools.com

The Swiss Group of International Schools (SGIS) has existed since the mid 1960s. It was originally founded to meet the needs of students, parents, teachers and administrators in international schools in Switzerland-for example, the need for exchange of information and ideas, for inter-school sports programs, for professional development programs for staff, and for a common representation to Swiss federal authorities and worldwide educational bodies.

INDEX

Index

Index

Index

Index

Index

Index

R

S

Index